POLITICAL IDEOLOGIES

POLITICAL IDEOLOGIES

Second Edition

H.B. McCullough

OXFORD
UNIVERSITY PRESS

Oxford University Press is a department of the University of Oxford.
It furthers the University's objective of excellence in research, scholarship,
and education by publishing worldwide. Oxford is a registered trade mark of
Oxford University Press in the UK and in certain other countries.

Published in Canada by
Oxford University Press
8 Sampson Mews, Suite 204,
Don Mills, Ontario M3C 0H5 Canada

www.oupcanada.com

Copyright © Oxford University Press Canada 2017

The moral rights of the author have been asserted

Database right Oxford University Press (maker)

First Edition published in 2010

All rights reserved. No part of this publication may be reproduced, stored in
a retrieval system, or transmitted, in any form or by any means, without the
prior permission in writing of Oxford University Press, or as expressly permitted
by law, by licence, or under terms agreed with the appropriate reprographics
rights organization. Enquiries concerning reproduction outside the scope of the
above should be sent to the Permissions Department at the address above
or through the following url: www.oupcanada.com/permission/permission_request.php

Every effort has been made to determine and contact copyright holders.
In the case of any omissions, the publisher will be pleased to make
suitable acknowledgement in future editions.

Library and Archives Canada Cataloguing in Publication

McCullough, H.B., 1944–, author
    Political ideologies / H.B. McCullough. — Second
edition.

Includes bibliographical references and index.
ISBN 978-0-19-902560-2 (paperback)

1. Political science—Textbooks. I. Title.

JA71.M332 2016   320.5   C2016-904358-4

Cover image: TablinumCarlson/Getty Images
Chapter opener image: © iStock/derrek

Oxford University Press is committed to our environment.
Wherever possible, our books are printed on paper
which comes from responsible sources.

Printed and bound in Canada

1 2 3 4 — 20 19 18 17

Contents

Acknowledgements vi

1. Introduction   1
2. Classical Liberalism   8
3. Conservatism   29
4. Reform Liberalism   55
5. Marxism   85
6. Democratic Socialism   107
7. Fascism and National Socialism   131
8. Pacifism   157
9. Anarchism   179
10. Neo-Liberalism and Libertarianism   203
11. Feminism   226
12. Environmentalism   252
13. Religious Fundamentalism   278
14. Secularism   313
15. Conclusion   331

Appendix A: Scatter Diagram of Political Ideologies   337

Appendix B: Comparing Political Ideologies   339

Glossary   342

Notes   362

References   407

Index   420

Acknowledgements

The author would like to acknowledge Trudy Govier for her suggestions in regard to feminism. Her measured opinion over many years has always been appreciated. In addition, thanks are due to Gillian Treschow, Barbara Sobol, and Ian Robinson for their dedication in tracking down articles on religious fundamentalism. And much appreciation is owed my research assistant, Ellen Sierakowski, for her painstaking efforts in the matter of further readings. In addition, the author would like to recognize the assistance of Wolfgang Depner, my co-editor of a book of readings on political ideologies, for his innovative ideas and recommendations. In addition, I would like to express my thanks to Kate Skene and Meg Patterson of Oxford University Press for their patience, guidance, and common sense during the writing of this book. And of course, much gratitude is owed Richard Tallman for his considered suggestions and meticulous copy-editing, which have substantially enhanced the quality of the writing. Lastly, many thanks are owed to my wife, Photini, for her steadfast support in listening to ideas aired in the pages that follow.

*In honour of friends and family in Kakovatos, Ilia, Greece
for their support over many years.*

1 Introduction

In his moving novel *Darkness at Noon* (1940), Arthur Koestler has the self-assured prison interrogator Ivanov say categorically, "I don't approve of mixing ideologies." Addressing the prisoner Rubashov, Ivanov the interrogator goes on to develop his idea by saying that there are only two conceptions of human ethics, and they reside at opposite poles. One of them is "Christian and humane," and "declares the individual to be sacrosanct." The other is utilitarian, and attaches itself to the principle that "a collective aim justifies all means." Ivanov calls the first of these "anti-vivisection morality" and the latter "vivisection morality." As he tells Rubashov, the mixing of these two conceptions—despite the attempts of "humbugs" and "dilettantes" to do so—is impossible.

There is some truth in what Ivanov has to say, at least when applied to political ideologies. He is correct that the adoption of some ideologies logically precludes the adoption of some others. In short, there is some truth to the idea that in political thinking one has to lay down one's money and take one's pick. For instance, opting for libertarianism and its market theory of value logically precludes one from simultaneously endorsing Marxism and its labour theory of value. And opting for conservatism and its view of the corrupted nature of persons logically precludes one from concurrently affirming anarchism and its view of the perfectible nature of human beings. These theories and the ideologies in which they are found compete for the same logical space. So much, then, for the truth of Ivanov's remarks.

It is equally evident, however, that Ivanov says something false by maintaining, as he does, that political ideologies are exhausted by Christian humanism on the one hand and what amounts to utilitarianism on the other. Political ideologies are much more sweeping and varied than Ivanov would have it, and the choices with which one is faced in confronting the human political condition are not limited to two.

As a first approximation, political ideologies include diverse perspectives such as classical liberalism, conservatism, reform liberalism, democratic socialism, Marxism, anarchism, fascism, libertarianism, fundamentalism, feminism, environmentalism, and pacifism. One can map these ideologies along an axis from left to right according to the level of government involvement in the life of the individual, ranging from very considerable involvement on the left to very little on the right.[1] And one can map these ideologies along an axis from top to bottom according to the role played by substantive justice in the ideology, ranging from significant on the top to insignificant on the bottom. It would be premature at this time to conceptualize any of these ideologies in this way; rather, we should let these ideologies speak for themselves. Only after looking at all of them would any mapping be appropriate.

Political ideologies are perspectives on the world that synthesize philosophical, scientific, economic, religious, political, and technological beliefs for the purpose of encouraging a course of action. The three components of each political ideology—descriptive, motivational, and incorrigible or unfalsifiable—are briefly discussed below.

- *Descriptive component.* The most straightforward element of political ideologies, the descriptive component, includes, but is not exhausted by, points of view on human nature, the origins of the state, the structural traits of government, the form of economic organization, the ends of government, the function of power, and the role of the community.[2]
- *Motivational component.* This less straightforward element of political ideologies prescribes a course of conduct, comprising beliefs that encourage the implementation of certain values, such as those of justice, equality, liberty, and human rights. All political ideologies aim at inducing people into either collective or individual action. Their function is to mobilize people into accepting a course of action, whether, for example, it be in support of or against government, in favour of one socio-economic class or another, in agreement with one gender or another, or in aid of one voluntary association or another. In this sense, political ideologies differ from political philosophies in that the latter aim to engage people in thought rather than action. Political ideologies are more like "rallying cries" to be made use of by those who shape politics than they are the deep and penetrating analysis of reflective thought. It is in this context that the prescriptive comments of Marx ("Working men of all countries, unite!")[3] and Hitler ("In the first place, our people must be delivered from the hopeless confusion of international convictions, and educated consciously and systematically to fanatical nationalism")[4] need to be understood. In promoting their ideologies of Marxism and National Socialism, respectively, they hold high in their hands the particular "truths" to which they subscribe and to which they wish others to lend their allegiance.
- *Unfalsifiable or incorrigible component.* This is the most elusive of the three elements. To be a political ideology, a set of beliefs with a prescriptive component that mobilizes people into action must also be held with a kind of passion that makes them irrefutable from the believer's point of view. Under this construction, ideologies turn out to be akin to secular religions, assuming the roles of dogmas, doctrines, or even myths. Some ideologies are so extreme that they quite naturally fit into the category of those things that most reasonable people would deem to be dogmas or myths, while others are more ambiguous and do not fit so readily into this category. Nonetheless, all the political stances assumed in the following chapters have been held by some of their supporters in an unfalsifiable or incorrigible way. Ultimately, even reasonably good political thought can be held onto past its breaking point, long after it should have been abandoned. In such cases the political thought crosses over into the domain of political ideologies.

The foregoing outline makes clear the three components of political ideologies. What it does not make clear is an important connection that obtains among all three: that the motivational component almost always necessitates a simplification of beliefs at the descriptive and prescriptive levels, a simplification that leads its adherents into holding onto these beliefs in an irrefutable, unfalsifiable, and incorrigible way. Unlike political philosophy, which does not require action, political ideologies aim at action and therefore cannot afford to pay attention to subtle distinctions between political, social, and economic alternatives. Political action, therefore, will often not take place unless matters are simplified and then defended tenaciously. This defence is accompanied by a particular "emotive tone" used by intransigent supporters, or **ideologues**, to articulate their beliefs and rally supporters; see the accompanying box for the characteristic emotive tones associated with specific ideologies.

With this understanding of the essence of ideologies we can now proceed to their importance. Political ideologies influence both domestic and foreign policies of governments. Domestic policies include the fields of education, the economy, transportation, health, immigration, criminal law, taxation, the environment, social services, employment, agriculture, bankruptcy, patents, copyrights, defence, navigation, shipping, broadcasting, and pensions. Foreign policy comprises the fields of trade, diplomacy, treaties, and military engagement. It would be fair to say that policy, both domestic and foreign, covers the multi-dimensional nature of human existence. Given that political ideologies influence policies of governments—that is, that political ideologies influence the multi-dimensional nature of our lives—their importance is self-evident. Further, given that these same ideologies are held in an incorrigible or unfalsifiable manner, policies based on them run the risk of being other than evidence-based. There is real danger in this, for it may result in governments closing their minds to facts and insisting on policy choices destined to make matters worse for the body politic. Clearly, then, political ideologies are both important and have the potential for negative impact in our lives.

In the following discussion, a wide range of political ideologies will be examined to give the reader a fair and frank understanding and assessment of each. Though most of these ideologies began in the West, some of them underwent change and flourished

Characteristic Emotive Tones of Political Ideologues

- Classical Liberal: reflective and detached
- Reform Liberal: moderate and tolerant
- Conservative: sanguine but guarded
- Marxist: iconoclastic and self-assured
- Fascist: bellicose, disdainful, proud, and arrogant
- Fundamentalist: self-righteous, self-confident
- Environmentalist: alarmist
- Pacifist: concerned, empathetic, non-violent, but willing to engage in selective civil disobedience
- Libertarian: strident, self-confident, self-absorbed
- Anarchist: buoyant and optimistic
- Democratic Socialist: engaged and constructive
- Feminist: indignant and energized

elsewhere, as in the case of Marxism in China and pacifism in India. Others, like anarchism and fundamentalism, originated in non-Western soil—in Russia and the Middle East, respectively. Still others are simply global ideologies, as in the case of feminism and environmentalism. The ensuing discussion will aim to provide not only an accurate description of the ideology in question, but also an evaluation that takes into account comparative propositions from competing ideologies with an end to determining which of these ideologies, if any, is credible or at least salvageable.

To attempt to remain sensitive to historic conditions, our starting point will be the seventeenth century and a study of the political ideology known as classical liberalism. The discussion begins here because of the three major developments that transformed European societies once and for all near the midpoint of that century: the rise of modern science, the aftermath of the Reformation, and the emergence of the nation-state. A brief examination of each of these is now in order.

The Rise of Modern Science

In 1543, just before his death, the Polish churchman Nicholas Copernicus (1473–1543) published his magnum opus, *On the Revolutions of the Celestial Spheres*. In this work, he introduced the concept of a moving earth—a concept that implied a new physics, and certainly one different from that put forth by the great Greek philosopher, logician, and scientist, Aristotle (384–322 BCE). Copernicus's book was one of revolutionary proportions, for it contained the germ of the idea that reached its zenith with Isaac Newton's ideas of modern physics.[5] Paralleling Copernicus, the Belgian physician Andreas Vesalius (1514–1564) published *On the Fabric of the Human Body* (1543), a book that provided an exact anatomical analysis of the human body.[6]

Copernicus and Vesalius were soon followed by other emerging scientists, including Galileo Galilei (1564–1642), who showed rather convincingly with the aid of a telescope that the astronomical system of Copernicus was not just a computing device but a theory that told us something about the real world.[7] It showed that the heliocentric theory of Copernicus was anchored in reality, and this in turn motivated the search for a physics that would apply to an earth in motion.[8] Galileo then published his findings on the new science of motion in arguably his greatest work, *Discourses and Demonstrations Concerning Two New Sciences* (1638). Among his findings was a formulation of the principle of inertia, a formulation that "awaited the genius of Isaac Newton (1642–1727) for its modern definitive formulation."[9]

Clearly, science gained momentum during the first half of the seventeenth century, but the establishment of the Royal Society of London for the Improvement of Natural Knowledge in 1660 and the establishment of the Académie des Sciences in France in 1666 cemented science in the landscape of a new age of man. These organizations professionalized science—a consequence, at least in the case of the Royal Society, of the efforts of men such as Robert Hooke, Thomas Sprat, and Robert Boyle. Iconoclasm reigned in the form of the experimental or empirical method,[10] and this more than any other factor turned these men away from the authority of Aristotle and the Scholastic tradition. Academics, clergy, and politicians alike were forced to reconsider their understanding of science. It is in this context that John Locke (1632–1704) appears, writes his groundbreaking work of philosophical empiricism, *An Essay Concerning Human Understanding* (1690), and develops the political component of the ideology called classical liberalism[11] in *Two Treatises of Government* (1690).

The year 1660, then, is a natural starting point for a study of modern political ideas, more so than the sixteenth or early seventeenth century. The creation of science as an organized activity, built around respected institutions that applied empiricism through the scientific method, was really something new in the history of mankind.

The Aftermath of the Reformation

Whereas the scientific revolution was in part a revolution against the authority of Aristotle, the Reformation was a revolt against the authority of the Catholic Church. Martin Luther (1483–1546) was not the first to lead a movement for Church reform,[12] but he was the first to bring about the creation of a church that existed outside the Catholic communion. In 1517 he posted his Ninety-Five Theses, a denunciation of abuses by the Catholic clergy, most notably the sale of indulgences as a legitimate form of penance. Luther's writings galvanized dissent within the Christian community, for "within the very generation that had seen the posting of the Ninety-Five Theses, there were organized dozens of churches or sects or denominations—Anglican, Calvinist, Anabaptist, and many others."[13] Unity in the Christian world had given way to fragmentation and pluralism.

This is not to suggest that Luther alone was responsible for this new pluralism. To be sure, he played a role in the erosion of Christian unity, but he was assisted in this matter by independent thinkers such as Ulrich Zwingli (1484–1531) and John Calvin (1509–1564) in Switzerland, the Huguenots (1500s) in France, John Knox (died 1572) in Scotland, the opportunist Henry VIII (reigned 1509–1547) in England, and the Anabaptists (1500s) in Northwestern Europe.

At the core of the Protestant movement in its various forms lay a commitment to the notion of justification by faith rather than good works, a commitment facilitated by the slow and progressive translations of the Bible into the vernacular. The authority and hegemony of the Catholic Church could not help but be eroded by the commitment to faith alone, and to the parallel notion of the priesthood of all believers, for these concepts made salvation a matter between individuals and their maker. Perhaps nothing symbolizes this failed hegemony better than English Civil War (1642–1651), in which Henry VIII's Anglican Church, itself an offshoot of the Catholic Church, was challenged by Oliver Cromwell's Puritans and their commitment to independent judgment based on conscience and Bible reading. Clearly, by the middle of the seventeenth century, the issue of who really did possess **authority**, conceived as power and **legitimacy**, was a very real one for all members of the body politic in Europe.

Faced with this challenge to authority, Thomas Hobbes (1588–1679) published his great work, *Leviathan* (1651), in which he attempted to defend, rather unsuccessfully, a version of **absolutism** that addressed the anarchy induced by sectarianism. In many ways, however, Hobbes looked backward. What was needed was someone who looked forward, who began to address issues of authority in a different way, and who veered away from absolutism. John Locke is this person, and so the latter part of the seventeenth century is a compelling point of departure for a study of political ideologies.

The Emergence of the Modern Nation-State

The third development affecting politics, in addition to the rise of modern science and the aftermath of the Reformation in the mid-seventeenth century, was the emergence of the modern nation-state. This was owing to the Treaty of Westphalia in 1648 that ended the Thirty Years' War. Among other things, this treaty granted the 300 small states of the Holy Roman Empire the right to form alliances with foreign powers as well as to wage war.[14] The resulting states had their own foreign services, as well as their own armies and finances.[15] Moreover, the resulting states had the appearance of political units, and saw the development of permanent institutions, including bureaucracies. In addition, these political units recognized the need for some form of authority to make binding decisions in cases of dispute.[16] These centralized structures of the modern state were consolidated over a period of time lasting from 1450 to 1648, but it was the Treaty of Westphalia that accelerated the gestation period of "an international system based on a plurality of independent states, recognizing no superior authority over them."[17]

The full impact of the change in European societies triggered by the emergence of the new nation-state would take years to work itself out. To be sure, it would take time for the new nation-state to be fully born—that is, for it to have the characteristics of territorial organization, popular sovereignty, secularity, social purposiveness, economic independence, and citizenship.[18] Indeed, the full birth of the modern nation-state would await the American Revolution (1776), the **French Revolution** (1789), and the **Industrial Revolution**.[19] Nonetheless, the Treaty of Westphalia did hasten this birthing process by upgrading the sovereign rights of some 300 smaller states. It is evident in the writings of both John Locke and Adam Smith (1723–1790) that each of them struggled in different ways to come to terms with this impact. Locke wrestled with representative government as well as executive functions; Smith struggled with the economic leverage of the modern state and its need to be less protective of its local industries as he advanced his ideas of the "wealth of nations" generated through the adoption of free trade principles at the expense of mercantilism and physiocracy. This is a story that must be addressed more fully in later chapters. Suffice it to say that the impact of the emerging nation-state was both immediate and long-lasting, and this shift in the structure of societies required new thoughts about the political role of people in a world that stood in magnitude between the Greek city-state and the Holy Roman Empire.

In sum, the argument for beginning our discussion of political ideologies in the seventeenth century is found in the convergence of the transformative forces of science, religion, and the nation-state that dislodged European societies from their normal beliefs about themselves and their relation to the world around them.[20] It was in this context that John Locke found himself. With the occurrence in England of the Civil War (1642–1651), the end of absolutism under James II and the Glorious Revolution (1688), and the victory of Parliamentary supremacy (1701), a new era of politics commences near the close of the seventeenth century. Although these events are not products of the scientific revolution, they are nonetheless manifestations of a new way of thinking that is consistent with and expressive of the open-mindedness of the empirical approach found at the heart of the scientific method. Politics was not immune to this approach, nor was political philosophy or ideology.

This study therefore begins with the first major political theorist to appear after the foundation of the Royal Society in 1660. Without any hesitation one can say that John Locke is this theorist. He created space for nascent **liberalism** as a political ideology that argues in favour of limitations of arbitrary government by representative government, and in favour of specified rights of the individual against governmental action. In *Two Treatises of Government*, Locke lays down the blueprint for a liberalism that would predate, by over a hundred years, movements that formed part of ideologies, such as nationalism, or ideologies such as conservatism and early socialism. **Nationalism**, however it may be defined, surfaced during the Revolutionary and Napoleonic periods of France.[21] **Conservatism** arose in the writings of Edmund Burke (1729–1797) in response to the French Revolution. And early **socialism** awaited the Industrial Revolution to make its presence felt. Not so with classical liberalism. It was carved out from scratch by John Locke much earlier than any of these ideologies.

Political Ideologies and Their Dangers

Before moving on to a description, analysis, and evaluation of modern political ideologies, one needs to draw attention to an incontrovertible fact: their tendency to be treated by their advocates as incorrigible and dogmatic. Attitudes of incorrigibility and dogmatism open up the possibility of cruelty. Marxism is not alone in this, and what is about to be said of it could, with little effort, be said at some point about other ideologies. That fact notwithstanding, one can add that at times the actions of those supporting ideologies is so exaggerated that they become illustrations of black humour.

One of the best of these illustrations is found in Aleksandr Solzhenitsyn's *The Gulag Archipelago*. Describing the political prison system in the Soviet Union under Joseph Stalin, Solzhenitsyn provides one vignette of that era. He describes a district Party conference underway in Moscow Province. At the conclusion of the conference, a tribute to Stalin was called for, which resulted in everyone standing to give "stormy applause." This applause, "rising to an ovation," continued for three, four, five, six minutes, with old people "panting from exhaustion." As Solzhenitsyn says, "It was becoming insufferably silly even to those who really adored Stalin." The question was, who would dare to be the first to stop applauding? In the event, after 11 minutes, the director of the paper factory assumed a business-like expression and seated himself. "To a man everyone else stopped dead and sat down." Solzhenitsyn then adds: "Where had the universal, uninhibited, indescribable enthusiasm gone?" Regrettably, claims Solzhenitsyn, that was how "they discovered who the independent people were." That night, the director of the paper factory was interrogated by agents of the KGB. After he signed the appropriate documents, "his interrogator reminded him: Don't ever be the first to stop applauding."[22]

That there is something bizarre, perverse, and pathetic in the characters and situation drawn from the pages of *The Gulag Archipelago* cannot be doubted. That it is alleged to have happened under the former Soviet Marxist regime is not the point. Rather, the point is that it illustrates the kinds of social pathologies to which political ideologies can easily give rise. No one in the study of this subject area should go gently into its dark night. Accordingly, the maxim should be the following: the best way to be forearmed is to be forewarned. Implementing this maxim necessitates an understanding of political ideologies.

2 Classical Liberalism

And it has been an article of faith in this country [the United States] that a rising tide lifts all boats.
— Paul Krugman, "For Richer" (2002: 67)

Learning Objectives

- To understand the role of the rights of life, liberty, and possessions in classical liberalism.
- To appreciate the explanatory role of the theory of the invisible hand in classical liberalism.
- To appreciate the role of reason in shaping the morality of classical liberalism.

Three figures in the development of **classical liberalism** are the Englishman John Locke (1632–1704), the Scot Adam Smith (1723–1790), and the German Immanuel Kant (1724–1804). We may summarize their contributions as follows:

- Locke develops a political philosophy that encompasses such wide-ranging themes as the state of nature, civil society, the social contract, rights of man, majoritarianism, and justifications for rebellion.
- Smith develops an economic perspective that focuses on free trade, the abolition of monopolies, man's motivation, the division of labour, the notion of money, mercantilism, physiocracy, and justice. Lingering just below the surface of these economic notions is the notion of inventiveness, generally of machines, but one rich enough to capture inventiveness associated with new technologies. Hence Smith's economic perspective is rich enough to capture the entrepreneurial (innovative) spirit of Meg Whitman and eBay, Steve Jobs and Apple computers, Larry Page and Google, and Richard Branson and Virgin Atlantic Airways.[1]
- Kant develops a moral philosophy centred on the categorical imperative and the ideals of freedom, equality, and autonomy. All of these ideas play a role in his affirmation of what he calls Enlightenment.

Though they are products of different generations, Locke, Smith, and Kant together establish a clear ideological position: classical liberalism.

Classical liberalism sets the stage in the seventeenth century for political discussions turning on institutional controls on arbitrary government and the **rights** of individuals. This ideology triggers a backlash in the form of conservatism in the eighteenth century by those wishing to preserve established institutions and practices threatened by the ideas of classical liberalism. Finally, this ideology, when coupled with the effects of the Industrial Revolution, gives birth to new problems in the nineteenth century: the class struggle, exploitation, and alienation to which Marxists, reform liberals, and democratic socialists react. What classical liberalism unleashes in the seventeenth and eighteenth centuries is a set of ideas, some of which are ideals, ranging from **representative democracy**, to human rights, to economic freedoms, and finally to constitutional polity.

As stated in the preceding chapter, the emergence of the modern state, beginning in 1450 and culminating in the seventeenth century at the conclusion of the Thirty Years' War, created a new political arrangement with the erosion of the power of the papacy and of the Holy Roman Empire. With this new arrangement came demands on the state at the domestic level.[2] An emerging question that needed to be addressed was the legitimacy of those who governed. Among modern ideologies, thereby excluding absolutism, classical liberalism was the first to address this question, and it did so domestically, initially in Britain and then in Europe, with considerable success. The challenge to clerical authority in general, and not just the papacy, meant a slow but perceptible historical drift towards a consideration of liberty as a right, at least in the field of religion, then of the **equality** of this liberty. This equality carried with it the implication that no person could claim "natural authority" over another.[3] And this in turn set the stage for the notion of the social contract as a new foundation for authority and legitimacy.

The **social contract**, as first introduced by Thomas Hobbes and then made use of by John Locke, turned out to be the philosophical undergirding of the evolving legal framework of **constitutionalism**. What classical liberalism introduced, conceptually and then practically, was constitutionalism, which over time came to comprise the following:

i. the limitation of government powers and arbitrary rule;
ii. the definition of law through written law, conventions, or common law;
iii. the recognition of the constitution as the supreme law; and
iv. the compliance with the constitution.[4]

Constitutionalism did not ride into Europe on the back of industrialization[5] but on the back of Locke and his successors. In so doing it brought with it principles of majoritarianism and representative government as fundamental aspects of the supreme law or constitution. But an understanding of the resilience and capaciousness of classical liberalism, and how it addressed the demands of the new political arrangement, can only be realized by a serious study of its founders, Locke, Smith, and Kant.

As we shall see in succeeding chapters, constitutionalism, the rule of law, and affirmation of what were believed to be universal principles by classical liberals have come under severe attack in recent years, in part from Chinese authoritarianism and Russian revanchism and dictatorship and in part from the rise of radical Islam.[6] There is a sense in China, Russia, Islamic states, and even Brazil that talk in the West about the rule of

> **Central Beliefs of Classical Liberalism**
>
> - Human nature is rational, self-interested, and acquisitive.
> - The origin of the state is the social contract.
> - Liberty as an ideal is the absence of government intervention.
> - The end of government is equivalent to the role of the night watchman.
> - Economic organization, at its best, is laissez-faire in nature.
> - The rights of humans are the rights to life, liberty, and property.

law and universalism is "laced with hypocrisy," decadence, and self-interest.[7] Others have maintained that "[b]road fissures have appeared in Western democracies themselves, further contributing to questions about the universality of liberal democracy."[8] In our study of the great contributions of Locke, Smith, and Kant, it is worth bearing in mind these most recent challenges to the influential ideas they advocate.

John Locke

In his chapter entitled "Of Slavery," in the *Second Treatise of Government*, John Locke distinguishes between the "natural liberty of man" and "the liberty of man in society."[9] The natural liberty of man consists in man being "free from any superior power on earth, and not to be under the will or legislative authority of man, but to have only the law of nature for his rule."[10] But Locke adds more colour to his initial description of the state of nature. Later in the *Second Treatise of Government*, he says that there are things lacking, wanting, in such a state: first, a settled and known law, received as the standard of right and wrong; second, a known and indifferent judge, with authority to resolve disputes according to established law; and third, the power to execute the judge's sentence when right. Further, Locke adds that in a pre-civil society man has two powers: first, the power to do what is fit for his own and others' preservation within the bounds of the law of nature; and second, the power to punish crimes committed contrary to the law.[11]

The Liberty of Human Beings in the State of Nature and in Civil Society

Locke provides a contrast between the liberty of human beings in a state of nature and the liberty of human beings in society. In a **state of nature**, persons are "under no other legislative power but that established by consent in the commonwealth, nor under the dominion of any will or restraint of any law but what that legislature shall enact according to the trust put in it."[12] Natural liberty is enjoyed in a state of nature—which, as it turns out, is not thought by Locke to be solitary, poor, nasty, brutish, and short, as it is thought to be by Hobbes.[13] Rather, the state of nature is a condition in which humans reside when there is no common judge to protect their rights of life, liberty, and possessions.[14] Locke makes clear that this state of nature is not to be confused with a state of war, as it is by Hobbes, though Locke readily admits that a state of nature—that is, a condition in which no constitutional power can be appealed to for the purpose of settling disputes—can degenerate into a state of war.

In **civil society**, by contrast, there is an appeal to a common power, fully constitutional, for the purpose of settling disputes. This civil state, the state of human beings living in society, can, like the state of nature, degenerate into a state of war. A state of war for Locke is "force without right upon a man's person . . . both where there is and is not a common judge."[15] According to Locke, then, the state of nature is logically distinct from the state of humans living in society, hereinafter called civil society, and the state of war is a condition into which each of these can degenerate. In a state of nature, people can harm others and invade their rights, and thereby declare war on them. So, too, in a civil society, people can invade the rights of others and by so doing put themselves in state of war with those individuals. In the latter case, Locke knew, with Hobbes, that if this violation were to occur on a widespread scale, the result would be civil war.[16]

Early on in the *Second Treatise*, Locke maintains that the state of nature has a law of nature. According to Locke, this law of nature obliges everyone—that is, it obligates everyone to abide by it. Moreover, in Locke's view, *reason* is this law of nature, and it teaches that no person ought to harm another, whether in life, health, or possessions, all of these being equal and independent.[17] Like the Stoics of ancient times, Locke equates this law with reason itself, and then goes on to focus on particular areas of one's life that ought to be respected. It soon becomes evident, however, that Locke wishes not only to speak of obligations that others have to fellow members of the state of nature, but also of rights or entitlements of members of the state of nature to a particular kind of treatment. The conception of rights that Locke works with here is a strong sense of entitlement—something to which all humans are entitled, and governments are obligated to protect. These rights comprise the right to life, the right to liberty, and the right to estates (possessions). Locke thinks of life, liberty, and estates under the general name of **property**. He says, much later in the *Second Treatise*, that "[t]he great and chief end, therefore, of men's uniting into commonwealths and putting themselves under government is the preservation of their property."[18] Clearly, Locke wishes to sweep three rights into one collective right to property, which government is obliged to protect. Constructs like that of the state of nature and civil society comprise a duality of ideas that help to contextualize this right (within which lie three distinct rights). It is to the relation between the aforementioned rights and the ideas of a state of nature and of a civil society that attention now turns.

Though Locke does not use the notion of a steady state in his political thought, the notion can serve a useful role in clarifying what he wishes to say. The state of nature does not function as a steady state; rather, it is much like a radioactive particle subject to decay. But unlike Hobbes, who holds that the state of nature is subject to decay owing to its being a state of war, Locke holds that the state of nature has within it certain *inconveniences*, which include the unreasonableness of humans being judges in their own case, humans' partiality, and humans' propensity to carry punishment too far. The upshot of all this is "confusion" and "disorder," and these, to return to the earlier analogy, produce a condition in which the radioactive state of nature is subject to decay.

Locke says that the "proper remedy" for this unstable situation is civil government, established "by their own consent,"[19] meaning by the consent of those in the state of nature. When Locke speaks here of the proper remedy for this situation, he means a remedy that is rationally defensible, one that is justifiable, as reflected in his general deference to what is "intelligible and plain to a *rational* creature" (emphasis added). Locke's veneration, when not heaped on God, is saved for reason, and so it is here. The rational or reasonable remedy for persons and their condition in a state of nature is for them to extricate themselves from it and move into a civil society by common consent. In effect, Locke says that in the event that persons were in a state of nature, it would be rational for them to leave it. Usually the reasons given by Locke for leaving the state of nature turn on inconveniences, but occasionally he lapses and says that "one great reason for putting themselves into society and quitting the state of nature" is "to avoid this state of war."[20] Though Locke frees himself of Hobbes's view of the state of nature, he is still haunted by it.

Nozick's Thought Experiment and the State of Nature

In outlining the transition from a state of nature to civil society, Locke provides only sketchy details. However, the Harvard philosopher Robert Nozick provides a more updated version of Locke's story. Nozick attempts to provide reasons for a person abandoning the state of nature, given that she is rational.[21] He believes that someone, faced with the difficulties unearthed by Locke, might very well join groups called **protective associations**, associations that also have inconveniences: the fact that everyone is on call, and the fact that any member, regardless of the frequency or time of day, may request help from the association. In the thought experiment provided by Nozick, one is only a hop, skip, and jump away from a dominant protective association. **Dominant protective associations** are those that prevail over other associations in protecting the interests and rights of those who are members of them. With suitable enrichment, the dominant protective association comes to have a monopoly on the use of force, and protects the rights and interests of all those persons within a specified territory. And behold, the state! Or at least, the minimal version of it, the **night watchman** state.

This version of a **state** has the advantage of conforming to current definitions of states in international law. Antonio Cassese has marked the general characteristics of states by saying that they include (i) a central structure capable of exercising effective control over a human community in a given territory, and (ii) a territory that does not belong to any other sovereign state.[22] The gap between Nozick's plausible interpretation of Locke's view of civil or political society and Cassese's view of the state is insignificant. Both views emphasize the notion of effective control over a given inhabited territory. And central to this control, especially in Locke's case, is the establishment of executive power that adjudicates the conflict inevitably arising in civil society.[23] In a state of nature, however, there is no common judge to adjudicate conflict, while in a political society there is. Locke never loses sight of the integral role played by conflict in politics.[24]

One of the attractions of Nozick's thought experiment is that it makes clear a defensible reading of Locke. This reading interprets Locke as providing a *justification* rather than an historical *explanation* of civil society and the state. Developing Nozick's ideas, one can say that once protective associations begin to establish themselves, the winnowing process of selecting out for the biggest and strongest will almost automatically ensue. A rational agent cannot afford the luxury of being left out of a protective association of some kind, and the association of choice will probably be the one most likely to win out over the rest. Rational agents will join such associations and will wish to see their associations made secure from the threats of others; failing this, they will join these other more successful associations.

The Right to Property

The rights protected by this newly emergent civil society or state are the right to life, the right to liberty, and the right to property. Locke does not shed much light on the first of these two, but he does have substantial things to say about the institution of property, by which he means more specifically "possession."[25] In his chapter "On Property," Locke lays down three criteria for the justifiable appropriation of property (possessions), though he fails to make clear whether these criteria function as necessary or sufficient conditions. The first of these is the labour limitation, the second the spoilage limitation, and the third the sufficiency limitation.[26] Property in the strictest sense starts with the ownership one has of one's body, and then expands outward to include that with which one mixes one's labour. This appropriate process can go on to include everything one can make use of, i.e., use before it spoils. Locke caps off this appropriation process by saying that one can appropriate in this manner because "there [is] still enough and as good left."[27] What he has in mind with respect to the third criterion is that appropriation can occur because the riches of the world are, practically speaking, inexhaustible.

It would seem from this that Locke refines his understanding of justifiable ownership as he works his way through the chapter. If this is true, then he could plausibly be construed as saying the three criteria function individually as necessary conditions, and function collectively as sufficient conditions for justifiable ownership. It is against this background that Locke says, "Thus in the beginning all the world was America, and more so than that is now . . . ."[28] Presumably, for Locke, "America" stood as a metaphor for a cornucopia of limitless opportunities for humans to advance themselves, provided they were industrious and rational.[29]

Locke no sooner lays down the above-mentioned restrictions on justifiable appropriation than he takes steps to transcend them. The introduction of money has the effect of endorsing unequal appropriation, for with money comes the introduction of something that does not spoil: money makes possible the inequality of property. Thus, the spoilage limitation is transcended. Money also facilitates, though Locke does not say this, the wage-labour system of economics, i.e., the alienation of one's labour for wage. Thus, by implication, the labour limitation is transcended. And finally, it creates the possibilities of a commercial economy, which creates markets for produce from previously unproductive land. And thus the sufficiency limitation is transcended.

But more to the point, the introduction of money creates the opportunity for Locke to abandon the **labour theory of value**, which claims that the value of manufactured goods is a function of labour time used to produce them. It creates an opportunity for Locke to replace the labour theory with the consent theory of value, which claims that value of goods is determined by the market. Within a few pages, Locke moves from saying "for it is labour indeed that put the difference of value on everything"[30] to saying "[g]old and silver . . . has its value from the consent of men, whereof labour yet makes, in great part, the measure."[31]

Has Locke abandoned the labour theory of value? It is difficult to tell. One is tempted to say that he has, but that he does not know he has. Whatever the truth here, it is clear that Locke is on the cusp of articulating the market theory of value: things have the value they fetch in the marketplace. Indeed, Locke even goes so far as to say that "[g]old, silver, and diamonds are things that *fancy* and agreement has put value on" (emphasis added).[32] He has come about as close to advancing the market theory of value as one could come without actually spelling it out.

With this proto-version of the market theory of value in his pocket, Locke can easily advance a defence of inequality, and hence he concludes that, with the introduction of money, "[I]t is plain that men have agreed to a disproportionate and unequal possession of the earth, they having, by a tacit and voluntary consent, found out a way how a man may fairly possess more land than he himself can use the product of."[33] Here Locke openly embraces inegalitarianism. Adam Smith, for his part, thinks that these comments led Locke to embrace not just inegalitarianism but mercantilism, the school of thought claiming that the wealth of a nation is measured by its gold and silver. As Smith says of Locke, "Gold and silver, therefore, are, according to him, the most solid and substantial part of the moveable wealth of a nation, and to multiply those metals ought, he thinks, upon that account, to be the greatest object of its political economy."[34]

The Social Compact and Majoritarianism

The foregoing provides one construct in Locke's political ideology. This construct makes use of the notions of a state of nature and of a civil society, together with its connection to the institution of property. No mention has been made of another of Locke's constructs, namely that of social agreement, an idea Hobbes canvasses in *Leviathan* when he discusses the social contract.

Under Locke's scheme, the body politic is formed when every human consents to establish a political association and submits to the "determination of the majority."[35] Locke really proposes an agreement that is unanimously endorsed but that has at its core the principle of majoritarianism. He sees that an agreement with a core principle of unanimity would be wholly impracticable.[36] This follows, thinks Locke, once it is understood what variety of circumstances might keep members of the body politic from being present at the "public assembly" (e.g., infirmities, health, business), and once it is understood what variety of opinions and interests would make unanimous agreement impossible.[37] So unanimity is out and majoritarianism is in. Once Locke admits the principle of majoritarianism, the rights he affirms become defeasible rights, that is, rights that can be overruled by majoritarian interests.

Further refinement of our understanding of majoritarianism is required. Who actually comprises the majority? To answer this question requires backtracking to the notion of unanimity, and this in turn requires clarification of the notion of consent—specifically, what it takes for a sufficient declaration of consent.[38] Locke then distinguishes between express and tacit consent. Express consent occurs when a declaration of a person entering society is made by that person, and tacit consent occurs when no such declaration is made but the person enjoys the protection of the government. Of the former, he says, "nobody doubts but an express consent, of any man entering into society, makes him a perfect member of society, a subject of that government."[39] In saying that such a consent makes a human being a perfect member of society, Locke is saying that there is nothing deficient with his membership. Of the latter, tacit consent, Locke says that it is attributable to anyone who "hath possessions or enjoyment of any part of the dominions of any government."[40] Such individuals must submit to the laws of the government of that territory, but this does not make "a man a member of that society."[41] Such individuals are like the denizens of Aristotle's polis: they are not perfect members of that society. Clearly, these individuals are not participants in shaping a unanimous agreement in the formation of the body politic. These individuals stand at the edge of the formation of the civil society, in contrast to the unanimous body that gives its express consent and from which the majority is drawn. Only those who give express consent, i.e., those who are perfect members of society, can be part of any majority.

Locke is quite clear in saying that those who enjoy the privileges and protection of government do not thereby become "subjects or members of that commonwealth."[42] It seems that one only becomes a member (i.e., a perfect member) of society by express consent, and by affirming with others unanimously that majoritarianism is the decision-making principle of those who have, as it were, signed up for membership. So the majority is drawn from the group that has registered unanimity. And what group is it? It is a group that has the protection of its property as the primary aim. In Locke's case, the principle of majoritarianism leads to the institution of property. The Canadian political theorist C.B. Macpherson has captured this point very nicely in saying that "[t]here is no conflict between Locke's two assertions of majority rule and property right, inasmuch as Locke assumed that only those with property were full members of society and so of the majority."[43]

Rebellion

The final construct in Locke's classical liberalism is his theory of rebellion against government. Locke provides two broad reasons to justify rebellion: unconstitutional alteration of the legislature, and a breach of trust on the part of the prince or legislature. He analyzes the first of these more fully than he does the second, saying that the legislature can be altered (unconstitutionally) when the arbitrary will of the prince is set up in place of the will of the legislature, when the prince hinders the legislature from assembling or from acting freely, when the electoral process is altered, when the people are delivered into subjection, and finally, when the supreme executive abandons its charge and effectively reduces all to a state of anarchy. Locke's analysis of the second general reason for rebellion against government reduces to his charge that a breach of trust results when the legislature attempts to invade the property of the subject. The reasons proffered by Locke here are self-explanatory. He argues for rebellion and the overthrow of government, not society, when the rule of law is set aside by the arbitrary power or by the violation of manner and form restrictions on the legislature. Against the charge that his theory of rebellion "lays a ferment for frequent rebellion," Locke says three things. First, his theory will not make this any more likely than any other theory; second, under his theory revolutions will happen only after a "long train of abuses . . . make the design visible to the people"; and third, his theory offers a "fence" against rebellion, for rulers will be reluctant to violate the constitution when they are faced with the prospect of revolution from those who are justifiably disgruntled.[44]

In effect, Locke offers a theory of rebellion premised on serious constitutional violations, and as such it is designed to appeal to rational creatures living under the rule of law. In the end, people cannot be blamed if they "have the sense of rational creatures and can think of things no otherwise than as they find and feel them."[45]

What Locke offers in his political ideology is a set of constructs aimed at casting light upon discernible forces that help to shape the political life of humans. He thinks critically of the state of nature, the anarchic condition in which persons live prior to the establishment of government and political society. He then puts forth his ideas on why human beings would decide to leave this condition of anarchy, the condition Hobbes feared so much. His reasons for leaving the state of nature centre on inconveniences. Acknowledging the existence of the rights to life, liberty, and possessions, Locke moves by covenant or agreement to a political society in which the fundamental principle is majoritarian rule. Along the way, and with the introduction of money, he affirms what might be called a proto-market theory of value and inegalitarianism, having apparently abandoned the labour theory of value. Finally, Locke offers a theory of rebellion, almost as an insurance policy for his theory of the social contract and constitutionalism. This is Locke's classical liberalism.

Adam Smith

The political ideas of John Locke fell on fertile soil in the last decade of the seventeenth century and during the entire eighteenth century in England. With the abandonment of absolutism both in theory and in practice, the emerging commercial class came to express the very ideas advanced by Locke. But it is not until 1776, with the publication of Adam Smith's *An Inquiry into the Nature and Causes of the Wealth of Nations*,[46] that the case is made unequivocally for free trade. Once it is made, the idea of **laissez-faire** and its corollary, the theory of comparative advantage, together with the theory of the invisible hand, are etched in the limestone cliffs of classical liberalism.

While the notions of free trade, comparative advantage, and the theory of the invisible hand stand at the centre of Smith's famous work, other notions are also located there. Four of these are: the notion of humans being driven to better their condition, the notion of the division of labour, the notion of money, and the dangers of religious sectarianism. A brief word on each of these is in order.

Four Preliminary Notions

Both in *The Theory of Moral Sentiments* and in *The Wealth of Nations*, Smith argues that humans strive ceaselessly to better their condition, and that this is fundamental to their life.[47] He says in *The Wealth of Nations*, by way of explaining why people save, that saving arises "from the desire of bettering our condition, a desire which, though generally calm and dispassionate, comes with us from the womb, and never leaves us till we go into the grave."[48] He adds to this in a resounding way, saying, "The uniform, constant, and uninterrupted effort of every man to better his condition, *the principle from which publick and national, as well as private opulence is originally derived*, is frequently powerful enough to maintain the natural progress of things toward improvement"[49] (emphasis added). And in *The Theory of Moral Sentiments*, Smith claims that humans are driven to better their own condition, and that, though this motivation is fundamental to their life, the drive is surrounded by the false belief—bordering on deception—that happiness will be achieved if they simply reach those things desired.[50] Unquestionably, Smith sees the wealth of nations as being based on the nature of humans, a nature defined by its restless desire for bettering its condition.

The second notion is the **division of labour**, and Smith presents the first hard-headed defence of it. In an example that is now well known, Smith argues that 10 persons could make 48,000 pins if they were to divide the labour, whereas one person working alone could make between one and 20. According to Smith, the increase in the quantity of work, i.e., the productivity increase, arises from the division of labour. The explanation for this in turn is threefold: the increase in the dexterity of each workman, the saving of time in passing from one kind of work to another, and, finally, the invention of a greater number of machines.[51]

The third notion, which is preliminary to a solid understanding of Smith, is the institution of money. Money is for Smith, as Rothschild and Sen say, "the universal instrument of commerce."[52] Smith has a marked preference for gold and silver money, as distinct from paper money with its Daedalian wings, and compares this hard currency to a highway when he says, "The gold and silver money which circulates in any country may very properly be compared to a highway, which, while it circulates and carries to market all the grass and corn of the country, produces itself not a single pile of either."[53] He acknowledges at the same time the importance of the labour theory of value, but denies that labour is that by which the value of commodities is commonly estimated.[54]

The fourth notion facilitating a better understanding of Smith is his recognition of the dangers associated with religious sects. He is particularly concerned with the unsocial nature of such sects, and goes on to propose two remedies for what is "unsocial or disagreeably rigorous in the morals of all the little sects into which the country [is] divided."[55] His first remedy for these maladies is the study of philosophy and the study of science. Of the latter he says, "Science is the great antidote to the poison of enthusiasm and superstition."[56] His second remedy, interestingly, is "the frequency and gaiety of publick diversions."[57] Public diversions, in the form of painting, poetry, music, and dancing, as well as "all sorts of dramatic representations," would dissipate all of the melancholy and gloomy feeling that engenders superstition and enthusiasm. As he concludes, "Publick diversions have always been the objects of dread and hatred, to all the fanatical promoters of those popular frenzies."[58]

It seems that at least one modern writer—Gore Vidal—has picked up on part of what Smith says here by recognizing the importance of entertainment being provided by leaders. He puts in the mouth of Julian the Apostate, the fourth-century Roman emperor, the following words: "I celebrated my fifth year as Caesar . . . I thought it wise to make a great event of this occasion. It is well known that I detest what goes on in hippodromes, whether games, fighting or the slaughter of animals. But there are certain things one must do in high places and the giving of games is one of the most important. If the games are a success, one enjoys the popularity of the mob. If not, not. It is as simple as that."[59] Evidently this notion of Smith's is still very much alive in contemporary historical novels. We are now in a position to look at the major themes running through his monumental treatise, *An Inquiry into the Nature and Causes of the Wealth of Nations*.

Central Notions: Freedom of Trade, the Invisible Hand, and Comparative Advantage

Smith turns to the subject of "Restraint upon the Importation from Foreign Countries of such Goods as can be Produced at Home." He asserts, without qualification and as a matter of fact, that "[e]very individual is continually exerting himself to find out the most advantageous employment for whatever capital he can command. It is his own advantage, indeed, and not that of the society, which he has in view."[60] What Smith offers here is a descriptive account of human motivation. He does not offer, protests notwithstanding, a normative account of human motivation.[61] Once assuring the reader of the self-interested nature of man's motivation, Smith continues by arguing in support of a convergence between self-interest and society's interest as whole.[62] "But the study of his own advantage naturally, or rather necessarily leads him to prefer that employment which is most advantageous to the society."[63] Whether the world is so happily arranged that self-interest and other interests dovetail is not the subject of the present inquiry, but suffice it to say that this is the very subject of the inquiry that reform liberals such as John Maynard Keynes launch 150 years later. This is a topic to be discussed in a later chapter.

At this juncture Smith introduces his **invisible hand** explanation. Intending only his own gain, the investor "promotes an end which was no part of his intention," namely, the interest or well-being of society.[64] The investor seems led by an invisible hand to promote society's well-being. In the event, the good that society experiences arises as the unintended consequence of a self-interested act. Succinctly, one could say: the well-being of society seems something aimed at when it is not. Self-interest, for Smith, turns out to be an engine for wealth in a nation. Let loose in a world of competition, that is, in a world in which monopolies are frowned upon, self-interest can help improve the fortunes of nations better than any other alternative. Regulation that facilitates the creation of monopoly must, he thinks, "in almost all cases, be either a useless or a hurtful regulation."[65] And regulations encouraging the acquisition of particular manufacturing in a nation have the effect of diminishing revenue. This gratuitous loss of capital Smith frowns upon. In place of regulations, which tend to introduce some degree of disorder into a state,[66] Smith argues for the use by countries of their natural advantages. This has come to be known as the principle of **comparative advantage**. Smith thinks nations should play on their strengths. If western Canada has an abundance of softwood lumber, it should play on this strength, while if Scotland has an adverse climate for the growing of grapes, it should not play on this economic weakness. Such, at least, is the consequence of this principle.

Smith works and reworks all of the foregoing ideas—including those of self-interest, public interest, the invisible hand, and the principle of comparative advantage—for the purpose of showing the lack of utility in supporting restraints on the importation of foreign goods. What is needed is free trade, for regulations discouraging it will be either useless or hurtful because they will protect local industry that is not in need of protection or they will force higher prices than are necessary on the buyer.[67] For Smith the maxim is: employ your industry in such a way that you have an advantage over your neighbours.[68] And for Smith, this leads to free trade. Time and again in his chapter entitled "Restraints upon Importation," Smith argues forcefully in favour of "restoring the free importation of foreign goods" and "restoring free trade."[69] He does acknowledge, however, that "[t]o expect, indeed, that the freedom of trade should ever be entirely restored in Great Britain, is as absurd as to expect that Oceana or Utopia should ever be established."[70] Two things work against this ever being realized—the prejudices of the public and the private interests of many individuals.

Mercantilism

In his effort to advocate the new free trade system, Smith takes aim at **mercantilism**. It should be noted that, notwithstanding other similarities between himself and John Locke, including an affirmation of the rule of law and of various rights, Smith distances himself from Locke's mercantilism. Mercantilism, Smith maintains, is the economic system that claims: (i) the wealth of a nation consists in gold and silver, and

(ii) those precious metals could be brought into a country that lacked mines only by balancing trade or by exporting more than was imported.[71] Hence, thinks Smith, the engines for enriching the country are, under mercantilism, restraints on importation and encouragements to exportation. Restraints are themselves subdivided, Smith argues, into (i) restraints on the importation of foreign goods that could be produced at home, and (ii) restraints on any goods originating in countries with which one had a negative balance of trade.[72] Exportation, on the other hand, is encouraged by drawbacks, bounties, advantageous treaties, and the establishment of colonies.[73] Smith takes issue with all of this.

The exact arguments Smith brings to bear against mercantilism do not need to be explored here, except to say that he attacks the principles that animated colonization. What motivates the establishment of colonies by countries such as Spain, France, Britain, and Portugal are, quite simply, gold and silver. But these are chimerical views. The wealth of nations, asserts Smith, is not founded on this mercantile dream, but on the progress of population and improvement.[74] It is not wisdom that motivates colonization, but folly and injustice.[75] Smith encourages the abandonment of monopolies, which form the backbone of this mercantile policy.[76] In its place he substitutes economic liberation, for "[t]o prohibit a great people . . . from making all that they can of every produce, or from employing their stock and industry in the way that they judge most advantageous to themselves, is a manifest violation of the sacred *rights* of mankind"[77] (emphasis added).

That Smith disagrees with Locke over the theory of mercantilism, there can be no denying. But this should not obscure what they hold in common: a passion for the rule of law, a respect for fundamental rights (including the right to life, liberty, and possessions),[78] and an affirmation of the virtues of industry and reason. There may be a temptation to think of Smith as the economist and Locke as the political and moral theorist. But this is a temptation to which one should not give way. Locke, after all, thinks of the economic institution of property as the primary objective of government, and Smith, one should recall, as Professor of Moral Philosophy at the University of Glasgow up until 1763, thinks of moral matters in an economic setting. Both of these great minds wrestle with economic ideas in a moral and political way.

That political power includes among the highest duties of the sovereign not only "defense of the commonwealth from foreign injury" but also the "protection of every member of society from the injustice or oppression of every other member of it" is a belief held by both Locke and Smith.[79] Moreover, Locke affirms the appropriation process by claiming that the world belongs to the "rational and industrious,"[80] while Smith "seeks to detoxify the pursuit of wealth and to provide a limited defense against Greek and Christian accusations that it destroys moderation, that it destroys martial spirit and thus jeopardizes liberty."[81] Finally, as seen above, both Locke and Smith subscribe at least initially to a labour theory of value that is slowly displaced by a quasi-market theory of value, value thus coming to depend upon the estimations of buyers. This shows the extent of the convergence of their political ideologies. Nor is this convergence deflected by Locke's inegalitarianism and Smith's belief in a commercial society that, through the division of labour, produces specialization and national opulence in which the worker shares. There is plenty of room in Smith's thinking for landlords, workers, and capitalists to get their just desserts without each of them getting the same thing. There is, therefore, no real deflection from convergence here.

Political Economy or Physiocracy

Near the conclusion of Book IV of *The Wealth of Nations* Adam Smith discusses an economic system, **physiocracy**, which he thinks is the "nearest approximation to the truth that has yet been published upon the subject of political economy."[82] While Smith ultimately rejects the theory behind this system, he was sufficiently impressed with it to consider dedicating his *Wealth of Nations* to its founder, François Quesnay.[83] As noted by Smith, the followers of this French physician were so taken with his ideas that one of the more "diligent" and "respectable" among them claimed that Quesnay's Economical Table was one of "three great inventions which have principally given stability to political societies."[84] With all of this in mind, Smith makes the following assertion regarding physiocracy: this system is correct in maintaining that the wealth of nations consists in the "consumable goods actually produced by the labour of that society," but is incorrect in believing that "the labour which is employed upon the land [is] the only productive labour."[85] And Smith continues by claiming that the capital error of physiocracy is its representation of artificers, manufacturers, and merchants as unproductive.[86] He believes that the physiocrats err in emphasizing agriculture at the expense of manufacturing. They bend the rod too far in the direction of agriculture and too far away from the activity carried on by inhabitants of towns.

Having presented his views on physiocracy, Smith ends this chapter with a drum roll in favour of liberalism. According to Smith, physiocracy, by representing "perfect liberty" as the only means of greatest possible production, turns out to be a doctrine that is both just and liberal. Nonetheless, Smith sees physiocracy and mercantilism, on their own, as subversive of the wealth of nations. In their place stands the "simple system of natural liberty" in which the sovereign has only three duties: (i) the duty to protect society from external assault; (ii) the duty to protect each member from injustices carried out by other members of the society; and (iii) the duty to erect and maintain public institutions that individuals in society cannot afford to erect.[87] This is Smith's liberalism: an economic system of equality, liberty, and **justice**.[88] It is a system of equality and justice, but most importantly of liberty considered as a "sacred right," at least in the economic domain. For this reason he asserts, "To prohibit a great people . . . from making all that they can of every part of their produce . . . is a manifest violation of the most sacred rights of mankind."[89] This comes as close as anything to Smith's credo or confession of faith in liberalism.

Immanuel Kant

There is no doubting the brilliance of the German Enlightenment philosopher Immanuel Kant. An outstanding student, he entered the University of Königsberg where, in 1755, he was granted permission to lecture as *Magister legens* or *Privatdozent*.[90] In that same year he established himself as both a scholar and scientist with the publication of the *General History of Nature and Theory of the Heavens*. The genius of his writings in this field was later vindicated by the similarity his account of the origin of the universe bore to that offered later by the famous French physicist Pierre-Simon Laplace. His emergence as a philosopher to be reckoned with did not occur until 1781, when he published the *Critique of Pure Reason*. He continued to write prolifically in the field of philosophy until his death in 1804, writing on topics as far ranging as epistemology, metaphysics, religion, morals, and, to a lesser extent, politics. Nonetheless, Kant's contribution to classical liberal thinking is significant, and his ideas on **freedom** helped to confront the notion of authority in a way in which Locke's ideas did not.

Kant's political contributions turned largely on his interest in finding philosophical principles on which a lasting world peace could be based, on which representative constitutional government could be vindicated, and on which respect for political rights could be guaranteed. His interests and thoughts in these areas proved influential but never terribly seminal in subsequent thinking. These ideas were worked out in better ways by others. Kant's political contribution was twofold: first, as an inspiration to the Enlightenment and the subsequent American and French Revolutions, and second, in cementing into the philosophic vocabulary of liberalism the notions of freedom, equality, and independence. A few words need to be said on each of these.

What Is Enlightenment?

In an essay by the same name, Kant answers the question posed above: what is **enlightenment**? His answer is: "Enlightenment is man's release from his self-incurred tutelage. Tutelage is man's inability to make use of his understanding without direction from another. Self-incurred is this tutelage when its cause lies not in lack of reason but in lack of resolution and courage to use it without direction from another."[91] What Kant advocates is freedom of reason in the arts and sciences that eventually results in freedom of action in the public domain. People are thus able to voice their opinions on the ways to draw up laws for the society of which they are a part. This seems to Kant to be the desirable outcome of enlightenment. But it is important to note here that the role of reason for Kant is not that role described by the sixteenth- and seventeenth-century rationalists (e.g., Descartes, Leibniz, and Spinoza). In other words, it is not the role of reason found in deduction and proof, but instead the role of reason found in "the model and patterns of contemporary natural science."[92] The underpinning of Kant's command, *sapere aude* (dare to know), is his confidence in natural science or natural philosophy, a philosophy that shows no inclination to laziness or indifferent acceptance. Kant challenges humanity to dare to know and confidently to make use of their reason in the realization of their freedom. It is for this reason that some have said, "Kant asserted the independence of the individual in the face of authority."[93]

From the foregoing it is easy to see that in the case of Kant, human freedom is "at the very core of his thought."[94] This notion of freedom of thought in the face of authority is fundamental to the Enlightenment[95] of which he was part. And the American and French Revolutions were facilitated, if not prepared for, by the very ideas of the Enlightenment. So there is a link, at least a loose causal link, between Kant's aspirations found under the rubric of his essay on enlightenment and these revolutions.

Freedom, Equality, and Independence

The fundamental moral principle is, for Kant, the categorical imperative: act in such a way that you always treat humanity, whether in your own person or in the person of another, never simply as a means, but always at the same time as an end.[96] When this principle is applied to law and politics in the form of a principle of right, it assumes the following formulation: every action which by itself or by its maxim enables the freedom of each individual's will to exist with the freedom of everyone else in accordance with a universal law is right.[97] In a state of nature, Kant thinks, along with Hobbes, human beings are in a state of war; however, in a state governed by the universal principle of right, the situation is quite different. In such a state, humanity exists in freedom, equality, and self-dependence. We have already addressed the issue of freedom in Kant's political thinking, so we shall now direct our attention to equality and independence.

While freedom is the first principal right of a citizen of the state, **equality** and autonomy are the second and third. According to Kant, if all individuals are free, they must of necessity be equal.[98] His reasoning in defence of this is simply that the freedom of individuals is "absolute and can only be universally and equally restricted by law."[99] Accordingly, individuals are equal before the law and therefore no exceptions can be made in the administration of the law, neither in defence of slavery nor in support of inferior status for some citizens. But it is important to note that, consistent with the classical liberal tradition already articulated by Locke and Smith, Kant only speaks of political and not economic equality, though he does acknowledge with Locke the right of people to own property. As for the principle of autonomy or self-dependence, Kant sees it as synonymous with the principle of freedom. This third principle affirms the right of citizens to participate in the government, at least indirectly through the franchise. But even here Kant is somewhat guarded, for in the end he extends the franchise only to active citizens or those who have real independence, and not to passive citizens such as women, servants, or employees.[100] All three principles of right—freedom, equality, and autonomy—Kant sees in the context of a social contract, an idea of reason (a regulative idea) that permits government to exercise the power of political action in order to encourage others to comply with the universal law.[101] Kant embeds these principles in a social contractarian tradition with an end to providing ample room for human dignity and moral capacity, both of which presuppose freedom.

Conclusion

Although they are writing about 80 years apart, both Locke and Smith contribute something distinct to classical liberalism. Kant, for his part, largely reaffirms their ideas, making them part of an ideological tradition. Locke contributes political insight, including the concepts of constitutionalism and majoritarianism, along with a defence of civil and political society as against a state of nature and anarchy. Smith, on the other hand, contributes economic insight, including the concepts of monopolies, colonies, division of labour, the invisible hand, comparative advantage, mercantilism, physiocracy, justice, and natural liberty. Given their respective proximity to the English Civil War and the unabated exploration of the New World, it is not surprising they have the perspective and orientation they do. Nonetheless, they provide Western thought with two sheets that can be riveted together into a single entity.

Both Locke and Smith affirm the importance of liberty,[102] equality, and justice. Smith even goes so far as to say that commerce can seldom flourish in the absence of confidence in the justice of government.[103] And he is critical if not contemptuous of the injustice of European governments in coveting the possession of the New World, whose "harmless natives, far from having ever injured the people of Europe, had received the first adventurers with every mark of kindness and hospitality."[104]

Kant picks up on the foregoing motifs and blends them into a rich tradition grounded in an affirmation of human progress and optimism about the future. Though sharing the ideals of liberty, equality, and justice, these thinkers share one tenet that binds them most firmly together, and that is the ideal of the freedom of the individual from the state. This notion of individual freedom is most energetically and imaginatively captured by Kant in his essay, "What Is Enlightenment?" It will fall to other writers to explore more deeply the notions embedded in this new ideology. Notable among these other writers are Jeremy Bentham, James Mill, and John Stuart Mill. But it is especially the last of these, John Stuart Mill, who mines the depths of one of the concepts highlighted by Locke, Smith, and Kant—namely, liberty. No one before Mill and no one since Mill has exposed the precious metals found in this notion as well as he does in his justly famous *On Liberty*. His contribution to the legacy of classical liberalism is substantial, but here it is simply acknowledged as the logical development of an ideology well sketched by Locke, Smith, and Kant.

How might one characterize the line of argument pursued by classical liberals? Clearly, the answer to this question must in part be given by saying that the locus of the argument never strays far from the notion of liberty, whether viewed as sacred or natural, political or economic. This may seem more apparent in the case of Locke and Smith than in the case of Kant, but it is true of him as well. With their respective ideas of liberty, each of these thinkers uses it to reach out and touch other notions such as equality under the law and proprietary rights. Common to all three thinkers is an adoption of the intrinsic value of freedom and an affirmation of the right that humans have to it. This is the key intuition of classical liberals, and it is this intuition that they use to construct their vision of a legitimate civil society.

Evaluation: The Strengths of Classical Liberalism

1. The overriding strength of classical liberalism, sometimes called classical **capitalism**,[105] is that it creates a wide berth for the liberty of the individual. This liberty is conceived broadly to include freedoms of religion, conscience, thought, expression, the press, and peaceful assembly and association, but it also extends to include freedom to engage in commercial activities. In most constitutional regimes, these rights have grown to become rights that trump legislative activity to the contrary. Locke, Smith, and Kant offer an ideology that provides ample room for individual initiative and commercial enterprise not unlike that envisaged by Mill. The result is an ideology that, when appropriated, affords considerable scope for individual growth (sometimes, enlightenment) and satisfaction, as well as scope for general economic prosperity. This seems to be borne out by the satisfaction individuals attain in capitalist societies, immersed as these individuals are in a state of general economic well-being.

2. Classical liberalism appropriately places an emphasis on the rule of law and constitutionalism. The replacement of absolutism by constitutionalism in Europe, beginning with Britain, clearly owes much to the force of classical liberalism. In effect, what this ideology offers is the rule of supreme law. This helps to curb the arbitrary will of government, not just in the area of human rights but also in the day-to-day activities of people. While Locke and Kant are perhaps more emphatic about this point than Smith, the latter also has a vivid concern with the "regular administration of justice" so that people come to feel secure in their possessions, have faith in contracts, and are confident about the payment of debts.[106]

3. The use of the notion of the social contract also has attractions. This is largely owing to the heuristic role it plays in explaining why a rational agent would join a protective association and how such an association would, perforce, through competition with other similar associations, strive to become a state. As will be seen later, a sensitive but forceful use of the social contract theory can function as the foundation of a formidable argument against anarchists. While it is true that among Locke, Smith, and Kant, only the first and last explicitly make use of the notion of a social contract, it should be pointed out that Smith does distinguish other animals from human animals by their propensity to truck, barter, and exchange one thing for another.[107] What stands at the base of all of this is contractual language: give me that which I want, and you shall have this which you want.[108] Smith recognizes the need on the part of man for co-operation and assistance of the great multitudes, "because man has almost the constant occasion for the help of his brethren."[109] He is therefore not far removed from the notion of the social contract.

Evaluation: The Weaknesses of Classical Liberalism

1. While the principle of division of labour has obvious advantages through increased productivity, it does have a real disadvantage: it engenders "gross ignorance and stupidity."[110] While Smith believes that the country labourer is a person of judgment, understanding, and discretion, the mechanic, by contrast, is a person incapable of judgment, courage, and sentiment. In other words, the mechanic stands at the crossroads of psychological mutilation.[111] The division of labour, thinks Smith, will in the case of the mechanical labourer be destructive of his well-being. As Smith says, "The torpor of his mind renders him, not only incapable of relishing or bearing a part in any rational conversation, but of conceiving any generous, noble, or tender sentiment, and consequently of forming any just judgement concerning many even of the ordinary duties of private life."[112]

   While it is true that Smith thinks the public, i.e., the government, ought to take it upon itself to educate these common people, whose minds have become corrupted and "mentally mutilated,"[113] the reality is that in countries in which classical liberalism has taken hold (in Europe, North America, New Zealand, and Australia), the effect has been quite different. The division of labour has created many jobs that are dull and monotonous and in which it is impossible for the worker to experience fulfillment or personal satisfaction. In a word, many workers—and now no longer only those acting as mechanical labourers—are alienated from their jobs. This is a subject on which Marx has a great deal to say. For the moment, we need only highlight as a troubling aspect of classical liberalism the fact that so many working people in capitalist societies—societies indulging in laissez-faire economics—find their jobs unrewarding. This is one of the first things a university student learns when taking on a summer job.

2. But it is not just alienation that is a negative consequence of classical liberalism. Another serious problem is vulnerability—especially the vulnerability of the worker. The two R's of rationalization and restructuring point this out. In the competitive environment of capitalism, in the environment of classical liberalism, workers are subject to downsizing and capitalist mobility. If profits are down, companies may decide to restructure,

resulting in job losses. If companies do not agree with government regulations pertaining to, say, pollution controls on pulp mills, the companies may decide to rationalize by moving "lock, stock, and barrel" to another, more friendly community. The result is job losses in one community and insecurity for the workers and their families. But not only are people and their employment, under such circumstances, made vulnerable. Clearly put at risk are any government policies that aim to protect the public interest at large, as, for example, pollution controls. And when these policies are put at risk, the public is put at risk. Just how damaging this can become to a classical liberal society will become evident in Chapter 12, which discusses environmentalism.

3. Notwithstanding Smith's opposition to monopolies, the fact remains that "enormous business corporations and conglomerates" dominate, if not control, many vital industries. Such conglomerates have resources and staying power that enable them to "squeeze out" smaller businesses. Indeed, many small businesses turn out to be very dependent on subcontractors to, or franchises provided by, these same enormous business interests.[114] "Large firms," says Peter Self, "have greater market power than small firms." Continuing, he notes that many small businesses are dependent on large companies.[115] This one can say with confidence, even though some dire predictions made in the nineteenth century by radical thinkers, critical of capitalism, have not come to pass. There does, therefore, remain a problem of monopoly or near monopoly control in many vital industries, a view affirmed by democratic socialists and environmentalists. In brief, the problem of domination or quasi-monopoly control is dysfunctional and results in diseconomies to classical liberal societies.

4. Classical liberalism fails to address the asymmetry of power not only between large conglomerates and smaller firms, but also between employers and workers. The asymmetry in power here goes to the heart of classical liberalism as viewed by Friedrich Hayek, a twentieth-century successor to Locke and Smith for the mantle of this ideology. Hayek's central claim is simply that markets are but a spontaneous, self-regulating system.[116] Clearly, an asymmetry exists between the bargaining positions of employers, especially large employers, and workers—a fact made evident by unequal share in profits. Smith is ever so aware of this asymmetry, in a way that Hayek seems not to be, but Smith does not take it to be a problem. According to Smith, between the two parties, masters and workmen, the former have the advantage in disputes owing to the fact that they are fewer in number and easier to organize and are not, unlike workmen, prohibited by law from organizing.[117] So Smith acknowledges the asymmetry but does not take it to be a problem. Hayek does not acknowledge the asymmetry, and therefore does not take it to be a problem. The claim here is that the asymmetry is a problem for all interpretations of classical liberalism, for it affects the initial liberty (spontaneity) of all bargaining agents. As a final point, it should be added that asymmetry is made evident by the inequality in the terms of trade between the manufacturing sector and the agricultural sector, as well as by the inequality in legal resources enjoyed by large conglomerates or businesses over small businesses or agricultural workers.[118]

5. Classical liberalism is inattentive to substantive justice. Supporters of this ideology, at least in Hayek's later neo-liberal version, admit that rewards in the marketplace

are not proportionate to what one merits or deserves.[119] Rather, these rewards seem to be a function of luck, inheritance, ability, and industry. The later neo-liberal view of Hayek and others, therefore, leaves little room for substantive justice, a form of justice that aims to arrive at a more level or equitable playing field for all concerned. But Smith, unlike his successor Hayek, does take into account some aspects of substantive justice, for Smith is concerned with the oppression of individuals. Hence he speaks of "[t]he second duty of the sovereign, that of protecting, as far as possible, every member of the society from the injustice or oppression of every other member of it, or the duty of establishing an exact administration of justice."[120] In addition, he acknowledges that justice—more or less represented in our legal system—is the main pillar that upholds the whole fabric of society.[121] Further, Smith opposes poverty, slavery, and colonialism,[122] thereby suggesting support for some substantive justice. He castigates Europeans for having committed, with impunity, "every sort of injustice in those remote countries,"[123] and (as alluded to earlier) says of Columbus's expedition to St Domingo: "The pious purpose of converting them [the inhabitants] to Christianity sanctified the injustice of the project."[124] This proposition—coupled with his commitment to the principles of liberty, equality, and justice—suggests that, for Smith, justice amounts to something more than procedural justice.

Alas, there is ambiguity in Smith's position, for while clearly being opposed to colonialism and slavery on both economic and moral grounds, he seems at times to reduce all considerations of justice to the adjudication of disputes over property or economic relationships.[125] The result is a somewhat ambiguous position on substantive justice. Whatever the presence of substantive justice in Smith, by the time classical liberalism has reached F.A. Hayek and *The Road to Serfdom* in 1944, anything resembling this kind of justice has been pushed to the margins. In the event, classical liberalism is left with no compelling answer to the question of tempered social justice: how is the disadvantaged individual to use her freedom in some meaningful way?[126] This is a question that, in the end, reform liberalism, democratic socialism, Marxism, and feminism will attempt to answer.

6. There is a marked tendency for classical liberalism to be paternalistic or dismissive of women. Locke is aware of a parental role for women, though strikingly he discusses this role under the heading "Of Paternal Power"[127] without stopping to address Maternal Power. And Smith, as others have shown, is largely neglectful of the role women play in the economy. In the words of Kathryn Sutherland, "[w]omen's labour is largely absent from the Smithian economy,"[128] though the pins made in Smith's invisible hand explanation would certainly have been constructed by women and for women.[129] As for Kant, in speaking of autonomy, he extends the franchise to active citizens who, interestingly, do not include women. The neglect of women by classical liberals raises the further question of whether this neglect distorted their view of human nature and its motivational elements.

7. Difficulties arise in connection with the notion of a social contract. These difficulties affect Locke and Kant in a way they do not affect Smith, who largely ignores the topic. For both Locke and Kant the social contract acts as a contractual political theory that uses consent to legitimize government. With the Reformation came the need for a new justification for political power, so that there might be such a thing as authority.

The social contract seems to fill this bill, but only in part. Since the social contract is not thought by Locke or Kant to have been a historical event, it can only function as a normative model for social justice. Most people never find themselves in the role of someone who explicitly consents to such a contract, and for them what Locke and Kant have in mind can only serve as a norm against which to measure the justice of government policies. But the details of this normative model are left undeveloped by Locke and Kant, except to say, in the case of Locke, that some pre-monetary restrictions (labour, sufficiency, spoilage) are transcended (at least in the case of Locke) with the introduction of money. This means that the social contract as developed by classical liberals is weak on principles used to interpret it.

The attempt to remedy this problem by squeezing out of the contract the Lockean proviso, to the effect that initial ownership cannot take place to make others worse off, is in the end inadequate for two reasons: (i) Locke sees it transcended by money; and (ii) nothing stops the Lockean provision from being pushed beyond the initial ownership to the next transaction, and again to the next, so that no transaction should be permitted that makes others worse off. But if (ii) is asserted, we end up with something quite different from the inegalitarianism of Locke, Smith, and Kant. As will be seen in Chapter 10, this point would even go so far as to undermine the attempt by libertarians (such as Nozick) to make use of the entitlement theory to defend inequality. For the present, it will suffice to point out that it undermines the normative interpretation of the social contract as presented by Locke and Kant.

Related Websites

Center for Independent Studies
www.cis.org.au/research/ideas-about-liberty/classical-liberalism

De Jasay, Anthony. "How Many Cheers for Classical Liberalism?" *Library of Economics and Liberty*, 6 Oct. 2014.
www.econlib.org/library/Columns/y2014/Jasaycheers.html

Gordon, David. "Ralph Raico on Authentic Liberalism." *Mises Institute*, 29 Mar. 2012.
https://mises.org/library/ralph-raico-authentic-liberalism

Williams, Garrath. "Thomas Hobbes: Moral and Political Philosophy." *Internet Encyclopedia of Philosophy*.
www.iep.utm.edu/hobmoral/

Lloyd, Sharon A. "Hobbes's Moral and Political Philosophy." *Stanford Encyclopedia of Philosophy*, 25 Feb. 2014.
http://plato.stanford.edu/entries/hobbes-moral/

Further Readings on Classical Liberalism

Adcock, Robert. *Liberalism and the Emergence of American Political Science: A Transatlantic Tale*. New York: Oxford University Press, 2014.
De Jong, Jan. *Rethinking Rational Choice Theory: A Companion on Rational and Moral Action*.

Houndmills, Basingstoke, Hampshire, UK: Palgrave Macmillan, 2012.

Deepak, Lal. *Reviving the Invisible Hand: The Case for Classical Liberalism in the Twenty-First Century*. Princeton, NJ: Princeton University Press, 2006.

Dryzek, John S., and Patrick Dunleavy. *Theories of the Democratic State*. Houndmills, Basingstoke, Hampshire, UK: Palgrave Macmillan, 2007.

Evrigenus, Inoannis D. *Images of Anarchy: The Rhetoric and Science on Hobbes' State of Nature*. New York: Cambridge University Press, 2014.

Galston, William A., and Peter H. Hoffenberg. *Poverty and Morality: Religious and Secular Perspectives*. Cambridge: Cambridge University Press, 2010.

Haar, Edwin van de. *Classical Liberalism and International Relations Theory: Hume, Smith, Mises and Hayek*. New York: Palgrave MacMillan, 2009.

Hay, Carol. *Kantism, Liberalism and Feminism: Resisting Oppression*. Houndmills, Basingstoke, Hampshire, UK: Palgrave Macmillan, 2013.

Hickson, Kevin. *The Political Thought of the Liberals and Liberal Democrats since 1945*. Manchester: Manchester University Press; New York: Palgrave Macmillan, 2009.

Hobson, John M. *The Eurocentric Conception of World Politics: Western International Theory, 1760–2010*. Cambridge: Cambridge University Press, 2012.

Kalyvas, Andreas, and Ira Katznelson. *Liberal Beginnings: Making a Republic for the Moderns*. Cambridge: Cambridge University Press, 2008.

Maliks, Reidar. *Kant's Politics in Context*. Oxford: Oxford University Press, 2014.

Muthur, Sanku. *Empire and Modern Political Thought*. Cambridge: Cambridge University Press, 2012.

Nozick, Robert. *Anarchy, State and Utopia*. New York: Basic Books, 1974.

Palmer, Tom G. *Realizing Freedom: Libertarian Theory History and Practice*. Washington, DC: Cato Institute, 2009.

Rasmussen, Dennis Carl. *The Pragmatic Enlightenment: Recovering the Liberalism of Hume, Smith, Montesquieu and Voltaire*. New York: Cambridge University Press, 2014.

Ruffin, Rixey J. *A Paradise of Reason: William Bentley and Enlightenment Christianity in the Early Republic*. New York: Oxford University Press, 2008.

Schulz-Forgen, Hagen, and Niklas Olsen. *Reinventing Western Civilization: Transnational Reconstructions of Liberalism in the Twentieth Century*. Newcastle upon Tyne, UK: Cambridge Scholars Publishing, 2014.

Seagrave, Adam S. *The Foundations of Natural Morality: On the Compatibility of Natural Rights and the Natural Law*. Chicago: University of Chicago Press, 2014.

Smith, George H. *The System of Liberty: Themes in the History of Classical Liberalism*. New York: Cambridge University Press, 2013.

Starr, Paul. *Freedom's Power: The True Force of Liberalism*. New York: Basic Books, 2007.

3 Conservatism

Learning Objectives

- To acknowledge the fundamental role of tradition in conservatism.
- To recognize views on the complexity of society and the intricacies of human nature in conservatism.
- To recognize the artificial and conventional role of justice in conservatism.
- To comprehend the affirmation of reform but not change in conservatism.

Adam Smith was certainly not alone, even as a Scot, in producing fundamental ideas that would help give shape to a new and emerging ideology in the eighteenth century. One only need think of the Scot David Hume (1711–1776) and the Irishman Edmund Burke (1729–1797) to realize that there is other gold to mine in the history of eighteenth-century ideologies besides that offered by classical liberals—gold that comes in the form of **conservatism**. While sharing some ideas with classical liberalism, conservatism is for the most part quite unalloyed, and quite capable of standing on its own feet as a type of precious metal. This is an ideology that turns its back on some of the central ideas of classical liberalism. The social contract is replaced by custom and convention, rights by obligations, and individualism by the organic whole of society.

Four political philosophers make the case for conservatism as clearly as any, and they are David Hume, Edmund Burke, Michael Oakeshott (1901–1990), and Roger Scruton (1944–). Attention now turns to these four. All of these thinkers affirm traditional practices and, in a sense, a politics that resists change. They advocate an ideology that even today is making a comeback in what used to be the safe social democratic environment of Western Europe.

Faced with unsettling economic news in 2009 and destabilizing immigration problems in 2015 and beyond, many Europeans are inching their way to conservatism. A case in point is the Dutch homosexual community, which 10 years ago constituted a solid left-wing bloc of voters; it now supports conservative parties on account of the dramatic rise in gay-bashings by immigrant Muslim youths.[1] The governments and societies of Poland and of Hungary in 2015 provide further examples of a swing towards the right. Their deference to tradition—religious tradition—as a reaction to the huge wave of Syrian

> **Central Beliefs of Conservatism**
>
> - Human nature is intricate, passionate, and corrupt.
> - Equality as an ideal is civil, and political equality is tinged with a strong flavour of social and economic inegalitarianism.
> - The end of government is the preservation of the wisdom of the species as captured by tradition.
> - Prudence takes priority over rights.

refugees attempting to enter those countries demonstrates quite clearly a conservative impulse. Prime Minister Ewa Kopacz of Poland is quoted as saying, "Christians, subject to barbaric oppression in Syria, deserve today for a Christian country like Poland to react quickly and come to their aid."[2] Instructive is that the Prime Minister says nothing about Syrian Muslim refugees. But the chairwoman of a private foundation called Estera, which facilitated the immigration of Christian Syrians, is alleged to have said of Muslim refugees in general that they "are in fact ISIS soldiers infiltrating Europe."[3] Other Poles, such as Andrzej Duda and Withold Waszczykowski from the opposition Law and Justice Party, have hinted that those Syrians admitted should be those who are "culturally close to us" and "Christian."[4] As for the Hungarian reaction to the Syrian refugees in 2015, it can best be summed up by noting that the Hungarian Prime Minister, Viktor Orbán, has adopted an uncompromising approach in saying Hungary has no obligation to accept

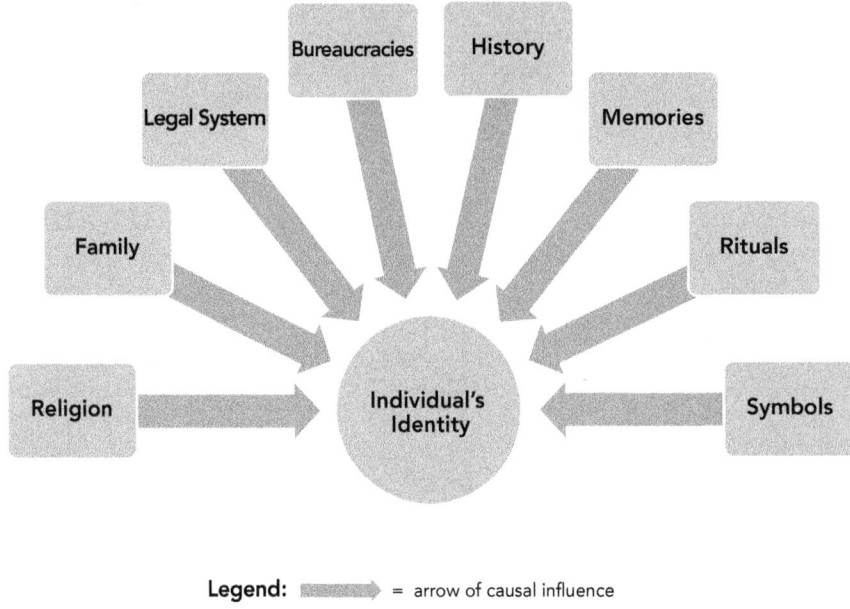

Figure 3.1 Conservatism's Model of Society

large numbers of Muslims and thereby endanger its traditional Christian values.[5] These examples, drawn from recent events in Europe, show a strong streak of deference to tradition and thereby an affirmation of a key part of conservatism. It is evident that conservatism is not passé.

But it is not just in Europe where conservatism has raised its head in respect to tradition. In what used to be multicultural-proud Canada, deference to "the way we do things here" and "old stock" raised its head during the 2015 federal election campaign. Central to debates about cultural matters during the election was the issue of wearing a **niqab** (face veil) by Muslim women during the Canadian citizenship ceremony. In 2011 Jason Kenney, then Immigration Minister, banned the niqab at citizenship ceremonies. Kenney's decision was recently successfully challenged before the Federal Court by Zunera Ishaq on the grounds of its unconstitutionality.[6] In the lead-up to the election of 19 October 2015, debates among the competing party leaders turned on their support or lack thereof for traditional ways of dressing at citizenship ceremonies.[7] That so much of the political narrative focused on traditional dress during such ceremonies shows unequivocally the staying power of conservatism and its deference for tradition.

To learn more about conservatism, then, we must now turn to one of the originators of this political ideology.

David Hume

One of the most remarkable philosophers of the English-speaking world, David Hume, helped shape the ideology of conservatism. Hume provides an analytical treatment of human nature in terms of understanding, passions, and morals, a fact often neglected by contemporary writers who see him solely as an epistemologist. In the third part of his definitive *A Treatise on Human Nature*, Hume is at pains to come to terms with the moral dimension of the life of human beings, especially as it relates to the social virtue, justice, thereby making it clear that moral issues are an integral part of his philosophy. The dominant questions, which he addresses in this part of the *Treatise*, are the following: Is justice a natural or artificial virtue? And, what is the origin of justice? It is to these questions, as posed and answered by Hume, that we now turn in order to better appreciate the ideological flavour of his position.

Justice as an Artificial Virtue

Hume first addresses the question of the natural or artificial nature of justice, and comes down quite unequivocally on the side of it being artificial. In contradistinction to justice as an artificial virtue stand the following natural virtues: meekness, beneficence, charity, and generosity. What separates these two kinds of virtue is only this: the good resulting from natural virtues arises from every single act, whereas the good from the artificial virtue of justice arises from the general scheme or scheme of action.[8] He says some virtues "produce pleasure and approbation by means of an artifice or contrivance, which arises from the circumstances of mankind. Of this kind I assert *justice* to be; and shall endeavour to defend this opinion."[9] Hume adds later that "when I deny justice to be a natural virtue, I make use of the word *natural*, only as opposed to *artificial*."[10] And then he continues: "Tho' the rules of justice be *artificial*, they are not *arbitrary*."[11] Accordingly, the rules of justice are devised but non-capricious, and arise from the circumstances of mankind.

In the preliminary discussions he undertakes on this subject, Hume is not clear about the nature of these circumstances, but he is clear that the original motive for justice cannot be regard to public interest or private benevolence. His reason for rejecting the first of these motives has to do with his observation that the motive of public interest is simply "too remote and too sublime to affect the generality of mankind."[12] From Hume's perspective there simply is "no such passion in human beings as the love of mankind, merely as such, independent of personal qualities, of services, or of relation to ourself."[13] As for the second motive—private interest or regard for the interests of the party concerned—Hume categorically denies that this can function as a motive for justice because it would lead to unreasonable conclusions. For example, it would create obligations to those whom one justly hated, and it would create obligations to a vicious man deserving of the hatred of mankind.

Without public and private motives for justice, it follows, according to Hume, that there is "no real or universal motive for observing the laws of equity,"[14] by which he presumably means the laws of justice. The upshot of this reasoning leads Hume to the conclusion that "the sense of justice and injustice is not deriv'd from nature, but arises artificially, tho' necessarily, from education and human conventions."[15] These two factors, education and human conventions, describe the circumstances previously alluded to, and it is to these that we must now turn to get a better understanding of what Hume thinks justice truly is.

Conventionalism versus Contractarianism

That Hume believes justice is artificial might incline us to think of him as a social contractarian, grounding justice in a social contract. But this he is not. Rather, he turns out to be a **conventionalist**,[16] one who subscribes to practices that have slowly evolved. According to this position, a person enters into a convention to make up for his or her infirmities in life and to meet the necessities of life.[17] The convention entered into in order to "bestow stability on the possession of those external goods"[18] is "not of the nature of a *promise*; for even promises themselves . . . arise from human conventions."[19] Hume believes that a resolution of the conflict over goods or possessions occurs when people mutually express a common sense of interest. In essence, what happens is that an agent recognizes a rule of conduct to be in the agent's interest: to leave another "in the possession of his goods, *provided* he will act in the same manner with regard to me."[20] That this rule of conduct evolves is no evidence for its not being a convention; to the contrary, Hume believes this shows that the sense of interest has become common, and "gives us confidence of the future regularity of their conduct."[21] Hume then draws an analogy between the convention for the maintenance of one's possessions and the convention for the construction of language: "in like manner are languages gradually establish'd by human conventions, without any promise."[22]

What, then, is the connection Hume envisages between the convention for the maintenance of one's possessions and the principle of justice? Hume answers this question in the following terms. Referring to the convention centred on possessions, Hume says, "After this convention, concerning abstinence from the possessions of others, is entered into, and every one has acquired stability in his possessions, there immediately arise the ideas of justice and injustice; as also those of property, right, and obligation."[23] Hume recognizes the existence of three kinds of goods: the internal satisfaction of the mind;

the external advantages of our body; and the enjoyment of those possessions we have acquired through industry and good fortune."[24] But only the third of these—our material possessions—is of interest to Hume so far as justice is concerned. He says, when speaking of persons in their early education, that they must seek a remedy to the disturbances in society by putting the goods of industry and fortune on the same footing as "the fix'd and constant advantages of mind and body."[25] In other words, Hume wishes respect to be given to the goods of industry and fortune when speaking of the convention that leads to justice—a convention that results from judgment and understanding rather than from what is "irregular and incommodious in the affections."[26] He does not want the goods of the mind and body to eclipse in importance those of the third type.

Inconveniences and Justice

The convention of justice that gives rise to society provides what Hume calls a remedy for three inconveniences: limited power, diminished abilities, and exposure to fortune and accidents. In a nutshell, justice remedies our limitations, but especially our exposure to fortune and accidents so far as these apply to external goods. For this reason, Hume moves immediately from talking about the convention concerning the abstinence from the possession of others, to talking about justice, and finally to talking about property. The linkage Hume makes between convention, justice, and property is meant to be very tight, for he says, "I have already observ'd, that justice takes its rise from human conventions; and that these are intended as a remedy for some inconveniences, which proceed from the concurrence of certain *qualities* of the human mind with the *situation* of external objects."[27] Once again, the focus is on external objects, those things that could become the property of someone. Hume sees these external objects as fitting into a matrix comprising selfishness, limited generosity, and the scarcity of such objects, inspiring Hume—Hume the skeptic—to make the following bold remark: "Here then is a proposition, which, I think, may be regarded as certain, *that 'tis only from the selfishness and confin'd generosity of man, along with the scanty provision nature has made for his wants, that justice derives its origin.*"[28]

It is tempting to believe that the connection Hume draws between justice and possessions or property is provisional and rather tentative, but such is not the case. Speaking in Part II of Book III of the *Treatise*, he says, referring to the imaginary state called the state of nature, that no such thing as justice or injustice is there to be found. The reason for this, as given by Hume, is simply that no such thing as property is there to be found, "and consequently cou'd be no such thing as justice or injustice."[29] Hume makes this same point a few pages earlier when, in stentorian fashion, he says, "'Tis very preposterous, therefore, to imagine that we can have any idea of property, without fully comprehending the nature of justice."[30] In brief, the rules of justice imply and are implied by the institution of property. This is how tight Hume makes the connection between justice and property.

It would seem, under the Humean analysis, that people first come to have possessions, which are held precariously owing to fortune and accident. Second, under this same analysis, these possessions only get anchored firmly in one's hands through the evolution of a convention or set of rules called the rules of justice, which in turn create the institution of property-keeping. According to Hume, experience (or in the idiom of Hume, "impressions") teaches us the rules of justice, or, put differently, teaches us that "the whole plan or scheme is highly conducive, or indeed absolutely requisite, both to the support of society, and the well-being of every individual."[31] Justice turns out to be an artificial virtue, when it is a character trait and not a rule, established upon reflection of one's own interest and the interest of the public. This leads Hume to say, "All our obligations to do good to society seem to imply something reciprocal. I receive the benefits of society, and therefore ought to promote its interests."[32] It is at the confluence of the two of these that justice is to be found.

Justice in particular, and morality in general, takes into account both self-interest and public interest, and these get built into their respective discourses—a point Hume comes close to making when he says that "our natural uncultivated ideas of morality, instead of providing a remedy for the partiality of our affections, do rather conform themselves to that partiality, and give it additional force and influence."[33] The language of morality is, then, according to Hume, constructed on the grounds of an ever-present respect for self-interest. But Hume does not stop there, for he admits that eventually we need to recognize a role for the satisfaction of the public interest if our private interest is to be satisfied. The interaction of these two interests, coupled with scarcity of goods, leads to a person's finally being driven relentlessly in the direction of a rule-governed society that nourishes a sense of interest common to all.[34] Thus, Hume says, "'Twas therefore a concern for our own and the publick interest which made us establish the laws of justice."[35]

Early Education and Justice

For Hume, early education teaches humans of the infinite advantages that result from the artificial virtue, justice, which is constructed on the basis of a convention.[36] So, too, do private education and instruction increase a person's esteem for justice, making parents aware of its usefulness and of the importance of conveying this lesson to their children. Principles of honesty and justice teach humans the principles for the establishment and survival of society, a claim not to be sneered at, given Hume's conviction that one's infirmities are all compensated by society.[37] So Hume presents justice as a virtue capable of establishing society, which mitigates a person's weaknesses and failings and affords the individual the opportunity of infinite advantages if, presumably, fortune smiles on him or her. In a sense, then, Hume does not see justice as simply a strategy for minimizing one's losses, but also as a strategy for maximizing one's gains.

Experience and Tradition

Hume says enough on the subject of justice and its role for society to mark him as a conservative. He clearly sees justice as deriving from a convention or practice or agreement without the interposition of a promise. According to Hume, justice has its origins primarily in possessions, and in a mutual recognition to respect those possessions. But this mutual recognition develops slowly, and not in a social contractarian way through some promise. The gap between Hume the conventionalist and Locke the social contractarian may indeed appear small, but one should not underestimate the differences. Conventions, for Hume, evolve slowly; in fact, Hume goes so far as to say the rule governing the stability of possessions "arises gradually" and "acquires force by a slow progression."[38] The analogies he uses here to illustrate his point are the establishment of languages, common measures of exchange such as gold and silver, and the pulling of oars on a boat. None of these practices, he argues, comes about through promises along lines suggested by social contractarians. To the contrary, what Hume envisages in each of these cases, as with justice, is a progression of confidence "of the future regularity of conduct."

What ties all these practices together is the simple fact that they are all founded upon *experience*. They have been tested over time and not found wanting. For Hume, a person's experience assures him or her that "the sense of interest has become common to all our fellows, and gives us a confidence of the future regularity of their conduct: And 'tis only on the expectation of this, that our moderation and abstinence are founded."[39] Nothing happens overnight for Hume; the species slowly comes to recognize some advantage in the principle of mutual recognition of possessions, and a custom is born. But all of what Hume says here is founded on a deference to experience rather than reason. Whereas the social contractarians provide ample room for reason to enter in, and Jean-Jacques Rousseau (1712–1778) is a good example here, the conventionalists (of which Hume is the prime example) provide room only for evolving practices that culminate in compliance. It would not be an exaggeration to say, in the case of Hume, that experience trumps reason in explaining our moral notions and practices.[40] Given this unconcealed deference to experience and evolving practices, a step from this to an affirmation of tradition is an easy matter. And once this is arrived at, the step to conservatism is a done deal.

What Hume affirms is the special, almost sacred character of the established order of things, including "property, contracts, courtesy, marriage, political authority, and the entire status and rank among men."[41] While one may not categorize Hume as a metaphysical conservative, such as T.S. Eliot (1888–1965)[42] and Eric Voegelin (1901–1985),[43] "he does in his own way share with them the conviction that established order has a sacred character and that this sacred character constitutes part of the authority of that order."[44] What Hume provides is a common-sense conservativism, the effect of which is "to endorse a deeply traditionalistic and conservative view of social and political order."[45] Moreover, in adopting common sense, Hume adopts a policy of guiding thought and action by empirical regularities. With common sense as his bastion, Hume wishes to head off revolutionary intrusion and its accompanying order of illusion, as well as to head off philosophical and religious fanaticism, which threatened both the constitutional system and the commercial and industrial society of Britain.[46] The stretch from the common-sense conservatism of Hume to the conservatism of Edmund Burke is a simple step. It is to Burke that we now turn.

Edmund Burke

In his influential work, *Reflections on the Revolution in France*, Edmund Burke outlines some of the central ingredients of what would become known as conservatism. Burke distinguishes between real rights and metaphysical rights, and goes on to affirm the relevance of the former and the irrelevance of the latter in civil society. Real rights appear, in Burke's case, to be rights rooted in convention or established practices, while metaphysical rights are rights thought up or imagined. The rights Burke affirms are the right to live by the rule of law, the right to justice, the right to the fruits of one's industry, and the right to the acquisitions of one's parents.[47] Clearly, the rights he has in mind are very tightly drawn, and do not begin to touch the rights of the French Revolution—namely, the right to liberty, equality, and fraternity. Moreover, it would not be unfaithful to the spirit of Burke to say the rights that he thinks real are quite distinct from the rights referred to in constitutional documents such as the Constitution of the United States, in its Bill of Rights, or an internationally recognized legal document such as the Universal Declaration of Human Rights. In effect, there is no talk by Burke of the right to freedom of religion, the right to freedom of the press, the right to freedom of speech, the right to freedom of association, or the right to freedom of expression. For Burke, metaphysical rights are **abstract rights**, and of very limited utility. He asks, "What is the use of discussing a man's abstract right to food or to medicine? The question is upon the method of procuring and administering them. In that deliberation I shall always advise to call in the aid of the farmer and the physician, rather than the professor of metaphysics."[48] With this sarcasm, Burke distances himself from those who would ground their political ideology in talk of rights.

Inegalitarianism

Before proceeding to an analytical treatment of Burke's ideology, we need to understand clearly Burke's inegalitarianism. Burke affirms that "all men have equal rights; but not to equal things."[49] The person who invests, say, five shillings in a partnership has as good a right to the partnership as the person who has invested five hundred pounds, but the former does not have a right to an equal dividend in the product of the joint stock. Similar things, Burke thinks, can be said for the share to which people are entitled with respect to power, authority, and management of the state.[50] And a similar inegalitarian position is expressed later in *Reflections* when he discusses the legislators who framed the ancient republics. These legislators, he claims, had to do with humans, and had to study human nature and to make allowances for diversities among persons with regard to birth, education, professions, the periods of their lives, their residence (town or country), ways of acquiring possessions, and the quality of their property.[51] Accordingly, the legislators broke up people into classes as though they were different species of animals.[52] There is no mistaking Burke's inegalitarianism, a position he thinks is based on "long observation" and "much impartiality."[53]

It is now time to look at Burke analytically. A full understanding of Burke's rejection of rights needs to be understood against a background of other claims he wishes to make. Among these are the following:

i. Civil society is the offspring of convention.
ii. Convention modifies the constitution formed under it.
iii. Government is not made in virtue of natural rights.
iv. Government is a consideration of convenience, something that follows from the positive limitation placed on rights.
v. While reform in a country's institutions is, at times, acceptable, change of them is not.

Some amplification of the meaning of each of these is in order.

Convention and the Social Contract

The first two propositions can best be addressed in the following terms. Speaking of the equality of "the civil social man," Burke says, "It is a thing to be settled by convention."[54] What does Burke have in mind here when he speaks of convention? He answers this question by distinguishing between conventions and constitutions, saying that constitutions are formed under conventions.[55] He means by this that constitutions, which provide for the legislative, executive, and judicial power, are creatures of convention. So conventions and constitutions are different for Burke.

What then, again, is a convention for Burke? His answer seems to be that it is a social contract. It seems that Burke not only affirms the existence of such contracts, but thinks of conventions and social contracts as one and the same. He claims that "society is indeed a contract" or partnership at the root of the state, which ought to be looked on with "reverence," and in this way it plays the same role as convention. Moreover, the contract is a partnership not only with those who are living but with those who are dead and those who are yet unborn.[56] Burke sees each contract of a particular state as mystically or religiously part of a "great primaeval contract of eternal society" that puts all physical and moral natures in "their appointed place."[57] Obviously, Burke's notion of the social contract is different from that of Locke, who talks of the social contract (compact) in terms of the unanimous voice of those who are present to express their preferences and who lay the groundwork for majoritarianism of the living.

Burke's view of the social contract or compact, then, is importantly different from that of Locke. But where does it stand in relation to Hume's convention? Recall that Hume thinks of the conventions for the running of society as analogous to the development of a language. They occur without any promise. Is Burke's social contract, like Hume's convention, so understood? It certainly lacks the promissory element, for it is not promises that tie together the partnership referred to by Burke but "an obligation" that stands above those who participate in the partnership, an obligation that requires the participants to "submit their will to that law," and this obligation is itself rooted in the "eternal society." Still, this is not enough to turn Burke's view of the social contract into Hume's view of convention. It is, however, enough to distinguish his view from Locke's, for it does incline to ground the authority of government in traditional religious belief rather than in the free consent of the living. It is more like intergenerational consent, and this seems at bottom to be a nod of endorsement in the direction of tradition, especially traditional religious belief.

Rights: Metaphysical and Real

As for proposition (iii), Burke draws a sharp distinction between what he calls metaphysic rights and real rights. He does not deny that metaphysic, or natural, rights exist. Indeed, he affirms that natural rights may exist in total independence of government, and affirms that they have clarity and perfection.[58] But according to Burke, therein lies their practical defect.[59] Metaphysic or natural rights, thinks Burke, enter into common life "like rays of light which pierce into a dense medium [and] are, by the laws of nature, refracted from their straight line."[60] When these abstract rights penetrate the medium of man's intricate nature and society's inherent complexity, they "undergo such a variety of refractions and reflections, that it becomes absurd to talk of them as if they continued in the simplicity of their original direction."[61]

Metaphysic or natural or abstract rights are also said by Burke to be "pretended rights," for though "they are metaphysically true, they are morally and politically false."[62] The real rights of humans are the refracted residue of metaphysic rights, and these refracted rights turn out to be advantages found in the balances and compromises that take place in choices one makes between good and good, good and evil, and evil and evil. Any real right, thinks Burke, must be consistent with virtue, which has prudence as its paradigm.

So when Burke claims, as he does, that "government is not made in virtue of natural rights," he means that it is not made in virtue of metaphysic or abstract rights because they have no purchasing power as "true moral denominations."

Burke thinks that, rather than starting with abstract rights, political thinkers should start with the proposition that "Government is a contrivance of human wisdom to provide for human *wants*."[63] Commencing elsewhere will result in political thinkers paying inadequate attention to two Archimedean points of Burkean conservatism: the fact that human nature is intricate and the fact that human society is complex. Leaning on these points, Burke concludes that government should be constructed on the basis of experience, not on the basis of a priori reasoning, and therefore it should not be constructed on "any abstract rule" such as natural or metaphysic rights.

Government and Convenience

Proposition (iv) asserts that government is a consideration of convenience, and this, as indicated above, follows from the positive limitation placed on natural rights. The words of Burke deserve to be quoted here, for they make the point he wishes to make with abundant clarity: "The moment you abate any thing from the full rights of men, each to govern himself, and suffer any artificial positive limitation upon those rights, from that moment the whole organization of government becomes a consideration of convenience."[64] Burke seems to be suggesting here that, in the construction of social life, there are two choices: (i) natural or metaphysic rights trump everything else, and individual anarchism or libertarianism prevails, or (ii) compromise and balance trump everything else, and prudence prevails. These two choices form a logical disjunction for Burke, and he concludes that reasonable individuals are driven to the second of the foregoing for the reason that some restraints on persons' liberties are essential for society. He thinks further that once some restraints on rights are admitted ("the moment you abate any thing from the full rights of men"), all rights are subject to negotiation in light of changing "times and circumstances" that "admit of infinite modifications," which "cannot be settled upon any abstract rule." Given the foregoing disjunction, Burke thinks the first is untenable, and thus goes on to affirm the second.

Reform versus Change

Proposition (v), which admits of reform but not change to extant institutions, can be gleaned from a reading of Burke's *Reflections*.[65] In his deference to the old-fashioned British constitution, the Church, and the sacred institute of the French National Assembly, Burke reveals his marked preference for the stability of the existing organic whole.[66] These are the sorts of institutions whose merits, Burke thinks, "are confirmed by the solid test of long experience."[67] Burke could have made use of the maxim "Don't alter that which works." This idea, after all, leads him to attack the French Revolution. As some have said, and accurately so, "For Burke, the [French] Revolution had been the embodiment of radical evil, produced by a conspiracy of atheistic intellectuals like Rousseau who had disturbed the natural tendency of society to move towards the organic unity."[68] For Burke, radical thinkers such as Rousseau run the risk of undoing that which has stood the test of time. They run the risk, it is said, of undoing "the wisdom of the species." And here Burke thinks of such institutions as the established church, the established monarchy, the established aristocracy, and the established democracy, all of which he says, "We are resolved to keep."[69]

It should be noted, however, that Burke admits to the reform, but not the change, of such institutions. In "A Letter to a Noble Lord" (1796), Burke draws attention to the manifest distinction between reform and change. Change, according to him, "alters the substance of objects themselves, and gets rid of all their essential good as well as of all the accidental evil annexed to them," while reform "is not a change in the substance or in the primary modification of the objects, but a direct application of a remedy to the grievance complained of."[70] Reform allows for the "slow but well-sustained progress" in which "[o]ne advantage is as little as possible sacrificed to another. We compensate, we reconcile, we balance."[71] Those who advocate not reform, but change, advocate "[v]iolent haste, and their defiance of the process of nature," and are thereby "[d]elivered over blindly to every projector and adventurer, to every alchymist and empiric."[72] So, for Burke, institutions represent the wisdom of the species, and should only be altered slowly through reform rather than shattered through radical change.

Reasons for Resistance to Change

There are two underlying reasons for Burke's resistance to radical change. The first is theological, and claims that "change is bad in so far as it threatens to disrupt the original perfection of creation, and man is singled out as especially liable to attempt such change. He is dangerous, because he is distinguished from the rest of creation by his capacity for deliberate evil."[73] Given Burke's defence not only of the church but of religion, this should not be dismissed as a minor reason for Burke's opposition to change. He does, after all, say quite categorically, "We know, and it is our pride to know, that man is by his constitution *a religious animal*; that atheism is against, not only our reason but our instincts; and that it cannot prevail long"[74] (emphasis added). So religion, in the form of Christianity, is a source of truth for Burke, and accordingly man is not to be trusted to embark on radical change.

The second reason for Burke's opposition to radical change is rooted in man's intricate nature and society's complexity. In spite of acknowledging man's "plastic nature," Burke says legislators, both old and new, are obliged to heed the diversities among men, according to "their birth, their education, their professions, the periods of their lives, their residence in towns or in the country, their several ways of acquiring and of fixing property, and according to the quality of the property itself, all of which rendered them as it were so many different species of animals."[75] The intricacies of human nature, with its plasticity, spill over into a society that inevitably is complex. Thus Burke maintains,

> From hence they [the legislators] thought themselves obliged to dispose their citizens into such classes, and to place them in such situations in the state as their peculiar habits might qualify them to fill, and to allot to them such appropriated privileges as might secure to them what their specific occasions required, and which might furnish to each description such force as might protect it in the conflict caused by the diversity of interests, that must exist, and must contend in all *complex* society.[76] (emphasis added)

Faced with the psychological truth that humans are intricate and confronted by the social truth that society is complex, Burke reasons in favour of "circumspection and caution [as] a part of wisdom" when we work only upon inanimate matter, and as "a part of duty" when we work upon sentient beings.⁷⁷ This same circumspection and caution drive Burke towards an affirmation of reform and a denunciation of radical change.

Institutions, Moderation, and Hume

A few other points still need to be addressed in rounding out the discussion of conservatism as advanced by Burke. First, Burke's staunch support for established institutions places him squarely in the camp of those who favour tradition over innovation. What is meant here by the term "tradition" is, at least according to Alasdair MacIntyre, "an argument extended through time in which certain fundamental agreements are defined and redefined."⁷⁸ This insightful definition allows one to see that Burke is bent on supporting a set of interconnected ideas, some of which constitute premises and others conclusions. In his case, the ideas are those that affirm the value of established institutions. Burke is not interested in offering an argument that is sound only in the present moment; rather, he is resolved to show that his arguments are valid and grounded on true premises that are durable.

Burke, then, is a traditionalist because he attempts to offer arguments—arguments sustainable over time—that affirm the value of established institutions.⁷⁹ These same institutions, one will remember, are the visible evidence of the wisdom of the species.

Second, there is more than a thematic connection between the great Scottish philosopher David Hume and the influential Irish literary figure Edmund Burke. Even in the *Reflections* Burke says, almost as an aside, "Hume told me, that he had from Rousseau himself the secret of his principles of composition."⁸⁰ Both Hume and Burke, while admiring Rousseau's literary skills, share a profound distrust for and dislike of his radical political ideology. This opposition is rooted in their adherence to the ideas of compromise and moderation, something already seen in the case of Burke. Hume's adherence to the same idea is nicely captured by Noel Sullivan when he says, "There is, that is to say, an ineliminable tension amongst the constituents of human happiness, and in this situation the greatest good for man is a spirit of moderation and compromise. The best representative of this school is, perhaps, David Hume."⁸¹

Michael Oakeshott

The analysis up to this point has concentrated on the political ideologies of Hume and Burke, both of the eighteenth century. It is instructive to fast-forward our study to a twentieth-century observer of conservatism—and an articulate and subtle one at that. Here I am thinking of Michael Oakeshott. The importance of Oakeshott in conservatism is ably captured in the words of Anthony Quinton: "Conservatism is a long-lasting body of political doctrine.... It is above all the political doctrine of Burke. But it goes much further back in English history, at least to Hooker, and, in the world as a whole, perhaps to Aristotle. Since Burke it has taken the form of a continuous tradition, culminating for the time being in Oakeshott."⁸² So it is appropriate that we focus on Oakeshott as a contemporary example of a conservative.

Oakeshott sometimes gives the impression that he does not believe conservatism is an ideology, for the simple reason that conservatives shun theory in dealing with politics, and ideology is theory.⁸³ But it would be fairer to say not that he denies its ideological status, but that he wishes instead to present it as a disposition to behave and think in certain manners.[84] What does this disposition amount to? In a nutshell, it amounts to a preference for the familiar to the unknown.[85] And this means, in turn, that the disposition amounts to adopting a certain attitude towards change and innovation, namely an attitude that is "correspondingly cool and critical in respect of change and innovation."[86] In this sense, the conservative embraces "rational prudence." But this rational prudence, stressed by Oakeshott, does not entail a belief in certain religious or moral beliefs, in natural law, in providential ordering reflecting a divine purpose in nature and human history, or in an organic theory of history.[87]

The Ritual of Government

Oakeshott says, when speaking of the conservative disposition and the above-mentioned beliefs pertaining to moral, religious, providential, or organic matters, that it "does not entail that we should hold these beliefs to be true or even that we should suppose them to be true."[88] What conservatism is linked to, he thinks, are "certain beliefs about the activity of government."[89] And these certain beliefs about government activity have nothing to do with natural law or providential ordering or morals or religion; rather, they have to do with governing being viewed as a "specific" and "limited" activity that provides general rules of conduct, "not as plans for imposing substantive activities, but as instruments enabling people to pursue activities of their own choice."[90]

Government, according to Oakeshott, begins not with a vision of another world, but with the self-government practised by persons of this world. The intimations of government are more likely to be found in ritual than in religion or philosophy, in seeking peace and order rather than truth or perfection. The ritual, however, is not one of passion, but of settled disposition that facilitates the resolution of disputes. The caretaker of this more precise and less easily corrupted ritual is government, and the rules it imposes come to be recognized as the law.[91] Finally, the conservative disposition in respect of politics comprehends that the business of government, far from being the inflaming of passions, is but the injecting of moderation into the activities of passionate men, and the restraining and reconciling of men's interests.[92] Oakeshott asserts, in conclusion, that the conservative disposition can better be learned from Michel de Montaigne, Blaise Pascal, Thomas Hobbes, and David Hume than from Edmund Burke and Jeremy Bentham,[93] a point that, at least in the case of Hume, was previously suggested.

Roger Scruton

Before giving an overview of conservatism, we should look at a contemporary conservative who boldly stakes out the terrain of this ideology. Here I am thinking of Roger Scruton. In innovative language, Scruton defines conservatism as "the maintenance of the social ecology."[94] In defending this political posture, he presents arguments in favour of the territorial nation-state and national loyalty (as distinct from nationalism), as against regional entities such as the experiment of the European Union (EU), the United Nations (UN), and the World Trade Organization (WTO). Next, he presents arguments in favour of seeing conservatism and conservation as aspects of a single long-term policy of husbanding resources; in favour of not abandoning our meat-eating habits but remoralizing them in keeping with the Judeo-Christian *tradition*;[95] in favour of the law withdrawing from direct involvement on moral issues on which society is deeply divided, as in the case of abortion or euthanasia; in favour of the aura of conventional marriage; and in favour of religion rooted in custom.[96] Finally, and in addition, Scruton attempts to launch an attack against the structuralists, post-stucturalists, deconstructionists, and postmodernists illustrated in the writings of Michel Foucault, Jacques Derrida, and Richard Rorty on the grounds that these movements and writers set out "to destroy the ideas of objective truth and absolute value," to be replaced by "political correctness as absolutely binding and cultural relativism as objectively true."[97] In pursuit of his attack against these movements, Scruton claims that the ruling postmodernist idea is that Western culture is a burden from which we need to be released, and that the propagation of this idea has required, so it is thought, a new critical language that collapses into gobbledygook.[98] It is worthwhile looking more closely at the various arguments he advances in support of some of these claims.

Social Ecology

Scruton appears to mean by "the maintenance of the social ecology" that conservatism is the conservation of shared resources, be they social, material, economic, or spiritual, as well as the resistance to all forms of social entropy.[99] He endorses the words of Lord Salisbury that "delay is life," then adds, "conservatism is the politics of delay,"[100] the purpose of which is to maintain in being "for as long as possible, the life and health of a social organism."[101] At least with respect to the West, Scruton believes that its life and health as an organism, as a civilization, lies in the preservation of its culture, where "culture" is defined as the accumulation of art, literature, and humane reflection that has established a tradition of reference and allusion. It is the culture of a civilization that provides it with an ability to be conscious of itself and to have a vision of the world.[102] Of particular concern to him in maintaining the social ecology of the West are the outside challenges from multiculturalism and from Islam.

Conserving Nations

According to Scruton, the nation-state is the only answer that has proved itself able to deal with the problems of modern government. The French, Russian, and Fascist revolutions ended in failures with the collapse of legal regimes at home, the mass murder of their citizens, and war with other nation-states. Better and wiser it would have been for these and other countries to have accepted whatever evolved and inherited political arrangements prevailed at the time, and to have improved on these by means of small adjustments. According to Scruton, transnational and universal aspirations that turn their back on the nation-state, such as the UN and EU, run the risk of unleashing despotism and then anarchy. He believes that we as citizens are powerless to reject the laws these entities enact, and that we as citizens find the legislators of these bodies unaccountable to us. Continuing, he claims that oikophobes, those who repudiate their inheritance and home, attack customs and institutions "associated with traditional and native forms of life."[103] Finally, there is reason to believe, he claims, that the forces of internationalism can be defeated. Whether one is talking about the UN, the EU, or the WTO, each lacks a military force, and therefore the cost of defying them would "rapidly be outweighed by the benefit." Free trade is neither possible nor desirable, and an open-door policy on immigration is problematic. Once again, the spectres of despotism and anarchy await us if we do not return to national loyalty, national sovereignty, and the conservation of the nation-state.

Conserving Nature

Consistent with his previous remarks, Scruton asserts that conservatism and conservation are but two aspects of a long-term policy of husbanding resources. On this account, conservatism and environmentalism turn out to be "natural bedfellows," both advocating political action in terms of trusteeship rather than enterprise. With the help of institutions, persons can extend their social concern not just to the environment but to the whole social organism.[104] Moreover, as Scruton claims, appealing to rational self-interest in discussing environmental decay will not work because of its accompanying problems: the prisoner's dilemma, the free-rider problem, and the tragedy of the commons. What is needed to advance the environmental cause is not so much a hereditary principle advanced by Burke, but something not quite as dated as Burke's suggestion, something that nonetheless rests on "a human motive that would appeal to people in general." What Scruton recommends as a human motive is national loyalty. Environmental conservation needs to begin here because it is only at the local level that one can realistically hope for any kind of improvement; this locale will define our home and motivate us to hold the environment in trust for our descendants. This is the best we can hope for, given that human beings are "creatures of limited and local affections."[105] Environmentalism leads to conservatism, according to Scruton, by travelling along the road of the limitations of human nature.

Marriage

The institution of marriage, according to Scruton, has both a social and spiritual function. It performs this "complex" function because it turns out to be more than a contract of mutual co-operation and more than simply an agreement to live together; owing to this, it has had, at least until recently, a "distinct social aura." Society takes a keen, even profound, interest in marriage because this is the institution in which children are socialized and become new members of society. Without marriage, children run the risk of being brought into the world as strangers.[106]

Since the time of the French Revolution, thinks Scruton, the West has seen a marked tendency in the direction of the "de-sacralization" of marriage such that what results are "rescindable civil unions." Such an institution can neither assure security to children nor call upon the support of society. Moreover, this transition from marriage to civil unions is a retreat from substantial ties to "a world of negotiated deals." The "indefeasible obligations," which stand at the heart of the vows of marriage, have been jeopardized by the state's eagerness to "refashion marriage for a secular age." These marriage vows, for Scruton, have at their heart sexual emotion: the desire for an incarnate person in whom self-consciousness shines. This sexual desire, conceived in these terms, amounts to a state of mind experienced only by human beings.[107] All of this vanishes as marriage is redefined in terms of contract. As a result, this newly defined marriage "has ceased to be a rite of passage into another and higher life, and become a bureaucratic stamp, with which to endorse our temporary choices."[108] People are less well placed to dedicate their lives to one another, or to their home, or to their children, for the reason that society plays down or diminishes the value and uniqueness of marriage. In short, the function of what is known as the traditional marriage is not able to be performed by the welfare state. Continuing, and in conclusion, Scruton says of gay marriage that its effect is to rob marriage of its social meaning: the blessing conferred by the unborn on the living. The same-sex union does away with the dramatization of sexual differences that stand at the heart of traditional marriage.[109]

Religion

While presenting interesting ideas on the subject of religion, Scruton's main ideas boil down to a few simple claims. He maintains that the first wave of secularization was characterized in Europe in the nineteenth century by the gradual erosion of faith and a general retreat of religious ideas. People attempted to support their social world—a world previously supported by religious belief—by establishing secular law and secular institutions. Scruton then maintains that the second wave of secularization was characterized by the violent destruction of religious symbols of the past and their replacement by man-made functional devices. This he dates as a development that gained momentum after World War II. The upshot of these two waves is that current human experience is transformed and human relations are "voided of the old religious virtues." Nonetheless, even this second wave of secularization has not eliminated the religious needs of our species: the species' hunger for the sacred remains.[110]

Postmodernism

Scruton sees postmodernism as a culture of repudiation that claims the appeal to reason is merely an appeal to Western ethnocentrism. The Enlightenment values of objectivity and universalism give way to intersubjectivity and particularism, not for the purpose of letting opinions in but to exclude the beliefs of old authorities and objective truth. For Scruton, Foucault and his ideas represent postmodernism in full dress. His is a philosophy that explains belief not as something that has truth or validity, but as something to be expounded in terms of a social context and thereby explained away. All discourse is therefore a function of power, and ends up being but an ideology. Scruton objects strongly to Foucault's position and to all of postmodernism, and says that it, too, is but a form of ideology. Moreover, Scruton claims that the ruling postmodernist idea is the following: Western culture is a burden that cries out for release and repudiation. This ruling idea, believes Scruton, is spelled out in words that amount to nothing much more than gobbledygook comprised of opaque language, invented words, and out-of-place technicalities. Against this, Scruton believes we should see culture as a repository of knowledge, not an ideology, and that we should go back to the basics: classics, ancient history, the Hebrew Bible, medieval poetry, and the legacy of Islamic philosophy. In different words, Scruton wishes to say that we should return to the principles of the Enlightenment to rediscover the oneness of the human condition.[111]

In summary, one can say that Scruton's arguments align very well with the spirit of Hume, Burke, and Oakeshott before him. Of the arguments he advances, possibly only the one dealing with the nonsense of the language of recent relativists sets him apart from the others, though even on this point one can well imagine that the clear-minded Hume, the articulate Burke, and the lucid Oakeshott would stand in agreement.

Conclusion

In attempting to give an overview of conservatism, Anthony Quinton summarizes the central components in terms of the following propositions: (i) it affirms traditionalism, thereby supporting the maintenance of existing institutions and practices, and is thereby suspicious of change; (ii) it adopts a skeptical attitude towards political knowledge, deferring instead to wisdom found in established laws and institutions; and (iii) it adopts a conception of human beings and society as being organically related.[112] How well does Quinton's summary capture the political ideas of Hume, Burke, Oakeshott, and Scruton? All of the foregoing writers endorse traditionalism and custom, as well as a deference to wisdom or prudence as found in institutions. As for the third proposition, Hume,[113] Burke, and Scruton embrace it, with Oakeshott apparently distancing himself from it. But there is more to the similarities of these thinkers than that which Quinton emphasizes: all of them, in their own words, endorse a politics of delay; all focus on the role of custom (which for some comes at the expense of any notion of a social contract); and all recognize the role of society as a whole in restraining one's unbridled desires. What conservatives favour, at the expense of rights, are customs and their associated obligations. And what conservatives favour, at the expense of the individual of classical liberalism, is society as an organic whole.

The line of reasoning found in Hume, Burke, Oakeshott, and Scruton is strongly deferential to experience, custom, and pragmatic considerations, all of which, when folded together, allow for the preservation of traditions in nuanced forms. All of these individuals shun a revisionary metaphysics or revisionary political stance that would produce change in the practices of the communities of which they speak. One does not see in conservatism an affirmation of the intrinsic value of liberty, whether natural or sacred; what one finds instead is an affirmation of everyday experience uncluttered by abstract principles or revolutionary ideals. To steal a phrase from Hume, what conservatives subscribe to is the "general scheme" or "system of action" that has arisen, not through some social contract but through some voluntary conventions that have become established just as a language or the use of money becomes established—in fits and starts. Slowly, ever so slowly, the community of users recognizes the advantageous nature of these emerging conventions. Morality, by all accounts, turns out to be something more felt than judged, and it is felt in the context of the tradition of which one is a part. The tradition is but the product of adherence to the conventions that have emerged, noteworthy among which is the convention of justice. Hume, Burke, Oakeshott, and Scruton would have us "consult common experience" in our search for the correct line of political and moral thinking and in our search for that which is indispensable to the very survival of society itself, without which none could survive. The "politics of delay" is the conservative's strategy for preserving what has allowed for the survival of society and the individual, and this "politics of delay," grounded in common experience, argues passionately in favour of the preservation of practices and institutions as the bearers of the "wisdom of the species." The conservative's line of reasoning and argumentation is clearly not one of abstractionism, but one of respectful consideration of common experience.

Evaluation: The Strengths of Conservatism

1. The emphasis conservatism places on the intricate nature of humans and the complexity of society—especially conservatism as defended by Burke—is a strength. To take each of these in turn, one can readily see that human nature is intricate. Whether one is talking about linguistic skills, mathematical skills, artistic skills, literary skills, athletic skills, musical skills, entertainment skills, and so on, it is transparent that any attempt to comprehend the nature of humans by understanding these skills is exceptionally difficult. What is it that makes one person a polyglot, another a Madame Curie, another a Shakespeare, another an Ingrid Bergman, another a Picasso, another a Nina Simone, and another a Henri Poincaré? Or to take an even more humble example, what explains the humour and wit of some people? We do not have, at this time, a convenient theory to explain such a humble example, and of course even less to say about the more celebrated cases. Moreover, if we leave the behavioural and psychological world behind and enter the world of neurophysiology, the story is just as difficult to tell. How exactly does the brain work? What are the changes in the brain that account for various mental diseases such as Parkinson's and Alzheimer's? To be sure, there is incremental progress in understanding these diseases and in understanding the origin of certain skills in persons, but progress for the most part is slow, creating a healthy respect for the subtlety of the workings of nature, no less when it is human nature. Burke's comment that the nature of human beings is intricate is about as true today as it was when he made it.

    As for the complexity of society, the story is similar to the one just told. The buoyant optimism of Auguste Comte in the nineteenth century with respect to positivism and the creation of the social sciences has, in many cases, produced much less than was hoped for. Of the social sciences today, economics stands as the one that has managed to quantify its findings in ways that allow for measured progress. In other fields, such as sociology and political science, progress has been much slower. The fact that in no social science is there to be found a Newton, a Galileo, a Copernicus, or a Kepler is evidence of how tough the going is. Comparative studies of societies and civilizations as undertaken by Arnold J. Toynbee[114] and Jared Diamond,[115] for example, offer promising insights into what makes a civilization or society survive and flourish and what makes it break down. That being said, no one is rushing to the gates of these studies to declare a victory for social studies. And why not? The explanation is ready to hand: the variety of human life and the multitude of circumstances in which it is placed lead one, at best, to a guarded optimism about any theory seeking to explain this life at the macro level. As A.C. Grayling remarks, "Merely to glance at a fully mature civil society is to see immediately the elaborate structures which create and sustain it, from government and a system of laws to the manners and customs which lubricate transactions between individuals, groups, genders and generations."[116] So the conservative has a point in saying that society is complex.

2. Conservatives raise an important point when they say that it is better to stick with the familiar than to lurch to the unknown. We should not, they counsel, be prepared "to drop the bone we have for its reflection magnified in the mirror of the future."[117] Here they come in conflict with political philosophies such as reform liberalism, democratic socialism, Fascism, and Marxism, to name but a few. When Hume,

Burke, Oakeshott, and Scruton take this position, they are adopting it on the basis of rational prudence and wisdom. Briefly, what the position amounts to is opposition to change, especially accelerated change. Scruton describes this, appropriately, as the "politics of delay." For the conservative, it is simply better to stick with the true and tested. The social experimentation of John Dewey and reform liberals, for example, is anathema.

While there are difficulties with conservatives' resistance to change, there is something in what they say that is worth close attention. To take two examples that illustrate the merit of their claim, let us focus on the institution of public education in Canada and in the United States. These are but two examples from the many that could be cited, not just in the field of education but in others as well.

Residential schools. Residential schools were established in Canada in the nineteenth and twentieth centuries for the purpose of assimilating Canada's Indigenous population into the predominantly English culture with which they were coming into contact.[118] The practice of sending Aboriginal children to residential schools is considered by almost everyone today as having been an unmitigated disaster: it did not result in successful assimilation; it did not facilitate closing the economic and social gap between the two cultures; it ripped children away from their parents; and it created a climate in which unsupervised religious authorities held sway over the lives of innocent children, resulting in sexual abuse and other acts of violence.

Desegregation busing. The American practice of busing black and white children from one school district to another was meant to facilitate racial integration. One of the best-known decisions to enforce busing was the result of a court order issued by a federal judge in Massachusetts, W. Arthur Garrity, in 1974. The order—one of several implemented across the country—was intended to put teeth into the Fourteenth Amendment. This amendment, which guarantees equal protection before the law, had been given a robust interpretation in *Brown v. Board of Education* (1954), the landmark case that had established desegregation in the United States.[119] Today, however, enthusiasm for busing as a way of solving racial strife in the United States is minimal. Busing did not work. Racial discrimination still occurs inside schools in America. The black ghetto has not been dismantled. Conservatives would say of this (as with the residential schools in Canada) that the judicial activism of the Warren Supreme Court in the 1950s, as well as the judicial activism of Judge Garrity in putting teeth into the *Board of Education* decision, was just social experimentation. Notwithstanding Dewey's protests to the contrary, conservatives would see such social experimentation as nothing other than "messing around." Judging by the results, one would be hard-pressed to disagree. There is therefore something to be said with sticking with that which is familiar.

3. Conservatism is correct, not in its rejection of, but in its suspicion of abstract political ideas. Burke, in particular, leads the charge against the use of abstract ideas—or metaphysics—in connection with political reasoning. He affirms that political reasoning is but computing: adding and subtracting, multiplying and dividing moral denominations.[120] Burke makes a persuasive case for seeing the science of constructing a commonwealth as something founded on experience. Speaking of rights and liberties, he says that they admit of infinite modifications and cannot be settled upon "any abstract rule,"[121] The constitution and the laws of the land have to be confirmed

"by the solid test of long experience"—and the wisdom derived from that experience—rather than by abstract ideas such as "the rights of man."

Support for Burke is illustrated by the apparently unsustainable position adopted by US Supreme Court Justice Antonin Scalia (1936–2016). Justice Scalia adhered to a strict "original intent" reading of the Second Amendment of the US Constitution, an amendment guaranteeing the "the right of the people to keep and bear arms." This reading of the Second Amendment, while perhaps not an illustration of abstractionism, is an interpretation that is not supported, certainly not in an obvious way, "by the long test of experience" and "wisdom" derived from experience. One might well ask how the right to bear arms entails the right to carry guns in modern society, to carry guns to lectures in universities, or to carry knives in a courtroom. Yet such are the conclusions of judges like Justice Scalia when wedded to "original intent" and when indifferent to "the long test of experience" and "wisdom." Yet such are the conclusions of judges working with rights freed from their historic context and engaging in abstractionism. Burke's point is well made. A couple of decades later, Jeremy Bentham, from a very different perspective, takes issue with some of the same abstractionism to which Burke takes offence. Bentham, it should be pointed out, construes natural rights as "nonsense upon stilts." So conservatism does raise genuine concerns about the misleading nature of some of the language of political theory.

4. Conservatism, in addition to its suspicion of abstractionism, is correct in its stinging criticism in modern times of structuralism, post-structuralism, deconstructionism, and postmodernism on the grounds of their manifestations of gibberish or gobbledygook. Scruton takes up this issue on behalf of conservatism, and rightly so, providing ample instances drawn from the humanities. And the writing of Alan Sokal and Jean Bricmont justifiably pokes fun at such intellectual impostors who use language in this way.[122] Scruton is correct in this criticism, and to his list of writers of obscurity he could have added the name of Judith Butler when she says, "If a deconstruction of the materiality of bodies suspends and problematizes the traditional ontological referent of the term, it does not freeze, banish, render useless, or deplete of meaning the usage of the term; on the contrary, it provides the conditions to *mobilize* the signifier in the service of an alternative production."[123] Scruton could have added, as well, the name of Jacques Derrida when he says that "the order of the signified is never contemporary, is at best the subtly discrepant inverse or parallel—discrepant by the time of a breath—from the order of the signifier. And the sign must be the unity of a heterogeneity, since the signified (sense or thing, noeme or reality) is not in itself, a signifier, a *trace*: in any case it is not constituted in its sense by its relationship with a possible trace."[124] Scruton rightly condemns this corruption of our thought and language.

5. At least as articulated by Scruton, conservatism is correct in its rejection of postmodernism as a culture of repudiation that seeks to "root out the secret meaning of cultural works, to expose their ideological pretensions, and to send them packing into the past."[125] In some way, the culture of repudiation is but an extension of the work initiated by Karl Marx over a hundred years ago. This culture of repudiation should itself be rejected, according to Scruton, because it is predicated on an undermining of all claims to absolute truth while upholding its own orthodoxy as absolutely binding.[126] Conservatives, like Scruton, see this predication as inconsistent, as

affirming a kind of relativism only to give its own position a privileged status; it is a paradoxical combination—relativism towards Western culture, absolutism in support of the undescribed alternative.[127] Speaking on behalf of conservatism, Scruton is correct in his attack on postmodernists: if postmodernism embraces absolutism, it can hardly criticize the principles of Western thinking that also embrace absolutism, and if postmodernism embraces relativism, it can hardly privilege itself unless it can develop an alternative global postmodernist view, which it has not done.[128] The secret meaning of "repudiation of the ideals of the Enlightenment" is thus disclosed and sent packing.

6. The social disruption that seems attributable to multiculturalism provides the foundation of a rebuttable presumption advanced by conservatives, such as Scruton, in favour of the status quo and the absence of change, but not reform, when it comes to social policy dealing with culture. While it may be true that some change is foisted on governments as a result of changing technology and economic collapse, among other things, it does appear that social solidarity or unity is compromised when governments move hastily and unnecessarily in the field of introducing new culture patterns into those long established. Indeed, it seems that this is at the root of the Dutch homosexual community's *volte-face* in abandoning its left-wing ideas in favour of conservatism in recent years, as mentioned at the beginning of this chapter. The values of immigrant Muslim youths have driven them in this direction. Reform liberals, such as Will Kymlicka, challenge this type of argument in discussing multiculturalism, as will be seen in the ensuing chapter, but their challenge seems largely unsuccessful in this one specific domestic policy sphere.

While it is undoubtedly true that multiculturalism enriches a society (in this, reform liberals are vindicated), too much of it can break the back of the reed supporting it, and in this conservatives such as Scruton are vindicated. The idea that too much multiculturalism can prove destructive of a society seems to be what motivated the public backlash in Ontario in 2005 over the proposal to permit "*sharia* law tribunals to settle family disputes."[129] And it is in this context that fears arise concerning the victimization of women through "honour killings" and other less severe methods of patriarchal control of women, practices from which liberal Muslims distance themselves.

Much the same point is made with great effectiveness in Laurent Cantet's movie *The Class* (2008), unsurprisingly a French movie, which dramatically presents the difficulty of pedagogy in France's multicultural environment. Undoubtedly, conservatives have difficulty in making this argument because it can easily be construed as "racist" or "xenophobic," but beyond this there is an empirical claim that conservatives rest their argument on—namely, that societies can take only so much multicultural stress before they begin to generate very unpleasant conflict leading to social decay. This is a claim that has force and strengthens conservatism, and should not, in fairness, be dismissed solely as racist or xenophobic nonsense.

Evaluation: The Weaknesses of Conservatism

1. While conservatism has a point when it says it is better to stick with that which is familiar, it introduces at the same time a dark side. If change and especially innovation

are to be shunned, what is one to do when faced with obvious social institutions that are unjust, such as slavery? If conservatives resist change even when talking about such a practice, then they can be accused of being not only morally insensitive but morally callous. On the other hand, if they allow for change when dealing with some institutions, such as slavery, then why not allow change in other areas of our lives where reason so dictates?

One of these areas could well be the institution of marriage. If those advocating conservatism choose to allow innovations with some institutions and not with others, they have one of two choices: either admit to being inconsistent, or provide a set of criteria that allow for a clear distinction to be drawn between circumstances in which change is acceptable and circumstances in which it is not. For his part, Oakeshott seems to opt for the second of these, but his distinctions are not clear. He allows that, in human relationships such as those between a master and servant, between an owner and bailiff, between a buyer and seller, and between a principal and agent, "some result is sought; each party is concerned with the ability of the other to provide it. If what is being sought is lacking, it is to be expected that the relationship will lapse or be terminated."[130] Would the master–slave relationship fall into this same group? If not, why not? If it would, what about the institution of marriage? These questions suggest very strongly that even one of the most articulate of conservatives, Michael Oakeshott, does not provide sufficient guidance to troubling aspects of his position on change: either too little is included in what could legitimately change, or too much.

Nor do other comments made by Oakeshott, measured though they be, provide a way around the just-mentioned dilemma. These other comments are as follows: (i) since innovation (read: "change") entails gains and losses, the onus of proof for a balance of benefit should reside on the would-be innovator; (ii) the more likely an innovation resembles growth, the less likely it will result in loss; (iii) an innovation designed for a particular problem is more desirable than one that aims at generality and perfection; (iv) slow change is better than rapid change; and (v) innovation is less likely to be corrupted when the projected change is limited.[131] However, even these guarded comments do not address the foregoing dilemma. Nor do the comments of Roger Scruton help much in this area. Talk of conservatism as the politics of delay and as the maintenance of social ecology does not provide much illumination on what change should be countenanced and what should not. In the result, either conservatism seems morally brutish, or its notion of acceptable change becomes so broad that the definition of conservatism loses its content as articulated by Hume, Burke, Oakeshott, and Scruton.

2. Conservatism, at least as advocated by Burke, is rigidly inegalitarian. Burke, in particular, affirms the legitimacy of classes, not just with respect to "antient republics" but with respect to his contemporary society. He speaks of the nobility at the time of the French Revolution "comport[ing] themselves towards [the inferior classes] with good nature."[132] As previously seen, Burke's class distinctions are based on such things as birth, education, profession, and methods of acquiring property. The best retort to Burke is given by no less a person than Adam Smith. In a very rarely cited passage from *The Wealth of Nations*, Smith says, "The difference of natural talents in different

men is, in reality, much less than we are aware of, and the very different genius which appears to distinguish men of different professions, when grown up to maturity, is not upon many occasions so much the cause, as the effect of the division of labour."[133] For Smith, unlike Burke, the division of labour creates genius, not the reverse. This line of thinking runs counter to and seriously challenges Burke's inegalitarian and aristocratic line of thinking. Supporting Smith against Burke is the simple fact that people, when given opportunities, frequently prove themselves—suggesting that humans have much in common, and implying that class divisions and inegalitarianism are not rationally defensible.

3. Conservatism also subscribes implausibly to the organic theory of human society. According to this theory, society is thought of as an organism and compared to the human body.[134] At best this is a weak analogy, and it does not provide the rational foundation for establishing a political ideology. While it might be true that societies break down into national cultures, and that it is not easy to export these cultures or the people from them, this truth does not shed much light on what public policies should be countenanced in a society. For example, it is difficult to see how the organic analogy helps one decide whether the government should adopt a tight fiscal policy, a new environmental policy, a tougher crime bill, or free daycare. The reed of organicism is simply too weak to bear this kind of weight. And certainly any attempt to use the arguments of organicism in confronting radicalism as argued by Compte, Marx, and Bentham would be sure to fail, for this would mean countering beliefs in favour of political levelling, economic levelling, and man's perfectibility on the basis of an analogy with the human body. How such counter-arguments would be developed is difficult to discern.

4. Conservatism seems also to have difficulty with issues raised by Thomas Paine and his *Rights of Man*. Whereas conservatives, like Burke, are loath to accept talk of rights, or are at the very least suspicious of it, Paine endorses this talk. Paine rejects, correctly, Burke's reasoning that would have rights trumped by the "authority of the dead" or "the vanity and presumption of governing beyond the grave."[135] The specific rights that Paine thinks of here are the right of English people to choose their own governors, their right to cashier them for misconduct, and their right to frame a government for themselves. Paine successfully makes the point that rights need to be taken seriously. At the very least, Paine argues effectively enough to show that if rights are to be rejected, they will have to be rejected by different arguments that are more persuasive than those offered by Burke and other conservatives.

5. Conservatism does not have a ready answer to the points made by John Stuart Mill in *On Liberty* when he says that while traditions and customs provide evidence of what experience teaches one, and as such have a claim to a person's deference, nonetheless (i) one's experience may be too narrow; (ii) the interpretation of one's experience may unsuitable to another; and (iii) the customs may be good as customs in themselves, but stultifying and unsuitable as far as education or development are concerned.[136] Mill rounds out his remarks on custom and tradition with this comment: "The despotism of custom is everywhere the standing hindrance to human advancement,

being in unceasing antagonism to the disposition to aim at something better than customary."[137]

6. As a conservative, Scruton argues on behalf of marriage as something with a distinct "social aura," and not something exhausted by a contract of mutual co-operation. He thinks that marriage ceases to be viewed as "a rite of passage into another and higher life" when contractually construed. One difficulty with Scruton's position here is that it seems to be based on a tacit religious view, which Scruton endorses when he talks about the "species' hunger for the sacred." But it is precisely this religious view of the world that many who endorse a non-higher life contractual understanding of marriage would challenge. Scruton does not show that marriage construed contractually cannot result in good child-rearing, nor does he show that marriage so construed runs the risk of children being brought into the world as strangers, nor does he show that homosexual marriages rob marriage of its social meaning. With respect to the last of these, Scruton owes us an account of social meaning.

7. Scruton makes use of the interesting notion of social ecology. But he does not show that multiculturalism is a threat to the well-being of social organisms as they exist around the world. He does not show, therefore, how the accumulation of art, literature, and humane reflection—what he calls culture—is threatened by multiculturalism. For some, particularly reform liberals, multiculturalism can add new life to traditional cultures, thereby energizing rather than enervating them.

8. Finally, there are counter-examples to offset the examples of residential schools and forced busing as found in the foregoing discussion of the strengths of conservatism. For instance, anti-discrimination statutes have been introduced in jurisdictions around the world, prohibiting unjust treatment on the basis of such factors as race, gender, age, sexual orientation, and disability. Furthermore, anti-smoking rules (e.g., no smoking in public buildings, no smoking in restaurants) have reduced tobacco consumption, a surprising result given that non-smoking legislation was motivated in large part by the effects of second-hand smoke. So, as the reform liberal John Dewey says, social experimentation cannot be dismissed as "just messing around." Sometimes, and not all that infrequently, the social designers get it right.

9. The principle of liberty articulated by John Stuart Mill is a principle of tolerance. In the vernacular, it is a rule that encourages all in a democratic society to tolerate any practice that does not cause harm to others. It could be argued plausibly that deference to custom and tradition blocks, in unreasonable fashion, the tolerance Mill espouses. Hence, contrary to what conservative ideology says, the wearing of the niqab during citizenship swearing-in ceremonies or the wearing of a turban in the RCMP (Canada's federal police force) should not be prohibited. Briefly, no harm, no restriction. Whether one agrees with this reasoning or not, the fact remains that anyone embracing Mill's thought will inevitably be driven to permitting the wearing of the niqab during these ceremonies and the wearing of turbans in the RCMP. For those supporting such practices with Mill's principle, these practices present no more problem than the introduction of unisex toilets—something once frowned upon but now widely accepted.

Related Websites

Cato Institute
www.cato.org/

The Conservative Citizen
http://theconservativecitizen.com/essay-the-conservative-ideology/

Heritage Foundation
www.heritage.org/initiatives/first-principles/conservatism

Internet Encyclopedia of Philosophy
www.iep.utm.edu/polphil/#SH3b

Kirk, Russell. "The Essence of Conservatism." Russell Kirk Center for Cultural Renewal
www.kirkcenter.org/index.php/detail/essence-1957/

Further Readings on Conservatism

Berkowitz, Peter. *Constitutional Conservatism, Liberty, Self-government, and Political Moderation*. Stanford, CA: Hoover Institution Press, Stanford University, 2013.
Brooke, Jeffrey. *Dismantling Canada: Stephen Harper's New Conservative Agenda*. Montreal and Kingston: McGill-Queen's University Press, 2015.
Burke, Edmund. *Revolutionary Writings: Reflections on the Revolution in France and the First Letter on a Regicide Peace*. Edited by Ian Hampshire Monk. Cambridge: Cambridge University Press, 2014.
Carsten, Jensen. *The Right and the Welfare State*. London: Oxford University Press, 2014.
Celis, Karen, and Sarah Childs. *Gender, Conservatism and Political Representation*. Colchester, UK: European Consortium for Political Research, 2014.
Farber, David R. *The Rise and Fall of Modern American Conservatism: A Short History*. Princeton, NJ: Princeton University Press, 2010.
Grove, John. "Calhoun and Conservative Reform." *American Political Thought* 4, 2 (Spring 2015): 203–27.
Horwitz, Robert Britt. *America's Right: Anti- Establishment Conservatism from Goldwater to the Tea Party*. Cambridge: Polity, 2013.
Huntington, Samuel P. "Conservatism as an Ideology." *American Political Science Review* 51 (1957): 454–73.
Kirk, Russell. *The Conservative Mind*. London: Faber and Faber, 1954.
Lloyd, Gordon. *New Deal and Modern American Conservatism: A Defining Rivalry*. Stanford, CA: Hoover Institution Press, Stanford University, 2013.
Maciag, Drew. *Edmund Burke in America: The Contested Career of the Father of Modern Conservatism*. Ithaca, NY: Cornell University Press, 2013.
———. "The Latest Remake of Edmund Burke." *Chronicle of Higher Education* 60, 34 (2014): B10–B12.
Morgan, Marietta. *A Citizen's Guide to American Ideology: Conservatism and Liberalism in Contemporary Politics*. New York: Routledge, 2012.
Nisbet, Robert. *Conservatism: Dream and Reality*. Milton Keynes, UK: Open University Press, 1986.

O'Hara, Kieron. *Conservatism*. London: Reaction Books, 2011.

Postell, Joseph W., and Johnathon O'Neill. *Toward an American Conservatism: Constitutional Conservatism in the Progressive Era*. New York: Palgrave Macmillan, 2013.

Robin, Corey. *The Reactionary Mind: Conservatism from Edmund Burke to Sarah Palin*. New York: Oxford University Press, 2011.

Scruton, Roger. *The Meaning of Conservatism*. Harmondsworth, UK: Penguin, 1980.

———. *A Political Philosophy*. London: Continuum, 2006.

———. *Culture Counts: Faith and Feeling in a World Besieged*. New York: Encounter Books, 2007.

———. *How to Think Seriously about the Planet: The Case for an Environmental Conservatism*. New York: Oxford University Press, 2012.

Thackeray, David. *Conservatism for the Democratic Age: Conservative Cultures and the Challenge of Mass Politics in Early Twentieth-Century England*. Manchester: Manchester University Press, 2013.

Tuck, Richard. *Natural Rights Theories: Their Origin and Development*. Cambridge: Cambridge University Press, 1979.

Von Mises, Ludwig. *The Anti-Capitalistic Mentality*. Princeton, NJ: Princeton University Press, 1956.

4 Reform Liberalism

Learning Objectives

- To appreciate the attempted refutation of laissez-faire principles in reform liberalism.
- To understand the important role of institutions in creating equal opportunities in reform liberalism.
- To acknowledge the restraints on liberty found in reform liberalism.
- To recognize the affirmation of change and non-violent radicalism in reform liberalism.

During the first half of the nineteenth century it became evident that serious social problems were arising, largely as a result of the Industrial Revolution and the ideological changes initiated by Adam Smith. In previous chapters it has been argued that the scientific revolution, the Protestant Reformation, and the emergence of the nation-state profoundly influenced modern history, but it would not be far from the truth to say that the Industrial Revolution was a fourth event that added to the shaping of modern history.[1] The Industrial Revolution, which piggybacked on top of the scientific revolution, along with the ideological perspective afforded by John Locke and Adam Smith, proved to be a mighty machine for transforming the social world. The writings of Charles Dickens (1812–1870) capture vividly the social forces at work during this time, forces created by industrial changes and the political ideology that went with them.

From the perspective of the history of ideologies, the nineteenth century can be viewed as a cluster bomb, comprising several miniature bombs: reform liberalism, Marxism, and democratic socialism. The first of these to be discussed, **reform liberalism**, is the offspring of classical liberalism, an ideology that failed to speak to the needs of the industrial age.[2] Those thinkers who fell within the ambit of this new ideology included the nineteenth-century writers John Stuart Mill (1806–1873) and T.H. Green (1836–1882); the late nineteenth- and early twentieth-century writers L.T. Hobhouse (1864–1929), J.A. Hobson (1858–1940), John Dewey (1859–1952), and John Maynard Keynes (1883–1946); and the mid- to late twentieth-century writers John Kenneth Galbraith (1908–2006), Ronald Dworkin (1931–), John Rawls (1921–2002), Pierre Trudeau (1919–2000), and Will

Kymlicka (1962–). In the ensuing discussion, only the works of Mill, Green, Hobhouse, Hobson, Dewey, Keynes, Rawls, and Kymlicka will be considered. All of these writers share in common a recognition of the importance of the individual and the individual's civil liberties, as well as a recognition of the importance of equality of opportunity coupled with a more egalitarian allocation of resources than that provided by the market alone. Reform liberals such as these thinkers are sensitive to market failures in a way in which Adam Smith and his followers were not. Undoubtedly the starting point for this discussion has to be the resourceful and independent philosopher, John Stuart Mill.

It is worthwhile bearing in mind that the political ideology advocated by those discussed here is the same ideology practised by many who currently are attempting to address the global economic meltdown. It is the ideology of many (though not all) countries in the G20 that pledged $1.1 trillion in new resources for the International Monetary Fund (IMF). It is the ideology of Nobel economics laureate Joseph Stiglitz, chair of a UN Commission of Experts on financial system reform, when he proposes such measures as making polluters of the financial system cover the costs of the economic cleanup, creating greater competition so as to prevent any institution from being too big to fail, making for greater transparency and simplicity and democratic accountability for the financial system, and ensuring that the regulators do not become captives of the institutions they are regulating.[3] And in many ways it is the ideology of US President Barack Obama, as found in the American Recovery and Reinvestment Act he signed in February 2009. Among other things, the Act aims to provide a tax cut for workers who earn the least, as well as to initiate health reform, which Obama claims is greater than any carried out in the United States in the last decade.[4]

That reform liberalism is making a comeback is evident in the writing and observation of Paul Krugman, widely known American economist. In the summer of 2015 Krugman wrote a brief but incisive article entitled "The M.I.T. Gang,"[5] in which he drew attention to the displacement of the "Chicago boys" by the "MIT gang," that is, the displacement of those economists, trained at the University of Chicago schooled in radical free-market laissez-faire economics, by the economists trained at the Massachusetts Institute of Technology in Keynesian economics. These two schools of thinking pitted the likes of Milton Friedman against John Maynard Keynes. According to Krugman, those from MIT following in the footsteps of Keynes, who recognized "the imperfections of markets and the role that monetary and fiscal policy can play in boosting a depressed economy,"[6] include Mario Draghi (President of the European Central Bank), Oliver Blanchard (Chief Economist of the IMF), Maurice Obstfeld (Blanchard's replacement), and Stanley Fisher (US Federal Reserve vice-chairman).[7] All of these individuals represent the ongoing influence of reform liberalism as articulated in economic terms by Keynes, and they represent

Central Beliefs of Reform Liberalism

- Human nature is rational and not self-sufficient.
- Liberty as an ideal is the opportunity to realize one's self.
- The end of government is the cultivation of the person.
- The rights of humans are mixed with consideration of utilities in determining government policy.

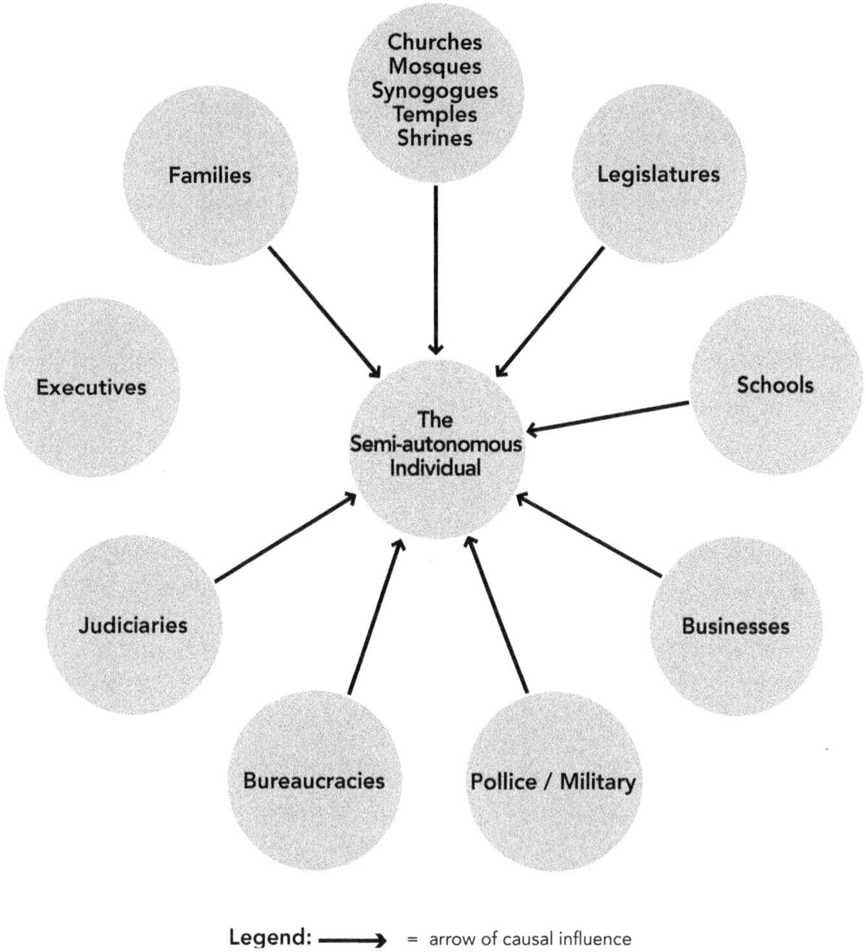

Figure 4.1 Reform Liberalism's Pluralistic Model of Society

those who maintained during the economic crisis of 2008 that "inflation and interest rates would stay low in a depressed economy, and that attempts to slash deficits too soon would deepen the slump."[8] Krugman is unrelenting in his attack on the ideological stance taken by the likes of Jeb Bush, former governor of Florida, who criticized Medicare in the United States and wished to phase out the program. According to Krugman, such individuals remind him of a Rip Van Winkle "who slept through everything since he left the governor's office."[9] In other words, Krugman believes such right-wing individuals as Bush are like zombies, denying the truth that evidently confronts them. Evidently, if Krugman is to be believed, the reform liberalism of Keynes is alive and well and living in the halls, not just of MIT, but of many important global institutions and in the text of successful government policies such as Medicare.

More evidence that reform liberalism is making a comeback is found in some of the proceedings of the Athens Democracy Forum of 2015 organized by *The International*

New York Times. Echoing the values attached to equality and democracy in some of the authors discussed below, the participants of the first panel of the Forum, including Paul Krugman (Nobel winner and *New York Times* columnist), Anna Diamantopoulou (former European Commissioner for Employment and Social Affairs and cabinet minister in the socialist government of Greece), and Alan Rousso (managing director at the European Bank for Reconstruction and Development [EBRD]), reached a consensus "that the levels of inequality today, even in developing countries, are hurting democracy and creating pressing challenges for policy-makers."[10] Linking equality and democracy, or the absence of the former and the diminishment of the latter, in this manner echoes the very ideas of some, if not all, reform liberals. Once again, there is ample proof that reform liberalism has traction among many current celebrated thinkers and influential players.

And so begins our journey with the first figure in the ideological tradition of reform liberalism.

John Stuart Mill

While it is possible to construe some of Mill's leading political ideas along lines that are quite compatible with classical liberalism and even at times with libertarianism, other remarks of his, especially those positive remarks dealing with socialism, suggest that the natural home for Mill—all things considered—is found at a point between classical liberalism and socialism. Such a position is reform liberalism. Of those ideas advanced by Mill, the one that stands above the rest is that of liberty. His work, by the same name, published in 1859, still remains the most impressive work on the subject in the English language. It is as refreshing today as it was in 1859.

It will be recalled that John Locke, in his *Second Treatise of Government*, places emphasis on the notion of the rights of man, specifically the rights of life, liberty, and possessions. Of these rights, the one he singles out for special attention is that of the right to possessions, which he generalizes as the right to property—property being, according to him, an institution of appropriation so essential to man's self-preservation that man is entitled to it. He proceeds to place limitations on this appropriation in a state of nature. The limitations are those of labour, spoilage, and sufficiency. Locke, however, does not provide a detail and equivalent analysis of the right to liberty. This job, or at least a part of this job, was left for John Stuart Mill.

One must say "at least a part of this job" for the simple reason that Mill, along with other utilitarians such as Jeremy Bentham (1748–1832), saw talk of natural rights as (in Bentham's words) "nonsense on stilts." Indeed, Mill goes so far as to distance himself from talk about rights when he says, "I forgo any advantage which could be derived from the idea of abstract right as a thing independent of utility. I regard utility as the ultimate appeal on all ethical questions."[11] So it was left to John Stuart Mill to undertake an analysis of the notion, if not the right, of liberty. This he fulfills in *On Liberty*, where he completes a detailed study of the "nature and limits of the power which can be legitimately exercised by society over the individual."[12] Mill's study of this subject is thorough: he sinks a shaft into the surface of an intellectual globe and extracts a core sample of the subject entitled "liberty," then proceeds to analyze it in detail.

Mill's moral philosophy is a kind of consequentialism, specifically **utilitarianism**. But it is a kind of utilitarianism that is different from Bentham's. Mill, unlike his predecessor Bentham, maintains that there are qualitative differences in pleasures (e.g., push-pin, a children's game, is not as good as poetry), and argues that the greatest aggregate happiness is not the same as the continual satisfaction of one desire after another, but is found in the individual's development of the self.[13] Whereas a rights-based theory such as Locke's leads to social contractarianism, Mill's utility-based theory leads away from it.[14] Mill's moral philosophy drives his political ideology, the fundamental value of which is self-improvement. Self-improvement, which displaces Bentham's happiness as the goal of Mill's consequentialism, is logically tied to freedom or liberty. For Mill, liberty functions as a necessary condition of self-improvement. So it is to his principle of liberty that we now turn.

The Harm Principle

In *On Liberty*, Mill makes clear that the object of his essay is to assert one "very simple principle" that is entitled to govern the dealings of society with the individual in the way of compulsion and control.[15] He then proceeds to state his principle in two versions: (i) the sole end for which mankind is warranted, individually or collectively, in interfering with the liberty of action of any of their number is self-protection; and (ii) the only purpose for which power can be rightfully exercised over any member of a civilized community, against that individual's will, is to prevent harm to others.[16] Since it is evident from other things Mill says that the second of these more accurately expresses what he wants to claim, hereinafter our attention focuses on this version.

Mill proceeds to examine his principle in light of (i) freedom of opinion and thought; (ii) freedom of tastes and pursuits, and, more generally, freedom of doing as we like; and (iii) freedom of association. Mill continues his discussion by analyzing in detail the essential role each of these freedoms plays in allowing the individual to choose her or his own path of self-improvement. His point in detailing this role is to underscore the logical link between self-improvement and freedom, the latter being a necessary condition of the former. It should be noted, however, that none of these comments by Mill actually addresses in direct form the Harm Principle. To tie this principle to his claim that self-improvement entails freedom, one needs to determine under what conditions Mill thinks harm is done to an individual. Only when this is understood will one be able to determine when Mill really thinks restrictions on a person's thoughts, actions, and associations are justified.

Two Maxims

To get a better handle on Mill's thinking here, we need to look at what Mill calls two maxims, which form the doctrine of the essay *On Liberty*. Maxim One states that an individual is not accountable to society for his actions, insofar as these concern the interests of no person but himself. Maxim Two states that for actions prejudicial [read: harmful] to the interests of others, the individual is accountable, and may be subjected to social or legal punishment, if society is of the opinion that one or the other is required for its protection.[17] These maxims put into relief some of the problems with the so-called "simple" Harm Principle. A very real difficulty occurs in connection with these maxims, and by implication with the Harm Principle: nowhere does Mill give either a clear account of the interests of others or a coherent account of harm to others. As has been said, "The obscurity of Mill's conception of human interests expresses a larger difficulty having to do with his account of harm."[18]

Obscurity notwithstanding, it seems that Mill wishes to construe these notions in a robust fashion, and not in a Lockean night watchman fashion. Thus, something like positive liberty is embraced by Mill, as distinct from the negative liberty embraced by Locke. **Positive liberty** includes the enhancement of opportunities for a person's exercising choice more effectively, while **negative liberty** means the absence of constraints, especially those of government, upon the person's decision to act in a particular way.[19]

This endorsement by Mill is evident in his comments on education and on poverty. In the case of the former, he is far from indifferent to the need of an education of a certain standard for "every human being who is born its citizen" (i.e., a citizen of the state).[20] This he takes to be "a self-evident axiom." It is this belief that inspires him to say it is a moral crime not to provide instruction and training for the young mind, a task the state must fulfill if parents prove negligent in their duty.[21] Clearly, Mill understands "harm" and "interests of others" in robust ways that open the door to government action of a positive nature in areas including but not restricted to the field of education.

As for poverty, in his posthumous *Chapters on Socialism* (1879), Mill decries the enslavement of the majority of people to poverty, "an evil equal to almost any of those against which mankind may have hitherto struggled."[22] What is called for, he suggests, under the circumstances, is an adaption or adjustment of the ideas of property to the improvement of human affairs. In fact, Mill goes so far as to say that socialists have successfully made their case that the poverty of the present economic order demands a consideration of those means by which the institution of property may be made to work (or changed) so as to be more beneficial to the large portion of society that presently gets the least share of its benefits.[23] Nor was this position of Mill's something that surfaced late in his writings. It is already present in his 1848 *Principles of Political Economy*, where he argues against the principle of apportioning the produce of labour in such a way that the largest portions go to those who have never worked and the least amount goes to those who engage in "fatiguing" and "exhausting" bodily labour.[24]

Whether talking of the institution of education or the institution of property, Mill recognizes the harm to one's interests that could occur, and in fact did occur, when institutions such as these were not structured to be compatible with a person's interest as a progressive being. Mill sees that reform of just such institutions is needed for harm to be avoided, for the progressive interests not to be frustrated, and for real liberty to be realized. One might say that Mill's liberalism consisted in his recognition of the dependence of individual intelligence and character on such political and social institutions.

One should add in passing here that Mill's concern for institutional support for the liberty of the individual extends not only to the institutions of education and property, but also to the institution of wealth and capital itself. In contrast to classical liberals such as Smith, with his notion of increasing productivity, trade, and wealth, Mill advocates "the stationary state of capital and wealth." He argues that while "riches are power" and the path to the attainment of wealth should be "open to all," the best state for humans is one in which no one is poor and no one desires to be richer—or fears being "thrust back" by the competitive efforts of others.[25] For Mill, the competitive world of classical liberalism seems to be but a "disagreeable symptom of one of the phases of industrial progress" and one from which he wishes to distance himself. Thus, institutional reform in the matter of wealth and capital is something Mill embraces in his notion of harm reduction.

What one can conclude about Mill is his commitment to an individualism that, in its liberty, is restrained by a robust notion of harm and the interests of others. This harm and these interests he sees as able to be mitigated by institutional reform.

T.H. Green

The core of T.H. Green's political ideology is captured by the notion of the state having as its role the removal of obstacles to the good life. While it is customary to find Green's political thought discussed in terms of his "Lectures on the Principles of Political Obligation," it is more promising to attempt to locate his political views in his much less well-thumbed lecture on "Liberal Education and Freedom of Contract." It is to this latter work that we shall now turn our attention.

Green, in discussing liberalism, quickly fastens on the notion of individual liberty or freedom. And while he admits that all would agree that freedom is the "greatest of blessings," he maintains that we need to be careful what we mean by it. Green makes clear straightaway that what liberals have in mind when they talk of freedom is not freedom from restraint or compulsion, but "a positive power or capacity of doing or enjoying something worth doing . . . we mean a power which each man exercises through the help or security given to him by his fellow-men."[26] Again, he says that "freedom . . . is valuable as an end. That end is what I call freedom in the positive sense: in other words, the liberation of the powers of all men equally for contributions to a common good."[27] Green goes on to sound the clarion call of reform liberals: late nineteenth-century British legislation with respect to labour, education, and health, involving as it does a manifest interference with freedom of contract, is "justified on the ground that it is the business of the state . . . to maintain the conditions without which a free exercise of the human faculties is impossible."[28]

With this clarion call—this justification for an active state—Green and his followers promoted a number of government policies in the UK: the development of public education, including adult education delivered through the Workers' Educational Association, as well as the development of social and community work such as the settlement houses in East London. In addition, Green and his followers aroused the conscience of the upper classes in Britain and influenced the slow elimination of the last vestiges of colonialism. All of this was done in the name of a new liberalism that saw the state removing obstacles to the good life as a precondition for the exercise of meaningful liberty. And again, all of this was undertaken in the spirit of a liberalism that opposes the class conflict of Marxism and aspires to a unified nation grounded in a moralized capitalism.[29]

Green clearly rejects the night watchman approach to freedom. The role of the state, in an even more pronounced form than Mill conceives, is to create conditions of rough equality so that all persons have the real opportunity through institutions, such as those of health, labour, and education, to do the things they choose to do and to develop themselves in their own way. What we have in the case of Green is a strong endorsement of positive liberty.

L.T. Hobhouse

According to the celebrated Marxist, C. Wright Mills, L.T. Hobhouse—in his frequently cited *Liberalism* (1911)—provides perhaps the best statement in the twentieth century of liberal ideals.[30] This statement of Mills is reason enough to include Hobhouse in a study of reform liberalism.

The State and the Individual

The liberalism endorsed by Hobhouse falls within the traditions initiated by Mill and Green, both of whom recognized a dynamic conception of the individual and society. Perhaps this linkage between the individual and society is best expressed in the case of Hobhouse by his acknowledgement that the function of the state is to provide for those conditions that enable the development of the mind and character. This view of the state and the right of the working man is owing to "an enhanced sense of responsibility" as well as "the teaching of experience." From these qualities, Hobhouse derives the principle that the individual simply cannot stand alone, and between him and the state there stands a reciprocal obligation. Among the obligations or duties of the state, he argues, is that of securing the conditions necessary for the self-maintenance of the normal, healthy citizen.

Central to Hobhouse's view of these conditions is a "living wage," which would be expected to cover the costs of food, clothing, and shelter for a family, as well as the risks of accident and unemployment, coupled with education and one's needs in old age. Meeting these conditions, he thinks, would provide a "substructure" for the normal individual that would enable him to "keep his head above water." This ties into the liberal notion of responsibility, Hobhouse believes, for if the state lifts the burden from the shoulders of individuals so that it is not too great to bear, individuals can better be charged with a fixed responsibility. The obligation or duty on the part of the normal person would be that of labouring to earn his or her own living, but this obligation needs to be seen, thinks Hobhouse, against the backdrop of society providing the means of earning by useful work all those necessities of a healthy and efficient life. This is required as a principle of economic justice.[31]

Socialism, Individualism, and Hobhouse's Liberalism

Hobhouse is conscious of possible confusion about his ideological position, and for this reason he acknowledges that many of his ideas, including that which boldly asserts an equation between social service and reward, make up the "framework" of socialism. However, he is quick to point out that socialism seems oblivious of the elements of individual right upon which he lays emphasis. Thus, he thinks that the liberalism he advances aims to do justice to both the social and individual factors in the workplace, and thereby distinguishes itself from socialism as well as rugged individualism. The delicate balance Hobhouse wishes to achieve between socialism and individualism is well caught when he says that "it is the right, in the same sense, of every person capable of performing some useful social function that he should have the opportunity of so doing."[32] Finally, it should be added, Hobhouse is emphatic—echoing Mill—that the rights of individuals are constantly defined in terms of the common good, which in turn is defined in terms of the welfare of individuals comprising society.[33]

J.A. Hobson

The reform liberalism of J.A. Hobson attempts to steer a course between the six-headed monster Scylla of classical liberalism and the whirlpool Charybdis of socialism. It does this by acknowledging the importance of the individual, his/her liberty, and the development of personality,[34] as well as by acknowledging an important role for the state in establishing bodies essential to the individual in the use of that liberty.[35]

Problems with Capitalism

Hobson's ground for rejecting classical liberalism and its endorsement of capitalism is that there is no tendency for buyers and sellers, in the bargaining process, to make an equitable gain or equal gain from the price at which they buy or sell. The inequality in outcome is attributable in large measure to the inequality in the bargaining powers between buyers and sellers. The outcome of this is a far cry from the distribution according to need, resulting instead in inequities in the midst of growing waste and disturbance.[36] In memorable words, Hobson goes on to say that "the economics as well as the ethics of capitalism have now been punctured," with the result that there is a need to displace the blind enterprise of profiteers by "some conscious ordering of industry under public control."[37] Evidently, Hobson remains deeply suspicious of the bargaining process at the root of capitalism. This, he thinks, is a bargaining process more suited to Robinson Crusoe than to fully engaged people of the twentieth century, owing to its very nature of inhibiting consideration of the good of others. In the result, self-interest of this sort involves a "hardening of the moral arteries" and a neglect of equity, kindness, and consideration, when one should be establishing "in all human institutions the education of a truly social personality."[38]

Problems with Socialism

For Hobson the true line of cleavage between socialism and individualism lies in the domain of the necessary productive qualities of the craftsman, artist, or skilled risk-taker.[39] Socialists wrongly assume, thinks Hobson, that they can maintain the liberty of those who participate in the skilled satisfaction of non-routine consumption as well as of those who engage in skilled creative work simply on the basis of a motive of social service.[40] But this is, according to Hobson, rather fanciful: it is to imagine that we already have the Kingdom of God on earth. It is to imagine that human nature can be changed here and now, peacefully and suddenly, and that people will freely accept those changes in human nature that will make them willingly engage in social service rather than in self-interested activity. But, as Hobson maintains, the difficulties here are many, including (i) the resistance most people would have to accepting the opinion of a dominant minority that their interpretation of human nature is sound, and (ii) evidence in the history of tyrants masking their desire for power under the label of public service.[41] Clearly, Hobson thinks that socialism fails the critical ethical test of any large socialist experiment: it cannot persuade most members of society to consider it fair and agreeable that they do their proper share of productive work and take their proper share from the general good.[42] For Hobson, a willing submission to "a single social will is simply not there" in ordinary times.[43]

Individualism

Hobson advocates that the state own a number of routine and key industries and that private individuals own others. In addition, he envisages all industries, public and private, being subject to public regulations in the matter of wages, hours, and prices. But he resists the idea that some standard of production could be justifiably used in the name of equality to cripple progress in economic activities and in the finer arts of human life.[44] Economic levelling has to be restrained in the name of individual liberty. Indeed, in the case of economic institutions, their ethical soundness depends on how effective they are as instruments of cultivation of personality and community, a cultivation that requires room for human liberty. Individuality and community are compatible values.[45] Generalizing beyond economic institutions, Hobson maintains that a goal in the establishment of all institutions is "the education of a truly social personality, and a sound community in which such social personalities may live and thrive."[46] Evidently, the individual is to be surrounded by those structures that enable her or him to lead a life worth living.

John Dewey

The starting point for any coherent presentation of reform liberal ideas in the United States is John Dewey, who was influenced by T.H. Green. In a rather short work entitled *Liberalism and Social Action* (indeed, a work based on lectures given by Dewey at the University of Virginia), and in a short article published in the same year in the *Journal of Philosophy*, entitled "The Future of Liberalism," Dewey outlines in some detail what he has in mind by "renascent Liberalism."

Individuality

According to Dewey, "Liberalism is committed to an end that is at once enduring and flexible: the liberation of individuals so that the realization of their capacities may be the law of their life."[47] True to the spirit of the earlier liberal tradition, Dewey emphasizes individuality and liberty as the focal point of reform or renascent liberalism. He believes that the old liberalism, the one that stands in need of reform, added the conception of natural laws to that of natural rights.[48] The natural rights to which he refers are those of the Whig movement and of John Locke: the right to life, liberty, and possessions. The natural laws are "economic in character," exemplified by the law of supply and demand. The "fundamental defect" of classical liberalism, according to Dewey, is its "lack of perception of historic relativity."[49] From this fundamental defect emerges a conception of the individual as complete and of liberty as a "ready-made possession" of each person.[50]

The upshot is a view of individuality and liberty thought to be good for all times and places. But, says Dewey, one is left with a pseudo-liberalism in need of elimination. Once eliminated, renascent liberalism can concentrate on the individual as something that is not fixed and ready-made. Knowing that social conditions may have an adverse effect on individuality, reform or renascent liberalism "takes an active interest in the working of social institutions that have a bearing, positive or negative, upon the growth of individuals who shall be rugged in fact and not merely in abstract theory."[51] In addition, liberalism, as advocated by Dewey, embraces the idea of historic relativity and what this implies—namely, "the content of the individual and freedom change with time."[52] This commitment to historic relativity entails a commitment to experimental procedure— "the positive counterpart of opposition to doctrinal absolutism."[53]

Experimentalism

Liberalism, for Dewey, embraces experimentalism. The experimentalism to which he refers keeps an open door to change, not just reform. Here the liberalism of Dewey diverges significantly from the conservatism of Burke, which allows for reform but not change. We should recall that Burke feels that change alters the substance of objects themselves, whereas reform is not a change in substance but the direct application of a remedy to a particular problem.[54] Dewey, contrary to Burke, openly embraces change. This is seen in his experimental procedure, which "carries with it the idea of continuous reconstruction of the ideas of individuality and of liberty in intimate connection with *changes* in social relations" (emphasis added).[55] Ultimately, the thoroughgoing social liberalism of Dewey is characterized by two essential things: (i) a realistic study of existing conditions as contextualized by historic changes, and (ii) developing policies for dealing with these conditions for the purpose of enhancing individuality and liberty.[56] Dewey is emphatic that the experimental method is "not just messing around." The experimental method implies, for Dewey, the adoption of a coherent body of ideas—a theory—that gives direction to the policy effort.

Radicalism

But Dewey carries his discussion of renascent liberalism further than this. He advocates, in addition, a liberalism that endorses radicalism, meaning a liberalism that endorses "the perception of the necessity of thorough-going changes in the set-up of institutions and corresponding activity to bring the changes to pass."[57] Dewey sometimes speaks of "drastic" rather than "thorough-going" social changes.[58] Either notion will suffice here, so long as one understands that he has in mind significant changes to institutions, but changes that are brought about through the "maximum reliance upon intelligence."[59]

For liberals the chief method of social change is, according to Dewey, rooted in intelligent action.[60] Here the liberal parts company, he thinks, with those who construe "radical" and "radicalism" to mean an endorsement of violence as the chief means of social change. While it is tempting to construe Dewey as meaning that violence is, in all its forms, decried, the more prosaic truth is that he denounces it as the chief method of social change. Ideologies he criticizes, such as Marxism and Fascism, have a marked tendency to rely on violence as the chief method of social change. Liberalism, as advocated by Dewey, stands apart from these movements. On behalf of liberalism, Dewey advocates a strong emphasis on intelligent action, and for this reason he maintains that "the first object of renascent liberalism is education."[61] It is perhaps helpful to see Dewey as an idealist in the sense in which Georg Hegel (1770–1831) was an idealist. Dewey believes in the efficacy of ideas, and he applauds the implementation of intelligent ideas through government policies. But these same intelligent ideas need nourishment inside institutions such as families, schools, and churches.[62] Importantly, however, these same institutions must themselves be subject to revision and change based on intelligent thought. So there is a kind of dialectical process at work in Dewey's argument.

Democracy

Dewey's interest in individuality, a linchpin of renascent liberalism, leads him to a discussion of democracy. Speaking of democracy, he claims that it is "the best means so far found, for realizing ends that lie in the wide domain of human relationships and the development of human personality."[63] Democracy is, for Dewey, a constitutional means of realizing the values of individuality and liberty. His affirmation of democracy is rooted in his "faith in the capacities of human nature; faith in human intelligence and in the power of pooled and co-operative experience."[64] Democracy, therefore, turns out to be a means, albeit a constitutional means, to an end: the cultivation of individuality or personality. This constitutional means, then, allows individuals, and individuals alone, the right to decide "the methods and means by which subjects may arrive at the enjoyment of what is good for them."[65]

Notice here that Dewey reaffirms points made earlier, notably that human intelligence stands at the foundation of democracy. Thought should precede action, even in a democracy. Thought and action are nested in an environment of legal and political equality, as part of the democratic credo. And on a practical note, Dewey observes that universal suffrage, together with recurring elections and the responsibility of those elected to the voters, is the means chosen to realize democracy. Claiming that no person is wise enough or good enough to rule others without their consent, Dewey argues for democracy as a constitutional regime that affirms universal suffrage.[66] And in conclusion and as corollaries, Dewey adds this defence of democracy: while democracy allows for participation by all citizens, its denial results in a lack of interest and concern of those "shut out," and this in turn leads to "a corresponding lack of effective responsibility."[67]

Wollheim and Dewey

One way of refining part of what Dewey has to say in defence of democracy is to look at six neatly crafted arguments in support of such a constitutional regime. These arguments were made by the British philosopher Richard Wollheim (1923–2003) some 50 years ago.[68] With these in mind, it may be possible to better understand the position advocated by Dewey. The arguments are as follows:

i. To enjoy political authority is to undergo a moral education and have an opportunity for self-improvement. Democracy extends this opportunity to all and therefore is the best constitutional regime.
ii. True opinion on political and moral matters is the privilege of the common person. Therefore, power in a community should reside with the common person, and this it does only in a democracy.
iii. The ordinary human being is the best judge of her or his own interests. Only by controlling government through a democracy do these best interests prevail. Therefore, democracy is justified.
iv. Since it is impossible for anyone to know the right course of action for, or know the true interests of, the community, everyone should be allowed to do what she or he wants to do where this is compatible with what is socially possible. This is only achievable in a democracy.
v. Since everyone has a natural right to control government and this right is recognized only in a democracy, it follows that democracy is justified.
vi. Democracy is the only working possibility, or, as the American psychologist and philosopher William James (1842–1910) might say, "live option," since no person in an emancipated industrial society will "put up with" political tutelage.

Dewey's argument in defence of democracy, as part of his renascent liberalism, shares some of these ideas. The notion of an opportunity for self-improvement through the cultivation of one's capacities, coupled with the belief that no human being is wise enough or good enough to rule others, drives one in the direction of democracy. This is vintage Dewey, echoing the substance of arguments found in (i) and (iii), and possibly (iv). Other arguments referred to by Wollheim are largely untouched by Dewey. He does not explore arguments in favour of democracy that are based on the privilege of the common person, or natural rights, or live options.

Without indulging in a criticism of Dewey's renascent liberalism, one can assert that he says practically nothing about some of the defects of democracy. Notable among these defects are the following: the danger that the majority opinion may not be representative of the *considered* opinion of the majority; the fact that owing to some technical difficulty in the electoral procedure (which is meant to be both rational and democratic, as discussed in the mathematically elegant and powerful conclusions of Kenneth Arrow), it may not be possible to represent accurately the wishes of the majority;[69] the real threat that the majority may disregard the interests of the minority;[70] and finally, the possibility that democracy may fall legally into the hands of an oligarchy.[71] With these visible shortcomings of Dewey's position before us, it is time to consider that other noteworthy figure of reform liberalism, John Maynard Keynes.

John Maynard Keynes

Writing in 1925, John Maynard Keynes outlines what he wants liberalism to become.[72] His concern in this essay is not with the historical context of liberalism, which included a long list of matters relevant to the nineteenth century. Some of these matters were civil and religious liberty, dominion self-government, the power of the House of Lords, graduated taxation of incomes and fortunes, and the lavish use of public revenues for "social reform," such as social insurance for sickness, unemployment, and old age, and public education, housing, and health. All of these are causes, thinks Keynes, for which liberalism in the UK fought successfully, and are now obsolete or the common ground of all political parties.[73] The direction of Keynes's thought is towards cultivating a political stance, possibly an agenda, that deals with matters "which are of living interest and urgent importance today."[74] The true destiny of new liberalism is to seek the solution to the enormous technical and political difficulties as society moves from "economic anarchy to a regime which deliberately aims at controlling and directing economic forces in the interests of social justice and social stability."[75]

There is much that Keynes shares in common with Dewey, notwithstanding the terminological differences separating them. Both support serious change, not just cosmetic reform of social systems, particularly as this significant change aims at institutional structures. And whereas Dewey talks about removing institutional impediments to the development of personality or individuality, Keynes talks about social justice. The difference between what each of them says is more apparent than real, for lurking just beneath the surface of Dewey's talk of liberalism taking an active interest in the workings of social institutions that have a bearing on the growth of individuals is a concern for social justice, or, in his own words, a concern for equality of opportunity.[76] In the case of Keynes, his desire for change is evident in his willingness to use—in the economic field, to give but one example—"new policies and new instruments to adapt and control the working of economic forces."[77] In their separate calls for change, both Dewey and Keynes stand distinctly apart from conservatives such as Burke and Hume.

New Liberalism

The details of Keynes's sketch of reform or renascent or new liberalism are provided in other things he says. A listing of the questions with which he believes new liberalism should be concerned shows a remarkable prescience on his part. Those matters he considers to have a "living interest" or "urgent importance" fall under five headings: peace questions, questions of government, sex questions, drug questions, and economic questions. Keynes deals with each of these summarily. Regarding questions of peace, he asserts that just as we have taken risks in the interest of war, we should now take risks in the interest of peace.[78] As for questions of government, he believes governmental tasks must be decentralized and devolved and placed in the hands of semi-autonomous corporations.[79] With regard to what Keynes calls sex questions, he says that new liberalism must begin to address issues related to birth control and the use of contraceptives, marriage laws, the treatment of sexual offences and abnormalities, the economic position of women, and the economic position of the family.[80] According to Keynes, the status quo in these areas is clearly unacceptable to any relevant political ideology, for he says, "in all these matters the existing state of the law and of orthodoxy is still medieval—altogether out of touch with civilised opinion and civilised practice and with what individuals, educated and uneducated alike, say to one another in private."[81] Further, Keynes is of the opinion that the position of wage-earning women and the project of the family wage raise serious social and economic questions. In particular, they raise questions of whether wages should be fixed by forces of supply and demand in the spirit of laissez-faire theories, or whether the freedom of the forces of supply and demand should be limited by what is considered "fair" and "reasonable."[82] Given what Keynes says in other writings about the untenability of orthodox laissez-faire ideas, he would seem here to be implying that new liberalism would have to go in the direction of the fair and reasonable.

Three Economic Epochs

The last question Keynes addresses is the economic one. This he considers the largest of the political questions. Keynes defers to the opinion of the American economist John R. Commons (1862–1945), who distinguishes among three epochs or economic orders, the last of which Keynes believed British people were entering in the 1920s. The first epoch is the era of scarcity, characterized by a minimum of individual liberty and the maximum of feudal control through physical control. The second epoch is the era of extreme abundance, with a maximum of liberty and the minimum of government control. This is the era of historic laissez-faire liberalism.[83] The third epoch is the period of stabilization. It is characterized by a diminution of individual liberty, enforced by governmental and economic sanctions through "concerted action, whether secret, semi-open, open, or arbitrational, of associations, corporations, unions, and other collective movements of manufacturers, merchants, labourers, farmers, and bankers."[84]

Laissez-faire under Attack

Keynes appears to accept this triad of economic epochs, and certainly does not aim to contest any part of it. In apparently accepting the ideas of Commons, Keynes, by implication, accepts the reality of the third epoch, that of stabilization. The defining feature of this era is its pluralism, which works to diminish individual freedom, at least as this was understood in the heyday of laissez-faire economics in the nineteenth century. We shall shortly see what independent reasons Keynes has for rejecting the laissez-faire ideology, but for the moment one need only note his belief that by the 1920s the philosophy of economic life, together with what is reasonable and tolerable, has changed in the UK. Economic anarchy is in the descendant, while a regime aiming to control and direct economic forces in the interest of social justice and stability is in the ascendant. Keynes endorses this. Coupled with what he has to say against the laissez-faire economic philosophy, this endorsement sums up a good part of his new liberalism.

Keynes acknowledges his intellectual pedigree by claiming, first, that it was J.E. Cairnes (1823–1875) who, in 1870, at University College, London, delivered a "frontal attack" on laissez-faire in general, and, second, that it was Alfred Marshall (1842–1924) who delivered a direct attack against a specific axiom of Adam Smith, namely, the doctrine of the invisible hand. According to Marshall, Keynes argues, private and social interest are *not* harmonious.[85] Keynes has a compendium of criticisms of laissez-faire economics, but before listing its contents he contextualizes what he wishes to say. He asserts that like other hypotheses in science, the ones in economics are chosen because they are the simplest, and not because they are nearest to the facts.[86] After attempting to explain how the principles of laissez-faire triumphed for so long, he launches into a compressed criticism of these same principles.[87] It is probably worthwhile to highlight each of these:

i. "It is not true that individuals possess a prescriptive 'natural liberty' in their economic activities."
ii. "There is *no* 'compact' conferring perpetual rights on those who Have or on those who Acquire."
iii. "The world is *not* so governed from above that private and social interest coincide."
iv. "It is not so managed here below that in practice they coincide."
v. "It is not a correct deduction from the principles of economics that enlightened self-interest always operates in the public interest."
vi. "Nor is it true that self-interest generally is enlightened; more often individuals acting separately to promote their own ends are too ignorant or too weak to attain even these."
vii. "Experience does *not* show that individuals, when they make up a social unit, are always less clear-sighted than when they act separately."[88]

Probably no economist or political economist has ever written so succinct a criticism of the basic ideas of Adam Smith. Not even Cairnes or Alfred Marshall manages the intellectual dexterity and analytical precision achieved here by Keynes. These are clearly such trenchant criticisms of laissez-faire principles that anyone wishing to resurrect Adam Smith, such as perhaps modern-day libertarians or, alternatively, Hayekians,[89] will have to deal with each of these in turn.

The Agenda

Keynes does not stop his exploration of his new liberalism with an attack on classical liberals; instead, he lays down what he thinks should be the Agenda of economists and politicians who stand, presumably, in this new camp of liberalism. He undertakes his exploration of the Agenda by looking at its two subject areas: the ideal size of organization of society and the tasks that government should assume.

With respect to the first, Keynes believes the ideal size for organization and control in society lies somewhere between the individual and the modern state. Accordingly, he believes that progress is predicated on both the growth and recognition of semi-autonomous bodies within the state.[90] Such semi-autonomous bodies, thinks Keynes, have the public good as their criterion of action and are bodies "from whose deliberations motives of private advantage are excluded."[91] What Keynes advocates is the existence of such autonomous entities as "the universities, the Bank of England, the Port of London Authority, even perhaps the railway companies."[92] Keynes adds another to this list—namely, joint stock institutions and their propensity to approximate to the status of public rather than private corporations once they have attained a certain age and size.[93] While decrying state socialism, Keynes seems to support the quasi-socialism of the universities, the Bank of England, and other semi-autonomous bodies. It is these bodies that stand between the state *and* the individual. And he prefers the "natural tendencies of the day" towards semi-autonomous corporations and away from the organs of central government.[94] Presumably, for Keynes, semi-autonomous bodies, together with government, assume the burden of doing those things in society "that are not done at all."

Regrettably, Keynes does not elaborate on his notion of semi-autonomous bodies, but the list he provides—including, as noted above, the universities and the Bank of England—gives an illustrative or extensional meaning. The fact that the Bank of England, the Bank of Canada, and the European Central Bank all exist at arm's length from governments, as do many public universities, is evidence of their autonomy. And their autonomy is evidence of the applicability of Keynes's notion in the present context.

With respect to the second subject area of the new liberal agenda, Keynes says the following: governments should not aim to do those things that individuals are doing, sometimes well and sometimes badly, but to do those things that "at present are not done at all." He then proceeds to "name some instances," three in fact, where government action is called for.

In the first instance, according to Keynes, "Many of the greatest economic evils of our time are the fruits of risk, uncertainty, and ignorance."[95] Out of these, he thinks, arise inequalities of wealth, unemployment, the disappointment of reasonable business expectations, and the reduction of efficiency and production.[96] The cure for these, at least in part, is to be sought in the control of currency and credit by a central institution (presumably, one that is semi-autonomous), as well as in the distribution on a wide scale of "data relating to the business situation."[97]

The second instance relates to savings and investment. Keynes claims that "some coordinated act of intelligent judgement," presumably government, is needed as to (i) the scale of savings desirable for a community; (ii) the scale on which local savings should be invested abroad; and (iii) whether the present investment market "distributes savings along the most productive channels."[98] In these matters, Keynes does not think private judgment and private profits should prevail.[99] The implication is that government should play a role.

The third example offered by Keynes is that of population. There are two aspects to what he has to say on this matter. The first, and the most pressing according to Keynes, relates to the national policy on the *size* of the population. He does not say, in the case of the UK, what size it should be, only that *expedience* needs to be considered in connection with size. The second aspect, and one reserved for later consideration, relates to the "innate quality" of its future members.[100] This second aspect seems more in keeping with conservatism than with reform liberalism, a fact that is odd given his castigation of the former ideology.[101]

In defining reform liberalism, then, Keynes offers us a society that has several players: the state, semi-autonomous entities such as the Bank of England and universities, private organizations and corporations, and individuals. Central to his vision is the job undertaken by semi-autonomous institutions, which should aim to mitigate the evils of inequalities in wealth, unemployment, and the disappointment of reasonable business expectations. The tools of mitigation are not only currency and credit control, transparency, and a savings and investment regime, but also a population regime. On the non-economic policy front, Keynes would have questions of peace be front and centre, sex issues resolutely confronted, and drug questions rationally confronted. All of these are contextualized in an environment of social stability and social justice. These focal points, then, represent reform liberalism for Keynes.

John Rawls

Rawls is an American social contractarian reform liberal. He aspires to show, first, that the principles of justice—justice being the fundamental social virtue[102]—are those that rational persons concerned to promote their interests would agree to as equals,[103] and, second, how these principles can be derived from a hypothetical condition he calls "the original position."

The **original position**, under Rawls's interpretation of the social contract, is one in which "no one knows his place in society, his class position or social status, nor does anyone know his fortune in the distribution of natural assets and abilities, his intelligence, strength and the like."[104] What this amounts to is a "veil of ignorance" that shrouds the agent involved in bargaining when forming a social contract. Rawls uses the idea of the original position to derive a criterion for evaluating different conceptions of justice, and this he thinks he is able to do because "the original position is the appropriate initial status quo which insures that the fundamental agreements reached in it are fair."[105] So, in assessing conceptions of justice, Rawls thinks that one must look at how acceptable its principles would be to someone in the original position.[106] Adopting the original position is the setting up of a fair procedure, according to Rawls, so that any principles agreed to will turn out to be just.[107]

Rawls imposes several qualifications on people in the original position. These qualifications include (i) assuming that all parties in the original position are equal in that they have the same rights in the procedure for choosing principles;[108] (ii) assuming that all parties are rational, in the way in which rationality is understood in social theory;[109] and (iii) assuming that all parties know the general facts about human society, understand political affairs and the principles of economic theory, the basis of social organization, and the laws of psychology.[110]

Constraints on Principles of Justice

Before deriving two principles of justice, the **liberty principle** and the **difference principle**,[111] Rawls describes five constraints on them:

i. These principles should be general, and hence he believes predicates used in their statement should express general properties and relations.[112]
ii. These principles should be universal in their application, and therefore should hold for everyone as moral persons.[113]
iii. The principles will be publicly known upon agreement in the social contract.[114]
iv. The principles must impose an ordering on claims involving conflict.[115]
v. Finally, the principles must be taken by the parties to the contract as "the final court of appeal in practical reasoning."[116]

Now attention needs to be paid to the two principles of justice derived from the social contract and located behind a veil of ignorance.

Principles of Justice

The principle of liberty reads:

> Each person is to have an equal right to the most extensive total system of equal basic liberties compatible with a similar system of liberty for all.[117]

The principle of difference reads:

> Social and economic inequalities are to be arranged so that they are both (a) reasonably expected to be to everyone's advantage, and (b) attached to positions and offices open to all.[118]

These principles apply in lexical order, and therefore priority is given to the first principle over the second.[119] In short, this means that civil and political liberties are given priority over economic ones.[120] This follows once it is understood that Rawls recognizes that the liberty principle defines and secures the equal liberties of citizens, while the difference principle specifies and establishes social and economic inequalities.[121] He includes the following liberties under the first principle: the right to vote, the right to hold office, freedom of speech and assembly, liberty of conscience and thought, freedom of the person along with the right to hold property, and freedom from arbitrary arrest and seizure.[122] He includes the following conditions under the second principle: distribution of income and wealth, as well as differences in authority and responsibility in the design of organizations.[123]

There are some complexities to Rawls's position, largely relating to the difference principle. Rawls's position seems to embrace the "trickle-down" theory of economics, a theory claiming that greater benefits to the wealthy trickle down to and thus benefit the less well-off. This seems to be a position advocated by classical liberals, possibly neo-liberals, and libertarians rather than reform liberals. Although this might seem to show that Rawls is a neo-liberal, this is not the case for three reasons, as Stephen Nathanson says. The difference principle does not entail "trickle-down economics" for the following

4 Reform Liberalism   73

...kes benefits for the less well-off individuals a
...ds for others. Second, the difference principle
...imize the well-being of people who are located
...nd third, the difference principle demands that
...of the poor simply to qualify as just, implying
...nded as ways of improving those who are least
...stification, Rawls's position is more appropri-
...ckle-down" theory. So Rawls's account should
...als, neo-liberals, and libertarians.

...rinciples of justice that Rawls uses, it is evi-
...While he does not use the expression "reform
...his is revealed in the early part of *A Theory of*
...bing his own theory, about the "liberal inter-
...eral conception" in the context of discussing
...l knowledge and skills should not depend on
...zed that this progressive or reform liberalism
...s present in his much later work, *The Law of*
...ok I consider how the content of *The Law of*
...ea of justice similar to, but more general than,
...*ry of Justice*" (emphasis added).[126] Rawls goes
...s of reasonable liberal conceptions of justice.
...s and liberties, a ranking of these rights, lib-
...ims of general good and perfectionism, and
...equisite primary goods to enable them to act
...[127] Rawls's attribution of these three princi-
...equivocally a reform liberal.

...young Canadian scholar began to make his
...Charles Taylor (1931–), another Canadian
...important political philosophers, and each
...r by taking seriously issues encountered in
...here.
...has been concerned to develop a liberal
...explicit and systematic way than is usually
...rection of an investigation of liberalism and
...his more recent work that the concern was
...terms of liberalism and multiculturalism.
...he one that stands out for present purposes
...discussion of liberalism beyond that found
...economic thinkers.

...en communitarianism and liberalism is a
...uralism claims in Western democracies.[129]

It should be remembered here that, for Kymlicka, communitarians dispute the autonomy of the individual and affirm the embeddedness of the individual in social roles and relationships, whereas liberals traditionally affirm the autonomy of the individual to decide on what constitutes the good life. Thus, Kymlicka rejects the idea that the debate on multiculturalism—the debate on the plurality of cultures—should be understood in terms of the dispute between those who affirm the importance of the community for the individual and those who simply affirm the importance of the individual. Rather, "the overwhelming majority of debates" concerning multiculturalism are "debates amongst liberals concerning the meaning of liberalism."[130] Thinking this way leads one to ask the question, what is the possible scope for, or role of, multiculturalism within liberal theory?

The question Kymlicka raises here is a very natural one to ask in the Canadian polity. As he understands only too well, the Canadian Charter of Rights and Freedoms, initiated by Pierre Trudeau in 1982, contains in section 27 a multicultural provision: "The Charter shall be interpreted in a manner consistent with the preservation and enhancement of the multicultural heritage of Canadians." So in querying "the possible scope for . . . multiculturalism within liberal theory," Kymlicka is asking a question that cries out for an answer in Canada.

How does he answer his question? His first step is to say that many liberals believe not just in state neutrality but in benign neglect. Accordingly, there should be a strict separation between the state and the church, for example, or, to take another example, there should be a strict separation between the state and ethnicity. This is what benign neglect amounts to—a general separation between the state and ways of life, including the use of language, history, literature, and calendar, of different groups.[131] But Kymlicka finds the theory of benign neglect to be "manifestly false"; it is not true, he thinks, that liberal-democratic states are indifferent to ethnic identities. He asserts that the model of benign neglect must be replaced with a "more accurate model."[132] This more accurate model argues that states are nation-building. Against this background the question for liberals then becomes, do majority efforts at nation-building create injustices for minorities? And do minority rights safeguard against these injustices? These are the questions Kymlicka throws at his own doorstep as a reform liberal.

Five Models of Multiculturalism

Rather than treat multiculturalism as an undifferentiated phenomenon, Kymlicka makes five distinctions within it. He asserts that there are five different types of ethnocultural minorities found within Western democracies: national minorities; immigrants; isolationist ethno-religious groups; metics (irregular migrants and temporary migrants); and racial caste groups.[133] Kymlicka then attempts to show what kinds of minority-rights claims have been made by minorities in response to nation-building, and how these claims relate to those principles considered liberal. Kymlicka presents a long and subtle discussion regarding these claims to rights and how they relate to the five foregoing groups. It is impossible to pursue the details of his discussion here, but suffice to say he claims categorically that neither concerns about (i) justice nor concerns about (ii) social unity in a democratic state can provide grounds for rejecting multiculturalism in general.[134] He finishes by asserting that the acceptance of liberal premises about the revisability and plurality of the ends of our actions will result in a liberal form of multiculturalism that challenges status inequalities (inequalities based on such things as gender, skin colour, lifestyle, sexual orientation) while affirming individual freedom.[135] In drawing attention to status inequalities, Kymlicka is at pains to emphasize that questions of status hierarchy are not reducible to questions of economic hierarchy.[136] In making this claim, he clearly marks out a terrain that is ideologically quite different from that occupied by Marx.

Kymlicka acknowledges in his discussion of multiculturalism that politics is almost always about identities and interests.[137] With respect to both of these subjects he begins to open the door on the subject of transnationalism.[138] Hence, implicit in Kymlicka's thinking is some linkage between multiculturalism and transnationalism. While much of what he says about transnationalism pertains to transnational institutions,[139] his ideas have implications for a new and challenging matter of concern to reform liberals—namely, the linkage between multiculturalism and transnational *identity*. In particular, his ideas have implications for what a reform liberal says regarding the connection between a policy of multiculturalism and the practice of immigrants and ethnic groups maintaining "ties with their real or imagined homelands."[140] Under the banner of multiculturalism the Canadian government initially encouraged "immigrants to engage in transnational social practices and to develop transnational social identities."[141] More recently, particularly in the past 10 years, "the Canadian government has advanced the notion of 'civic multiculturalism' with the goal of creating a sense of belonging and attachment to Canada among immigrants."[142] These changes in the Canadian government's approach to multiculturalism, seen against the backdrop of Kymlicka's thinking, raise the important question for reform liberals of just how far the reed of multiculturalism can be bent before it breaks. How far, reform liberals might well ask in light of Kymlicka's writing, can something like dual citizenship go before serious issues of loyalty arise? This question becomes all the more acute when considered in light of the reaction of societies, particularly North American societies, to the events of 11 September 2001, an event that has triggered a backlash of racism, anti-immigration, and anti-multiculturalism.[143] While Kymlicka does not explore issues of multiculturalism and transnationalism with this event in mind, for the reason that the publication of his ideas and 9/11 occurred about the same time, nonetheless his ideas provide a context for further thinking by reform liberals on this important subject, amplified as it is by considerations of transnationalism.

Conclusion

What unites Mill, Green, Hobhouse, Hobson, Dewey, Keynes, Rawls, and Kymlicka as liberals is their affirmation of individualism and their contextualizing of individualism in the middle of social structures. At the heart of each of their political ideologies stands the fundamental freedom or liberty of individuals, but all are in agreement that this liberty needs to be nourished by actions of the state to enable citizens "to make intelligent and effective use of their freedoms."[144] While there is no agreement among these liberal thinkers on whether the principle of justice should be utilitarian (as in the case of Mill) or social contractarian (as in the case of Rawls), there is agreement that the principle of justice requires the creation of genuine opportunities for people to exercise their freedom. In all cases, what is aspired to here falls short of creating conditions of social and economic equality; instead, what is aspired to is creating conditions in which individuals can meaningfully aspire to their progressive interests.

Needless to say, the articulation of this ideological position is not given by all in terms of human rights. Mill, for one, rejects appeals to abstract rights, emphasizing utility instead; Green engages in some talk of human rights,[145] and presents an argument for positive liberty that is independent of rights. Hobhouse makes reference to individual rights, but defines them in terms of the common good. Hobson acknowledges a role for rights, at least in the case of property rights, but tempers them by consideration of equity. Dewey avoids talk of rights and replaces it by considerations of usefulness and pragmatics. Keynes rejects talk of perpetual rights, at least in the field of economics, and substitutes talk of "living interest" and "urgent importance." And Rawls dismisses the utilitarian tradition and unabashedly emphasizes these rights in his first and second principles of justice.[146] Finally, Kymlicka gives a nuanced view of human rights by focusing on minority rights and claims associated with them in multicultural environments. In the thinking of all eight of these intellectuals one sees the inextricable link between self-improvement and freedom. To make this link, "without qualifying it in a way that destroys it, is to have the faith called liberalism."[147]

The general line of argument used by reform liberals places overriding value on positive liberty, the kind of liberty that allows an individual to put into effect those decisions she or he has made. The ideal of liberty takes a front seat to the ideal of equality. Nonetheless, in their arguments, reform liberals acknowledge that economic inequalities and status inequalities can act as impediments to one's freedom, and for that reason these inequalities need to be reduced. Here reform liberals see the role of institutions and social conditions. This position is reflected in the writings of Mill, Green, Hobhouse, Hobson, Dewey, Rawls, Keynes, and Kymlicka. These liberals aim to expose the causal line of support running from institutions and social conditions, when they are healthy, to positive freedom. This exposition is undertaken in various ways by each of these theorists, with some, like Dewey, focusing on educational institutions and others, like Keynes, focusing on economic institutions (such as saving and investment practices and rules to eliminate economic uncertainty). Other of these reform liberals focus on social conditions: Hobson recognizing unequal bargaining positions between buyers and sellers; Kymlicka emphasizing the role and scope of multiculturalism in the building of nation-states; Keynes pointing the finger at population size. So institutional support and favourable social conditions play a central role in the reform liberals' argument of positive liberty. It is the assignment of a central role to this support and these conditions by reform liberals that separates them from classical liberals.

Evaluation: The Strengths of Reform Liberalism

1. A compelling point raised by Mill, Green, Hobhouse, Hobson, and Dewey is the importance of the liberation of individuals in the realization of their capacities in life. Mill correctly recognizes that this liberation embraces an opportunity for individuals provided by social support, in the form of education and financial support. With respect to the second of these, Mill goes so far as to talk about how inimical to liberty is the excessive wealth of the rich and the plight of the poor. Much the same could be said of Green. Dewey carries Mill's and Green's ideas further. He sees, in ways that classical liberals did not and in ways only implied by Mill and Green, that individuals are not "ready-made," but instead are constantly being constructed and reconstructed on the basis of the social institutions that surround them.

    When Dewey speaks of "historic relativity" in this context, he means not relativism in values, but the impermanence of institutions and the need to be mindful of them in creating a favourable climate in which the individual can flourish. One might even say that Mill, Green, Hobhouse, Hobson, and then Dewey argue in favour of positive liberty as the new credo of liberalism. Positive liberty, so understood, contrasts with negative liberty. The former means an enhancement of opportunities for a person's using her freedom more effectively, while the latter means simply the absence of constraints, especially governmental, upon the person's freedom to act in a way of her choice. So the compelling point made especially by Dewey is simply that institutional support is necessary to the individual in her self-realization, or, what amounts to the same thing, in her search for well-being.

Though Dewey says little about what he has in mind by "institution" here, there is every reason to believe that he means what every social scientist of his day meant, and they include legal entities, educational bodies, economic undertakings, public health practices, religious ceremonies, and recreational activities, to name but a few. Of these, educational institutions capture his greatest attention. Mill, Green, Hobhouse, Hobson, and Dewey might well say here that humans are not islands unto themselves, but rely extensively upon others through formal structures such as families, schools, and businesses. The evidence supporting their position confronts one every day: children raised in fragmented families, owing to violence, drugs, disease, or mental problems, are disadvantaged. Individuals who drop out of school at an early age are handicapped. Individuals who lack the financial resources to feed and house themselves are open to a host of problems, ranging from ill health to lack of meaningful employment. And, of course, those individuals who lack institutional guidance—whether from the family, church, school, or work environment—are exposed to problems related to criminal and civil law.

One might add, by way of conclusion, that Dewey's renascent liberalism, with its active interest in the working of social institutions and the bearing they have on the life of the individual, is completely opposed to the nineteenth-century liberalism of the British philosopher Herbert Spencer (1820–1903). Spencer laments the intrusion of government into the life of the individual as a threat to individual freedom.[148] Dewey actively encourages institutional involvement, both government and non-government, for he sees it as promoting individuality through a robust freedom.

2. Reform liberalism, as offered by Hobhouse, Hobson, and Dewey, is willing to embrace by non-violent means thoroughgoing changes in the organization of institutions. Setting aside reform liberalism's reference to non-violence, something needs to be said about its embrace of thoroughgoing changes in the set-up of institutions. Previous discussions, especially in the chapter on conservatism, have shown that some institutions, such as slavery, are so odious that they need to be dismantled wherever they are—dismantled at once and completely. The same could be said of **apartheid**, the South African policy that enforced the racial segregation of blacks, "coloureds," Asians, and whites from 1948 to 1994. It is the willingness of reform liberalism to embrace thoroughgoing changes that makes Dewey think of his ideology as radical. Radical or not, reform liberalism is correct in its willingness to embark on institutional change—change that is dramatic—when institutional structures stand in the way of freedom and individuality.

3. Reform liberalism also affirms democracy and pluralism. This is reflected somewhat in Mill's writings, but more so in those of Dewey and Rawls. Dewey sees democracy

as a constitutional means that allows individuals the right to decide the methods and means by which subjects can arrive at what is good for them. He sees a plurality of positions being taken by individuals on their conception of the good, and believes democratic constitutions facilitate the realization of human values in a particular society. Dewey appropriately emphasizes universal suffrage as a mechanism for arriving at these values. The picture thus painted by Dewey is one of democracy by universal suffrage, and pluralism by virtue of the multiple conceptions of the good that citizens hold.

This position is not all that different from the one promoted by Rawls many years after Dewey, except that, while they both affirm the value of democracy, Dewey addresses pluralism in a concrete setting, whereas Rawls addresses it in a hypothetical and abstract setting. Nonetheless, both of these philosophers maintain that there is "a plurality of different and opposing, and even incommensurable, conceptions of the good."[149] They both part company, it seems, with the univocal conception of the good as laid down by Plato, Aristotle, St Thomas, and St Augustine.

Reform liberals, such as Dewey and Rawls, are correct in affirming democracy and universal suffrage, for the reasons cited by Wollheim in this chapter. Furthermore, reform liberals are correct in affirming pluralism for the reason that there is no convergence of opinion on what the good or the good life consists of. While it is tempting to say "happiness" or "well-being" as a rebuttal, the fact remains that reform liberals say, and are correct in saying, that there is no agreement on how this is to be achieved. In this sense, reform liberalism presents a strong claim to the effect that pluralism rules.

4. Reform liberalism correctly maintains that organized society, in the form of the state, "must use its powers to establish conditions under which the mass of individuals can possess actual as distinct from merely legal liberty."[150] This is a point made by Dewey and reinforced by Rawls in his difference principle. It is obvious to those who have eyes to see that state intervention is required for purposes other than national defence. The night watchman approach of Locke and Hayek will not suffice when it comes to addressing social ills such as poverty, violence in the home, and environmental decay, and it will not suffice in addressing some of the items mentioned on Keynes's political agenda, including economic risk, uncertainty, savings and investments, and the growth of domestic and global populations. These are policy areas over which the private sector has no interest and no power to solve.

In response to those who would say that state initiatives in these areas are unrealistic and utopian, two points need to be made: (i) Adam Smith, in *The Wealth of Nations*, admits that even his scheme of laissez-faire is utopian, and yet this has not discouraged those on the right, e.g., neo-liberals and libertarians, from trumpeting Smith's ideal; and (ii) even if "[c]omprehensive social justice is impossible, [one should aim at] more modest and incremental measures . . . guided by the liberal principle of helping disadvantaged individuals to use their theoretical freedom in a meaningful way."[151]

5. Reform liberalism as found in Keynes delivers a brief but blistering attack on the metaphysical principles of laissez-faire. Without going into a deep analysis of the points he makes, suffice it to say that most if not all of his points are quite telling:

- He openly challenges the claim to a prescriptive natural liberty in one's economic sphere, a challenge that is appropriate given that the alleged liberty is simply laid down by fiat by classical liberals such as Locke, and was not argued for by them.
- Even if there is such a thing as a social compact or contract, none of this speaks to the issue of perpetual rights that allegedly cannot be trumped under any circumstances by the state. Indeed, if Rawls is correct, some trumping must occur to level the playing field for the disadvantaged.
- There is no reason to believe that some transcendent power ensures the convergence of private and social interest. If there is, where is the proof of such a power?
- No government on the face of the earth ensures the convergence of these interests.
- Economic theory does not show that enlightened self-interest always operates in the public interest. Mistakes in judgment can occur, even when collectively engaged in.
- Self-interest is not always enlightened. People can be incredibly stupid in the things they decide to do.
- Lastly, the evidence at hand does not show that collective opinion is less intelligent than individual opinion. While the majority of citizens may believe that dangerous chemicals should not be dumped in the water table, nonetheless some individuals insist in believing otherwise.

Each of Keynes's points more or less speaks for itself. But ample evidence for each of these claims could be provided by almost any reflective person who has lived a bit in the world.

6. Reform liberalism, as spelled out by Keynes, affirms the important role played by semi-autonomous entities such as central banks and universities. This position, curiously, is supported by a motley crew of different ideologues, including Aristotle, Mill, and Friedrich Hayek. Roughly speaking, all of these support the principle of subsidiarity or, roughly, decentralization when possible. There simply are some jobs that government should not do, for a variety of reasons, not all dealing with efficiency. Some of these are tasks the private sector should also refrain from doing. At least with respect to tasks the government should not take on, universities provide a healthy example. It is highly unlikely that the situation for the body politic would be as good were the government to run universities as they do colleges, by issuing directives and by appointing all board members. The intellectual life of the community is preserved and enhanced by giving it this measure of independence. Similar claims could be advanced in the case of hospitals and central banks.

7. Reform liberalism as advanced by Hobhouse is respectful of the potential danger of this ideology collapsing into a version of socialism. In the end, however, the reform liberals distinguish their position from socialism by emphasizing the individual and the individual's talent, risk-taking, artistic creativity, initiative, energy, and personal independence, "of which socialism appears oblivious."[152] What reform liberals aim at is a harmonization of divergent interests: those of the state and those of the individual. Socialists are likely to see this attempt at harmonization as "half-hearted" and "illogical," and to a great extent unachievable. They would be more inclined to defer to the state. Reform liberals think otherwise, whether this is through the radical changes in institutions that Dewey suggests, or through the creation of semi-autonomous

bodies as Keynes suggests. These are not meant as coercive bodies in the model of the state, but as bodies that are respectful of the liberty and independence of the individual. In short, these bodies are thought to create opportunities for the individual, not to create centres of power that constrain the individual. And finally, as Hobson says, modern-day liberals would be unwilling to follow the line proposed by socialists in trusting a minority to define the new human nature necessary to sustain the changes envisaged under a more robust plan of state action.

8. Reform liberalism as advanced by Kymlicka correctly embraces multiculturalism. This is in keeping with the liberalism of John Stuart Mill, who says two things are necessary for human development: freedom and variety of situations. Multiculturalism provides this "variety of situations." Those having the good fortune of living in a pluralistic culture have the opportunity of making contact with new and varied "situations" through exposure to ethnic cuisine, ethnic music, ethnic dress, and ethnic humour. So Kymlicka stands in good company when he includes multiculturalism on the liberal agenda. But it is not just that he is correct to include it; he is correct in thinking that exposure to a plurality of cultures enriches one's life.

9. Kymlicka's reform liberalism makes a useful distinction among five different types of ethnocultural minorities found in Western democracies. He effectively distinguishes national minorities, immigrants, isolationist ethno-religious groups, metics (irregular migrants and temporary migrants), and racial caste groups. These distinctions, plus other observations of Kymlicka, facilitate the transition to a new and invigorating discussion of multiculturalism and transnational identity. This discussion is well underway, largely arising from the events surrounding 9/11 but also more recently from the events surrounding the massive exodus of people from war-torn Syria. These events have created a climate in the United States and Canada as well as in most parts of Europe in which liberal reform values can play a useful role by highlighting the importance and enriching power of tolerance.

Evaluation: The Weaknesses of Reform Liberalism

1. Reform liberalism (at least according to Rawls and, it seems, Kymlicka, though not according to Mill, Green, Hobson, Hobhouse, Dewey, or Keynes) is grounded in the notion of a social contract. That Rawls is able, through the clever use of the idea of the original position and the veil of ignorance, to tease out a couple of principles of justice—namely, the principle of liberty and the principle of difference—is commendable. These principles do give weight to considerations of equality and efficiency.

   There are two objections to Rawls's approach here. First, as J.L. Mackie has argued, choosing principles from behind a veil of ignorance is a less adequate guarantee of fairness than establishing principles from a compromise acceptable from every viewpoint.[153] In short, principles chosen from behind a veil of ignorance—though rationally chosen—need not be fair. Second, the rights-oriented social contractarianism of Rawls is not clearly related to the consequentialism, specifically utilitarianism, of Mill, and to a lesser extent Dewey. Assuming that these two ways of talking about moral and political questions, the way of rights and the way of utility, give rise to two levels of talking about morality and politics, how "is it possible to prevent the two levels of morality from seeping into one another?"[154] And how is tension between these two ways of talking to be resolved? This is a problem for reform liberalism, embracing as it does both figures like Mill and figures like Rawls. It does no good to sidestep this problem by saying there is no internal inconsistency in either Mill or Rawls. The point is that they do belong to a single tradition, reform liberalism, and the tradition has tension embedded deep in its soul.

2. Reform liberalism, notwithstanding its claim to be radical, frequently finds itself powerless to effect these policy changes when confronting large corporations. For example, reform liberals may wish to introduce serious environmental legislation to curb pollution or to preserve scarce resources, but may be unable to act owing to the capacity of large firms to engage in capital strikes. A capital strike occurs when those with capital assets invested in a community threaten to withdraw these assets if particular government policies adverse to the corporations' interests are introduced. Faced with the flight of capital, community officials and voters then protest against government policies and the environmental legislation is stopped dead in its tracks.

It thus appears, in the end, that Dewey's faith in human intelligence and in the power of pooled and co-operative experience is sometimes overly optimistic. Human intelligence and derived power are not sufficient to trigger the thoroughgoing changes of which Dewey speaks. Occasionally, the good but inefficacious intentions of reform liberals surface in a particularly memorable way. Such was the case when Robert McNamara, outgoing president of the World Bank, addressed the issue of global poverty in a heart-rending and tearful speech before that body in 1980. It is obvious that neither the global community nor the World Bank has since made a serious effort to address this problem. Hence, one must conclude that the radical nature of reform liberalism is sometimes more apparent that real.

3. Reform liberalism mistakenly gives priority to political and civil matters over economic ones, even if this mistake is somewhat muted in the case of Hobson, Hobhouse, and Keynes. Of course, once this brand of liberalism, like all brands of liberalism, gives priority to the individual person, political and civil matters will stand at the head of the list. Economic and social issues, in the reallocation process, will come a distant second, and this seems to be confirmed by Rawls's notion of lexical priority, in which he gives special treatment to political and civil liberties under the liberty principle before moving on the difference principle. In emphasizing this weakness, one does not thereby adopt a Marxist ideology, even if Marxists would be in agreement with the criticism. The point of the criticism is simply to draw attention to the unmistakable role played by economic issues in shaping the interests of the dominant class. These interests ensure that priority is given to political and civil issues rather than redistributive economic ones. There are two problems with this: (i) it is difficult to see how radical change of the type to which Dewey refers can take place given Rawlsian lexical priority; and (ii) it is difficult to see how nasty aspects of liberal societies—such as homelessness and the "mental mutilation" of tedious work (to use Adam Smith's phrase)—are to be addressed.

4. Reform liberalism does not come to grips with the logical tension between democratic ideals and market ideals. Democratic ideals, as advocated by Dewey, largely entail

a bargaining process (with shades of the bargaining of the social contract) undertaken through universal suffrage and resulting in "a substantial collective sphere of social responsibility and action";[155] market ideals, as advocated by Hayek, largely consist of a "spontaneous, impersonal, and largely self-regulating system."[156] It is not at all clear how these are to be integrated. Democratic ideals and collective responsibility may in fact not result in economic efficiencies, whereas market forces, if left unchecked, will swamp democratic concerns. The dance between these two partners could result in both of them falling down.

5. Reform liberalism, while suited to the needs of the middle classes of the already industrialized and democratic nations of capitalism, is not an ideology with much to say to the vast majority of mankind living in conditions of poverty, famine, ignorance, disease, war, and environmental catastrophes. This criticism can be best summed up in the words of C. Wright Mills, written in 1962: "The most grievous charge today against liberalism and its conservative varieties is that they are so utterly provincial, and thus so irrelevant to the major problems that must now be confronted in so many areas of the world."[157]

6. Reform liberalism as articulated by Kymlicka does not confront in a serious fashion the following question: Against the background of social unity, how far can the rod of multiculturalism be bent before it snaps? Put differently, one might ask, how much cultural pluralism can a nation (which is being built) accommodate? Kymlicka is correct that there is nothing in general that makes multiculturalism objectionable to social unity, but this says nothing about particular difficulties that may arise and says nothing about ways to address these in a liberal society when they do arise. For example, if ethnic quarrels begin to spill over into a multicultural community, this may be a signal to the body politic in question that multiculturalism as a policy of the government is moving too quickly. Kymlicka does not seriously consider this potential difficulty and does not suggest ways, e.g., education, in which it might be addressed.

7. Finally, reform liberalism as advanced by Kymlicka does not take full stock of the inability of liberal body politics to address the accommodation of Indigenous peoples by majorities even while these same politics embrace multiculturalism. A conservative such as Roger Scruton would undoubtedly be critical of Kymlicka's reform liberalism, which promotes multiculturalism but offers no real solution to the full acceptance of First Nations peoples.

Related Websites

Foss, Jerome C. "John Rawls; Theorist of Modern Liberalism." Heritage Foundation, 13 Aug. 2014.
www.heritage.org/research/reports/2014/08/john-rawls-theorist-of-modern-liberalism

Horowitz, Asher. "Liberalism, Democracy, and John Stuart Mill." *Perspectives on Politics*, Department of Political Science, York University, Toronto.
www.yorku.ca/horowitz/courses/lectures/39_mill_liberalism_democracy.html

Kent, Tom. "Paul Martins's Moment of Choice—Liberal Opportunism or Reform Liberalism." *Policy Options*, 1 Mar. 2004.
http://policyoptions.irpp.org/issues/realignment-on-the-right/paul-martins-moment-of-choice-liberal-opportunism-or-reform-liberalism/

Plank, Barbara. "John Stuart Mill." Liberal International.
www.liberal-international.org/editorial.asp?ia_id=685

Starr, Paul. "The Modern Liberal Theory of Freedom's Power." *Freedom's Power*, 10 Jan. 2007.
www.freedomspower.com/2007/01/modern-liberal-theory-of-freedoms-power.html

Further Readings on Reform Liberalism

Alnes, Harald Jan, and Manuel Mendez Toscano. *Varieties of Liberalism: Contemporary Challenges*. Newcastle upon Tyne, UK: Cambridge Scholars Publishing, 2014.

Banerjee, Kiran. "Rawls on the Embedded Self: Liberalism as an Effective Regime." *European Journal of Political Theory* 14, 2 (2015): 209–28.

Bankovsky, Miriam. *Perfecting Justice in Rawls, Habermas and Honneth: A Deconstructive Perspective*. London: Continuum, 2012.

Bavetta, Sebastiano, and Pietro Navarra. *The Economics of Freedom: Theory, Measurement and Policy Implications*. New York: Cambridge University Press, 2012.

Bercuson, Jeffrey. *John Rawls and the History of Political Thought: The Rousseauvian and Hegelian Heritage of Justice as Fairness*. New York. Routledge, 2014.

Bevir, Mark. *Modern Pluralism: Anglo-American Debates since 1880*. Cambridge: Cambridge University Press, 2012.

Brink, David Owen. *Mill's Progressive Principles*. Oxford: Oxford University Press, 2013.

Congleton, Roger D. *Perfecting Parliament: Constitutional Reform, Liberalism, and the Rise of Western Democracy*. Cambridge: Cambridge University Press, 2011.

Davidson, Paul. *John Maynard Keynes*. Houndmills, Basingstoke, Hampshire, UK: Palgrave Macmillan, 2007.

Dworkin, Ronald. *A Matter of Principle*. Cambridge, MA: Harvard University Press, 1985.

Fawcett, Edmund. *Liberalism: The Life of an Idea*. Princeton, NJ: Princeton University Press, 2014.

Finlayson, James Gordon, and Fabian Freyenhagen. *Habermas and Rawls: Disputing the Political*. New York: Routledge, 2011.

Fitzpatrick, John R. *John Stuart Mill's Political Philosophy: Balancing Freedom and the Collective Good*. London: Continuum, 2006.

Giovanelli, Alessandro. *Aesthetics: The Key Thinkers*. London; New York: Continuum, 2012.

Kotz, David M. *The Rise and Fall of Neoliberal Capitalism*. Cambridge, MA: Harvard University Press, 2015.

Lehning, Percy B. *John Rawls: An Introduction*. Cambridge: Cambridge University Press, 2009.

Olssen, Mark. *Liberalism, Neoliberalism, and Social Democracy: Thin Communitarian Perspectives on Political Philosophy and Education.* New York: Routledge, 2010.

Rosen, Frederick. *Mill.* Oxford: Oxford University Press, 2013.

Ryan, Alan. *The Making of Modern Liberalism.* Princeton, NJ: Princeton University Press, 2012

Wall, Steven. *The Cambridge Companion to Liberalism.* Cambridge: Cambridge University Press, 2015.

5 Marxism

Learning Objectives

- To understand the primitive role of class struggle played in Marxism.
- To acknowledge in Marxism the affirmation of violence as a tool to effect social change.
- To recognize the overall explanatory force of economic factors in Marxism.

By 2008, what started as an American economic crisis had become a global debacle, fuelled by a number of factors: the lax oversight of the US financial sector, the use of large quantities of debt and leverage, the triggering of a housing and mortgage credit bubble, the quadrupling of the US credit-market debt, and the combining of administrative incompetence with greed and dishonesty.[1] This global financial crisis has led to a renewed interest in Karl Marx and his writings, a point made persuasively by writers such as Leo Panitch and Christopher Hitchens.[2] What is of interest here, however, is not so much what Panitch and Hitchens go on to say as the fact that such distinguished individuals[3] arrive at the same conclusion: that Marx is deserving of attention in the present economic climate.

One person who has made use of Marx's ideas in a recent context is Yanis Varoufakis, the former Greek Minister of Finance in the Syriza government of Alexis Tsipris. Faced with a mounting economic crisis that necessitated a rescue package of $94 billion from the troika of the IMF, the European Commission, and the European Central Bank in exchange for the government's accepting additional severe austerity measures,[4] the former Finance Minister refused to bend in his attempt to make the troika present more favourable terms in the form of debt forgiveness, which thereby would reduce the severity of the austerity measures. The trump card, from Varoufakis's perspective, was that Greece could threaten to leave the eurozone, something he believed other eurozone members would dislike. When it became clear in the summer of 2015 that the troika was itself unwilling to bend, Prime Minister Tsipris had little choice but to either follow through with what came to be known as the Grexit, the exit of Greece from the eurozone, or the removal of Varoufakis as his Finance Minister. Tsipris chose the second of these options. There are many interesting aspects to the negotiating positions of Varoufakis and the troika, but one aspect that should not be forgotten is the Marxist framework within which Varoufakis's thinking takes place. He happily makes use of Marx's ideas that "capitalism strives to turn us into automata and our market society into a Matrix-like dystopia."[5] He echoes Marx again in asserting "it is capital that has usurped the role of the primary force shaping our world, including our will."[6] And again, he echoes Marx in affirming booms and busts as the two parallel dynamics in capitalism.[7] The point here is not to demonstrate that Varoufakis is a Marxist, which he may or may not be, but to demonstrate the influence of Marx and his ideas in current European politics. The Greek economic crisis, particularly in the first half of 2015 and Varoufakis's role in it, make this point clear.

To speak of **Marxism** is to speak of Marx. During his life, Karl Marx (1818–1883) wrote extensively as a political economist and journalist. With his philosophic and legal background, Marx proceeds to undertake an analytic investigation of the deep forces at work in shaping human societies. While his desire for constructing a theoretical scheme, a grand theory, sometimes leads him astray, and while his predilection for Hegelian categories sometimes leads him into undue simplification, his analytical and rhetorical skills make him—along with Charles Darwin (1809–1882) and Sigmund Freud (1856–1939)—one of the three most influential intellectuals of the nineteenth century. While his friend and collaborator Friedrich Engels (1820–1895) certainly helps to complement his writing and insights, Marx is the one who makes the lion's share of a contribution to the formation of Marxism, an ideology that—along with reform liberalism and democratic socialism—attempts to address some of the troubling issues and problems raised by the Industrial Revolution.[8] It is therefore to his writings, and only a selected portion of these, that attention now turns.

Several writings provide deep insight into Marx's thought. These are: *On the Jewish Question* (1843); *Contribution to the Critique of Hegel's Philosophy of Right: Introduction* (1843); *The Economic and Philosophic Manuscripts* (1844); *The Communist Manifesto* (1848, with Engels); *A Contribution to the Critique of Political Economy* (1859); and *Capital* (1867–94, with the second and third of three volumes edited and published by Engels after Marx's death).[9] These are the writings that will be the primary focus of the ensuing discussion.

Central Beliefs of Marxism

- Human nature is plastic, socially dependent, and highly influenced by modes of production and property relations. The origin of the state is class conflict, itself rooted in property relations.
- Communitarianism takes priority over individualism.
- Economic organization, at its best, is the result of central planning.
- The rights of humans are projections of bourgeois class interests.
- Power ultimately is proletarian power, though this is realized historically only through violent revolution in the overthrow of the bourgeoisie.
- The end of government is the classless society that results when the state withers away.

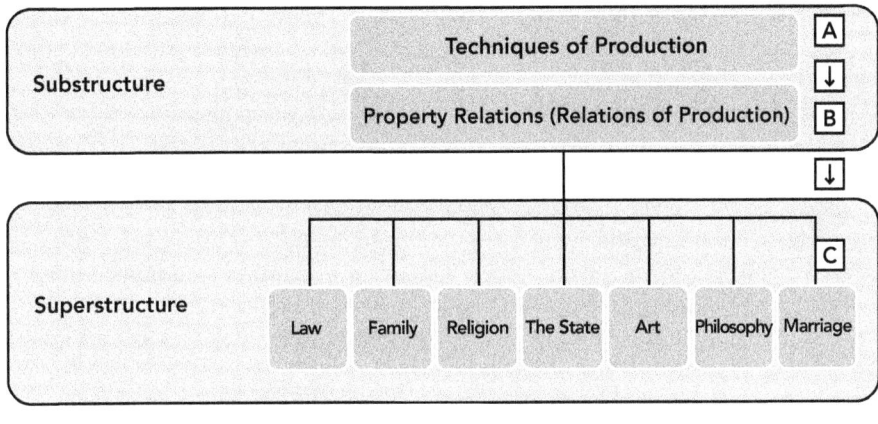

Figure 5.1 Marxism's Monistic Model of Society

Political and Social Emancipation

In one of his earliest publications, *On the Jewish Question*, Marx takes on a topic that undoubtedly was important to him both as a Jew and as a social critic. The topic is that of political emancipation—sought after, in this case, by the Jews of Germany. The question of the Jews is the question of their political emancipation.[10] Marx's points of departure in this essay are the comments by the German theologian and philosopher Bruno Bauer (1809–1882), who writes, thinks Marx, with clarity, wit, and profundity. According to Bauer, emancipation or freedom from religion is a condition for the Jew who seeks political emancipation as well as for the state, which should free him and be itself freed.[11] Marx wishes to carry this idea forward, which he does by likening the religion of the Jews and the Christians to stages in the development of the human mind that should be shed like snake skins.

Marx draws a distinction between political emancipation and human emancipation. He is of the opinion that political emancipation is not the final form of human emancipation, for the simple reason that it forces persons to live a double existence, a bifurcated existence, one within the political community and one within civil society.[12] Life within the political community is life within the ambit of the state, and life within the community is life within the ambit of society. The double existence of a human is that of a public person under the rule of the state and of a private person within society.[13] Religion is relegated, under political emancipation, to the private world—or, as Marx would say, it is relegated to the world of private whim or caprice, to the world of individual folly.[14] Thus, in a perfected democracy, religious consciousness or religious awareness is, according to Marx, without any political significance, and is but an affair of the heart withdrawn from the world. For Marx, religious consciousness keeps company with egoism, independence, and other private whims, all under the rubric of civil society, while citizenship and morality fall under the rubric of the political community.[15] Together, political community and civil society constitute political emancipation.

But Marx seeks more than political emancipation, more than what we might call a bifurcated emancipation. He seeks human emancipation, which is a restoration of humans to themselves. He then says that human emancipation, not political emancipation, will only be complete when the abstract citizen (including his or her rights) has been absorbed into the real individual, with the result that the real individual's powers become social powers. It should be added that, in passing, Marx refers approvingly to the rights of citizens. On the matter of rights, Marx therefore appears to be a social contractarian, and distances himself from naturalism of the natural law tradition.[16] The appropriation of the abstract citizen to the very soul of the individual results, for Marx, in a transformation of human nature. This transformation is a change in human nature from a state of political emancipation to human emancipation. The implication this holds for Jews is the question Marx then puts to his readers.

There are three steps to Marx's argument regarding the emancipation of the Jew. The first is that the everyday Jew is defined by the profane basis of Judaism. This profane basis comprises practical need, self-interest, and the worldly cult of huckstering, with a focus on the god of money.[17] Thus the everyday Jew is defined by the cult of bargaining and haggling and money. Jews have become, thinks Marx, devotees of the god of money. The second step is that the emancipation of the Jews is nothing other than the emancipation of mankind from Judaism, and presumably therefore the god of money.[18] Finally, the third step is that the emancipation of the Christian occurs with the emancipation of the Jew. For Marx, the abolition of huckstering and the god of money means the end of Judaism and the Jew and, presumably, the end of Christianity and the Christian. Like old snake skins, they simply fall away and cease to have any utility. Once society succeeds in abolishing the conditions of huckstering, the Jew and the Christian will melt away and they will find themselves not in religious opposition but in a scientific and human relationship. This will mean not the political but the social emancipation of both Jew and Christian. Thus, Marx thinks, the entrails of civil society, the Jew and the Christian, will both disappear.

The Criticism of Religion

Marx returns to the motif of religion in *Contribution to the Critique of Hegel's Philosophy of Right*, where he expresses his reservations about the young Hegelians and their criticism of religion. He begins in a categorical fashion by saying, "For Germany *the criticism of religion* has been essentially completed, and criticism of religion is the premise of all criticism."[19] The criticism of religion to which Marx refers is a criticism that begins with Hume and Kant, is developed by Hegel, and is rounded out by the stinging indictments of David Strauss (1808–1874) and Ludwig Feuerbach (1804–1872).[20] Feuerbach, in his *Essence of Christianity* (1841), reduces religious belief to a projection made by man, a dream of the human mind. Man is a creature, thinks Feuerbach, capable of self-transcendence, and religion turns out to be manifestation of this self-transcendence as man attempts to objectify his own essence. What Feuerbach offers is a nineteenth-century version of twentieth-century deconstructionism.

Strauss, for his part, engages in a different kind of attack on conventional Christianity, for he is among the first scholars to ask serious questions concerning the historicity of Jesus. The effect of his study is to lead him to downplay the historical importance of the Gospels and to overplay their aesthetics and philosophical importance. What intrigued Strauss was the extent to which a mythological explanation of the Holy Scripture, especially the

New Testament, could be sustained. Unlike other scholars of his time, Strauss does not shrink from a sustained application of this type of explanation to the Gospels. His reason for taking this stand has to do with the fact that, according to Strauss, there is no evidence to prove that the Evangelists were eyewitnesses to the events associated with Jesus, and no evidence that they stood in relation to such eyewitnesses. In the result, historic material gets intermixed with myth. Strauss is less concerned with whether God-manhood has been realized in Jesus and more concerned with the fact that the idea of God-manhood "is now alive in the common consciousness."[21] Whatever the social effect of the ideas of Feuerbach and Strauss, their intellectual effect is to eliminate the historic significance of religious belief, especially of Christian religious belief.

It is here that Marx picks up the attack on, and new evaluation of, religion. For him, the effect of the ideas of Strauss[22] and Feuerbach is disillusionment, in the sense of losing one's illusions. Thus Marx says, "The criticism of religion disillusions man so that he will think, act and fashion his reality as a man who has lost his illusions and regained his reason."[23] Continuing in this spirit, Marx says, "The immediate task of philosophy, which is in the service of history, is to unmask human self-alienation in its secular form now that it has been unmasked in its sacred form."[24] There is much being said by Marx in these comments. First, he makes clear that philosophy is subordinate to history, then he makes clear that the task of this subordinate discipline is to unmask or disclose the presence of human self-alienation in mundane contexts now that it has been disclosed in "holy" contexts. Philosophy thus turns out to be a tool of reason, with both serving in the interests of history. Philosophy and reason have the capacity to help humans move towards self-understanding, but this movement, to be complete, must be realized through an application of reason to the secular world. This only happens if humans examine their situation in terms of their mundane world, including their law and politics. The picture with which one is left is that of Marx imploring those around him to bring to bear all their reflective skills on non-religious themes. Stated this way, the door is opened for the establishment of a secular social science.

The Bourgeoisie and the Proletariat

With his ideas of the unmasking of human self-alienation in its holy form now fully digested, Marx delivers in *The Communist Manifesto* a set of ideas that generally converge on a position called **dialectical materialism**. Under this metaphysical scheme, Hegelian laws of the **dialectic** are applied in a materialistic way. The exact meaning of this scheme will become clearer once we turn our attention to Marx's comments in *A Contribution to the Critique of Political Economy*; for the moment, however, it suffices to understand that Marx's scheme converges on a set of principles having as their foci historical forces that originate in matter rather than ideas, and that react against and with each other according to Hegel's laws of the dialectic: the transformation of quantity into quality, the unity of opposites, and the negation of the negation. In the *Manifesto*, Marx's attention begins to shift towards the unmasking of the human self-alienation in its unholy form. It is perhaps in this work above others that Marx writes with a bluntness and clarity that he otherwise never achieves. Gone are any efforts to convey ideas in Hegelian terms, or to convey ideas with a thousand qualifications. Here, Marx speaks categorically and, seemingly, prophetically, about the then extant European social system. What follows is a summary of some of these seminal ideas, ideas that Marx delivers in machine-gun fashion.

First, the history of hitherto existing society is defined as the history of the **class struggle**.²⁵ Marx continues by saying that the earlier epochs of history, characterized by a complicated arrangement of society into various groups, are now replaced by a simplified arrangement into two hostile groups: the **bourgeoisie** and the **proletariat**. The former class, the capitalist class, plays a revolutionary role by doing away with idyllic relations and resolving personal worth into exchange value.²⁶ One might say that Marx believes the economic system of the bourgeoisie helps humans get rid of their illusions. This is just part of the process of unmasking human self-alienation, an unmasking that Marx thinks he helps initiate with his criticism of religion. Both have the effect, or at least lead in the direction, of making humans come to their senses. These illusions include a belief in the holiness of occupations, the sentimentality of the family, and the idiocy of rural life.²⁷

Marx carries his analysis further than a few definitional points in the *Manifesto*. In keeping with his desire to approach the study of societies in a scientific way, Marx undertakes to offer some predictions about capitalist societies—predictions he believes are rationally grounded. Most striking in this respect is an argument he gives at the very end of Chapter 2 in the *Manifesto*. Roughly, the argument is as follows.

i. The existence of the bourgeois class implies the accumulation of wealth in the hands of private individuals (i.e., it implies the augmentation of capital in their hands).
ii. Capital and its augmentation imply wage labour.
iii. Wage labour implies competition between labourers.
iv. Therefore, the existence of the bourgeois class implies competition between labourers. (Derived from premises i, ii, and iii.)
v. Labourers form associations. (This occurs as the advance of industry replaces the isolation and competition of workers by their revolutionary combination.)
vi. Therefore, the bourgeois class falls. (Derived from conclusion iv and premise v.)

The validity of this argument cannot be questioned. It follows the standard pattern of a *modus tollens* argument in logic. Of course, the soundness of it may be questioned in the form of doubts one may have about the truth of the premises, but its form cannot. This argument allows one to appreciate the connection among a cluster of ideas that Marx advances, and helps explain the confidence he has in the "inevitable" victory of the proletariat and the fall of the bourgeoisie.

The *Manifesto* also carries in it a strong undercurrent of philosophical **materialism**. Responding to attacks made by others on **Communism**, Marx clips the wings of his opponents by charging, "Your very ideas are but the outgrowth of the conditions of your bourgeois production and bourgeois property, just as your jurisprudence is but the will of your class made into a law for all, a will, whose essential content is determined by the material conditions of existence of your class."²⁸ Matter trumps ideas. Materialism displaces idealism. And Hegel is indeed turned on his head.²⁹ By relativizing political ideas, including the prevailing ones of classical liberalism, Marx wishes to lampoon the idea that there are "eternal truths" or "eternal laws" governing property, family, law, and even philosophy. From Marx's perspective, Locke's emphasis on the right to life, liberty, and possessions is a consequence of a selfish conception of the world, itself a product of modes of production of, in this case, the Industrial Revolution. Marx thinks this selfish conception is one that the bourgeoisie shares with every ruling class.³⁰

There are, in addition to the foregoing, many other ideas in *The Communist Manifesto*. He provides a unique definition of history in terms of the history of class struggle.[31] He recognizes the discovery of America and the rounding of the Cape of Good Hope as opening up fresh ground for the rising bourgeoisie.[32] Further, he acknowledges the exploitation by the bourgeoisie of the proletariat,[33] and anticipates the evolution of the class struggle from a veiled civil war into a violent attempt to overthrow the bourgeoisie.[34] In addition, Marx expects the **immiseration of the proletariat** under capitalism,[35] and predicts the end of national differences.[36] Finally, Marx thinks of the proletariat as a revolutionary class pitted against the bourgeoisie in violent confrontation for the purposes of producing a forcible overthrow of all existing social conditions.[37]

Modes of Production and Property Relations

By the time Marx writes *A Contribution to the Critique of Political Economy* in 1859, his ideas have hardened into a credo. The *Critique* marks another phase of Marx's thought, and one where he develops ideas expressed in the *Manifesto*. In the *Critique*, Marx presents a summary of his thought to that time, and he does this in terms that deserve to be quoted at length:

> The study of this [the political economy of civil society], which I began in Paris, I continued in Brussels, where I moved owing to an expulsion order issued by M. Guizot. The general conclusion at which I arrived and which, once reached, became the guiding principle of my studies can be summarised as follows. In the social production of their existence, men inevitably enter into definite relations, which are independent of their will, namely relations of production appropriate to a given stage in the development of their material forces of production. The totality of these relations of production constitutes the economic structure of society, the real foundation, on which arises a legal and political superstructure and to which correspond definite forms of social consciousness. The mode of production of material life conditions the general process of social, political, and intellectual life. It is not the consciousness of men that determines their existence, but their social existence that determines their consciousness.[38]

Here one sees the credo of a radical thinker persecuted by authorities. The credo is grounded in metaphysical materialism, namely modes of production, upon which rests the ideological forms of man's consciousness. These ideological forms are legal, political, religious, artistic, and philosophic, and help comprise a superstructure. Mediating the materialistic **substructure** and the **superstructure** stand relations of production or property relations, and these represent the legal rules of ownership.[39] For Marx, the foundations are shaken when conflict occurs between the **modes of production** and **property relations**. In effect, according to Marx, property relations at some point cease to keep pace with the changes in the methods of production. The property relations turn out to be the "fetters" on the productive forces, but these fetters are thrown aside as the productive forces develop.

The ideas discussed by Marx in his *Critique of Political Economy* reveal a maturity in thought from the days of the *Manifesto*. Marx's earlier idea of history, being the history of class struggle, is modified to allow for a more settled materialistic interpretation of history. Under the new scheme, history is driven by modes of production, which in turn affect property relations. Property relations are those relations that determine what classes own the tools of production, and what classes are employed by those who own the tools of production. The class struggle overlays the forces of production and is subject to its seismic shifts. During periods of relative stability in modes of production, social stability ensues. During periods of dramatic changes in production, social instability results. Proprietary interests must try to ride out these seismic waves.

Two other thoughts of Marx in the *Critique of Political Economy* are worthy of comment in the present context. One of these relates to religion and the other to consciousness or self-understanding. Hitherto we have seen how Marx acknowledges the unmasking of human self-alienation in its sacred form, and thereby indirectly acknowledges the work of neo-Hegelians like Feuerbach and Strauss. In *Critique of Hegel's Philosophy of Right*, Marx recognizes the need to unmask human self-alienation in its secular form, and proceeds to do this by showing how man's **alienation** occurs in the context of law, politics, art, and philosophy. In different words, he applies the insights of the likes of Feuerbach, Strauss, and himself on religion to other human practices that share with religion the feature of being a part of the superstructure. It is Marx's understanding of religion in 1843 that allows him to walk across the bridge to his understanding of the secular world, first in 1848 and then more decidedly and self-confidently in 1859.

The other idea in need of discussion relates to his comments on consciousness. In bold fashion, one that clearly anticipates Freud's view that the mind is not self-translucent, Marx claims, "Just as one does not judge an individual by what he thinks about himself, so one cannot judge such a period of transformation by its consciousness, but, on the contrary, this consciousness must be explained from the conflict existing between the social forces of production and the relations of production."[40] Not all of what Marx says here is new. Aristotle, in *Politics*, makes the comment concerning people and their judgment that "[m]ost people, as a rule, are bad judges where their own interests are involved."[41] Nonetheless, Marx carries the discussion further by effectively claiming that self-understanding is reached through social science, not by self-reflection. An understanding of one's self is achieved by looking at the productive forces that shape the individual, by coming first to understand the world and then the self.[42] Such an interpretation of Marx comports very nicely with the view that Marx sees himself doing science by dealing with that which "can be determined with precision."[43] Self-reflection is set aside in favour of economic materialism, subjectivity in favour of objectivity. At least, so he thinks.

The Use of Demographics

Marx's final work, *Capital*, is often thought to be dry and turgid. Though this charge has some merit, it is more fittingly applied to the section of this work dealing with what Marx calls "the form of value." His discussion of value theory is, in the end, rather tortuous and one not likely to grip the minds of people today. This said, there is much else in *Capital* that deserves acknowledgement, including his discussion of surplus value, the transformation of money into capital, the industrial reserve army, and capitalist accumulation. And there remains in the last few pages of this work a defiant and confident prognostication of the demise of capitalism, very reminiscent of what he says by way of argument in the *Manifesto*. There is a difference in the way he expresses himself on this point in his final work. Instead of emphasizing the revolutionary role of the proletariat, which short-circuits the bourgeoisie by co-operating instead of competing, Marx emphasizes the monopoly of capitalism and the centralization of the means of production. He believes that monopolies and centralization are incompatible with "their capitalist integument." And Marx concludes, based on this incompatibility, that "[t]he knell of capitalist private property sounds. The expropriators are expropriated."[44] The effect of this comment and others dealing with value theory is to sharpen much of what Marx has already said in earlier writings, and to which attention has already been given.

There is, however, something quite new in *Capital*, and that is the inclusion of considerable **demographic information** to support Marx's position. An intimation of his reliance on demographic statistics is given in the Author's Preface to the first edition. Defending his deference to England as the chief illustration of his theoretical ideas, Marx says, "The social statistics of Germany and the rest of Continental Western Europe are, in comparison with those of England, wretchedly compiled."[45] Though acknowledging Malthus's recognition of the importance of demographics to a study of modern industry,[46] Marx places an even greater emphasis on statistics that are either about the population or about matters affecting the population. Hence he forms opinions based on statistical matters dealing with mortality rates,[47] levels of grain imports and exports from the United Kingdom,[48] death rates from pulmonary infections,[49] annual increases in the population of England and Wales in decimal numbers,[50] augmentation of the rent of land subject to taxation,[51] distribution of incomes in England, Wales, and Scotland,[52] and details of cottages of agricultural labourers in a dozen counties in England.[53] In addition, *Capital* is replete with historical examples relevant to the study of political economy, as well as historical examples relevant to the study of industrial legislation in England, such as the various Factory Acts. Marx's interest in statistical and historical details helps provide a better understanding of him, for his interest in these matters reveals his methodology. Wanting to be scientific,[54] he deliberately adopts an empirical method roughly equivalent to the method used today by most social scientists. So, while *Capital* further develops ideas earlier discussed by Marx, his methodology should capture our attention.

Normative Discourse

With the foregoing in mind, it is time to direct attention to Marx's use of **normative discourse**. In referring to the normative dimension of his thought, one refers to the acceptable principles of obligation and general judgments of value used to determine what is morally right, wrong, or obligatory. Schools of normative thought include, even if they do not comprise, utilitarianism and deontologism. The main difficulty with determining Marx's normative position is the following: he does not appear to adopt any obvious utilitarian or deontological position, but he does at the same time write "as though his pen were dipped in molten anger."[55] However, while offering no explicit moral theoretical framework in which to assess his position, he remains outraged, even indignant, at the human self-alienation present in capitalist societies. But it is difficult, if not impossible, to make sense of this outrage or indignation without supposing that Marx thinks that the world should conform to some pattern, that people's conduct should be measured against a standard, and that some patterns of conduct are acceptable and some not. Put differently, it is difficult to make sense of Marx's "molten anger" without assuming that he holds some normative position.[56]

One way around this difficulty would be to deny the alleged anger, sarcasm, and indignation customarily attributed to Marx, thereby denying the need for a normative ethical theory. Read in this way, Marx could not be construed as a revolutionary, and his ideas could not be understood as more supportive of proletarian than capitalist causes, of Third World countries than advanced industrialized societies, of workers than management, or of impoverished individuals than wealthy ones. Further, if Marx is understood in this non-normative way, then one would be faced with the task of explaining how so many people were influenced by his writings along revolutionary and socialist lines. And finally, if one reads Marx in this value-free way, one would be faced with the task of explaining why he invests so much time dissecting the economic conditions of the proletariat. This is especially true given that the opportunity costs of so doing included harassment by the police in Belgium, France, and Germany, his fleeing Continental Europe, and the impoverishment of his own family while in England.

The better explanation is that Marx is filled with an anger based on his normative convictions—convictions, it should be added, that are never clearly articulated in a utilitarian or deontological way.

The evidence for the normative interpretation of Marx is rather compelling. Speaking in *Capital*, Marx takes a nasty swipe at those who believe that social capital is a fixed magnitude of a fixed degree of efficiency by saying, "But this prejudice was first established as a dogma by the arch-Philistine, Jeremy Bentham, that insipid, pedantic, leather-tongued oracle of the ordinary bourgeois intelligence of the nineteenth century."[57] And in speaking of the power that workmen have at their fingertips in the form of numbers, Marx says, in the *Inaugural Address of the Working Men's International Association* (1864), that "if [these numbers] are united by combination and led by knowledge," workmen will possess an element of success.[58] He is, however, quick to add the normative remark: "Past experience has shown how disregard of that bond of brotherhood which ought to exist between workmen of different countries . . . will be chastised by way of the discomfiture of their incoherent efforts."[59] And in *The Civil War in France* (1871) Marx says, "All the more it is our duty to make again accessible to the German workers these brilliant proofs, now half-forgotten, of the farsightedness of international working-class policy."[60] Still later in the same work he speaks of "the war of the enslaved against their enslavers, the only justifiable war in history."[61]

These comments all bespeak a normative commitment on the part of Marx. Other comments made by him imply the same commitment. Such is the case when he says of the Paris Commune that it will be forever celebrated "as the glorious harbinger of a new society. Its martyrs are enshrined in the great heart of the working class. Its exterminators history has already nailed to that eternal pillory from which all the prayers of the priests will not avail to redeem them."[62] And such is the case when he relates the following in the Speech at the *Anniversary of the People's Paper* (1856). In it he says that during the Middle Ages there existed the practice in Germany, by a secret tribunal (called the *Vehmgericht*), of painting a red cross on a house where the misdeeds of the ruling class needed to be revenged. He then adds, "All the houses of Europe are now marked with the mysterious red cross. History is the judge—its executioner, the proletarian."[63]

These extracts from both the young and mature Marx reveal an indignation and righteousness anchored in a normative world of duty and obligation. It is this that explains his use of notions like "ought" and "duty" and "justifiable." It is frequently easy to lose sight of these value-laden notions in Marx because of his variability in style, which facilitates the hiding of his explicitly normative position behind his deeply held emotions. In the above extract from *The Civil War in France*, there is no doubt on whose side Marx stands when he claims that the Paris Commune will be forever celebrated as the harbinger of a new society, with its martyrs enshrined in the great heart of the working people and their exterminators nailed to the eternal pillory. Nonetheless, even here, he shies away from using normative language as the emotional content seeps through the page. Still, one would be very hard-pressed to construe Marx as thinking anything other than that it is a very good thing that the prayers of the priests will not avail those who are nailed to the eternal pillory. So, even on those occasions when Marx does not explicitly use a normative vocabulary (e.g., ought, duty, justifiable), his remarks are predicated on implied normative beliefs. The unavoidable conclusion is that Marx is immersed in a discourse of normative thought and presuppositions.

The Role of Justice

There remains a residual issue that bears upon the foregoing discussion, and that is the role of **justice** in Marx's thought. One might think that, since Marx saves his analytical invective for capitalism, it would be an easy matter to gain an understanding of his conception of justice from what he says. Indeed, one might well think it possible, with Marx's help, to draw a line from capitalism to injustice and from communism to justice. Alas, the matter is not nearly so straightforward. As stated by others, Marx does not attempt in his works to argue that capitalism is unjust, nor does he explicitly say that capitalism is unjust. There is even, at times, an intimation that Marx considers capitalism just.[64]

With this in mind, what can be said with certainty is that Marx never says very much about justice, and that his few comments on it are opaque. Nonetheless, one can attribute the following views on justice to Marx:

i. Justice is for him a way of speaking about social facts from a juridical viewpoint.[65]
ii. Justice is a way of measuring the rationality of social acts and institutions from the juridical viewpoint.[66]
iii. Marx considers the notion of justice in the context of "its function within a given mode of production."[67]
iv. Justice is a standard, by which "each mode of production measures itself."[68]
v. Marx rejects "a formal conception of justice," but embraces a conception made up of the concrete requirement of "a historically conditioned mode of production."[69]
vi. Finally, "[f]or Marx, a transaction is just on account of its function within the whole."[70]

These opaque remarks can be summarized in the following terms. According to Marx, justice is the norm essential to the dominant mode of production in a given society. In other words, norms receive juridical expression in those laws that have as their function the preservation of the modes that have produced them.[71] Such norms, then, aim to preserve the status quo and are inherently conservative.

The upshot of all this is that justice, as thought of by Smith, Hume, Dewey, and Keynes, is not the concern of Marx. As Allen Wood says, all of this "should convince working class parties not to fill their programs with ideological trash about rights and justice."[72] Marx's concern is elsewhere; it is with servitude, exploitation, and, finally, alienation. And for Marx a line can be drawn from capitalism to these three degrading states of being. Wood argues that, according to Marx, exploitation is not a form of injustice but rather a form of servitude.[73] By "servitude," Wood says, Marx means "'productive activity which . . . is itself alienated from the producer and appropriated by someone or something external to him, standing over against him."[74] So even if capitalism does exploit the worker, which it certainly does, according to Marx, it would be incorrect to say on this basis that it is unjust. What one could say instead is that capitalism is characterized by "disguised exploitation, unnecessary servitude, economic instability, and declining productivity."[75] Moreover, Wood adds, these constitute "good reasons for condemning it."[76]

However, something more should be said about Marx's exclusion, or alleged exclusion, of a principle of justice from his normative discourse. This topic demands a rehearsal, albeit brief, of the kinds of arguments sometimes given in defence of the claim that Marx has no interest in a normative notion of justice. Moreover, we need to rehearse these arguments slowly to avoid unnecessary confusion.

Wood suggests that two such arguments of Marx are aimed at excluding a principle of justice from normative discourse. The first maintains that justice is a moral good, and that it is open to all the successful criticisms that can be made against morality as such. These include the fact that morality is ideological (it subverts self-understanding and preserves the status quo), the fact that it demands the impossible (e.g., the impartial treatment of everyone's interests), and the fact that morality can have no rational basis or justification outside its role in the social system. The second maintains that class interests and their recognition exclude us from taking justice, as an evaluative principle of distribution, as a fundamental matter of concern.[77] R.G. Peffer has responded to these arguments and attempted to demonstrate the logical compatibility of Marx's thought with a principle of justice. But he does not demonstrate that Marx actually embraces such a principle. To the contrary, and here Wood seems correct, almost everything Marx says about justice is critical of it, because he sees justice as relative to class and therefore not objective. Is there a way of teasing out something of interest in these two positions of Wood and Peffer? The answer is affirmative, and found in the words of Friedrich Engels.

Briefly, Engels thinks that morality (presumably including any principle of justice) has always been class-based:

> We therefore reject every attempt to impose on us any moral dogma whatsoever as an eternal, ultimate and forever immutable ethical law on the pretext that the moral world, too, has its permanent principles which stand above history and the differences between nations. We maintain on the contrary that all moral theories have been hitherto the product, in the last analysis, of the economic conditions of the society obtaining at the time . . . morality *has always been* class morality.[78] (emphasis added)

Engels's comments make it appear as though he, who co-authored books with Marx, believes morality (and therefore justice) is always related to class. But a closer reading reveals that he acknowledges only that morality *has always been* class morality, implying that this is the way it has been in the past. Moreover, Engels suggests that the distinction between morality in the past and future is not trivial:

> That . . . there has . . . been progress in morality, as in all other branches of knowledge, no one will doubt. But we have not yet passed beyond class morality.

A real human morality which stands above class antagonisms and above any recollection of them becomes possible only at the stage of society which has not only overcome class antagonisms but has forgotten them in practical life.[79]

Engels acknowledges much here. He acknowledges that morality is a branch of knowledge, presumably implying that moral claims are truth-bearing claims and capable of objectivity. He acknowledges that morality has experienced progress, presumably implying that our knowledge of moral claims has become refined or improved upon. And finally, he acknowledges that a real human morality becomes possible only after the cessation of class struggles and the realization of a collective amnesia with respect to memory of these struggles. These three things Engels acknowledges.

Putting these findings together with Engels's earlier remark, one reaches the conclusion that Engels believes that, while morality is currently class-based and hence not objective, it can be freed of its class roots at some time in the future. Provided one takes Engels's comments to be an accurate reflection of Marx's own beliefs,[80] one can say that they capture very nicely the positions of Wood and Peffer. Looking backward, one sees only ideological struggle and class conflict and hence only a subjective morality; looking forward one sees the end of class conflict and the very real possibility of morality, including a principle of justice. Looking backward, Wood is correct. Looking forward, Peffer is correct. In this way, something of interest is drawn out of the positions of Wood and Peffer, and in this way, Marx appears more consistent. With this clarification of Marx's position on justice, we need to address other topics that have a moral dimension but that Marx addresses in his typical non-moral way. These topics include exploitation, servitude, and alienation.

Without being a card-carrying utilitarian,[81] Marx nonetheless finds capitalism offensive, for reason of its effects. These effects include exploitation, servitude, and alienation. But there seems a logical link among these three that allows the first two to be defined in terms of the latter. Exploitation is, for Marx, a kind of servitude. And servitude is, for Marx, simply productive activity alienated from the producer. Hence exploitation is logically tied to alienation. Marx has a propensity, therefore, to talk of alienation rather than justice. A word or two is in order on his concept of alienation, given that it is intended to pull so much theoretical freight.

The best insight offered by Marx into the topic of alienation is provided by his 1844 work, *The Economic and Philosophic Manuscripts*, in which he specifies clearly what constitutes the alienation of labour:

i. Alienation of labour consists in the fact that labour is external to the worker, that it does not belong to his essential being.[82] As such, the product of his labour functions as an alien object "exercising power over him."[83]
ii. Alienation of labour consists in self-estrangement, or the experience of the worker confronting his own working activity as alien, as not belonging to him, as emasculating, and as turned against him.[84]
iii. Alienation of labour consists in the collapse of persons understanding themselves as members of a species into persons understanding themselves as individuals. In other words, it consists in man losing sight of "those potentialities which mark man off from other living creatures."[85]
iv. Finally, alienation of labour consists in the estrangement of man from man, especially as found in the conflict between himself and the man who owns the product he has

produced. Accordingly, the labourer stands separated not just from his product, but from the capitalist who has dominion over him.[86]

The notion of alienation, or estrangement, consists in these four points. Exploitation and servitude are thus tied to the estrangement man experiences in relation to the objects he produces, to others, and to himself. This turns out to be the normative focus of Marx.

That Marx holds strong normative views on alienation is implied by his remarks on private property.[87] Marx says, while explicitly addressing the fact of estrangement, that

- "the worker loses reality to the point of starving to death";[88]
- "the worker is robbed of the objects most necessary not only for his life but for his work";[89]
- "the life which he has conferred on the object confronts him as something hostile and alien";[90]
- "the worker becomes a slave of his object";[91]
- estranged labour produces hovels, deformity, and "idiocy and cretinism for the labourer";[92]
- and, finally, wages, being the direct consequence of estranged labour, result in "better payment for the slave."[93]

Communism turns out to be, for Marx, the positive transcendence of private property, or human self-estrangement.[94] And communism, even in its crude form, shows the *vileness* of private property.[95] It is the institution of private property, intertwined with alienation or self-estrangement, that Marx sees as morally hateful. It is impossible to read Marx without seeing his moral indignation in spite of his carefully tiptoeing around blatant moral categories of good, bad, right, wrong, just, and unjust. So while it may be true that servitude, exploitation, and alienation replace justice in Marx's scheme of things, they do not replace implied normative discourse. Norms emerge through his terminology.

Conclusion

As Marx makes clear in his *Critique of Political Economy*, he is a staunch believer in economic determinism, with the techniques of production or modes of production influencing property relations (class structures), and both of these influencing the broad outlines of institutional structures such as law, government, family, philosophy, education, religion, and aesthetics, which appear at the superstructural level. With sweeping strokes of his pen—"dipped in molten anger"—Marx provides an energetic and iconoclastic view of history and society, especially bourgeois society. There is no doubt in reading Marx that one is reading someone who is passionate and original in his thinking. This passion and originality, coupled with what many consider Marx's deep insight into the workings of capitalist society, give rise to the political ideology of Marxism, an ideology that became almost a secular religion or myth in its own right, and something that, through much of the twentieth century, carried with it revolutionary appeal. This ideology would inspire **Bolshevism** and the Russian Revolution under Lenin, and then Stalin; it would inspire the Chinese Communist Revolution in China under Mao Zedong; and it would inspire many others, such as Pol Pot in Cambodia and Fidel Castro in Cuba. The proletarian revolution of which Marx speaks would have to wait for these ideologues to enter the stage to implement his ideas.

The line of argument of Marxism, as exemplified by Marx, is one of social science acting as the rational foundation of a social revolution. Marx, throughout his writings, thinks of himself as a scientist applying the same techniques or methods to society that the physicist and naturalist apply to their domains. Having seen humanity's alienation unmasked by scholars such as Strauss and Feuerbach in the religious world, Marx was eager to apply the same critical method, itself grounded on scientific method, to the non-religious or unholy worlds. Strauss and Feuerbach demythologize religion (particularly Christianity, but not only Christianity), and Marx is truly inspired by this, for it opens the door to his understanding Judaism and ultimately human emancipation in non-mythological ways. Buoyed by the success of Strauss and others, Marx seeks evidence for his economic or materialistic determinism, and is persuaded that he has found it and that it has confirmed his overall social theory. Clearly, at this point, Marx reaches out well beyond an affirmation of common sense in the spirit of Hume or Burke; rather, Marx theorizes, and seeks empirical evidence to justify his theory. Once convinced of its truth, Marx implicitly jumps in his reasoning from providing an explanation for the way the capitalist world works to providing a justification for its destruction. This move from explanation to justification forms the backbone of Marx's spirited denunciation of capitalism and of his general line of argument.

Evaluation: The Strengths of Marxism

1. Marxism has breadth. It says something about most aspects of human social and economic life, and does so in an organized and original way. One of the most important features of a good explanation is that it tells us something new and surprising. And this is what Marx's theory does. It links together legal, religious, familial, artistic, state, and educational practices, and aims to show how these are causally related to economic practices. Therein lies the scope of his theory. The surprise in all of this is simply that no one prior to Marx, except perhaps Feuerbach and Strauss, had seen the illusory nature of these practices. What was illusory in these practices was simply that they represented interests different from those that appeared on the surface. Religion, according to Marx, represents the interests not of the practitioner, but of the ruling class. By disclosing to us the illusory nature of our lives, Marx joined Darwin the sociobiologist and Freud the psychotherapist as a genius of social studies in his day. Even if one rejects Marx's analysis of the causal role played by economic forces on various institutions comprising the superstructure of society, it is possible to see a coherent picture emerge. At the end of the day, Marx then gives us a theory that is sweeping and surprising. One should note how different this is from the position advocated by Dewey on behalf of reform liberalism. As a pluralist, the most that Dewey can do is indicate vaguely that the individual is surrounded by institutions upon which she or he is reliant for personal development. But how these impinge on the individual and what the connection is between and among the institutions is unclear. For Marx, this obscurity is replaced by a causal explanation based on modes of production and property relations.

2. Marxism recognizes, in a way reform liberalism does not, the deep reluctance on the part of the elite and privileged to relinquish wealth or power. In a sense one could say, adopting some of the imagery from *Darkness at Noon*, that Marxism embraces a vivisection morality, and does so out of necessity. It is not that Marx and his followers are interested in engaging in gratuitous evil by eliminating anyone who gets in their way, but rather that they are interested in removing evil and will do so by means of violence in the event that those who are privileged do not make concessions. There is sober thinking in this position, a point one is reminded of when examining the futile efforts of reform liberal governments to establish the Just Society or reallocate wealth in a given society. Marx knows that inequalities in wealth and power in a capitalist society will not be addressed without a struggle—and a violent struggle at that.

3. Marxism acknowledges the significant role of alienation in the life of modern man. What does alienation mean for Marx? Bertell Ollman has provided the best exegesis of Marx in this area, saying, "Alienation can only be grasped as the absence of unalienation . . . and for Marx, unalienation is the life man leads in communism."[96] Communism is the social system that results after the proletarian revolution, and it results in the "free development of each [being] the condition for the free development of all."[97] As a consequence, the alienated person is the one who fails to experience his or her freedom at the same time it is experienced by others. The effect of this, at least under capitalism, is to separate workers from their work, their fellow human beings, and themselves. What human beings experience with this separation or cleavage is the following: they play no part in deciding what to do or how to do it, they have no control over what they make or what becomes of it afterwards, and they have "been reduced to performing undifferentiated work on humanly indistinguishable objects among people deprived of their human variety and compassion."[98]

There is no need to agree with Marx's attempt to define alienation in terms of its distance from communism in order to appreciate the value of this important notion. What Marx has done is simply to draw attention to the estrangement a human being feels in relation to his or her work, his or her fellow human beings, and finally himself or herself. In many ways, Marx's notion of estrangement parallels the existentialist notion of forlornness, but Marx provides a social setting to this notion by inserting it in the life of the everyday person and his or her social and economic conditions. As such, it is easy to see the radical separation of much of the proletariat in industrialized societies: assembly line workers, restaurant workers, office clerks, workers in natural resource extractive industries, bottle collectors, waste management workers, housewives, office cleaners, truck drivers, salespersons, and employees in meat-packing plants. Few of these jobs have high social status or are financially very rewarding. More important, however, is the fact that the jobs are inherently tedious and allow very little room for initiative or creativity. Marx's own words are deserving of quotation here: "All these consequences follow from the fact that the worker is related to the product of his labor as an alien object. . . . The more the worker exerts himself, the more powerful becomes the alien objective world which he fashions against himself, the poorer he and his inner world become, the less there is that belongs to him."[99] Marx alerts us to the fact that something was lost, a sense of participation in our own future, as we moved from the Agricultural Era into the Industrial Era in the nineteenth century. This is a problem that is still with us today, but it is to Marx's credit that he draws the point to our attention with force and clarity.

4. Marxism correctly emphasizes exploitation in capitalist societies. In the *Manifesto*, Marx makes clear that he is eager to see the end of bourgeois freedom and bourgeois individuality—the kinds of things Locke and especially Mill describe so ably.[100] He is eager to see the end of these kinds of things owing to the conditions that must exist for such freedom and individuality to thrive. The conditions he deplores and that facilitate the things so cherished by Locke and Mill are the conditions of capitalism, from which derives exploitation. What is exploitation for Marx? Plamenatz sums up concisely Marx's definition when he says, "Exploitation, as Marx defines it, is the appropriation of surplus-value, the taking away from those who produce value of part of the value they produce."[101] This must be understood against the background of the labour theory of value, to which Marx subscribes. Accordingly, only human labour can create value. By his labour power, the worker produces a product that has a greater value than that for which he is paid. This so-called "surplus value" is appropriated by the dominant class, the capitalist class. Hence, Marx says the worker is exploited.[102] One does not have to subscribe to the labour theory of value, however, to find merit in Marx's intuition—which surely must be an intuition of fairness (maybe even in Rawls's sense of justice as fairness). One could subscribe to a market theory of value and still feel that the worker was not getting his or her just desserts. And indeed, there are many occasions in our society where one senses that those doing the "dirty" work are not getting their share of the pie. It is to the credit of Marxism that it draws a line in the sand with respect to this latent moral idea.

5. Class analysis, as emphasized by Marxism, is a vehicle for understanding not only history but societies. The fruitfulness of the notion of social classes, thanks to Marx, has given birth to a theoretical position called the "class perspective," according to which "individual actions and organizational interests must be understood via the societal contradictions inherent in the class relations comprising a mode of production."[103] From this perspective the state is biased in its actions, biased in favour of capitalists or those who own the means of production. The state's actions are a function of the class struggle, a struggle that is sometimes open and sometimes covert. From this perspective there is no public interest, but only class interests in a capitalist society. Finally, from this perspective there can be no rational planning of social investments, for the simple reason that capitalism operates on the basis of profitability—a basis that is irrational for social production. This results in an increasing gap between what could be produced socially and what is produced.[104] This theoretical perspective is indebted to Marx and his innovative thinking. That such a perspective has established itself in social theory as one of the three or four best theories (alongside pluralism, the managerial perspective, and the public choice perspective) is a credit to Marx.

Evaluation: The Weaknesses of Marxism

1. A peculiar contradiction stands at the heart of Marxism. Marx subscribes to economic determinism. This is found in his dialectical materialism, according to which modes of production, not ideas, through property relations, cause a particular

superstructure to emerge. The superstructure includes such institutions as the law, the state, the family, philosophy, marriage, and arts. As an economic determinist, Marx is eager to press the point that Hegel's dialectical idealism is turned on its head: ideas are not causally efficacious when it comes to tracing the broad outline of history. All the while Marx is pressing home this point, he spends time in the library at the British Museum gathering demographic information to support his conjectures and theories on capitalism.

The question to ask at this point, simple though it is, is, why did Marx work so hard at this research? Why, in other words, did he work so tirelessly to discover ideas and to pass them on to others—namely, the working class? This seems a particularly important question for the reason that his time doing research took him away from his home life—a home life that was in need of financial help and support. Marx made great sacrifices with his family in order to complete his research. But why? Given his adherence to economic determinism, surely it is appropriate to claim that he should have understood that the class struggle, which he so ably described, would go its merry way quite independently of his writings. His writings were, after all, only ideas, and the changes in the modes of production—triggered by the Industrial Revolution—were real, concrete things. While the tension between Marx's actions here and his economic determinism do not amount to a formal logical contradiction, it does point to something like a practical paradox. One might wonder in the end whether Marx, for all his bravado, did succeed in turning Hegel on his head.

2. Marxism suffers from an inability to understand just how responsive and resourceful capitalism can be when faced with social circumstances to which it has to adapt. Here one thinks of its adaptation to the existence of labour unions, or what Adam Smith and Marx call "combinations." Marx predicts the demise of capitalism and the bourgeois class owing to the formation of combinations, which would destroy the necessary competition that lies at the heart of this particular economic system. Alas, combinations did not prove so united or so universal.

It can be argued that unions simply became part of the corporate structure, along with government and big business. The level of co-operation among these three entities has given rise to a completely different theoretical perspective called corporatism, a theory that stresses the social nature of people and their need for order, in place of opportunities for competitiveness. One does not have to embrace corporatism to see that the capitalists have not been overthrown. Corporatism simply shows one plausible way in which capitalists have made adjustments to pressure from the working class when it has organized itself into unions. Whatever conclusions one wishes to draw in this area, whether corporatism prevails over pluralism,[105] it remains perfectly clear that Marx is simply incorrect when he says that the bourgeoisie produces its own gravediggers. The formation of unions has simply not led to the elimination of capitalism.

3. Marxism is guilty of a hasty dismissal of nationalism. Marx, in a rather buoyant moment, claims that national differences and antagonisms between peoples are disappearing owing to the bourgeoisie.[106] There is something prescient in Marx's comment here inasmuch as the "unconscionable" free trade, as he calls it, has definitely helped to create something like a global village and thereby helped to dilute nationalism.

Nonetheless, nationalism—a movement that promotes ethnic messages, memories, and symbols in social communication and uses its ethnic identity as a basis for promoting its right to existence as a state[107]—was, along with democratic socialism, one of the two main currents of thought in the nineteenth century. "In the twentieth century, [it] has had unparalleled success, its importance growing by leaps and bounds in Europe directly before and after the First World War, and then, particularly after the Second World War, in Asia and Africa. Some of this, though by no means all of it, was due to the disintegration of two large multinational states, to wit, the Ottoman and Habsburg Empires."[108] In more recent years, spilling over from the twentieth to the twenty-first century, nationalism has raised its head yet again—this time in the former Yugoslavia, with Croatia, Slovenia, Montenegro, and even Kosovo seeking and sometimes attaining state status internationally. And to this list of national movements can be listed the Kurds, the Tamil Tigers, the Québécois, the Basques, and the Chechens of the former Soviet Union. Clearly, nationalism is not dead. And as Alter says, "we must recognize the inability of Pan-movements to place any significant brake on the march of nationalism since the nineteenth century."[109] Whether supranational joint efforts at a regional level, such as the European Union and the North American Free Trade Agreement, will eventually be foundation stones upon which we can build co-operation across national boundaries—the vision of Adam Smith—is something quite unknown. Suffice it to say, we are not by any means at that point in our global village. And Marx is quite wrong to think that nationalism is a spent force.

4. Marxism hastily subscribes to the inevitability of the immiseration or impoverishment of the proletariat. There is no need for further comment on this point, except to say that Marx believes the proletarian worker will sink deeper and deeper until he or she eventually stands below the conditions for the existence of his or her own class. This is a phenomenon that has not occurred inside advanced industrialized capitalist states. In fact, viewing it in somewhat Machiavellian terms, one might say it has not happened simply because capitalists realized that it would not be in their interest to let it happen. This possible explanation aside, the fact remains that it has not happened in the aforementioned states, a matter acknowledged by Eduard Bernstein,[110] R.H. Tawney,[111] and Alec Nove[112] (all three of whom will be discussed in Chapter 6, "Democratic Socialism"). A thin element of truth in Marx's position here might be that the immiseration has been displaced onto the workers in the Third World, where employment conditions (wages, health and safety standards, and job security) are low, and for this reason it has not occurred inside advanced industrialized capitalist societies. While this is possible, even plausible, it does not change the fact that Marx is simply incorrect in his prediction of the immiseration of the workers in capitalist societies. Thus, the objective conditions for class conflict have not been realized. Faced with this, one might ask rhetorically, did Marx not attempt "artificially" to warm up the class conflict through his writing?

5. Marxism incorrectly predicts a class-based violent revolution by the proletariat. This anticipation is precariously perched on top of the phenomenon just discussed: the immiseration of the proletariat. Assuming a causal connection from immiseration to open violent revolt, the absence of the former more or less dooms the second. In any

event, there has been no violent revolution in any industrialized capitalist society, and so Marx turns out simply to be incorrect in this prediction.

6. Marxism makes use of a vague and uncertain notion of the economic base. C. Wright Mills, one of the distinguished authorities on Marx, has this to say: "Exactly what is included and what is not included in 'economic base' is not altogether clear, nor are the 'forces' and 'relations' of production precisely defined and consistently used."[113] The looseness of these terms, as Mills says, lends a kind of imprecision to Marx's model of society as a whole.[114]

7. Marxism's economic determinism is too hastily endorsed. Perhaps Yanis Varoufakis, Greece's former Finance Minister, is an example of this when he says, as cited at the beginning of this chapter, "it is capital that has usurped the role of the primary force shaping our world, including our will."[115] C. Wright Mills says, quite correctly, that economic means are but one means of power, others being military and political means.[116] Still others might be legal means as well as moral means. The truth in the domain of social theory seems somewhat more prosaic than that envisaged by the irate Marx. In some societies at specific times economic determinism may hold sway, but things can change so that at another time in the same society military means or political ones carry the day. What one must conclude is that the "causal weight of each of these types [of determinism] is not subject to any historically universal rule."[117] Consequently, Marx's monistic theory of society is unsustainable.

8. Marxism expects too much from the proletariat. Setting aside inconsistencies in Marx between his economic determinism and his view of history being the history of class struggles—that is, setting aside the inconsistency between saying that modes of production determine history and saying that class struggle determines history—one should note that Marx is quite mistaken in thinking that the wage workers will be the main political actors in the decline of capitalism. First of all, capitalism has not yet declined, notwithstanding the many problems it faces. And second, wage labourers have not proven to be the catalyst for change in advanced industrialized capitalist societies. Rather, organizations of workers have been drawn into both national and international capitalism. Part of this undoubtedly is owing to the precarious nature of the worker and his/her limitation of resources, such as time and money. But it also results from how capitalism has changed and from the model of capitalism with which Marx works. Wage labourers, as a result, have not proven to be a revolutionary class, and there is no expectation that this is about to change. Marx is just mistaken in his belief to the contrary.

9. Marxism is naive in thinking that the **dictatorship of the proletariat** will be short-lived. The evidence is incontrovertible: where people applied Marx's ideas in societies such as the USSR and China, power calcified in the hands of a new ruling elite. Moreover, with its new power, unchecked by constitutional restrictions, or a free press, or a free people, the dictatorship of the proletariat misused its powers. A good example of this occurred in Stalin's Soviet Union, where millions of people died at the hands of his regime. Other examples include Mao Zedong's China and Pol Pot's Cambodia.

These examples reflect badly not just on those who applied Marx's ideas but also badly on Marx's ideas themselves, for in the case of the latter they show that there was no provision in Marx's theory for elimination of the dictatorship of the proletariat. This is a point that the anarchists Pierre-Joseph Proudhon and Mikhail Bakunin (to be discussed later in Chapter 9) were both keen to make, notwithstanding Marx's protests to the contrary.

Related Websites

In Defence of Marxism
www.marxist.com/

McLellan, David T. "Marxism." *Encyclopedia Britannica.*
www.britannica.com/EBchecked/topic/367344/Marxism

Ollman, Bertell. "What Is Marxism? A Bird's Eye View." *Dialectical Marxism: The Writings of Bertell Ollman.* New York University.
www.nyu.edu/projects/ollman/docs/what_is_marxism.php

Prychitko, David L. "Marxism." Library of Economics and Liberty.
www.econlib.org/library/Enc/Marxism.html

Further Readings on Marxism

Backan, Abigal B., and Enakshi Dua. *Theorizing Anti-Racism: Linkages in Marxism and Critical Race Theories.* Toronto: University of Toronto Press, 2014.

Berlin, Isaiah, and Henry Hardy. *Karl Marx.* Princeton, NJ: Princeton University Press, 2013.

Béteille, André. *Marxism and Class Analysis.* New Delhi and New York: Oxford University Press, 2007.

Breckman, Warren. *Adventures of the Symbolic: Post-Marxism and Radical Democracy.* New York: Columbia University Press, 2013.

Cohen, G.A. *Lectures on the History of Moral and Political Philosophy.* Princeton, NJ: Princeton University Press, 2014.

Drake, Richard. *Apostles and Agitators: Italy's Marxist Revolutionary Tradition.* Cambridge, MA: Harvard University Press, 2009.

Eagleton, Terry. *Why Marx Was Right.* New Haven: Yale University Press, 2011.

Geuss, Raymond. *A World without Why.* Princeton, NJ: Princeton University Press, 2014.

Hal, Richard. "The Implications of Autonomous Marxism for Research and Practice in Education and Technology." *Learning Media and Technology* 40, 1 (2015): 106–22.

Hall, Lauren K. *Family and the Politics of Moderation: Private Life, Public Goods and the Rebirth of Social Individualism.* Waco, TX: Baylor University Press, 2014.

Henry, Michel. *From Communism to Capitalism: A Theory of Catastrophe.* Translated by Scott Davidson. London and New York: Bloomsbury Academic, 2014.

Hobsbawm, Eric J. *How to Change the World: Reflections on Marx and Marxism.* New Haven: Yale University Press, 2011.

James, Ryan. *Lenin's Terror: The Ideological Origins of Soviet State Terror.* Abingdon and New York: Routledge, 2012.

Laclau, Ernesto. *Politics and Ideology in Marxist Theory: Capitalism, Marxism and Populism.* London and New York: Verso, 2011.

Lucardie, Paul. *Democratic Extremism in Theory and in Practice: All Power to the People.* New York: Routledge, 2014.

McLellan, David. *Karl Marx Selected Writings.* London: Oxford University Press, 2001.

Marcuse, Herbert. *Marxism, Revolution and Utopia.* Edited by Douglas Kellner and Clayton Pierce. London: Routledge, 2014.

Nimtz, August H. *Lenin's Electoral Strategy from Marx and Engels through the Revolution of 1905: The Ballot, the Streets—or Both.* New York: Palgrave Macmillan, 2014.

Tabak, Mehmet. *Dialectics of Human Nature in Marx's Philosophy.* New York: Palgrave Macmillan, 2012.

Tally, Robert T., Jr, and Frederic Jameson. *The Project of Dialectical Criticism.* London: Pluto Press, 2014.

Waldron, Jeremy, ed. *"Nonsense upon Stilts": Bentham, Burke, and Marx on the Rights of Man.* London and New York: Methuen, 1987.

Welch, Stephen. *The Theory of Political Culture.* London: Oxford University Press, 2013.

6 Democratic Socialism

What counts today, the question which is looming on the horizon, is the need for a redistribution of wealth. Humanity must reply to this question, or be shaken to pieces by it.
—Frantz Fanon, *The Wretched of the Earth* (1967: 78)

Learning Objectives

- To comprehend the special role that the ideal of equality plays in democratic socialism.
- To acknowledge the rejection, in most instances, of the use of violence in democratic socialism.
- To ensure the important role played by the state through regulations and the distribution of scarce commodities in democratic socialism.

The cry of the French Revolution—"liberty, equality, and fraternity"—proved an unsettling motto to Edmund Burke as he strove, in *Reflections on the Revolution in France*, to articulate the conservative ideology as a bastion against those who would overturn the state and society. There is something prescient in Burke's political thought, for he sees something that others do not: the French Revolution fired a salvo across the bow of conventional and traditional life in Europe. What he does not see, however, is how this event is entangled in the rise of science and industrialization, but entangled it is, as shown by a new ideology—**democratic socialism**—that emerges in the early part of the nineteenth century. Indeed, in the course of time, the very ideals of liberty, equality, and fraternity would constitute the core values of this new ideology, an ideology that became acutely aware over time of the revolutionary character of industrialization and of its linkage to the emergent economic order of capitalism.

By the middle of the nineteenth century, socialism had already inched its way onto the political ideological spectrum. Evidence of this is found in a neglected chapter of Marx and Engels's *Communist Manifesto* (1848), a chapter entitled "Socialist and Communist Literature." It is here that Marx takes aim at socialism in its various kinds: reactionary socialism, conservative or bourgeois socialism, and critical-utopian socialism.[1] His purpose in dissecting versions of socialism is to demonstrate once and for all that communism is distinct from socialism. No one describes the emergence of the new ideology of socialism better than the agitated Marx, and so it is to his comments—pithy and scathing though they be—that we now turn.

Marx divides the first kind of socialism, reactionary socialism, into three streams: feudal socialism, petty-bourgeois socialism, and German or "true" socialism. According to Marx, feudal socialism developed when—owing to its historical position—the aristocracy in France and England in the early nineteenth century responded to a call to arms against the new bourgeois society by writing pamphlets condemning this new class. The pamphleteers included French Legitimists, a group of aristocratic landowners longing for the restoration of the Bourbon dynasty, and Young England, a group embracing Tory writers and politicians such as Thomas Carlyle (1795–1881) and Benjamin Disraeli (1804–1881). These same pamphleteers, in Marx's opinion, offered nothing but half lamentations and half lampoons to little or no effect as they rushed out in apparent defence of the interests of the working class while in reality they sought to preserve the old order of society—a feudal order in which their reactionary interests were protected.

However, according to Marx, the feudal aristocracy apparently was not alone in being ruined by the ascending star of the bourgeoisie. Also affected was the petty bourgeoisie, including medieval burgesses and small peasant proprietors, as well as those who fluctuated between the dominant classes of the bourgeoisie and proletariat but whose fate was ultimately that of being hurled down into the abyss of the proletariat on account of competition. Petty-bourgeois socialism, again according to Marx, laid bare some of the consequences and contradictions of modern production: the disastrous effects of machinery and the division of labour, the concentration of capital in a few hands, the problem of overproduction, the misery of the proletariat, anarchy in production, inequalities in the distribution of wealth, industrial wars of extermination, and the dissolution of old moral bonds of families and nations. But this same version of socialism aimed to solve these contradictions by reverting back to old property relations, resulting in corporate guilds and patriarchal relations in agriculture. This ideology, in Marx's words, suffered from "a cowardly fit of the blues."

In speaking of German or "true" socialism, Marx castigates it on the following grounds: (i) it abandons the idea of class struggle, and (ii) it replaces the vocabulary of French socialists by substituting the requirements of Truth for true requirements, the interests of Human Nature and Man in general for the interests of the proletariat, and the language of fantasy for the language of reality. German socialism, in the end, turns out to be "the bombastic representative of the petty-bourgeois Philistine."

The second kind of socialism, conservative or bourgeois socialism, is that of Pierre-Joseph Proudhon as found in his *Philosophie de la Misère* (1846). What this advocated was a redressing of social grievances, as experienced by the proletariat, for the purpose of maintaining the existence of the bourgeoisie. Those supporting this kind of political ideology included "economists, philanthropists, humanitarians, improvers of the conditions of the working class, organizers of charities, members of the societies for the prevention of cruelty to animals, temperance fanatics, and reformers of every imaginable kind."[2] Marx objects to Proudhon's socialism on the grounds that it constrains the proletariat so that the proletariat remains within the bounds of the existing bourgeois society.[3] He further condemns a variant on this kind of socialism that depreciates every revolutionary movement at the expense of "administrative reforms." Then, with a sneer, to finish off what is left of bourgeois socialism, Marx says this kind of socialism gives free trade for the benefit of the working class, protective duties for the benefit of the working class, and solitary confinement for the benefit of the working class. It is obvious that this is Marx speaking at his ironic best.

The third and final kind of socialism discussed by Marx is critical-utopian socialism. This is the socialism of Henri de Saint-Simon (1760–1825), Charles Fourier (1772–1837), and Robert Owen (to be discussed below), and it is they who see "the class antagonism, as well as the decomposing elements in the prevailing form of society."[4] They believed that the material conditions were not yet right for the emancipation of the proletariat, and they accordingly sought a new social science to create these same conditions. Advocates of this kind of socialism considered the class struggle as undeveloped and aimed "to improve the conditions of every member of society."[5] Moreover, according to Marx, "they reject all political, and especially all revolutionary action; they wish to attain their ends by peaceful means, and endeavour by small experiments, necessarily doomed to failure, and by the force of example, to pave the way to the new social Gospel."[6] The upshot is that, notwithstanding acute observations by this group of socialists—observations on the abolition of contradictions between town and country, of the family and of private profit—they nonetheless attempted to deaden class struggle and to reconcile antagonisms. Inevitably, this group "sink[s] into the category of the reactionary conservative socialists depicted above."[7] All political action is strongly opposed by these same socialists.

The foregoing overview represents Marx's views on socialism at the middle of the nineteenth century. These views throw into sharp relief a contrast between socialism, in its different varieties, and communism as advocated by Marx. Setting aside quibbles as to whether Marx has fairly represented the socialism in question, suffice to say that he is correct in asserting a marked propensity on the part of all socialists to avoid class struggle and to avoid revolutionary (violent) action. This aversion to violence Marx seems to attribute to naïveté or conservatism. In any event, he draws a line in the sand to separate socialism (which has an aversion to the use of violence) from communism (which has no aversion to the use of violence in the class struggle). Moreover, this line in the sand seems justified in light of the observations one can make of two adherents of socialism—namely, Robert Owen and Eduard Bernstein.

The foregoing account of how Marx represents the emergence of socialism should not mislead us into thinking socialism is a thing of the past. Recent developments in Europe and the United States make clear the contemporary relevance of this ideology. Here one has only to think of the emergence of left-wing parties in Europe, parties such as Syriza in Greece, Podemos in Spain, and the Labour Party (under the new leader Jeremy Corbyn) in the United Kingdom, all of which place an emphasis on equality.[8] As stated by one of the best-known socialists in Canada, to wit, David Lewis, and echoed by his son, Stephen Lewis, "the equality of men and women is the socialist watchword."[9] So too with these parties. They are at their very core socialist parties.

But it is not just in Europe that this left-wing ideology is making its presence felt. In the United States, Senator Bernie Sanders, a self-avowed socialist, became a serious contender for the Democratic nomination for President of the United States. As the only socialist in Congress, "he believes capitalism is screwing over 99 per cent of Americans and, moreover, that the resultant 'grotesque levels of income and wealth inequality' are no accident."[10] His agenda called for the abolishment of corporate funding of elections,

Central Beliefs of Democratic Socialism

- Human nature is decent and corrigible.
- Liberty as an ideal is understood as positive liberty.
- Equality as an ideal embraces political, civil, economic, and social equality.
- Justice is fairness in both a procedural sense and a substantive sense.
- The end of government is the fulfillment of both the individual and the community.
- Utility takes priority over rights.

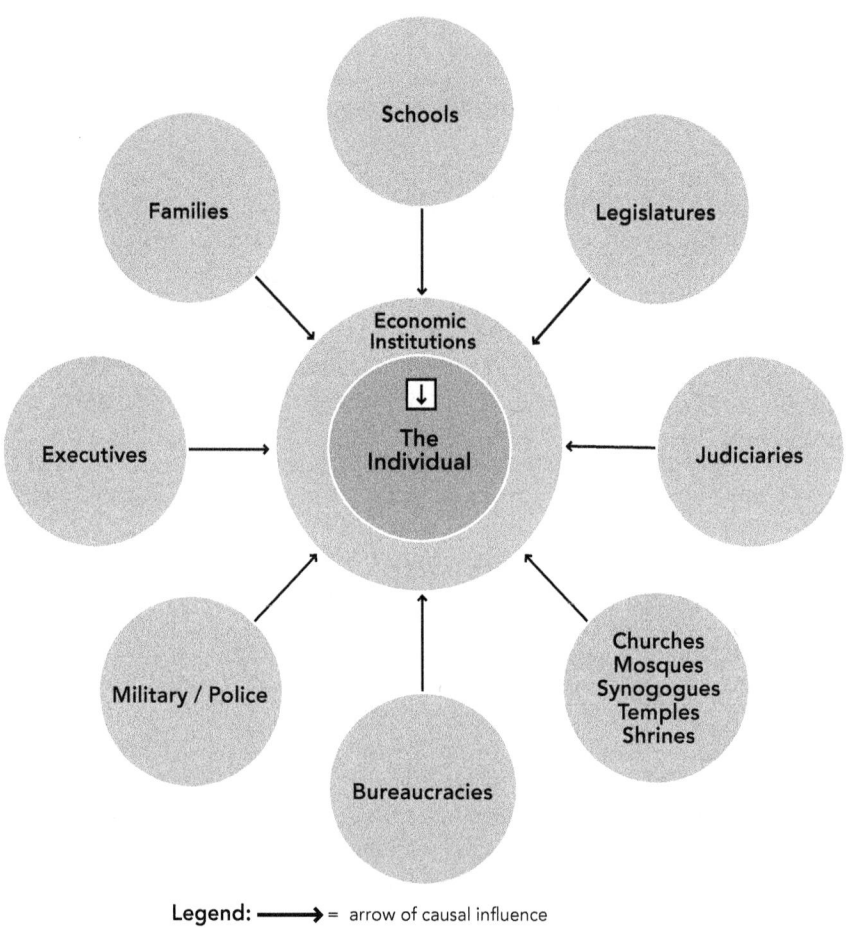

Figure 6.1 Democratic Socialism's Pluralistic Model of Society, with Priority Given to Economic Influences

the nationalization of health care, the breakup of the banks, free college education, and the conversion of outstanding student debt into soft loans paid by a Wall Street tax.[11] Moreover, Sanders's candidacy for the Democratic nomination for President amounted to more than talk. During the three months leading up to October 2015, Sanders had raised $25.5 million as compared to $28 million raised by Hillary Clinton.[12] Sanders, appealing to individuals for small contributions, succeeded in putting money where his mouth was.

Bearing in mind Marx's account of the emergence of socialism as well as the mark this ideology is currently making on politics in Europe and the United States, it is time to turn our attention to two influential socialists, Robert Owen and Eduard Bernstein, first separately and then together.

Robert Owen

Robert Owen (1771–1858) was one of 13 children and began working at the age of nine. He became a wealthy factory owner and, unlike most British industrialists, was deeply concerned with the working conditions faced by his employees, many of whom were young. He devoted considerable time and energy to improving their work environment, so much so that his cotton mills at New Lanark, Scotland, on the Clyde River, became famous as model work sites where Owen reduced work hours, improved housing and schooling, forbade alcohol, and organized pensions and a sick-pay system.

Owen was, after a fashion, a Benthamite, believing that the best government is the one that produces the greatest amount of happiness for the greatest number. In addition, Owen was a curious kind of Gnostic, for he laid the blame for the great and leading evils of Britain squarely on the shoulders of ignorance, the chief error of which is the belief that individuals form their own characters.[13] According to him, one need only apply intelligence in tracing the origin of evil, and then administer the appropriate remedies. Conspicuous in all of this is Owen's commitment to social change by means of peaceful institutional change; there is no mention of revolutionary (violent) activity. Also conspicuous is Owen's recognition of the role of industrialization in transforming the lives of many people—and in many cases transforming these lives in a calamitous fashion. Moreover, Owen refrains from speaking of class struggle.

Eduard Bernstein

Eduard Bernstein (1850–1932), a German proponent of evolutionary socialism, "contends that a socialist party enrolling a major section of the electorate and linked with trade unions and cooperatives can achieve socialism within a democratically constituted polity by use of constitutional means—that is, without a revolution."[14] Seeing a whole series of objections to certain claims of Marx as irrefutable, Bernstein develops his version of democratic socialism, and this turns out to be a political ideology advocating the use of the intellect rather than emotion and of constitutional and legislative reform rather than revolution. Bernstein sees in Marx's thinking an untenable dualism[15] in which Marx combines scientific thinking with doctrinal posturing.[16] Furthermore, Bernstein subscribes to politics as a movement rather than a teleological exercise: "to me that which is generally called the ultimate aim of socialism is nothing, but the movement is everything."[17] In addition, Bernstein rejects the notion of the immiseration of the proletariat advanced by Marx—a notion that predicts extensive downward mobility caused by capitalist competition and economic cycles, and also predicts the constant shrinkage in the number of capitalist magnates.[18] Finally, Bernstein recognizes the consequences of capitalism as a system that produces a class of people "whose members live under crowded conditions, are badly educated, and have uncertain and insufficient income."[19] As such, he believes capitalism must be overcome—through non-violent means.

Owen and Bernstein

Our examination of the democratic socialism of Owen and Bernstein shows that Marx is correct in drawing a line in the sand separating various kinds of socialism from Marx's communism. Though one could examine other socialists (among them utopian socialists, ethical socialists who appealed to principles of reason, and trade union socialists), Owen and Bernstein are representative of the best in the tradition of socialism in the nineteenth century. Grasping this point firmly allows one to see that democratic socialism is distinct from communism (Marxism), especially in its rejection of the use of violence or revolution and its embracing of constitutional, legislative, and institutional change as the means to the advancement of the proletariat. Furthermore, it is clear that democratic socialism has its roots in the industrialization of the nineteenth century. Without an appreciation of these roots, one cannot understand democratic socialism, including the versions offered by Owen and Bernstein. Without an appreciation of the industrial background to this political ideology, one cannot make sense of the concerns of Owen in reducing the work week or improving working conditions, or the concerns of Bernstein regarding the working class. Democratic socialism has its roots in the Industrial Revolution.

The foregoing shows an intellectual, moral, and spiritual reaction located at the foundation of democratic socialism. It also shows that socialism stands apart from Marx's communism. What it does not show is how socialism is distinct from reform liberalism. Reform liberalism, one recalls, follows the lead of John Dewey in embracing radicalism but rejecting the use of violence. Accordingly, it is anything but clear in what way socialism stands distinct from reform liberalism. What characteristics does socialism possess that allow it to be wedged meaningfully between the ideologies of Marxism and reform liberalism? It must be so wedged, otherwise it will simply collapse into a form of Dewey's political ideology. Any answer to this question requires a close examination of the positive content of socialism over and above the content already exposed in hiving socialism off from communism. What, then, of its positive content? With an end to answering this question, we shall look at five major socialist thinkers of the twentieth century: R.H. Tawney (1880–1962), C.A.R. (Anthony) Crosland (1918–1977), Alec Nove (1915–1994), Stuart Hampshire (1914–2004), and finally Anthony Giddens (1938–) .

R.H. Tawney

Not until the twentieth century did the sharp outline of democratic socialism become visible, and among its chief advocates is the deservedly famous historian, R.H. Tawney. In analyzing with wit and charm the main ingredients of democratic socialism, Tawney points back to the watchwords of the French Revolution: liberty, equality, and fraternity. While saying little about the last of these, he does have more to say about liberty and equality, acknowledging in very candid terms the way in which they have been perceived in England in an antithetical way.[20] From the perspective of his political ideology, Tawney is much less interested in the conventional classification of communities by "the character of their constitutional arrangements"[21] than in the more robust classification of their economic and social structure. Among those distinctions that fall under the robust scheme is that which divides communities where economic initiative "is widely diffused, and class differences small in dimensions and trivial in their effects, from those where the conditions obtaining are the opposite—where the mass of mankind exercise little influence on the direction of economic enterprise, and where economic and cultural gradations descend precipitately from one stratum to another."[22] Tawney, as a democratic socialist, goes so far as to say that this distinction is indeed the most fundamental. In his opinion, discussion about responsible government, representative institutions, and universal franchise conceals important differences of spirit and quality between democracies in which class divisions play a comparatively small role and those in which they play an all-pervasive role.[23]

Equality and Liberty

It is apparent from reading just a few pages of Tawney that his analytical skills plus his historical understanding elevate the discussion concerning democratic socialism several notches above that of Owen or, for that matter, Bernstein. Perhaps, however, one should acknowledge that in political studies, as in scientific studies, far-sightedness necessitates standing on the shoulders of giants. Tawney certainly has the advantage of standing on the shoulders of Bernstein, who sees himself as offering to the study of social democracy what Kant offers to the study of pure reason.[24]

With flourish and passion and considerable insight, Tawney throws himself into working out a nuanced relation between the ideals of equality and liberty in a way that he thinks is defensible. Central to his thinking is the idea that equality is at odds with a particular interpretation or construction of liberty, one that today would be called "Friedmanian" or libertarian. But he wishes to prove that other constructions of liberty are logically compatible with equality. Quoting A.F. Pollard in *The Evolution of Parliament* (1920), Tawney says that the liberty of the weak depends on the restraint of the strong, of the poor on the restraint of the rich, and of the simpler-minded on the restraint of the sharper.[25] In his eagerness to develop a coherent political ideology in an industrial age that has passed beyond the first phase of industrialization, he asserts categorically that when the economic scales are "so unevenly weighted, to interpret liberty as a political principle, which belongs to one world, the world of politics and government, while equality belongs—if, indeed, it belongs anywhere—to another world, the world of economic affairs, is to do violence to realities."[26] For Tawney, liberty and equality belong to one world. Absent this construction, freedom for the pike means death for the minnow. Liberty, for Tawney, turns out to be equality in action.[27]

In Tawney's case, a larger metaphysics surrounds his democratic socialism, particularly his principle of equality. This metaphysics is the Christian perspective, and it leads him to assert that "in order to believe in human equality it is necessary to believe in God."[28] But the equality of which he speaks is not that all men are equal in their natural endowments.[29] Indeed, he thinks this interpretation blinds us to a very different meaning of equality. Instead of affirming that "men are, on the whole, very similar in their natural endowments of character and intelligence,"[30] Tawney wishes to affirm that, notwithstanding the profound differences as individuals in character and intelligence, "they are equally entitled as human beings to consideration and respect, and that the well-being of a society is likely to be increased if it so plans its organization that, whether their powers are great or small, all members may be equally entitled to make the best of such powers as they possess."[31] The equality of which he speaks is therefore not that "of capacity or attainment, but of circumstances, institutions and manners of life."[32] Accordingly, what Tawney advocates is that, owing to the fact that humans are humans, social institutions (property rights, the organization of industry, and the systems of health and education) should be designed to emphasize the common humanity that unites them rather than the class differences that divide.[33] It is clear that Tawney's notion of equality extends from the political to the economic.

Corporate Economic Power

Tawney's democratic socialism highlights the urgency of extending liberty from the political to the economic sphere.[34] And this extension must be fully sensitive to the corporate economic activity carried on "by groups which are endowed by the State with a legal status, and the larger of which, in size, complexity, specialization of functions and unity of control, resemble less the private enterprise of the past than a public department."[35] The significance of this for the ordinary individual is captured, thinks Tawney, by the words of US Supreme Court Justice Louis D. Brandeis when he says, "The main objection to the large corporation is that it makes possible—and in many cases makes inevitable—the exercise of industrial absolutism."[36] So when Tawney looks at the coercive power of economic structures he thinks primarily of the modern corporation and its influence over consumers and workers alike.

The common motifs of Tawney's democratic socialism are those of the French Revolution, with an emphasis on liberty and equality. These he inserts in the modern-day corporate world, over which he vigilantly keeps watch in order that the general public interest and not that of a minority is safeguarded.

C.A.R. Crosland

According to Crosland, the basic socialist aspirations are both ethical and emotional, and partly negative and partly positive. He summarizes these in terms of five different ideas: (i) a protest against the material poverty and squalor produced by capitalism; (ii) a wider concern for social welfare and for the interests of those in need; (iii) a belief in equality and the classless society; (iv) a rejection of competitive antagonism and an ideal of cooperation; and finally (v) a protest against the inefficiencies in capitalism, particularly its inclination to mass unemployment.[37] After listing these five elements of socialism, he hastens to add that he intentionally mentions only the economic and social aspirations, but that underlying them is a passionate belief by socialists in liberty and democracy.

Crosland believes that the foregoing five elements characterize the main aspirations of socialism as it has evolved to the middle of the twentieth century, but he is eager to reformulate these aspirations in light of change that has overtaken the doctrine.[38] He wishes to reformulate the goals of socialism in such a way that its ethical and emotional content is preserved. In the opinion of Crosland, at least in the British context, the first and the last of the five points—the protest against material poverty and physical squalor, and the protest against the inefficiencies of capitalism—have lost their relevance. He chooses to concentrate on the remaining three positive ideals: concern for social welfare, desire for a classless society, and rejection of competitive antagonism and embracing of fraternity and co-operation. To each of these we now turn.

The Co-operative Aspiration

Crosland chooses to discuss the co-operative aspiration first because he thinks it is difficult if not impossible to reach "a definite conclusion" about its contemporary relevance. He thinks that matters bearing on co-operation are much less clear-cut than they were during the nineteenth century, owing to two reasons: (i) much moderation in the excesses of competition has occurred, and (ii) competition is now understood to have some compensating advantages. Moreover, Crosland admits that a psychological conversion in people, from acting from self-regarding motives to acting from other-regarding motives, is unlikely. Also unlikely is an alteration in institutions that create a better outlet for social motives. Furthermore, the application of the co-operative ideal in the workplace setting seems an unattainable ideal. Whatever groups exist, they may not be characterized by altruism with respect to other groups; in fact, their behaviour may be largely selfish and lead to a worsening of relations with management and to a fostering of resentment and discontent in place of harmony and common purpose.

In the result, Crosland believes that, while the co-operative ideal has been partially achieved, most people still work for personal gain rather than the social good. Finally, he admits to much agnosticism concerning the effect of the co-operative ideal that suppresses the motive of personal gain, an agnosticism that reaches the effect of co-operation or communal activity on (i) personal contentment, (ii) attitudes to work, (iii) the quality of our society, (iv) privacy, (v) individuality, (vi) personal independence, (vii) equality of opportunity, and (viii) standard of living.[39]

The Welfare Aspiration

Socialists, thinks Crosland, give high priority to the relief of social distress or misfortune—the welfare aspiration. Within this concept are embraced all of the following: secondary poverty, natural misfortune, physical or mental illness, the decline in the size of the family, and shortcomings in social capital. The shortcomings in social capital include (i) ugly towns, (ii) mean streets, (iii) slum houses, (iv) overcrowded schools, (v) inadequate hospitals, (vi) under-staffed mental institutions, (vii) too few homes for the aged, and (viii) a general lack of social amenities. For Crosland, socialists are those who, on humanitarian and compassionate grounds rather than egalitarian grounds, give priority in social expenditure to addressing such distress and squalor.[40] Put somewhat differently, Crosland believes that, for socialists, priority in the distribution of national output should be given to the poor, the unfortunate, and generally those who are in need.

The Equality Aspiration

Crosland is emphatic in saying that the belief in social equality—the equality aspiration—remains the "most characteristic feature of socialist thought today." Accordingly, what the socialist seeks is a distribution of rewards, status, and privileges that is sufficiently egalitarian to minimize social resentment, to secure justice, and to equalize opportunities. It seems, too, that Crosland wants to embrace the notion of a classless society in the bosom of his egalitarian ideal, and by so doing he hopes to rid society of the associated feelings of envy and inferiority as well as those barriers to uninhibited mingling between classes.[41] Finally, it should be added, Crosland feels that the ideal of social equality has much less to do with the economic realm than with something social. For Crosland, this ideal has much more pertinence in the international sphere than in the domestic sphere in Great Britain. In other words, for democratic socialists, egalitarian issues have more salience for social issues between Great Britain and the Third World than they have within Great Britain.

In conclusion, what one sees in Crosland's democratic socialism is an affirmation of the ideals of equality and welfare, as well as a recognition of the possible importance of fraternity and co-operation.

The previously recognized ideological space of democratic socialism allows us to look beyond Crosland at later twentieth-century and early twenty-first-century democratic socialists: Alec Nove, Stuart Hampshire, and Anthony Giddens. The first of these was a noted economist and the second a highly respected philosopher; the third is an established social scientist. To these we now turn.

Alec Nove

Alec Nove, late Emeritus Professor of Economics at the University of Glasgow, was raised in the social democratic environment of the Russian **Mensheviks**. He rejects both the Marxism of the USSR and the neo-liberalism of the Chicago School and Milton Friedman. In *The Economics of Feasible Socialism*, he expresses his belief that "the basic assumptions of liberal capitalism are ceasing to be true,"[42] while recognizing the resurgence of "New Right" thinking.[43] Nove is no fool, and recognizes that democratic socialism is "only conceivable on condition that a majority of the population desire it."[44] While he is not optimistic about the realization of democratic socialism, he nonetheless admits to its desirability in order to circumvent the problems of scale and specialization in capitalist societies.[45]

Nove is adamant that no social system can work that is based exclusively on free contracts and in which everyone is guided by the utilitarian interest of making money. As an alternative, Nove attempts to construct a feasible socialism that bears in mind the unattractive elements in capitalism: monopoly power, vulnerability, and alienation. These elements surface in connection with (i) corporations and trade unions, each of which may gain power via specialization; (ii) large-scale units that are run by unknown bosses; and (iii) the substitution of capital for labour (e.g., the bulldozer replaces the labourer). It is in this context that Nove explains the socialist's response to **externalities**, where externalities are viewed as effects on third parties that surface from transactions in the capitalist market. He maintains that these are effects socialists should emphasize and, presumably, capitalists do not, and they include pollution, ugliness, congestion, size, noise, and species elimination through the use of insecticides.[46] In what follows, we shall examine Nove's proposal for a feasible socialism—one in which socialism is thought of as an alternative to a society largely based on private ownership and private profit.

Feasible Socialism

Nove's definition of feasible socialism involves a state of affairs that could come about in "some major part of the developed world within the lifetime of a child already conceived without making implausible assumptions." Moreover, Nove assumes the continued existence of the state, with its important political and economic functions, and assumes a division between the governed and governors.[47] It is obvious from this that Nove is not imagining some Kropotkin-like, anarchistic state of affairs. As a political assumption, Nove postulates a multi-party democracy with elections to a parliament. Pivotal to his thinking are the categories of producers of goods and services. And, while he admits that consumer preferences must predominate in determining what to produce, he believes that to avoid alienation, the producers' preferences must be taken into consideration. The categories of producers are briefly as follows: centralized state corporations, state-owned enterprises with full autonomy, co-operative enterprises, small-scale private enterprises, and individuals.[48] While acknowledging that his ideas are open to challenge, Nove adds the following elements to his feasible socialism:

i. Central management of current microeconomic affairs would be confined to sectors where economies of scale make this necessary.
ii. A preference would be shown for small scale as a means of maximizing participation and a sense of belonging.
iii. Current output and distribution of goods and services should be determined by negotiations. This would imply competition as a precondition of choice.
iv. Workers should be free to determine the nature of their employment.
v. The state would have vital functions in determining income policies, levying taxes, intervening to restrain monopoly power, and setting the ground rules of a competitive market.
vi. Moral incentives would be encouraged and inequalities consciously limited.[49]

These six elements fairly represent Nove's thoughts on feasible socialism. He presents these ideas of democratic socialism in order to carve out an ideological position distinct from that advocated by latter-day Marxists and distinct from that advocated by Friedmanians (one could also add Hayekians) of the Chicago School. The position he carves out is that of democratic centralism.

Before wrapping up this discussion of Nove's version of democratic socialism, we should keep in mind that Nove acknowledges, in the Preface to *The Economics of Feasible Socialism*, that while a section of his book deals with "transition" and the need to be vigilant in protecting against extremist policies (he admits to the dangers of centralized planning leading to centralized despotism), he has no idea of how to bridge the gap between transition and his feasible socialism.[50] This is a matter to which I shall return in the criticism. For the moment, however, one can see that Nove has gone a long way towards describing an up-to-date socialism, and has given a picture of this ideology that is much more detailed than those suggested by Bernstein or Tawney. It is now an opportune moment to consider the thoughts of another socialist.

Stuart Hampshire

Hampshire affirms straight off that "I have always been a Socialist,"[51] although he is quick to add that he distrusts the element of British socialism that he calls the "pure-minded element." Such an element or approach has suffered, in his opinion, from a marked tendency to conceal the split in morality between virtues of innocence and virtues of experience, and as such this approach suffered from an inability to confront Machiavelli's problem: what is the relation between virtues in the private lives of persons and hardness and deceit that seem necessary in government?[52] The socialism Hampshire offers is intended to be robust enough to apply to situations filled with the ambivalence of the public and private, the gentle and the hard, and integrity and deceit.

Fundamental Concepts

Hampshire works with four fundamental concepts: the good life,[53] substantial justice, procedural justice, and equality. Conceptions of the good life vary, thinks Hampshire. These are attached to different social roles as well as to the individuality of persons.[54] Many of these conceptions of the good (life) are defensible, he believes, by means of reasonable arguments that draw on both personal experience and historical evidence. Some conceptions of the good (life) are simply indefensible, being based on error (factual or logical), and some conceptions of the good (life) are "absolutely evil" because they violate the principle of procedural justice.[55]

Hampshire leans on the idea of **substantial justice**, as well as on ideas of distributive justice, corrective justice, and social justice. The substantial conception of justice is derivable from the conception of the good.[56] In addition, a minimal and procedural sense of justice is indispensable if there is to be peace and coherence in society; this procedural sense of justice, moreover, is independent of specific conceptions of the good.[57] **Procedural justice** gets its sense from a minimum fairness found in established procedures for settling conflicts (national and international) by arguments and negotiations.[58] According to Hampshire, therefore, there is a logical connection between the good and substantial justice, but no logical connection of the good with procedural justice; nor does procedural justice imply substantial principles of justice.[59] Common decency, on this line, is found in procedural justice, and this provides the answer to Machiavelli in addressing innocence and experience and in locating a foundation of public morality. And, in uncompromising language, Hampshire asserts that there is a universal requirement of procedural justice "in virtue of practices without which any form of shared human life is unimaginable."[60]

Equality versus Substantial Justice

Of the four concepts mentioned above, three of these have been discussed. But nothing has been said of the principle of **equality**. It is in this context that Hampshire develops his thoughts on socialism. Hampshire believes that, though the demands of the dispossessed have often been given in terms of substantial justice, in the last two centuries these demands have been expressed in terms of greater freedom or greater equality.[61] Since the days of Rousseau, Robespierre, and the Jacobin tradition, socialists have drawn on the concept of equality as a product of their particular conception of the good. Hampshire thinks that socialist parties in Europe have been mistaken in grounding their moral appeals in the ideal of equality or the ideal of liberty rather than substantial justice. He believes the disagreements between conservatives, liberals, and socialists—disagreements with regard to poverty, property, and property rights—will be clearer if they take place under the aegis of substantial justice and its connection to different conceptions of the good. Rather than follow the thought of French revolutionaries—liberty, equality, and fraternity—socialists should follow the implicit moral appeal of Marx as he argues against the unfairness of the distribution of property.[62]

The particular injustice that seems to play a prominent role in Hampshire's thinking is that of the unfairness of the distribution of property. For this reason he singles out the injustices of the dispossessed, stretching from the nineteenth-century factory worker and agricultural labourer, to slaves in the ancient world, to conquered populations everywhere, to untouchables, to ethnic minorities, to landless peasants, and to those who are completely and utterly dispossessed.[63] According to Hampshire, these dispossessed have no alternative but to organize themselves so as to present an effective demand for justice. For Hampshire this is a demand for substantial justice, which should lead to "serious negotiation." In the event that those who are dispossessed and who seek substantial justice—a justice related to the distribution of absolute goods and to the avoidance of evils[64]—are denied this justice by being denied a fair consideration of their claims, they are justified in resorting to violence.[65] For Hampshire, then, procedural justice underwrites our discussions of substantial justice and the distribution of the rewards of labour. Nonetheless, he firmly holds on to the conviction that it is the idiom of substantial justice through which socialists should advance their claims.

Hampshire's contribution to the discussion of socialism is quite different from that of Nove. The latter, as an economist, focuses quite naturally on the distribution of property and the means of production as seen through the eyes of monopoly control, vulnerability, and alienation. Hampshire, for his part, wants to do two things: (i) establish rational room for the socialist in a pluralistic world of competing substantial views of justice, and (ii) show the exact point of unacceptable unfairness as residing in a denial of procedural justice, the very justice that is the glue of civilized society. To be sure, there are differences between their approaches to socialism, but these differences should be seen as a function of the job each scholar sets for himself. In the end, their positions are complementary. And to see that these positions are complementary one needs only to look at Nove's endorsement of Vilfredo Pareto's comment, "Une société d'où la justice et la morale seraient bannies ne sauraité videmment subsister"[66]—an endorsement with which he introduces his whole book on feasible socialism. With these fully modern views on socialism in tow, we can now turn to a consideration of a contemporary democratic socialist.

Anthony Giddens

The final democratic socialist to be considered is, in the fullest sense of the word, a contemporary. At the very end of the twentieth century, Giddens outlined five dilemmas facing democratic socialists. These include questions concerning (i) globalization, (ii) individualism, (iii) left and right, (iv) political agency, and (v) ecological problems.[67] Giddens proposes to find a framework of thinking and policy-making about these questions that stands apart from—or between—old-style, top-down, state-driven social democracy and new-style liberal capitalism. And this he proposes largely owing to the reason that "the world has changed fundamentally over the past two or three decades."[68]

While it is impossible to give a nuanced account of all aspects of Giddens's "Third Way," one can present its main values in direct fashion: equality, protection of the vulnerable, freedom as autonomy, no rights without responsibilities, no authority without democracy, cosmopolitan pluralism, and philosophic conservatism. A word or two on each of these is in order.

Equality

The new politics of Giddens defines **equality** as inclusion and inequality as exclusion. Inclusion, accordingly, refers to citizenship, civil and political rights and obligations, and genuine opportunities that members of society should have. Two forms of exclusion are involuntary and voluntary, the former referring to those who are unwillingly cut off from the mainstream of opportunity offered by society, and the latter referring to the withdrawal from public institutions by affluent members.[69]

Protection of the Vulnerable

It is the **welfare state**, a favourite of democratic socialists, that Giddens sees providing protection for the vulnerable. He correctly notes that the origin of the welfare state in Great Britain is attributable to Sir William Beveridge,[70] who, incidentally, picked up the idea from Bismarck's Imperial Germany.[71] But Giddens would replace the welfare state with the welfare society, and as such expenditure on welfare would be generated and distributed by both the state and other agencies (including businesses) working in combination. The negative welfare defined by Beveridge would be replaced by the positive welfare of Giddens. Beveridge speaks of *want*, Giddens speaks of *autonomy*; Beveridge of *disease*, Giddens of *active health*; Beveridge of *ignorance*, Giddens of *education*; Beveridge of *squalor*, Giddens of *well-being*; and Beveridge of *idleness*, Giddens of *initiative*.[72] Clearly, Giddens thinks of welfare along social lines rather than economic ones. In the event, Third Way socialism encourages investment in human capital rather than direct economic maintenance.

Freedom as Autonomy: Rights and Responsibilities

Giddens says little on the subject of freedom or liberty. What he does say can be captured in the following few observations. Equality and individual freedom have the potential to conflict. At the same time, the range of freedoms afforded an individual can be enhanced by egalitarian measures. To social democrats, freedom should mean nothing short of autonomy of action, something that of necessity requires the involvement of the social community. In its abandonment of collectivism, democratic socialism looks for a new relationship both between the individual and the community and between rights and obligations.[73]

Democracy and Authority

The Third Way, as outlined by Giddens, affirms categorically that there is no authority without democracy. Tradition and custom, contrary to conservatism, are losing their hold on the minds of people, and consequently the only live option, as William James would say, to establishing authority is by means of democracy. Whatever individualism is affirmed by democratic socialism does not "corrode" authority, but this individualism must be based on participation. But there is, thinks Giddens, a crisis in democracy.[74] Moreover, he believes this crisis can only be addressed by decentralization, by greater transparency and the creation of new safeguards against corruption, by elevating administrative efficiency, by experiments with democracy (e.g., by electronic voting and citizens' juries), by improving risk management so as to include the opinions of persons other than experts, and by making the state have an outward cosmopolitan outlook as well as an inward civil society-renewal outlook.[75]

Cosmopolitan Pluralism

Giddens's Third Way suggests some interesting though somewhat opaque ideas in connection with the cosmopolitan nation, a nation that is active and has an open and reflexive construction of national identity.[76] Here the new nation no longer espouses xenophobic nationalism, but instead embraces tolerance of multiple affiliations and embraces the idea of citizens with a sense of global citizenship.[77] Cosmopolitanism, as Giddens sees it, carries the Third Way of democratic socialism in the direction of cultural pluralism, indeed, in the direction of multiculturalism. Finally, he asserts that cosmopolitanism is a necessary condition of multiculturalism.[78]

Philosophic Conservatism

What Giddens has in mind when he talks about philosophic conservatism is not at all clear. It appears, however, that some understanding of this term can be had by listening to what he has to say about the approach of new politics to the question of the family. After listing multiple reasons for the implausibility of returning to the traditional family as a model of family life today, Giddens asserts that the present family is becoming democratized, and that the single most important aspect of family policy should be the protection and care of children.[79] As a basic institution in civil society, the family needs to be reassessed by renewed democratic socialism in order to steer a course between neo-liberalism and old-style democratic socialism. At least, so thinks Giddens. Beyond this, Giddens seems only to have the following suggestions to make, of a philosophically conservative nature, regarding the new family. It should allow for shared responsibility between men and women for child care, and it should allow for the separation of contractual commitments to children from the institution of marriage, resulting in both unmarried and married fathers having the same rights and obligations. Finally, Giddens asserts that the new democratic family must have life-long parental contracts, negotiated authority over children, and obligations of children to parents, and should be characterized by social integration.[80] This is what he has in mind in speaking of philosophic conservatism in regard to one key institution.

Conclusion

Looking back on socialism in its various guises (reactionary, conservative and bourgeois, utopian, and others advocated by Bernstein, Tawney, Crosland, Nove, Hampshire, and Giddens), what general features emerge as representative of this ideology in the twenty-first century? Over the long haul, what general features does it have?

Two things should be noted before drawing up a list of general features of democratic socialism. The first is that democratic socialism staggered on its feet in the early part of the twentieth century largely owing to the inability or unwillingness of the industrial workers to join forces in opposing World War I; second, it floundered badly during this same time owing to the spiritual hijacking of many of its ideas by the Russian Revolution.[81] Once these points are firmly anchored in one's mind, one will more easily understand why this ideology has morphed into different forms of socialism.[82] It has had to do this in order to survive in "different times and places" and in a way that is "congruent with a belief in freedom, diversity and experiment." This makes generalizing difficult, though not impossible. Helpful suggestions along this line can be made by focusing on the ideas of ethical socialism, a socialist economy, and the socialist state and society.[83] A word on each of these is in order.

Ethical Socialism

Ethical socialism draws on Protestantism, especially Methodism, but also on the Baptist confession of individuals like the Canadian Tommy Douglas (1904–1986), and on humanism. In what we have seen above, this kind of socialism surfaces in the thought of R.H. Tawney. It does so in his notion of equality—a robust version of equality indeed. This same ideal finds its way into the cant of the French Revolution—liberty, equality, and fraternity. While it is true that Tawney and others, such as Crosland and Giddens, see this robust notion of equality as fundamental, they also see that it is logically tied to the other two ideals of liberty and fraternity (sisterhood). Moreover, at least in Tawney's case, he sees all three of these as being understood and analyzed not just in a constitutional and political context but also fundamentally in an economic one.

While it may be true, in light of ethical socialism, that, as Peter Self says, "the egalitarian value is undeniably the most exclusively socialist one and following some disillusionment with state ownership of industry, it became elevated for a time into the key objective of socialism,"[84] there is reason to wonder if this is the case in light of Stuart Hampshire's questioning whether this is the correct objective for socialism to have. Hampshire maintains that socialist parties in Europe have been misguided in grounding their moral indignation in the principle of equality rather than that of justice.[85] Which principle provides the key objective of socialism: that of equality or that of justice? The truth would have it that both equality and justice are essential objectives of democratic socialism, and both provide key objectives.[86]

The Socialist Economy

As for the socialist economy, Alec Nove agrees with Bernstein, Crosland, and possibly Giddens against Marx, that the polarization of capitalist society into a small group of monopoly capitalists and dispossessed proletarians has not been realized. Nove shares with other socialists, such as Crosland, a recognition of the need to counter monopoly control, deal with vulnerability, and subdue alienation through a preponderance of state, social, and co-operative property and an absence of large-scale private ownership of production techniques. The socialist sees the priorities of the capitalists' world as topsy-turvy. Wastefulness, inefficiencies, massive unemployment, and externalities such as pollution, ugliness, congestion, noise, and the overuse of insecticides are given little attention in the presence of growing economies or greater gross national products (GNP). And, of course, the dispossessed are almost completely neglected. The socialist economy plans, along lines suggested by Nove, allow for a plurality of production techniques so long as large-scale private ones are excluded. Competition and private ownership will be allowed, and small-scale enterprises will be favoured over large ones. All of this is to be democratically endorsed by responsible and duly elected assemblies.

Socialist State and Society

Finally, democratic socialists must wrestle with the relationship between the socialist state and society. Indeed, this is reflected in Alec Nove's version of feasible socialism when he speaks of the predominance of state ownership of the means of production.[87] While much of this state ownership will be in the form of centralized state corporations, some will be in the form of state-owned yet autonomous socialized enterprises, and some will be in the form of co-operative enterprises.[88] Democratic socialists of a modern guise are faced with two problems: (i) the problem of over-centralization, and (ii) the problem of the voluntary transformation of society.

The first of these problems arises in connection with the obvious failure of highly centralized economies found in Eastern Europe under the Communist Party banner. The second of these problems arises in connection with the difficulty of persuading people to endorse democratically socialist ideas. Nove, Giddens, and other socialists are cognizant of both of these problems and their interconnectedness; nonetheless, Nove presses for a central management of microeconomic affairs, at least in the case of sectors where informational, technological, and organizational economies of scale make this a necessity.[89] So the first problem—namely, over-centralization—is meant to be addressed by restricting centralization to that which is necessary, a point with which Giddens seems to agree. And the second problem is meant to be addressed by presenting political ideas in a democratic setting—ideas that present genuine alternatives on the subject of economic policies, priorities, and strategies. Among the alternatives would be the creation of autonomous economic entities that help to minimize the feeling of worker alienation.[90] So by permitting individual preferences to realize themselves in elected assemblies, the problem of the voluntary transformation of society is partly addressed. The rest of the job in this respect would fall to education as provided by schools and by political parties.

Ultimately, the modern democratic socialist meets the historic failure of democratic centralism (i) by restricting the amount of centralization and (ii) by emphasizing smallness to maximize participation and to ensure a sense of belonging (fraternity, to use a term of the French Revolution). Moreover, the democratic socialist meets the transformation problem by deferring to education through political parties. In this way the democratic socialist hopes to address the two foregoing problems.

Ethical socialism, the socialist economy, and the state and society are themes of democratic socialism as it addresses private monopoly control, vulnerability, and alienation. This is the direction in which the early utopian socialists carry us, but it is also the direction reflected in Bernstein and then in a string of British Labourites and quasi-Labourites, including R.H. Tawney, C.A.R. Crosland, Alec Nove, Stuart Hampshire, and Anthony Giddens (renewed democratic socialist).

Untouched in the foregoing discussion of democratic socialism is the role played by this ideology in the British Labour Party in the twentieth century, particularly under Clement Atlee (1883–1967) and his four able colleagues: Ernest Bevin (1881–1951), Stafford Cripps (1889–1952), Hugh Dalton (1887–1962), and Herbert Morrison (1888–1965), individuals who had a fairer distribution of wealth, social welfare, economic planning, and nationalization as their objectives for Britain.[91] Untouched also is the current difficulty of the Social Democrats in Germany, as part of the Grand Coalition, in losing ground to groups further to the left on the ideological spectrum, such as Die Linke, over issues related to solidarity, freedom, internationalism, and equality.[92] And finally, untouched is the erosion in the last 20 years of democratic socialism in Israel, as witnessed by the decline of the Labour Party as well as the decline of the Zionist secular dream of concrete and cement, and untouched are the implications these declines hold for peace with Palestinians.[93] Though we have not addressed these current political issues, the foregoing analysis of democratic socialism provides a rich context in which they can be understood. With this in mind and as a final concluding remark, it is time to turn to the argumentative form used by democratic socialists of all stripes.

The line of argument pursued by democratic socialists distinguishes itself from that of reform liberalism and Marxism. Whereas it shares with reform liberalism the idea of the individual being surrounded by institutions and social conditions that, in varying ways, aid or hinder the individual in her or his aspirations, it distinguishes itself from reform liberalism in giving a special place to the causal economic role of these institutions and social conditions among the various causal roles of these institutions and social conditions. In the words of John Rawls, one could say that democratic socialism gives "lexical priority" to economic factors in the causal story. And whereas democratic socialism shares with Marxism the idea of economic factors trumping other factors, it distinguishes itself from Marxism by distancing itself from the use of violence. This can be said notwithstanding the position adopted by Hampshire that a denial of procedural justice for those seeking substantial justice justifies resort to violence. The Marxist's response to the failure of substantial justice turns out to be precipitous, whereas the democratic socialist's response turns out to be measured.

It should also be added that the democratic socialist's line of argument is predicated on the study of society in a scientific way. The lexical priority socialists give to economic considerations is based on their belief that the empirical evidence shows compellingly the debilitating side to poverty, misfortune, and neediness. This is a common story among all socialists, whether they discuss their ideology in terms of vulnerability, exploitation, mean streets, slum houses, overcrowded schools, inadequate hospitals, understaffed mental hospitals, or too few homes for the aged. Moreover, this is a common story, whether it is told by a socialist who emphasizes equality or one who emphasizes substantial justice. Clearly, for democratic socialists, equality and substantial justice, when aided and abetted by fraternity, help give sustenance to liberty understood as positive liberty.

Evaluation: The Strengths of Democratic Socialism

1. A strength common to the various versions of democratic socialism is its attention to human well-being. Whether one is talking about Tawney's ethical socialism or Alec Nove's feasible socialism, democratic socialists are one in thinking that "their system would distribute goods in a way that maximizes their usefulness in promoting human well-being."[94] Democratic socialists correctly claim that the diminishing marginal utility of wealth, coupled with capitalism's tendency to produce gross disparities of wealth, "show that a roughly equal distribution would produce the highest overall level of human well-being."[95] Of course, as Peter Self remarks, things could be different if the vision of the market was to feed the hungry, provide decent housing for the homeless, raise health and education standards, and create a better natural environment.[96] Alas,

things are not different, and these are not the goals of the free market. It is thus open to democratic socialism to step in and occupy the moral high ground in the matter of humans' overall well-being.

2. A separate, though related, strength of democratic socialism is the connection it makes between liberty and equality. This ideology thereby asserts correctly that the guarantee of equal shares of the social product would empower many people who would gain "the resources to make a larger selection of actions possible."[97] There are really two separate points being made here on behalf of democratic socialism: (i) people are entitled to substantive (not just procedural) equality, and (ii) substantive equality plays a causal role in enhancing people's freedom.

With respect to (i), Hobbes's comments still seem the most telling of all: "If nature therefore have made men equal, that equality is to be acknowledged: or if nature have made men unequal; yet because men that think themselves equal, will not enter into the condition of peace, but upon equal terms, such equality must be admitted."[98] Hobbes alerts us to the dual nature of equality: the ethical side and the practical side. People either really are equal, or, at the very least, people think they are equal. Democratic socialists simply give their normative blessings to this affirmation of equality as articulated by Hobbes, and they are correct to do so both on ethical and practical grounds.

As for (ii), it is simply too late in the day to deny that the needs of people must be addressed before they can meaningfully have any liberty, before they can cultivate their personality, or before they can develop (as Mill would have it) their individuality. It is not by chance that the slogan of the French Revolution linked "liberty" to "equality," a point not lost on democratic socialists. And Tawney in his own way gives expression to this when he says that the liberty of the weak depends on the restraint of the strong, of the poor on the restraint of the rich, and of the simpler-minded upon the restraint of the sharper.[99] It can also be said that Hampshire gives expression to this when he draws the attention of socialists back to substantial justice and the unfairness of the distribution of property. While Hampshire is reluctant to address socialist issues in terms of equality, nonetheless the troubling aspect of inequality seems to be smuggled into the discussion under the heading of substantial justice and different conceptions of the good.[100]

3. Rather than adopt an unstructured pluralistic account of industrial societies as presented by reform liberalism, democratic socialism recognizes correctly the primitive, that is, the fundamental, role played by economics in the domain of politics. Where politics is defined as the study of who gets how much of what, economics turns out to be central. And when politics is thought of as the study of the distribution and redistribution of scarce resources, economics turns out be to be critical. What democratic socialism offers is a highly plausible explanation of how human society operates, and central to this explanation is the role played by economics—transcending in importance other considerations. In a nutshell, democratic socialism offers two attractions: (i) a structured account of causal influences shaping society, and (ii) a recognition of economics as the central causal agency of change. This is a point made successfully by Bernstein and Nove.

4. Democratic socialism has the capacity to absorb within it much of what is said by other persuasive ideologies. What are the current movements that have moral appeal? Setting aside those that seem to be dysfunctional, such as nationalism and religious fundamentalism, three ideologies of the modern world with wide appeal are those of environmentalism, reform liberalism, and feminism.

Of these three ideologies, environmentalism appears to have the greater global reach. It would not be difficult for democratic socialism to embrace ideals of environmentalism, as made evident in the writings of Nove and Giddens. While some of the ideals of the deep ecology movement may be too extreme for a functioning democratic socialism, most ideals of the larger movement of environmentalism would not.[101] Democratic socialism would have no difficulty in agreeing with environmentalism in diagnosing the causes of environmental destruction: the joint effects of high levels of consumption and rapid population growth, coupled with the misuse of technology.[102]

As for reform liberalism, it will be recalled that population growth is considered a major problem by Keynes, and that positive liberty is endorsed by Green, Hobson, Hobhouse, and Dewey. Democratic socialism, therefore, can accommodate ideas from reform liberalism, recognizing as it does that capitalism is inimical to rational environmental goals in at least two respects: (i) market forces work within a time frame that discounts future scarcities or overuse of resources, and (ii) the drive for continuous economic growth, as measured in the positive change in the GDP of a nation, works largely through the increase in consumption of the already affluent.[103]

Not only can democratic socialism accommodate much of what is said by environmentalism and reform liberalism, it can also accommodate much of what is said by feminism: political, civil, economic, and social equality as advocated by many feminists would easily be endorsed by most democratic socialists. Moreover, it can also accommodate feminism's rejection of violence against women and children, as well as its affirmation of the important role that justice plays in the family.[104] The capacity of democratic socialism to absorb and develop the ideas of other competing ideologies, therefore, shows it in a favourable light.

Evaluation: The Weaknesses of Democratic Socialism

1. Notwithstanding the title of Alec Nove's book to the contrary, Nove and other socialists have not shown that it is feasible. The first sign of difficulty in this respect comes when Nove admits that he has no idea how to move from the transition period of democratic socialism to "feasible socialism."[105] Notwithstanding the detailed overview of feasible socialism he provides, beginning with the point about central management of current microeconomic affairs being confined to sectors where economies of scale make this necessary and ending with the point about moral incentives being encouraged and inequalities consciously limited, Nove is at a loss as to how to bridge the gap from transitional socialism to applied democratic socialism. This shows that there is a deep weakness in his position that needs to be addressed.

The depth of this difficulty is in part revealed in Joseph A. Schumpeter's *Capitalism, Socialism, and Democracy*, originally published in 1942. Schumpeter, ever aware of the limitations of capitalism, turns his attention eventually to the question, can socialism work? Notice here that Schumpeter is interested in workable socialism rather than transitional socialism. Nonetheless, his answer is instructive for the problem facing Nove. Schumpeter's answer is unequivocal: "Of course it can [work]."[106] He then proceeds to assert that there is no doubt about this once we assume, "first, that the requisite range of industrial development has been reached, and, second, that the *transitional* problems can be successfully resolved" (emphasis added).[107]

With an end to proving that socialism can work based on these assumptions, Schumpeter draws a meaningful distinction between commercial and socialist societies. The former he defines by an institutional pattern with two elements: private property in the means of production and regulation of the productive process by private contract. The latter, socialist societies, he defines by an institutional pattern in which a central authority is vested with control over the means of production and over production itself.[108] This definition excludes guild socialism and other types, and is intended to exclude "the existence of a plurality of units of control such that each of them would on principle stand for a distinct interest of its own, in particular the existence of a plurality of autonomous territorial sectors that would go far towards reproducing the antagonisms of capitalist society."[109]

With respect, Schumpeter does not prove his second assumption, that transitional problems can be resolved. In this sense, and notwithstanding his "socialist blueprint," in which he outlines his version of workable socialism, Schumpeter does no better than Nove, who comes after him. Schumpeter does not show how his socialism can be made to work. Not even Schumpeter's highly ingenious notion of "creative destruction" can step into the breach and help us here, and nor can his Heraclitus-like observation that capitalism can never be stationary owing to the new consumer goods, new methods of production, and new forms of organization that capitalism produces.[110] In short, while Schumpeter does an effective job in showing that capitalism has incurable ills, he does not show that this leads to the victory of democratic socialism. Schumpeter fails to show the workability of socialism because he fails to show that there is a solution to the problem of transition. So Nove is left with his problem and Schumpeter with his. We are left with a very real weakness in this ideology: neither the transitional nor workability problems are satisfactorily addressed.

2. A further weakness in democratic socialism, though clearly one related to the previous one, is its inability to displace the prevailing ideology of liberalism (either classical or reform). The argument here is simple: the capitalists have economic and legal power and the middle class enjoys a reasonably comfortable life. In short, class antagonisms are not so great as to motivate the middle class to use its time to try to change the system. The capitalists are aware of this and can take ameliorating measures to mitigate damage against their interests. The working class does not have the financial resources or the resource of abundant time to invest in trying to bring some justice to the situation. Faced with the adaptability of the capitalist, an adaptability that Marx did not foresee, the democratic socialist is forced to concede that the capitalist will remain in what is, invariably, as feminists would correctly point out, his position of privilege. As such, democratic socialism is left on the outside looking in when it comes to ideological success.

3. Democratic socialism fails to address satisfactorily the question of productivity. Human nature, while not being solely driven by self-seeking goals, is to a very

considerable extent motivated by concerns people have for themselves, their families, and their friends. This is a point made long ago in the history of philosophy, but in modern times it is given an endorsement by Adam Smith when he says, "It is not from the benevolence of the butcher, the brewer, or the baker, that we expect our dinner, but from their regard to their own interest. We address ourselves not to their humanity but to their self-love . . . ."[111] Given this psychological profile, the possibility exists that "economic equality [would be] self-defeating because it would make everyone worse off."[112] The reasoning here is that socialism would make people less motivated, since the rewards for themselves and their friends would be diminished. The effect of this is that productivity would decline and would tend to make everyone worse off.[113]

To be sure, this argument against democratic socialism has weak premises. People are not all or always self-seeking, and they can be educated into changing their motivations. Still, the fact that these are possibilities does nothing to counter, once and for all, the misgivings that reform liberals and classical liberals, to say nothing of libertarians, have of democratic socialism. So long as serious doubts remain about humanity's psychological profile—that is, so long as doubts remain about how other-interested people can become—doubts will remain about the attractiveness of democratic socialism. A person will not very willingly give up his or her enjoyment of high levels of productivity in exchange for equality, especially for others, if the loss of productivity is such as to produce inconveniences and a lack of variety and stimulation in life. This is undoubtedly a problem that the democratic socialist must take seriously.

4. While it is true that democratic socialism has morphed over the years owing to its need to adapt to freedom, diversity, and experiment, one has a sense in the case of Anthony Giddens's Third Way that what is advocated comes dangerously close to being nothing but reform liberalism. Giddens abandons the idea that there is any alternative to capitalism: "No one any longer has any alternatives to capitalism—the arguments that remain concern how far, and in what ways, capitalism should be governed and regulated."[114] Here he seems to part company with Bernstein, Tawney, Nove, and Crosland, and possibly other democratic socialists. So the question might genuinely be asked whether he is even a democratic socialist. Is what he offers a renewal of democratic socialism or its abandonment? Perhaps the former, simply because he affirms the fundamental role of economics in explaining social systems, because he affirms the fundamental role of equality in the political ideas he advances, and because he defends the interests of those who are vulnerable. However, the case is not clear, especially in light of his affirmation of such values as autonomy, decentralization, cosmopolitanism, and cultural pluralism. It would seem a small step from this to the explanatory pluralism of John Dewey, who sees the individual as influenced by several institutional constraints.

One might find plausible the ideas of the famous British historian Richard Pares (1902–1958), who claimed that there are at least four or five variables that influence social systems: climate, war, religion (possibly), technology and science, and conditions of production.[115] Giddens, in his affirmation of pluralism, does not seem far removed from Pares, and this would tend to blunt the claim that Giddens is any longer within the democratic socialist tradition. If this is true, it might show that democratic socialism cannot be made adaptable to the twenty-first century.

Related Websites

Democratic Socialist Perspective
www.dsp.org.au/

Schweikart, David. "Democratic Socialism." *Encyclopedia of Activism and Social Justice.* 24 Mar. 2006.
http://orion.it.luc.edu/~dschwei/demsoc.htm

Whitehorn, Alan. "Social Democracy." *The Canadian Encyclopedia/Historica Canada.*
www.thecanadianencyclopedia.ca/en/article/social-democracy/

Democratic Socialists of America
www.dsausa.org/what_is_democratic_socialism

Further Readings on Democratic Socialism

Bevir, Mark. *The Making of British Socialism.* Princeton, NJ: Princeton University Press, 2011.
Bratton, John, David Denham, and Linda Bell Deutschmann. *Capitalism and Classical Sociological Theory.* Toronto: University of Toronto Press, 2009.
Brockman, Johanna. *Markets in the Name of Socialism: The Left Wing Origins of Neoliberalism.* Stanford, CA: Stanford University Press, 2011.
Deflem, Mathieu. *Sociology of Law: Vision of Scholarly Tradition.* Cambridge: Cambridge University Press, 2008.
Derman, Joshua. *Max Weber in Politics and Social Thought: From Charisma to Canonization.* Cambridge: Cambridge University Press, 2012.
Elliot, Gregory. *Hobsbawm: History and Politics.* London and New York: Pluto Press, 2010.
Ghosh, Peter. *Max Weber and the Protestant Ethic: Twin Histories.* London: Oxford University Press, 2014.
Huo, Jinging. *Third Way Reforms: Social Democracy after the Golden Age.* Cambridge: Cambridge University Press, 2009.
Jones, Pip, Liz Bradbury, and Shaun LeBoutillier. *Introducing Social Theory.* Cambridge: Polity Press, 2011.
Karger, Howard Jacob, and David Stoesz. *American Social Welfare Policy: A Pluralist Approach.* Boston: Pearson, 2014.
Kivisto, Peter. *Social Theory: Roots and Branches.* New York: Oxford University Press, 2011.
Kleven, Thomas. *Equitable Sharing: Distributing the Benefits and Detriments of Democratic Society.* Lanham, MD: Lexington Books, 2014.
Lane, David Stuart. *The Capitalist Transformation of State Socialism: The Making and Breaking of State Socialist Society, and What Followed.* Abingdon, Oxen, UK: Routledge, 2014.
Lucardie, Paul. *Democratic Extremism in Theory and Practice: All Power to the People.* New York: Routledge, 2014.
Malleson, Tom. *After Occupy: Economic Democracy for the 21st Century.* New York: Oxford University Press, 2014.
Mill, John Stuart. *On Socialism.* Buffalo, NY: Prometheus Books, 1987.
Orum, Anthony M., and John G. Dale. *Introduction to Political Sociology: Power and Participation in the Modern World.* New York: Oxford University Press, 2009.

Sandbrook, Richard. *Reinventing the Left in the Global South: The Politics of the Possible*. Cambridge: Cambridge University Press, 2014.

Self, Peter. *Political Theories of Modern Government: Its Role and Reform*. London: Allen and Unwin, 1985.

———. *Rolling Back the Market: Economic Dogma and Political Choice*. New York: St Martin's Press, 2000.

Stedman Jones, Gareth, and Gregory Claeys. *The Cambridge History of Nineteenth-Century Political Thought*. Cambridge: Cambridge University Press, 2011.

Steiner, Phillip. *Durkheim and the Birth of Economic Sociology*. Translated by Keith Tribe. Princeton, NJ: Princeton University Press, 2011.

Wu, Yiching. *The Cultural Revolutions at the Margins: Chinese Socialism in Crisis*. Cambridge, MA: Harvard University Press, 2014.

7 Fascism and National Socialism

Learning Objectives

- To acknowledge the totalitarian nature of Fascism and National Socialism.
- To understand the wide berth given to the use of violence in Fascism and National Socialism.
- To recognize the endorsement of justice as the interest of the stronger (a view held by Thrasymachus in Plato's *Republic*) in Fascism and National Socialism.
- To comprehend the rejection of reason and affirmation of emotion in Fascism and National Socialism.
- To heed the explicit racism, anti-Semitism, and intolerance of minorities in Fascism and National Socialism.

The ideological movements of Benito Mussolini (1883–1945) and Adolf Hitler (1889–1945) can be classified as paradigmatic instances of **Fascism** and National Socialism. There are enough similarities between these two schools of thought to justify calling it a single ideology, and one that contains a mélange of ideas that renders it unique in the history of thought. This ideology (hereafter simply referred to as Fascism) can be studied beneficially under a number of headings, including anti-liberalism and anti-Marxism, the veneration of the nation and state, the leadership principle, racism, the rejection of procedural and substantive justice, autarky (self-sufficiency), and corporativism. These will be examined in turn, and discussed largely through the positions adopted by their most influential and powerful exponents. Before discussing these topics, however, brief mention should be made of current manifestations of Fascism or quasi-Fascism to show that, at least among some, the ideology still has purchasing power.

The present-day National Democratic Party (NPD) of Germany, with some 7,000 members, comes close to being appropriately described as a Fascist party. It is alleged to be racist, anti-Semitic, revisionist, and anti-democratic, with designs on forming a Fourth Reich. And neo-Nazism in Germany is still "alive and kicking." Among other developments, neo-Nazis staged a silent march in the eastern part of the country on 14 February 2009 to protest the Allied bombing during the World War II.[1] These developments have prompted one prominent analyst of the far right at Berlin's Free University to remark that the neo-Nazi scene, both inside and outside of the NPD, is becoming stronger, especially in its influence on racist attitudes and the use of violence.[2]

A very different example, drawn from the Republic of India, also illustrates a drift towards the extreme or quasi-Fascist right. Such is the case of Narendra Modi, the Chief Minister of the state of Gujarat, who advocates a prosperity gospel and a virulent Hindu-based nationalism. In 2007, Congress Party president Sonia Gandhi described Modi as a *maut ka saudagar*, or merchant of death, and this statement was not made lightly. Five years earlier, a six-week riot in Gujarat (ironically, the birthplace of Mohandas Gandhi) resulted in the death of 1,800 people, most of whom were Muslims. The Indian Supreme Court has finally ordered an investigation into Modi's role in the riots, for which he remains unapologetic.[3] Modi appears to combine racism with his nationalism, and in so doing shows that he adopts a quasi-Fascist position.

A third example is drawn from Hungary, in which, on 23 February 2009, a deadly attack occurred on members of the country's Roma (gypsy) minority. The home of a Roma family, the Csorbas, was attacked by right-wing fanatics using a Molotov cocktail. The door of the home was blown open. In their attempt to escape, two members of the Csorba family, including a five-year-old child, were killed by gunfire. Although police reportedly dragged their feet in investigating these murders and other attacks on and killings of Roma, four men were later arrested and convicted, and three were sentenced to life in prison. Observers suggest that these racist manifestations fit in with a general move to the right advocated by a new party, Jobbik, headed by Krisztina Morvai, a party with which the perpetrators had become involved.[4] Under her leadership, this party launched an initiative that shows little tolerance for the Roma people. The party promotes a distinction between "our kind" and "their kind," the latter of which seems to include Jews, Roma, liberals, and socialists. And in the wings supporting Jobbik stands the Magyar Gárda, the Hungarian Guard, a uniformed paramilitary organization created by Jobbik.[5] The similarities between the ideology of Jobbik and Fascism are quite striking.

A fourth and more current example involves comparisons that some make between the politics of Donald Trump, a Republican hopeful for the presidential nomination, and Hitler. While claiming that comparing Trump to Hitler is inaccurate, Marsha Lederman has nonetheless recently written that "Mr. Trump has earned his comparisons to Hitler with his open racism and scapegoating, divisive lowest-denominator politics and unapologetic, even gleeful inflammation of anger and incitement to violence."[6] Lederman then goes on to add that Trump is a "xenophobic, sexist, boorish, unsophisticated bully . . . [who] has talked about his desire to punch a protester in the face . . . and warned there could be riots if he doesn't get the Republican nomination."[7] Whether the comparison between Trump and Hitler can be sustained is questionable, but what is not questionable is the traction that this comparison gained in the media. And what this shows is the purchasing power Fascism motifs have in North American media. Curiously, lost in this discussion by Lederman and others is the position not only of Trump but also of Democratic presidential hopeful Bernie Sanders, and increasingly of Hillary Clinton, that free trade agreements are not good. Or at least not nearly so good as libertarians and neo-liberals might think. Here the direction of Trump and possibly Sanders is towards more American self-sufficiency in the field of trade, thereby endorsing the old dream of Johann Gottlieb Fichte (1762–1814) of autarky, precisely the position advocated by National Socialists in Germany. So there are some comparisons

Central Beliefs of Fascism and National Socialism

- Human nature is emotional and irrational.
- The origin of the state is power, coercion, and social fitness.
- Equality as an ideal is a delusion.
- Justice is the interest of the strongest and fittest.
- The end of government is the advancement of the superior people (e.g., Aryan) or state (e.g., Italy) for the purpose of advancing imperialism.
- Dictatorship is the best form of government.
- Economic organization is at its best in corporativism.
- Rights are delusions and at best only manifestations of the interest of the stronger.

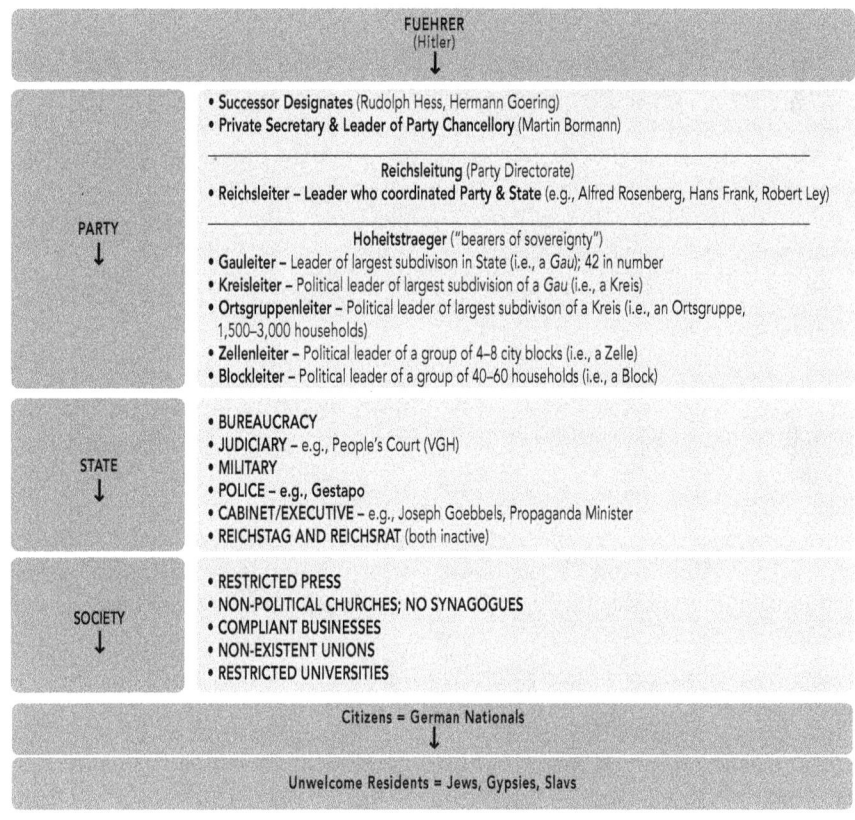

Legend: ↓ = arrow of subordination, indicating the leadership principle

Figure 7.1 National Socialism's Model of Society, State, and Party

The information on the party in this diagram comes from one source: *The Nizkor Project: Nazi Conspiracy & Aggression*, Vol. I, Chap. VI, "The Organization of the Nazi Party & State," http://www.nizkor.org/hweb/imt/nca/nca-01/nca-01-06-organization.html. The balance of the information comes from Alan Bullock, *Hitler: A Study in Tyranny* (Harmondsworth, England: Pelican Books, 1962).

between the politics of Fascism and current American politics that are deserving of further investigation.

The four foregoing examples illustrate the ongoing presence of Fascist ideas and their effect on people's lives. So, far from its being the case that Fascism is dead, this ideology remains a threat to civilized democracies everywhere. Perhaps no recent writing makes this point clearer than *Night Train to Lisbon*, the fictional work of Pascal Mercier that describes in dramatic way the effect of Antonio de Oliveira Salazar's Fascist regime in Portugal from 1932 to 1968.[8] This novel reveals the sadistic nature of the actions of the Salazar regime in repressing and torturing a people. Made clear by the novel are the tangled lives, broken dreams, and unfulfilled personalities brought about by the Fascist Salazar and his supporters. In brief, the story is a compelling example of how precarious life is when tyranny prevails, when authoritarian regimes get the upper hand, and when civilized practice is pushed to the margins.

With these examples in mind, it is time to turn the most influential articulations of Fascism as found in Italy and Germany in the years leading up to World War II.

Mussolini and Hitler

Two pivotal events set in motion the establishment of Fascism and National Socialism in Europe. The **March on Rome** (27–29 October 1922) led to Mussolini taking power in Italy with the help of the *squadristi*, or Blackshirts, while the **Enabling Act** of 1933, passed by the German Reichstag, allowed Hitler to assume full power in that country. Once entrenched, the implementation of Fascism could begin, putting into action the concepts and ideas now to be discussed in detail.

The Rejection of Liberalism

Fascism first has to be understood through and through as a reaction against two ideologies of the nineteenth and early twentieth centuries: liberalism and Marxism.

Conditions existed in Germany and Italy in the latter part of the nineteenth and early part of the twentieth centuries that made it possible for liberal ideas to be victimized. In the case of Germany it was the fact that, even by the 1890s, German liberalism, such as it existed, was "adulterated by extreme patriotism and elitism,"[9] and that by 1928, on the cusp of the Great Depression, "liberalism as a socio-cultural force had failed to put down healthy roots."[10] In the case of Italy, liberalism was tarred by the brush of neutrality in the Great War at a time when nationalists expected "substantial territorial gain from the eventual peace settlement,"[11] and liberalism in Italy proved to be out of touch with the social and economic crisis that came in on the heels of the army's demobilization.[12]

Evidence of Fascism's rejection of liberalism is found in remarks by Mussolini and Hitler. In an effort to lay out the political and social doctrine of Fascism in 1933, and in the only statement by Mussolini on the philosophical basis of Fascism, he clarifies the position of Fascism in relation to the era of liberalism, an ideology that, in Mussolini's opinion, "accumulated an infinity of Gordian knots."[13] Mussolini undertakes to disqualify liberalism as a living ideology.[14] And he aims to do this by attacking several of its component parts: the ideal of perpetual peace,[15] universalism, and democracy. In denouncing perpetual peace,[16] Mussolini affirms war as something that brings human energy to its highest tension. Here, by implication, he distances himself from the pacifism of Keynes and the non-violent radicalism of Dewey. As for universalism, Mussolini rejects it, presumably out of lack of trust—and one cannot help but think that he has in mind the League of Nations as one species of universalism. Finally, Mussolini rejects democracy on the grounds that the majority has no right to rule. In turning his back on perpetual peace, universalism, and democracy, he rejects those ideals and methods of governing that rationalist-oriented political philosophies embrace and that date back, in some respects, to the Enlightenment. It was the pre-eminent spokesperson of the Enlightenment, Immanuel Kant, who single-handedly introduced the very notion of perpetual peace, a notion that Mussolini happily discards.

It should come as no surprise that Hitler, who modelled himself on Mussolini, is equally contemptuous of liberalism. This is made evident by culling some of his remarks from speeches made during the 1920s. For example:

- 22 November 1926: "Unfortunately, the contemporary world stresses internationalism instead of the values of the race, democracy and the majority instead of the worth of the great leader. Instead of everlasting struggle the world preaches cowardly pacifism, and everlasting peace."[17]
- 2 April 1928: "The first fundamental of any rational **Weltanshauung** [world view] is the fact that on earth and in the universe force alone is decisive."[18]
- 22 September 1928: ". . . our people must be delivered from the hopeless confusion of international convictions . . . . we educate the people to fight against the delirium of democracy . . . to tear it away from the nonsense of parliamentarianism . . . to deliver the people from the atmosphere of pitiable belief . . . such as the belief in reconciliation, understanding, world peace, the League of Nations, and international solidarity. We destroy these ideas."[19]

While Hitler, in these speeches, did not mention the word "liberalism," he nonetheless attacks, in an unmistakable fashion, its values and ideals. From the days of Locke, democracy and representative government have been touchstones of liberalism, and at least since the days of Adam Smith, so has internationalism, at least in the form of free trade. And all liberals, from classical liberals like Kant to reform liberals like Dewey and Keynes, have placed a premium on peace and have shunned violence as a last resort. In attacking these ideals, Hitler repudiates liberalism and replaces the rule of law with the rule of force, going so far as to say, "Force is the first law."[20]

All of these remarks are from speeches Hitler delivered on his way to becoming Chancellor, but things did not change after he assumed this position, a point well made by Roger Griffin when he says, "Once Hitler had been appointed Chancellor on 30 January 1933 he immediately set about destroying liberalism and eroding pluralism through the same insidious blend of sham legality, pressure and violence that he had used so masterfully to turn Weimar's post-1930 constitutional crisis to his advantage."[21]

The Rejection of Marxism

In addition to Fascism's rejection of liberalism, there stands its rejection of Marxism. Mussolini thinks, correctly, of Marxism as comprising two pillars: first, that class war is the preponderant force in the transformation of history, and second, that changes in the means and instruments of production are sufficient to explain history. Fascists, according to Mussolini, deny both of these. The materialism of Marxism is false, he thinks, because the economic conception of history adhered to by Marxists is "not sufficient to explain the history of humanity."[22] And the inadequacy of this conception of history erodes the credibility of class war theory. Hence, Mussolini says, "And if the economic conception of history be denied . . . it follows that the existence of an unchangeable and unchanging class-war is also denied."[23]

As for Hitler and his opposition to Marxists, perhaps his actions speak louder than his words. Following the Reichstag fire of 27 February 1933, Hitler issued a decree described as "a defensive measure against Communist acts of violence."[24] Article 5 of the decree instituted the death penalty for crimes of high treason, poisoning, arson, and sabotage. This article had the effect of allowing Hitler and his second-in-command, Hermann Goering (1893–1946), to do pretty well whatever they wanted to their opponents—notably the Communists, whose 81 Reichstag deputies would be shortly arrested or at least prevented from attending the Reichstag on the day of the passage of the important and crucial Enabling Act of 23 March 1933.[25] Perhaps Hitler's opposition to Marxism is best captured by Alan Bullock when he says, "Hitler regarded the Marxist conception of class war and of class solidarity cutting across frontiers as a particular threat to his own exaltation of national unity founded on the community of *Volk*."[26] In both Mussolini and Hitler, then, there is to be found considerable antipathy to Marxism.

While it might be tempting to say, as others suggest,[27] that Mussolini and Hitler reject liberalism and Marxism on account of the reliance these ideologies have on reason and rationalism, the truth is more prosaic. Fascists cherry-pick: they use reason when it suits them and disregard it when it gets in their way. Science, in some bastardized form, is used by National Socialists to foster social Darwinism. It could hardly be said that National Socialists turn their backs on Darwin and biology, even if they misapply him and the principle of natural selection. Indeed, National Socialists openly practise eugenics in trying to preserve what is thought by them to be "the master race." And of course both Italian Fascism and German National Socialism are prepared to make use of new scientific discoveries and inventions to strengthen their military machine, as in the case of the successful development of the V2 rocket and the efforts to develop an atomic bomb. All of these scientific efforts have, as their desideratum, social change and the resolution of social problems.

The more probable explanation for the rejection by Fascism and National Socialism of liberalism and Marxism lies elsewhere. Liberalism holds doctrines, both economic and social, that Fascists think false or untenable. This would certainly be true in the case of Adam Smith's notion of free trade, or laissez-faire, and in the case of Dewey's notion of equality. Fascists reject both of these notions. And this would be true in the case of Marxist doctrines that allow no room for the hero in history, the charismatic leader or spiritual master, or, indeed, little or no room for the efficacy of any ideas. One might say correctly that Marxism is a denial of spiritualism, and hence a denial of that which is affirmed by Fascism, "holiness and heroism." And of course Marxism undercuts nationalism and the "volk" by limiting analysis to classes. Fascism and National Socialism have no patience with any of this because they think Marxism is incorrect in its analysis of history. What can be concluded from this brief foray into liberalism and Marxism is that Fascism's rejection of these ideologies has much less to do with the rejection of reason by Fascism and much more to do with other ideological differences.

Veneration of the Nation and State

Though Hitler and Mussolini, as will be seen, formally disagreed on which had priority, the state or the nation, in their actions they both treated the state as supreme. Moreover, they both subscribed unwittingly to a kind of spiritual monism: a belief that what shapes countries are spiritual and moral facts. This is a conclusion that needs to be teased out of what they say on other subjects.

Perhaps the best entry to the topic at hand is Mussolini's comment that "whoever says Liberalism implies individualism, and whoever says Fascism implies the State."[28] Setting aside his comment on liberalism, what is one to make of his remark as it bears on Fascism? Mussolini is unequivocal in saying that the foundation of Fascism is "the conception of the State, its character, its duty, and its aim."[29] In contrast to the liberal state, which Mussolini thinks of as a force limited to recording results, the Fascist state is conscious, with a will and personality that act as a guiding force for the play and development of the collective body in both material and spiritual ways.[30] For the Fascist, the state is not a guardian, an organization with material aims, or a political organization divorced from contact with the complex life of individuals and people as whole, but rather a spiritual and moral fact, "since its political, juridical, and economic organization of the nation is a concrete thing: and such an organization must be in its origins and development a manifestation of the spirit."[31]

Some equation seems to be drawn here between the state and spirit that gives rise to organization. It is up to the state, thinks Mussolini, to educate its citizens in civic virtue, to create their consciousness of their task, and, very importantly, to weld them into unity and organize them into a nation. Moreover, the state leads men from the primitive life to the highest expression of human power, namely Empire.[32] In addition, it is the job of the state to preserve the memory of those who have died for its existence and who have brought it glory. Finally, the Fascist state is nothing less than embodied will to power and government whose aspiration is that of having an Empire.[33] Evidently, for Mussolini, the equation between the state and the spirit implies a connection between the state and calculated and determined aspirations of the leaders of a nation, aspirations that include imperialism as a goal and aspirations that are defined by the heroic endeavours of those who have preceded the present people. This is Mussolini's spiritual explanatory monism.

The situation with Hitler and his veneration of the **nation** is a bit more complicated. First, one must distinguish between the rhetoric and the practice. Hitler's rhetoric certainly held the nation, but not the state, in the highest regard. Running through *Mein Kampf* (1925–6) is a long list of tributes to the nation. The roots of these tributes can be traced through the Weimar Republic all the way to a *volkisch* nationalism that appeared in Imperial Germany and aimed to maintain and strengthen the German way of life in Germany and in the diaspora.[34] But it was not until 1923 that the phrase "Third Reich" was coined by Arthur Moeller van den Bruck and applied to a wide array of ethnic German communities abroad, including those in Austria, Sudetenland, and other Eastern and Western European countries.[35] It was this idea that Hitler attempted to implement in 1938.

As for Hitler's nationalistic comments in *Mein Kampf*, the following are but a small sample:

- "For this reason my instinct of national self-preservation caused me even in those days to have little love for a representative body in which the Germans were always misrepresented rather than represented."[36]

- "If now, after so many years, I examine the results of this period, I regard two outstanding facts as particularly significant: First, I became a nationalist. . . . Second, I learned to understand and grasp the meaning of history. Old Austria was a state of nationalities."[37]
- "To win the masses for a national resurrection, no social sacrifice is too great."[38]
- "Without the clearest knowledge of the racial problem and hence of the Jewish problem, there will never be a resurrection of the German nation."[39]
- "The fact of the non-existence of a nationality of unified blood has brought us untold misery."[40]
- "Science, too, must be regarded by the folkish state as an instrument for the advancement of national pride."[41]

All of this culminated in a world view of fanatical nationalism, something Hitler championed.

For Hitler, the nation turns out to be a folkish entity, the bearer of cultural values as personified in the **Aryan** race. This definition, with all its vagaries, allows him a free hand to pretty well define the Germany of his choice and, when coupled with a doctrine of *lebensraum* ("living space"), was the perfect recipe for turmoil and death in Europe in the 1940s. But there is a bit more to be said on the subject, in particular how his talk on the nation and nationalism relates to his practice as the head of state. How are the state and nation conjoined for Hitler?

Clearly, in the rhetoric, the state was the nation's junior partner, but the political reality was a different story. Hitler, like Mussolini, was a master at using the instruments of the state, in the form of the military, police, judiciary, and bureaucracy, to further the ends of his folkish entity. Whereas Mussolini openly venerated the state, Hitler kept his audience focused on the myth of the nation, and exploited its emotional attachment to the nation by carefully and skilfully leading it in the direction he chose. Fanatical nationalism was definitely part of the National Socialist agenda, but it was furthered, as in the case of Mussolini, by the tools of the modern state. With these tools to guide the emotions associated with nationalism, Hitler was well on his way to establishing a **totalitarian** state. In doing so, he merely beat Mussolini at his own game.

The Leadership Principle

In a nutshell, the leadership principle—otherwise called the **Fuehrerprinzip**—makes the leader's authority absolute, and, at least in the case of Hitler, is inspired by his respect for the army.[42] The justification for this principle is the incorrigibility of the leader. Hence, Mussolini says, in both the first and second versions of "The Fascist Decalogue", "Mussolini is always right."[43] In this form, the principle is completely antithetical to the principle of liberals, who claim that the individual is the best judge of his or her interests. Under the *Fuehrerprinzip*, a "massive quantitative expansion of leadership roles in society" occurs.[44] This expansion is readily seen in Hitler's case, less so in Mussolini's. The leadership principle in Italy functioned as a cult of personality in that Mussolini "presented himself and the Fascist Party as the only forces able to unite all Italians and to make them great."[45] Of course, Mussolini's claim that he was always right, and the deference to the leadership principle, did not serve to dislodge completely the role played by either King Victor Emmanuel or the Constitution. Nonetheless, the claim of Mussolini seems to have been grounded in two needs: first, his personal need to establish his leadership as one of the dominant features of every Italian's life, and second, the need to focus attention on Il Duce's attributes rather than on those of the flawed regime.[46] In the event, the role of the leadership principle in Italy was much more muted, as will be seen, than in Germany. But one can say that there was an attempt to invoke this principle under Fascist Italy, especially in light of the successful Italo-Ethiopian War (1935–6), though it never resulted in the Olympian detachment found in the case of Hitler's Third Reich.[47]

In the case of National Socialism in Germany, the Nazi party used its own organization as a model for a huge pyramid of sub-leaders, stretching from the Reich level to the street block leader, all with the blessings of the leadership principle. Although the implementation ran into difficulty in the civil service, it did play a symbolic role in the adjudication of disputes internal to it. Other institutions, including big business and the churches, also resisted the full application of the principle.[48] And of course the army had a special kind of autonomy from it. Notwithstanding these exceptions to the principle, the overall effect of it was that "[m]illions of Germans now had the opportunity to experience the personal responsibility and absolutism of a Fuehrer."[49]

It is worth pausing to trace the historical roots of the *Fuehrerprinzip*. The fundamental law of Hitler's regime was the Enabling Act, otherwise referred to as the Law for Removing the Distress of People and Reich (*Gesetz zur Behebung der Not von Volk und Reich*).[50] And it is in this law that the roots of the leadership principle are to be found. This bill, which altered the German Constitution, required a majority of two-thirds of the Reichstag for passage. On 23 March 1933 the Reichstag assembled in the Kroll Opera House to consider the bill.[51] The debate over the passage of the bill was acrimonious, and as others have said, "It needed courage to stand before this packed assembly ... and tell Hitler and the Nazis to their faces that the Social Democrats would vote against the Bill."[52] Otto Wels and other Social Democrats opposed five clauses that comprised the bill. The first and fifth clauses granted the government the power to make laws for four years independent of the Reichstag. Effectively, these clauses legitimized the transfer of constitutional power from the legislative body to the executive body. The second and fourth clauses asserted that the power of government "should include the right to deviate from the Constitution and to conclude treaties with foreign States."[53] The effect of these clauses was to free the government of constitutional restraints. And finally, the third clause stated that the Chancellor, i.e., Hitler, should first draft the laws that would subsequently be enacted by the government. What occurred here was a transfer of power from the government to the Chancellor. When these clauses were combined, they yielded the total transfer of power from the Reichstag and Reichsrat (Imperial Council) to the Chancellor. Behold, the leadership principle!

The historical and ideological components of the *Fuehrerprinzip* are revealing of the way in which Hitler established himself. But it would be remiss to leave things here. Two other points should be made. First, it took Hitler some time after March 1933 to establish himself as a dictator, though by the summer of that year he was "complete master of a Government."[54] And it would not be until the summer of 1934 that he would finally get the *Sturmabteilung* (SA) under control, get rid of its leader, Ernst Roehm, and finally settle the question of the need to remodel the army by turning the SA into soldiers (the infamous "storm troopers").[55] All of these were necessary conditions of establishing a functioning leadership principle. Second, Hitler did not have to make use of the enormous powers he had, for often he could rely solely upon the masses' attraction to force and success.[56]

Hitler's confidence in his being able to win over the majority of Germans with this combination of success and power led him to pass the law of 14 July 1933 introducing the concept of plebiscites, as well as to publish the following announcement in the *Official Gazette*:

> The German Government has enacted the following law, which is herewith promulgated:
> Article 1: The National Socialist German Workers' Party constitutes the only political party in Germany.
> Article 2: Whoever undertakes to maintain the organizational structure of another political Party or to form a new political Party will be punished with penal servitude up to three years or with imprisonment up to three years, if the action is not subject to a greater penalty according to other regulations.[57]

Hitler's confidence in the *Volk*, as well as his removal of Ernst Roehm, consolidated leadership. When the leadership principle is so understood, one can better see how it served as a force quite opposed to both the anonymity and absence of personal responsibility that so characterized the Weimar Republic in its parliamentary and bureaucratic life.[58]

Racism

The notion of racism has to be understood, in part, against the background of **social Darwinism**. And while it is not the time to engage in a detailed analysis of this background, suffice it to say that Darwinism stood at its foundation. Charles Darwin had introduced, in his *On the Origin of Species* (1859), the principle of natural selection. According to this principle, plants and animals exhibit variations, some of which provide the organism with an advantage in the struggle for life. Furthermore, organisms with favourable characteristics, because they survive, pass them on to their offspring. In addition, Malthusian-like pressures ensure that populations produce more than their environments can sustain, and hence the proportion of favourable variants that survive will be larger than the proportion of unfavourable variants. In this way, a population undergoes evolutionary change.[59]

The application of the principle of natural selection as so understood outside the biological context, in such areas as culture, economics, and society in general, came to be known as social Darwinism. And indeed, it "became a means of explaining the difference between races and classes. It showed great flexibility in the attitudes it could express to these questions."[60] Intellectuals of considerable repute lent an air of respectability to this social stance. Such intellectuals included William Graham Sumner (1840–1910), a Yale economist; Houston Stewart Chamberlain (1855–1927), the Anglo-German writer and race theorist; and Karl Pearson (1857–1936), a statistician who became the first Galton Professor of Eugenics at University College, London. But the application of Darwin's ideas to society in general, especially in light of its flexibility, meant that sooner or later it would be applied not just to populations, but to so-called races. Purity of race became, for some, the touchstone of truth.

Houston Chamberlain celebrates explicitly the entrance of the Jews and Teutonic races in world history.[61] In fact, he goes further by challenging those who question the existence of distinguishable races:

What is the use of detailed investigations as to whether there are distinguishable races? Whether race has any worth? How is this possible? And so on. We turn the tables and say: it is evident that there are such races: it is a fact of direct experience that the quality of race is of vital importance.[62]

The biologist T.H. Huxley (1825–1895), in contrasting whites and blacks, says of the latter:

it is incredible . . . that [he] will be able to compete successfully with his bigger brained and smaller pawed rival in a contest which is to be carried on by thoughts and not by bites.[63]

The celebrated historian and philosopher Oswald Spengler (1880–1936) asserts:

It is high time that the "white" world, and Germany in the first place, should consider these facts. For behind the world wars and the still unfinished proletarian world-revolution there looms the greatest of all dangers, the coloured menace, and it will require every bit of "race" that is still available among white nations to deal with it.[64]

And the philosopher and economist Eugen Duehring (1833–1921) boasts:

Society is in many places so paralysed by the moral poison that it can no longer stir its limbs to reaction. . . . Where the Jews are to the fore, there is there most corruption.[65]

So the motif of race was well embedded in the intellectual and literary communities of the European world in the latter part of the nineteenth century and early part of the twentieth century, and this theme of race inevitably spilled over into the political world.

While Fascism in Italy did not emphasize race in the way that National Socialism did in Germany, nonetheless even Mussolini found occasion to make use of this category for political purposes. He maintains,

The principle that society exists solely through the well-being and the personal liberty of all the individuals of which it is composed does not appear to be conformable to the plans of nature, in whose workings *the race* alone seems to be taken into consideration, and the individual sacrificed to it.[66] (emphasis added)

But the role of race was more emphasized by National Socialists in Germany than by Fascists in Italy. Nowhere is this truer than in the case of Hitler's "**Twenty-Five Points**," which he delivered on 24 February 1920. Point No. 4 runs as follows,[67] when structured in a way compatible with Aristotelian logic:

i. All citizens are members of the nation.
ii. All members of the nation are Germans.
iii. No Jews are Germans. (missing premise)
iv. Therefore, no Jew may be a member of the nation, and so no Jew may be a citizen.

Nor is this racial argument of Hitler a one-off argument. Other statements of his continued along these lines in the late 1920s and early 1930s. Hence, in 1927, he said, "The value of man is determined in the first place by his inner racial virtues; second, by the ability of the race to bring forth men who in turn become the leaders in the struggle for advancement."[68] And one year later he added, "Whatever man possesses today in the field of culture is the culture of the Aryan race."[69] *Mein Kampf*, moreover, was riddled with racism. In his book one finds the following racial slurs directed against Jews: "[t]heir whole existence is based on one single great lie, to wit, that they are a religious community while they are actually a race."[70] Again, "Thus, the Jew lacks those qualities which distinguish the races that are creative and hence culturally blessed."[71] And again, "Thus the organizing principle of the Aryan humanity is replaced by the destructive principle of the Jew."[72] Hitler's racism attributed German national decadence to the Jews. It advocated racial regeneration in Germany to overcome the strictures of the Treaty of Versailles. And it argued in favour of uniting all ethnic Germans into a German state.[73] The effect of racism in Hitler's Germany was to establish the **Third Reich**, a constitutional regime, based not only on the leadership principle but also on the primacy of the ***Volk***, or *Volksgemeinschaft* ("people's community").[74] It was the principle of the *Volk*, as a racial concept, that stood as a spiritual principle opposed to "the rootless, egotistical individualism and the materialist class struggle of the Weimar society."[75]

The culmination of Hitler's racial views was, as is well known, the "**final solution**": the physical extermination of more than six million Jews. The events leading up to this liquidation—the **Holocaust**—are all well known, but bear repetition. According to the transcripts of the trial of Adolf Eichmann, on 31 July 1941 Reinhard Heydrich, SS understudy of Heinrich Himmler, received a letter from Reichsmarschall Hermann Goering, Commander-in-Chief of the Air Force and Hitler's Deputy of State, to the effect that Heydrich was to prepare a general solution to the Jewish question and to submit a general proposal for the final solution of the Jewish question.[76] A few weeks after receipt of this letter in Berlin, Heydrich summoned Eichmann to his office and said, "The Fuehrer has ordered the physical extermination of the Jews."[77] Though oaths of secrecy were sworn, the truth in the matter of the killing of millions of Jews began to emerge long before the war reached its conclusion. Some of its perpetrators were dealt with at the **Nuremberg tribunals**, charged with committing crimes against humanity, and finally sentenced to death for these crimes.

Though the role of race was more emphasized by National Socialists in Germany than by Fascists in Italy, race became a more important factor in Mussolini's Fascism after 1936. The closer relationship between Germany and Italy in this year brought "ominous developments within Italy over racial policy."[78] At this time the "shifting diplomatic balance allowed a new climate of European race-thinking to work on Italian fascism."[79] Faced with ideological competition from Germany, it was thought desirable to broaden key elements in Fascist ideology to include not only extreme nationalism and the belief in a subordinate role for women,[80] as well as the need for a higher birth rate, but also "measures that served to protect a supposedly pure Italian race from various forms of 'contagion' from other races."[81]

By 1937 Mussolini was moonstruck by National Socialism's mechanized barbarism and racial intolerance, and as a result he "abandoned Italy's traditionally tolerant attitude towards the Jews in favour of a vicious and discreditable persecution campaign."[82] The campaign against the Jews began in earnest in July 1938 with publication of *The Manifesto of Fascist Racism.* This publication, coupled with a government decree, restricted the rights of foreign Jews to live in Italy and revoked the citizenship granted to foreign-born Jews after January 1919.[83] In September 1938, government decrees banned Jewish students and teachers from schools, banned their participation in the National Fascist Party (PNF), forbade mixed marriages, and purged Jews from cultural, professional, and academic associations.[84] And as the final salvo of racism, the Fascist government enacted the Law for the Defence of the Race, which prohibited mixed marriages between Jews and non-Jews. The racial laws and decrees in Italy under Fascism, enacted in emulation of Hitler's anti-Semitic **Nuremberg Laws** of 1935, included Jews who had become Catholic converts. This inclusion of Catholics exceeded the discrimination of the Church against Jews, and was correspondingly viewed by the Church with suspicion.[85]

The Rejection of Procedural and Substantive Justice

The story of the rejection of procedural and substantive justice is best told in connection with National Socialism, for in this form of the ideology the most egregious violations of justice occurred.

That clouds would soon gather over the judicial world in Germany following the passage of the Enabling Act in 1933 should come as no surprise, and in fact these clouds would result in the thorough Nazification of the law courts.[86] One of the first signs of trouble occurred in connection with Carl Schmitt (1888–1985), professor of law at the University of Cologne in 1933 and one who owed his appointment in part to the efforts of Hans Kelsen, a brilliant Jewish jurisprudence authority of the first half of the twentieth century. Goering was responsible for having Schmitt appointed to a chair at the University of Berlin, and Schmitt became the mentor of the leading National Socialist professors of constitutional law. In 1934 Schmitt wrote a legal and moral defence of the murders committed by the Nazis in purging the party of Roehm and his supporters, and two years later Schmitt, who was called the constitutional theorist of the new Reich, remarked, forgetting conveniently the efforts of the Jewish Kelsen on his behalf, that Jews were parasitical, tactical, commercial, and different from his [German] kind.[87] As an enemy of the liberal principles found in the Weimar Constitution, Schmitt aimed to restructure the whole legal profession: judges were not to be independent, but rather extensions of the executive, while prosecutors were to be politically subordinate and defence counsel silent. As a critic of the liberal principles of war, Schmitt embraced the demonization of political adversaries, ridiculed the laws of armed conflict, and advanced the idea of "law-free" zones as a counterweight to the senseless and counterproductive idea of guaranteeing legal rights to an enemy.[88]

But once we move beyond Carl Schmitt and other individuals in the German legal circles, such as Ernst Forsthoff, Ernst Rudolf Huber, and Theodor Maunz, one can best see the depth of corruption in German justice by examining what happened to and in the courts. Of primary importance in understanding justice under the Third Reich is the People's Court, or *Volksgerichtshof* (VGH), founded on 24 April 1934, which had exclusive jurisdiction over treason, high treason, attacks on the President of the Reich, major cases of destruction of military property, and assassination or attempted assassination of members of the national or state government.[89] This date, falling as it does after the ascendancy of Hitler to the Chancellorship, suggests that the People's Court was his invention. The evidence indicates otherwise, however. The Court was the idea of Kurt Eisner, the first

Prime Minister of the Free State of Bavaria. His purpose in introducing the Court on 16 November 1918 was the trying of cases that arose in the aftermath of the revolution of that same period.[90]

Before proceeding further in an examination of the actions of the People's Court, we need to understand in a more sensitive fashion the preoccupation of many Germans with attacks upon the state, especially those that could be called treasonable attacks, as well as the preoccupation of at least some Germans with assassinations or attempted assassinations. To begin with treasonable acts, one is reminded that many Germans, not only Nazis such as Hitler, believed that Germany had lost the Great War owing to treason—a position first articulated, it seems, by the British general Sir Neill Malcolm. He not only coined the phrase "stab in the back," but attributed the German army's failure to the "treason of the German revolutionaries" and the apathy of German civilians.[91] When knowledge of this "treasonable" act was coupled with Hitler's own knowledge of the Kapp Putsch of 1920, and his own failed Beer Hall Putsch of 1923, the stage was set for a concerted effort by the state, in this case the Third Reich, to minimize the chances of treason and assassinations. All of these factors conspired to give rise to a chain of command that naturally encouraged loyalty to Hitler and the state as a supervening duty.[92] The People's Court was simply one of the state structures that helped ensure compliance with this duty.

The two names most commonly associated with the People's Court are those of Otto Thierack (1889–1946), in charge of the Court during its "constitutional period" from 1936 to mid-1942, and the notorious Roland Freisler (1893–1945), who headed the Court during its bloodthirsty period (August 1942–February 1945).[93] Some examples of their jurisprudence are in order. One case involved Ernst Niekisch, a member of the German resistance. Charged in 1937 with making preparations for high treason, Niekisch had written an essay critical of Hitler prior to 1933 and had in the ensuing years collected evidence that the SA had broken the law and used force in terrorizing Jews and non-Jews. He received a life sentence from Thierack's court, to be served in the Brandenburg prison. Though he was liberated in 1945, he had suffered the loss of his eyesight and the use of his legs owing to experiments performed on him while imprisoned.[94] In another case, Thierack conspired with Heydrich to get a quick sentence, punishable by death, for Alois Elias, head of the protectorate of Bohemia and Moravia, for his having had contact with Czechs living in exile in France. To facilitate a speedy conviction, Heydrich had Elias face charges raised by the SS rather than the public prosecutors attached to the People's Court as provided under the Constitution. Lacking proof for the major charges against Elias, the Court nonetheless sentenced him to death after but a four-hour trial.

The statistics demonstrate that things became worse under Freisler, with more people being executed than in the period prior to 1942. In 1940 and 1941, under Thierack, there were 52 and 102 death sentences, respectively, issued by the People's Court. This stood in sharp contrast to the figures of 1942 (1,192 executions), 1943 (1,662 executions), and finally 1944 (2,709 executions).[95] Freisler is perhaps most famous for sentencing the young members of the non-violent resistance group the "White Rose" (including siblings Hans and Sophie Scholl) to death by beheading. Another of Freisler's infamous cases involved the sentencing to death of the pianist Karlrobert Kreiten for comments made to a long-time friend of his mother while they had a meal. At that time, Kreiten is reputed to have said of Hitler that he was "brutal, sick, and insane," and that the Nazis would soon lose the war.[96] In still another case, as the presiding judge in the trial of one of those responsible for the unsuccessful coup and attempt on Hitler's life, Freisler berated, mocked, and vilified the accused so much that even the minister of justice, in a report of the trials to Martin Bormann, admitted that the gravity and dignity of the People's Court had suffered as a result of the way Freisler conducted himself.[97]

As these examples illustrate clearly, the moral decay found in Hitler's *Mein Kampf* began to work its way gradually but perceptively into the judicial system, particularly the VGH. This development was paralleled by the death of the spirit of the Enlightenment that had fought so hard to establish itself on German soil. A beachhead for the Enlightenment was established pre-eminently by Immanuel Kant, but preparations for this landing had been provided earlier by Gottfried Leibniz (1646–1716), Christian Wolff (1679–1754), and both Johann Jakob Moser (1701–1785) and his son Friedrich Karl von Moser (1723–1798).[98] However, the development of the VGH by the Third Reich saw the disintegration of these intellectual and cultural achievements. Gone was the rallying cry of the French Revolution, "Liberty, equality, and fraternity," a cry that would inspire succeeding generations in Europe. In its place was subordination to the *Volksgemeinschaft*, as articulated by Ernst Rudolf Huber (1903–1990), professor of jurisprudence at Kiel, the most authoritative of academic lawyers in Nazi Germany. In his words, "The civil rights of the individual vis-à-vis the state are incompatible with *volkisch* law. There is no personal freedom of the individual prior to the state and outside the state which the state is obliged to respect."[99]

Reproached were those who advocated "bourgeois constitutionalism," with its accompanying ideals of democracy, liberalism, equality before the law, and tolerance of differing political opinions. At the heart of this so-called bourgeois constitutionalism stood the principle **nulla poena sine lege**, no penalty without a law, which when expanded stood for the following: nothing could be prohibited retroactively, nothing could be prohibited by analogy, nothing could be left unclear, and the rights to impose punishments were to be left exclusively to the judiciary.[100] The independence of the courts, including the VGH, was further eroded by Clause 7 of a Prussian statute, which made it quite clear that Gestapo[101] decisions were not appealable, and that persons acquitted by the courts could be rearrested by the Gestapo.[102] With the erosion of these procedural safeguards, it was inevitable that substantive justice—the allocation of rewards or punishment in an equitable way—would be depleted if not completely lost. This erosion of procedural and substantive justice was recognized by General Ludwig Beck, the Chief of Staff, in 1938 when he tried unsuccessfully to persuade Hitler to end the brutal Gestapo methods and restore law and justice in the country.[103]

The evidence suggests quite strongly that by the end of the 1930s the principle of justice, both procedurally and substantively, had become depleted in the Third Reich. What remained was a legal regime lacking in principles of fairness, respect for rights, proscriptions on double jeopardy, due consideration of evidence, and clarity of law. Already by 3 March 1933, in the aftermath of the Reichstag fire, there was a hint of what was to come. Goering, speaking in Frankfurt, said, "Here I don't have to worry about Justice: my mission is only to destroy and to exterminate; nothing more."[104] In another telling remark, Goering said, "I am proud of not knowing what justice is."[105] Finally, the comment of Hitler in the summer of 1934, after his elimination of Ernst Roehm, is instructive: "If anyone reproaches me and asks why I did not resort to the regular courts of justice, then all I can say to him is this: in this hour I was responsible for the fate of the German people, and thereby I became the supreme Justiciar (*oberster Gerichtsherr*) of the German people."[106] Hitler had obviously moved beyond the principles of justice and beyond the rule of law.

What was left of justice in the Third Reich after 1933? Precious little, as is aptly captured by Goering himself when on 3 March 1933, in the address in Frankfurt quoted above, he said, "My measures will not be crippled by any judicial thinking."[107] Impartiality gave way to subjectivity and deference to the **Fuehrer**. Fairness was abandoned in the rejection of principles of equality. The Reich Ministry of the Interior, through Wilhelm Stuckart and Hans Globke, asserted, "National socialism stands opposed to the theories of equality of all men . . . [but adheres to] the harsh but necessary recognition of the inequality of men and the differences between them based on the laws of nature."[108] And Huber, professor of jurisprudence, maintained, "Formal equality before the law cannot be the deciding factor for the law-giver."[109] Respect for the rights of persons, moreover, was narrowed to the right of men, thereby excluding women as well as non-Aryans. Perhaps the Fascist attitude towards justice is best expressed by those who helped form the resistance to Hitler in Germany, when they said, "Badly outnumbered, we were faced with an unscrupulous, unprincipled, amoral enemy who respected no law and no rules except force."[110]

In summary, one can say that Fascists adhered to a conception of justice that lacked impartiality, that constrained fairness to the selected few, and that rejected respect for rights of all but the elite. And even in the case of the elect and the elite, as famed Field Marshal Erwin Rommel was to discover, there was very little room for error, while respect for their rights proved a very ephemeral thing. After the attempted assassination of Hitler in July of 1944, the Fuehrer was informed that enough evidence had been gathered to implicate Rommel in the plot. In October of that year, Hitler presented Rommel with two options: suicide or trial by Freisler's VGH.[111] Rommel chose suicide

In the result, for Nazis, the principle of justice is depleted to the point where it retains practically nothing of its original meaning. Justice continues to carry with it the idea of obligations, but obligations that realize themselves in loyalty to the Fuehrer, with all the partiality and subjectivity that this entails. In the spirit of Thrasymachus, the strident figure in the early pages of Plato's *Republic*, Fascists reduce justice to the interest of the stronger. In rejecting justice, Fascists embrace nihilism.

Autarky and Corporativism

The last topics that should be covered in any analysis of Fascism and National Socialism are those of autarky and corporativism.

Autarky is the economic theory advocating self-sufficiency for a country and, by implication, the reduction of imported goods. Another way of teasing out the main ingredients of the theory is to say that it is against free trade, for free trade makes a nation reliant on another and therefore makes it vulnerable to coercion. Self-sufficiency, on the other hand, makes the nation-state impervious to outside influence. Understanding autarky is important for present purposes for the reason that "[i]nsofar as fascist economic theory was coherent it revolved around the central principle of economic autarky."[112]

While the principle of autarky has classical roots, dating back as far as Aristotle and his polis,[113] we need to be concerned with the economic ideas prevalent in Germany in the nineteenth century. Several German thinkers stand out as contributing to the development of the principle of autarky: Johann Gottlieb Fichte, Adam Müller, Johann Gottfried Herder, Friedrich List, and Friedrich Naumann. Some of these will now be discussed.

Johann Gottlieb Fichte, a leading German intellectual in the nineteenth century, "was totally hostile to the Adam Smith theory of economics,"[114] and accordingly sought to eliminate commercial anarchy and the importation of essential goods. These opinions were shared by other German intellectuals, such as List, in the nineteenth century, and then Naumann, in the early twentieth century. Friedrich List (1789–1846) denounced Adam Smith and free trade as undermining Germany's ability to protect itself through its military.[115] And Friedrich Naumann (1860–1919) advocated a mélange of "nationalism, economic autarky, and imperialism in a geopolitical framework [that] proved irresistibly attractive to his contemporaries and to Germans in the inter-war years."[116]

Opposition to free trade and the laissez-faire spirit of Adam Smith, while being weak in England, was strong in Germany, notwithstanding the battery of English thinkers who weighed in on the other side. These included the likes of Richard Cobden, John Bright, David Ricardo, James Mill, and Thomas Malthus.[117] The German Eugen Duehring, for his part, saw things quite differently from these individuals. He claimed that the doctrines of egalitarian free economics (including free trade), as developed by David Hume and Adam Smith, were used by Jews to achieve a monopoly in the economic sphere.[118] In developing a strong anti-free trade stance, coupled with anti-Semitism and a doctrine of *lebensraum* whereby neighbouring states were turned into colonies, Nazis in Germany placed themselves squarely in opposition to the ideological stance of classical and reform liberals. Fascists in Italy, while standing passionately opposed to liberalism, never emphasized in the same way the principle of autarky, or, as already indicated, the principle of racism. Rather, Mussolini's antagonism to liberalism was based more on disagreements pertaining to pacifism, democracy, and universalism rather than autarky, racism, and *lebensraum*. Undoubtedly there are endorsements of each of these last three by Mussolini, but they are often cosmetic in nature and therefore distinctively different from remarks by Hitler. It is plausible to account for this difference in tone between Hitler and Mussolini on the grounds that autarky was a clear-cut economic policy believed to be immediately implementable, and that Hitler, unlike Mussolini, was "[a]rmed with a radical **palingenetic** myth which could be translated much more readily into immediate decisions and medium-term strategies than Mussolini's."[119] And though autarky helped form a major plank of National Socialist economic planning, its results were "dismal travesties of the claims made for them in propaganda."[120]

Fascist Italy stood well behind Germany and France in its advocacy of autarky. Inasmuch as the principle of autarky was implemented in Italy, however, it had the effect of holding back Italy's technological revolution.[121] And Italy, unlike Germany, proved ill-equipped to extend the doctrine of autarky in the most logical way—namely, by implementing a doctrine of *lebensraum*. Try though it did, Italy never succeeded in its project of colonization in East Africa the way Germany did in Central and Eastern Europe.

Corporativism is the economic component of Italian Fascism. Fascists believed that the corporate state stood as a third way, between capitalism and communism.[122] As early as 1929 the Grand Council in Italy was urged to establish a National Council of Corporations. By 1930 this National Council comprised seven large sections bringing together both employer and worker organizations.[123] These large sections—embryonic corporations—covered the main branches of the economy. By 1934 the National Council was empowered by law to create 22 corporations "for the productive cycles of the major sectors of industry, agriculture, and services," and these corporations could "fix prices of goods or rates for services in their own areas and issue norms to regulate economic relations."[124]

It became clear in the development of Italian Fascism that corporativism was intended to be a new political and social order, an alternative to the dysfunctional and socially unjust liberal capitalism as well as the state collectivism found in the Soviet Union.[125] During the years of the Depression, an economic collapse that put corporativism under renewed examination as the instrument to deal with this collapse,[126] most of the government's economic measures were "proclaimed as advances of the corporative economy."[127] The truth was more prosaic inasmuch as most of these economic measures were emergency and non-corporative measures.[128] One of the by-products of corporativism was the imposition of wage cuts between 1933 and 1934, and the introduction of the 40-hour work week. What finally undid the corporative system was the Fascist government's military and imperialistic foreign policy, coupled with its autarkic economic policy.[129]

Conclusion

Fascism and National Socialism represent the ideology of men with a strong desire for a new order, domestically and internationally. In their eagerness to destroy the old, supporters of this ideology rejected not only liberalism, as seen above, but also, importantly, conservatism. This they did at least in theory, if not in practice. They stood as ideological critics of the conservatism of Hume and Burke in their eagerness to introduce the new man and a new civilization. Institutions did not represent for them, as they did for Burke, the wisdom of the species. Like Marxists, Fascists saw institutions as the fabrications of the liberal order, with all its Gordian knots representing bourgeois interests. These needed to be cut in the spirit of Alexander the Great who, with one mighty stroke of his sword, sliced through the knot. But, of course, Fascists distanced themselves from Marxism owing to its materialism. Spiritualism, emotion, and myth were the touchstones of truth for Mussolini, Hitler, and their supporters. And cast in the waste bin of history were the icons of Karl Marx and Friedrich Engels, and with them went such ideas as material goods equitably distributed and reason applied in a dialectical and scientific way. Fascism represents a new ideology, rooted in its palingenetic (new creation) myth, that stands against and in contrast to classical liberalism, conservatism, reform liberalism, and Marxism.

The line of argument adopted by National Socialism and Fascism is steeped in emotion and rhetoric. It plays upon the xenophobia and ethnocentrism of Germans and Italians, and encourages a marked emotional and superficial interpretation of history and ideas. As an ideology it takes as self-evident the inerrancy of its leader and the supremacy of its culture and race; these beliefs are not so much argued for as simply asserted and then used as axioms from which to derive other beliefs or policies of the central authorities of the state. There is, then, a kind of internal logic to National Socialism and Fascism, but the logic's fundamental premises are sweeping (e.g., Il Duce is always right) and largely unsupported. Advocates of this ideology are prepared to make use of science when it suits them and just as prepared to reject and corrupt science, as in the case of social Darwinism, when it does not. In many ways the line of argument of this ideology makes extensive use of the strategy of telling people things they wish to be told about themselves. In this way, National Socialism and Fascism prove to be rhetorically successful, especially when things unfold in a way that confirms the views on destiny that their respective leaders hold.

Evaluation: The Strengths of Fascism and National Socialism

1. Alan Bullock offers one strength of National Socialism. Under Hitler, this ideology, with its breakdown of law and order, was a profound shock to a German society already suffering from depression and unemployment, but the violence it introduced captured the spirit of a revolutionary idealism that attracted many young people.[130] For the youth of Germany, the National Socialists represented hopes, new possibilities, overcoming frustration, new initiatives and action, pride, self-confidence, and a place in the world.[131] What Fascism and National Socialism offered in both Italy and Germany was a reason for optimism about the future. While the regimes of the past represented progressive decadence, decline, and decomposition as a result of the anarchic tendencies of liberalism,[132] the new ideologies of Fascism and National Socialism represented a new beginning or new birth.

    Roger Griffin quite ably points out the foregoing by claiming that, notwithstanding the untold millions of victims of Nazi violence, the mythic power of Nazism was such that it acted as a symbol of rebirth and national awakening and the end of the Weimar liberalism. Evidence of this is found in the writings of the jurist Carl Schmitt, as well as in the writings of men such as Gottfried Benn (1886–1956), the German expressionist who was penalized by the Nazis despite his holding of right-wing views; Martin Heidegger (1889–1976), the German existentialist who, while the rector of Freiburg University in the 1930s, was instrumental in furthering Nazi policies; Richard Walther Darré (1895–1953), the Nazi Reich Minister of Food and Agriculture who called for the creation of a German aristocracy of soil as a new ruling class; and Alfred Rosenberg (1893–1946), the German Nazi ideologue of cultural racial history and cultural anti-Semitism.

    It is important to note here, however, that the mythic power of Nazism did not operate only at the intellectual level but, very importantly, at the emotional level. And for this reason it could be identified with by millions of citizens in helping to establish a national community.[133] A similar story could be told in connection with Italy. There, the squadrista myth led an affirmation of the new ideology by articulate hierarchs and ideologues such as Giovanni Gentile (1875–1944), who encouraged the idea that they were the facilitators of a new Italy born in a new image.[134]

2. Fascism openly rejects the simplicity of the materialistic conception of history. This entails a rejection of two theses of Marxism: (i) the economic conception of history, and (ii) the class-struggle conception of history. Fascists are correct that the first of these theses is false on the grounds that political, legal, moral, and scientific concerns, and history itself, to name a few, function as independent variables and as causally efficacious factors in influencing the direction of history. The monistic explanation cannot stand up to a pluralistic criticism. As for the second thesis regarding history and class conflict, it is simply unsustainable and unhelpful. It is unsustainable owing to the fact that classes do not exist in such a clearly defined way and, even if defined, do not operate to influence political decisions in this straightforward fashion. So Fascists seem correct so far as they go in their criticism of Marxism.

3. There may be a sliver of truth to the claim of Fascists like Mussolini that war alone brings human energy to its highest tension. An idea sympathetic to Mussolini's is

reflected in Machiavelli when he says, speaking of ancient Rome, that it became a great city by creating an empire and destroying the surrounding cities.[135] The Roman Empire evidently did quite well for itself by keeping people on their toes owing to the use of violence through war. One can only assume that Germans and Italians, and for that matter the Romans, would have found this claim of Mussolini to be more persuasive when the war was being waged successfully, and far from home (e.g., in Ethiopia) than when it was going badly and being waged inside Italy (or Germany), with their adversaries knocking on the door.

It may also be said in support of Fascism that war, by bringing human energy to its highest tension, ratcheted up the use of science and technology—and, in one case, with positive results. As has been pointed out, the Fascists and Nazis used science to further the cause of empire, strengthening their "military machine" with the development of weapons such as the V2 rocket. If not for the V2 program, however, man might not have walked on the moon. The brilliant physicist and engineer Wernher von Braun (1912–1977), who was central to the development of the V2, became the architect of the US space program, where his Saturn V rocket sent Apollo missions on their way.

Evaluation: The Weaknesses of Fascism and National Socialism

1. National Socialism and Fascism were unspeakably cruel. The millions of people who were victimized by it—Jews, Slavs, Russians, Roma, the infirm and the "different," and many, many others—are testimony to this. Whether one is speaking of the six million Jews who were systematically exterminated, or of the 20 million Russians who lost their lives as a result of Hitler's *lebensraum* and imperialistic policies, or of the Yugoslavs who lost their lives, or of the atrocities committed in Greece when the Germans came to that country to salvage a botched operation initiated by the Italians, the story remains one of unimaginable evil. Similar though not identical charges can be laid at the doorstep of Fascism in Italy. Here one only needs to think of Italy's unprovoked attack on Ethiopia and its ridiculing of Haile Selassie before the League of Nations, or of the unprovoked and fiendishly cruel bombing raid that the German Condor Legion, together with a handful of Italian planes, undertook in 1937 on the defenceless Basque village of Guernica (immortalized by Pablo Picasso in a painting of the same name), for this point to be made with force.

2. Mussolini's criticism of pacifism seems crude and completely insensitive to the natural urge most people have for a pacific state of affairs. In attacking pacifism, he attacks people's natural inclination towards the Kantian ideal of perpetual peace. This repudiation seems based on the unsupported claim that "war alone brings up to highest tension all human energy and puts the stamp of nobility upon the peoples who have the courage to meet it."[136] It seems plausible to say that a crisis such as a war has a remarkable capacity for concentrating one's attention, but from this it does not follow that war alone puts the stamp of nobility upon people with courage. There are noble people and there are courageous people. Neither attribute seems logically or psychologically to entail participation in war. To be noble is to show greatness of

character, and such a trait can be found even in those who are defeated or exploited. To be courageous is to be willing to face danger without being foolish. War is not a prerequisite of this virtue.

3. National Socialism and Fascism also launch a rather vapid attack on democracy. Fascism attacks the idea that the majority is entitled to govern by virtue of being the majority, and both National Socialism and Fascism affirm the inequality of mankind. On these two grounds they distance themselves from democracy. In response, the liberal can persuasively argue that the ordinary person is, in most cases, the best judge of his or her own interests, and, since these interests prevail only under a government run on majoritarian principles (what other possible principle is there?), democracy is justified. As for the principle of equality, the right response is to say that the principle applies to political and civil equality, and possibly to economic and social equality, but that it does not apply to physical or mental equalities. In addition, the counter to Fascism on this point of equality is simply that made by Hobbes in *Leviathan*: "If nature therefore have made men equal, that equality is to be acknowledged: or if nature have made men unequal; yet because men that think themselves equal, will not enter into conditions of peace, but upon equal terms, such equality must be admitted."[137] Another way of making Hobbes's point here is to say that democracy is the only working possibility, since no person in an emancipated industrial society, barring false consciousness, will put up with political tutelage.

4. As a final point in favour of democracy and against Fascism, one can echo Griffin's comment to the effect that a strength of liberal democracy, but not of Fascism and National Socialism, is that the former allows for constitutional mechanisms that facilitate the change of the head of state and cabinet without recourse to violence.[138] The case with Fascism and National Socialism is quite different. As Griffin says, "With a major programme of social engineering the charisma of a fascist movement can, in Max Weber's phrase, be 'routinized' to some extent after it seizes power. But the growing senility and eventual death of a fascist leader could only mean the dissolution of the regime which he incarnated: the 'movement' would grind to a halt."[139] For anyone well versed in the political philosophy of Hobbes, Locke, or even Robert Nozick, this has to be seen as a huge advantage of democracy over National Socialism and Fascism.

5. National Socialism and Fascism suffer from an inability to see all the political options. They reject Marxism and liberalism and affirm totalitarian principles on the basis of its rejection of the other two. But in his argument, Mussolini (and the same could be said of Hitler) never seriously examines democratic socialism as another option. So his argument is faulty from the outset, because the denial of liberalism and Marxism does not imply the truth of either National Socialism or Fascism. But even were one to restrict the options in this way, Mussolini's attack on liberalism has to be placed in a more robust context. It is simply not true, even if Marxism is rejected, that liberalism (of either variety) has "accumulated an infinity of Gordian knots."[140] What it has accumulated around it are the following problems: the problem of alienation, the problem of exploitation, and the problem of monopolies. Other problems that might be added to the list are those of environmental decay and imperialism.

But this list is hardly infinite, and Fascism offers no compelling reason for saying that liberalism cannot find solutions to these problems. So Mussolini and Fascism are precipitous in saying that "the Liberal faith must shut the doors on its deserted temples."[141] Though this has a Nietzsche-like ring to it, it is still unsupported on the balance of the evidence.

6. Fascism concedes too much in its conception of the state as absolute. For Mussolini this means control over juridical, political, and economic organization of the nation. More accurately, it means control by Mussolini in Italy, or Hitler in Germany, over these three kinds of organizations, and, effectively, over the lives of individuals in regard to "useless or possibly harmful freedom."[142] But in the absence of the rule of law, why should a rational individual trust anyone to decide which freedoms are useless or possibly harmful? Rhetorically, one might well ask, if individuals are not good judges of their own interests, what reason is there to believe that a Mussolini or a Hitler would be a good judge of everyone's interest? The skepticism in the one case would inevitably spill over to skepticism in the second case. The dangers inherent in totalitarian rule seem so great that the inconveniences of democratic rule seem a small price to pay by way of comparison.

7. National Socialism and Fascism fail to present a credible defence of their views on racism. By way of a metaphor, one might say that this card has been used by many in playing the political and social game. Alas, there is no reason to believe it has any credibility. The comments of Duehring, Huxley, Spengler, and others cited above now look quite absurd from our perspective of the twenty-first century. One can attribute racist beliefs to xenophobia and to ethnocentrism in particular societies. That these two psychological attitudes can exist among educated and privileged people should come as no surprise. As for viewpoints that lean on the arguments of Herbert Spencer in developing social Darwinism, one can only say that there is nothing in biology and its principles to justify taking the biological notion of natural selection and applying it outside its biological context to a political or economic one. Nothing in Darwin's principle of natural selection justifies one in saying that an Andrew Carnegie, Paul Mellon, or Bill Gates is socially selected to rule. Faced with these criticisms, racists would do better to seek out the explanations for their own beliefs now that *justifications* are wanting.

One remaining matter with respect to race concerns the argument Hitler makes use of in his "Twenty-Five Points" speech. As we recall, Hitler claims that being a citizen in Germany entails being a national, that being a national entails being German, and that being Jewish entails being non-German. From this he concludes, validly, that being Jewish means being a non-citizen. Whether this argument is sound, as well as valid, depends on whether its premises are true. And whether the premises are true depends on the definition one assigns to the word "nation." Since a scientific definition of "nation" is impossible,[143] and can take at least two non-scientific forms (first, the form of *political* nation that centres on the idea of individual and collective subjective commitment to the state, and second, the form of *cultural* nation that centres on a common cultural, historical, and linguistic heritage and more or less objective criteria),[144] the truth of Hitler's claims depends on which of these one accepts. There are precedents in international law for each of these, respectively distinguished as *jus soli* (law of the soil) and *jus sanguinis* (law of blood).[145] For the premises to be true, one must accept the second notion of the nation, to wit, the cultural view of the nation (the law of blood). Presumably, tucked slightly below the surface of this view is that the people making up the nation share the same blood, or, in modern terms, belong to the same gene pool. Taking this as our definition, it is arguably the case that Hitler's second premise is true: the Jewish Germans and the non-Jewish Germans belonged, for the most part, to different gene pools, and only the second of these were German in the true sense—in the historical and cultural sense. But even granting this much to Hitler, there is no reason to think that citizenship entails only this version of nationality. Why could it not entail being a national in the first sense of nation, of belonging to the political nation, involving as it does a subjective commitment to the state? So viewed, there was no reason whatsoever for saying that Jews in Germany did not make this commitment to the state. They played a role in business, in professions, in education, and in government. If anything, their mistake was to make too much of a commitment to the state. One could fairly say that citizenship entails being a national in at least one of two senses of the term. In the result, Hitler's first premise is false and his argument proves unsound. Jews, on this reading, would be members of the nation in one sense but not in the other. For Hitler's argument to be sustainable it would have to show that Jews could not be members of the nation in either sense.

8. National Socialism and Fascism, in their abandonment of principles of procedural and substantive justice, provide a recipe for the disintegration of society. Where substantive justice is fairness in the distribution of scarce resources and procedural justice is fairness in treating like cases alike, an abandonment of the former is much less serious than an abandonment of the latter. However, as the remarks of Goering make clear, Fascism in Germany took this low road and abandoned not just substantive justice but procedural justice as well. This is evident in Goering's comment, "I don't have to worry about Justice."[146] It is also evident in Hitler's comment in response to tepid criticisms of the execution of Roehm before he was tried: "And everyone must know for all future time that if he raises his hand to strike the State, then certain death is his lot."[147] It is difficult to imagine a more complete abandonment of procedural justice than this. And to those who would question the gravity of this consequence, he should be reminded of the words of Vilfredo Pareto: "Une société d'où la justice et la morale seraient bannies ne saurait évidemment subsister."[148]

9. National Socialism and Fascism, in their support for economic autarky, are unsustainable. In Italy under Mussolini, autarky, or self-sufficiency, was to generate dynamic industrial and agricultural growth. This resulted in tariff barriers, an effort to boost agricultural output, a program for land reclamation, and the creation of many state-owned monopolies for the purpose of exploiting new mineral resources, developing natural fibres, maximizing the efficiency of the petrochemical industries, and diminishing the dependency on oil and coal through hydroelectric plans.[149] The results of these autarkic initiatives, however, were dismal: wasted resources and inefficiencies in a stagnant manufacturing sector, as well as the elimination of bargaining rights for workers without providing for their integration into production and decision-making.[150] As for the success of autarky under National Socialism, this was parasitic upon the success of the *lebensraum* doctrine. Hitler's ambition was to turn Eastern Europe into what List called client-states, or *Ergänzungsgebiete*, whose resources would

make for German self-sufficiency. Here was a blend of nationalism, imperialism, and economic autarky.[151] But just as the Russians proved the *lebensraum* doctrine unsustainable, so did the Russians prove autarky to be unrealizable for the Nazis.

10. Both Hitler and Mussolini, as advocates of what they thought of as the high culture of a racially superior stock, adopted an unsupportable, condescending, and sometimes hateful attitude towards the culture of other peoples. This seemed particularly true in the case of their attitudes towards the musical culture or subculture of black people. Hitler, for his part, thought of the tango as the dance of apes, and profoundly disliked jazz music. But this Nazi campaign against *Entartete Musik* ("degenerate music") was only part of a larger campaign against *Entartete Kunst* ("degenerate art"). Although directed against Jewish composers and musicians from Felix Mendelssohn to Kurt Weill, it also attacked African-American music forms, notably jazz. The poster for the *Entartete Musik* exhibition shows a caricatured black jazz musician (wearing, incidentally, a Star of David on his lapel).[152]

Whether Mussolini felt the same way towards black culture as did Hitler is difficult to discern, but at least officially he took steps to suppress jazz music. "Jazz music was censored in Italy during the fascist regime."[153] Though Benito Mussolini preferred classical music, jazz did make its way into the very home in which he raised his children. In the result, one of his sons, Romano, came to have a love for jazz, and in the fullness of time released a record entitled *Jazz Allo Studio 7*, which was acclaimed throughout the international community. By the 1960s, Romano had become "one of Italy's foremost jazz musicians."[154] One can only conclude that Fascists and Nazis had difficulty in making their cultural elitism believable in their own homes. Perhaps realizing, as did Plato, "that rhythm and harmony sink more deeply into the soul than anything else,"[155] Hitler and Mussolini sought to control black music, but they could not stop the appreciation of the natural beauty that the world found in it. In this sense, their position on black music is unsupportable.

To repeat, Fascism's attack on art, especially in Germany, was an attack on all non-Aryan art in many forms. These forms included non-Aryan paintings, sculptures, and the famed Bauhaus design school, as well as music such as jazz and dances such as the tango. Thousands of offensive artworks were seized from German galleries and either burned or put on display with captions such as "Nature as seen by sick minds." Exhibitions comprising such art travelled throughout Germany and Austria under the aegis of Adolf Ziegler, the appointee of Minister of Enlightenment and Propaganda Paul Joseph Goebbels (1897–1945). The attempted elimination of these many art forms under Fascism is testament to a perversion at the heart of this ideology. It was this perversion that loyal German jazz fans recognized, even during the reign of Nazism, by going underground to keep jazz alive in a kind of cultural resistance movement,[156] and this perversion that artists, architects, and graphic designers recognized by fleeing for their lives.

Related Websites

Gentile, Giovanni. "The Doctrine of Fascism: Benito Mussolini (1932)." World Future Fund.
www.worldfuturefund.org/wffmaster/Reading/Germany/mussolini.htm

Our Legacy of Truth. "National Socialist Studies."
https://www.stormfront.org/posterity/ns/

Reisman, George. "Why Nazism Was Socialism and Why Socialism Is Totalitarian." Mises Institute, 5 Nov. 2005.
https://mises.org/library/why-nazism-was-socialism-and-why-socialism-totalitarian

Richman, Sheldon. "Fascism." The Library of Economics and Liberty.
www.econlib.org/library/Enc/Fascism.html

Soucy, Robert. "Fascism." *Encyclopedia Britannica.*
www.britannica.com/EBchecked/topic/202210/fascism

Further Readings on Fascism and National Socialism

Baratieri, Daniela, Mark Edele, and Giuseppe Finaldi. *Totalitarian Dictatorship: New Histories.* New York: Routledge, 2014.

Bialas, Wolfgang, and Lothar Fritze. *Nazi Ideology and Ethics.* Newcastle upon Tyne, UK: Cambridge Scholars Publishing, 2014.

Bosworth, R.B.J. *The Oxford Handbook of Fascism.* London: Oxford University Press, 2009.

Champagne, John. *Aesthetic Modernism and Masculinity in Fascist Italy.* Abingdon, Oxon, UK: Routledge, 2013.

Corner, Paul. *The Fascist Party and Popular Opinion in Mussolini's Italy.* London: Oxford University Press, 2012.

Ebner, Michael R. *Ordinary Violence in Mussolini's Italy.* New York: Cambridge University Press, 2011.

Eley, Geoff. *Nazism as Fascism: Violence, Ideology and the Ground of Consent in Germany 1930–1945.* New York: Routledge, 2013.

Ferrari, Chiara. *The Rhetoric of Violence and Sacrifice in Fascist Italy: Mussolini, Gadda and Vittorini.* Toronto: University of Toronto, 2013.

Gregor, James A. *Totalitarianism and Political Religion: An Intellectual History.* Stanford, CA: Stanford University Press, 2012.

Ihrig, Stefan. *Atatürkin the Nazi Imagination.* Cambridge, MA.: Belknap Press of Harvard University Press, 2014.

Kertzer, David I. *The Pope and Mussolini: The Secret History of Pius XI and the Rise of Fascism in Europe.* London: Oxford University Press, 2014.

Lavelle, Ashley. *The Politics of Betrayal: Renegades and Ex-Radicals from Mussolini to Christopher Hitchens.* New York: Palgrave Macmillan; Manchester: Manchester University Press, 2013.

Lucardie, Paul. *Democratic Extremism in Theory and Practice: All Power to the People.* New York: Routledge, 2014.

Motadel, David. *Islam and Nazi Germany's War.* Cambridge, MA: Belknap Press of Harvard University Press, 2014.

Nicosia, Francis R. *Nazi Germany and the Arab World.* New York: Cambridge University Press, 2014.

Petropoulos, Jonathon. *Artists under Hitler: Collaboration and Survival in Nazi Germany.* New Haven, CT: Yale University Press, 2014.

Steber, Martina, and Bernard Gotto. *Visions of Community in Nazi Germany: Social Engineering and Private Lives.* London: Oxford University Press, 2014.

Ward, David. *Piero Gobetti's New World: Antifascism, Liberalism, Writing*. Toronto Italian Studies. Toronto: University of Toronto Press, 2010.
Weeks, Jessica L.P. *Dictators at War and Peace*. Ithaca, NY: Cornell University Press, 2014.
Weisman, Tama. *Hannah Arendt and Karl Marx: On Totalitarianism and the Tradition of Western Political Thought*. Lanham, MD: Lexington Books, 2014.
Woodley, Daniel. *Fascism and Political Theory: Critical Perspectives of Fascist Ideology*. London and New York: Routledge, 2010.
Zox-Weaver, Annlisa. *Women Modernists and Fascism*. Cambridge: Cambridge University Press, 2011.

8 Pacifism

Learning Objectives

- To comprehend the religious roots in pacifism.
- To understand Gandhi's notion of *satyagraha* and its distinction from passive resistance, civil disobedience, and non-co-operation in pacifism.
- To appreciate the role of *ahimsa* or harmlessness in pacifism.
- To acknowledge the significant intellectual heritage of individuals like Tolstoy, Russell, Huxley, Franklin, and Einstein in pacifism.

At least since the time of Mohandas K. Gandhi and his *satyagraha* doctrine, and perhaps earlier, **pacifism** has had the defining features of an ideology: it carries with it a view of human nature, of justice, of the state, of liberty, and of political power. Although, in some cases, pacifism has had anarchistic roots—as in the case of the Doukhobors, the Russian Christian sect discussed later in Chapter 9—it has enough autonomy to stand as an ideology in its own right. And as seen in the previous chapter and as made perfectly clear by Mussolini in his repudiation of pacifism, it stands as a foil for Fascism.

The definition of pacifism seems fraught with difficulties. Some have suggested, helpfully, that there are different types of pacifism: just war pacifism, absolute pacifism, pragmatic pacifism, Gandhian non-violence pacifism, utopian pacifism, and the pacifism of the categorical imperative.[1] Teichman has argued that, differences aside, what these have in common is anti-warism.[2] While there is something to be said for this position, it does in the end seem unnecessarily constrained, and somewhat insensitive to the sweeping political stance of Tolstoy, Thoreau, and Gandhi. For this reason it is suggested here that we define it more inclusively in terms of its non-violent opposition to the use of violence[3] and injustice in any form. So construed, pacifism and terrorism, rather than the just war, stand related to each other as two ends of a very long stick, in the middle of which lie the just war and the just war doctrine.[4]

This chapter will examine the ideological content of pacifism as it has occurred over the years. However, one should not infer from this historical analysis that pacifism is a thing of the past. As evidence of more recent political actions based on pacifism, one can cite not only the example of Martin Luther King Jr and his "Letter from Birmingham Jail"

> **Central Beliefs of Pacifism**
>
> - Human nature is corrigible.
> - The origin of the state is the protective instinct and the thirst for power.
> - Equality as an ideal is civil, political, economic, and social.
> - Communitarianism takes priority over individualism.
> - Justice is procedural and substantive fairness.
> - The end of government is peace.
> - Rights are subordinated to utility in the name of peace.

in the 1960s, but the pacific protests in 2007 of the 10,000 monks in Yangon, Myanmar (formerly Rangoon, Burma), in support of the detained pro-democracy leader Aung San Suu Kyi,[5] as well as protests in Tokyo in 2009 in support of the pacifist charter of the Constitution of Japan.[6] Moreover, the issue of pacifism at the core of the Japanese Constitution has even more recently proved relevant to the politics of Japan. Prime Minister Shinzo Abe in the summer of 2015 attempted to circumvent Article 9 of the Constitution, which asserts that the Japanese people "forever renounce war as a sovereign right of the nation and the threat or use of force as a means of settling international disputes."[7] Realizing the difficulty of acquiring the two-thirds majority in both houses of the Japanese Parliament for a constitutional amendment in regard to Article 9, Prime Minister Abe unilaterally declared a reinterpretation of the Constitution. The reinterpretation permitted the enactment, by simple majority, of security-related bills that have effectively allowed the Japanese government to find a way around the constitutional restrictions normally associated with pacifism.[8] What this shows is that pacifism as an ideology continues to play a role in political discourse in the twenty-first century.

And while it may come as a surprise to many readers, pacifism in the form of nonviolence has a home in the political ideology of the Muslim Brotherhood. The recent resort to violence among the young as a means of settling political disputes in Egypt alarmed Brotherhood officials, who maintain that "the group still opposes violence as immoral and counter-productive."[9] The resort to the use of violence among young Brotherhood members created a generational split in the organization.[10] While this development certainly challenges the pacifism that lies at the heart of old-style Brotherhood ideology, it does not show its irrelevance in present-day political considerations in Egypt and elsewhere in the Middle East where the Muslim Brotherhood is strong. To the contrary, it shows that at least up to the present, pacifism has had a role to play in the strategy of the Brotherhood. The motto of the Brotherhood still appears relevant: "peacefulness is stronger than weapons, and violence is the reason for defeat and demise."

Religious Figures and Movements

Pacifism has religious and anarchistic roots. As for its religious roots, they surely must include these sayings of Jesus as given in the **Sermon on the Mount**: "Love your enemies, do good to those who hate you, bless those who curse you, and pray for those who treat you badly. As for the man who hits you on one cheek, offer him the other as well"

(Luke 6:27–9). The Sermon on the Mount also opens with the Beatitudes, in which Jesus says, "Blessed are the peacemakers, for they will be called sons of God" (Matthew 5:9). As Peter Brock says, the teaching of Jesus seems unmistakably to be one of love, non-retaliation, and a rejection of violence.[11] By the time we reach early Church fathers such as Tertullian (c. 160–c. 220 CE) and Origen (185–254 CE), the ideas of Jesus had congealed into anti-militarism. For this reason Origen had to respond to the pagan philosopher Celsus, who maintained in 178 CE that the Roman Empire's security was imperilled by Christianity's attempt to subvert society, undermine family life, and create dissatisfaction among the subjects of the Empire.[12] Celsus's real concern was that Christians lacked a sense of civic loyalty to an empire whose benefits they enjoyed[13]—and this loyalty embraced an affirmation of the common beliefs regarding the gods and, undoubtedly, military service.[14] As Frend observes, when one attends to Tertullian's assertion that "nothing is more foreign to us than the state" and to Tertullian's claim that the Christian soldier's duty was desertion, one soon understands the magnitude of Celsus's problem.[15] Whether Tertullian and Origen satisfactorily countered the criticisms of Celsus is not our present concern; what is of significance is that the anti-militarism of the early Church did not end until Constantine (272–337 CE) was converted to Christianity. Indeed, as some have said, Christianity could only have become a state religion by getting rid of its pacifism.[16]

The Christian ideas of pacifism did not emerge again, and then only briefly, until the time of the Waldenses, in southern France, near the end of the twelfth century. This sect refused to take human life, and opposed secular states that waged war and executed criminals.[17] Following the Waldenses, it was not until the early 1400s that another Christian religious group, the Taborites, took up the pacifist position, albeit for a short while. After the Taborites—apart from the pacifist philosophy of Petr Chelčický (c. 1390–c. 1460), a Hussite—pacifism fell on infertile ground, at least within Christendom. Chelčický himself stood at odds with the rest of his Hussite brethren, who adopted militancy in the practice of their faith.[18] The heritage he passed on to his brethren in Bohemia was that of a nascent anarchist who rejected the state and embraced non-resistance. The group that carried on his thought was the Unity of Czech Brethren, which originated around 1460 but split apart 30 years later as it tried in vain to accommodate itself to the world.

The Anabaptists were the next group to adopt a similar pacifist philosophy. Though apparently owing no historical influence to the Unity of Czech Brethren, this group also embraced non-resistance and was inspired in so doing by the teachings of Jesus. Closely related to the Anabaptists were the Mennonites, under the leadership of the Frisian Menno Simons (1496–1561), and it was he who articulated over time a message of non-violence in response to war and then in response to crimes that normally resulted in torture or hangings. One could go further and say that Menno Simons's position evolved into a general principle of non-resistance.[19] Another group that should be mentioned here were the Hutterites, who were connected—if only loosely—with the Mennonites. The Hutterites came from Moravia in the first half of the sixteenth century and proved themselves to be pacifists who embraced **communitarian** values as well as the principles of non-resistance.[20]

Before turning to the last of the Christian sectarian pacifist groups—namely, the Quakers—the opportunity should not be lost to summarize the pacifism of the foregoing groups, ranging from the Waldenses to the Hutterites. Though a central part in their pacifism was opposition to militarism as conducted by the state, this was not the only part of their ideological stance. This is evident when one remembers that their opposition extended not only to the taking up of swords but also to torture and the execution of criminals. It would accordingly be a misrepresentation of Christian sectarian pacifism—at least during the second millennium—to construe it as solely concerned with anti-militarism or anti-warism. Christians such as Mennonites and Quakers were quite aware that violence occurred in other contexts, which they also opposed even if their focus turned out to be violence conducted by the state.

It would be incorrect to say that the **Quakers**—the Religious Society of Friends—were a sectarian group of a completely different colour from those examined above, but they were different just the same. Though there were "peripheral influences" that the Anabaptists and Mennonites had on the Quakers, the Quakers represented a rediscovery of pacifism rather than its continuation.[21] The inspiration for this latter group came more from the New Testament itself than from the Anabaptists and Mennonites—from the same source as that which had inspired Tertullian, Origen, and Chelčický years before. What the Quakers, under the leadership of the English cobbler George Fox (1624–1691), gleaned from the New Testament was the necessity of adopting non-violence so as to "out-live all wrath and contention." And while again the focus of this in their peace testimony seemed to be on distancing themselves from militarism, there was more to their ideology: they were committed to good neighbourliness and justice and, in the case of William Penn (1644–1718), the Quaker founder of Pennsylvania, practised a humanitarian tradition in the work of the Friends.[22] So the pacifism of the Quakers under Penn extended beyond a rigid interpretation of pacifism as anti-warism and embraced a more general form of non-violence by the individual and the state.[23] It is not surprising, therefore, to find the most articulate Quaker theologian of the time, Robert Barclay (1648–1690), arguing that the teachings of Jesus as found in the Sermon on the Mount resulted in "a new dispensation that excluded his [Jesus'] followers [individually and collectively] from warring and fighting, binding them instead to suffer and to repay evil with good."[24] While the peace testimony issued by Fox and Richard Hubberthorne in 1661 focused on the repudiation of war, Barclay's theology clearly pointed Quaker thinking to something that was more encompassing—a prohibition on violence in general. It is not surprising that in the course of time, other Quakers saw this as grounds for a campaign to eliminate the cruel treatment of the insane.[25]

Thus far our attention has been on what otherwise could be called sectarian pacifism—more specifically, Christian sectarian pacifism. While this has an interest in its own right, there is more to the story of pacifism than that which is confined to Christian sectarianism. One person stands out in this regard: Henry David Thoreau. This American writer, philosopher, and naturalist in turn had his own influence on two other non-sectarian figures, Leo Tolstoy and Mohandas Gandhi.[26] It will be evident from a discussion of their ideas that pacifism is not restricted to anti-warism or anti-militarism, but also embraces non-violent opposition to many injustices.

Henry David Thoreau

Perhaps best known for *Walden* (1854), his account of the two years he spent living more or less alone in a woodland cabin at Walden Pond near Concord, Massachusetts, Thoreau (1817–1862) wrote one of the great classics on non-violent **civil disobedience**. Published in 1849, his "Civil Disobedience" made a forceful case opposing the US war against Mexico, as well as opposing the institution of slavery. In protesting the Mexican war, Thoreau refused to pay his taxes and as a consequence was sent to jail. Before his friends paid his taxes (contrary to the wishes of Thoreau), resulting in his being released from jail, Thoreau's friend Ralph Waldo Emerson visited him in jail and demanded to know what Thoreau was doing there, to which Thoreau is reported to have said, "What are you doing out there?"[27] No doubt in saying this he was relying on his own words in the aforementioned essay: "Under a government which imprisons unjustly, the true place for a just man is also in prison."[28]

Besides protesting the Mexican war,[29] Thoreau argued against the institution of slavery in the United States, and he counselled in favour of revolution and rebellion: "When a sixth of the population of a nation which has undertaken to be the refuge of liberty are slaves . . . I think it is not too soon for honest men to rebel and revolutionize."[30] But the rebellion and revolution of which he speaks is something new. It is not the rebellion or revolution countenanced at times by the classical liberal John Locke, nor that repudiated by Edmund Burke, nor that recommended by Karl Marx, nor that rejected by John Dewey. It is, to the contrary, a non-violent revolution in which parties to the practice or institution "withdraw from their copartnership" and do so for the purpose of being put in jail in order to make the system collapse. It is clear that with Henry Thoreau, the pacifism of the early religious leaders has moved beyond anti-militarism to a more embracing pacifism. It is not just opposition to the Mexican war that bothers this pacifist, but other unjust practices. In short, here is a pacifist who opposes non-violently both violence in the form of war and violence in another guise.[31] In this context, Jenny Teichman's claim—that the doctrine of the just war is the most important philosophical response to pacifism—seems simply too crude and not properly nuanced enough to cover non-sectarian pacifism.

Leo Tolstoy

Author of the epic novel *War and Peace* (1869), Leo Tolstoy (1828–1910) was born a Russian noble and progressive landowner, but became a pacifist-anarchist and was deeply concerned with the welfare of his peasants and peasants in general.[32] An integral part of his anarchism was his commitment to the words of Jesus as found in the Sermon on the Mount, as well as his bitter opposition to the institutional Christian Church in its various guises (Orthodox, Catholic, and Protestant).

Tolstoy's opposition to the Christian Church is less relevant to present considerations than his affirmation of the principles of the Sermon on the Mount. It is here that Tolstoy found "the Christian teaching in its full meaning," and in which he found "the law of non-resistance."[33] So Tolstoy drew a line from the Sermon on the Mount to the principle of non-violence, in much the same way in which earlier individuals, such as Origen, Tertullian, Chelčický, Fox and the Quakers, and Thoreau had done. This principle, the principle of non-resistance to evil by violence, amounts to the claim that "the mutual interaction of rational beings upon each other should consist not in violence . . . but in rational persuasion; and that consequently, towards this substitution of rational persuasion for coercion all those should strive who desire to further the welfare of the world."[34]

What this means is that the method of combatting social evil should be non-violent, persuasive rather than conflictual. But there is more to what Tolstoy has to say. While it looks as though he wishes to apply this principle solely to evils caused by violence, he also sees it as a principle that can be represented as proscribing a right to dominate or use coercion over fellow human beings.[35] For this reason he embraces the ideas of the American abolitionist William Lloyd Garrison (1805–1879) and staunchly attacks slavery.

It is obvious from this that Tolstoy's pacifism goes well beyond anti-militarism, though to be sure his pacifism embraces that, too. But Tolstoy, in his pacifism, advances a line of thinking much like Garrison's, that non-violent resistance[36] should be used to combat social injustices such as slavery.[37] Indeed, Tolstoy's principle of non-violence embraces a variety of social injustices, from imprisonment in foul-smelling cells[38] and seizure of chattels for debt, to whippings, running the gauntlet, and burnings at the stake[39]—in short, many different types of injustice, not just those that are blood-curdlingly violent.

Many other writers are deserving of attention as individuals attracted to pacifism owing to the events of war. Two of these undoubtedly are Wilfrid Owen (1893–1918) and his acquaintance, Siegfried Sassoon (1886–1967), both of whom wrote compelling poetry about the pathos of war. But with Thoreau and Tolstoy firmly etched in our minds, it is now time to turn to perhaps the most famous of all pacifists: Mohandas Gandhi. It is Gandhi, more than anyone else in the history of pacifism, who develops its theory and practice most fully.

Mohandas Gandhi

Mohandas Karamchand Gandhi (1869–1948), otherwise known as Mahatma, or the Great Soul, was the leader of the Indian independence movement and advocate of the doctrine of *satyagraha*. This doctrine can be traced to the ideal of karma yoga in the Bhagavad-Gita, as well as to Jesus's Sermon on the Mount and to the more recent writings of Thoreau, John Ruskin, and Tolstoy.[40] In Gandhi's own words, *satyagraha* is "holding on to the Truth and it means, therefore, Truth-force."[41] Gandhi is insistent that this principle or doctrine excludes the use of violence, for the reason—among other reasons—that man is not competent to punish.[42] The unconditionality of Gandhi's exclusion of violence should be cemented in our thoughts, for he says, "Satyagraha excludes the use of violence in any shape or form, whether in thought, speech, or deed."[43] In saying this Gandhi makes clear that his principle and philosophy go well beyond anti-militarism. It would be a mistake, in light of this, to construe his pacifism as being primarily focused on anti-militarism.[44] H.J.N. Horsburgh captures the meaning of *satyagraha* very nicely when he says that in Gandhi's estimation this principle is more than an attitudinal change. It means, for the individual, a way of life, whether or not he is combatting a large-scale social injustice in society. It means, for the community, the continuous attempt to utilize and transform social conflict.[45]

Satyagraha

Gandhi provides considerable insight into the full meaning of *satyagraha*, which he does by tracing its relationship to passive resistance, civil disobedience, and non-co-operation. He says *satyagraha* is distinguished from passive resistance in that the latter is considered a weapon of the weak and does not rule out—except for armed resistance—the use of violence.[46] *Satyagraha* is not conceived as a weapon of the weak, and does exclude the use of violence. Civil disobedience and non-co-operation are, however, species of *satyagraha*.

To begin with the first of these, civil disobedience was, in the opinion of Gandhi, an expression coined by Thoreau, and represents a civil breach of immoral statutory enactments.[47] From Gandhi's perspective, however, Thoreau was not a paradigmatic champion of non-violence, for he seems to have restricted his breach of statutory law to the payment of taxes. By 1919, civil disobedience, again in Gandhi's opinion, had evolved to cover a breach of any law that was statutory and immoral, where the violator of the law both invoked the sanctions of the law and willingly suffered imprisonment.[48] Jail-going is a special non-resistance activity in a civil disobedience program.[49] Non-co-operation implies withdrawing from the state when the state has been, in the view of the non-co-operator, corrupt. Non-co-operation may include strikes, walkouts, hartal,[50] and resignation of offices and titles.[51] However, non-co-operation is not as "fierce" as civil disobedience, and can also be practised by children and the masses. Civil disobedience, on the other hand, can only be undertaken as a last resort and by "a select few."[52]

Four Essential Characteristics

Gandhi acknowledges that any *satyagraha* campaign requires discipline. Four characteristics stand out as essential to this discipline: courage, self-reliance, patience, and freedom from covetousness. Great courage is required to meet violence with resolute non-violence; patience is needed to trump impatience, which will threaten the civil resister's will to resist non-violently; self-reliance is needed to help in creating fearlessness; and, finally, freedom from covetousness is needed to eliminate anxiety, fearfulness, and violence.[53] But it is clear that this discipline will be, in Gandhi's opinion, a very slender reed upon which to put much weight in the absence of a "highly developed religious life." The religious life to which reference is hereby made is to prayer, meditation, and fasting.[54] And it is this religious life that Gandhi uses to strengthen himself—to give him the resolve necessary to cultivate courage, patience, self-reliance, and freedom from covetousness. This religious life allows him not only to develop a political ideology, but to live an ideology that affirms a pledge of non-violence, and nonetheless a pledge that does *not* require the civil resister to "crawl on our bellies or to draw lines with our noses or to walk to salute the Union Jack or to do anything degrading at the dictation of officials."[55]

Truth, Non-Violence, and Self-Suffering

Gandhi's concern in facing the British in South Africa and in India was to develop a philosophy of conflict appropriate to his times.[56] The philosophy he ends up with is characterized by truth, non-violence, and self-suffering.[57] Each of these has corollary elements. In the case of truth it is ethical humanism.[58] In the case of non-violence it is social service. In the case of self-suffering it is sacrifice and the preparation for sacrifice—even death.[59] At the practical level and over time, Gandhi's *satyagraha* came to mean something quite specific for the individual as an individual, as a prisoner, as a member of a unit, and as a participant in communal struggles. As an individual, a *satyagrahi* or civil resister will do the following: harbour no anger, suffer his opponent's anger, not retaliate to his opponents' assaults, submit to arrest, refuse to surrender property in his possession, not swear or curse, not insult his opponent, not salute the Union Jack, and protect officials from attack. As a prisoner, the civil resister will behave courteously to prison officials, make no distinction between an ordinary prisoner and himself, and not fast for want of conveniences whose deprivation does not involve any injury to his self-respect. As a member of a unit, a civil resister will obey all orders issued by the leader of the corps, carry out these orders in the first instance and then appeal them later, and expect no maintenance for his dependants. As a participant in communal struggles, he will not intentionally become a cause of communal quarrels, not take sides, avoid occasions that give rise to communal quarrels, and not wound religious susceptibilities of any community in a procession.[60]

Gandhi's commitment to non-violence, it should be noted, embraces something more transformative than first meets the eye, a point noted curiously by Albert Schweitzer in his study of Indian thought.[61] Non-violence, or **ahimsa** in Hindu, Jain, and Buddhist ethical precepts, means not so much "action based on the refusal to do harm" as "the renunciation of the will to kill or to damage."[62] In this renunciation of one's will to kill or do damage, Gandhi finds not a policy for seizing power but a way of transforming relationships so that a peaceful transfer of power can occur.[63]

It is clear that Mohandas Gandhi, the Great Soul, has spelled out the details of pacifism in a more theoretical and advanced way than his predecessors, and has exposed its practical details in a way unseen before him. While George Fox and the Quakers and Thoreau and Garrison and Tolstoy had worked their way through some of these theoretical and practical difficulties, Gandhi worked his way through them with much more acuity and ingenuity. Perhaps this point is best made, at least in the case of Tolstoy, by recalling how he responded to those who thought his non-resistance was absurd. He purportedly said, "I am Tolstoy, but I am not Tolstoyan," thereby indicating that he was unable to live up to the full logic of his argument. The same could not be said of Gandhi, who not only worked out the logic of his theoretical and practical argument, but lived it. It is a propitious moment to move on to consider three final advocates of pacifism, Aldous Huxley, Bertrand Russell, and Ursula Franklin.

Aldous Huxley

Aldous Huxley (1894–1963) offers a refreshing approach to the study of pacifism. For the most part this approach is one of anti-militarism, and so in that respect is not new; what *is* new is his application and consideration of pacifist principles to the twentieth-century military machine. In this application and consideration Huxley sheds new light on a range of topics in his small but engaging book, *An Encyclopaedia of Pacifism*.[64] We will consider only a sample of the topics he addresses, but enough to give us a sense of the direction of Huxley's thinking.

Constructive Pacifism

There are particular targets of Huxley's pacifism, and they include capitalism, the church, and imperialism. But before looking at his comments on some of these, we need to have a grasp of the positive comments he makes about pacifism. He affirms, to begin with, that constructive pacifism is not just opposition to war but rather "a complete philosophy of life,"[65] and this philosophy carries with it implications that are political, sociological, and economic. Further, he adds that pacifism is opposed to inter-tribal conflicts, to large-scale conflicts,[66] and to the exploitation of the consumer. Pacifists believe that good means are more important than good ends, for the reason that good means can only result in good ends. Further, he maintains that pacifism is democratic and non-violent,[67] and the moral equivalent of war. As such, it is "a way of living which calls out endurance, bravery and self-forgetfulness, but for constructive ends and not for destruction."[68] Then he adds, by way of analysis of morality, that pacifism is but the application of principles of individual morality to the problems of politics and economics.[69] In brief, Huxley believes that we work with two systems of morality: one that applies to individuals and one that applies to communities. Loyalty to the community serves to justify and excuse the individual "in committing every kind of crime."[70] This loyalty seems to license individuals to swindle, lie, steal, and murder, precisely the kinds of things condemned under individual morality. But, thinks Huxley, this can no longer continue for the simple reason that science has now given war-makers such a power of destruction that its deployment will be the ruin of European civilization. In the event, the costs of the resultant "lunacy" and "wickedness" are so excessive that nations simply cannot afford to behave except as moral human beings. In other words, the morality of communities must return to the morality of the individual.[71]

Unilateral Disarmament

Huxley is interested in cultivating a pacifism that has implications for conflicts that engage the body politic, whether domestically or internationally. For this reason he asserts that a pacifist gesture of unilateral disarmament would "profoundly affect public opinion throughout the world and would lead to a measure of general disarmament."[72] The effect of unilateral disarmament would short-circuit the rationalizations of most governments in their piling up of armaments as a precaution of defence against a possible aggressor. Huxley believes that unilateral disarmament would short-circuit this rationalization by relieving international tensions, allaying fears and suspicions, and calming those who feel that their prestige and status demand a military as big as that of the next country.[73]

To those who suggest that pacifism should be opposed on the grounds that civilization is built on force, Huxley contends that the word "force" has no single definite meaning.[74] So far as one can talk about it, however, one can say the forces that accomplish most are those that are psychological (persuasion, loyalty, social tradition, good example), whereas the force of modern armies is "morally unjustifiable and is not even likely to secure its object, for the simple reason that these weapons are so destructive that a war cannot preserve any of a nation's vital interests; it can only bring ruin and death to all who come within its range . . . ."[75]

Ahimsa

In pre-Aryan India, Huxley sees a theology and doctrine of immanence in which the soul of the individual is thought of as a portion of the divine soul. Huxley believes that pacifism and humanitarianism are corollaries of this doctrine.[76] According to Huxley, both of these principles were acted upon by the followers of Jainism and Buddhism, who also practised *ahimsa* ("the renunciation of the will to kill or to damage")—a practice lived, as we saw earlier, by Gandhi. Huxley contrasts the bloodlessness of Buddhism with atrocities of Christianity, inspired as it is by "the savage literature of the ancient Hebrews."[77] None of this means that Huxley sees in Jesus's words the words of a pugilist. To the contrary, like Tertullian and Origen, like the Quakers and Hutterites, Huxley sees in the Sermon on the Mount and other words of Jesus a message of love and reconciliation that would be used to "undercut Gentile hostility by means of non-violence."[78]

But how far does Huxley carry this philosophy of non-violence? Those who are opposed to him, he understands, will be only too willing to deploy the following rhetorical question to erode his confidence in pacifism. What would you do if you saw a stranger break into your house and try to violate your wife? To this question Huxley replies: "... it is quite likely that I should become very angry and try to knock the intruder down or even to kill him."[79] It is obvious from this that Huxley is not advocating a pacifism as encompassing as that of Gandhi, or of Jesus; instead, this pacifism is largely anti-militaristic. Continuing his answer to the previous question, and in the spirit of the present discussion, Huxley adds, with respect to the intruder just mentioned, "I should certainly not send my brother to go and poison the man's grandfather and disembowel his infant son."[80] In Huxley's mind there is a profound and unqualified disanalogy between his hypothetical reaction to an intruder (which is, he thinks, justifiable) and war (which, he thinks, is entirely unjustifiable). War, after all, consists of murdering all kinds of persons who have never done one any kind of injury.[81] Huxley then provides his analysis of war, to which we now turn.

War

Endorsing the War Resisters' International Peace Pledge, Huxley affirms the following: war—to defend the state, to preserve the existing order of society, and on behalf of the oppressed proletariat—is a crime not to be supported in any of its manifestations. Accordingly, war resisters must recognize and strive for the removal of all causes of wars, including differences between races, differences between religions, differences between classes, and differences between nations, and in misconceptions of the state.[82]

As for the political implications of pacifism, according to Huxley, they can be summed up as affirming the need for democratic institutions, decentralization, local and professional government, improvement of social services and extension of educational facilities, disarmament, and the removal of barriers to international trade. Finally, as for the economic implications, they can be summed up as being opposed to capitalism in its present form: militaristic, exploitive, and socially irresponsible. Huxley suggests that pacifism endorses co-operation rather than competition and conflict. For this reason pacifism endorses co-operative movements and other efforts, such as the London Transport Board as well as the Port of London Authority, to limit the opportunities for private profit-making, and to protect the consuming public.[83]

Imperialism

Needless to say, Huxley's pacifism excludes **imperialism**, a hegemonic practice that empowers certain nations, such as Great Britain, France, Belgium, Portugal, the Netherlands, and Italy.[84] His conceptual map for understanding imperialism in discussing pacifism is given by his explanation of the three causes of war: (i) the pursuit of wealth, (ii) the pursuit of glory, and (iii) the advocacy of a creed. In modern times the main cause is found in the first of these, which in turn, according to Huxley, is best understood as comprising the competition between states for markets and raw materials and the competition between classes regarding the distribution of raw material.[85] But these factors are what make up imperialism.[86] Hence, on Huxley's own terms, it would seem that pacifism is at logical odds with imperialism as one of the sources of war.

More Than the Philosophy of Origen

One can see from the above that pacifism is, for Huxley, something more than anti-militarism. It is, as he says, "a complete philosophy of life."[87] Indeed, Huxley hints at this, more by accident than design, when he says that the conscientious objection movement in Britain that occurred in 1914, many years after the pacifism of Doukhobors, Mennonites, and Quakers, "necessitated a deeper consideration of the issues involved than has ever been given to them since the days of Origen."[88] What Huxley offers, in the form of pacifism, is something more constrained than that offered by Gandhi; he offers a subtle and sensitive analysis of the economic, social, and political forces surrounding war. So while anti-warism is the focus of his philosophy of life, many other issues are found at the edges of this philosophy. In brief, Huxley is not simply a modern-day Origen, for Huxley, unlike Origen, does not restrict himself to anti-militarism.

With Huxley's position in train, it is an appropriate moment to look, albeit briefly, at the pacifism of Bertrand Russell. Perhaps there is no better place to commence this discussion than with Russell's *Which Way to Peace?*, a work that Huxley refers to approvingly while discussing pacifism.[89]

Bertrand Russell

The pacifism of Bertrand Russell (1872–1970) is not the capacious pacifism of Gandhi, but something closer to that of Huxley. It is worth bearing in mind that their two works—*An Encyclopaedia of Pacifism* and *Which Way to Peace?*—were written within a year of each other and just before the outbreak of World War II. There is, therefore, in both writings, a sense of urgency. In Russell's case, this urgency is found in his preoccupation with militarism.

Pacifism: Partial and Complete

Russell divides pacifism into two forms: partial and complete. The former entails a refusal to fight on some occasions when there is considerable provocation, but not on all such occasions.[90] Since Russell believes that partial pacifism is unsustainable, he is interested in considering only complete pacifism, though again he thinks of this, at least initially, only in the context of war and not in the context of other forms of violence such as muggings in the park or murders in the cathedral. He is, he says, thinking of pacifism not as a principle deduced from Christ's teachings or as a principle deduced from Kant's categorical imperative, but as a course of action recommended by common sense.[91]

Russell, as an atheist, eschews explicitly any attempt to base his argument for pacifism on religious grounds, which he thinks is the "short road" to anti-militarism.[92] While he respects the Society of Friends for their pacifism and anti-militarism, he does not base his moral opinion on similar religious beliefs, but rather on the consequences of the actions.[93] He does not say, *simpliciter*, that war is wicked, but rather that modern war is sure to have worse consequences than an unjust peace.[94] In a nutshell, Russell's argument for pacifism comes to this:

> If you, at great expense, prepare the means of killing large numbers of other people, they will certainly, unless they have been convinced by our argument, make equal preparations to kill you. They will, feeling themselves innocent, consider

you wicked on account of your preparations; you, convinced that you intended only self-defence, will think them wicked. Each side will then be persuaded that the other side is capable of a treacherous attack, and will therefore become itself capable of the very thing that it suspects.[95]

Obstacles to Pacifism: Fear, Pride, and Greed

Perceptively, Russell lists three things that stand in the way of the pacifism he advocates: fear, pride, and greed.[96] With respect to the first of these, he says that fear should promote unilateral disarmament rather than the swashbuckling and ferocity usually cultivated, carefully and industriously, by the militarists of all countries,[97] because "if we do not disarm it is highly probable that we shall suffer all the horrors of attack from the air, with no better consolation than the enemy will suffer in like manner."[98] Hence fear, according to Russell, needs to be redirected into something constructive rather than something destructive. Otherwise, the mutual fear that exists before a war will be greatly increased during a war, and will lead to the blindness of war—making it impossible for people to see the illusory nature of the good to be achieved by war.[99]

According to Russell, pride plays a different role. Writing in 1936, he notes that England has colonies and considerable influence in the world, and clearly disarmament would mean the loss of this influence and empire. But only pride stands in the way of relinquishing these through unilateral disarmament, and thereby being able to "substitute a civilized standard of values for the primitive lust of dominion."[100] The last of the trio that Russell considers is greed, or, as Plato would call it, *pleonexia*. Russell admits that England's economic system is bound up with the Empire, the loss of which would entail a loss of income—gold from the mines of the Transvaal, jute from India, oil from Persia, and rubber from the Straits Settlements. This loss, he thinks, will be tiny compared to the cost of the next war.[101] In his opinion, this war will bring with it widespread destruction, depleting the nation's energies and requiring a lengthy period of restoration.

Given the negative side of the balance sheet and calibrating the destructive capacity of the next war when grounded in fear, pride, and greed, Russell reaches the conclusion that complete pacifism is the wisest policy.[102] Then, in crescendo-like fashion, he caps off utilitarian common sense argument in favour of complete pacifism in the coming war by issuing the following credo to all war resisters: to abstain from fighting, and from all voluntary participation in war between civilized states; to use every effort to persuade others to do likewise; to bring all possible influence to bear to prevent the participation of his country in war; and, within the limits of his capacity, to aim at similar results in other countries also.[103]

Two Residual Issues

But this is not quite the end of Russell's pacifism. Two other elements need to be discussed. The first pertains to what Russell thinks the individual can do if the individual wishes his or her country to disarm, while the second pertains to what Russell thinks the connection is between military violence and other forms of violence, especially that which is rooted in an economic system. To each of these important issues we now turn.

Russell does not think he is subscribing to a visionary's dream and endeavouring to apply the Sermon on the Mount to real life. Just the same, he is faced with the hard question: what can be done by an individual who accepts pacifism?[104] Russell acknowledges that the forces arrayed against the individual are colossal, organized, and secretive.[105] The psychological effect on the individual is one of "despairing impotence" as he faces government, business, and other groups. To this Russell counters with an example drawn from nineteenth-century politics—namely, the anti-slavery movement. Here was a movement that managed to convert "cynical old Tories" to the idea of the abolition of the slave trade.[106]

The options Russell gives the individual who wishes to confront a government heading for war are two: (i) combinations, and (ii) conscientious objection. With respect to combinations, Russell believes a war resister should ally himself with organizations pledged to complete pacifism in order to help alleviate the feeling of despairing impotence. With respect to conscientious objection, Russell admits that practising this in the next war may be a recipe for execution, but that it may nonetheless have the effect of making public opinion more skeptical of the value of war and armaments and stimulating resistance to any increase in the armed forces.[107] Again, writing in the mid-1930s, Russell says that the best one can hope for as a conscientious objector is that the idea of war resistance will spread fast enough to keep Great Britain neutral in the next war.[108] As fate would have it, that next war was World War II.

In tracing the connection between military violence and other forms of violence, Russell offers a more expansive interpretation of pacifism. Admittedly, these thoughts are the thoughts of a young Russell, but such as they are, this is what he maintains, speaking in 1917. He affirms unconditionally that the spirit of pacifism does not stand simply against the act of killing or the use of violence. Rather, the spirit of pacifism seems rooted more in a love that has as its aim the well-living of others. Accordingly, pacifism will oppose slavery, tyranny, the division between rich and poor, male chauvinism, and elements of criminal law that are unjust.[109] Among these opponents of pacifism he singles out the economic system, which produces division between rich and poor. He believes that the same principle of brotherhood that has inspired pacifists to take a stand against war will perforce lead them to think of its implications for a just economic system.[110] There is no doubt whatsoever that the economic system he criticizes is capitalism, for he says, "The very same spirit of freedom which makes the active pacifist find war intolerable must also lead him to oppose the power of the landowner and the capitalist."[111] Further, he argues, "It is impossible to doubt that the abolition of the capitalist would be a tremendous step towards the abolition of war, and ought therefore to be supported, if it becomes feasible, by those who aim at establishing a secure peace throughout the world."[112] So Russell's pacifism is somewhat more encompassing than first meets the eye, and to be fair, it does not remain constant over the years. At the core stands his anti-militarism, and this he shares with figures discussed earlier, such as Origen and Tertullian. There are times, however, when he sees a connection that carries his pacifism to other areas of violence. Slavery is possibly the clearest example of this, but the younger Russell is unquestionably opposed to the violence of the rich against the poor and of other forms of exploitation, such as sexism, that have only a veneer of respectability covering their own kind of violence.

Russell offers us an insight on pacifism from the perspective of a logician, mathematician, and philosopher standing with his feet in World War I and in the period just before the eruption of World War II. An unmistakable sense of iconoclasm in Russell's writings makes clear his unwillingness to have anything to do with the so-called glories and heroism of war. To him these stand as passé relics of the Age of Chivalry and have no place in the modern world—a conclusion he thinks is reachable on the basis solely of common sense. But this common sense is backed, as we have seen, by his deployment of argumentation. To those who would disagree with his stand he would marshal other arguments, those dealing with the intrinsic evils of war, the ethical uselessness of punishing a nation, and the practical impossibility of destroying by force what is of real value in a nation's life. The intrinsic evils include the massive destruction and misfortune visited upon humanity—a misfortune analogous to but worse than the Black Death. The uselessness of punishing a nation is grounded in the failure of defeat in war to be remedial. And the practical impossibility of destroying what is of real value is manifest in the things of the spirit—which are not subject to force.[113]

To stop at this point in our discussion of Russell would be inexcusable, for in the years following World War II he became actively involved in the Campaign for Nuclear Disarmament (CND). In fact, to say that Russell was "involved" in this movement does a disservice to his participation, for he was the figurehead and tactician of the CND. However, prior to his assuming leadership of the CND, he collaborated with Albert Einstein on a remarkable document, the *Russell-Einstein Manifesto*. This document was issued in London on 9 July 1955 as a forerunner to the Pugwash Conferences, and amounted to a plea by its two advocates of the urgency in renouncing war. The declaration says in unqualified terms:

> Here, then, is the problem which we present to you, stark and dreadful and inescapable: Shall we put an end to the human race; or shall mankind renounce war? People will not face this alternative because it is so difficult to abolish war.[114]

Both Russell and Einstein see the dangers posed by nuclear war as being so real and so catastrophic for the human race that they argue in favour of abolishing war entirely. Neither of these individuals believes that global wars, if started, can avoid degenerating into nuclear wars. The hope that they can is, according to the *Manifesto*, "illusory." In the *Russell-Einstein Manifesto* one sees a position adopted with respect to war that is not unlike that advocated by Origen and Tertullian, except that in the case of Russell and Einstein a new reason for opposing war is given: the universal death of the human race will occur unless war is renounced.

Within a year of the *Manifesto*, Russell took his position as head of the CND and became "a key figure in the nuclear disarmament movement as it emerged at the end of 1957."[115] Little known now is the fact that he used his position as an éminence grise and leader of the CND to write personal letters to Soviet Premier Nikita Khrushchev and US President Dwight D. Eisenhower on the dangers of nuclear war between their nations. To the astonishment of most, Russell received a lengthy reply from Khrushchev and, though he received no reply from Eisenhower, he did receive one from Secretary of State John Foster Dulles on behalf of the President.[116] Russell, in his writings at this time, remains suspicious of the fanaticism found in both camps (Soviet and American) that had nuclear weapons, and is appalled that anyone could believe in the ideology of Communism. But lest one think that his criticism of ideology stops there, one needs to be reminded that he is equally concerned about the growing tendency in the United States at that time to combat one fanaticism with another.[117] There is an urgency in Russell's pacifism in these early heady years of the Cold War, an urgency that eclipses that felt by Russell even during the dark days of World War I and the interwar years.

Ursula Franklin

A professor of metallurgy and materials science at the University of Toronto for more than 40 years, Ursula Franklin (1921–) is a Canadian pacifist, feminist, and environmentalist. She was born in Germany of a Jewish mother and German father, where she was imprisoned in a Nazi forced labour camp and experienced the bombing of Berlin as well as the Soviet occupation of East Germany. Owing to her experiences there, she was persuaded early on of the dysfunctionality of war and began to contribute to Quaker thinking on the subject of war and peacemaking and on a better understanding of violence.[118] Her pacifism can be summed up in the following terms: only a commitment to ethical means and non-violence in all human actions can address the problems of society and lead to a peaceful, just, and egalitarian world.[119] Her pacifist views are wide-ranging and touch such diverse topics as women and militarism, nuclear peace, justice and modern technology, green energy, and the Montreal École Polytechnique massacre of 1989. It is impossible to do justice to the range of Franklin's pacifist thought, so the intent below is to direct our attention to some of its fundamentals.

Belief Systems and Fundamentals

Franklin contends, correctly, that all religions and all belief systems reconstitute the world for their followers, providing a cultural interpretation of life and death as well as an explanation of the world and what it ought to be. She admits that troubles arise for believers when there is a contradiction between the principles and teachings, on the one hand, and the world, on the other. She goes on to describe three ways in which these contradictions can be resolved: (i) behaviour in the world can be made to conform to the belief system; (ii) the belief system can be made to conform to the conduct in the world; or (iii) the belief system and principles of conduct can be generally abandoned in favour of individual and situational practices and decisions. She believes that Quakerism leads one to choose the first of the above options, and to immerse oneself in the world and to conduct one's life on the basis of Christian principles. This, she believes, separates Quakers from Mennonites and the Czech Brethren whom, she believes, tend to isolate themselves from the world they think is evil.[120]

Franklin says that Quakerism practises discernment according to the "Advices and Queries" of the Religious Society of Friends. She believes that the following precepts from the "Advices and Queries," the spiritual and personal guidance presented at the Society's annual national meetings, illustrate an internally consistent value system as advocated by the Quakers. These include: (i) bring the whole of your daily life under the ordering of the spirit of Christ; (ii) live adventurously; (iii) exercise imagination and sympathy with others; (iv) make your home a place of peace and happiness; and (v) maintain your witness against all war as inconsistent with the spirit and teachings of Christ.[121]

Putting together what Franklin says about belief systems, consistency, and Quaker values, it is clear that she believes anti-militarism flows from the spirit and teaching of Christ. Her Christian belief, therefore, leads her to practise pacifism.

Women and Militarism

In a highly ingenious fashion Franklin makes a connection between women's rights and opposition to militarism. She claims these are but "two sides of the same coin."[122] Her reason for saying this is not hard to locate: there is a link, she believes, between militarism and the hierarchical structures that oppress women. Moreover, in her opinion, this linkage is something perceived by many of the leading advocates of women's rights, including Jane Addams (1860–1935), Sylvia Pankhurst (1882–1960), and Clara Meyer-Weichmann, all of whom were pacifists.[123]

Militarism she defines as the undue prevalence of the military system and as "the ultimate expression of the threat system."[124] She believes that feminist analysis of social structures has revealed to women how hierarchical systems "can threaten any opposition with social and psychological isolation, with economic penalties, and with political blackmail."[125] Since women understand threat systems, they are in a good position to object to them. Franklin sees an unmistakable connection between pacifism and feminism in their desire to rid the world of the noxious beast of militarism and its associated propensity for domination.

Inclusion and Exclusion Caused by Technology

It is important to understand that Franklin's pacifism rejects the participation in war as well as the use of violence for any cause.[126] But her pacifism seeks not just peace but also justice,[127] and for this reason we need to understand what she has to say about difficulties in the access to justice manifested in the involuntary inclusion or exclusion from particular social activities caused by technology. On the side of involuntary inclusion of individuals and its connection with injustice, Franklin notes modern warfare and its technology, which draw no line between soldiers and civilians. People who are entirely innocent and defenceless are treated unjustly. She also notes the insidious role of pollution caused by modern technology and the way it affects everyone, even those who are, once again, quite innocent. So here we have two cases of involuntary inclusion that seem unjust.[128] On the side of involuntary exclusion caused by technology, she draws attention to the displacement of workers caused by machines, dating from the time of the Industrial Revolution. She correctly notes how the democratic socialist, Robert Owen, wrestled with this issue, and the way it impacted principles of justice. She could have added more recent cases, which she does not, in which robots have come to replace assembly-line workers at car manufacturing plants. These examples of involuntary exclusion, from the early days of the Industrial Revolution to the present, Franklin sees as caused by technology, and such exclusion results in injustice to which she, as a Quaker in search of peace and justice, must give attention.

Conclusion

From Origen and his disagreement with Celsus down to Ursula Franklin, there has been an articulate philosophy of pacifism. Not explored here is an element of pacifism as found in Eastern philosophy and religion—for example, that found in the ethics of Jainism, Lao Tzu's *The Way and Its Power*, the Dhammapada, and the Bhagavad-Gita. Predominantly, and notwithstanding these instances to the contrary, pacifism is a political ideology that has been applied with success in India and in various parts of Europe and North America. It would be a mistake to think of it as a Western attitude or ideology, especially when one thinks of figures such as Jesus, Tolstoy, and Gandhi. While it is clear that, since the time of Martin Luther King Jr, this ideology has taken a back seat to the Cold War, the

Vietnam War, the Contra War, the Gulf War, the Iraq War, the Afghanistan War, and many, many others, nonetheless there has remained—largely through groups like the Hutterites, Mennonites, and Quakers—an enduring interest in it. What is evident is that, through the works of recent commentators and advocates in the field, notably through the works of Ursula Franklin as well as Robert Holmes and Barry Gan,[129] a keen and growing interest in ways to resolve conflict peacefully so as to avoid violence of any kind is making its presence felt.

The line of argument pursued by pacifists is a mélange of utilitarian and deontological considerations. It starts with a basic assumption of the intrinsic value of human life and then focuses on militant acts of violence against it. Pacifists slowly widen the focus to include many, if not all, acts of violence, and reject them *in toto* on the largely utilitarian grounds that the cost of such violence exceeds by a wide margin the benefits. While pacifists originally backed up their argument with metaphysical beliefs of a religious nature, modern-day pacifists such as Russell and Huxley have often abandoned such beliefs and instead base their computations in more secular calculations. It should also be pointed out that the line of argument employed by pacifists has changed somewhat in the last 60 years. Ever since the experiences of Hiroshima and Nagasaki, pacifists have been eager to point out the devastating and cataclysmic nature of present-day weapons, a nature that easily works in favour of the denunciation of any military action that would increase the likelihood of their use. What all of this makes clear is that the line of argument pursued by pacifists is multi-dimensional. It includes an axis that distinguishes military violence and non-military violence, another axis that distinguishes the sacred from the secular, and another that distinguishes conventional weapons from nuclear weapons. The line of argument pursued by pacifists is thus varied and nuanced.

Evaluation: The Strengths of Pacifism

1. Pacifism offers a counterweight to both violent conflict (e.g., war) and non-violent conflict. Leaving aside minor conflicts, it is obvious that war has proven to be devastating for humankind. Two developments have contributed to this devastation: (i) professional armies have given way to mass armies, and (ii) technological innovation (think here of Adam Smith's praise of such innovation) has created new deadly weapons of destruction. With respect to the first of these points, one can say that at least between 1648 and 1789 wars tended to occur between professionals, with minimal involvement of civilians. However, following the French Revolution and especially during the Napoleonic Wars, wars became total conflicts and enveloped all citizens. This effectively meant that Rousseau's image of war as a relationship between state and state was negated, and Carl von Clausewitz's image of war as events involving the whole population was triumphant.[130] On the second point, one can say that the inventions of the machine gun, the tank, mines, cluster bombs, nuclear bombs, missiles, aircraft, submarines, chemical and bacteriological weapons, and today drone warfare have radically altered the character of war. Among other things, these technological changes have increased the devastation caused by war and have blurred the lines in casualties between civilians and military personnel, so that in recent years death and injury among civilian populations is euphemistically accounted for by the Orwellian term, "collateral damage." In this context one has only to think

of the bombings of Hiroshima and Nagasaki. Accordingly, war has become a major problem for the species—how to contain it, how to avoid it, and how to bring a resolution to the conflict.

Against all of this stands pacifism. This ideology can say, with conviction and justification, that the destruction of war is so great that it is never justified. This is what motivated the distinguished Aldous Huxley, the celebrated Bertrand Russell, the brilliant Albert Einstein, and the tireless Ursula Franklin to subscribe to anti-militarism. As Huxley says, "The advocates of a policy of unilateral disarmament believe that a genuinely pacifistic gesture by one of the great powers, would profoundly affect public opinion throughout the world and would lead to a measure of general disarmament."[131] In the result, pacifism offers a very different model to be followed in conducting international affairs, at a time when the present model is so fraught with violence.

2. Pacifism, at least in its *satyagraha* form as advocated by Gandhi and as adopted by Martin Luther King Jr, can be effective. Gandhi was successful in using non-violence to combat large-scale social injustice in society and to dislodge the British from India. His philosophy of truth, non-violence, and self-suffering was causally efficacious in producing the desired result. A similar story could be told in the case of King and his use of non-violent resistance to racial discrimination in the United States. In his "Letter from Birmingham Jail," King speaks of the steps he followed in his non-violent campaign on behalf of the blacks of the United States and the injustices to which they were subjected. He speaks of (i) the collection of facts to determine whether injustices exist; (ii) negotiation; (iii) self-purification; and (iv) direct action.[132] His leadership and his method, as outlined in his letter, eventually led to the elimination of state-sponsored social injustices in the form of racial discrimination. Clearly, pacifism can be effective, so much so that in the course of recent human history it has altered the social landscape in countries, as far away from each other as India and the United States, in a dramatic fashion. Other more recent examples could be added to the above list if we include the non-violent resolution of conflict in Eastern Bloc countries as they sought release from the yoke of the Soviet Union. Here one thinks of Poland, Czechoslovakia, Romania, and East Germany.

3. Thinking of the anti-militarism in pacifism, we should consider the following. It is reputed that Einstein once wrote to Sigmund Freud asking him to explain the occurrence of war. Freud's explanation, in response to Einstein's query, was that war was caused by the natural propensity of humankind to violence and inequality.[133] But as Grayling says, Freud's answer is "neither real diagnosis nor real cure. It assumes the naturalness of man's violence towards man, and sees collective aggression as the sum of individual aggression. But neither assumption is convincingly explored."[134] Moreover, it appears that, apart from humans, animals do not prey on each other in a systematic way. So it would seem that whatever explains the occurrence of war has to be sought in areas other than biology, such as psychology, economics, and politics, and the search for wealth, power, and control. All of this works in favour of the pacifism of those opposed to war, because it suggests that war is not inevitable. People as diverse as Thomas Hobbes in the seventeenth century and, as seen in the chapter on reform liberalism, John Maynard Keynes in the twentieth century, have seen peace

as a laudable and achievable goal. As Keynes says, we have taken risks in the interest of war; perhaps it is time to take risks in the interest of peace. This is something with which pacifists from Origen to Ursula Franklin could agree.

4. Pacifism is not logically incoherent, despite protests to the contrary. To see this we need to look at an argument that aims to show that pacifism is incoherent and then refutes it.

Jan Narveson has presented such an argument.[135] According to Narveson, "the pacifist is generally thought of as a man who is so much opposed to violence that he will not even use it to defend himself or anyone else."[136] Narveson continues by asking what we are claiming when we maintain that violence is morally wrong or unjust. He answers by asserting the following: "To say that it is wrong is to say that those to whom it is done have a right not to have it done to them."[137] But according to Narveson, "a right just is a status justifying preventative action. To say that you have a right to X but that no one has any justification whatever for protecting people from depriving you of it is self-contradictory."[138] A few pages later Narveson asks rhetorically, "If a right isn't an entitlement to protection, then is it anything at all?"[139] Linking these claims together, Narveson believes, spells disaster for pacifism. The reason is simple: pacifists believe the use of violence is wrong, and this entails that those to whom it is done have a right not to have it done to them. However, since having a right justifies its bearer's engagement in preventive action—at least enough to stop the violation of the right—it follows, thinks Narveson, that even the pacifist must allow for the use of some violent force, there being some individuals who simply cannot be reasoned with.

What is one to think of Narveson's argument? He is certainly correct in asserting that the pacifist is one who is opposed to the use of violence and will not use it to defend himself or anyone else. In fact, from Origen to Chelčický, the Taborites, the Mennonites, the Quakers, Thoreau, Tolstoy, Gandhi, Huxley, Russell, and Franklin, one hears the refrain that violence is wrong and that it is one's duty not to engage in the use of violence at all. But this would seem to mean both that (i) people have a right not to have violence done to them, and (ii) that people (not just pacifists) have a duty or obligation not to use violence to stop violence. However, if people have a right not to have violence done to them, this means they have a right to engage in preventative action. This much seems correct about Narveson's argument. Civil authorities can be challenged by preventative action such as strikes, walkouts, hartal, and resignation of offices and titles. If they are mugged in a dark alley they can cover their heads and curl up in the fetal position to minimize damage done to them. However, it does not follow that the right not to have violence done to one entails a right to inflict violence on others when this right is violated. This requires a further argument from Narveson, which he does not give. To this extent, then, pacifism has not been shown to be logically incoherent.

As a final point to Narveson's argument, pacifists could respond to Narveson in terms other than human rights, speaking in terms of consequences instead. Here the pacifist could argue that Narveson's rights argument should be set aside and replaced by utilitarian considerations. Simply put, the pacifist would say that violence is not a good strategy: the risks are too high, and the gains too few. Certainly the devastation caused by conflict, especially conflict in war, plausibly supports this claim.

5. Ursula Franklin shows convincingly that pacifism reaches out to touch, surprisingly, the ideology of feminism as well as the role of technology in modern-day society. She recognizes that pacifism is sensitive to hierarchical structures that lead to injustices associated with sexism. She properly points out, on behalf of pacifism, that the tentacles of technology are far-reaching and often the source of deep injustices. Showing that pacifism has the capacity to deal with something other than the historical bread and butter issue of pacifism, namely war, Franklin reveals two theoretical strengths in this ideology: surprise and breadth. In all, Franklin makes a convincing case in favour of ridding society of domination and violence in all its forms.

6. The arguments of Russell and Huxley, coupled with the practical examples of Mohandas Gandhi and Martin Luther King Jr, show that there is much more room for the practice of pacifism than is commonly assumed. Russell and Huxley show persuasively that on a cost/benefit basis there is much to be said, at least in the modern world of high technology, for peaceful approaches to conflict. In other words, the arguments of these two renowned thinkers show that reason supports a great deal more of pacifism than is customarily assumed. Gandhi and King show, through their actions, that pacifism can work and that this ideology does not expect more from human nature than is possible. So, on the basis of reason and human psychology, pacifism is much more defensible than normally assumed.

7. Even in the world of international politics, pacifism has a role to play. This is evident in the actions of former Canadian Prime Minister Lester B. Pearson (1897–1972), who, as a strong advocate of diplomacy and peace, received the Nobel Peace Prize for his work in helping to resolve the Suez Crisis in 1956. His reputation was somewhat sullied when in the early 1960s he bowed to US pressure and allowed Bomarc missiles—which carried nuclear weapons—to be placed on Canadian soil.[140] Later, however, he openly challenged the wisdom of the US war policy in Vietnam in a famous speech at Philadelphia's Temple University in 1965. Though severely and patronizingly chastised by US President Lyndon B. Johnson for this speech, Pearson, in the grand scheme of things, was vindicated years later when former US Secretary of Defense Robert McNamara, who served under Presidents Kennedy and Johnson, admitted that the war in Vietnam was a mistake.

Evaluation: The Weaknesses of Pacifism

1. Pacifism has limited efficacy. While it is true that Gandhi and King were successful in their use of lessons from the Sermon on the Mount, their success seems in part owing to the particular social and constitutional settings in which their pacifism was applied. It is difficult to imagine effective passive resistance when facing the Nazis in Germany, Pol Pot in Cambodia, Joseph Stalin in the Soviet Union, Idi Amin in Uganda, Saddam Hussein in Iraq, or Augusto Pinochet in Chile. It would seem at first blush that the list of situations where it could be practised successfully would be much shorter than the list of situations where it would fail. And a similar story could be told at the local level and outside the field of large-scale international or domestic politics. Even in dealing with the bully on the block, one would be hard-pressed to find many bullies who would respond to the gentle touch of passive resistance as

found in Gandhi's doctrine of *satyagraha*. And, of course, it seems quite implausible to think that the method of *satyagraha* would be effective in combatting those who use violence in promoting prostitution, drug trafficking, or the sex slave trade. While it might be true that some individuals engaged in these activities would be open to changing their attitude towards the world and other people when confronting someone practising the lessons of the Sermon on the Mount, relying on this outcome would not very often be a reliable strategy.

2. The pacifism of Gandhi, King, the Mennonites, the Hutterites, and Franklin suggests that it is linked to religious belief, so much so that it would falter without the belief. This is, of course, not true of the pacifism of Huxley and Russell, who were critical of such belief, but it is true of those listed above. Pacifism so construed becomes problematic in a world of secularism and humanism. It would seem, therefore, that as religious belief diminishes, the appeal of pacifism shrinks.

Related Websites

Cady, Duane L. "Pacifism Is Not Passivism." *Philosophy Now* (June–July 2015).
https://philosophynow.org/issues/105/Pacifism_Is_Not_Passivism.

Moseley, Alexander. "Pacifism." *Internet Encyclopedia of Philosophy.*
www.iep.utm.edu/pacifism/

"Pacifism." *Stanford Encyclopedia of Philosophy.* 14 Aug. 2014.
http://plato.stanford.edu/entries/pacifism/

Pacifist Nation
www.pacifistnation.net/

Peace Pledge Union. "Pacifism."
www.ppu.org.uk/pacifism/

Further Readings on Pacifism

Amster, Randall, Elavie Ndura-Oedraogo, and Michael N. Nagler. *Exploring the Power of Nonviolence: Peace, Politics and Practice.* Syracuse, NY: Syracuse University Press, 2013.

Bellamy, Alex J., and Paul Williams. *Providing Peacekeepers: The Politics, Challenges and Future of United Nations Peacekeeping Contributions.* London: Oxford University Press, 2013.

Betts, Alexander, and Phil Orchard. *Implementation and World Politics: How International Norms Change Practice.* London: Oxford University Press, 2014.

Chenoweth, Erica, and Maia J. Stephan. *Why Civil Resistance Works: The Strategic Logic of Nonviolent Conflict.* New York: Columbia University Press, 2011.

Cockburn, Cynthia. *Anti-Militarism: Political and Gender Dynamics of Peace Movements.* Basingstoke, UK: Macmillan, 2012.

Cracraft, James. *Two Shining Souls: Jane Addams, Leo Tolstoy, and the Quest for Global Peace.* Lanham, MD: Lexington Books, 2012.

Dudouet, Veronique. *Civil Resistance and Conflict Transformation: Transitions from Armed to Nonviolent Struggle*. London: Routledge, 2015.

Genser, Jared, and Bruno Stagno Ugarte. *The United Nations Security Council in the Age of Human Rights*. New York: Cambridge University Press, 2014.

Higgs, Robert. "Tolstoy's Manifest on the State, Christian Anarchy, and Pacifism." *Independent Review* 19, 3 (2015): 471–9.

Hintjens, Helen M., and Dubravka Žarkov. *Conflict, Peace, Security: Theories and Methodologies*. Abingdon and New York: Routledge, 2015.

Hunt, Charles T. *UN Peace Operations and International Policing: Negotiating Complexity, Assessing Impact, and Learning to Learn*. London: Routledge, 2015.

Jahanbegloo, Ramin. *The Ghandian Movement*. Cambridge, MA: Harvard University Press, 2013.

Llewellyn, Jennifer J., and Daniel Philpott. *Restorative Justice, Reconciliation and Peacebuilding*. London and New York: Oxford University Press, 2014.

Paupp, Edward Terrence. *Redefining Human Rights in the Struggle for Peace and Development*. New York: Cambridge University Press, 2014.

Smith, Jackie, and Ernesto Verdeja. *Globalizations, Social Movements, and Peace Building*. Syracuse, NY: Syracuse University Press, 2013.

Sotomayer, Arturo C. *The Myth of the Democratic Peacekeeper: Civil–Military Relations and the United Nations*. Baltimore: Johns Hopkins University Press, 2014.

Staur, Carsten. *Shared Responsibility: The United Nations in the Age of Globalization*. Trans: Steven Harris. Montreal and Kingston: McGill-Queen's University Press, 2013.

Tonge, Jonathon. *Comparative Peace Processes*. Cambridge: Polity Press, 2014.

Wallensteen, Peter, and Anders Bjurner. *Regional Organizations and Peacemaking: Challengers to the UN?* London and New York: Routledge, 2015.

Whalan, Jenny. *How Peace Operations Work: Power, Legitimacy, and Effectiveness*. London: Oxford University Press, 2013.

9 Anarchism

And the lie of Authority
Whose buildings grope the sky:
There is no such thing as the State.

—W.H. Auden, "September 1, 1939" (2007: 95–7)

Learning Objectives

- To appreciate the deep suspicions of the institution of property found in anarchism.
- To understand the radical rejection of the entire apparatus of the state in anarchism.
- To reflect on the rejection of coercion in any form in anarchism.
- To see the antipathy towards Marxism found in anarchism.

In a recent article on voting habits in Canada published in a public policy journal, the author quotes from writings of the anarchist Emma Goldman (1869–1940): "If voting changed anything, they'd make it illegal."[1] This makes clear that anarchism as an ideology still resonates in the minds of some social critics and social activists. The point will become more obvious in what follows, but first we need to learn a little about the background of anarchism.

While **anarchism** shares some common themes with pacifism, the former has distinguishing features that make it a distinctive ideology. Pre-eminent among these are an affirmation of the decency of persons, a thirst for individual freedom, and a complete rejection of domination.[2] Celebrated anarchists, discussed below, are William Godwin (1756–1836), Pierre-Joseph Proudhon (1809–1865), Mikhail Bakunin (1814–1876), Peter Kropotkin (1842–1921), Emma Goldman, and Paul Goodman (1911–1972). The ancestors of these anarchists were the peasants of England and Germany in the fourteenth and sixteenth centuries, respectively, who denounced property and sought equality, albeit of a communal kind. But the pedigree of anarchism also includes within its ambit a cult of individual personality, which appeared in Italy in the fourteenth century, such as in the writings of Dante, and, later, in the work of Protestant reformers, such as the Quaker George Fox, who placed a new emphasis on the value of the individual.[3]

By the seventeenth century, certainly in England, these forces all conspired to advance anarchist ideas in the aftermath of the English Civil War. Central to these ideas were those of individual freedom and authority, the former to be advanced and the latter to be curtailed. The main anarchistic group that existed at this time in England was not the frequently cited **Levellers**, called "Switzerizing anarchists" by a pro-Cromwell pamphleteer,[4] but the **Diggers**, who—as victims of economic recession—sought social and economic goals rooted in equality and directed against the corrupting nature of authority. The Diggers were led by Gerrard Winstanley (1609–1676), an old soldier of the English Civil War, whose own modicum of success in pamphleteering was "fuelled" by the expansion of literacy in England at this time.[5] The Digger doctrine turned out to be a "precursor" of later social ideologies and in its own way anticipated some of the ideas of the first anarchist to be discussed, William Godwin.

Notwithstanding the importance of the historical background of anarchism, it would be a mistake in our study to think of it as an ideology that is long dead. To illustrate this we need only reference and briefly describe the manner in which a kind of anarchism took over the universities in Greece, especially in Athens, after 1973.[6] During the last few months of the Greek dictatorship of the colonels from 1967 to 1973, the regime moved to crush a protest at the Polytechneio on 17 November 1973. Dozens of Polytechneio students were killed by government troops. When the regime fell eight months later, "student radicalism was widely tolerated."[7] What emerged from this tragedy nine years later was legislation passed by the Greek parliament in the form of an asylum clause that "explicitly guaranteed the protection of academic spaces from police incursions."[8] By 1983 a real effort was made by the Rector of the University of Athens to "harmonize the demands of the [student] revolution with the need for continuity and order at Greece's leading university."[9] Nonetheless, as described by a leading Greek journalist, Yannis Palaiologos, in 1985 on the twelfth anniversary of the Polytechneio uprising, tension erupted in violence between police and anarchist students resulting in the death of a 15-year old boy who was shot by police.[10] This was followed by the occupation of the old chemical building by anarchists at the University of Athens, an occupation that ended only with the temporary suspension of the asylum clause of the 1982 higher education law. A similar event occurred 10 years later, in 1995, at the National Technical University, again on the anniversary of the 17 November 1973 uprising at Polytechneio. The 1995 anarchist

Central Beliefs of Anarchism

- Human nature is innocent but corruptible.
- The origin of the state is the lust for power.
- Liberty as an ideal is understood best as negative liberty.
- Equality as an ideal is the equality in the treatment of interests.
- The end of government is its annihilation.
- The right to liberty from the state takes priority over all other considerations.

activities resulted in the vandalizing of "administrators' offices, the School of Fine Arts, laboratories, and classrooms."[11] Once again, the asylum law was temporarily suspended and police were called in to clear the Technical University of its 600 anarchistic occupiers. More could be told pertaining to the legacy of this story, but it is sufficient to note that the above events make evident the role played by those subscribing to a kind of anarchism in universities in Athens.

With the historic overview of anarchism in mind and with the late twentieth-century manifestations of anarchism among the youth in Greek universities in front of us, we can now turn our attention to William Godwin.

William Godwin

Though Digger doctrine was similar to the ideas presented by William Godwin in his *Enquiry Concerning Political Justice* (1793), Godwin himself seems not to have been aware of this fact. Thus, it would be too much to say that the ideas of the Diggers influenced Godwin; at most we can say there is a thematic connection. The Diggers prepared the soil in which the fertile ideas of Godwin sprang to life. Godwin advocated all of what would become the central ideas of anarchistic doctrine, although he did not call himself an anarchist. These ideas included the following: a rejection of a social system that depended on government; an affirmation of a decentralized society with minimal authority; and an affirmation of the voluntary sharing of goods.[12] At the root of these ideas stood a deep and settled hostility to authority and despotism, a point reflected in the poetic words of his equally famous disciple and son-in-law, Percy Bysshe Shelley (1792–1822), who, in his "Song to the Men of England," says,

> Men of England, wherefore plow
> For the lords who lay you low?
> Wherefore weave with toil and care
> The rich robes your tyrants wear?[13]

Shelley captures succinctly the objectionable nature of the "life-destroying propensities of authority," authority that Godwin so vociferously opposed.

Godwin's own life was characterized by much change. Though born the son of a minister of a rural Independent congregation, Godwin over time became a passionate atheist. By 1790 he abandoned his Christian beliefs altogether. Three years later he published his *Enquiry Concerning Political Justice*, and within a few years he married the feminist writer Mary Wollstonecraft (1759–1797). Their daughter, Mary Godwin (later to become famous as the author of *Frankenstein*), subsequently married Percy Shelley. In elucidating Godwin's thought, we shall focus on a few central ideas drawn from *Political Justice*.

Humans' Social Capacity

Godwin wishes to establish the form of political society most beneficial for humankind. How is society to be organized such that it contributes most to personal security, to the general improvement and happiness of individuals, and to the preservation of each individual's operation? These are the questions he asks, almost in the spirit of Rousseau and *The Social Contract*. While not embracing the idea of a social contract,[14] Godwin does embrace, on utilitarian grounds, the idea of society as the most desirable condition of the human species.[15] Human beings seem, to Godwin, to be social animals. Nonetheless, he believes that history shows humans to be the most formidable enemies of each other, a fact demonstrated convincingly by the institution of war.[16] Moreover, Godwin believes that political institutions have a powerful and extensive influence on the character of people, but he seems to hold educational institutions as of even greater importance in this matter.[17] Education shapes the opinions of men and women, and these in turn shape their voluntary actions; in fact, in this respect, Godwin goes so far as to say that in all cases voluntary actions originate in opinion.[18] So Godwin holds educational institutions in high regard in the matter of shaping the characters of people. In their social capacities, therefore, persons appear modifiable.

Government

Nowhere does Godwin present his views on government more clearly than he does in the "Summary of Principles" that guided his work. Therein, Godwin maintains that government arose not from a social contract but from the injustice and violence of men in a social condition. Further, in keeping with his views on voluntary actions and their being rooted in opinion, he asserts that government arises from people's vices, which, for the most part, are rooted in ignorance and mistake. And he adds that while government was initially intended to eliminate injustice, the concentration of force in its hands allows for "wild projects of calamity," oppression, despotism, war, and also conquest. By sustaining the inequality of property, furthermore, government fosters injurious passions and encourages robbery and fraud. Finally, he remarks, by way of rounding out his comments, that government evidently embodies and perpetuates injustice. Though the purpose of government is security, the method employed by government to achieve this objective results in an abridgement of one's independence. Owing to this, Godwin concludes that the most desirable condition for humankind is one that maintains security, but with minimal intrusion upon individual independence.[19]

Property

The subject of property is an integral part of Godwin's conception of political justice. He is convinced that the more nuanced our ideas of this subject are, the more understanding we shall have of, in his words, "a simple form of society without government."

For this anarchist, on the subject of property, two questions arise. The first is: who is the person morally entitled to the use of any particular article? And the second is: who is the person in whose hands articles will be most justly and beneficially vested? To the first of these, Godwin confidently responds in utilitarian language: the person in whose hands a greater sum of benefit or pleasure will result than from any other course of action. To the second, Godwin appears to say three subordinate things: first, the person to whom a greater sum or benefit will result; second, the person who has laboured on the object; and third, the person who is legally empowered to dispose of those things produced by the labour of others. Yet, one must be careful in reaching a conclusion on what exactly Godwin means here. A complete reading of his words shows that he stands by the first general utilitarian point, but that he embraces only the first and second subordinate points and forcefully denounces the third. In other words, he denounces persons who, through renting land, exercising patents or monopolies, or government control of manufacturing, control the products produced by others' labour.

But how, one might ask, does Godwin's talk of property tie into his general anarchistic philosophy? The answer here is ready to hand, in a two-step way. First, he admits that the object or goal of government is the right of private judgment, or, as Godwin sometimes calls it, the right of the exercise of a person's "own discretion." Second, he adds that the idea of property is nothing but a deduction from the right of private judgment. So, like building blocks, private property is built on private judgment, which in turn is built on government, suggesting very strongly that for Godwin private property is built on government. What this seems to imply is that, for Godwin, the institution of private property is rooted in the liberty of thought of a person, a liberty or discretion that is the precondition of virtue and happiness, which in turn is somehow rooted in government. But however much he may defer to this much of the institution of property, he is careful to keep the lid on the institution, and this for the reason that the administration of property can easily degenerate into a spirit of servility, a spirit of fraud, and a spirit of oppression.[20] His reservations about government are greater still. This is evident in his remark that mankind can look forward to the auspicious time of the dissolution of government, the perennial cause of mankind's vices. These same vices are not removable except by the utter annihilation of political government.[21]

How is one to make sense of Godwin's comments on property and government, where he sometimes claims that government is to be done away with but that property, which requires government, is to be preserved? This apparent contradiction can be resolved along the following lines. A residue of the institution of property is to be retained along egalitarian lines, rooted in utilitarian considerations, and grounded in considerations of one's own industry. Beyond this, the institution of property is unjustifiable. But within these narrowly circumscribed boundaries, the institution does not require the venal presence of government. At most it requires a loose federation of independent parishes, each extending its authority over a small territory.[22] About the only apparatus of the modern state that Godwin seems to affirm is that of the jury in order to resolve conflict and, importantly, to attend to offences against justice.

Marriage

Radical anarchistic ideas on the institution of marriage are customarily associated with the name of Emma Goldman, but long before she wrote on the subject William Godwin offered some iconoclastic ideas of his own. Godwin understands marriage as a species of cohabitation, something he sees as destructive of a person's ability to form intellectual operations independent of the operations of other persons.[23] For him, cohabitation has the consequence of shaping persons' opinions into a common mould, something to which he objects with passion. His objection to cohabitation reaches its zenith in his critical attack on the institution of marriage, which he sees as evil and filled with delusions and unrealistic expectations. The institution is, in his opinion, an institution of fraud and monopoly control, the former because it necessitates husband and wife shutting their eyes to the realities around them under the guise of "eternal attachments," and the latter because it facilitates the despotic and possessive treatment of women. Godwin, in fact, criticizes marriage under these terms as the "most odious selfishness."[24]

Pierre-Joseph Proudhon

Following closely on the heels of William Godwin in the history of anarchism is the paradoxical Pierre-Joseph Proudhon, a French thinker of the nineteenth century who contributed seminal ideas on the subjects of property, revolution, and federation. The first of these topics he addresses in 1840, but the events leading up to that year are noteworthy. In July of 1830 the monarchy of Louis-Philippe had been founded amid much liberal fanfare, including the hope that the aims of the French Revolution could be achieved. The expectations at this time in France were that the bourgeoisie as the third estate, as well as the workers, would prosper under the principles of liberty and justice.

For a time, the words "Enrich yourselves"—spoken by François Guizot (1787–1874), leader of the conservative constitutional monarchists—seemed to ring true. But by 1839 unmistakable signs of an economic downturn began to emerge. This resulted in an assassination attempt on the life of Louis-Philippe, the pursuit of Guizot's policies to preserve political stability and bourgeois hegemony, and dismal working conditions for the proletariat. It seemed that the principles of liberty and fraternity were readily converted into principles of egoism on the part of the ruling elite under the influence of Guizot.[25] One of those who came passionately to oppose Guizot was Karl Marx, who considered Guizot—along with Pope Pius IX, Czar Nicholas I, the Austrian politician and diplomat Prince Metternich, French radicals, and German police spies—as constituting the force aimed at exorcising the spectre of communism. But someone else who set his sights on the apologist of the French constitutional monarchy was Pierre-Joseph Proudhon.

Property

In almost Socratic style, Proudhon calls himself by the name Seeker of Truth. In seeking the truth he pronounces his famous words, "Property is theft." This he thinks is the answer to the question, "What is property?" Moreover, he feels there is some parallel between the questions "What is slavery?" and "What is property?" Both questions can be answered without having any appeal to a long explanation. In the case of the former the answer is "murder," for the power over thought, will, and personality is the power over life and death. The analogue to "murder" in the case of the second question is "theft." In almost poetic fashion Proudhon gives us some idea of the method he uses in his search for the truth. He sees himself, as a member of the human race, as a builder of the temple of science, a science that includes both man and nature. Truth reveals itself to everyone, to the Newtons and Pascals of this world today and to shepherds and workers tomorrow, with each adding a stone to the temple under construction. For Proudhon, eternity precedes each of these individuals and eternity follows them all, and "between these two eternities, what is the significance of one mortal that the age should inquire about him?"[26] This rhetorical question is Proudhon's way of disarming those who might be resistant to the unconventional truth he hopes to reveal, applying a method of common sense and making use of an empirical approach.[27]

Early on in his work on property, Proudhon makes clear that the institution of property is defensible only on the ground of justice, and that this leads inevitably to consideration of equality. But this last consideration, thinks Proudhon, leads to the negation of property.[28] There is a prosaic side to the poetic remark "Property is theft," according to Proudhon. Humans are, he thinks, entitled to the things they produce, but not the means of production. Whether one is talking about the hunter, the cultivator, or the fisherman, all are proprietors of their products, but none is the owner of the means of production.²⁹ He says, "The right to the produce is exclusively *jus in re* whereas the right to the means is common, that is *jus ad rem*."³⁰ He later asserts that the labourer retains, even after receiving his wages, a natural right to property—i.e., ownership of that which he has produced.³¹

What Proudhon objects to is the use of property for the exploitation of others, not the right to property (i.e., ownership) in that which one has worked on. Exploitative property he condemns for the simple reason that, as an institution, it does not work, for the following reasons:

i. It demands something for nothing.
ii. It leads to production costs that are more than the property is worth.
iii. It violates the idea that production is proportional to labour, not property.
iv. It is equivalent to homicide.
v. It causes society to devour itself.
vi. It leads to tyranny.
vii. It causes itself to turn against production.
viii. Its power of accumulation is infinite, while exercised over finite quantities.
ix. It is powerless against property.
x. It is the negation of equality.³²

Since, as we have seen, justice is integrally related to equality, the undoing of equality leads to an undoing of justice and hence to the condemnation of property. Property, so construed, turns out to be theft.

Revolution

In 1851 Proudhon published his work *The General Idea of the Revolution in the Nineteenth Century*. In it he argues that the French Revolution of 1789 left its task unfinished, leaving in place of liberty and industrial equality the legacy of authority and political subordination.³³ For the **revolution** to be complete, it is necessary, thinks Proudhon, for people to take seriously the idea of there being no government; hence he believes the question should not be, Monarchy or Republic? But, Government or No-Government?³⁴ In pursuing the idea of anarchy, or no-government, Proudhon defers to reason, where reason is defined as an agreement between intuition and experience. This same reason, when applied politically, results in the formation of the social contract, but a social contract quite distinct from that put forward by Rousseau.³⁵ The social contract Proudhon advocates is not a contract of association in the sense advocated by Rousseau, but a contract of exchange. Moreover, it adds to the liberty of the individual citizen. What Proudhon describes as the incurable misanthropy of Rousseau's contract is replaced by that which completes the revolution: the triumph of reason. This same triumph, through the contract of exchange between people as producers, results in humanity being led to a new system in which there is no government, neither direct nor simplified.³⁶

To summarize Proudhon's view of the Revolution, one can say that he sees the fall of the monarchy in 1789 as the signal for a social revolution that, little by little, led to the substitution of an economic or industrial system for a governmental, feudal, and military system. The industrial system, so understood, is not a form of government, but a constitution of society having economic forces as its organizational basis.[37] Proudhon wholeheartedly supports this new industrial system, grounded as it is on the social contract between free individuals. What results is a society constructed neither on the back of a theory of divine right of kings nor on the back of Rousseau's social contract, both of which are rooted in authority construed as force. This, thinks Proudhon, is a contradiction. Liberty, equality, and fraternity can only be guaranteed by a system of contracts, that is, a network of voluntary agreements among free individuals, which is substituted for a system of laws. When reason prevails in this way, the Revolution will be complete.

Federation

In very innovative terms Proudhon introduces his reflections on constitutions. One should recall that this is a topic well canvassed by philosophical greats such as Plato and Aristotle, and echoed and re-echoed down through the ages in the writings of Machiavelli, Hobbes, Locke, Rousseau, and Montesquieu, to name but a few. But Proudhon's contribution is different—one may say quite original, in fact. He says, in unmistakable terms, that among the constitutions there is but one that reconciles the various demands of justice, order, liberty, and stability. In epigrammatic fashion, he remarks that truth, like nature, is one such constitution, and that it would be odd if this were not so for the mind and for its great work, society.[38] The constitution that stands out above others is that of a **federation**. But to understand what it entails and how Proudhon positions it in the general scheme of constitutions, more needs to be said.

Proudhon is clear in his beliefs regarding political order. It rests on two contrary principles, authority and liberty. These principles are manifest in four, and only four, forms of government: monarchy, communism, democracy, and anarchy.[39] The first two of these are authoritarian regimes, while the second two are liberal regimes. Proudhon clearly favours the second two and, as seen above, favours the anarchic form most of all. In this type of constitutional arrangement, political functions are reduced to industrial functions, and the social order, as a result, emerges solely from transactions and exchanges.[40] In other words, social order emerges from a social contract, distinct from that of Rousseau, in which heads of families, towns, cantons, and provinces or states undertake bilateral and commutative obligations. For Proudhon, in contrast, the contract is made so as to reserve more for oneself, in the form of rights and liberty, than one abandons to others.[41] Such a political contract is what Proudhon calls a federation. He goes so far as to say that "the social contract *par excellence* is a federal contract."[42] Then, to round out his discussion on this new constitutional arrangement, Proudhon makes the following claim: the freest and most moral government is one in which powers are best divided, administrative functions best separated, the independence of groups most respected, and more regional authorities best served by some central authority.[43] Economically, Proudhon's ideas amount to agro-industrial federation; politically, they amount to decentralization. Liberty expands and authority diminishes, with the former fulfilled in the constitutional arrangement of federation.

Mikhail Bakunin

It is in *Statism and Anarchy*, published in 1873, that one best learns of the main ingredients of Mikhail Bakunin's view on anarchism. In fact, this is the only major work he ever managed to complete, other writings of his constituting a bewildering array of letters, speeches, essays, and pamphlets. Contributing to this unevenness in his publications was the fact that Bakunin was pre-eminently an activist anarchist. It was Marx who commented, "Philosophers have hitherto interpreted the world, the point is to change it." But Bakunin, more than Marx, actually lived this slogan.

Perhaps nothing better demonstrates his commitment to a life of action, sometimes foolish action, than his participation in a protest in Dresden, Germany, by Saxon insurgents against the King of Saxony. The protest was based on the desire of the people of Dresden for a federated constitution. While Bakunin had no strong feelings in favour of the protest, he did dislike the King of Saxony and what his regime stood for. Hence, persuaded by no less a person than the composer Richard Wagner, he threw in his lot with the people of Dresden. This impulsive little gesture landed Bakunin in prison, first in Germany, then in Austria, and finally in Russia, where he waited out a sentence that lasted some six years. During this time he developed scurvy, lost his teeth, and became bloated. It is a credit to his iron physical disposition that this prison sentence did not break him.

In time he was permitted by Czar Alexander II to spend his life in exile in Siberia. He spent some four years there before, in his own way, launching on his peripatetic philosophic career by escaping from Russia, travelling to Japan, San Francisco, and New York, and finally London. These exploits and travels, including his escape from Siberia, turned Bakunin into nothing less than a legendary figure, so much so that when he attended the inaugural Congress of the League of Peace and Freedom held in Geneva in 1867, a congress sponsored by John Stuart Mill, Bakunin was received on stage with the applause of some 6,000 delegates.[44] Two years later, in 1869, the conflict between Bakunin and Marx, which had been festering for a number of years, came to a head at the Basel Congress of the International. The difference between these two revolutionary figures centred immediately on the issue of the right of inheritance, with Bakunin demanding its abolition and Marx adopting higher death duties during a transitional phase. But these small differences concealed the real difference between these two influential characters: Marx was an authoritarian socialist, while Bakunin was an anarchistic socialist. These brief historical remarks provide a sufficient background to two important themes of his major work, *Statism and Anarchy*: criticism of Marxism, and fundamental anarchist principles.

Criticism of Marxism

Bakunin's attack on Marx and Marxism is direct and uncompromising. Its core is simply one of asserting a marked propensity on the part of Marx and his followers to be the state's most ardent defenders. As doctrinaire revolutionaries, thinks Bakunin, Marx and his followers have as their objective the overthrow of existing governments and the creation of their own dictatorships on their ruins.[45] Bakunin, in prescient fashion, sees this response of Marx as being almost an act of treachery, for, at a time when sincere revolutionaries ought to be uniting against all states that are filled with malicious self-preservation, Marx and his followers take the side of the state and its supporters against popular revolution.[46]

In addition to critical comments directed against Marx's ideas, Bakunin also directs comments against Marx as a Jew. As a thoroughly political man, Marx, according to Bakunin, is vain, quarrelsome, intolerant, absolute, and "vengeful to the point of madness," as was "Jehovah, the Lord God of his ancestors." So there is perhaps a streak of anti-Semitism in Bakunin's views here. This is echoed again when he compares Marx to the French politician Louis Blanc (1811–1882), saying that "the diminutive Frenchman" influenced Marx "in his threefold capacity as an Hegelian, a Jew, and a German." Bakunin adds that both Blanc and Marx were "hopeless statists" advocating state communism. So while getting in his dig at Marx's statism, Bakunin embellishes this with the rather gratuitous and impliedly negative comment about religion and ethnicity. But Bakunin is quick to point to a list of positive characteristics of Marx to complement the foregoing negative ones. He sees Marx as highly intelligent, learned, voracious in his reading, and correct in advancing the truth that economic fact precedes legal and political right.[47]

Once Bakunin has assessed Marx in these terms, he goes back once again to his concern with a "flagrant contradiction" at the heart of Marx's thinking. The popular government that Marx strives for is nothing but government of the people by a small number of individuals who are elected by the people.[48] For Bakunin, the end is still "the same dismal result: government of the vast majority of the people by a privileged minority."[49] But this privileged minority is, thinks Bakunin, nothing but a dictatorship, which, like all dictatorships, has no other objective than the perpetuation of itself. This so-called "people's state" is nothing but a yoke that creates a form of despotism and slavery. The "people's state" will not be coloured with the desire to liberate the proletariat from the yoke of the bourgeoisie. Bakunin's response to this unpalatable Marxist outcome is simply to declare that liberty will only come from liberty, in other words, from an insurrection of the people and the voluntary organization of the workers from below. In contrast to this vision of Bakunin stands that of Marx, someone Bakunin sees as a Jacobin whose favourite dream is that of a political dictatorship.[50]

Fundamental Anarchist Principles

For Bakunin and his fellow anarchists, the existence of a state necessarily implied domination and slavery. Then, in words reflecting his basic ideas, Bakunin adds, "A state without slavery, open or camouflaged, is inconceivable—that is why we are enemies of the state."[51] In line with other anarchists, Bakunin takes aim at the state. But what is the state for Bakunin? He has a number of answers to this question. On one account the modern state is a military state and an aggressive state. For this reason the modern state has to be big and expansive. But this circular definition of Bakunin's is quickly replaced by a non-circular and sophisticated account that could rival any presented by modern-day Marxists or Marx himself. On this second account, the modern state is military, police, and bureaucratic centralization.[52] All that is lacking in this view of the state to make a fully modern one is the addition of an executive and legislative body, with both of which Bakunin was perfectly well familiar.

So the first plank of Bakunin's anarchism is anti-statism. Another plank in Bakunin's thought is his belief in the irreconcilability of the wild, hungry proletariat, striving as it does for truth, liberty, justice, equality, and fraternity (including some of the ideals of the French Revolution), and the well-fed, educated, and privileged classes defending the state and the military, police, and law that facilitate their class role as economic exploiters.[53] For Bakunin, this irreconcilability means that there is no middle ground, and that doctrinaire revolutionaries such as Marx who wish to have both state structures and revolution are only deluding themselves, and us with them. Such individuals are reactionary by working in the end to consolidate the political and economic privileges of the governing minority and the political and economic domination of the masses. This irreconcilability means that, since revolution from above along Marx's lines means oppression from on high, revolution from below must take its place.[54]

Another plank, a final one, in Bakunin's anarchism, is his deference to the inexhaustible depths of life. Accordingly, Bakunin believes that life trumps abstract thought, and that accordingly not even the abstract thought of the specialized scientist should be used as a blueprint for how society should be organized. Rather, individuals can be happy and free only when they are allowed to create their own lives through the organizing of independent and completely free associations. As a consequence, idealists such as metaphysicians, those who venerate science, and doctrinaire revolutionaries must step aside and give a wide berth to the ship of experience—and, one might add, common sense. Progress for the labouring proletariat will come not by book learning, but only by the accumulation of experience and thought.[55]

With the discussion of Bakunin now complete, it is a favourable moment to pass on to another Russian anarchist, one who would be as troublesome to Lenin as Bakunin was to Marx.

Peter Kropotkin

Peter Kropotkin stands alongside Mikhail Bakunin and Emma Goldman as another famous Russian anarchist. Though he was the son of a high-ranking officer in the Russian military and attracted the favourable attention of Czar Nicholas I for obtaining a place at the most exclusive Russian military school, Kropotkin's promising military career came to an early end as he witnessed in Siberia the sickening effects of autocratic government: salt mines and gold mines where convicts and Polish rebels worked in conditions that produced tuberculosis and scurvy. This experience, coupled with other events he had witnessed, led to his resignation from the Czarist army. Following his resignation, he eventually found his way to Switzerland, which had become the centre of Russian radicals, including those associated with Bakunin. One of Bakunin's followers, Nicholas Zhukovsky, put him in touch with future Bakunin biographer James Guillaume (1844–1916). Guillaume, in turn, directed Kropotkin towards anarchistic ideas in the early 1870s. Though it took several years after this for Kropotkin's ideas to begin to consolidate, by 1877, after time spent in Russia and England, his anarchistic inclination would take on the form of a moral philosophy and move beyond being just a program of social change.[56] This moral philosophy, in a nutshell, affirmed the following propositions:

i. Government is evil.
ii. Society as a whole needs to be transformed.
iii. Free communism needs to replace a system dominated by the state and wage labour.
iv. Capitalism is evil.[57]

When boiled down, these propositions can be discussed under two headings: anti-statism and anti-capitalism. Once these are discussed, something needs to be said about Kropotkin as a man of action.

Anti-Statism

In his *Memoirs of a Revolutionist* (1899) and in *Mutual Aid* (1902), written as a corrective to the point of view advocated by T.H. Huxley, Kropotkin marshals arguments against the state, the police, and central authority and organization. A key focus of his attack on the state is that it has led to the absorption of all social functions, which in turn has "necessarily favoured the development of an unbridled, narrow-minded individualism."[58] Kropotkin sees anarchism as a political ideology that functions as the means "by which justice (that is, equality and reciprocity) in all human relations could be established throughout the world of humanity. This could best be achieved by the complete elimination of the state and all government processes, and their replacement by a free and spontaneous co-operation among individuals, groups, regions, and nations."[59] Kropotkin argues against the spirit of Malthus[60] and Huxley in his advocacy of **mutual aid**, which he believes can be rescued by having recourse to society as a natural phenomenon. This natural entity, when its laws are observed, will allow man to live "without the need for artificial regulations."[61] Kropotkin fears that as the obligations to the state increase, the obligations of citizens to one another decrease, with the result that "men can, and must, seek their own happiness in a disregard of other people's wants."[62] This rugged individualism is one logical outcome of the thinking of Hobbes, Malthus, and Huxley: the struggle of each against all is the leading principle of nature.[63] And Kropotkin sets himself the task of undermining this very principle by showing "the immense part which the mutual-aid and mutual-support principles play even now-a-days in human life,"[64] in addition to the immense role it plays in the animal kingdom: "If we knew no other facts from animal life than what we know about the ants and the termites, we already might safely conclude that mutual aid . . . and individual initiative are two factors infinitely more important than mutual struggle in the evolution of the animal kingdom."[65] By undermining the principle of the struggle of each against all, Kropotkin thinks society as a whole can be transformed, and that free communism can replace a system dominated by the state and wage labour. "For him only spontaneous, self-organised communes, now fashionably known as participatory democracy, based on mutual aid and respect for each person's individuality and person, are practical and realistic."[66]

Anti-Capitalism

Kropotkin's attack on capitalism is oblique. This comes as a surprise from someone who knew Marx as well as he did. Nonetheless, that he rejects capitalism can be seen from the following. He admits that the "movement in favour of communal possession runs badly against the current economical theories."[67] Clearly, his brand of communal ownership represented in mutual aid relationships stands at odds with other competing economic models, which must have included the pre-eminent economic theory of capitalism. And Kropotkin must have seen the linkage between those economic theories that ran counter to communalism, especially capitalism and its industrialization. Hence his attack on industrialization is implicitly an attack on capitalism. Kropotkin remarks, "But as the value of land was increasing, in consequence of the growth of industries, and the nobility had acquired, under the State organization, a power which it never had had under the feudal system, it took possession of the best parts of the communal land, and did its best to destroy the communal institutions."[68] In condemning industrialization Kropotkin is condemning capitalism, for he believed that the emergence of proprietary rights with respect to land, aided by the Industrial Revolution, had the effect of undermining communalism and mutual aid. This is Kropotkin's oblique criticism of capitalism.

Man of Action

Peter Kropotkin was a man of ideas, though it would be going too far to claim, as does Ashley Montagu, that these ideas made Kropotkin's *Mutual Aid* "one of the world's great books."[69] Nonetheless, Kropotkin was indeed a man of ideas, and—just as importantly—a man of action and a man bent on empirical discoveries. To give an illustration of this, one can cite the connection between Kropotkin and the religious movement of the Doukhobors of Russia. A little known fact is that, in 1897, Kropotkin visited Canada for the purpose of attending a meeting of the British Association in Toronto, subsequently travelling to the West and finally reaching Victoria.[70] Some 30 years before this he had visited the Doukhobors on the Amur River in Russia and "admired their mutual aid."[71] When the Doukhobors, who had suffered under the oppression of the Czar's regime, sought refuge in the 1890s in a new country other than Cyprus (a refuge that had proved inhospitable), Kropotkin and Vladimir Chertkov wrote letters to James Mavor, a professor of political economy at the University of Toronto, for the purpose of persuading him to back their idea of settling the Doukhobors in Canada. Mavor, as it turns out, was a "friend and admirer of Kropotkin and Tolstoy."[72] Kropotkin, for his part, emphasized the matters on which the Doukhobors would require assurances: the absence of interference in the internal organization of the sect, the right not to perform military service, and, finally, block land grants similar to those that had been provided to the Mennonites.[73] The support of Chertkov, Tolstoy, and Kropotkin for the Doukhobors encouraged Canada's Minister of the Interior, Clifford Sifton, to accede to their requests for admitting Doukhobors to Canada in October 1898.

Of course, the kind of communal arrangement the Doukhobors practised in Saskatchewan, Alberta, and finally in British Columbia was not the same as that spelled out in Kropotkin's *Mutual Aid*, but nonetheless in this arrangement there were to be found practical intimations of what he had talked about so theoretically in his book. In Canada, the long arm of the state, through its military, was to stand some distance from the Doukhobors. The state treated them in such a way that the Doukhobors became economically self-sufficient through large land grants where they lived in close proximity to each other, and they were given a right to be consulted in the matter of their children's education. Putting all of these together does not result in an association existing in a federated way with other associations, as advocated by Kropotkin in his anarchism; still, there was a partial realization of some of his ideas. One can see from this that Kropotkin has both a theoretical and a practical side to his anarchism, the latter of which reached out and touched Canada.

Emma Goldman

Any survey of anarchism would be incomplete without a discussion of Emma Goldman, who was born in the Russian Empire (in present-day Lithuania) of Orthodox Jewish parents, immigrated to Rochester, New York, at the age of 16, and lived a peripatetic life of political revolutionary activism—editing magazines and papers, pamphleteering, and not infrequently being arrested and imprisoned. Though attracted to the communist anarchism of Peter Kropotkin, she presents a different version of anarchism. It is said of her that she combines his ideal of a society with a strong Nietzschean individualism.[74] Goldman opposes the state, government, church, big business, conventional marriage, and male sexism; she supports the people, unions, and freedom.

Opposition to Big Business, the Church, and the State

One finds in Goldman, as in Kropotkin, a fusion of ideas and actions. This fusion is evident in her rejection of three institutions: big business, the church, and the state. Goldman's courage in taking on big business in the United States is exemplified by the support she gave the workers of the Amalgamated Association of Iron and Steel Workers at Homestead, Pennsylvania, in its dispute in 1892 with the Carnegie Steel Company of Andrew Carnegie, who had turned the entire management of the company over to Henry Clay Frick. With strikebreakers in tow, heavily armed Pinkerton security men opened fire on a number of Homestead men, killing several. Goldman then conspired with her friend and lover, Alexander (Sasha) Berkman (1870–1936), to kill Frick. Their efforts were unsuccessful, but it did not prevent her from being hunted and arrested by authorities.[75]

Goldman's opposition to the church is evident in her comments when she was interrogated after being incarcerated. She remarks, "I was just as opposed to the Catholic as to the other Churches. I considered them all alike, enemies of the people."[76] And it is evident in her comment made at a public rally: "I do not believe in God, because I believe in man. Whatever his mistakes, man has for thousands of years past been working to undo the botched job your God has made."[77]

In addition to her iconoclasm in the field of religion, one can find outright attack upon the state by her willingness to endorse assassination of some rulers, such as the Russian Czar. As her notoriety grew throughout the United States in the latter part of the 1890s, so did her fame as she delivered lectures on the New Woman, the Absurdity of Non-Resistance to Evil, the Basis of Morality, Freedom, Charity, and Patriotism.[78] And her passionate defence of liberty against the state is seen in her remark following the passage of the federal anti-anarchist immigration law: "Too late did the lukewarm liberals realize the peril of this law to advanced thought."[79] Passed in 1903 in the aftermath of the assassination of President William McKinley, an assassination for which she was briefly implicated, this law would have the effect of excluding the likes of Tolstoy and Kropotkin from the shores of America.[80]

Radicalism on Social Issues

Added to the foregoing list of items in Goldman's anarchism are the following radical positions on social issues: opposition to war, promotion of freedom in love, endorsement of birth control, as well as the approval of homosexuality.[81] Illustrative of only the first of these was her effort to lead the anti-conscription campaign expressing her opposition to the declaration of war by the United States during World War I. For her opposition she was charged with treason, and her response to her official treatment at the hands of the state was typical: "We did not believe in the law and its machinery, and we knew that we could expect no justice."[82] In the result, Judge Julius Mayer sentenced Goldman and other anarchists to two years in jail and a $10,000 penalty. In issuing his judgment, Mayer made clear, "In this country of ours [the United States] we regard as enemies those who advocate the abolition of our government and those who counsel disobedience of our law by those of minds less strong."[83] The judge was focusing on Goldman when he said these words, so one can conclude that it was not just her anti-war ideas that made her a pariah of the state, but evidently her vocal opposition to the state's laws, its legal system, its government, and in fact the state itself with all its repressive elements.

Perhaps nothing better illustrates Goldman's view of the pathological nature of the state, exemplified by her adopted country, than her comment on the reaction of authorities there after America entered the Great War. She says, almost as an aside,

> America, only seven months in the war, had already outstripped in brutality every European land with three years' experience in the business of slaughter. Non-combatants and conscientious objectors from every social stratum were filling the jails and prisons. The New Espionage Law turned the country into a lunatic asylum, with every State and Federal official, as well as a large part of the civilian population, running amuck.[84]

In fact, it was under this Espionage Act that Goldman, Berkman, and others were arrested and jailed in 1917 for their outspoken views against military conscription. But Goldman's opposition to the state was not limited to her opposing the American state: shortly after her release from prison in 1919 she was deported to the post-revolution Soviet Union, where she became disillusioned with what she saw and proclaimed, "In no country have the anarchists ever begged favours from the government, nor do they believe in loyalty to the State."[85] It is small wonder that, notwithstanding her close ties to Lenin, she progressively distanced herself from the state he went on to construct. Her anti-statism enveloped all states, democratic and totalitarian. In later years she travelled widely and spoke in support of radical causes in England, France, and Canada, and soon after the Spanish Civil War broke out in 1936, and shortly after Berkman died, she went to Spain to join the Spanish anarchists in their fight against the Nationalist forces of the state. After some time back in England, she moved to Canada in 1939, where she died the following year in Toronto.

Paul Goodman

It would be remiss, in any discussion of anarchism in the last century, not to mention the name and ideas of Paul Goodman. During the mid-twentieth century in the United States he contributed innovative ideas on civil disobedience and decentralization in the field of education, as well as the physical planning of communities. All of these are tinged with anarchistic thinking. His views on the physical planning of communities will be discussed below, with an attempt to tease out of his comments the flavour of his anarchistic thinking. One must proceed somewhat tentatively here for the reason that his major work, *Communitas* (1947), reads more like a community planning guide than a treatise on anarchism. Nonetheless, there is always a hint of anarchism in his suggestions, and the practical aspect of his thinking, especially as an anarchist, makes it worthy of at least some attention. The following examination of Goodman's thought is based on his ideas expressed in *Communitas*, as well as two essays, "Reflections on the Anarchist Principle" and "Anarchism and Revolution."

The Conditions of Planning

According to Goodman, every community plan is based on technology, standard of living, political decision, and the geography and history of the place. He contends that unless all these conditions are analyzed together, a plan will fail.[86] Special emphasis is placed on technology, at least in the present context, for technology has changed into what Goodman calls surplus technology, which is characterized by plasticity and flexibility. Technology is plastic if it embraces a variety of productive capacities, and it is flexible if it changes and improves rapidly. Surplus technology is different from surplus economy, yet the former contributes to the latter and itself is connected to the notion of standard of living.[87]

Goodman's deep conviction is that two things, coupled with a lack of "direct relationship" between them, have contributed to making much of external life "morally meaningless." These two things are (i) the multiplication of commodities and the false standard of living, and (ii) the complication of economic and technical structure in which one works at a job.[88] Goodman seems to want planned societies directed towards a standard of minimum subsistence, the very point of which is to free people so they can make selective choices on how they will regulate their time. While Goodman favours making government's business as minimal as possible, he does acknowledge that meeting the minimum subsistence level might require political decisions that are somewhat coercive, as in the case of having a universal labour service that would be like periods of military training. Goodman is of the firm belief that if freedom is the aim, which he thinks it is, then community planning should eliminate everything beyond the minimum, where the minimum would produce and distribute the following: food sufficient in quantity and kind for health, uniform clothing for all seasons, shelter, medical services, and transportation.[89] Anchoring this minimalism is Goodman's commitment to what seems an anarchistic principle: the rejection of intermediary services, of expenditure that is neither production nor consumption, and of time wasted in transportation that has no other advantages.[90]

Valuable Behaviour and Freedom

For Goodman, anarchism is rooted in the following proposition extracted from his "Reflections on the Anarchist Principle": "valuable behaviour occurs only by the free and direct response of individuals or voluntary groups to the conditions presented by the historical environment."[91] He goes on to assert that anarchism proposes that more harm than good is done by coercion (found in top-down direction, central authority, states, bureaucracy, jails, conscription, standardization, and excessive planning), and, owing to this, anarchists wish to increase "intrinsic functioning" and diminish "extrinsic power." Moreover, he sees this coercion in multiple areas of human affairs—religious, political, economic, military, moral, and pedagogic.

Goodman thinks that the aforementioned anarchist principle of free and direct response, as opposed to coercion, far from being a principle predicated on "utopia" or a "glorious failure," is largely vindicated. In his opinion, it has proven itself in the free enterprise of joint stock companies in the mercantile period, the Jeffersonian Bill of Rights and independent judiciary, Congregationalist churches, progressive education, the free cities in the feudal system, and the civil rights movement of the 1960s in the United States.[92] For Goodman, in their time and in their place, all of these developments were anarchistic. Goodman subscribes to, in his words, a relativistic view of anarchism, meaning he believes that all of these anarchistic instances were thought by their opponents to be ushering in chaos. They were once thought to be anarchistic, but no longer are so perceived. Therein rests anarchism's relativity.

Freedom

Goodman construes freedom as the absence of coercion. But he is quick to point out that freedom, so defined, is not safeguarded by "eternal vigilance." Something else—the extension of freedom—is required. His point is simply that unless freedoms are extended, no amount of vigilance will help. The reason for this, as found in Goodman's "Anarchism and Revolution," is that those in positions of power (e.g., the authorities of the state, military, bureaucracy, church, or corporation) "always have the advantage of organization and state resources."[93] Those in positions of power have access to new technologies (e.g., computerized Interpol), to co-opted labour leaders, and to a triumphant science. The result of this is that we shall always have new freedoms to fight for, and in the present context this may include a right to a functioning and healthy natural environment.[94] Goodman recognizes that anarchists have disagreed about the conditions that encourage freedom. Bakunin, he believes, relied on the unemployed and alienated, while Kropotkin relied on the competent, independent, and highly skilled. Goodman favours moving more in the direction of Kropotkin's anarchism in his examination of the conditions that encourage freedom.

The foregoing provides a brief overview of the position Goodman takes in three representative works. In *Communitas*, Goodman writes deliberately from a dialectical perspective (with questions and possible answers),[95] so it is difficult to pin down exactly what he wishes to assert there. In this respect he is much more elusive than other anarchists. Nonetheless, as he addresses community planning, Goodman seems to echo anarchistic themes of freedom, minimal government, mutuality, and smallness. His later publications, "Reflections" and "Anarchism and Revolution," spell out more clearly his anarchistic understanding of freedom as absence of coercion, his understanding of the linkage between valuable behaviour and absence of coercion, and his belief that anarchism has been successful at different times in human history. Given this appreciation of Goodman, one can see that implicit in *Communitas* is a rejection of excessive community planning. Clearly, in all of this, Goodman leans towards a Kropotkin-like optimism with respect to the potential of human beings.

Conclusion

The themes emphasized by the anarchists discussed here, from Godwin to Goodman, include an affirmation of human decency and human freedom together with a categorical rejection of domination and coercion. The first of these three themes is manifest in Godwin's deference to man's social capacity and the importance and efficacy of education, in Proudhon's optimism about human reason, in Bakunin's endorsement of the inexhaustible depth of human life, in Kropotkin's relentless support of social causes, in Goldman's commitment to social organizing and activism, and in Goodman's willingness to tackle community planning issues using the dialectical (question and answer) method and in his consideration of valuable behaviour and freedom. The themes of human freedom and rejection of domination and coercion are tied together and dealt with by each of the anarchists, sometimes in terms of the institution of property, sometimes in terms of voluntary agreements of exchange, and quite often in terms of an open and undiluted criticism of the very existence of states and governments. Clearly, for anarchists, property, governments, and states function as structures of authority that dominate humans, and for this reason they reject these social structures. Freedom, by contrast, is promoted, they believe, by transactions conducted between individual workers. Hovering in the background for many, though not all, of these anarchists is a rejection of big business, capitalism, marriage, and the church, as well as a clarion call for federalism, free love, acceptance of homosexuality, and minimal subsistence. What these anarchists offer by way of a political ideology is something more sweeping than the democratic socialist societies imagined and constructed by Robert Owen and something much more radical than the proletarian society put forth by Karl Marx.

The line of argument pursued by anarchists is predicated on individual freedom, and this notion is used to justify unwillingness to comply with the directives of the state or any other organization wielding authority. Liberty or freedom trumps everything else in anarchism even more so than it does in libertarianism. The latter ideology shows deference to the minimal state, whereas the former does not. The latter ideology shows deference to law and order, whereas the former does not. This line of thinking is replete throughout anarchist literature. Further, there is a general assumption within anarchism that humans have within themselves all those attributes that make them capable of living in peace and freedom. As for tactics to be used by anarchists who appeal to this line of argument, the term that comes to mind is "direct action." This notion embraces, for the anarchist, the general strike, as well as resistance to military service and, in the case of some anarchists, violence. Certainly, when workers use direct action in their confrontations with government, they are employing a weapon of anarchism.[96] Such was the case during the winter of 2009 on the French island of Guadeloupe in the Caribbean, where protestors ransacked shops and burned vehicles as a general strike verged on outright revolt. And such was the case in France itself, where 2.5 million people took to the streets on 29 January 2009 as part of a general strike aimed at persuading President Nicolas Sarkozy to better protect jobs and consumers during the global economic meltdown.[97] What makes the general strike and violence of the French protests a part of anarchist activity is the fact that, whether talking about mass action or individual action, "they are based on direct individual decisions."[98]

Evaluation: The Strengths of Anarchism

1. Anarchism challenges conventional thought regarding the virtues of the state. If anything, it forces one to think seriously about the questions of why we have government and why we have state structures at all. It forces one to think of questions of authority and legitimacy in the spirit of those in the seventeenth century who had to come to grips with these questions with the demise of the divine right of kings. Thinking about authority and legitimacy is essential if government and state structures are not to be corrupted. Furthermore, thinking about each of these is a way of re-energizing

the commitment of citizens to their body politic. For instance, today in most democratic states, voter turnout is diminishing. Few social commentators see this as a good or healthy sign, yet they seem equally helpless in offering solutions on how this trend is to be reversed. It is suggested here that until such time as we think seriously about the kinds of issues raised by anarchists, apathy among the electorate will likely continue. Somehow, then, to steal a turn of phrase from Marx, democracy seems to carry within it the seeds of its own destruction. The remedy for this is, in part, a thorough examination of why we should (or should not) support government and the state. And anarchism undertakes this very examination.

2. Transparency and accountability are considered, by modern-day critics of democratic states, to be traits of a healthy democracy. The emphasis all anarchists place on mutual aid groups (Kropotkin) or groups established by voluntary agreements (Proudhon), which in turn are federated in a loose kind of way (Proudhon and Godwin), free of false standards of living (Goodman), and not subject to the directives of some distant authority (Bakunin and Kropotkin), allows for a practical and direct way of realizing these traits. As anyone who has lived in a village knows, transparency and accountability tend to be features of small communities. In such communities everyone knows everyone else and, consequently, anonymity is simply lacking. Instead, one has transparency, not because of the virtues of the people involved, but simply because of the difficulty of concealing the truth. With this demographic openness comes a kind of demographic accountability. The pedophile or thief is not only more readily detected, but also more easily held accountable by the community for crimes committed.

3. The importance anarchists place on the institution of property as a force that influences the shape of societies and the connection anarchists make between this institution and government are quite in order. It has been said by a celebrated figure of the past, "Wherever there is great property, there is great inequality," and "Where there is no property . . . civil government is not so necessary."[99] One would be excused if she thought this the remark of Jean-Jacques Rousseau rather than the father of economics, Adam Smith. This aside, one can say quite confidently that Proudhon, Bakunin, Kropotkin, and Godwin would be quite supportive of Smith's line of thinking. They would, of course, go further and denounce the institution, but inasmuch as they agree with Smith they affirm something that has come to be widely accepted even outside anarchistic circles.

4. Anarchists are correct, too, in holding that individuals in general are the best judges of their interests. For this reason most, if not all, anarchists want government off their backs and individuals free to make their own decisions. Hence Kropotkin talks about mutual aid, Proudhon talks about voluntary exchanges by labourers, and Godwin speaks of the loose federation of parishes, all in the name of preserving the freedom of the individual. Once again, this position enjoys considerable support, from Adam Smith to John Stuart Mill. Smith claims, "But the law ought always to trust people with the care of their own interest, as in their local situations they must generally be able to judge better of it than the legislator can do."[100] And Mill claims, "Speaking generally, there is no one so fit to conduct any business, or to determine how or by

whom it shall be conducted, as those who are personally interested in it."[101] So the anarchists, in their view of human nature and their confidence in persons' ability to judge correctly in things affecting themselves, are in good company.

5. There is a prescience in anarchistic thinking that challenges societal conventions such as marriage, monogamous sex, contraception, anti-abortion, and fear of homosexuality. From Godwin to Goldman, there is a persistent tendency for most, if not all, anarchists to question traditional customs and beliefs associated with these areas. It is clear that with respect to a sexual revolution, their views have been largely vindicated in the case of abortions and contraception. Huge strides have also been taken with respect to combatting prejudice against homosexuals. As for the institution of marriage, the longevity of contemporary persons and the unrealistic expectations that are formed when young couples enter matrimony make this institution vulnerable. This was seen long before the anarchists. Surprisingly, John Locke made the point in 1690 when he said, "But tho' these ties upon mankind, which make the conjugal bonds more firm and lasting in man, than the other species of animals; yet it would give one reason to enquire, why this compact, where procreation and education are secured, and inheritance taken care for, may not be made determinable, either by consent, or at a certain time, or upon certain conditions, as well as any other voluntary compacts, there being no necessity in the nature of the thing, nor to the ends of it, that it should always be for life."[102] Once again, anarchists of the ilk of Godwin and Goldman are in prestigious company. Deferring to reason, anarchists ask, in the spirit of Locke, why this compact of marriage should always be for life.

6. Kropotkin's theory of human nature, sometimes resonating in Godwin, Goldman, and Goodman, appears evidentially and ethically more attractive than the egoistical individualism of Hobbes and libertarians who have followed in his wake. Kropotkin recognizes correctly that humans who are independent, skilled, and competent have considerable potential both as individuals and as members of a community, and that there is plenty of room for mutual aid.

Evaluation: The Weaknesses of Anarchism

1. Anarchism suffers from too much optimism. It is difficult not to admire Kropotkin's intellectual tenacity in combatting the ideas of Malthus and Darwin and Huxley with their concomitant pessimism. Nonetheless, there are problems with his optimism that, after a century, force us to be less shrill when speaking of him. It is to the credit of Mancur Olson, a public choice theorist, that he shows the necessity of sounding a more mellow note when he traces a thematic connection between public choice thinking and that of anarchists like Kropotkin, Godwin, and Proudhon. Writing from the perspective of the public choice school, a school to be examined in Chapter 10, Olson makes the following observation that bears upon anarchistic thinking. He says, "The anarchistic assumption that in the absence of the oppressive state a natural, spontaneous unity would spring up to take its place is now regarded as evidence of a hopeless eccentricity."[103]

   It would appear Olson is hasty in his remark. While it might be overly optimistic to assume that spontaneous, robust, morally sensitive associations would spring up, it is not rash to assume that protective associations of the like suggested by Robert Nozick would come into being.[104] One would not have to assume a world as wholly venal as Hobbes's state of nature to believe that protective associations would evolve. If a warlike group such as the Vikings or Huns were to spring into action out of predatory motives, this would be sufficient to lead other rational individuals to seek membership in some protective association. So Olson is correct that it is far-fetched to assume that some kind-hearted communal association necessarily would develop once the state was overthrown, but it would seem incorrect on his part to think that no protective associations would appear. Indeed, if social contractarians of the past were correct in anything at all, it was in asserting that rational agents would be driven to form protective associations. This is, in fact, the position of political thinkers as diverse as Hobbes, Locke, and Rousseau.[105]

Consideration of Olson's view of anarchists is of assistance in advancing the discussion. Olson helps to show that the anarchist is probably correct in his or her belief of the emergence from a state of nature to a minimalist mutual aid society, but that the anarchist is incorrect in asserting the inevitability of a robust, morally sensitive version of these. Emma Goldman spent her entire life working for anarchistic causes, but only in her last years, when she entered the cause of Spanish anarchists during the Spanish Civil War, did she encounter communal, collectivist, and mutually supporting comradeship. This may happen or it may not happen. But nothing makes it inevitable. However, none of what Olson says delivers a knockout punch to anarchism. None of this shows the preference of the modern democratic state to the mutual aid societies of Kropotkin or the loose federation of parishes of Godwin. What would show this?

The compelling argument in favour of the modern state can be stated as follows. Predatory protective associations have existed in the past; the Vikings and Huns are good examples of these.[106] In the past, such predatory associations could be met with force through the use of collaborative or federative protective associations, as in the Iroquois Confederacy. These did not make use of professional or standing armies. However, with the rise of modern science and the accompanying industrial and informational revolution, protective associations of a predatory nature can only be resisted by standing military machines. In present history, only the most ardent pacifist would be prepared to lay down all his military might and trust his fate to the National Socialists' Wehrmacht, Idi Amin's troops, Saddam Hussein's military guard, or Stalin's Red Army.

What tips the balance in favour of the modern state—in spite of the success of the anarchist movement in southern Italy and in Andalusia and Catalonia in Spain, as well as those listed by Goodman (Congregationalist churches, joint stock companies, the free cities in the feudal system, and the 1960s civil rights movement in the United States)—is the fact of our living in an industrial and technological era in which the predatory motive is abetted by vast military resources. What this shows, I suggest, is that a rational person is driven in the present context to prefer the modern democratic state to Kropotkin's mutual aid associations or Godwin's loose federation of parishes. It is the mix of predation and industrialization that tips the balance in favour of the modern state over mutual aid associations and loose federations of parishes. The rational equilibrium point is not that of a loose federation of mutual aid associations, but the modern industrialized democratic state.

But what is this modern political state that trumps so ably the federation of associations envisaged by anarchists? It is a political arrangement characterized by legalism, military power, bureaucracy, parliamentary and executive branches, and control over the major levers of the economy. Each of these needs to be explained to show how the state—a democratic state—captures the high ground in competition with a Proudhon-like federation of associations.

Legalism is understood as comprising a system in which:

i. Law has a paramount sanctity.
ii. The individual is a citizen in the sense of enjoying rights to life, liberty, and property.
iii. Culpability is personal.
iv. Some limitation is placed on the ruler.
v. A distinction is drawn between private and public law.
vi. Individuals are empowered to sue the Crown or state.[107]

Military power means a standing army. Bureaucracy refers to the administrative arm of government responsible for implementing the law enacted by the legislative body. Parliament refers to a body of government, elected by citizens, and an elected executive is the nerve centre of government. Finally, control over the economy does not mean control over the private sector in all its transactions, but it does mean the existence of a central bank with monetary control. This is what is meant by a democratic state, which captures the high ground in competition with the anarchists' federation of associations. Given predation and industrialization, a rational person will be drawn to a protective association of this type. This is the line of reasoning that ultimately leads to the undoing of anarchism.

2. The preconditions for anarchist success are insurmountable.[108] Notwithstanding the success stories that Goodman speaks of (e.g., the Congregationalist church, joint stock companies, free cities under feudal law), and that others speak of (Andalusia and Catalonia in Spain), there is little or no reason to believe in the demise of hierarchical and coercive state-like structures. Unquestionably, the modern-day state—the state that emerged with the signing of the Treaty of Westphalia—is challenged by a number of issues (economic, environmental, and human rights, to name three); this is no reason, however, for believing that its coercive power is seriously impaired and about to be replaced by co-operative organizations in parishes (Godwin), or mutual aid societies (Kropotkin), or some federated arrangement of such parishes or societies (Proudhon). Furthermore, if there is any impairment of state coercive power, it is at the hands of super-sovereign entities like the European Union in Brussels or the North American Free Trade Agreement (NAFTA), with its commissions in Dallas, Montreal, and Mexico City. In short, if there has been a "piercing of the veil of sovereignty" of states, it shows no sign of significantly empowering civil society at the expense of governing structures. Some modest impairment of state power can be attributed to civil society through its use of social media, as occurred in the Arab Spring in Egypt in 2011, as well as in British Columbia in 2015 and 2016 in the matter of the Northern Gateway oil pipeline. But these are, at best, modest achievements. The Arab Spring did not manage to bring

permanent change to state power in Egypt but only a brief interlude, after which it was "business as usual." As for the civil resistance to the Northern Gateway, this has perhaps blocked the export of oil from Alberta through BC, but the jury is still out regarding what will eventually be done with tar sands oil. So, while the "veil of sovereignty" has been pierced this is largely attributable to super-sovereign entities rather than to civil society.

Related Websites

Bufe, Chaz. *Anarchism: What It Is & What It Isn't*. See Sharp Press.
www.seesharppress.com/anarchismwhatis.html

Chomsky, Noam. "Notes on Anarchy" (1970).
www.chomsky.info/articles/1970----.htm

Ehrlich, Carol. "Socialism, Anarchism and Feminism" (1977). The Anarchist Library.
http://theanarchistlibrary.org/library/carol-ehrlich-socialism-anarchism-and-feminism

"William Godwin." *Stanford Encyclopedia of Philosophy*. 13 May 2013.
http://plato.stanford.edu/entries/godwin/

Panarchy: A Gateway to Selected Documents and Web Sites
www.panarchy.org/indexes/anarchy.html

Further Readings on Anarchism

Avrich, Paul, and Karen Avrich. *The Anarchist Odyssey of Alexander Berkman and Emma Goldman*. Cambridge, MA: Belknap Press of Harvard University Press, 2012.
Bader, Ralf M., and John Meadowcroft. *The Cambridge Companion to Anarchy, State, and Utopia*. Cambridge and New York: Cambridge University Press, 2011.
Carter, April. *People, Power, and Political Change: Key Issues and Concepts*. London and New York: Routledge, 2012.
Davies, William. *The Limits of Neoliberalism: Authority, Sovereignty and the Logic of Competition*. London: Sage, 2014.
Davis, Laurence, and Ruth Kinna. *Anarchism and Utopianism*. Manchester: Manchester University Press; New York: Palgrave Macmillan, 2009.
Dixon, Chris. *Another Politics: Talking Across Today's Transformative Movements*. Foreword by Angela Y. Davis. Berkeley: University of California Press, 2014.
Evrigenis, Ioannis D. *Images of Anarchy: The Rhetoric and Science in Hobbes's State of Nature*. New York: Cambridge University Press, 2014.
Gornick, Vivian. *Emma Goldman: Revolution as a Way of Life*. New Haven: Yale University Press, 2011.
Jensen, Richard Bach. *The Battle against Anarchist Terrorism: An International History, 1878–1934*. Cambridge and New York: Cambridge University Press, 2014.
Kazmi, Zaheer. *Polite Anarchy in International Relations Theory*. New York: Palgrave Macmillan, 2012.
Klausen, Jimmy Casas, and James R. Martel. *How Not to Be Governed: Readings and Perspectives from a Critical Anarchist Left*. Lanham, MD: Lexington Books, 2011.

Laudani, Raffaele. *Disobedience in Western Political Thought: A Genealogy*. Cambridge and New York: Cambridge University Press, 2013.

Leeson, Peter T. *Anarchy Unbound: Why Self-Governance Works Better Than You Think*. New York: Cambridge University Press, 2014.

Morrow, James D. *Order within Anarchy: The Laws of War as an International Institution*. New York: Cambridge University Press, 2014.

Perry, Lewis. *Civil Disobedience: An American Tradition*. New Haven: Yale University Press, 2013.

Scott, James C. *Two Cheers for Anarchism: Six Easy Pieces on Autonomy, Dignity, and Meaningful Work and Play*. Princeton, NJ: Princeton University Press, 2012.

Shantz, Jeff. *A Creative Passion: Anarchism and Culture*. Newcastle upon Tyne, UK: Cambridge Scholars, 2010.

———. *Active Anarchy: Political Practice in Contemporary Movements*. Lanham, MD: Lexington Books, 2011.

———, and Dana M. Williams. *Anarchy and Society: Reflections on Anarchist Sociology*. Leiden, The Netherlands: Brill, 2013.

Smith, William. *Civil Disobedience and Deliberative Democracy*. Milton Park, UK: Routledge, 2013.

10 Neo-Liberalism and Libertarianism

Learning Objectives

- To comprehend the basic principle that all coercive action of government is limited to general rules of just conduct in neo-liberalism.
- To acknowledge the basic principle that all actors are rational utility maximizers, especially in the public choice version of neo-liberalism.
- To recognize that virtually all welfare state benefits are deliverable as private goods, especially in the New Right version of neo-liberalism.
- To appreciate the self-interested and rational presuppositions found in the anti-statism of libertarianism.
- To engage the idea that contractarianism, which rejects intuition and utilitarianism, is foundational for morality in libertarianism.

Whereas anarchism rejects the state in its entirety, seeing it as venal and destructive, neo-liberalism and libertarianism affirm the state, albeit a minimalist one. **Neo-liberalism** tends to direct its attention towards the market, while **libertarianism** tends to focus on the rights of individuals, especially property rights, in defining the minimalist state. From this it is evident that neo-liberalism carries one in the direction of economic considerations and libertarianism leads one towards legal and political issues. Nonetheless, these differences of emphasis should not obscure the common thread running through both of them, that is, their opposition to a large role played by the state in the lives of individuals. In this respect, Jan Narveson is correct when he says, "Libertarianism is one kind of liberalism."[1] Indeed, in the political world one sometimes sees these two ideologies coming together, as in the case of Mark Sanford, the former Republican governor of South Carolina who, in espousing economic libertarianism, threatened to reject the US Congress's $700 million stimulus bailout for his state.[2] Sanford's case makes clear that, owing to their emphasis on minimalism, these ideologies deserve to be considered together. But not just in the United States does one see the impact of neo-liberalism and libertarianism. The same is readily found in Canada. This is a point made in convincing fashion by Nora Loreto in an engaging article in the *Monitor* in 2015, a publication by the Canadian Centre for Policy Alternatives.[3] She argues that neo-liberal attacks have proven to be relentless over the past 30 years, leaving no public service or civil employee untouched. And she echoes quite explicitly the position taken by Paul Verhaeghe, writing in the *Guardian* newspaper, who asserts the success of neo-liberal policies in changing the norms and values that help define who we are. Loreto ends by saying the consequence of enduring neo-liberal policies in Canada is, among other things, a reduction in voter turnout by young people as well as reduction among these same people in participating in formal democratic structures.

There is more to the Canadian story than the above words suggest. Speaking of the recent libertarian Conservative government of Stephen Harper, Heather Mallik notes that it resulted in lowered consumption and income taxes, pushed through mandatory minimum jail sentences, escalated the war on drugs, created a more expensive military, eliminated the long-form census, killed the long-gun registry, undermined environmental rules, eliminated accountability, and was well on the way to eliminating the Canadian Broadcasting Corporation and eviscerating the national health-care system.[4] Whether these observations by Loreto and Mallik are correct is not the point of the present line of thought. Rather, it is to show that neo-liberal and libertarian ideas are in the air and that this ideology plays a significant role in the political narratives now being told, not just in the United States but also in Canada.

The starting point for our discussion is neo-liberalism, an ideology that in so many ways is a throwback to the days of John Locke and Adam Smith. To say this is to say that neo-liberalism is a return to classical liberalism and the night watchman approach to politics, with its emphasis on negative liberty. The meaning of **negative liberty** employed here is the one famously developed by Isaiah Berlin (1909–1997) in his "Two Concepts of Liberty"; it is the area within which a person can act unobstructed by others.[5] Following this definition, a person is free if and only if she is not interfered with by others in the activity she pursues, and accordingly a person lacks freedom (or liberty) only if other humans prevent her from attaining her goal. Negative liberty is contrasted, says Berlin, with **positive liberty**: making decisions based on oneself and not on external forces of any kind.[6] The difference between these two senses is the difference between the freedom of not being prevented from choosing as one does by other people, and the freedom of being one's own master.[7]

There is not much doubt but that the negative liberty championed by neo-liberals has held sway over the last 30 years. But how this came about should be briefly reviewed, if only to provide a context for what follows. The context is best provided by backing up to the nineteenth century and the liberalism of John Stuart Mill. Mill, in his later writings, was sympathetic to setting limits on the operation of the marketplace in defence of the well-being of the individual. Mill's liberty was a positive liberty and placed considerable emphasis on the cultivation of personality and individuality. In the latter part of the nineteenth century, British liberalism was cut in two.[8] Liberals such as Herbert Spencer, who advanced the ideal of negative liberty, stood opposed to liberals advancing the ideal of positive liberty. This opposition is ably captured by Spencer himself in his *The Man versus the State* when he says, castigating the new liberals, "They have lost sight of the truth that in past times liberalism habitually stood for individual freedom versus State-coercion."[9] Pressing for the ideal of positive liberty in the liberal camp, and very much against Spencer, were reform liberals such as T.H. Green, J.A. Hobson, and L.T. Hobhouse. Alas, the coming of the Great War took much of the wind out of the

Central Beliefs of Neo-Liberalism and Libertarianism

- Human nature is acquisitive and self-interested.
- The origin of the state is the social contract.
- Liberty as an ideal is exhausted by negative liberty.
- Equality as an ideal is restricted to civil and political equality.
- Individualism takes priority over communitarianism.
- Justice is exhausted by procedural justice.
- The end of government is equivalent to the role of the night watchman.
- Economic organization, at its best, is market-driven.
- Rights take priority over utility.

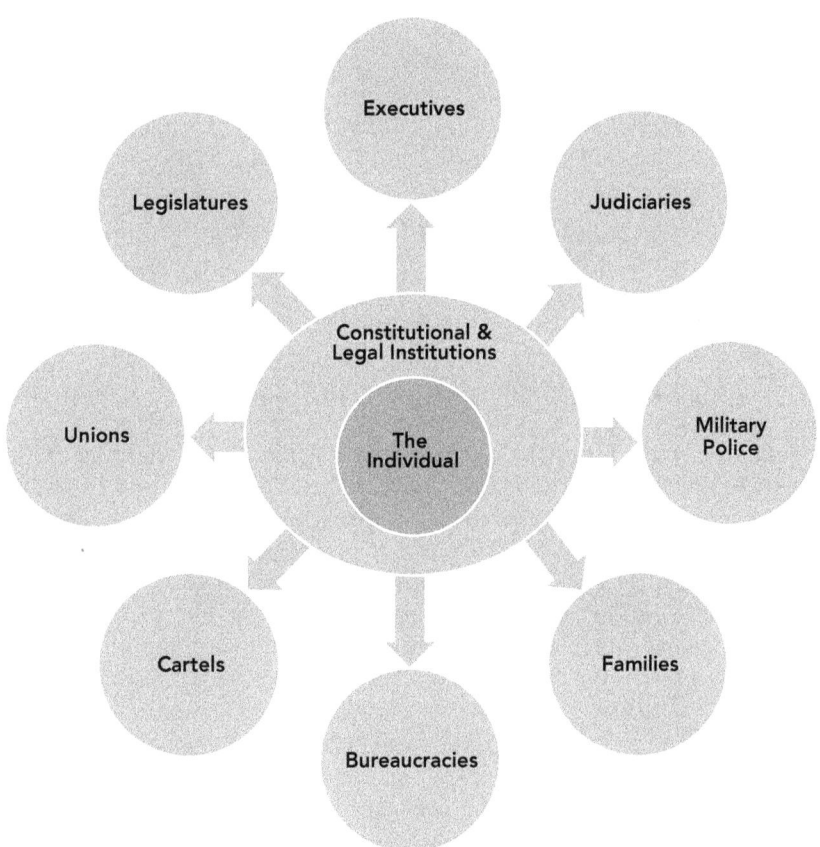

Legend: ▬▬▶ = arrows representing causal protection of the freedom of the individual from external institutions

Figure 10.1 Neo-Liberalism/Libertarianism's Model of Society

sails of this side of the liberal camp, especially given its internationalism and aspirations for peace and progress.[10] It would not be until the Great Crash of 1929 that serious questions would be raised once again about the confidence that should be placed in the marketplace; until that time the ghost of Herbert Spencer was to be seen both in the United States and in Great Britain.

Near the end of World War II, the Austrian economist Friedrich Hayek (1899–1992) published *The Road to Serfdom*, a work that seemed to have more influence the more time elapsed. During the 1980s, under the rule of Margaret Thatcher (1925–2013) in Britain and the tenure of Ronald Reagan (1911–2004) in Washington, a new political orthodoxy was established; it was an orthodoxy of free markets and limited government,[11] but it was an orthodoxy that was very indebted to the work of Hayek. Indeed, one could say that Hayek made a very substantial contribution to the success enjoyed by the neo-liberals. Indeed, Hayek should be thought of as an initiator of the invasion of political science by economists—at least by economists who stand in the neo-classical tradition.[12] It is not surprising, therefore, that by the time one reaches Thatcher, one of her chief economic advisers would be Madsen Pirie (1940–), the head of the Adam Smith Institute. Classical liberalism had returned with a vengeance.

Friedrich Hayek

It would be inappropriate to attempt a review of Hayek's *The Road to Serfdom* (1944), but it would not be inappropriate to highlight some of its main ideas. These include Hayek's views on individual spontaneity, merit and fortune, capitalism and democracy, and the limits of coercive action.

Individual Spontaneity

Lamenting the fact that the prevailing view in society no longer supports individual spontaneity, Hayek says, "We have in effect undertaken to dispense with the forces which produced unforeseen results and to replace the impersonal and anonymous mechanism of the market by collective and 'conscious' direction of all social forces to deliberately chosen goals."[13] Evidently, spontaneity is a big thing for Hayek. Further, Hayek adds, "the liberal argument is in favour of making the best possible use of the forces of competition as a means of co-ordinating human efforts, not an argument for leaving things just as they are."[14] Hayek believes that one of the best arguments in favour of competition is that it does away with the need for any conscious control.[15] He admits that in a competitive society our freedom of choice "rests on the fact that, if one person refuses to satisfy our wishes, we can turn to another."[16] In part, Hayek founds his economic position on an epistemological one—namely, the limits of our knowledge. His economic position is one of individualism, but an individualism that does not assume egoism.[17] This individualism "merely starts from the indisputable fact that the limits of our powers of imagination make it impossible to include in our scale of values more than a sector of the needs of the whole society."[18] Hayek concludes from this that individuals should be allowed to follow their own values within defined limits. Presumably, these defined limits are specified by the rule of law.[19] Social ends are, for Hayek, none other than the coincidence of individual ends. "Common action is thus limited to the fields where people agree on common ends."[20]

Merit and Fortune

Hayek also has some interesting things to say about merit and Machiavelli's old friend, *fortuna*. He admits openly that it is "impossible to foretell who will be the lucky ones or whom disaster will strike, that rewards and penalties are not shared out according to someone's view about the merits or demerits of different people but depend on their capacity and luck."[21] In the result, Hayek thinks the choices in front of us in choosing our political ideology are not between one of absolute and universal standards of right and one where the individual shares are allotted solely on the basis of good or bad luck. Rather, he thinks the choice is between a system in which a few persons decide who gets what and one where it depends in part on the ability and initiative of the person as well as on fortune.[22] Finally, Hayek concludes his book with the remark that our guiding principle is that a policy of freedom for the individual is the only progressive policy, a fact as true of the twentieth as of the nineteenth century.[23]

Democracy and Capitalism

Some 30 years after writing *The Road to Serfdom*, Hayek reaffirmed many of its basic contentions in a speech on "Economic Freedom and Representative Government."[24] It is worth reviewing some of what he says in this speech so as to comprehend fully his position. In it he acknowledges that he was initially concerned about the dangers to personal freedom caused by visible collectivist tendencies on the part of government.[25] Hayek reluctantly comes to agree with Joseph Schumpeter (1883–1950) that an irreconcilable conflict exists between capitalism and democracy, a conflict that Hayek thinks is rooted in a particular form of democracy that will result in a "progressive expansion of governmental control of economic life even if the majority of the people wish to preserve a market economy."[26] Hayek reasons that the unlimited power of the legislature will force the government of the day, in order to maintain the continued support of the majority, "to use its unlimited powers in the service of special interests."[27] The result of this is that, while the majority wishes to preserve the market economy, special interest groups demand exceptions in their favour (for special traders or for certain regions of the country), and this has the effect of undermining the market economy. Hayek seems to believe that such inroads against the market economy are but the thin end of the wedge, for once they are made, differential treatment is requested by many groups "on the pretext of a pretended principle of social justice or of public necessity."[28] It is at this point that Hayek claims, "Once such discrimination is recognized as legitimate, all the safeguards of individual freedom of the liberal tradition are gone."[29]

The Limits of Coercive Action

But Hayek has still more to say in his speech that clarifies his earlier position in *The Road to Serfdom*. He reaffirms the basic principle of neo-liberalism: all coercive action of government must be limited to the enforcement of general rules of just conduct. Hayek believes that this principle does not preclude government from offering other services for which it need not rely on coercion, apart from the raising of money.[30] He acknowledges that increased wealth and increased density of population have "enlarged the number of collective needs which government can and should satisfy."[31] He believes that such government services are compatible with liberal principles, provided:

i. government does not claim a monopoly and new methods of rendering services through the market are not prevented;
ii. the means are raised by taxation on uniform principles and taxation is not used as a means of redistributing income; and
iii. the wants satisfied are collective wants and not those of a particular group.[32]

Pulling together the observations made by Hayek in his 1944 book as well as his comments made in the speech 30 years later, one can sum up his position in the following terms: markets in their spontaneous and impersonal way are largely self-regulating; government actions, when they go beyond general laws, are arbitrary and destructive of personal liberty.

With the foregoing understanding of negative liberalism as personified by Friedrich Hayek in mind, one can now turn to a second neo-liberal, this time in the public choice tradition.

Mancur Olson

Mancur Olson (1932–1998) is probably the paradigmatic advocate of a neo-liberal economic theory—namely, **public choice theory**—and he certainly is at the forefront of the invasion of economists in the neo-classical tradition into the domain of political science. Olson's contribution provides the logic of collective action as one particular version of public choice theory. For his part, Olson's reduction of politics to economics takes the following form: individuals or organizations only join to form interest groups when they aim at some collective benefits or **public goods**, which are **indivisible** and **non-excludable**.[33] The relevance of Olson's comments in a study of political ideologies lies in his addressing public goods and in developing a theory of groups; both of these are relevant to ideologies in trying to understand why persons engage in collective action and how persons deal with goods that are deemed public. These themes have haunted the pages of the great political thinkers from Plato's day down to our own.

Public Goods and Group Activity

In his definitive study, *The Logic of Collective Action*, Mancur Olson develops, in a sophisticated way, a position on public goods and group activity. He says, in the early pages of his monograph, that group activity is best understood in terms of organizations and their purpose.[34] According to Olson, implicit in the literature about organizations is the belief that they exist to further the common interests of groups of people, presumably of groups that comprise the organization.[35] Olson takes issue with those who would collapse the difference between small and large organizations, for he believes there is not only a quantitative difference but also a qualitative difference between the two. Among qualitative differences between the two are the following: small groups have the capacity to work without inducements or coercion, whereas large groups do not,[36] and small groups are better than large groups at providing themselves with a collective good.[37] The import of Olson's observations is greater in what he has to say about large organizations, such as the state, and indeed he mentions early on in his monograph that his main focus is on large groups.[38] The implications of Olson's observations for the political state and citizens are what concern us here.

Rational Utility Maximizers

In Olson's model, both large and small interest groups aim to provide collective goods. Accordingly, they confront the problem of persuading members to contribute. Under the public choice model of collective action, articulated by Olson, all actors are rational utility maximizers who join the group only on condition that the benefits exceed the cost.[39] Accordingly, each actor must: "(1) establish her individual welfare gain if the group exists and is successful, (2) multiply this net benefit by the likelihood that her personal contribution to the group will be decisive in achieving its objectives, and (3) compare this discounted net benefit with the undiscounted costs of joining up."[40] When these considerations are advanced simultaneously, what results is the **free rider problem**, especially among large groups like the state: rational individuals will let others make the sacrifices and do the work, while they enjoy the non-excludable goods. This puts the lie to the claim that, if a group had some reason for organizing to further its interests, rational individuals who are members of that group would be rationally driven to support the group.[41] For large groups at least, rational and self-interested persons will not voluntarily act to achieve the common interest. This position of Olson, originally defended by him in 1971 in *The Logic of Collective Action*, is reaffirmed by him in 1982 in *The Rise and Decline of Nations* when he says that large groups, in the absence of special arrangements, will not act in their group interests when composed of rational individuals.[42]

The rational constraints on group members, when they are striving for collective goods, are such that these same members will tend to realize a result characterized by sub-optimality or inefficiency. The implications for the political state include the rather unmistakable conclusion of the state achieving much less than it is capable of achieving and of citizens being surrounded by this inefficiency, in spite of the state having emotional resources such as patriotism, nationalism, common religion, and language at its fingertips.[43] This at least seems to be the conclusion if the state is incapable of exercising a pretty thoroughgoing kind of coercion and packaging of incentives to achieve the public good. And, of course, democratic regimes, while perhaps having some coercive devices—such as the ability to tax—to fall back on, generally lack those found in other regimes such as a dictatorship, theocracy, or timocracy.

The upshot—though this is not spelled out clearly by Olson or other public choice theorists who advance the model of the logic of collective action—is that the free rider problem will lead people, at least rational agents, to be less inclined to "buy into" the idea of a public good. As Olson says, three factors keep larger groups from advancing their own interests: (i) the larger the group, the smaller the fraction of the total group benefit any person in the group receives; (ii) the larger the group, the less likely an individual will gain enough from the collective good to merit bearing his small burden; and (iii) the larger the group, the greater the costs of the organization.[44] All of this suggests, though Olson does not say so explicitly, that rational agents as utility maximizers will tend to disengage from the pursuit of collective goods, in the absence of coercion. Clearly the state is affected by this.

In *The Rise and Decline of Nations*, Olson has gone on to criticize interest groups that promote their own issues at public expense. The groups that he has in mind are either small interest groups that do not have to rely on coercion and incentives for advancing the interest of the group, or large ones that do. Either way, they challenge the state—at least in its democratic, and presumably enfeebled and bureaucratic, version. They do this as "rent-seekers," looking out for themselves very much at the public expense. Faced with the foregoing and the impact that such groups have on economic growth of a democratic state, Olson favours a smaller government, as well as limitations on its spending and taxing powers.

Olson both affirms the classical laissez-faire liberal ideology and distances himself from it. He affirms, in his later publication, the value of markets, but he distances himself from those in the laissez-faire ideological camp who think that markets alone will solve the economic problem if government leaves them alone. Since the government is not the only source of coercion or social pressure, distributional coalitions need to be confronted by repealing all special interest legislation or regulation and by applying antitrust legislation to all types of cartels and collusions that use their power to obtain prices or wages above competitive levels.[45] In the result, laissez-faire thinking leaves something out of the equation when it focuses exclusively on the evils of government; it needs also to focus on the evils of special interest groups.

Though Olson is emphatic in distancing himself from the conventional classical liberal position, it is important to note not only his unbridled support for the market, but also his affirmation that government needs to be disengaged from those interest groups (business, union, and others) that attempt to skew the market. In other words, Olson really argues for two things: (i) the ending of government legislation that helps special interest groups, and (ii) the application of government legislation that ensures real competition. What results is a mitigated night watchman approach to politics. As a night watchman, the government, for Olson, should ensure that no groups get a special legislative deal, and that cartels and collusions (sometimes called "distributional coalitions") are neutralized. Only in this way can we reasonably expect economic growth, full employment, coherent government, equal opportunity, and social mobility.[46]

Residual Thoughts on Anarchism

Olson makes a few interesting observations concerning anarchism, especially regarding the anarchism of Bakunin and Kropotkin. Given his position on the logic of collective action (a position that categorically affirms that rational individuals will not voluntarily act to achieve the interest of the group to which they belong), Olson believes that group behaviour is plagued with inefficiency or sub-optimality, thereby falling short of the group's interest. With this conclusion firmly in mind, Olson says confidently that the anarchistic assumption is wrong in affirming the spontaneous birth of a mutual aid group in the absence of the oppressive state.[47] One might say that for Olson interest groups are underachievers, while for anarchists they are overachievers. Olson's comments here are less important in signalling something true or false about anarchism, and more important in signalling to us that his neo-liberalism rubs shoulders with anarchism, even if it is distinct from it. This same rubbing of shoulders also occurs, as we shall see, in the case of libertarians.

New Right Theorists

A somewhat newer version of public choice theory takes a different tack than that adopted by Olson. This version is the New Right model, which shares with Olson's model the primacy of the rational actor, but differs from it in denying that the main objectives of groups turn on non-excludable public goods. According to the New Right model, most groups seek benefits that could be supplied, through market mechanisms, as divisible and excludable goods. Under this model of public choice, constraints triggered by the rule of law—which bar overt discriminatory action by government—explain, in Western societies, why government-provided goods are not more excludable and divisible. But there is more to this model, for it goes on to say that virtually all welfare state benefits are deliverable as private goods, including the following benefits: health care, education, employment insurance, public housing, and state-subsidized transport. Under the terms of the New Right theory, these services could in principle be provided more cheaply when marketed privately and have similar benefits to those marketed publicly. In the result, the New Right theory contends that very few products and services supplied by government are truly public goods, exceptions being national defence and mechanisms needed to safeguard the legal foundation of society.[48]

The foregoing neo-liberal positions of Hayek, Olson, and the New Right represent an application of economic notions to the field of politics. All argue in favour of tight constraints on government action in the field of public policy so as to minimize the size and role of government in particular and of the state in general. Though some would be tempted to say that the pedigree of this neo-liberal position is John Locke, it seems more appropriate to say that it goes back to Adam Smith. It was Smith, more than Locke, who used his economic insights to construct an emerging political ideology. What helps to make the connection between Smith and the neo-liberals is their use of economic notions and ideals to circumscribe space for the freedom of the individual. To say this, however, is not to say there are no differences between the classical liberal Smith and contemporary neo-liberals. In *The Theory of Moral Sentiments* and in *The Nature and Causes of the Wealth of Nations*, Smith, as a classical liberal, espouses reason, humanity, justice, equality, equity, generosity, kindness, and hospitality, and abhorrence of mental mutilation. Neo-liberals, on the other hand, are preoccupied with liberty or freedom, as seen through economic eyes, in such a way that little if any attention is given to these other matters addressed by Smith. In the result, what distinguishes classical liberals like Smith from neo-liberals is that the latter have a hard edge to their political ideology that is noticeably lacking in the case of Smith's position.

It is time to turn to those writers who have, in the latter part of the twentieth century, raised the torch of libertarianism. With an emphasis on rights, especially property rights, libertarians can rightly trace their pedigree to John Locke. They share with neo-liberals an affirmation of a right to economic freedoms, but their interest in freedoms is wider than that, ultimately touching social practice. One could say, without being misleading, that neo-liberals make use of a notion of freedom that largely focuses on economic transactions, whereas libertarians' notion of freedom is more general and applicable to whatever we do. Both emphasize freedom of the individual, but the libertarian is somewhat more anti-statist than the neo-liberal. Hence one could say that the libertarians to be examined are more anti-statist than neo-liberals like Hayek, Olson, and others.[49]

Robert Nozick

In 1974 Robert Nozick (1938–2002) wrote *Anarchy, State, and Utopia*—the most influential book on libertarianism in the twentieth century, and possibly of all time. Several key ingredients in Nozick's libertarianism include the notion of a protective association, state of nature, ultraminimal state, minimal state, and an invisible hand explanation. Nozick pursues a logical development of ideas, and in this respect the starting point must be the notion of an invisible hand.

Invisible Hand Explanation

Adam Smith coined the expression of an "invisible hand" to refer to how individuals can promote an end that was not part of the original intention.[50] Nozick believes that, if he can provide an **invisible hand** explanation for the existence of the state, he will have provided a fundamental explanation. A fundamental explanation is, for Nozick, one in which a realm (of discourse) is explained entirely by another realm. In the case of political ideology this means explaining the political in terms of the non-political. He wishes to give a fundamental explanation for the existence of the state, and this he attempts to do using an invisible hand explanation. This explanation, as outlined below, is quite different from the explanation envisaged by Hobbes, Locke, and Rousseau, for whom the origin of the state is the social contract. The social contract, interestingly, does not provide an invisible hand explanation.[51]

Protective Associations

Following Locke, Nozick makes use of the notion of a state of nature, a pre-political condition, in which inconveniences arise, including the invasion by some individuals of the rights of others. This leads to further problems, such as the bias involved in persons ascertaining the damage done to themselves when their rights are violated, feuds that develop through ongoing retaliation, and the inability of some to enforce their rights at all. Out of this situation Nozick believes mutual **protective associations** may plausibly arise not only in different geographic territories, but in one and the same territory. Over time, the overlap of protective associations brings its own inconveniences and problems, and this is only resolved by the birth of a dominant protective association. But is this dominant group the equivalent of a state? asks Nozick. Is it a minimal state? To follow Nozick's reasoning here it is useful to keep in mind three distinct concepts he employs: private protective association, ultraminimal state, and minimal (night watchman) state.

Is a private protective association a state? At first blush, the answer appears negative, and for two reasons: (i) the private association lacks a monopoly of power in the enforcement of rights, and (ii) the private association does not protect all individuals in its geographic territory. The night watchman state of classical liberalism does not fail in either of these two ways (let us call them the monopoly way and the redistributive way). In the night watchman state, both those who have paid to be protected and those who have not paid to be protected receive protection from the state, which turns out to be the only protective agency. But what of a protective association? Is it a state? A protective association, say a **dominant protective association**, that satisfies only the monopoly way is described by Nozick as an ultraminimal state, not a state. It does not satisfy the redistributive way. To move beyond the ultraminimal state to the minimal state, Nozick argues in favour of side constraints. These side constraints are the rights of other persons that constrain one's actions. These side constraints are grounded in "the fact of our separate existences."[52] The fundamental idea here is that different individuals have different lives, and therefore no one may be sacrificed for others; this leads to the libertarian idea that prohibits aggression.[53] These side constraints, when respected, help move a dominant protective association along from an ultraminimal state to a minimal state.

The Minimal State

Self-interested and rational persons in a Lockean state of nature, thinks Nozick, will inevitably be driven to protective associations and then ultraminimal states. The move from the ultraminimal state to the minimal state is justified by respecting the side constraints (the rights of others), something accomplished by providing compensation to those who are non-clients of the protective association. In constructing his minimal state, with its monopoly of power and redistributive feature, Nozick thinks he has satisfied the two necessary conditions for a protective association that is dominant in a geographical territory being called a state. Moreover, he believes he can answer the individualist anarchist who condemns such a state on the grounds of its being immoral. Nozick thinks the anarchist can be answered by demonstrating that such a monopoly and redistribution are morally legitimate when the principle of compensation is made use of and directed at non-clients of the protective association. In this way Nozick thinks he has discharged his task of explaining how a minimal state—but a state just the same—could arise from a Lockean state of nature without at the same time trespassing on anyone's rights. What Nozick offers us, in his opinion, is an invisible hand explanation (which is also a fundamental explanation) of monopoly control by morally acceptable means without violating anyone's rights.[54]

Beyond the Minimal State

It would be surprising if Nozick, as one advocating libertarian principles, were in favour of moving beyond the minimal state. In fact, he is not. His reasoning in support of his position is based on the claim that any state more extensive than the minimal state violates the rights of people.[55] Of particular interest in understanding Nozick in the matter of his opposition to a more extensive state is what he has to say about distributive justice. Distributive justice is, he thinks, too often mistakenly construed as patterned, and thereby allocates goods (the supply of things) on the basis of such criteria as moral merit, needs, marginal product, effort, or some combination of these. This he finds morally unacceptable because, among other things, it separates production and distribution as two separate issues, when they are not.

Nozick argues in favour of an alternative theory of distributive justice: the entitlement theory. Briefly, it claims the following: whoever makes something, having bought or contracted for the necessary resources used in the process, is entitled to it. If a person acquires something justly, he or she is entitled to it and entitled to transfer it accordingly. What Nozick presents is a historical entitlement theory, not a patterned theory, of distributive justice.[56] Once distributive justice is defined along historical lines in the spirit of the entitlement theory, the argument in defence of the minimalist state is more than made. This is Nozick's vindication of libertarianism: rights trump utilitarian considerations. The autonomy or separate existence of the individual is preserved.

With this understanding of Nozick in mind, we can now turn our attention to another defence of contemporary libertarianism, but one grounded on contractarian considerations in a way that Nozick's account is not.

Jan Narveson

In a masterful way, Jan Narveson (1936–) has presented a rigorous and highly reflective argument in favour of libertarianism. He does this by seeking to establish a position that will underwrite libertarianism, given that intuitionism (as found in Rawls's writing) and utilitarianism are rejected. This position he calls contractarianism, which aspires to generate moral principles for societies solely from the non-moral values of individuals. This, Narveson considers, is the most important feature of contractarianism.[57]

Contractarianism

A word or two on what Narveson means by contractarianism is in order. Roughly, contractarianism is a theory asserting the following: principles of morality are, or should, direct every person's conduct in a manner that it is reasonable for all to accept. Morality, on this theory, turns out to be a set of demands to make everyone better off if they are met by everyone. Making use of the constrained maximization notion put forward by David Gauthier (1932–), which states that one co-operates if and only if the other does as well, Narveson argues that problems normally associated with the **prisoner's dilemma**, which show that the rational thing for persons to do is not to co-operate, are overcome: co-operation among like-minded individuals is in and non-co-operation is out. Morality, so framed, is not the result of a "literal contract," thinks Narveson; rather, it is more like an artificial construct or rational convention.[58]

Narveson defends contractarianism on the grounds that "no other view can serve the requirements: namely of providing reasons to everyone for accepting it [morals], no matter what their personal values or philosophy of life may be."[59] According to him, contractarianism offers a view that avoids the obfuscation of intuitionism, and avoids the difficulties of utilitarianism with its use of the Rawlsian "veil of ignorance" and the rather arbitrary principle that one person's utility should count the same as that of another.[60] So contractarianism rules out intuitionism and does not serve as a foundation for utilitarianism. So far so good. In addition, Narveson says that contractarianism "offers an intelligible account both of why it is rational to want a morality and of what, broadly speaking, the essentials of that morality must consist: namely, those general rules that are universally advantageous to rational agents."[61] Intuitionism being abandoned and utilitarianism being rejected, contractarianism offers some hope in generating "moral principles for societies out of the nonmoral values of individuals."[62] Narveson offers some trenchant criticisms of intuitionism and utilitarianism. Faced with these criticisms, Narveson is correct in saying that contractarianism is an attractive and plausible option.

Rationality

In elaborating on contractarianism, Narveson speaks of rational agents and asks why it is rational for persons to want a morality. Early in *The Libertarian Idea* he indicates that he will operate for the most part with the "everyday, intuitively manageable concept of rationality."[63] The only refinement he provides to this understanding comes much later in his work when he distinguishes between interpretive rationality and reflective rationality. By interpretive rationality he means the readiness of a person to use available information to satisfy one's current desires, and by reflective rationality he means the willingness of a person to make immediate sacrifices for the sake of distant gains.[64] The contractarianism that Narveson develops encompasses both of these senses of the term.

Elements in Libertarianism

More clearly than most contemporary philosophers, Narveson has laid out the fundamental elements of libertarianism, which he treats as an ideology.[65] These elements involve each person having personal resources and the negative right[66] to use these resources, provided that she or he does not violate a similar right held by someone else. What this amounts to, when it is put more bluntly, is this: "our sole basic duty is to refrain from utilizing the fundamental resources of others without their consent."[67] Narveson teases several *implications* out of his essentially "moral" assumptions:

i. the absence of a fundamental general duty to "provide others with such goods as the necessities of life, let alone some particular proportion of all the socially distributable goods there are";
ii. the presence of a duty "not to interfere with the operations of the 'market', so long as it is a truly free market";
iii. a preference for "voluntary social arrangements to involuntary ones";
iv. a severe restriction on governments "in what they may properly do."[68]

An air of negativity is tied to Narveson's view of libertarianism, as seen in the above, and this is confirmed by his statement to the effect that libertarianism has generally been identified with the claim that the fundamental moral rights of persons are exclusively negative.[69]

Contractarianism and Libertarianism

Narveson is keen to establish a sound rational basis for libertarianism, which turns out to be—according to him—contractarianism. Hence he lays down as the subject of his present inquiry whether we could retrieve libertarian principles on a contractual rather than intuitive footing.[70] Another way of representing Narveson's position is in terms of a bridge that allows us to reach a promised land safeguarded from the depredations of others and filled with opportunities for co-operation. The bridge in this case is contractarianism, and the promised land is libertarianism. Hence Narveson asks the question he later answers affirmatively: "What prospect is there that the outcome of the widest possible general 'social contract' will be essentially the libertarian principle?"[71]

The linkage between contractarianism and libertarianism Narveson spells out in terms of what he calls the linchpin of the argument, which is as follows. First, contractarianism (or contractualism) is considered a voluntary undertaking, "that is, each agrees, without coercion, to whatever is accepted in the outcome of this 'bargain,'"[72] and, second, libertarianism maximizes individual freedom by considering "each person's person as that person's own property . . . that is compatible with everyone else's having such rights."[73] The trick in all of this is walking across the bridge from the first of these to the second, or as Narveson says, getting from Hobbes to Locke.[74] Narveson aims to walk across this bridge by showing that the libertarian principle leads to Pareto-dominance.[75] In other words, the libertarian principle leads us to prohibit the use of force and fraud, leaving us free to pursue co-operative ventures in such a way that not only are persons not worse off, but everyone is better off than they would have been had the agent not existed.[76] Under Narveson's scheme, the moral contract turns out to be a general-purpose commitment for social life that rational agents are driven to accept; moreover, it is a contract that, when actually implemented, turns out to be the incarnate version of libertarianism. According to Narveson, not only does this achieve Pareto-superiority, but Pareto-dominance in which each individual "gets the best possible deal."[77] Accordingly, thinks Narveson, "we must argue not only that no one is worse off but that everyone is better off, and strikingly so."[78]

Rationality and Libertarianism

The foregoing is a rough outline of Narveson's defence of libertarianism. However, he carries the discussion a bit further by maintaining (i) that rational agents would want prima facie the libertarian principle, and (ii) that objections to this principle are more apparent than real. In what follows I shall address only the comments of Narveson that bear on the first of these claims. Narveson seems to argue in the following terms: the libertarian principle is justified if and only if the life of constraint is preferable to the life of predation. Put differently, Narveson seems to argue that the libertarian principle is justified if and only if the Lockean proviso of constraint is preferable to the Viking life of predation. Indeed, Narveson goes so far as to say that the Gauthieran constraint, which for all practical purposes is the same as the Lockean constraint, takes predatory collective action as the chief obstacle to libertarianism being universally accepted as the hallmark of justice.[79] In other words, one is left with the impression that Narveson believes libertarianism is vindicated if it deals with the matter of collective action.[80] So what are the problems of collective action?

Narveson is of the opinion that the vulnerability of human beings in the state of nature drives them in the direction of a life of morals. However, he believes that group depredations, or collective action of a predatory kind, are a horse of a different colour. As he says in the case of groups, "it is not easy to demonstrate that [they] will always do better to be peaceable."[81] And of course if they will not do better, then the libertarian position—being one of constraint and co-operation—will be invalidated.[82] This follows once one remembers that the libertarian principle is justified if and only if the life of constraint is preferable to the life of predation. If group depredations or ravages lead to a life that is non-peaceable yet preferable for those who so act, then libertarianism, as a general principle, is falsified. So Narveson is eager to counter the claim that this is a probable outcome. To this end he makes four claims:

i. The military superiority of groups, such as nations, is impermanent ("evanescent") owing to military technology that can be possessed by even smaller groups.
ii. A predatory war will offer a higher return than peace only on the condition that a high value is placed on glory—but emphasis on glory at the expense of comfort, security, travel, the arts, and higher mathematics is unsustainable.
iii. Gains from military predation will always be less than gains from peaceable trade.
iv. Those wishing to discredit the liberalism of Locke must show either that war is preferable to peace (a position that is already discredited), or that Lockean liberalism is hopeless, as Marx tried (unsuccessfully) to show, or that some other set of ideological

principles is preferable to liberalism (which it is not when such topics as the market, the state, redistribution, the welfare state, and freedom and information are consulted).[83]

Narveson concludes on the basis of this that libertarianism is not only not invalidated, but validated.

Conclusion

Neo-liberals and libertarians share beliefs. They both affirm the fundamentality of individuals—something reflected in Hayek's and Nozick's political philosophies. And both neo-liberals and libertarians share the primitive role that rationality plays in constructing our political stances—something reflected in Olson's and Narveson's thinking. Moreover, both neo-liberals and libertarians emphasize the role of rights, with each focusing on the right to liberty. But this connection between neo-liberalism and libertarianism can be made sharper by drawing out the specific connection between the two versions of public choice theory and libertarianism. To this we now turn.

It will be recalled that the invasion of political science by economists resulted in two different versions of public choice theory. The first, as analyzed by Mancur Olson, concentrates on the objectives of groups as non-excludable public goods. The second, the New Right model, concentrates on the objectives of interest groups as divisible and excludable goods. What the New Right model retains from the logic of the collective action model is the rational actor.[84] The New Right model sees the discussion of excludability as unhelpful, if not bogus, and wishes to concentrate its firepower on goods in the marketplace—including all welfare benefits such as "health care, employment insurance, education, public housing, and state subsidized housing"[85]—believing that the private provision of such services can occur, presumably in a Pareto-dominant way.

Clearly, libertarianism as developed by Nozick and Narveson is directly connected with both of these versions of the public choice theory. It affirms the rational agent in constructing the dominant protective association or social contract, then uses this agent and either the invisible hand or contract to walk across the bridge to libertarianism, which affirms the principle of Pareto-dominance (i.e., welfare exchange ought not to leave any individual worse off) as the principle of rational agents living life together. This principle, according to Narveson, offers the best prospect to the rational person.[86] Nozick adds to this by introducing the entitlement theory, which gives further definition to the direction this rationality should take.

Both Nozick and Narveson believe libertarianism can be sustained when applied to the empirical policy arena of the market, redistribution, insurance schemes, freedom and information, and public space.[87] It is evident that the libertarianism of Nozick and Narveson fits hand in glove with the two versions of the public choice theory. In the result, when the neo-liberal ideas of not only the public choice advocates but also of Hayek are combined with those of libertarians such as Nozick and Narveson, one confronts an arresting political ideology.

The line of argument pursued by neo-liberals and libertarians is a mixture of rational and empirical considerations, largely viewed from a self-focused perspective. Each of these drills down deeply inside the notion of economics and the notion of rights, and extracts bore samples they proceed to analyze with great care and attention, both rationally and empirically. To steal a phrase from Marx, which he uses in describing his own methodology, one could say of neo-liberals and libertarians that they examine the minutiae of economics and rights that "are of the same order as those dealt with in microscopic anatomy."[88] The reasoning of neo-liberals and libertarians is of a no-nonsense kind that aggressively pursues the logic of rationality to the limits of cost and benefit and does so without regard to values rooted in sentimentalism. In this disregard of sentimentalism, neo-liberalism and libertarianism are at one with Marxism. Where the ideology of neo-liberalism and libertarianism parts company with Marxism, and irreversibly so, is at the point where they begin with the postulate of the individual and Marxism begins with the postulate of the class. Neo-liberalism and libertarianism argue their case from the perspective not of the community or class, but from the perspective of a self-absorbed individual. Rationality, for the ideology under study, gets its cadence from egoism. These are the considerations that set in motion the whole line of argument used by neo-liberals and libertarians.

Evaluation: The Strengths of Neo-Liberalism and Libertarianism

1. Both neo-liberalism and libertarianism, in their rejection of utilitarianism and in their affirmation of rights-based ethics, offer a crispness and clarity often lacking in ends-based political ideologies. With Hayek's emphasis on freedom in the marketplace, Olson's resolve to ban those forces such as cartels that collude in such a way as to upset the freedom of the marketplace, Nozick's talk of side constraints, and Narveson's affirmation of negative rights, the anti-statism of their position emerges as a position that is pointed and clear.

2. The invasion of politics by economists has brought a robustness to the subject matter of political science and political ideology that in other respects is lacking. The introduction of such notions as sticky wages, involuntary unemployment, free riders, Pareto-optimality, rent-seekers, non-excludability, indivisibility, collusion of cartels, and the prisoner's dilemma have reinvigorated a discussion that dates back to Plato and Aristotle. The invasion by the economists does not mean the conquering of the high terrain occupied by these distinguished philosophers and their descendants such as Locke and Hobbes, but it does mean that some of the terrain is not so securely held, or that some of the terrain needs new defences in light of economic notions that incorporate game theory. Neo-liberalism and libertarianism force us to rethink our position and, to steal a phrase from Kant in thinking of Hume, shake us from our dogmatic slumber.

3. Both neo-liberalism and libertarianism, though especially the latter, have a methodological attractiveness in attempting to ground their moral theory on non-moral considerations. This is especially true of Nozick and Narveson, the one aiming to find fundamental explanations in the field of political ideology through his invisible hand explanation, and the other seeking to find the non-moral values of individuals as the foundation of the moral values of society through his contractarianism. And

in a different but somewhat similar vein, Olson attempts to provide an explanation of group behaviour—the logic of collective action—in terms of individual rational choices, but in a way that is at first counterintuitive. So he, too, seeks something like a fundamental explanation that, as it happens, takes into account the view of Keynes and the view of monetarists.

4. Nozick's thought experiment of protective associations as minimal states, at least in their dominant condition, is explanatorily helpful. It does seem that early humans, with their developing sense of rationality, must have stumbled along his historical path in some such way. So this is an explanatory point in favour of Nozick. Related but separate from this is Nozick's belief that the consolidation of group interest in the form of a protective association, and the evolution of this institution, must have occurred in a non-contractual way in much the way that money did, or, as Hume says, language did. This seems a much more promising approach than the contractual way suggested by Narveson, though perhaps when Narveson has finally watered his contract down to a "rational convention," the differences between him and Nozick are minimal.

Evaluation: The Weaknesses of Neo-Liberalism and Libertarianism

1. Neo-liberalism overemphasizes maximum efficiency in producing social wealth, and is neglectful of diseconomies such as pollution, ugliness, congestion, noise, and the killing of animals through the use of insecticides, as well as its neglect of efficiencies for third parties in the matter of efficient urban transportation and reliable postal services.[89]

2. Contrary to the claims of neo-liberals, the linkage between capitalism and civil and political liberties is weak. Hayek would have it that a necessary connection exists between these two, with capitalism being a necessary condition for these liberties. However, as Will Kymlicka remarks, at most this connection is contingent, "for history does not reveal any invariable link between capitalism and civil liberties."[90] Some countries, such as Chile and Argentina, have enjoyed the free market and capitalist system while having a bad human rights record. Likewise, some socialist countries such as Sweden have an enviable record of human rights.

3. Both neo-liberalism and libertarianism are insensitive to the possibility that capitalism and democracy might very well be incompatible. The name of Joseph Schumpeter is normally associated with this line of thinking. Writing in 1942, Schumpeter claims, "[t]he very success of capitalist enterprise paradoxically tends to impair the prestige or social weight of the class primarily associated with it and . . . the giant unit of control tends to oust the bourgeoisie from the function to which it owed that social weight."[91] Again, he adds, "Thus the capitalist process pushes into the background all those institutions, the institutions of property and free contracting in particular, that expressed the needs and ways of the truly 'private' economic activity."[92] For Schumpeter, capitalism is dying almost from its own success, and

an integral process of this decline or evolution is democracy, which facilitates the existence of monopolistic controls. So there is a logical tension between capitalism and democracy. We have already seen above that Hayek himself, writing 30 years after *The Road to Serfdom*, acknowledges the logical tension between capitalism and democracy. Hayek's acknowledgement of this really amounts to the undoing of his thesis in *The Road to Serfdom*, a work that saw economic liberty as a necessary condition for democracy. Schumpeter's observations come back with a vengeance to haunt Hayek. And Olson recognizes a similar tension when he acknowledges that collusion can exist among cartels to such a degree that it will lead to the undoing of the competitive market. Freedom of association can actually lead to the erosion of the competitive market. Once again there is tension between a basic premise of capitalism and democracy.

4. The public choice version of neo-liberalism is problematic. As Peter Self observes, "the public choice theorists apply the logic of market behaviour to the political realm."[93] Voters thus have their analogue in consumers, pressure groups in political consumer associations, political parties in entrepreneurs, political propaganda in commercial advertising, and government agencies in (public) firms.[94] But a battery of criticisms can be made against these analogies:

   i. Individuals as rational egoists normally are defined narrowly to cover only individuals seeking private material gain. But this definition is not robust enough for political theories, being insensitive to other motives of individuals, such as a concern for reputation and duty.[95]
   ii. Rational egoism, when expanded to include values such as maximization of income, deference, and safety, makes prediction difficult owing to the contradictory nature of the goals.[96]
   iii. Rational egoism, to be robust, might be expanded to include the pleasure of helping others, or the duty to help others. So expanded, the notion seems to have embraced altruism and thereby robbed itself of meaning. At the very least, rational egoism, so defined, is much transformed from its meaning in the context of the market, and most assuredly provides a poor foundation for prediction based on utility maximization.[97] Indeed, one could add that the rationality of public choice theorists is much more limited in practice, and competes with motives of self-expression, civic duty, and group loyalty.[98]
   iv. Self-interest, when based on rational individualism or egoism, and in a world of functional interdependencies tending towards the loss of natural and social resources, will often result in the problem of the tragedy of the commons such that people would be better off if they were restrained, notwithstanding the fact that no one gains on her or his own by individually exercising self-restraint.[99] Hence the rationality of rational self-interest based on the marketplace is called into question.
   v. Public choice theorists neglect the ambiguity and confusion in the minds of voters whose information, emotional aptitude, and cognitive skills are inadequate for making nuanced calculations over public goods or collective goods or public policies. Utility calculation modelled on the marketplace seems a slender reed upon which to put so much weight. This fact, coupled with the ambiguity it

raises in the minds of voters against a background of agenda-setting which they little understand, means that the public choice theorists adopt a rather "unrealistic procedure of logical choice" in shaping the understanding of politics.[100]

vi. The public choice theory, in both its versions, focuses on the collective result when individuals pursue their own self-regarding interests. There is thus a strong tendency on the part of this theory to disregard, unjustifiably and implausibly, "the possibility of individuals making responsible judgements which take account of the welfare of others and of society generally."[101]

vii. The public choice theory, especially in its New Right version, tends to move beyond its task of pursuing a "scientific inquiry" by engaging in an implied normative discourse of privatization and deregulation. The theory, inasmuch as it aims to be explanatory, should limit itself to the non-normative. In the event that it wishes to move beyond this, it needs to make clear what aspects of its theoretical foundation imply the position of neo-conservatism, neo-liberalism, or libertarianism.[102]

5. Libertarianism suffers from its insensitivity to animal rights. A serious objection to contractarianism, and one that Narveson does not treat, is that of duties that one may have to animals, especially those that are sentient. If rights are generated, according to contractarianism, from the reciprocal laying down of one's liberty, then animals that are sentient but not rational are left out of the moral equation. Narveson does not appear to grasp fully the force of this point. He simply adds that if the contractarian theory is correct, "any creature can acquire rights."[103] But this is false, for sentient but non-rational animals, such as horses, cannot engage in the reciprocal laying down of their liberty.

While Narveson does address the issue of infants and their vulnerability in this context, he does not completely grasp the problematic nature of sentient but non-rational animals. Infants can, in some analogical fashion, be said to have rights. They are close enough to persons in the fully developed sense to say that it is rational to extend charity in their direction. We can look forward, for instance, to the time when they extend their appreciation for having their potential recognized in the present. The same cannot be said for the animals hitherto described. They do not have the potential to enter into reciprocal agreements. And so they function as a serious objection to contractarianism and therefore to libertariansm, at least as developed by Narveson.

Nozick's treatment of animals is somewhat different than Narveson's; at least he appears to wrestle with the issue more than does Narveson. Nozick does explicitly distance himself from the maxim "utilitarianism for animals; Kantianism for humans."[104] And he denies that the extra benefits people get from eating animals justify the practice.[105] Notwithstanding these statements by Nozick, he does have a serious problem fitting animals into his side constraints for the simple reason that they do not play any rational role in the emergence of a protective association of persons. So, though Nozick has more to say about animals than Narveson, neither of them says enough to allow for what would seem to be "intuitively" a morally defensible role in the context of the state. Obviously, non-human animals are not political animals; nonetheless they play a role in civil society, and even if some may deny that this is true, they have to have something morally defensible to say about animals. It is unlikely in the extreme that this "something" will emerge from contractarian talk or even watered-down contractarian talk.

6. Then there is the problem of the "thin end of the wedge" argument. The four strong points made by Narveson against group depredations, discussed above under the heading, "Rationality and Libertarianism," tilt the discussion in a direction that runs from contractarianism through to libertarianism. But they stop short of demonstrating that libertarianism is true. While Narveson correctly highlights the importance of collective action of a predatory kind being a *possible* counter-example, he does not give sufficient attention to another source of difficulty. Typically, libertarians acknowledge the need for a national defence policy, including a military, and the need for a national health policy—as it pertains to epidemics, for instance. It is difficult to understand how libertarians can acknowledge the legitimacy of these forms of force or governmental power in the life of the individual while denying the legitimacy of full-scale medical plans, public education, and a general social safety net as advocated by full-scale reform liberals of the ilk of John Maynard Keynes and John Dewey.

    It seems that once the "thin end of the wedge" is permitted to play a role here, it will prove quite difficult to stop the wedge from entering further. Once libertarians acknowledge the importance of the Lockean proviso, to wit, that "you can acquire so long as you don't worsen the situation of others,"[106] they open the door to greater involvement by the state in such fields as education, health, the environment, and the economy in general. Many in our society or our societies would be worse off if the state did not redistribute benefits through taxation. Certainly it could be argued that the obvious beneficiaries of this redistribution qualify in this respect. But it could be argued with plausibility that even those from whom the government takes its taxes would be worse off if it did not do so, for the same reasons that are often cited in the case of the need for national defence and minimal health protection. So the problem with Narveson's presentation of libertarianism is that it opens the door to a possible return of reform liberalism or democratic socialism.

7. Neo-liberalism and libertarianism, though especially the latter, suffer from an aversion to confronting empirical issues. One is left with the lingering impression that, notwithstanding the subtlety of neo-liberalism as found in the public choice theory and in libertarianism as articulated by Nozick and Narveson, many of the crucial issues affecting its motivation, if not its truth, remain empirical in nature. This is a point made with unavoidable bluntness by Kymlicka when he says that today's divide between the political right and left turns on "several essentially empirical questions" and not on appeals to libertarian principles of self-ownership or property rights.[107] The empirical issues, recognized by many[108] but especially by Kymlicka, include the following:

    i.   Is poverty a function of misfortune or bad choices?
    ii. Has the welfare state facilitated the escape from poverty or created a culture of welfare dependency?
    iii. Should welfare assistance be predicated on proof of the assumption of individual responsibility?
    iv. Does the state have the capacity to remedy serious social problems like poverty

and homelessness? If it does, will it just worsen the situation by attempting to so remedy these problems?[109]

These questions suggest a promising direction in which to carry the research program initiated by public choice theorists such as Mancur Olson. The promising direction is empirical in nature, suggested by Kymlicka, and will help us escape the orbit of an ideological chant that is getting "long in the tooth." Here I am thinking of neo-liberalism in its various guises (the public choice model, the New Right model, and libertarianism) when it is presented evangelically in the absence of hard evidence.[110] The shortcomings of neo-liberalism and libertarianism become apparent when considerations of the need to enter the empirical domain more energetically are combined with considerations of (i) the deep concerns about the narrowing of rationalism to self-interest in public choice theory and (ii) deep concerns about the libertarian and public choice neglect of the impact of externalities involved in any economic transaction. The invasion of economic ideas into the field of political science has not resulted in a final victory for the forces of economics. Much work in the field must be done before a final assessment can be made.

8. At least the version of libertarianism provided by Nozick, which embraces openly the entitlement theory of property and holdings, needs to be challenged. While it is no doubt an exaggeration to claim with Proudhon that property is theft, it seems no less a distortion to subscribe to the claim that the entitlement theory is morally correct or sustainable. There are two distinct points to be made against entitlement theory.

    First, the appropriation of "unheld things," in the case of land (i.e., the concept of terra nullius, or "land belonging to no one"), may not leave enough as good land for others, contra Locke. This can result in the marginalization of those left out of the enclosure system that develops, too often resulting in what the Aborigines of Australia call "terror nullius." Nozick tries to guard against this criticism by admitting into his theory of justice in acquisitions (which is what his entitlement theory is) the Lockean proviso: "a process normally giving rise to a permanent bequeathable property right in a previously unowned thing will not do so if the position of others no longer at liberty to use the thing is thereby worsened."[111] But even with this proviso, it is difficult to see how the entitlement theory could possibly be *administered* in such a way that it would result in a fair distribution of goods. It would seem that epistemological quarrels would result concerning the worsening or non-worsening of someone's position, so that no one could say with reasonable certainty whether the Lockean proviso had been complied with. When seen through administrative eyes, the neatness and tidiness of the entitlement theory begins to vanish.

    Second, the entitlement theory does not take into consideration the Machiavellian notion of *fortuna*. Lady luck can smile on someone so that successive crops are bumper crops, but just as readily she can cast a dark spell across your land and these same crops can be consumed by locusts or destroyed by hail. Such is the nature of the world in which we live: when you win, you often win big; when you lose, you just as often lose big. And there is no holding you back on the one hand and there is no redeeming you on the other. It seems that only a callous society would, in the spirit of entitlement theory, attribute this just to the luck of the draw and have no interest in having the state provide relief for those who suffer.

9. Neo-liberalism, which trumpets minimalism, is the driving force behind international trade treaties such as NAFTA and the TPP (Trans-Pacific Partnership). These treaties have the effect of interfering with individual choices, such as the choice to preserve one's own culture. In the result, the minimalism of neo-liberalism turns out be more apparent than real.

10. Neo-liberalism has hung around its neck the global economic crisis—a crisis deeply rooted in deregulation and privatization, two pillars of neo-liberal thinking. Deregulation, in particular, has led to some of the serious problems associated with the present financial crisis, including hedge funds, derivatives, and two instruments—the mortgage-backed security (MBS) and the asset-backed security (ABS). Financial capitalism, in the spirit of neo-liberalism, took upon itself (and, as it turns out, the rest of the world) a multiple gamble: lax oversight of the US financial sector, using massive amounts of debts and leverage, creating a housing and mortgage credit bubble, magnifying several fold the US credit-market debt, and engaging in incompetence and quantitative negligence.[112] These results show unmistakably the indefensibility of minimal regulatory schemes in the public domain and in the banking and investment worlds. To this extent neo-liberalism and, very likely, libertarianism show themselves in an extremely dubious light.

11. Finally, with respect to Narveson's position, especially as found in point (ii) under "Rationality and Libertarianism" discussed above, one can say that radicalized religious zealots of any faith may be prepared to seek glory at the expense of comfort, security, travel, the arts, and higher mathematics. Such individuals may see this as a rational course of action, especially with their belief in an afterlife. And with respect to his position under point (iii), military predation will undoubtedly be seen as a rational strategy for the corporate elite at the heart of the military-industrial complex. Each of these examples is problematic for Narveson's libertarianism.

Related Websites

Bourdieu, Pierre. "The Essence of Neoliberalism." *Le Monde diplomatique*, Dec. 1998.
http://mondediplo.com/1998/12/08bourdieu

Heidemen, Paul. "Bulletproof Neoliberalism." *Jacobinmag*.
https://www.jacobinmag.com/2014/06/bulletproof-neoliberalism/

Humphries, Liz. "Thinking through David Harvey's Theorization of Neoliberalism." An Integral State: Notes on Marx and Gramsci, 13 Sept. 2014.
http://anintegralstate.net/2014/09/13/david-harveys-theorisation-neoliberalism/

Martinez, Elizabeth, and Arnoldo Garcia. "What is Neoliberalism?" Corpwatch.
www.corpwatch.org/article.php?id=376

Shah, Anup. "A Primer on Neoliberalism." *Global Issues*, 22 Aug. 2010.
www.globalissues.org/article/39/a-primer-on-neoliberalism

Further Readings on Neo-Liberalism and Libertarianism

Armstrong, Elisabeth. *Gender and Neoliberalism: The All India Democratic Women's Association and Globalization Politics*. New York: Routledge, 2014.

Block, David, John Gray, and Marnie Holborow. *Neoliberalism and Applied Linguistics*. Abingdon; Oxon and New York: Routledge, 2012.

Conolly, William E. *The Fragility of All Things: Self-Organizing Processes, Neoliberal Fantasies, and Democratic Activism*. Durham, NC: Duke University Press, 2013.

Dardot, Pierre, and Christian Laval. *The New Way of the World: On Neoliberal Society*. Trans. Gregory Elliot. New York: Verso Books, 2013.

Davies, William. *The Limits of Neoliberalism: Authority, Sovereignty and the Logic of Competition*. London: Sage, 2014.

Gilbert, Jeremy. *Common Ground: Democracy and Collectivity in an Age of Individualism*. London: Pluto Press, 2014.

Gill, Stephen, and Claire A. Cutler. *New Constitutionalism and World Order*. Cambridge and New York: Cambridge University Press, 2014.

Goodman, Robin Truth. *Gender Work: Feminism after Neoliberalism*. New York: Palgrave Macmillan, 2013.

Harvey, David. *Seventeen Contradictions and the End of Capitalism*. New York: Oxford University Press, 2014.

Major, Aaron. *Architects of Austerity: International Finance and Politics of Growth*. Stanford, CA: Stanford University Press, 2014.

Marttila, Tomas. *The Culture of Enterprise in Neoliberalism: Specters of Entrepreneurship*. London: Routledge, 2013.

Olssen, Mark. *Liberalism, Neoliberalism, and Social Democracy: Thin Communitarian Perspectives on Political Philosophy and Education*. New York: Routledge, 2010.

Parr, Adrian. *The Wrath of Capital: Neoliberalism and Climate Change Politics*. New York: Columbia University Press, 2013.

Peck, Jamie. *Constructions of Neoliberal Reason*. Oxford: Oxford University Press, 2010.

Peters, Michael. *Poststructuralism, Marxism, and Neoliberalism: Between Theory and Politics*. Lanham, MD: Rowman & Littlefield, 2001.

Petras, James, and Henry Veltmeyer. *Beyond Neoliberalism: A World to Win*. Farnham, UK and Burlington, VT: Ashgate, 2011.

Phelan, Sean. *Neoliberalism, Media and the Political*. Houndmills, Basingstoke, Hampshire, UK and New York: Palgrave Macmillan, 2014.

Sandbrook, Richard. *Reinventing the Left in the Global South: The Politics of the Possible*. Cambridge: Cambridge University Press, 2014.

Ward, Steven C., *Neoliberalism and the Global Restructuring of Knowledge and Education*. New York: Routledge, 2012.

11 Feminism

Learning Objectives

- To gain an understanding of the history of feminism.
- To recognize two main ethical theories in feminism: an ethic of care and an ethic of justice.
- To appreciate the non-Anglo dimension of feminism as found in French, Dutch/Somali, and German writers.
- To understand the logical connections between feminism and environmentalism and between feminism and its opposition to religious fundamentalism.
- To recognize a sustained high level of innovative thinking in all forms of feminism.

Though considered by many to be a modern movement, **feminism** has ancient roots. Indeed, these roots can be traced back to Plato and the view he expresses in the *Republic* that women should form part of the guardian or ruling class. Less remotely, the roots of feminism are found in Christine de Pisan (1364–c. 1430) and her book, *City of Ladies*, published in 1405 in Italy;[1] in the writings of Mary Astell (1666–1731) and Lady Damaris Masham (1658–1708) in the seventeenth century;[2] in Mary Wollstonecraft (1759–1797) and her 1792 work, *A Vindication of the Rights of Woman*, the feminists' answer to Thomas Paine's *The Rights of Man*; and in Harriet Taylor Mill (1807–1858) in her 1851 volume, *The Enfranchisement of Women*. And of course one should not forget to mention *The Subjection of Women*, the celebrated contribution of John Stuart Mill (Harriett's husband) in 1869.

The period following Wollstonecraft is thought of as the first wave of feminism. What it focused on was parity of political and legal rights between men and women, especially as these rights were to be found in **suffrage**. In 1848 the **Seneca Falls Convention**, held in Seneca Falls, New York, marked the start of the American women's movement. Inspired by the American Declaration of Independence, convention attendees adopted the Declaration of Sentiments, which demanded female suffrage. The suffragette movement, as it was called, flourished in Western democracies in the late nineteenth and early twentieth centuries under the leadership of a number of women and supportive men: Elizabeth Cady Stanton (1815–1902), principal author of the Seneca Falls Declaration of Sentiments; Richard Pankhurst (1834–1898) and his wife Emmeline (1858–1928) in Great Britain; and the "Famous Five" of Nellie McClung (1873–1951), Louise McKinney (1868–1931), Irene Parlby (1868–1965), Emily Murphy (1868–1933), and Henrietta Muir Edwards (1849–1931) in Canada. There is a strong temptation to telescope the achievements of women such as Elizabeth Stanton, the Pankhursts, and Nellie McClung so as to give the impression of the inevitability of female suffrage and equanimity on the part of society concerning this new right. But this temptation should be resisted.

Female suffrage was first introduced in 1893 in New Zealand, as well as in the Cook Islands, a British protectorate in the South Pacific, and in Colorado, but this fact was largely eclipsed and forgotten by events elsewhere. In Great Britain, women received the franchise in 1918, largely owing to "direct action" taken by the Pankhursts; however, only 10 years later did women in that country actually have equal voting rights with men.[3] In the United States, Amendment 19, ratified on 18 August 1920, extended the franchise to women, stating that "[t]he right of citizens of the United States to vote shall not be denied or abridged . . . on account of sex."[4]

In Canada, in 1916 the right to vote was extended to women in Manitoba, Saskatchewan, and Alberta, and slowly thereafter universal suffrage came to other provinces. By 1918, with the passage of the Women's Franchise Act, women in Canada were given the right to vote federally, ahead of their counterparts in Britain and, as far as federal politics is concerned, the United States.[5] But progress on suffrage did not come evenly, even in a country like Canada. For instance, it was not until 1940 that Quebec women were able to vote in provincial elections. Moreover, a host of other issues of a legal nature prevented women from achieving parity with men in Canada. This seemed particularly true in Quebec, where the legal status of a married women under the Civil Code meant that "until 1955 a women could not seek a separation on the grounds of her husband's adultery, and until 1964 had no right to carry on a trade without her husband's consent."[6] Only in 1930, after a legal challenge, were women declared "qualified persons" within the meaning of section 24 of the British North America Act. This legal challenge by the Famous Five—brought forward in the case of *Edwards et al. v. Attorney General of Canada* (known as the Persons case)—enabled women to be appointed to the Canadian Senate, as they were recognized as "persons" by the Judicial Committee of the Privy Council in London, at that time Canada's court of last appeal.[7] So the temptation to see the suffrage movement as achieving success all at once is misleading.[8] The movement did indeed accomplish its goal, but only after many tries at kicking in the door. Even then, it seems, additional related legal issues confronted the suffragettes.

The second wave of feminism can be dated to the 1953 English translation of *The Second Sex*, by Simone de Beauvoir (1908–1986), first published in 1949, and to the publication of *The Feminine Mystique* (1963) by Betty Friedan (1921–2006). Both of these works recognize that political and legal changes of the past, though beneficial to women, did not bring forth the full freedom sought by women. Being unburdened from the tyranny of political and legal constraints did not mean being unburdened from the tyranny of social constraints. In a sense, the recognition of this by the women's movement was an acknowledgement of something admitted 100 years earlier by John Stuart Mill, namely, the tyranny of society, as distinct from the tyranny of the state, over self-regarding interests.[9] Writers such as Friedan and de Beauvoir spoke against the artificial constraints under which women lived, a point made with poignancy by de Beauvoir when she asserted, "one is not born, but rather becomes a woman."[10]

De Beauvoir saw the influence of society on women, daring to assert that it could be otherwise and that women could dethrone the myth of femininity and begin to affirm their independence: there was no essence of womanhood to which women must conform.[11] With less poignancy, but perhaps with more practicality, Betty Friedan spoke of the influence society had on women in terms of "the problem with no name." The effect of this second wave of feminism was to open the door to a deeper assessment of women. Following on the heels of de Beauvoir and Friedan were figures like Kate Millett (1934–), who wrote *Sexual Politics* (1970), Germaine Greer (1939–), who wrote *The Female Eunuch* (1970), and then many others. These figures wrote on various topics, but ones that stand out are:

i. domination and patriarchy;
ii. the distinction between gender and sex;
iii. the difference between the public and private worlds;[12]
iv. an ethic of care;
v. the political role of the family;
vi. need and dependency;
vii. justice in the family;
viii. experience as interpreted by women;
ix. feminism and ecological thinking;
x. women and subordination in religions;
xi. sexual equality;
xii. sexual assault law; and
xiii. sexism in political theory.[13]

The ensuing discussion will not address all of these topics. Nor will it attempt to pigeonhole various feminists into categories like liberal, socialist, radical, and postmodern. Instead, a select group of feminists will be examined on the basis of their clarity of thought and originality. This group comprises Alice Schwarzer, Luce Irigaray, Carol Gilligan, Susan Okin, Martha Nussbaum, Val Plumwood, Nel Noddings, and Ayaan Hirsi Ali. The intent here is to give a sample of opinions that exist among feminists on these various topics without presuming to deal with any topic or perspective in a complete way. Feminism as an ideology is simply too varied to permit such an undertaking.

Worth bearing in mind in the ensuing discussion is the self-evident fact that feminism is a current and evolving ideology that shows its relevance in multiple areas of global politics. New German feminist writers, for instance, advocate a feminism much

Central Beliefs of Feminism

- Human nature is **androgynous**.
- Equality as an ideal is gender-neutral.
- Justice is rooted in equality, including gender equality.
- The end of government is fulfillment of human beings, something that can only be accomplished through gender inclusiveness.

less interested in an evaluation of male-dominated society and much more interested in assisting women to deal with their sexuality and everyday lives.[14] And in the past two years rapes that resulted in the death of victims have produced a spontaneous backlash by women, with thousands of women protesting inaction by the state in protecting women, first in India, and most recently in Turkey, where women have demanded the death penalty for the perpetrators.[15] More recently, the vicious killing of an Afghan woman by a Kabul mob of men has renewed calls for authorities to ensure women's rights to equality and to protect them from violence. On 19 March 2015 men in Kabul beat a female religious scholar to death and then threw her body off a roof before running over it with a car and then setting the body on fire. This resulted in a huge outcry among the public and the carrying of her body by women activists who went against the tradition of men-only pallbearers.[16] And then there is the story of Mona Eltahawy, a radical Muslim feminist in Cairo who, in 2011, was arrested and sexually assaulted by Egyptian police while working as a reporter in Tahrir Square. Subsequently, while she was in jail, her right arm and left hand were broken. Undeterred, she has spent the past two years writing her book, *Headscarves and Hymens: Why the Middle East Needs a Sexual Revolution*, in which she argues that in Muslim countries the state, the street, and the home work in consort to keep girls and women down.[17] To this story can be added the story of Guadalupe [full name unavailable], an El Salvador woman who, upon having a miscarriage, was sentenced to 30 years in prison after being wrongly accused of having an abortion, something illegal in El Salvador. Amnesty International intervened on her behalf and she was granted a pardon.[18] When these events are coupled with the attempt by Iceland's women to find a female solution to the "man-made" financial crisis of 2008[19] and with the fact that women in the United States were predicted to become the chief breadwinners during this same recession,[20] one can see that feminism as a movement and ideology is getting traction in the international community. It is time to turn our attention to various perspectives of feminism that will undoubtedly act as a foundation for future ideological development.

Alice Schwarzer

Feminists sometimes draw upon anarchists and Marxists in constructing their ideology. From the former they are inspired to challenge the structures existing in representative democracies and they aim to find methods of decision-making in politics that differ from the controlling manner found in male-dominated societies.[21] From Marxists they are inspired to see capitalism as constructing an environment that is antagonistic to women's interests, and as a result they see Western institutions as eroding the freedom of women. The German feminist Alice Schwarzer (1942–) is one who, in part, fits into this latter category. But Schwarzer also draws on the ideas of Simone de Beauvoir and the Canadian feminist Shulamith Firestone (1945–2012). She agrees with de Beauvoir that women are not born but shaped into the persons they become, and she agrees with Firestone that the goal of the feminist revolution is not simply the elimination of male privilege but of the sex distinction itself.[22] Importantly, Schwarzer does not restrict her vision to capitalism and Marxism or to the ideas of de Beauvoir and Firestone. In more recent years, she has begun a serious critique of Islam and its impact on the rights and freedoms of women. The following discussion will not pick up on this theme, leaving it instead for later consideration in connection with the writings of Ayaan Hirsi Ali.

Vaginal Orgasm and Sex Monopoly

With clarity and care, Alice Schwarzer examines the function of sexuality in the oppression of women. Writing in 1975, she laments the inability of men to come to grips with the need for the emancipation of women. Even in progressive circles, she believes men are resistant to accepting masculinity and femininity as products of culture rather than nature.[23] Schwarzer's interest is people, not men and women. Her claim is that masculinity and femininity represent dominance and subjection and, hence, the absence of emancipation for women.[24] So she takes issue with those who claim that the **petite difference**, namely, the male sex organ, justifies dominance and subjection by men of women. Hence, she calls not for the elimination of the biological difference between men and women but of its ideological consequences.[25] While her focus tends to be on women, Schwarzer affirms that the stigma of masculinity and femininity "confines and defines us."[26] Her interest in gender, something culturally determined, is rooted in her belief that nothing determines life as much as gender and that gender must be eliminated for men and women to be truly emancipated.[27] Note here what she calls for is the elimination of something cultural, not biological. Gender, for Schwarzer, sows fear, dependence, distrust, and powerlessness in the hearts of women, which in turn creates victims (women) and then victims of victims (men) in the long run.[28]

What, then, is Schwarzer's solution to these problems encountered by women? She quickly reasons that male penetration of women provides men with an uncomplicated and comfortable way of practising sex but damns women to passivity.[29] Since she believes that for men power is pleasure, she seems resigned to accepting this as part of the explanation for why sexual norms have evolved the way they have, in spite of the fact that male pleasure does not explain why half of humanity, the female half, suffers under the weight of these same norms.[30] She argues that a **myth of vaginal orgasm**, which ensures the sexual monopoly of men over women, brings with it the considerable burden of contraception: the horror of unwanted pregnancies and abortions, the side effects of the pill, and inflammation caused by the diaphragm. Since the myth of sexual monopoly, tied to the myth of vaginal orgasm, is the foundation on which rests men's emotional, social, and economic monopoly, this monopoly must be addressed if women's emancipation is to be achieved. Schwarzer's solution can be summed up this way: heterosexual penetration would no longer be a form of lovemaking but would be reserved for procreation. The little difference of the male sex organ, in the end, would be of no significance and the result would be freer individuals practising sex in a way of their own choosing. The result would be a world of individuals dealing with each other as people rather than as bearers of masculinity or femininity.[31] "Gender would no longer be destiny."[32]

Compulsory Heterosexuality and the Political

Schwarzer has more to say. She asserts that male sexual monopoly is predicated not only on the myth of vaginal orgasm, but also on the myth or **dogma of heterosexuality**. Only the latter, not female homosexuality, allows for penetration along with all its side effects, and this cluster of side effects induces power, privilege, and pleasure in its male actors. So heterosexuality is affirmed while homosexuality is rejected. According to Schwarzer, the world could be different if procreation were not seen as the primary impulse for sexuality. In such a case, homosexuality, heterosexuality, and sex with one's self would be taken as behaviour compatible with the free development of the individual.³³ Echoing some of the words of Shulamith Firestone, Schwarzer goes on to say heterosexuality is political: people are first and foremost people and only secondarily male and female. The latter is the heart of gender and as such is simply a cultural product that privileges heterosexuality.³⁴

Luce Irigaray

Standing in the tradition of psychoanalysis and steeped in the tradition of Plato, Aristotle, Kant, Hegel, and Derrida, the French writer Luce Irigaray (1930–) attempts to "expose the foundations of patriarchy and in particular to show it at work in what has traditionally been taken to be the high discourse of universality and reason: philosophy."³⁵ In her effort to expose the foundations of patriarchy, Irigaray fluctuates between complexity and simplicity, opacity and clarity. Whatever difficulties one may encounter in reading her work, diligent pursuit of her ideas reveals new ways of understanding these foundations. This French philosopher is leery of accepting the "terms of the system currently in force" for she believes this will result in women becoming "men."³⁶ Hence, equality, for Irigaray, does not mean "becoming like men."³⁷ It would seem that, for Irigaray, the system currently in force is very much the product of the Enlightenment, the Western philosophic period of the eighteenth century that focused on the male atomistic individual who participated in the social contract. In addition to the foregoing bias in favour of the male sex, the Enlightenment, for Irigaray, "underestimates the non-rational elements of the human mind and its will to power, to control, manipulate, and destroy in the name of the rational."³⁸ Irigaray has at least two objections to the Enlightenment: first, it fallaciously models reason on the male individual, and, second, it overestimates the emancipatory promises of reason by underestimating the non-rational elements of the human mind.³⁹ She aims to move beyond principles of the Enlightenment, and so it is to her substantive contribution on feminism that we now turn.

Discourse and the Subordination of the Feminine

Irigaray sees philosophy and its discourse as "the one thing that has to be questioned" in ascertaining sexual **difference**.⁴⁰ The presuppositions of philosophy, at least as found in the West, underlie the patriarchal system that Irigaray sees as so noxious. These philosophical presuppositions stand at the foundation of psychoanalysis, something practised by Irigaray and something she believes provides the discourse on truth so far as female sexuality is concerned. To put the matter somewhat differently but preserving this French philosopher's meaning: patriarchy can be exposed by psychoanalysis but since this practice borrows the distortions of Western Enlightenment philosophy, psychoanalysis itself must be exposed by looking at its own discourse as well as that of its underlying philosophy. Irigaray believes if one stops with psychoanalysis, one is stuck with the feminine occurring only within the models and laws devised by male subjects.⁴¹ Thus, we are left with no difference but only sameness between men and women. Irigaray, on the other hand, is resolute about affirming the difference between men and women. She wishes to "secure a place for the feminine within sexual difference."⁴² So any philosophy, or psychoanalysis built upon this philosophy, must be re-examined so as to recognize this very difference.

Irigaray does not wish to say that the effectiveness of psychoanalysis is exhausted;⁴³ rather, she wishes to say that some of its implications are not at present operative or in service.⁴⁴ Freud's failure, in his discipline of psychoanalysis, is his failure to recognize that he is heir to an ideology that he does not challenge and his consequential failure to examine the metaphysical (read: philosophical) presuppositions of his very own discourse of psychoanalysis.⁴⁵ In short, Freud uses philosophical discourse to give a priori value to Sameness, thereby modelling the feminine on the masculine. Irigaray, for her part, is insistent that we can only avoid limiting ourselves to marginal issues by challenging the philosophical discourse that stands at the base of all discourses, and philosophy, after all, constitutes the discourse on discourse.⁴⁶

But what is this philosophical discourse? Irigaray takes a step in addressing this question when she speaks of the "figures" of philosophical discourse and then lists the following notions: idea, substance, subject, transcendental subjectivity, and absolute knowledge.⁴⁷ She is critical of the alleged oppositions in philosophy between the empirical and transcendental, the perceptible and the intelligible, and matter and idea, oppositions she claims help shape a "hierarchical structure" that puts the feminine in "a position of inferiority, of exploitation, of exclusion with respect to language."⁴⁸ She wants to reopen these philosophical notions and "pry out of them" what they have borrowed that is feminine. However, it seems that, for Irigaray, the main philosophical presupposition is simply making the masculine the sexual model and being negligent of difference between the sexes. This presupposition she sees carried over into Freud's thinking and affirmed there, but its origin, according to this French writer, lies in philosophy. Patriarchy, then, rests on psychological mechanisms and structures identified in Freud's psychology, but these mechanisms are previously affirmed in the prevailing philosophy of Plato, Rousseau, Kant, and others.

Women and Use-Value

Irigaray asserts that women have traditionally been simply a commodity among men. That is to say they have been seen as having simply a use-value for man.⁴⁹ This use-value, for Irigaray, is an exchange value. And she uses this notion of "exchange" to help define Western culture: "the society we know, our own culture, is based upon the exchange of women."⁵⁰ But the system of exchange that we speak of here is that found in patriarchal societies, and in these societies the production of women is always referred back to men. For Irigaray, this amounts to a social life or culture that depends upon a monopoly of homosexuality. In this monopoly the circulation of women among men establishes the way society operates. The presuppositions of this society include the following: man's appropriation of nature; the transformation of nature according to criteria defined by men; the reduction of material qualities to man's practical activity; equality of women only among themselves; and the establishment of women as "objects" in a world of men.⁵¹ According to Irigaray, homosexuality is required for the socio-cultural order.⁵² Any transcendence of this patriarchal socio-cultural structure requires a re-examination of the philosophical foundations on which it rests. Irigaray thinks that the **phallomorphism** of present patriarchal societies must be re-examined in light of the substructural philosophical discourse that prevents women from discovering woman.⁵³

Carol Gilligan

In 1982 the American psychologist and theorist Carol Gilligan (1936–) published *In a Different Voice*, and it became known as "the little book that started a revolution."

Translated into 17 different languages, Gilligan's book centred on an alternative to an ethic rooted in justice and replaced it with an ethic rooted in care. This is the principal notion discussed below.

An Ethic of Care

It is largely owing to Carol Gilligan that an interest has been awakened in the moral reasoning of women as distinct from the moral reasoning of men. According to her, women develop an **ethic of care**, a morality of care and responsibility, whereas men develop an ethic of rights. In Gilligan's own words, "The morality of rights is predicated on equality and centred on the understanding of fairness, while the ethic of responsibility relies on the concept of equity, the recognition of differences in need."[54] This morality of care, it is claimed, differs from the morality of justice in three ways: (i) it turns on different moral concepts—responsibility and relations, rather than rights and rules; (ii) it ties itself to the concrete rather than to the formal and abstract; and (iii) it is equivalent to an activity rather than to a set of principles.[55] In addition, Gilligan criticizes the theory of development of moral judgment advanced by Lawrence Kohlberg (1927–1987).

According to Kohlberg's moral theory, moral understanding is the basis for the motive to act morally.[56] Moreover, moral understanding, on which motivation rests, undergoes development in six stages. These six stages move from the simple to the complex through a process of integration, differentiation, and conflict resolution.[57] Higher stages of moral reasoning, in this theory, enable the person to resolve moral conflicts more adequately than lower stages. Finally, in Kohlberg's theory, the higher stages are Kantian in nature, and are characterized by "universality" and "principled judgment."[58]

As indicated above, Gilligan takes issue with Kohlberg's theory on the grounds that it does not get to the heart of the moral reasoning in women. Thus, in dissecting the responses of a male subject in Kohlberg's study and comparing them with the responses of a female subject in her own study, Gilligan says, "Thus while Kohlberg's subject worries about people interfering with each other's rights, this woman worries about the possibility of omission, of your not helping others when you could help them."[59] In Gilligan's words, Kohlberg's male subject identifies morality and justice (fairness, rights, the Golden rule),[60] whereas the female in Gilligan's study identifies morality with having "a very strong sense of being responsible in the world."[61] According to Gilligan, it follows that the Kantian model and Kohlberg's account are to be rejected. In place of the latter she proposes a morality of care, i.e., "an ability to find an equilibrium between connectedness and empathy on the one hand and the feeling of being an autonomous self on the other."[62] It should be noted that Gilligan believes these two modes of moral reasoning, these two voices, are fundamentally incompatible.[63]

The two voices to which Gilligan refers are captured by the expressions "justice" and "care and relationship." Kohlberg's subject identifies morality with justice, while Gilligan's subject identifies it with care and relationships. The former defines himself by the Kantian golden rule, while the latter "defines [herself] in a context of human relationships but also judges [herself] in terms of [her] ability to care."[64] It is evident that Gilligan's position becomes more sharply defined a few years after the publication of *In a Different Voice*. Writing in 1986, she claims there are two moral predispositions—one towards justice and one towards care—and that they arise from the human experience of (i) inequality, and (ii) attachment found in the relation between child and parent. Moreover, these two predispositions are the foundations for two forms of responsibility: one a commitment to obligations, the other a responsiveness to relationships.[65]

Whether an ethic of care is truly distinct from an ethic of justice is something to which we shall return in the evaluation. Suffice it to say that Gilligan has raised an issue that is interesting and intriguing. It is an appropriate moment to turn to feminism viewed through different eyes.

Susan Okin

In her 1979 work, *Women in Western Political Thought*, the New Zealand-born Susan Okin (1946–2004) examines the existing tradition of political thought to see whether it can "sustain the inclusion of women in its subject matter."[66] In determining the outcome of this examination, Okin looks at four philosophers: Plato, Aristotle, Rousseau, and Mill. She reaches two different conclusions from the study of these philosophers: (i) the most important factor influencing the philosophers' view about women has been their views about the family, and (ii) the constricted role of women is thought by these philosophers to be dictated by women's very nature.[67]

Ten years later in *Justice, Gender, and Family*, Okin seeks to build on her earlier findings, especially findings of a liberal kind as found in John Stuart Mill, whom she sees as "a rare exception to the rule that those who hold central positions in the tradition almost never question the justice of the subordination of women."[68] But, after praising Mill, Okin goes on in this book to focus on the liberal views not of Mill, but of another liberal, the late John Rawls.

Troubles with Rawls's Theory

Okin criticizes Rawls's work, *A Theory of Justice* (1971)—with its two principles of justice (the principle of equal liberty and the principle of difference)—on the grounds that it reveals a "blindness to the sexism of the tradition in which Rawls is a participant."[69] Though acknowledging the brilliance of Rawls's central idea of the original position, a hypothetical position discussed above in our consideration of reform liberalism, Okin has doubts about how this theory of justice, a liberal theory of justice, treats women, gender, and the family.[70] Okin objects to the way Rawls treats sex, as a morally irrelevant and contingent characteristic. She especially objects to this being said in a society such as ours, which is so visibly structured by gender.[71] Her point is not that sex (a biological fact) and gender (a social construction)[72] are one and the same; they are not. Rather, given the unjustifiable role that gender plays in our society, it is incumbent on any theory of justice to pay attention to sex as a morally relevant and essential characteristic. Okin's criticism of Rawls's view of gender is really rooted in what he says about the family. Okin believes that in Rawls's theory, the family is barely visible, and that the theory fails to subject the family to the aforementioned principles of justice.[73] In addition, Okin believes that "the family is the linchpin of gender," and that "Rawls neglects gender."[74] Given that, in Okin's opinion, Rawls treats the family superficially, it is not surprising that she is less than impressed with his few or non-existent comments on gender.

The Feminist Potential of Rawls's Method

Notwithstanding Okin's criticism of Rawls's theory of justice, she thinks the theory has considerable potential for feminist thinking. In particular, she believes Rawls's theory of the original position, with its accompanying veil of ignorance, "is a powerful concept for challenging the gender structure."[75] She believes that once we rid ourselves of some liberal assumptions about public versus domestic as well as political versus non-political spheres of life, one can use Rawls's theory as a tool that enables one to think about justice between the sexes, in the family, and in society at large.[76] The point of entry into an understanding of Okin's feminist interpretation of Rawls's theory is her understanding of **gender**.

By "gender" Okin means "the deeply entrenched institutionalization of sexual differences." Gender turns out, for Okin, to be a social construction. However, she leaves unresolved the issue of the causal role played by biological differences between the sexes in the construction of gender. Once she has defined "gender" in this way, Okin goes on to say that a major justice issue in contemporary society arises from "the issues of gender." These issues—issues of public policy—that surface in a patriarchal society include: sex discrimination, sexual harassment, abortion, pregnancy in the workplace, parental leave, child care, and surrogate mothering.[77] Gender thus becomes a matter of considerable importance in contemporary society because it involves, in very deep way, issues of justice.

Because Okin believes that the family is the linchpin of the gender structure,[78] it is not surprising that she would place an emphasis on the family in her attempt to construct a Rawlsian-inspired theory of justice that aims to build a society without gender. Okin is of the firm belief that the removal of gender from the family would mean the end of many injustices to women and children, and would make the family a much better place for children to develop a sense of justice.[79] With an end to moving away from gender, from this social construction and its accompanying injustices, Okin says that public policies and laws should assume no social differentiation of the sexes. Such public policies would remove injustices, and result in shared parental responsibility for child care, major changes in the workplace for the purpose of helping families, and the elimination of gender-structured marriages.[80] The traditional family is not benign because it is riddled with inequality and discrimination rooted in gender. Since "a just future is a future without gender,"[81] the humanistic family needs to rid itself of the social construction called "gender."

In summation, Okin's theory of what one could call humanistic justice would result in increased justice for women and children to the benefit of all society. Okin believes that, whatever the long-term costs of moving in the direction of a genderless society, the long-term benefits would outweigh them, keeping in mind that the family is the most intimate social grouping and that it is the institution in which justice is first learned.

Martha Nussbaum

In her presidential address to the Central Division of the American Philosophical Association in 2000, Martha Nussbaum (1947–) spoke on the subject of feminism and liberalism.[82] While criticizing the liberalism of Rawls and Kant, she goes on to endorse an Aristotelian liberalism that focuses on a definable list of capacities. The two central themes of her address are discussed below.

Need and Dependency

According to Nussbaum, a central fact for feminism is human need and dependency, a fact she believes is not easily accommodated under the umbrella of the social contract theory. Locke, Kant, David Gauthier, and Rawls have all presented their liberalism in the context of this same contractarian tradition, and because of this she thinks that any defensible liberalism must be revised to offer an account of political justice.[83]

Rather than pursue a political conception of the person that is Kantian in flavour, Nussbaum recommends pursuing an Aristotelian political conception of the person. Morality, she thinks, has the obligation to provide for human neediness and dependency, especially in nonage and dotage, but also when physical or mental misfortune strikes at other times in our lives. The Kantian conception of morality fails in this regard because it is based on the idea of humans being split into rational persons and animal dwellers; it therefore obscures the fact that the dignity of humans simply is the dignity of a certain kind of animal, wrongly denies that animals have a dignity, creates the illusion among humans of self-sufficiency, and creates the illusion of atemporality among humans. Crucial here to understanding Nussbaum is her protest against the Kantian conception on the grounds that it obscures the neediness and dependency that humans have in relation to others, especially when young or old, but at other times as well. Since Nussbaum does not think social contracts constructed on rational considerations undertaken in the "original position" are sensitive to neediness and dependency, she aims to provide a non-contractarian view that is liberal in spirit and sensitive to these aspects. Her proposed view is Aristotelian.[84] But what is this view?

Her guiding Aristotelian conception of the human being sees the person as both capable and needy. Central human capabilities are, she thinks, in a liberal scheme, to be nourished by institutions so that all citizens are given an opportunity to develop "the full range of human powers."[85] Among these capabilities she lists the following: bodily health, bodily integrity, senses, imagination and thought, emotions, practical reason, affiliation, other species, play, control over one's environment, and material.[86] But this says nothing about the "needy" part of the conception that Nussbaum is constructing here. It seems her answer to neediness is provided in the following: "All persons deserve support for a wide range of capabilities," presumably because citizens have "needs for a wide range of capabilities."[87] So the needs and capabilities go together. Hence the basic structure of society has to be built around institutions that positively influence a person's life chances from the start, and this is done by satisfying the needs for cultivating one's capabilities. What marks off Nussbaum's Aristotelian approach from the Kantian or Rawlsian approach to justice and social institutions is that it draws particular attention to dependence in our society, including that of the young and old as well as those who suffer various physical or mental challenges. There is little room for such individuals or for animals in a social contractarian philosophy, but there is room for these in Nussbaum's caregiving and care-receiving system of social justice.

Justice in the Family

When it comes to commenting on women's equality, Nussbaum says that in this matter the most difficult problem for a liberal theory is that of the family. From her perspective the family is one of the most significant areas in which people pursue their conception of the good, suggesting in liberal theory that those who constitute a family should be given considerable freedom to do as they please. Offsetting this is, of course, the fact that the family is a non-voluntary social institution in which occur some of the most egregious acts of sex-based violence, humiliation, denial of equal opportunity, and sex hierarchy. Unlike Rawls, Nussbaum sees the family as very much a creation of state action, and heavily influenced by law in a way that is deeper than the influence of law on other associations.[88] But though the family is, from her perspective, a creation of the state, she believes there are some legal limits to state intervention in the family and they include various liberties and rights of persons. Examples of such rights and liberties are associative liberties, as well as the right to be free from unwanted search and seizure.[89] Otherwise, state involvement in the family should be framed by those public policies that can best promote the human capabilities inside the family. The family, in her terms, has no special status as a "natural" entity or "mystical" entity to block state action in this regard.

Distancing herself from Rawls's approach to the family, she says informatively and categorically, "In my approach, at the basic level we have only the capabilities to consider and we may consider any institutional grouping that will promote them."[90] And again, as if to emphasize her position: "In my approach, the central capabilities always supply a compelling interest for purposes of government action."[91] She is clearly not as deferential to the autonomy of the family as either Kant or Rawls. Her non-contractarian view of justice turns out to be one of caring for others by keeping a vigilant eye on institutional roadblocks or practices that might impede the cultivation of capabilities. Hence she is quite prepared to have the state intervene in the name of caring justice to prevent those practices in the family that, for example, disfigure the lives of girls and women.[92] Therefore, as we shall later see, Nussbaum would have little difficulty in supporting the line of argument pursued by Hirsi Ali in Muslim communities concerning Muslim women and girls.

Val Plumwood

Ecofeminism is one strand of feminist theory that deals with the ways sexism, heteronormativity, racism, colonialism, and ableism support speciesism.[93] One of the better-known advocates of this strand is the Australian Val Plumwood (1939–2008). What she has emphasized in her writings is the link between women's oppression and the domination of nature, thereby tying together sexism and speciesism. Another way of looking at ecofeminism is to see it as the search for an "integrated framework" in the critique of two kinds of domination, namely that of humans and that of nature.[94] Plumwood presses her argument further by maintaining that women have an interest in escaping ancient domination, notably gender domination, and have an interest in a "sound and healthy planet." But then she adds, "gender is a major part of the problem that needs to be addressed to have a different human relationship to the earth."[95]

In developing her position, Plumwood addresses an array of topics, including: dualism, Plato and the philosophy of death, Descartes and the dream of power, mechanism and the mind/nature dualism, rationalism and the ethical approach, and, finally, deep ecology and the denial of difference. In what follows only the last two topics and related themes will be discussed. First to be discussed is Plumwood's view of mainstream environmental ethics, which focuses on the Kantian approach to ethics and is grounded in rationality and reason. Second to be discussed is Plumwood's view of deep ecology and denial of difference. These discussions will be sufficient to bring out themes in Chapter 12:

Environmentalism, and the topic of difference will raise, once again, themes found in the writings of Luce Irigaray. It is to the subjects of Kantian reason in ethics and deep ecology and the denial of difference that we now turn.

Kantian Reason in Ethics

Plumwood wishes to move environmental ethics in the direction of biocentrism, and this she thinks is best done by developing an ethic of care, in the spirit of Carol Gilligan, and then grounding this ethic of care in virtue ethics—ethics that favours people doing what they want to do rather than what they are "constrained to do by duty."[96] The ethic of care favoured by Plumwood stands in stark contrast to the ethic of Kant and its privileging of reason.[97] Plumwood objects to the privileging of reason, in consideration of human behaviour, because, in the case of environmental ethics, it turns respect for nature into a cognitive affair. The Kantian inclination to give special treatment to reason leans, thinks Plumwood, on the old dualism of reason/emotion dating back as far as Plato. Leaving aside Plumwood's general dislike of dualisms, her opposition to Kant's dualism in ethics is rooted, in part, in her belief that this "disguises and denies the dependency of ethical judgement on empathetic elements."[98] But Plumwood also opposes the privileging of reason in this Kantian way because it has led to a bias in favour of men at the expense of women, lower-class men, minorities, and animals.[99] And she also opposes the Kantian practice of privileging reason because it attempts to lead to a universality that "cancels difference,"[100] the very difference that, as we saw above, Irigaray wishes to preserve and affirm. Finally, it can be said that this Australian feminist philosopher opposes the appeal to reason in the Kantian spirit and as emulated by John Rawls in his *A Theory of Justice* because its marked tendency towards Kantian reason and universalization leads away from a nuanced account of ethics, with its appreciation of *difference* as noted by Irigaray and *care* as noted by Gilligan. Left out of the Kantian account of ethics grounded in reason are such practices and concepts as care, respect, gratitude, sensitivity, reverence, and friendship.[101]

Deep Ecology and Denial of Difference

Crucial to understanding Plumwood's overall ethical stance as a feminist is appreciating her affirmation of difference. Instructive in this respect is the following remark of hers: "The failure to admit difference is characteristic of the colonising self which denies the other through the attempt to incorporate it into the empire of the self, and which is unable to experience sameness without erasing difference."[102] So how, one might ask, does this claim tie into deep ecology? Simply in this way. Deep ecology fails to acknowledge difference. Rather, in the spirit of Arne Naess and Warwick Fox,[103] deep ecology cultivates the idea of an expanded self so as to allow for a wider set of concerns that in the end eliminate difference. What we are left with in the case of deep ecology, thinks Plumwood, is "an enlargement and expansion of egoism."[104] More specifically, we are left with an expansion of rational egoism, with all the accompanying problems associated with Kantian reason and rationality. The result is an emphasis once again on universalism, abstraction, and detachment from particularity and the personal and a neglect of difference. Hence the failure to admit difference, so it is thought by Plumwood, results in a colonizing self with an empire of the self. Plumwood wishes to build an account of ecological morality, not on

Kantian reason, but on an ethics of virtue. This ethics of virtue would give pride of place to such concepts as care, respect, gratitude, sensitivity, reverence, and friendship. These are moral concepts that involve cognitive, ethical, and emotive elements and are resistant to analysis along the lines of reason/emotion dualism. This ethics of virtue, she believes, is nuanced and thereby able to accommodate difference and able to combat gender issues and environmental issues in one fell swoop.

Plumwood aims to reject the master story of Western culture, a story of **phallocentrism**. She aims to do this by attacking dualisms,[105] importantly, the dualisms of reason/emotion and reason/nature. By so doing, and by attaching importance to the multi-dimensional aspects of ethical thinking, including the rational and emotional, Plumwood aspires to create room for difference, and in the process she expects to link gender considerations with environmental ones. Virtue ethics and the role of care, as espoused by Carol Gilligan, are used by Plumwood to carve out a new, non-instrumental way of considering ethical problems. In this way, she believes, the masculinity of Western culture can be dismantled more effectively. It is fair to say, in conclusion, that the ecofeminism of Plumwood emphasizes the need to pay attention to context over universal judgments, to care in addition to justice, and to emotion alongside of rationality when discussing the intersecting structures of power that impact women and the environment.[106]

Nel Noddings

Writing in 1989, the American feminist Nel Noddings (1929–) attempts to address the problem of evil in the world from the standpoint of women, not of male interests and masculine experience.[107] Noddings treats evil as anything that harms or threatens to harm humans, and although the problem is usually formulated in a theological context, she does not aim to formulate it this way but rather simply to look at the kinds of things that harm or threaten to harm us (e.g., pain, helplessness, war, terrorism, torture, and psychological abuse) and to analyze these things from a woman's perspective. The ensuing discussion of her thinking will be directed to only one of these evils: war. I will first outline her ethical theory and then discuss her analysis of war in light of this feminist theory of morality.

Relational Ethics

The ethical theory adopted by Noddings is said to be different from traditional individualistic ethics.[108] The first difference is that Noddings's theory does not judge acts on the basis of conformity with a rule or principle, or with the likelihood of increased happiness; rather, it judges acts by the feelings and responses of others. Relational ethics springs from natural caring, as illustrated in maternal caregiving. However, according to Noddings, natural caring is different from ethical caring inasmuch as the latter is dependent on, but not superior to or higher than, the former. In contrast, traditional ethical theory, such as Kant's, contends that the moral or ethical view is higher and more admirable. Relational ethics and natural caring are intertwined and distinct from traditional ethical theory.[109] Noddings leaves open the real possibility that a relational ethic, one with the caring relation at its heart, may be feminine.[110]

Noddings is eager to develop her relational ethics by drawing out the main elements of care theory. To this end she denies that care theory does not imply or posit a strict dualism between feminine and masculine. Instead, what Noddings argues for in care theory is paying attention to the differences in experience and language between men and women and an ethic of giving. She is not concerned with pride of place, but rather with place as it affects women's experience and language. While she thinks some of these differences may be accounted for by evolutionary biology in an essential way, she does not wish to affirm that biology accounts in an essential way for all the differences between men and women. In the end it would seem, according to Noddings, that there are differences between experiences and language of men and women, and that some, but not all, of these differences can be explained through evolutionary biology.[111] Regardless of the presence or absence of biological origins, the differences between the feminine and masculine give rise to two different paths to morality: one of care and one of justice and inequities.[112]

Women and War

Noddings claims that modern cultures typically acknowledge war to be a great evil.[113] She recognizes that, nonetheless, war and warriors have been glorified in many places and times.[114] However, this feminist wishes to move the discussion forward, and she does this by focusing not on the problems associated with conducting war but on ways of preventing it.[115] Early on in her discussion, she directs our attention to the practice of striving, whether for war or pacifism, poverty or wealth, and she locates this emphasis on the *agon* or contest in the masculine trait of striving. To reach the extremes by choice through striving is to show the mark of manhood.[116] This is not to say that Noddings wishes to totally condemn striving but that she wishes to help us understand and control it so that we have "a totally different way of looking at life, and we want to see what can be said of war when we take this perspective."[117]

Pervasive individualism that supports the warrior model stands in sharp contrast to the relational model of women. The former fits snugly into the masculine ethos of war, while the latter fits nicely into the care ethics of feminists. She wishes to look at war through the eyes of someone not "enchanted by the individualistic or tribal conception of striving," meaning she wishes to look at it through the relational ethics of care.[118] This ethic of care asks questions such as the following: How should I behave to maintain appreciation or respect? How can I get disagreeing parties to put aside their differences so that we can have a pleasant meal? How can I, without using violence, protect my children from violence?[119] Raising these questions, she thinks, leads us to developing practical skills, such as learning how to pay attention to people's feelings and to the ways these feelings are often manipulated for personal or group interests.[120] Care ethics, she thinks, being relational, can begin to shed light on the ways to prevent war by first getting at the root of rivalry and competition, predicated as they are on striving. We now turn to her suggestions on what can be done in schools to help create a favourable climate that turns students away from striving, rivalry, competition, and war.

In Noddings's opinion, schools have been sites for rivalries and competition for some time. In fact, she believes "competition seen in schools is not merely a mirror image of natural phenomena that the culture has not yet mastered; it is calculated preparation for a competitive way of life."[121] Moreover, she asserts that an ideology of individualism supports the competitive and adversarial way of life, and this individualism pervades our politics, sports, religion, and ethics.[122] What can schools do to move away from this ideology and from competition, rivalry, striving, and war? This will be accomplished, on Noddings's line of reasoning, by getting rid of ignorance in the human heart, not ignorance in the head, by attending to the transformation of affect and experience. One suggestion she has for this change in pedagogy is for students to engage in some sort of community service work as an apprenticeship in caring. Further, by getting rid of artificial separations in the school system, that is, by getting rid of grades, honours, competitions, summative evaluations, rankings, and the authority of hierarchical positions, the result will be an elimination of those things that "cripple caring relations" and sow the seeds of ignorance in the human heart.[123] Further, Noddings adds, teachers need to study human relations (not just the psychology of learning), teachers need to understand the tragic sense of life, and finally, teachers need to know something about ways to create various kinds of relations (e.g., projections, association and dissociation, rhetoric, and the use of oaths). In addition, Noddings says teacher–student relations have to concentrate on how our moral behaviour depends on the moral worth we give to others.[124] All of these pedagogical initiatives Noddings sees as contributing to a caring ethic that will serve to reduce competition, rivalry, enmity, and striving. From the perspective of women, she thinks, all of these, though particularly striving, constitute an evil or near evil. In conclusion, we can say that Noddings believes the cultural evil of war has at its root the neglect of relation.[125] By emphasizing care and relational ethics in education, Noddings wishes to "elevate positive female traits and encourage both boys and girls to hate, not love, war."[126]

Ayaan Hirsi Ali

Any discussion of feminism would be incomplete without a consideration of the thoughts of Ayaan Hirsi Ali (1969–), a Somali-born "lapsed" Muslim who presently lives in the United States and who wrote the screenplay for the provocative short film *Submission: Part I*, directed by Theo van Gogh. (Van Gogh, it should be noted, was murdered by a Dutch Muslim for having made this film about Islamic attitudes towards women barely two months after it aired in 2004 on Dutch television, and Hirsi Ali, at the time a Dutch legislator, went into hiding and was given security protection.) Hirsi Ali's trenchant criticisms of the faith in which she was raised offer a unique perspective on Islam and the life of Muslim women. Her discussion about Islam in her wide-ranging 2006 book, *The Caged Virgin*, presents many engaging ideas, only a few of which can be discussed here. Hirsi Ali investigates whether the roots of hatred, particularly hatred directed at the United States as made clear in the attacks of 9/11, can be traced to Islam. On the way to trying to answer this question, Hirsi Ali outlines three important features of Islam that had not struck her before she came to live in Europe. These were, first, that a Muslim's relationship with Allah his God is one of fear; second, that Islam recognizes only one moral source, the Prophet Muhammad, who is infallible; and third, that Islam is dominated by tribal Arab sexual values dating from the time of the Prophet.[127]

Hirsi Ali has been outspoken in her criticism of aspects of Islam; of particular note is her outspokenness concerning the way Muslim women are treated inside the Muslim community. She outlines four reasons in attempting to justify her position. To begin with, she says that she wishes to end the degrading treatment of Muslim women and girls by using her knowledge of Islam. Next, she believes that without the emancipation of Muslim women, which presumably her criticism would enhance, the socially disadvantageous position of Muslim women in Western countries will persist. Further, she feels that Muslim women need someone to speak on their behalf given the dearth of social organizations and political parties that speak for them. Finally, as a passionate believer in human rights, Hirsi Ali argues that someone must take aim at the emphasis placed on Muslim identity and its corresponding "group rights" because, in the end, this is detrimental to Muslim women. In this last reason, Hirsi Ali makes a point of expressly agreeing with Susan Okin, discussed above, in Okin's criticism of multiculturalism, which, it is argued, incubates and protects differences in power and repression of women.[128] Making a concerted effort to advance the position of Muslim women, Hirsi Ali first describes in detail the condition of contemporary Muslim women and then encourages the development of Enlightenment ideas in the Muslim world to advance the position of these same women. To these two themes we now turn.

The Caged Virgin

Prescient remarks that bear close examination are made by Hirsi Ali near the end of her chapter titled "The Caged Virgin." She asserts, "The Islamic world is in a great crisis that also constitutes a threat to the West, a threat that consists not only of terrorism but also of streams of migration and of the risk that civil wars will break out in the Middle East."[129] Her words have proved prophetic: terrorism is evident in the actions of **Boko Haram** in Nigeria; in the attack by ISIS supporters on the offices of the satirical magazine *Charlie Hebdo* in Paris on 7 January 2015; in the attack by ISIS supporters on the Bataclan Theatre in Paris on 13 November 2015; and in the attack by ISIS supporters on Zaventem airport and the subway in Brussels on 22 March 2016; and civil war and terror are evident in the conflict involving multiple state and insurgent groups in Syria and the so-called Islamic State group in Syria and Iraq, as well as in Libya. At the same time, the flood of approximately a million refugees and migrants from the Middle East has swamped the European Union. To be sure, these developments are beginning to make their mark on the twenty-first century as we know it. For Hirsi Ali, the plight of the Muslim woman in Islam has to be understood against the background of a religion that produces these fanatical movements. To appreciate this more we need to grasp more fully what she has in mind by the **caged virgin**.

Hirsi Ali believes strongly, based on the evidence she has gathered, that Arab and non-Arab countries that have "embraced" Islam are "in many ways far behind the West."[130] This leads her to ask what is blocking or preventing the progress of Muslims. From her perspective, Muslims are religious believers who are often faced with aggression, economic and scientific stagnation, repression, epidemics, and social unrest, and that these act as a drag on progress in Muslim states.[131] Why, she asks, is this so? She acknowledges that a complex combination of factors contribute to these social abnormalities, but the one she singles out for particular attention is the sexual morality of Islam, a morality that, in her opinion, was "originally a tribal morality that has been elevated within Islam to the status of a dogma."[132] If this is so, and considering the view advanced in Chapter 1, the dogmatic features of Islam begin to turn it into an ideology—an ideology that Hirsi Ali wishes to criticize.[133]

Hirsi Ali acknowledges that the obsession with the mastery over the sexuality of women is not limited to the Muslim faith. It is also, she claims, present in the Christian, Jewish, and Hindu faiths.[134] But she believes this obsession has hindered Muslim adherents more than it has hindered those of other faiths. She describes the social costs to Muslim women arising from the obsession with virginity, the obsession of protecting Muslim girls' hymens before marriage.[135] The measures taken to ensure the protection of the hymen are, according to Hirsi Ali, "all aimed at [Muslim] girls."[136] These measures include girls covering themselves, living a life of house arrest by being sentenced to domestic work indoors, being kept in separate quarters indoors from non-family members who may be present, and finally, the most extreme measure, female "circumcision," which is prevalent in African Muslim communities, with Somalia having the highest rate of female genital mutilation. In describing the last in this list, she writes, "The process involves the cutting away of the girl's clitoris, the outer and inner labia, as well as the scraping of the walls of the vagina with a sharp object . . . and then the binding of her legs together so that the walls of the vagina can grow together."[137] To this list of measures taken to protect Muslim girls' virginity, Hirsi Ali adds the measure taken by Muslim men to prevent cheating by Muslim women after marriage: denying women access to the outside world. Accordingly, a married Muslim woman must have the husband's permission or accompany the husband when she goes outside her home. All of these measures of control constitute, for Hirsi Ali, the virgin's cage.[138]

Hirsi Ali carries the discussion further by adding, "the virgins' cage is, in fact, a double cage," comprising the one previously described as well as a larger cage "in which the entire Islamic culture has been imprisoned."[139] It is her belief that by caging women for the purpose of guarding their virginity, frustration and violence ensues, and leads to "socioeconomic backwardness for the entire community."[140] This backwardness results from the ignorance of the women involved, who are kept isolated and away from education and, consequently, are able to pass on only limited knowledge to their children, thereby "perpetuating a vicious cycle of ignorance from generation to generation."[141] Hirsi Ali believes that when this ignorance is coupled with fear and violence against children and women, and with the unattainability of some of the values of the Qur'an (e.g., reconciling the belief that the faithful must strive after knowledge and the Qur'an is the source of all knowledge), confusion and contradictions result that inevitably become "pathological" in both Muslim men and women.[142]

Breaking out of the cage(s) in which Muslims are imprisoned and in which they have imprisoned Muslim women, people of this faith, according to Hirsi Ali, must practice self-criticism and begin to evaluate the moral values they extract from the Qur'an.[143] Moreover, she is convinced that Muslims (both men and women) who live in the West can take a critical look at their own faith because in the West, unlike in their countries of origin, they have access to libraries and universities where they can gain knowledge. Hirsi Ali believes that many Muslims (men and women) are waiting for an enlightenment to occur in Islam, but she does not believe this enlightenment can occur without men and women thinking differently about sexuality. To underscore this point, she adds, in uncompromising terms, "Instead of devoting energy and money to the development of an even larger atomic bomb . . . the Islamic world would be better employed in critically examining its own sexual morality and the suffocating effects of its own cultures and societies, and devising proposals for change."[144] Clearly, Hirsi Ali believes self-criticism of the larger and smaller cages can only occur by looking seriously at the pathological aspects of the impact of Islam's sexual morality, at the centre of which stand Muslim women and Muslim girls.

Enlightenment and Islam

Following the events of 9/11, Hirsi Ali thinks that many people in the West began to ask questions about Islam. In particular, she suggests, they began to ask whether Islam is compatible with a system of constitutional democracy and whether Islam should strive for enlightenment and modernization.[145] Put more bluntly, Hirsi Ali asserts that people began to ask if Islam needs a **Voltaire** to help rid itself of superstition.[146] For her part, she wishes for a Muslim Voltaire capable of ridding Islam of its superstition.

Hirsi Ali, who renounced her faith and became an atheist in 2002, appears to think that all or most of the following beliefs help comprise this superstition: Allah is almighty; man is his slave; Muslims are superior to other religious peoples; men are superior to women; children must obey parents; individuals who do not comply with the above rules are to be humiliated or murdered in the name of Allah; life on earth is temporary; and spiritual entities (saints, ghosts, angels, little demons, jinn, spirits of the dead, Satan) play a role in this earthly world.[147] She asserts that Muslims all over the world are brought up with "similar beliefs in the supernatural" and in the existence of an afterlife. She thinks it is a "short step" from these same beliefs to thinking that paradise is achieved through martyrdom. She then adds that this results from a mindset far removed from reason, in other words, far removed from the spirit of Voltaire who saw superstition at odds with reason and common sense.[148] These considerations drive Hirsi Ali to conclude that present-day Islam needs a reason-centred enlightenment, in the spirit of Voltaire, to take Islamic societies away from the Dark Ages with their superstitious prejudices directed against women, Jews, and homosexuals. In brief, her critique calls for a heavy dose of self-criticism among all Muslims.[149] From Hirsi Ali's perspective, the role of reason must be restored in the Muslim world. In other words, religion, which she thinks offers no solution to poverty, violence, political instability, economic malaise, and human suffering, must be driven back to the places where it belongs (mosque and home) and replaced by rational and scientific analysis.[150] While it is true that Hirsi Ali is concerned about the need for an enlightenment in Islamic societies to address a wide range of social ills, she is especially concerned with those that target women in a way that fails to recognize universal values such as the freedom of the individual and the equality of men and women.[151]

In her most recent work, *Heretic*, Hirsi Ali has restated much of the above by claiming that Islamic doctrine must be amended in five ways to make "being a Muslim more readily compatible with the twenty-first-century world."[152] These doctrinal amendments strike at the following core concepts in Islam:

- the status of the Qur'an as the last and immutable word of God and the infallibility of Muhammad as the last divinely inspired messenger;
- Islam's emphasis on the afterlife;
- the claims of *shariah* to be a comprehensive system of law governing both spiritual and temporal realms;
- the obligation on ordinary Muslims to command right and forbid wrong;
- the concept of jihad.[153]

The amendments of these beliefs constitute, for Hirsi Ali, a Reformation in Islam. While her focus in *Heretic* is on the overall social impact of Islam in its present form on Muslims and the world generally, her attention frequently shifts back to the impact of Islam today on Muslim women in their cage(s).[154] The Reformation she calls for is clearly meant to benefit the religion itself, but one should not lose sight of the fact that Hirsi Ali means for it to benefit Muslim women in a very significant way. In the conflict between traditional Islam and women's rights, she asserts that the former must give way to the latter. The two cages—the cage of the virgin and the cage of traditional Islam—must both be broken.

Conclusion

As is evident in the preceding discussion, generalizations on what this ideology stands for are hard to come by. While it might be tempting to say that the second wave of feminism as ushered in by Simone de Beauvoir and Betty Friedan split into different strands, it is more accurate to say that many voices are heard under the heading of "feminism." Schwarzer speaks of the vaginal orgasm and sex monopoly, echoing some of the things previously said by Shulamith Firestone, while Luce Irigaray attacks principles of the Enlightenment, affirms difference between men and women, and attacks the phallomorphism of present patriarchal societies by examining the substructural philophical discourse. Gilligan affirms difference and introduces the idea of an ethic of care, a theme that re-emerges in the writings of Noddings and, to a less marked degree, in the writings of Plumwood, who speaks of an ethics of virtue. Interestingly, Irigaray speaks critically of the omission in philosophy of the emotional part of the soul, a point made with some vigour by Plumwood. Okin, for her part, places emphasis on Rawls's notion of justice and the social contract and criticizes multiculturalism, a point with which Hirsi Ali agrees. Nussbaum reverts back to Aristotelian ethics, emphasizing capacities and needs. In this she perhaps stands with some of the above writers in rejecting the principles of Kantianism and the Enlightenment. Ultimately, no common thread runs through feminism, except this: all feminists object to the marginalization of women.[155] Some develop their ideas around language, some around ethics, and some around politics.

The line of argument pursued by feminists is based on a frank assessment of the traditional role of women. This assessment is rooted in the overwhelming empirical evidence of discrimination of women along gender lines, which works its way into practices of domination, patriarchy, institutions, and the prevailing ethics of justice. While largely empirical in its method of exposing these various modes of discrimination, the constructed ideology of feminism is normatively iconoclastic. Its form of argument sees little merit in the is/ought distinction, but moves along from descriptive idioms to normative ones as though there were a seamless connection between the two. Its method shares with Marxism its spirit of iconoclasm and disrespect for tradition (think here of its rejection of the virgin in the cage), and it distances itself from libertarianism in its affirmation of communitarian values (think here of Plumwood's position on the environment). The exact emphasis placed on these values varies from feminist to feminist. In all forms of feminism, the line of argument is meant to be prodding and unsettling, if not radical and revolutionary. Interestingly, this line of argument is anything but one enveloping spirit of equanimity.

Evaluation: The Strengths of Feminism

1. Feminism as a political ideology has transformed itself into an encompassing and versatile school of thought. It is not, contrary to the opinion of some, an ideology of white, middle-class North Americans, as found in Betty Friedan's *The Feminine Mystique*. It is keenly interested in vertical and horizontal power structures that work against the interests of women. It argues convincingly against domination by men

of women that occurs in most, if not all, societies. It argues successfully, throughout the world, in favour of mechanisms to guarantee support for women and children for the purpose of protecting them from violence inside the family.[156] It argues effectively against poverty that results from the inequality between men and women in the workplaces around the globe. Feminism has established convincingly that the exploitation and oppression in all societies (not just North America, Europe, Australia, and New Zealand) and in all classes (not just white middle-class ones) must be abolished by dismantling cages of domination.

2. Feminism, quite properly, alerts us to an ethic of care. In so doing, it alerts us to the importance of developing moral dispositions, seeking responses that are appropriate to particular cases, and placing some emphasis on responsibilities and relationships. Does this mean that the ethic of care is distinct from an ethic of justice? The answer here is not clear. What can be said is that, at the very least, points made by Gilligan, Noddings, Plumwood, and Nussbaum show the need to construct an ethical theory that is rich enough to capture the foregoing aspects of an ethic of care. Liberals, in their theory of justice, are often accused by feminists of being insensitive to these aspects. An example of such a liberal, it is claimed, is John Rawls, when he assumes—in his magnum opus, *A Theory of Justice*—that family institutions are just.[157] Whatever the failures on this score of liberals like John Rawls, the present point is not that feminists are correct in talking about "two voices" and two theories, but that at the very least they have demonstrated a need for advocates of theories of justice to prove that these theories can respond to feminists' criticisms by encompassing an ethic of care. Clearly, an ethic of justice has to have something to say about, for example, responsibilities and relationships. A lingering thought remains, however, that Gilligan and others may be correct in affirming the existence of "two voices." An ethic of care, which includes placing a premium on responsibilities and relationships, comes very close to an ethic of benevolence and maximalism, while an ethic of justice, at times, seems to come closer to rule-compliance and an ethic of minimalism. It could be argued that therein lie the two voices identified by Gilligan and others.

3. Feminism, quite appropriately, places an emphasis on relationships, in developing an ethic of care. In articulating this conception of morality, Gilligan asserts that it centres "moral development around the understanding of responsibility and relationships."[158] Gilligan is not alone in emphasizing relationships. In *Letters to a Young Poet*, Rainer Maria Rilke, in his discussion of love and death, comments, "We are only just now beginning to look upon the relation of one individual to a second person without prejudice and realistically, and our attempts to live such associations have no example before them."[159] Feminists, in their own words, are picking up on this theme of relationships and placing it front and centre in their ethic of care. Given that relationships provide meaning in one's life, that meaning entails disclosure, and that disclosure entails exposure, it would seem that feminism draws attention to a pivotal part of any interesting theory of ethics. It is to the credit of feminists that they raise this theme articulated by Rilke.[160]

4. Martha Nussbaum offers a plausible defence of a liberal version of feminism. She does this by avoiding the pitfalls with Rawls's contractarianism, including the difficulty

it has in accommodating infants and animals. Moreover, she very cleverly offers a reinvigorated Aristotelian approach to issues associated with need and dependency, thereby putting in modern dress ideas that were canvassed pretty thoroughly in the nineteenth century by John Stuart Mill. In addition, Nussbaum recognizes the limitations with Rawls's treatment (or lack of treatment) of the family. She is quite correct that this is a non-mystical institution in which governments have a right to intervene in the absence of proper nurturing of the needs of an individual. She thereby provides for a reinvigorated kind of liberalism, through feminist eyes.

5. The distinction Okin makes between gender and sex is clearly articulated. Okin, in particular, makes a persuasive case for saying that gender is a morally indefensible social construct, and that the family is the linchpin of this social construct. She makes a compelling case for ways in which Rawls's notion of the original position and the veil of ignorance can be exploited by feminists to advance issues of women.

6. Many feminists correctly point out the importance of the family as a bearer of values for future generations. Gilligan, Nussbaum, Okin, Noddings, Plumwood, and Hirsi Ali have emphasized that the family must be examined with an eye to establishing either a just or a caring society. It is clearly recognized by most feminists that acts of violence against women and children occur frequently in the confines of the family.

7. Schwarzer and Hirsi Ali have identified the totem-like role that phallocentrism and a dogma of virginity play in modern societies. Domination by men of women and the loss of freedom for women are alleged to be the product of these totem-like practices. This allegation is effectively argued by feminists in general, but especially so by Schwarzer and Hirsi Ali.

8. Feminists include individuals who, as advocates of care ethics, have presented a reasonable defence of the claim that emotions should not be left out of ethical considerations. In taking this position feminists mount a successful initial attack on a Kantian presupposition, namely, that ethics is about universal principles discernible by reason alone. It is the undiluted belief in the autonomy of reason—so passionately defended by Kant and others in the Enlightenment—that feminists subject to a relentless attack.[161]

9. Some feminists, notably Irigaray, alert us to the possibility that the deep philosophical presuppositions of our thinking about humans are fraught with a strong bias in favour of masculinity. Irigaray traces this bias back to Plato and Aristotle and extends it to the period of the Enlightenment inspired by Kant. Irigaray's irreverence is, in its own way, both courageous and healthy: courageous because it runs against the opinion of so many, but in an original way; and healthy because it forces any serious political philosophy to re-examine its foundations.

10. Hirsi Ali persuasively makes the case against cultural relativism by pointing out that talk of human rights has to be universalized to apply across cultures and not just to Anglo or European ones. By so arguing, Hirsi Ali shows the incompatibility of feminism with ethical relativism. This demonstration gives additional plausibility and

relevance to feminism, an ideology some have thought to be Western in its implications. Hirsi Ali, it is argued, disarms those who would restrict feminism to European and English-speaking societies.

Evaluation: The Weaknesses of Feminism

1. While Schwarzer successfully attacks sexual monopoly, the myth of vaginal orgasm, and the support these notions give to men's emotional, social, and economic monopoly, her solution to the problems they create for women is extreme. We should recall that her solution calls for the end to heterosexual penetration except for the purpose of procreation. This sounds more like a solution dated to a period prior to the contraceptive pill.

2. Irigaray ingeniously makes some bold and original observations about the linkage between phallomorphism and the patriarchal society. She carries this discussion correctly in the direction of philosophy as the discourse on discourse. What she does not make clear is how this philosophical discourse creates a hierarchical structure that puts the feminine in a position of inferiority and exploitation. Further, and importantly, she does not make clear how this errant philosophical language can be corrected in such a way that it preserves difference between the sexes without making use of this same language. Putting the matter in a metaphorical way: the ship can be rebuilt on the high seas but it has to be rebuilt plank by plank to avoid loss of all the cargo.

3. The ethic of care, so ably articulated by Gilligan and endorsed by others such as Plumwood and Noddings, arguably is implicit in the writings of Adam Smith when he speaks, not just of the virtue of prudence in one's own case, but also of the virtue of benevolence in the case of others. Smith, in his *Theory of Moral Sentiments*, numbers compassion, pity, and sympathy among the principles that direct a person to take an interest in the fortune of others.[162] Moreover, Smith does not see the virtue of benevolence as identical with that of justice, for he says, "The virtues of prudence, justice, and beneficence have no tendency to produce any but the most agreeable effects."[163] So it could be argued that Gilligan does not give credit where it is due when she hives off an area of ethics—namely, care—and fails to acknowledge its pedigree in Smith's notion of benevolence. Of course, none of this shows Gilligan et al. to be in error in what they assert, but it does imply a myopia on their part with respect to the philosophical roots of care ethics.

4. Okin does a good job in making suitable adjustments to Rawls's theory of justice, inspired as it is by Kantian ideals, and goes on to argue somewhat convincingly that the family is the linchpin of the gender structure and that the latter should be removed in order to establish justice for women and children. Okin's ethics is grounded in a theory of justice, not care. But whereas Okin's theory leaves no room for gender except as a social construct, care ethics, it seems, allows room for it as biologically rooted. Noddings, a supporter of relational and care ethics, concedes that some aspects of essentialism are true—biological evolution, at times, influences cultural evolution. Hence the maternal instinct influences cultural manifestations.[164] This seems to be an

affirmation of gender as something other than a social construct, at least under some circumstances. None of this shows that Okin is incorrect in what she says, but it does show that there is unresolved tension between her and some other feminists, notably Noddings, that needs resolution.

5. Nussbaum offers a refreshingly different approach from that proposed in the political philosophy of Kant or Rawls. Her emphasis on the nourishing of capabilities, which include a full range of human powers, is attractive and robust. Her biggest difficulty in adopting an Aristotelian approach to ethics and political philosophy is simply the absence of an agreed natural law theory on which her ethics has to be based. The rejection of contractarianism means the rejection of a form of positivism in keeping with the spirit of realism—a spirit that seems to infuse our times. With the rejection of contractarianism, Nussbaum is left to defend some kind of naturalism that runs the risk of sinking into subjectivity. This is by no means a fatal objection to what she says, but it does place a burden on her to deliver a higher-level defence of her normative judgments.

6. For her part, Plumwood aims to reject what she calls the "master story" of Western culture—phallocentrism. She might have considered extending this criticism, in the spirit of Hirsi Ali, who speaks of phallomorphism, to non-Western cultures as well. A more serious difficulty with Plumwood's foray into feminism and environmentalism is simply that, in her eagerness to adopt a kind of biocentrism and a non-instrumental way of thinking of the environment, she may well find herself unable to defend the "difference" between the feminine and the masculine that she, along with Irigaray, desperately wishes to preserve. The problem is simply that in homogenizing feminism and environmentalism, Plumwood will be unable to defend difference.

7. A different approach is taken by Noddings. She suggests that the evil of war—demonstratively a great evil—can be partially undone by adopting a relational ethics of care in certain fields, notably education. It would seem that, while there is merit in changing some of our educational practices so as to diminish the importance of competition and striving—said by Noddings to be the source of war—it strains credulity to think that significant inroads on war can be made in this way. To begin with, the entire capitalist system in both Eastern and Western cultures is predicated on innovation and competition. Consequently, even if some pedagogical success could be had to reduce the importance of competition, it seems unlikely that this would be effective in reducing conflicts around the globe. At most, people would only be slightly less inclined to resolve disputes this way. Long before approaching the reduction of war in this way, it is more plausible to say it could be reduced by educating people about their petty nationalisms or religions. A further problem arises when one thinks just how deeply embedded competition is in our lives: games, leagues, music competitions, Olympics, job searches, career paths, military appointments, judicial appointments, administrative appointments, contract awards on closed bids, and ethnic competition.

8. When Hirsi Ali calls for a Voltaire to come forth in the Muslim world, she affirms the principles of the Enlightenment. This stands in sharp contrast to the criticisms made

by Irigaray of the principles of this Kantian age. What this shows is a heightened tension among feminists, a tension that needs to be resolved if this ideology is to function in a coherent and consistent pattern.

9. Hirsi Ali attacks the notion of the caged virgin in Islamic societies. In her enthusiasm to support enlightened practices in the West, she misses an opportunity to show that Western women sometimes find themselves in cages. The feminist Kate Millett has explored the notions of power and domination in several literary works by Norman Mailer and Jean Genet.[165] Genet uses the metaphor of three cages to illustrate vividly the loss of freedom humans experience at the hands of (i) authority figures, such as judges, generals, and clerics, (ii) the police state, and (iii) the institution of sex—a cage in which all others are enclosed.[166] Hirsi Ali could have strengthened her account by making use of some of Millett's ideas as they apply in Western societies.

10. For historical accuracy, Hirsi Ali has an obligation to demonstrate that the sexual morality of Islam was originally a tribal morality that was subsequently elevated to the status of a dogma. Two factors were clearly at work in the cultural evolution that occurred in Arabia at the time of Muhammad. One of these was **Islamization** and the other was **Arabization**. Hirsi Ali needs to discuss these in depth to make her case more convincing, especially as it applies to virginity and sexual morality.[167]

Related Websites

Feminist Majority Foundation
www.feminist.org/

"Feminist Political Philosophy." *Stanford Encyclopedia of Philosophy.* 1 Apr. 2014.
http://plato.stanford.edu/entries/feminism-political/

The Feminist Wire
http://thefeministwire.com/

Offen, Karen. "The History of Feminism Is Political History." American Historical Association, *Perspectives on History,* **May 2011.**
https://www.historians.org/publications-and-directories/perspectives-on-history/may-2011/political-history-today/the-history-of-feminism-is-political-history

Further Readings on Feminism

Abbey, Ruth. *The Return of Feminist Liberalism.* Montreal and Kingston: McGill-Queen's University Press, 2011.

Anderson, Kristin J. *Modern Misogyny: Anti-Feminism in a Post-Feminist Era.* London: Oxford University Press, 2015.

Armstrong, Elisabeth. *Gender and Neoliberalism: The All India Democratic Women's Association and Globalization Politics.* New York: Routledge, 2014.

Bracke, Maud. *Women and the Reinvention of the Political: Feminism in Italy, 1968–1983.* New York: Routledge, 2014.

Collins, Dana M. *New Directions in Feminism and Human Rights*. New York: Routledge, 2011.

Coogan- Gehr, Kelly. *The Geopolitics of the Cold War and Narratives of Inclusion: Excavating a Feminist Archive*. New York: Palgrave Macmillan, 2011.

Eswaran, Mukesh. *Why Gender Matters in Economics*. Princeton, NJ: Princeton University Press, 2014.

Galtry, Judith. "Susan Miller Okin: A New Zealand Tribute 10 Years On." *Women's Study Journal* 28, 2 (2015): 1–93.

Gardiner, Rita H. *Gender, Authenticity and Leadership: Thinking with Arendt*. Basingstoke, UK: Macmillan, 2015.

Hague, Ros. *Autonomy and Identity: The Politics of Who We Are*. New York: Routledge, 2011.

Hannam, June. *Feminism*. Harlow, UK and New York: Longman, 2012.

Haussman, Melissa, Marian Sawer, and Jill Vickers. *Federalism, Feminism, and Multilevel Governance*. Burlington, VT: Ashgate, 2010.

McAfee, Noëlle. *Democracy and the Political Unconsciousness*. New York: Columbia University Press, 2008.

McBride, Dorothy E., Amy Mazur, and Joni Lovenduski. *The Politics of State Feminism*. Philadelphia: Temple University Press, 2010.

Mojab, Shahrzad. *Marxism and Feminism*. London: Zed Books, 2015.

Phipps, Alison. *The Politics of the Body: Gender in a Neoliberal and Neoconservative Age*. Cambridge: Polity Press, 2014.

Redhead, Robin. *Exercising Human Rights: Gender, Agency, and Practice*. New York: Routledge, 2015.

Richards, Rebecca S. *Transnational Feminist Rhetorics and Gendered Leadership in Global Politics: From Daughters of Destiny to Iron Ladies*. Lanham, MD: Lexington Books, 2015.

Tickner, Ann J., and Laura Sjoberg. *Feminism and International Relations: Conversations about the Past, Present, and Future*. New York: Routledge, 2011.

Wahab, Stephanie, Ben Anderson-Nathe, and Christina E. Gringeri. *Feminism in Social Work Research: Promise and Possibilities for Justice Based Knowledge*. New York: Routledge, 2015.

12 Environmentalism

They are all gone now. During our visit Claire and I saw not one fishing vessel at work on all the vast sweep of salt water bordering southwestern Newfoundland. Those once astoundingly fecund waters have been so drained of life that there is no longer any profit to be made from them.

—Farley Mowat, *The Farfarers: Before the Norse* (1998: 307–8)

Learning Objectives

- To understand the multi-faceted nature of the debate in environmentalism.
- To appreciate the historical lineage of present-day discussions in environmentalism.
- To learn about the *World Scientists' Warning to Humanity*.
- To recognize the complexity of the issues pertaining to population, land use, water availability, energy, climate change, toxic chemicals, forests, biodiversity, and oceans.

Near the site of a great nesting of the passenger pigeon in 1871, the following words are inscribed: THIS SPECIES BECAME EXTINCT THROUGH THE AVARICE AND THOUGHTLESSNESS OF MAN. Such are the words on a monument erected in 1947 by the Wisconsin Society for Ornithology in Wyalusing State Park.[1] These jarring words need to be read with an understanding of there having been well over a billion passenger pigeons in one flock in the early part of the nineteenth century.[2] The unmistakable effect of these words combined with an appreciation of the magnitude of the extinction—migrating flocks of many millions of passenger pigeons were said to block out the sun for hours on end—is one of pessimism, if not deep gloom, for the future of humans and their environment. Humans appear as a venal beast in this story of the passenger pigeon. But humans are fighting back against activities that contribute to the venal beast image, and they are doing so in many different ways. And just over the horizon, though not discussed below, are intimations of the possibility of de-extinction by means of genetic sequencing and synthetic biology.[3] Could the woolly mammoth or the passenger pigeon be resurrected as a species? This question has always appeared to have a self-evident negative answer, but new ideas drawing on genetic sequencing are beginning to challenge the "self-evidence." Clearly, a deeper answer to this question lies in the future. At present, it is worth our while to keep in mind the idea of de-extinction as we work our way through the thoughts of the writers and events discussed below.

On 5 June 2005, the Bhopal Medical Appeal (BMA), a project of Pesticides Action Network UK, took out a full-page ad in the highly respected English newspaper, *The Observer*, soliciting financial support for the victims of an accident at the Union Carbide factory in Bhopal, India, on 2–3 December 1984. A testimonial description by one of the victims of this accident, named Sanno, reads as follows:

> Our water began stinking years ago. It had a fiery taste, sometimes it was brown in colour. We told the authorities but nothing was done. The problem was the nearby Union Carbide factory. After that horrible night when the factory killed thousands, Carbide left without cleaning it. They left tons of chemicals. Far away in America, they denied they were poisoning our water. Their own company papers show that they knew otherwise. When they put fish in the water from the factory, all the fish instantly died.[4]

This testimonial highlights a tragedy that began over 30 years ago when highly toxic methyl isocyanate gas leaked from a Union Carbide factory, killing thousands and maiming up to 200,000.[5] As the BMA makes clear, this tragedy has been compounded by inaction on the part of Union Carbide down to the present time. It "calls on Union Carbide's owners Dow Chemical to act responsibly, clean their factory and the underground water." And it goes on to request that "the local government . . . obey the Supreme Court order and provide clean water."[6] The fate of the residents of Bhopal casts a dark shadow over corporations and local governments in the matter of their insensitivity to the environment and its impact on people. This dark shadow, along with others elsewhere, helped awaken the sensitivities of those advocating the ideology of **environmentalism**.

The Bhopal gas leak was just one of several environmental disasters that occurred around the world within a particularly troubling decade.[7] There seems little point in cataloguing those disasters here. Rather, what needs to be done to understand environmentalism as an ideology is, first, to trace its historical roots and, second, to analyze different versions of it: proto-ecologism, reform environmentalism, transitional environmentalism, deep ecologism, transpersonal ecologism, socialist ecologism, and anarcho-ecologism. Conceptualizing environmentalism in this way allows for different perspectives on the environment, each of which deserves analysis. For this reason, the foregoing positions will be studied as though on an ideological continuum. We now turn to the historical roots of this ideology, an ideology that US President Barack Obama has adopted in part by moving his nation towards a clean energy economy.[8] His action and advocacy have the potential of giving this ideology an even higher profile than it would otherwise have had.

Ramachandra Guha has argued that there have been two waves of environmentalism, one beginning around 1860 and the other around 1960.[9] It is useful to see the first wave as comprising several phases, possibly three, including a moral and cultural phase, a scientific conservation phase, and a wilderness phase. Once this wave had passed, talk about the environment began to congeal, around 1960, into something more ideological, and something that was qualitatively different from what preceded it. This marked the beginning of the second wave.

As Guha says, "The first wave of environmentalism proceeded step-by-step with the Industrial Revolution, itself the most far-reaching process of social change in human history."[10] The people who made up the first phase of this wave comprised those who engaged in a moral and cultural critique, otherwise called the back-to-the-land idea; those who favoured scientific conservation; and those who favoured a combination of morality, science, and aesthetics, otherwise called the wilderness idea.[11]

Back-to-the-land advocates included the poet William Wordsworth (1770–1850), who is said to have walked many miles throughout England,[12] as well as the art critic John Ruskin (1819–1900), who thought man had *desacralized* nature by turning every river in England into a sewer.[13] It also included the poet, designer, architect, and socialist William Morris (1834–1896), who decried the growth of London with its smoke-laden sky and befouled river,[14] as well as the socialist poet Edward Carpenter (1844–1929), who gave up his Cambridge mathematics fellowship and holy orders to move "back to the land" to set up a commune.[15] Of course, Henry David Thoreau, whom we met in Chapter 8, made famous the idea—and the idyll—of going back to the land when he lived in the woods at Walden Pond and wrote in lucid detail of his observations. One later proponent of this back-to-the-land movement was Mohandas Gandhi, who rejected the industrial model for India as well as modern civilization's fascination with the multiplication of wants.[16] Influenced by Carpenter and Ruskin, Gandhi was prescient in his perception of the "damaging effects on nature of the industrial economy and the consumer society."[17]

The back-to-the-land phase of environmentalism was followed by the phase of scientific conservation. The list of individuals who made a contribution to the international conservation movement includes George Perkins Marsh (1801–1882), whose *Man and Nature: Or, Physical Geography as Modified by Human Action* (1864) was recognized by Lewis Mumford as the "fountainhead of the conservation movement";[18] Dietrich Brandis (1824–1907), a German forester employed in India by the British to undertake tropical forest management;[19] Alexander von Humboldt (1769–1859), a German geographer who studied the changing levels of a lake in Venezuela;[20] Gifford Pinchot (1865–1946), the founder of the United States Forest Service, who illustrated that "scientific conservation was an ideology that was at once apocalyptic and redemptive";[21] and the Mexican, Miguel Ángel de Quevedo (1862–1946), known as "Mexico's apostle of the tree," who lobbied for the protection of parks and tree nurseries in the cities as well as for the compilation of inventories for forests.[22]

Following the phase of scientific conservation came the phase of the wilderness idea and the conservation of wild species and wild habitats, marked by the establishment of the first national parks in the United States (Yellowstone, 1872) and Canada (Banff, 1885). The first-ever international conservation endeavour took place at a conference in London in 1900, which resulted in the signing of the Convention for the Preservation of Animals, Birds, and Fish in Africa.[23] This Convention was followed by the initiatives of figures such as South African statesman Jan Smuts,[24] who helped create the Dongola Botanical Reserve (now Mapungubwe National Park).

In the United States, conservation ideas were advocated by John Muir (1838–1914), a lecturer, writer, and mystical pantheist who founded the Sierra Club in 1892. While sensitive to the economic value of the forest, he also ascribed to it an "independent, non-utilitarian" value.[25] The spirit of Muir was partially echoed in Aldo Leopold (1887–1948), a forester who went on to teach ecology and game management

> **Central Beliefs of Environmentalism**
>
> - Human nature is largely biological and best understood in ecological terms.
> - The origin of the state is natural selection.
> - Liberty as an ideal is freedom extended to all sentient beings.
> - Equality as an ideal is the equal consideration of interests.
> - Justice is fairness in the treatment of all forms of life.
> - The end of government is the encouragement of the diversity of life in all its forms.
> - Economic organization is at its best in a regulated economy.
> - Rights are subordinated to environmental considerations.

at the University of Wisconsin in the 1930s and became a founding member of the Wilderness Society. Some maintain, with plausibility, that his posthumously published *A Sand County Almanac* (1949) is "the intellectual touchstone for the most far-reaching environmental movement in American History."[26] The difference between Muir and Leopold, however, lay in the fact that Muir adopted a defensive attitude towards the wilderness, thereby showing a kind of indifference towards what happened outside the wilderness area. Leopold, on the other hand, thought that human behaviour outside the national parks "was perhaps even more important than the protection of wild species within them."[27] Finally, it should be added that Leopold's intellectual development moved from protection of species to protection of habitats, and on to protection of biodiversity.[28]

By the time the 1960s arrived, environmental thinking was beginning to congeal into ideological camps, and it was this that launched the second wave of environmentalism. Far and away the person who most famously represented this new start was Rachel Carson. What she articulated was more theoretical, more scientifically based, and more ideological than any previous environmental statements or writings.

Proto-ecologism: Rachel Carson

The effect of World War II on the environmental movement was to refrigerate it. And it was not until the 1960s that a thaw occurred and there appeared the second wave of environmentalism, largely inspired by Rachel Carson (1907–1964). A biologist and employee of the US Fish and Wildlife Service, Carson published her widely read and enormously influential *Silent Spring* in 1962.[29]

In *Silent Spring*, Carson alerts her readers to the assault of humans on the environment through the contamination of air, earth, rivers, and seas with dangerous and even lethal materials.[30] She emphasizes that in addition to "the possibility of extinction of mankind by nuclear war, the central problem of our age has therefore become the contamination of man's total environment with such substances of incredible potential for harm."[31] Her deep concern is that life is being forced to make adjustments not only to natural chemicals washed out of rocks and carried into the rivers, for instance, but also to the synthetic creations of humankind's inventive minds—creations such as 2,4-D and DDT, brewed in laboratories and having no natural counterpart. It is not hard to imagine how repelled Carson would be by the Union Carbide disaster of 1984 and its ongoing legacy of destruction.

Insecticides, Herbicides, and Pollution

Carson is concerned with the elixirs of death, as she calls the new synthetic insecticides, which have enormous potential not only to poison but to enter into vital processes of the body and alter them in "sinister" ways.[32] Whether the insecticides are chlorinated hydrocarbons or organic phosphorus insecticides, the result is the same: people are poisoned accidentally through drifting spray, or are poisoned during the application of sprays for agricultural or other purposes. The result seems to be the same in connection with herbicides. In Carson's measured opinion, herbicides contain dangerous chemicals that, if used carelessly, can have dangerous results.[33] In addition, Carson is concerned about the rapid pace of water pollution, blaming it on substances entering waterways from radioactive waste, fallouts from nuclear explosions, domestic wastes from municipalities, and chemical wastes originating in factories.[34] However, Carson points out that it is not just waters (both salt and fresh) that are adversely affected by herbicides and insecticides; soil, too, is impacted owing to the interwoven lives that are found beneath our feet and that are essential to the breaking down of organic material that makes the soil.[35] The manufacture and use of chemicals such as 2,4-D, DDT, aldrin, lindane, and arsenic can all result in poisoning the soil, and these toxins eventually can be absorbed in plant tissues and then consumed by humans.

Needless Havoc

In a splendidly titled chapter, Carson talks about the "needless havoc" humans have caused, first in recent centuries with the slaughter of the buffalo, the massacre of shorebirds, and the near elimination of egrets, and then in more recent times through the senseless use of insecticides and the killing of birds, mammals, fish, and "practically every form of life." Carson packs much into what she wishes to say here, but three of her important points are the following: (i) humans seem bent on "the conquest of nature," together with its destruction; (ii) this inclination is done without thought; and (iii) the citizen who wishes to confront the question of wildlife lost must come to terms with the conflict between control agencies that deny there has been a severe loss of wildlife and conservationists who affirm such a loss. The chapter heading seems to echo again the words of Albert Schweitzer, to whom she has dedicated her book: man has lost the capacity to foresee and forestall. Humans, she thinks, have been victimized by the "soft sell" of the use of contaminants, which have introduced, in a "haphazard" way, foreign chemicals with cancer-producing consequences into our environment. One such chemical is DDT. As she points out, what follows the introduction of such chemicals is a slow realization, on the part of humans, of the consequences of their use. And what follows this slow realization is still slower remedial action taken by humans to bring them under control.[36] Humans' ability to create such chemical monsters outstrips their legislative and legal ability to control them. And Schweitzer, the medical missionary and philosopher whose core belief was the need for a "reverence for life," in Carson's view, is vindicated.

Changing Our Philosophy

Carson echoes the views of a Canadian entomologist, G.C. Ullyett, who warned that "[w]e must change our philosophy, abandon our attitude of human superiority."[37] This she thinks we must do because the path of conquest and destruction is counterproductive. Two things stand out in this regard in the case of insecticides. First, the effective control of insects is produced by nature itself, and second, insects, like other species, have an "explosive power" of reproduction. In all of this Carson sees a balance of nature that sometimes works in favour of humans and sometimes against. Without bearing in mind this natural balance, which so characterizes nature, and by wedding themselves to conquest and destruction, humans run the very real likelihood of opening a Pandora's box over which they will have little control. Instead, Carson recommends that humans change their philosophy to account for the forces of life in such a way as to guide them into channels that are favourable to themselves,[38] and to abandon the philosophy that seeks vainly and arrogantly to "control" nature on the basis of ideas that date from the Stone Age of science.[39]

Reform Environmentalism: Gro Harlem Brundtland

In 1987, the World Commission on Environment and Development published its report, *Our Common Future*. The head of this commission was Gro Harlem Brundtland (1939–), the Prime Minister of Norway (1981, 1986–9, 1990–6). The key concept of the report is **sustainable development**, defined as "development that meets the needs of the present without compromising the ability of future generations to meet their own needs."[40] This version of environmentalism wishes to anchor the notion of development on a secure foundation; accordingly, it does not threaten the general policies pursued by industrialized economies, including those that are capitalist. It aims simply to redirect capitalist development so that it is less hostile to the environment. The spirit here is reflected in reform liberalism: compromise and adjustment. Some of the major ideas discussed in the report follow.

A Threatened Future

The Brundtland report begins with the sober claim that many regions of the world face irreversible damage to the environment, and that this damage threatens human progress.[41] The report is emphatic that this damage represents failures attributable to (i) poverty and (ii) the short-sighted way in which humans have pursued prosperity, often with unintended environmentally destructive consequences. The Commission acknowledges the bountiful dimensions of nature, but it also is cognizant of the fragility and balance of nature. In practice, this means that certain thresholds in our environment must not be crossed on pain of endangering the integrity of the whole system.[42] The Commission reminds us that, in light of these facts, we must be "mindful" of endangering the very survival of life on earth. Among threats to the environment listed initially are the greenhouse gas effect, the depletion of the ozone layer, air pollutants, desertification, and nuclear war.

Strategic Imperatives

From the notion of sustainable development, the Commission arrives at some critical objectives for environmental and developmental policies. These objectives aim to promote harmony among humans and between humanity and nature. Among the objectives are the following: reviving growth; changing the quality of growth; meeting the essential needs for jobs, food, energy, water, and sanitation; ensuring a sustainable level of population; conserving and enhancing the resource base; reorienting technology; and merging environment and economics in decision-making. But the Commission acknowledges that the achievement of these objectives requires institutional change, largely in the political and economic arenas. Such changes would include those that secure effective citizen participation, generate surpluses on a self-reliant basis, respect the obligations to preserve the ecological base, search for new solutions, sustain patterns of trade and finance, and support administrative flexibility.[43]

The Focus on Policy Sources

There is gravity in the tone of the Commission's report, for it emphasizes—after canvassing the multitude of problems connected with population and food resources, food security, ecosystems, energy, industry, and urban issues—that "the next few decades are crucial for the future of humanity."[44] And it acknowledges that pressures on the planet are now unprecedented and accelerating.[45] Faced with these daunting problems, the Commission recommends a shift in the way governments and individuals approach environmental and developmental issues. Rather than focusing on environmental effects, the Commission recommends focusing on policy sources, and to this end it advocates giving central agencies of government a mandate to ensure compliance with environmental protection and sustainable development. In effect, the Commission recommends getting on top of the problem of environmental decay by crafting firm policies focused on the sources of the effects, rather than by dealing with the effects of environmental decay once it has occurred.[46]

Transitional Environmentalism: The World Scientists' Warning

In 1992, in the shadow of the Brundtland report, over a thousand internationally known scientists signed a document produced by the US-based Union of Concerned Scientists entitled the *World Scientists' Warning to Humanity*.

Collision Course

The *World Scientists' Warning to Humanity* (henceforth *The Warning*) draws to global attention the collision course between human beings and the natural world order. In a nutshell, *The Warning* points out the often irreversible damage to the environment caused by human activity, which jeopardizes the future interests of humanity. It goes further by pointing to specific environmental degradation, including degradation of the atmosphere, water resources, oceans, soil, forests, and living species. In effect, *The Warning* reaffirms the litany of environmental despoliation discussed above. In addition, it affirms the need to put limits on human population growth, which, according to a World Bank estimate in 1992, will not stabilize until it reaches 12.4 billion. Given the finite ability of the earth to provide food and energy, the conclusion reached is that we are reaching the earth's limits.[47]

What Must Be Done

The Warning affirms five things that need to be done if "vast misery" is to be averted: environmentally damaging activities must be brought under control; resources must be managed more effectively; human population must be stabilized; poverty must be reduced and eliminated; and, finally, sexual equality must be ensured.[48] Having spelled out these five areas that require action, the scientists endorsing *The Warning* affirm that "a new ethic is required."[49] *The Warning* was signed by 1,670 scientists, including 104 Nobel laureates. The list of signatories includes Murray Gell-Mann, Stephen Hawking, Dorothy Crowfoot Hodgkin, Stephen Jay Gould, Lynn Margulis, Gennady Mesiatz, Ernst Mayr, Linus Pauling, John Polanyi, Carl Sagan, Susumu Tonegawa, Edward Wilson, Roger Penrose, and Jan Tinbergen.

Green Political Theory: Robert E. Goodin

Writing in 1992, the American-born and Oxford-educated philosopher Robert E. Goodin (1950–) was one of the first analytical thinkers to carve out a coherent and clear statement that stands midway between shallow ecologism, which asserts that things only have value to humans or for humans, and deep ecologism, which asserts that things have value separate from conscious valuers. Central to his position is the Green theory of value, to which we shall turn shortly, once we have examined what he has to say about the program of the Green Party.

Green Political Program

Goodin believes that, in their program, Greens tackle the following basic question: How can Greens further biocentric wisdom in all spheres of life?[50] With this pre-eminent value in mind, Goodin constructs the basic elements of the program in terms of technology, the economy, social relations, and foreign relations. Greens, according to Goodin, are not single-issue parties, but wish instead to be radical and "to shift the focus of discourse in the political community as a whole."[51] As such, they want to make the issue of saving the planet the real test of political parties.

Green theory encourages one to view technology as a mixed blessing, recognizing on the one hand that technology has increased levels of production but also that some of its products are agricultural poisons or unsafe (e.g., nuclear) power. Green theory calls for the use of "appropriate technology" so that there is a fit between the technology used and the end uses to which it is put and the purposes for which it is employed.[52] It seems that Goodin would embrace on behalf of Greens the idea put forward by E.F. Schumacher, which advocates the use of "intermediate technology." The hope is that the use of such technology would be more sensitive to the environment, and would avoid ridiculous outcomes such as "cutting butter with a chainsaw."[53]

Green theory encourages one to view suspiciously the focus of present economics. According to Greens, the present economic system overvalues the material side of the standard of living. In addition, it focuses on consumption rather than conservation, on competition rather than co-operation, and on open-ended economic growth rather than the quality of life. In a sense, the Greens move away from the economics of Adam Smith and in the direction of Aristotle's self-sufficiency.[54]

Green theory encourages one to cultivate social relations along egalitarian lines. But in the case of Greens, according to Goodin, the egalitarianism takes a new twist. It encourages a kind of solidarity that takes us well beyond the fraternity of the French Revolution and all the way to a oneness with the earth, with the poor, and with future generations. Oppression and exploitation, along with discrimination, are rejected for the reason that these are responsible for social instabilities.[55]

Green theory encourages one to adopt the same principles internationally and domestically. These principles include egalitarianism, respect for diversity, and non-violence.[56] Some advocates of Green theory have come up with ingenious strategies for discouraging the use of weapons of mass destruction, one such strategy being sending one's children to the country of your adversary and vice versa.[57]

A Green Theory of Value

Goodin's Green theory of value runs as follows. Things can have value only in relation to humans, but this is different from claiming, as do shallow ecologists, that things only have value to us or for us.[58] Goodin's position, however, is also different from the deep ecologist in denying that things have value quite separately from any conscious valuers.[59] Instead, Goodin takes a middle-of-the-road approach, asserting that values presuppose valuers and humans are the only beings on earth for this purpose. Goodin subscribes to a natural resource-based theory of value, which he distinguishes from the neo-classical welfare economic (capitalist) theory of value as well as from the Marxist theory of value. The welfare economic theory attributes the value of an object to the value people derive in partaking of it, i.e., to their preferences. The Marxist theory, on the other hand, attributes it to the values people impart to things as they are made, i.e., to their labour. The Green theory of value differs from the first of these by arguing that the values lie in the objects themselves (e.g., the cedar trees in Cathedral Grove, BC; humpback whales in the Pacific Ocean) rather than in the mental states, i.e., preferences, of humans. It differs from the second by arguing that the values are natural rather than functions of human activities, i.e., labour. The Green theory of value attributes the value of a thing to naturally occurring properties of the thing itself. Put differently, Goodin says that, under Green theory, what makes something valuable is its very naturalness, i.e., the fact that it has been produced by natural processes rather than the artificial ones of humans.[60] Some of the corollaries of this theory of values are, according to Goodin, post-materialism, irreplaceability, sustainability, futurity, liberation, and authenticity.[61]

The Greening of Social Theory: John Barry

In recent times, a British political scientist and activist, John Barry (1966–), has given structure to environmentalism by identifying a particular theory—ecologism/green social theory—and placing it in one of two different categories. In doing so, he adds considerable clarity to the types of disagreements one is likely to encounter in literature dealing with social theory and the position of environmentalism in these debates.

Barry divides social theory into mainstream and critical categories. Within the mainstream category, he places conservatism, neo-classical economics, sociobiology, and social Darwinism. Within the critical category, he places Marxism/socialism, feminism, ecologism/green social theory, and postmodernism.[62] By making use of this framework, one can see the position of ecologism in the overall scheme of social theory. What we shall discuss below are features of just one such social theory—namely, ecologism/green social theory. It should be kept in mind that what Barry offers here is a tempered form of ecologism—something less than Arne Næss's deep ecology, with its affirmation of the intrinsic value of all forms of life[63]—for the pragmatic reason that, in Barry's opinion, Næss's deep ecologism will not be able to garner widespread support.[64]

Principles of Green Social Theory

According to Barry, the main principles of ecologism/green social theory are: (i) the rejection of the separation of humanity and the environment; (ii) an emphasis on the biological embodiedness and ecological embeddedness of humans; (iii) the acceptance of social–environmental relations as constitutive of human society; and (iv) a claim that social–environmental relations are of moral concern.[65] These principles imply that humans are not a species that stands at the top of a "great chain of being" but rather a species that exists in web-like relation to other species, that Homo sapiens as a species of animal is embodied in its species-specific characteristics, that the natural contexts and dimensions of society are a central part of materialistic social theory more fundamentally materialistic than Marx's social theory, and that our moral theory should extend beyond the species barrier.[66]

Beyond these principles lie three supplementary aspects of these same principles. Barry calls these "three dimensions of the greening of social theory": (i) the extension of the social theory along temporal lines so as to extend into the future, thereby taking into consideration the interests of future generations; (ii) the adoption of an international and global perspective; and (iii) the consideration of the "well-being" of other species and the biosphere in general.[67]

Barry acknowledges what he takes to be a circularity at the heart of ecologism/green social theory: the study of human nature leads to an examination of the environment, which in turn "obliges us to return inwards towards an examination of 'human nature' and its place in social theory."[68]

Deep Ecologism: Arne Næss

Before analyzing some of the main ingredients of **deep ecologism** as represented in the writings of the Norwegian Arne Næss (1912–2009), one should pause for a moment to point to the thematic connectedness between earlier environmentalists and Næss. A kind of cascade of connectedness occurs when Muir's intimated notion of reverence for life surfaces in Schweitzer's principle of the same name; when Schweitzer inspires Carson's writing of *Silent Spring*; and when Aldo Leopold, writing in the 1930s, is remembered in the preface of E.F. Schumacher's 1973 *Small Is Beautiful*—a treatise on environmentally Buddhist economics—with a quotation from Leopold's inspirational words, using the metaphor of the exquisitely beautiful Spanish gardens of the Alhambra:

By and large, our present problem is one of attitudes and implements. We are modeling the Alhambra with a steam-shovel, and are proud of our yardage. We shall hardly relinquish the shovel, which after all has many good points, but we are in need of gentler and more objective criteria for its successful use.[69]

Arne Næss's deep ecology is just the culmination of ideas expressed by Muir, Schweitzer, Carson, Leopold, and Schumacher. His ideas are merely better and more completely formulated in such a way that they constitute an ideology. In this sense, Næss has the benefit of being carried to shore on the first and second waves of environmentalism. And it is he who, having arrived on shore, firmly plants the flag of deep ecologism. Things will not be the same again.

The Deep Ecology Credo

Næss offers eight points that comprise the basic views of the deep ecology movement:

i. The flourishing of human and non-human life on earth has intrinsic value.
ii. Richness and diversity of life forms are values in themselves.
iii. Humans have no right to reduce this richness and diversity except to satisfy vital needs.
iv. Present interference with the non-human world is excessive.
v. The flourishing of human life and cultures is compatible with a substantial decrease of the human population.
vi. Significant change of life conditions for the better requires change in policies.
vii. The ideological change is mainly that of appreciating *life quality*.
viii. Those who subscribe to the foregoing points have an obligation to participate in the attempt to implement the necessary changes.[70]

Næss's version of ecologism is of a no-nonsense kind. It is quite inconsistent with the status quo, and has the effect of fleshing out the ideas of Muir, Schweitzer, Leopold, Carson, and Schumacher. Unlike reform environmentalism as found in the Brundtland report, Næss's ecologism does not presume that there can be such a thing as sustainable development. For deep ecologists like Næss, sustainable development is to a very real extent a contradiction in terms and points to the failure of reforms to understand just how serious the ecological situation is. Instead, Næss's ecologism advocates an ideological change in the same spirit in which Carson urges a change in philosophy, but with this difference: Næss has a program that contains a call for action. It affirms the intrinsic value of all life, it affirms the intrinsic value of diversity, and it affirms the need for population control. Not since Thomas Malthus and John Maynard Keynes has the subject of human population control been raised (and Næss precedes the *World Scientists' Warning* by some 15 years). Finally, Næss's program calls for those who accept the credo to participate in attempts to implement it.

So there is something new in what Næss, as a deep ecologist, advocates: there is a clarion call for action and a strategy and program for dealing with it. In this sense Andrew Dobson is correct when, while speaking of Carson's book, he says, "[it] can only inform ecologism rather than be 'it' due to the absence of any overriding political strategy for dealing with the problems it identifies."[71] Næss, on the other hand, embodies ecologism by offering an overriding political strategy that reduces human population, changes governmental policies, emphasizes life quality, and imposes obligations on persons to attempt to implement the necessary changes to preserve the environment.

Ecologism: Andrew Dobson

The British scholar Andrew Dobson (1957–) draws a distinction between environmentalism and ecologism that sheds light on the direction of his political ideology. He is in favour of ecologism, which he thinks is an ideology, and not in favour of environmentalism, which he thinks is not an ideology. The differences between these, as viewed by Dobson, together with his defence of ecologism, are something to which we must now turn.

Environmentalism and Ecologism

In Dobson's view, an ideology has three characteristics: (i) it provides an analytical description of society, enabling its users to navigate in the political world; (ii) it prescribes a particular form of society; and (iii) it provides a plan of action, a program, for political endeavours.[72] He distinguishes environmentalism from ecologism on the grounds that environmentalism adopts a managerial approach to environmental issues, believing these issues can be addressed without adopting fundamental changes in our values or habits in production or consumption, whereas ecologism believes that a sustainable and fulfilling existence requires radical changes in our dealing with the non-human world.[73]

In elaborating on the first of the three points, Dobson says, "it is important to stress that whatever problem is being confronted by any given ideology, it will be analysed in terms of some fundamental and (as it were) necessary feature of the human condition."[74] Once the first point is cashed out in these terms, it is easy to see why Dobson denies that environmentalism is an ideology—it believes that environmental problems can be solved without fundamental changes in values or habits. Ecologism, on the other hand, endorses such changes by calling for radical action. For Dobson, the reformist mode of environmentalism simply "reinforces conspicuous consumption and certain sorts of technology rather than calling them into question."[75] This stands in sharp contrast to ecologism, which challenges these consumption patterns and calls for a fundamental change in the relationship between human beings and the non-human world.[76] Another way of understanding the contrast here is that ecologism takes seriously the finitude of the planet and asks what kind of practices (economic, political, and social) are possible and desirable in light of this, while environmentalism does not do either of these things.[77]

Anthropocentrism

In Dobson's opinion, the one thing underpinning the range of objections that radical green theorists have to current human behaviour is their opposition to anthropocentrism: the error of giving arbitrarily preferential treatment to human interests over the interests of other beings. He distinguishes between a weak and a strong sense of anthropocentrism, allowing that even in a respectable ecological position there could be room for the former. By weak anthropocentrism, Dobson means "human-centredness" or "a philosophy of respect held by humans," while by strong anthropocentrism Dobson means "human instrumentalism" or "instrumentally using the non-human world" in an unfair and unjust way.[78] He accepts weak anthropocentrism because the questions being asked, and the behaviour that comes from asking these questions, are human (i.e., it is a human search), but he rejects strong anthropocentrism for its endorsement of human instrumentality. In his words, "There is evidently a reasonable green rejection of human instrumentality."[79]

A Problem in Environmental Ideology?

While not elaborating on it, Dobson makes clear that the most obvious feature of ecologism is "its failure to make itself practical."[80] For Dobson this must be sincerely troubling owing to the fact that he has already said that ecologism is an ideology, unlike environmentalism, and that what in part makes it so is the fact that it provides a plan of action for political endeavours. So the question with which he leaves his readers near the end of *Green Political Thought* is revealing of some ambivalence in his thought regarding the ideological nature of ecologism. There, he says that we find ourselves back at square one: the radical green calling into question today's industrial order but not knowing for sure how to go about changing it.[81] He is unsure whether the greening of people, industries, governments, and retailing will be enough to secure a sustainable future.[82]

Ecologism and Beyond: Warwick Fox

The Australian philosopher Warwick Fox (1954–) aims to carry the green debate beyond deep ecology into the domain of transpersonal ecology,[83] and still later into the domain of a general theory of ethics that embraces (i) inter-human ethics; (ii) ethics of the natural environment; and (iii) ethics of the human-structured environment.[84] With respect to the first of these, Fox wishes to explore the possibility of an approach to ecology that goes beyond the egoic, biographical, or personal sense of self.[85] With respect to the second, Fox wishes to develop a theory of ethics that carries one well beyond the ethics of Aristotle and his inter-human ethics, or the animal rights ethics of Peter Singer, to ethics that also embrace things constructed by or built by humans. Such a theory of ethics carries us beyond the implied reverence for life principle of Muir or the explicit reverence for life principle of Schweitzer. Needless to say, since the theory of transpersonal ecology and the general theory of ethics are subtle, lengthy, and complicated, we can only manage a few brief observations concerning them. Four topics should be addressed: the transpersonal approach, transpersonal ecology and identification, the definition of a theory of responsive cohesion, and the key points of this theory.

The Transpersonal Approach

Fox makes it clear that the transpersonal approach to ecology is indebted to Næss, and that it is not an anthropocentric approach. Instead, it is a way of viewing the world that is concerned with "realizing one's ecological, wider, or big Self."[86] Alternatively, one may say that it is concerned with a this-world realization of the most expansive self possible. Fox is interested in thinking of the self in a robust way so that it moves beyond the tripartite model (rational, desiring, and normative self)—which is, according to him, atomistic and particle-like—to the wide, expansive, and field-like conception of the self. Under the transpersonal theory, the expansive view of the self brings with it a revolution in ethics in that it renders ethics superfluous. It does this, Fox believes, because one will naturally protect the unfolding of the expansive self (the ecosphere and the cosmos).[87] What this amounts to is an elaboration of Næss's theory that care naturally follows once the self is expanded: self-realization simply renders morality superfluous.

At this stage Fox's ideas are captivating but largely intuitive. One has a "sense" of what he is talking about, but not a "good idea." What can be said is that he wishes to develop an ethic that is this-world oriented and is deeply connected to the notion of an expanded self. As we shall see below, his later research leads him to develop his theory of ethics by thinking of the self in terms of human relationships that expand outward to embrace the natural and created environment. But these ideas are just around the corner, and await the publication of his later work in 2006.

Varieties of Identification

The immediate question facing one in connection with transpersonal ecology is Buddhist in nature: how does one come to have as expansive a self as possible?[88] Fox's answer on behalf of transpersonal ecology is: through identification or the experience of commonality. And Fox identifies the three bases of identification as personal, ontological, and cosmological.[89] Personal identification refers to the experiences of commonality brought about through personal involvement (e.g., family members, friends, our homes). Ontological identification refers to experiences of commonality through the realization of the fact that things are (e.g., that there is something rather than nothing). Finally, cosmological identification refers to experiences of commonality through the realization that we are aspects of a single unfolding reality (e.g., the philosophy of Spinoza, Taoism, the world view of some North American Native peoples).

Transpersonal ecologists want to place personal identification in the context of ontological identification, then place ontological identification in the context of cosmological identification. Though the first of these identifications has positive features, it also has negative ones, including egoisms, attachments, greed, exploitation, war, and ecocide. Only by setting the first of these (personal identification) in the context of the other two (ontological and cosmological identification) is one led to impartial identification with all entities and to treading lightly upon the earth. Presumably, when one identifies with the creatures of the earth, one wishes to protect them, and earth, from harm. This larger context also allows for the promotion of actions that respectfully but resolutely aim to alter the views of those who suffer from delusions of self-realization through personal identification, e.g., through family, friends, or homes.[90]

The Definition of a Responsive Theory of Cohesion

The flavour of Fox's ideas in his transpersonal ecology theory are expanded and enriched in his general theory of ethics. In the latter, Fox attempts to discover the foundational value in the world, in other words, the most basic form or source of value that we can discover.[91] This value would underpin or provide the foundation for all other values. In developing his idea Fox affirms that the foundational value "consists in a basic cohesion."[92] Fox's comments here are, initially at least, rather opaque, but persistence will reveal some light at the end of the tunnel. The **responsive theory of cohesion** is a theory about relations (relationships) or forms of organization, of which there are three types: fixed cohesion, responsive cohesion, and discohesion.[93]

We might say that Fox, in passing, is giving further definition to Rainer Maria Rilke's idea of relationships when Rilke speaks of them in these terms: "We are just now reaching the point where we can observe objectively and without judgement the relationship of one individual to a second one. Our attempts to live such a relationship are without a model."[94] Fox is interested in a theory of ethics that considers the connection (relationship) persons have with persons, their connection with the natural environment (e.g., animals, plants, rain clouds), and their connection with the intentionally organized, artificial, built, or constructed environment (e.g., buildings, roads, cars).[95] This definitely carries the discussion beyond Schweitzer and Næss. Two last points should be added, namely that for Fox "cohesion" means "coherence" or "hanging together," whereas "discohesion," a neologism, means "disorder" or "chaos."[96] By "fixed cohesion" he means "a cohesion that is fixed, rigid, frozen, tired, or dead," in contrast to a "responsive cohesion," by which he means "a cohesion that is fluid, adaptive, organic or creative."[97]

The Key Points of the Responsive Theory of Cohesion

In a nutshell, the key points of Fox's responsive theory are as follows: (i) there are three kinds of relational qualities: fixed cohesion, responsive cohesion, and discohesion; (ii) the relational quality of responsive cohesion is best; (iii) the relational quality of responsive cohesion is the most basic value there is, and thus the foundational value; (iv) therefore, we ought to live by the value of responsive cohesion; and (v) all forms of responsive cohesion are valuable. Nonetheless, biophysical responsive cohesion trumps mind-sharing responsive cohesion, and mind-sharing responsive cohesion trumps compound material (human-constructed) responsive cohesion.[98]

Fox thinks the biophysical realm is the primary context, followed respectively by the mind-sharing and compound material (human-constructed) realms.[99] His reason for so thinking is that the human-constructed realm depends on the mind-sharing realm, which in turn depends on the biophysical realm. The responsive cohesion theory takes us beyond life forms to artificially constructed things, and allows for a diminishing level of obligations as we move from humans to other animals and plants, to material artifacts. This theory does not deny the intrinsic value of non-human forms of life or of constructed things, but the diminishing levels of obligations do suggest that the intrinsic value of these levels of being are more defeasible the further one descends down the levels of obligations.

Fox argues that the relational quality (or form of organization) of responsive cohesion is the foundational value, because it lies at the basis of the best approaches to "an extremely wide range of domains of interest," from science, to psychology, to government, to personal relationships, to sports and arts, to the natural environment, and to the human-constructed environment.[100] As for the justification of the claim that the relational quality of responsive cohesion is best, Fox says that no one set reason across a domain of interests will explain this. Sometimes the reason has to do with pleasure, sometimes with truth, sometimes with what is workable and fair, sometimes with what has dramatic flair, and sometimes with what makes us feel more alive. But, thinks Fox, the relational quality of responsive cohesion underpins each of these evaluative notions.[101]

According to Fox, the responsive cohesion is flexible, fluid, free within bounds, adaptive, creative, semi-predictable, interesting, and alive; the fixed cohesion is rigid, regimented, structured, stuck in a rut, predictable, mechanical, and dead; and discohesion is chaotic, all over the place, turbulent, orderless, structureless, illogical, unpredictable, and non-patterned.[102] History has shown us that people have claimed to know things on the basis of (i) authority, (ii) tradition, (iii) revelation, (iv) intuition, and (v) reason. However, he thinks, informed judges generally think the last of these, when coupled with observation and the interplay between them, leads to the best way of knowing the world.[103] Reason is in, the others are out. This is really, for Fox, what drives him to accept responsive cohesion as the foundational and best value.

What are the policy implications of this for Fox? The answer comes in the form of a credo: In living your life, you should do what you reasonably can do to preserve examples of the relational quality of responsive cohesion, regenerate examples of this cohesion, and through your undertakings reflect and reinforce this cohesion. At the practical level this means, for Fox, accepting the primacy of self-defence in ethical matters and, importantly, making the whole planetary ecosystem the largest context that should be prioritized.[104]

Socialistic Ecologism: Rudolf Bahro

The name most commonly associated with a left-of-centre interpretation of the ecology crisis is Rudolf Bahro (1935–1997). Though raised in Germany under the National Socialists, he joined the Communist Party of the German Democratic Republic in 1952. Years later, after writing his famous *The Alternative in Eastern Europe* (1977, translated 1978), he was imprisoned for eight years for publishing state secrets, and then, upon his early release in 1979, fled to West Germany. From that point on, Bahro gravitated towards the new ecological movement, without rejecting the utopian aspects of the socialism he had inherited from Marx and that were, earlier still, reflected in the writings of environmentalist and socialist William Morris.[105] Some aspects of Marxist thought he did reject, including the pre-eminence given to class, but otherwise he seems to have remained a socialist. Bahro's thinking is rich and varied, so only a few of his ideas can be discussed below.

The Ecology Crisis and Socialists

Without abandoning his commitment to socialism, Bahro sees in ecologism a hope for avoiding a crisis of human civilization that applies to people of every colour of skin, every social class, and every continent. The crisis he envisages is one triggered by a population that multiplies and falls upon a certain territory, much like the locusts referred to by the prophet Isaiah in the Bible, only to strip it bare of its resources and then succumb itself.[106] Bahro argues that unless the ecology crisis—that is, the crisis that puts in question the very existence of human civilization—is addressed, the possibility of the socialist goal, the emancipation of human beings, becomes an illusion.[107] He sees a need to adopt the position held by utopian socialists,[108] namely, taking the interest of the species, rather than a particular class, as the fundamental point of reference in order to address the ecological crisis.[109] For Bahro, taking the interest of the species as a fundamental starting point is a way of initiating a social transformation that will lead humanity away from the illusion that the progress of industry, science, and technology will solve humanity's social problems.[110]

What the Greens Propose

For Bahro, the greens are not single-issue individuals; those who think they are cannot see the forest for the trees. Rather, the greens are multi-issue advocates who cast a wide enough net to be called supporters of an ideology. They maintain that the ecology crisis is insoluble without:

i. overcoming the confrontation between East and West, which fuels the arms race;
ii. a new economic order on the North–South axis;
iii. social justice in the industrially developed countries, necessitating an adjustment favouring those who received a bad deal in what is a capitalist society;
iv. human emancipation;
v. conversion and a high degree of cohesion brought through reason and the end of capitalism.[111]

When each of the above points is examined, Bahro's belief shines through. Such things as the arms race, exploitation and suppression of one part of humanity by another, social injustices within and between countries, the lack of self-realization and self-transcendence, and the presence of capitalism all prevent the elimination of the ecological crisis. And it should be kept in mind that for Bahro this crisis is really nothing less than the survival of civilization itself.

Eco-anarchism: Murray Bookchin

Leaving behind proto-ecologists and deep ecologists, we now come to the American anarchist, Murray Bookchin (1921–2006), someone who takes a different, specifically anarchistic tack. A clear thinker and excellent writer, Bookchin develops his own ideas on the environment, a couple of which will be examined below.

Social Ecology

Writing in the tradition of Peter Kropotkin and inspired by the ideas of Aristotle and Hegel, Bookchin takes from Kropotkin his emphasis on local initiatives and mutual endeavours, and from Aristotle and Hegel insights of dialectical thinking. The importance of these notions will emerge in due course. To commence, we need to get a grip on Bookchin's understanding of nature, which in its broad sense includes "everything around us," but which in a more specific sense includes first and second nature. First nature, for Bookchin, refers to the cumulative evolution of the natural world, especially the organic world, whereas second nature refers to the evolution of society.[112] Bookchin argues that second nature—that is, a cultural, social, and political nature—is the outcome of first nature. He adds further that by "second nature" he means human culture, with a variety of institutionalized human communities, symbolic languages, and managed sources of nutrients.[113] In other words, it is a product of natural evolution.[114] Looked at this way, one can see that second nature is synonymous with society and human internal nature, and it emerges out of organic evolution.

Bookchin sees nothing unnatural with the emergence of second nature from first nature. In fact, to the contrary, he sees this emergence as quite natural.[115] Indeed, it is in terms of the relation between these two—the concept of **social ecology**—that he wishes to explain the present ecological crisis. In his opinion, and an original one at that, the ecological crisis we face is a result of the emergence of society out of biology, of the second nature from the first. Still, putting it this way does not quite do justice to his point, which perhaps can be put more straightforwardly by saying that the ecological crises we face are a result of social problems such as the rise of hierarchy, domination, patriarchy, classes, and the state.[116] It is, as it were, as though the whole labour of evolution works to produce humanity, but that humanity's own evolution necessitates its going down numerous culs-de-sac (domination, classes, the state, etc.), many of which produce environmentally unfavourable results.

From Bookchin's perspective, natural evolution—the evolution of Darwin—has conferred upon human beings "a clear responsibility toward the natural world," and has thus made them moral agents.[117] Only because humanity has unique attributes—attributes that no other species has—can it use its ability to think conceptually and to feel empathy for the world of life in order to reverse "the devastation it has inflicted on the biosphere and create a rational society."[118]

Bookchin carries his ideas a bit further, revealing an element of Kropotkin's thinking as well as of the dialectic of Aristotle and Hegel. He believes that ecological thinking, along social lines, has the capacity to cleanse European thoughts of teleological thinking, of its denigration of the physicality, and of its preoccupation with the human soul. Ecological thinking has the capacity to lead to a transcendence of first and second nature, and thereby to a domain of free nature comprising rational humanity—a humanity that would wilfully cope with conflict, contingency, waste, and compulsion.[119] Here both Kropotkin's optimism and attachment to reason and Hegel's (if not Aristotle's) dialectic between first and second nature make themselves evident.

Biocentrism and Anthropocentrism

Bookchin takes issue with deep ecology in what it has to say about biocentrism and anthropocentrism. He also takes issue with deep ecology for the lamentable, foggy world into which it leads us. Those who would advocate **biocentrism** would place all life forms on the same ethical plateau, and would therefore condemn anthropocentrism, which places man at the centre of ethical considerations in the cosmos. Bookchin challenges this reasoning on the grounds that biocentrists and anti-humanists can hardly have it both ways. Either humanity is a special moral agent, and so can practise stewardship of nature, or it is one with the whole world, in which case it has all the rights that any other creature has to look after its own ends. So, thinks Bookchin, either humanity has a particular moral responsibility to look after nature, or humanity and everything else reverts to a Darwinian jungle.[120] It is clear from what he says here that Bookchin does not subscribe to the belief held by some that non-human animals have rights. Rights, he thinks, are the products of customs and traditions, of social relationships, and more immediately of the mind. In this he would seem to be at one with social contractarians such as Thomas Hobbes and Jan Narveson. Furthermore, Bookchin distances himself from Næss's affirmation as a deep ecologist, namely the claim that other sentient beings have intrinsic value. Bookchin claims, to the contrary, that "the intrinsic worth of [the] human being is thus patently exceptional, indeed extraordinary."[121]

Conclusion

Concern for the environment has changed over the past 150 years, from the days of William Wordsworth, John Ruskin, Edward Carpenter, George Perkins Marsh, and Aldo

Leopold, to Albert Schweitzer and his reverence for life, to Rachel Carson and her concern with pesticides, to Gro Harlem Brundtland and her notion of sustainable development, to the Union of Concerned Scientists and their warning of environmental collapse, to Arne Næss and his deep ecology, to the views of Robert Goodin, John Barry, and Andrew Dobson and their interpretations of green theory, to Warwick Fox and his transpersonal ecologism and his general theory of ethics, to Rudolf Bahro and his socialistic ecologism, and finally to Murray Bookchin and his eco-anarchism. Sentimentalism aside, there is a progressive sophistication in the kinds of ideological questions asked by these individuals. And while there is no unanimity on what exactly the correct ideological approach should be to the study of the environment, Aldo Leopold's comment, that our problem is one of attitude and implements, seems to capture the spirit of the foregoing individuals. Leopold reminds us that we should rethink whether we want or need to change the garden of Alhambra.

The line of argument pursued by these thinkers, under the general heading of environmentalism, comprises an ample body of scientific evidence in defence of normative judgments. Environmentalism's argumentative style is largely scientific—consider, currently, the exhaustive scientific reports of the Intergovernmental Panel on Climate Change—but it seeks to carry this scientific message further by advocating normative conclusions that carry one well beyond normal scientific detachment. In crossing from the descriptive and explanatory to the normative, environmentalists embark on a line of thinking that is ambitious and rather intolerant of the lax policies and practices that the human species has advanced and engaged in, especially since the Industrial Revolution but also, to a lesser extent, since the rise of modern science. A sense of urgency colours the line of argument pursued under this ideology, as evidenced, for example, in the Club of Rome's 1972 volume, *The Limits to Growth*, which used computer modelling to examine such variables as economic and population growth, resource depletion, and environmental degradation. This urgency, from the beginnings of environmentalism, has been derived from observations of the varied and comprehensive forms of destruction to nature. Environmentalism never confronts any is/ought division in its thinking, but assumes that the scientific evidence is sufficient, presumably coupled with common sense, to carry one from the "is" side of this division to the "ought" side in one fell swoop. So, while much of the line of argument pursued by those discussed here is scientific in a hard empirical sense, there seems to remain a latent assumption that what is scientifically discovered is sufficient to win the day in terms of challenging current domestic policies and international activities that run counter to the environment.

Evaluation: The Strengths of Environmentalism

1. The testimonial of the World Commission on Environment and Development offers compelling *secondary* support for the proposition that the earth's environment is being seriously compromised in a way detrimental to human interests. The Commission had 20 members, including the chair, Gro Harlem Brundtland, from about the same number of countries, members who came with distinguished portfolios either in government or in the private sector or both. Moreover, the Commission received advice from thousands of individuals, institutes, and organizations all over the world, most of which were distinguished individuals, institutes, or organizations in their own

right. Five years later, the *World Scientists' Warning to Humanity* enumerated five areas in which humans must make changes in dealing with the environment, noting that humans must adopt a new ethic if "vast misery" is to be averted. When the testimonial from the Brundtland report is coupled with the testimonial of the established and in many cases famous world scientists, a rebuttable presumption is established regarding the urgency of humans acting in a concerted fashion to address environmental decay. Does any of this show that green theory or environmentalism or ecologism is the correct ideology? Not quite, but it does show that the problems these theories are addressing are real and urgent, as the Suzuki Foundation and Greenpeace continue to point out. This is no trivial matter in the assessment of theories.

2. A substantial body of evidence offers *primary* support for the proposition that the earth's environment is being seriously compromised. This evidence is extensive and compelling, and is largely supportive of all versions of ecologism short of its deep ecology version. It should be noted that none of this evidence addresses in depth the environmental issue of climate change, for the simple reason that the case for climate change has been won in the minds of both government and the public at large.[122] There follows a list of the extensive and compelling evidence of environmental degradation. This evidence demonstrates that green theory, ecologism, and environmentalism are addressing a real and urgent problem. It is very much a strength of any theory that it recognizes the problem and draws attention to it. Regardless of which of the views on the environment one considers, they all recognize an urgency in regard to environmental destruction and to the consequences this holds for humanity. This is true whether one is talking about reform environmentalism, deep ecology, transpersonal ecology, socialistic ecologism, or anarcho-ecologism. All share the belief that there is an urgent problem. In this they are surely correct, as the following evidence compellingly demonstrates.

There are at least nine subject headings in discussing environmental problems. These are as follows: population; land use and property rights; water availability and water quality; energy; air quality, climate change, and atmospheric issues; toxic chemicals; forests, wilderness, and wildlife; oceans, fisheries, and aquatic life; and biodiversity.[123] Within the confines of the present study, it is not possible to explore any of these headings in detail. Only a brief statement on each can be given. Combined, however, they show rather convincingly the gravity of the environmental situation in the world today.

i. *Population.* From Thomas Malthus, to Keynes, to the Brundtland Commission, much concern has been raised about the geometric expansion of the human population. Work done by the Club of Rome and by Paul and Anne Ehrlich suggests very strongly that the earth is overshooting its carrying capacity.[124]
ii. *Land use and property rights.* Since 1945, 11 per cent of the earth's vegetated land surface has been degraded. Further to this, in many parts of the world, per capita food production is decreasing.[125]
iii. *Water availability and water quality.* The threat to freshwater systems comes, in part, from dams and dikes. The number of dams throughout the world was 5,000 in 1950, as compared to 45,000 today. Dams alter the timing and quantity of river flows, water temperature, and nutrient transport. Another threat comes from

uncontrolled pollution, which diminishes water quality.[126] One example of such pollution occurred in 1998 in connection with the accidental release of toxic sludge containing high levels of heavy metals following a spill from a pyrite mine in Aznalcollar, Spain, that drained into watercourses. The sudden drop in pH resulting from this spill contributed to the death of 37 metric tons of fish and a significant increase in levels of zinc and cadmium in the soil.[127] In addition, the threat to watershed sustainability is now present in connection with the Aberjona Watershed in Massachusetts, the Tama Watershed in Japan, the Toess Watershed in Switzerland, and the Atibaia River Watershed in Brazil.[128] The human-caused disappearance of vast bodies of water, such as the Aral Sea in Central Asia and Lake Chad in Africa, have impacted the lives and livelihoods of millions of people.

iv. *Energy*. The International Energy Agency (IEA) of the Organization for Economic Co-operation and Development (OECD) has claimed that, while energy sources are adequate to meet demand over the next three decades, problems exist on the horizon, including: (i) security of energy; (ii) investment in energy; (iii) environmental damage attributable to energy; and (iv) inequities in the accessibility of the world's population to energy.[129] There are serious problems in each of these areas, but to single out (iii) for special attention, one can say greenhouse gas emissions are attributable to the burning of the three fossil fuels: coal, oil, and gas, with the biggest culprit being coal. Germany, France, and China are pressing ahead with more coal-fired energy, clearly taking us in the wrong direction. And the extraction of oil from the tar sands of Alberta is having an adverse effect on both the natural and human environment.[130]

v. *Air quality, climate change, and atmospheric issues.* The United Nations Convention (1992) and Kyoto Protocol (1997) on Climate Change focus on the problem of gases such as carbon dioxide and methane gas resulting from the burning of fossil fuels. It is now widely agreed that these are now changing the earth's climate by trapping heat in the earth's atmosphere.[131] A specific example of air pollution being a serious problem occurred in connection with an area of Europe covering northern Bohemia, southern Saxony, and a part of lower Silesia called "The Black Triangle." Through joint efforts by various governments in the region, a noticeable reduction of air pollutants has taken place.[132]

vi. *Toxic chemicals*. One example[133] that stands out involving freshwater and the effect of toxic chemicals is the Sandoz warehouse fire of 1 November 1986 in Basel, Switzerland. This fire resulted in 859 metric tons of organophosphate insecticides and 11 metric tons of mercury compounds seeping into the Rhine River and forming a toxic trail some 70 kilometres in length. Some 150,000 eels were killed, as well as much of the fish population of the river.[134]

vii. *Forests*. Illegal logging undercuts government attempts to manage forests, a matter that is particularly acute in Brazil, Cameroon, and the Philippines, where illegal harvests of tropical rainforests run as high as 80 per cent in Brazil, 50 per cent in Cameroon, and 33 per cent in the Philippines.[135] Furthermore, greenhouse gas emissions, which contribute to climate change, are in part caused by tropical deforestation. Such deforestation contributes 15 per cent of the CO_2 of greenhouse gas emissions.[136]

viii. *Biodiversity*. Harvard University's famous ecologist E.O. Wilson estimates that the extinction rate of species is 10,000 times the rate it was before humans started practising agriculture. And population experts Anne and Paul Ehrlich claim that, if the present trends continue, half of the earth's species might be extinct by 2050.[137] An article by Boris Worm and David VanderZwaag of Dalhousie University discusses the difficulty depleted fisheries face in attempting to recover using current management practices. The cumulative consequences of overfishing include a loss of marine biodiversity—in other words, the loss of the richness of a genetically unique population.[138]

ix. *Oceans.* Ship-sourced pollution has led to two international legal conventions being signed, the London Dumping Convention of 1972 and the Marpol Convention of 1973/1978. Both before and after these international agreements, serious shipping accidents resulted in the leakage of crude oil into the ocean. These accidents, together with the size of their oil spills, included: the sinking of the *Torrey Canyon* (1967, with a loss of 117,000 tons of crude oil); the grounding of the *Oceanic Grandeur* (1970, releasing 2,000 tons); the grounding of the *Amoco Cadiz* (1978, with a spill that stretched eight miles long and 18 miles wide); the highly publicized grounding of the *Exxon Valdez* (1989, with a spill that damaged 1,000 miles of Alaskan shoreline); and the sinking of the *Kirki* (1991, with the escape of 20,000 tons of crude oil).[139]

3. Warwick Fox's theory of responsive cohesion offers a consistent and comprehensive general ethical theory that recognizes the layers of ethical considerations encompassing the biophysical realm, the mind-sharing realm, and the compound material (or artifact) realm. Fox's theory, which moves beyond ecologism, offers a structured way of understanding and coming to grips with environmental problems. His theory has several strengths: (i) it identifies its foundational or primitive value, namely responsive cohesion; (ii) it spells out responsive cohesion in terms of relationships, something to which Rilke drew attention; (iii) by layering ethical considerations and including the biophysical realm, it creates logical space for Schweitzer's notion of reverence for life (flora and fauna), as well as for Næss's and Barry's notion of intrinsic value, and it suggests a way to solve the problem of whose interests take priority; (iv) it provides a framework for discussing ethical issues as wide-ranging as abortion and the destruction of natural wonders such as mountains or caverns; and (v) it provides ample room for discussing what Goodin takes to be the fundamental question: how can greens further biocentric wisdom in all spheres of life?

4. Murray Bookchin presents a common-sense approach to problems of ecology. He recognizes the incontrovertibly special role that humans, as reflective and consciously creative creatures, have in the environment and in addressing ecological issues. He is correct, in presenting his ideology of social ecology, to argue that either humanity is a distinctive moral agent in the biosphere, and can therefore practise ecological stewardship, or humanity is just one with the whole world, with no special obligations to the rest of the biosphere. In this latter case, if leopards can be predators, then so too can humans. In this respect, Bookchin offers a robust interpretation of an ecological ideology. Furthermore, both he and Goodin make a persuasive case for saying that talk of rights, duties, and self-realization only exists because there are intelligent beings, valuers, who can think reflectively and critically on the world and give it value.

5. John Barry persuasively argues for biological embodiedness and ecological embeddedness of human beings in any social theory, both of which facilitate overcoming the separation of society from the environment. This is a desirable outcome. Furthermore, Barry presents a green theory that looks to future generations of humans, looks beyond the nation-state and globalization, and looks beyond the species barrier. As a theory, therefore, it helps to cure us of perverse kind of myopia.

6. The intuitions of early environmentalists such as Carpenter, Marsh, Leopold, Smuts, Quevedo, Gandhi, and Ruskin, as discussed by Guha, are vindicated in the ideas and theories advanced by Barry, Goodin, Fox, Bahro, and Dobson. These ideas include "desacralized nature," "independent and non-utilitarian value," "back to the land," and "the damaging effects of industry."

7. Whether one is talking about the crisis in energy, rising greenhouse gas emissions, or species elimination, environmentalists have something compelling to say.[140] The position taken by the foregoing environmentalists is very largely consistent with the position adopted by Thomas L. Friedman in *Hot, Flat, and Crowded*, his assessment of the environmental crisis in the United States. Friedman's work is a compelling read; its convergence with environmentalism supports the latter.[141]

Evaluation: The Weaknesses of Environmentalism

1. Andrew Dobson has highlighted one of the basic problems with ecologism: its failure to make itself practical. Since ideologies aim not only to describe but to give normative direction and a program of action to address political concerns, ecologism's failure to motivate individuals, corporations, societies, nations, and the international community is a weakness on its part. This is undoubtedly truer of the deep ecology movement of Arne Næss than it is of the proto-ecologism of Rachel Carson or of the line taken in *Our Common Future*. In the case of deep ecologism, it remains unclear what rhetorical devices could be introduced that would persuade people to adopt such a radical ideology. But the problem is more serious than this, for motivation is an issue even in the case of the more tepid reform environmentalism of the Brundtland report. The problem with the report is not in what it says, or in what it does not say. The problem lies simply in the fact that 30 years after the report's publication, the global environmental situation has worsened. Notwithstanding many of its sound recommendations and clarion calls, the report has not moved people, states, and corporations in sufficient numbers to do anything.

   The fact that in international law, according to Antonio Cassese, we have general principles, customary rules, soft law, treaties, enforcement mechanisms, and institutional bodies, all of which aim to protect the environment, does not in the end amount to a vindication for the idea of sustainable development.[142] The reality is that, as a species, we seem remarkably capable of putting teeth into the notion of development and only lip service into the notion of sustainability. As a species, we seem quite capable of short-sightedness grounded in greed, and quite deficient in far-sightedness grounded in wisdom. Hobbes captured this idea well when he said, "For all men are by nature provided of multiplying glasses (that is their passions and self-love) through which, every little payment appeareth a great grievance; but are destitute of those prospective glasses (namely moral and civil sciences) to see afar off the miseries that hang over them, and cannot without such payments be avoided."[143] The plight of reform environmentalism is the plight of reform liberalism all over again, and this is largely owing to the fact that reform environmentalism is simply the environmental policy of reform liberalism. It should therefore come as no surprise that reform environmentalism, as represented by Gro Harlem Brundtland, is unable to deliver the goods it speaks of. This seems no more likely in the field of the environment than it does in another field such as global poverty or Third World indebtedness. The simple reality is that very rarely are reform liberals prepared to make the very real sacrifices they must make to bring about the desired change. Sustainable development founders, as it were, in its own goodwill and best intentions.

2. A problem for the socialist version of environmentalism is its attribution of environmental problems to capitalism. Bahro goes too far in saying that industrialization is solely a result of capitalism. Whatever the etiology of industrialization, its role in socialist countries is as deep and penetrating as it is in capitalist ones. The industrial disasters that have occurred in socialist countries or owing to socialist policies—such as the Chernobyl nuclear catastrophe, the environmental and cultural problems resulting from construction of the Aswan Dam in Egypt, the loss of the Aral Sea to Soviet Union irrigation projects, and problems caused by the building of China's Three Gorges Dam, begun in 1994—all implicate socialism in a serious way.

3. While Fox's theory of transpersonal ecology and his theory of general ethics are interesting and, one might say, dynamic, Fox does not show through argument how these theories are to be applied to the position held by a contractarian like Jan Narveson or a libertarian like Robert Nozick or a public choice theorist like Mancur Olson. While one's heart might be with Fox in this intellectual battle, one needs more than feelings here to tilt the balance of the argument in Fox's favour and away from those who might simply view the biotic world instrumentally. At the very least, Fox needs to provide reasons why one should go down the route he describes as involving ontological or cosmological identification. Put somewhat differently, Fox needs to provide reasons why, among other things, humanity should affirm cosmological identification rather than personal identification as spelled out in the Brundtland report. In this respect, Fox's hortatory remarks—that one living at the cosmological level of identification should act to persuade one living at the personal level of identification—seem less than compelling.

Related Websites

Eisenberg, Sheryl. "Is Environmentalism a Religion?" Natural Resource Defense Center. 2011.
http://thisgreenblog.com/2011/02/is-environmentalism-a-religion.html

International Society for Environmental Ethics
http://enviroethics.org/

Property and Environment Research Center. "Free Market Environmentalism."
www.perc.org/about-perc/what-fme

Stroup, Richard L. "Free Market Environmentalism." Library of Economics and Liberty.
www.econlib.org/library/Enc/FreeMarketEnvironmentalism.html

Suzuki, David. "Why Environmentalism Has Failed." David Suzuki Foundation, 12 May 2012.
www.davidsuzuki.org/blogs/science-matters/2012/05/the-fundamental-failure-of-environmentalism/

Further Readings on Environmentalism

Anderson, Terry L., and Gary D. Libecap. *Environmental Markets: A Property Rights Approach*. New York: Cambridge University Press, 2014.
Armiero, Marco, and Lise Sedrez. *A History of Environmentalism: Local Struggles, Global Histories*. London: Bloomsbury Academic, 2014.
Attfield, Robin. *Environmental Ethics: An Overview for the Twenty-First Century*. Cambridge: Polity Press, 2014.
Baskar, Roy, Karl G. Hoyer, and Petter Naess. *Ecophilosophy in a World of Crisis: Critical Realism and the Nordic Contributions*. London: Routledge, 2012.
Betsill, Michele, Katherine Hochstetler, and Dimitris Stevis, eds. *Palgrave Advances in International Environmental Politics*. Houndmills, Basingstoke, Hampshire, UK: Palgrave Macmillan, 2007.
Bowen, Frances. *After Greenwashing: Symbolic Corporate Environmentalism and Society*. Cambridge: Cambridge University Press, 2014.
Cook, Deborah. *Adorno on Nature*. Montreal and Kingston: McGill-Queen's University Press, 2011.
Doherty, Brian. *Environmentalism, Resistance and Solidarity: The Politics of Friends of the Earth International*. Houndmills, Basingstoke, Hampshire, UK: Palgrave Macmillan, 2014.
Dryzek, John S. *The Politics of the Earth: Environmental Discourses*. London: Oxford University Press, 2013.
——— and Hayley Stevenson. *Democratizing Global Climate Governance*. Cambridge: Cambridge University Press, 2014.
Gioelli, Robert R. *Environmental Activism and the Urban Crisis: Baltimore, St. Louis, Chicago*. Philadelphia: Temple University Press, 2014.
Gupta, Aarti. *Transparency in Global Environmental Governance: Critical Perspectives*. Cambridge, MA: MIT Press, 2014.
Hironaka, Ann. *Greening the Globe: World Society and Environmental Change*. New York: Cambridge University Press, 2014.
Hostettler, Nick. *Eurocentrism: A Marxian Critical Realist Critique*. New York: Routledge, 2012.
Lejano, Raul P., Mrill Ingram, and Helen M. Ingram. *The Power of Narrative in Environmental Networks*. Cambridge, MA: MIT Press, 2013.
Martinez, Michael J. *American Environmentalism: Philosophy, History and Public Policy*. Boca Raton, FL: CRC Press, 2014.
Morin, Jean-Frédéric, and Amandine Orsini. *Essential Concepts of Global Environmental Governance*. New York: Routledge, 2015.

Musil, Robert K. *Rachel Carson and Her Sisters: Extraordinary Women Who Have Shaped America's Environment*. New Brunswick, NJ: Rutgers University Press, 2014.

O'Lear, Shannon. *Environmental Politics: Scale and Power*. New York: Cambridge University Press, 2010.

Rosewarne, Stuart. *Climate Action Upsurge: The Ethnography of Climate Movement Politics*. New York: Routledge, 2014.

Steinberg, Paul F. *Who Rules the Earth? How Social Rules Shape Our Planet and Our Lives*. New York: Oxford University Press, 2015.

Wood, Mary Christina. *Nature's Trust: Environmental Law for a New Ecological Age*. New York: Cambridge University Press, 2014.

13 Religious Fundamentalism

And for ferocity there is nothing on earth to equal a Christian bishop hunting "heresy," as they call any opinion contrary to their own. Especially confident are they on that subject where they are as ignorant as the rest of mankind. I mean death.

—Gore Vidal, *Julian* (1976: 14)

Learning Objectives

- To discover various perspectives in religious fundamentalism.
- To recognize the reactionary character of all versions of religious fundamentalism.
- To acknowledge the rejection of reason and affirmation of faith in fundamentalism.
- To comprehend the impact on public policy—both domestic and foreign—of fundamentalism.
- To appreciate fully the high level of intolerance in fundamentalism.
- To understand the logical tension between liberal values and those of fundamentalism.

In the nineteenth century Friedrich Nietzsche (1844–1900), in *Thus Spoke Zarathustra*, spoke of the death of God, a prediction that seemed credible in light of Darwin's theory of evolution, Freud's psychoanalysis, and Marx's materialism, but in the latter part of the twentieth century and early part of the twenty-first century, religious belief has come back by storm in the form of **fundamentalism**. Here fundamentalism is thought of as a strict adherence to the social and moral codes of revealed religion and the promise it holds for a life lived by faith as grounded in sacred and infallible texts such as the Torah, New Testament, Qur'an, and Veda and Bhagavad-Gita. Some have correctly described such fundamentalism as "a political ideology of the twentieth century that recruits members based on their shared ethno-religious characteristics,"[1] but this analysis of the ideology hardly goes far enough. What must be added is that it is an ideology upheld by those who subscribe to what are taken to be infallible religious texts. Further, it is an ideology whose subscribers treat the literal interpretation of these texts as beacons that shed light upon the crises of modernity and who persistently act to promote public policies that reflect the values and beliefs of these texts.[2]

Religious fundamentalism, evident in North America, Europe, the Middle East, Pakistan, and India, is practised by some—but by no means all—believers of Islam, Christianity, Judaism, and Hinduism. It is important to note that fundamentalists in each of these religions comprise only a part of the respective religion, often not even the largest part. What distinguishes fundamentalism in each religion is not its confession of faith, which it shares with the majority of the faithful, but its literalism and commitment to bring change to public policies, either in the international or domestic arenas. Other features of fundamentalism include:

i. its rejection of secularism (to be discussed in Chapter 14);
ii. its rejection of pluralism;
iii. its rejection of the values of the Enlightenment;
iv. its submission of humans to the authority of a divine being and that being's earthly representatives, whose truth and commands have been permanently revealed;
v. its rejection of uncertainty in policy debates;
vi. its distrust of human reason; and
vii. its interest in establishing a theocratic or theocratic-like society that conforms to divinely inspired absolutes.[3]

Bearing in mind that only some of the adherents to each of the religions referred to are fundamentalist, we can move on to providing a brief overview of the various kinds of fundamentalism found in each. We shall look at the various kinds in the following order: Islamic fundamentalism, Christian fundamentalism, Jewish fundamentalism, and finally Hindu fundamentalism. Progressing in this way we shall begin with the ultra-conservative views of the most recently founded religion and end with the ultra-conservative views of the oldest religion. As a first approximation, it is useful to think of each of these as manifesting themselves in these terms:

- In Islam, fundamentalism manifests itself in **Sunnism**, particularly in the Muslim Brotherhood as founded by Hassan al-Banna (d. 1949) in Egypt and Wahhabism founded by the Sunni scholar Muhammad ibn 'Abd al-Wahhab (1703–1792) in Saudi Arabia. More recently its tentacles have stretched further to Africa, especially in Nigeria under the influence of **Boko Haram** and in Somalia and Kenya under the influence of **Al-Shabaab**. It also shows itself in **Shi'ism**, particularly under the guidance of Ayatollah Khomeini (1902–1989) in Iran and Muqtada al-Sadr (1973–) in Iraq.
- In Christianity, fundamentalism manifests itself in movements such as the Moral Majority in its struggle against legalized abortion, same-sex marriage, humanistic textbooks, evolutionary theory, the failed Equal Rights Amendment, and embryonic research. And it manifests itself in publications such as *Under Orders: A Spiritual Handbook for Military Personnel* (2005), a book written by Major William McCoy, a US Army chaplain, and endorsed by David Petraeus, the then senior commander in Iraq. In his book, McCoy seeks to counter the alleged anti-Christian bias in the United States by making an argument for the necessity of religion—preferably Christian—for any properly functioning military unit.[4]

- In Judaism, fundamentalism manifests itself in that part of the faith called Hasidism and Orthodoxy, as well as in the **Gush Emunim** and **Chabad Lubavitch** movements. These movements stand at odds with Zionism, which sees no relevance to the religious-messianic world of Gush Emunim and, presumably, Chabad Lubavitch.
- In Hinduism, fundamentalism manifests itself in Hindu nationalism, in particular as this nationalism has shown itself under the leadership Narendra Modi, the current Prime Minister of India. His government was tarnished, when he was leader of the state of Gujarat, in the anti-Muslim riots that occurred in that state on 27 February 2002 after 60 Hindus were burned to death as a result of a fire on a train near Godhra. Accusations were made that the fire was caused by arsonists who were Muslims. Owing to these rumours and accusations, anti-Muslim protests occurred, resulting in the death of somewhere between 790 and 2,000 Muslims. Rumours persisted that the Modi government of that day did nothing to prevent these killings.[5]

Currently, events in different parts of the world make it clear that these ideologies are very much alive and in need of the attention of domestic and international bodies. The enmity between Muslims and Hindus confirms this in present-day India. The influence of Boko Haram in Nigeria, which kidnapped 276 girls from a girls' school on 14 April 2014 and frequently has attacked small villages in northeast Nigeria, establishes this as part of the political landscape in that part of Africa.[6] And the 2 April 2015 attack of Al-Shabaab on the Garissa University College campus in northeast Kenya, resulting in the death of 148 Christian students, makes the political relevance of this fanaticism self-evident.[7] Finally, the Gush Emunim Jewish settlers in the occupied territories,[8] by their very presence in Palestine, create a tense and unsustainable situation involving Jews and Palestinians. When these actions are combined with the ideologically motivated actions of the so-called Islamic State in Iraq and Syria (ISIS), the outcome can only be guessed at. Any talk of quick fixes in connection with any of these self-proclaimed fundamentalist groups is simply far-fetched.[9] This has become more evident in recent years. No longer is the radical Arabic Middle East characterized only by **Hamas** on the Gaza Strip (under the influence of the Muslim Brotherhood) and **Hezbollah** in Lebanon (under the influence of non-Arabic Iran). Today, the Wahhabi-inspired self-styled **ISIS caliphate** controls and terrorizes large swaths of Iraq and Syria, despite extensive American-led air strikes against this group that, arguably, only strengthen ISIS resolve and aid in the group's sophisticated global recruitment and terror strategies. And in North Africa more acts of terror have occurred in Libya and Tunisia under the ISIS banner. The unmistakable impression one is left with is that diplomacy is in disarray and a game of Russian roulette is underway—perhaps especially since 2015 with Russia's entry into the Syrian fray on the side of the brutal Bashar al-Assad regime.

The dust created by the ideological tension and confusion surrounding religious fundamentalism should not make us lose sight of something that ties all of these together. The commonality of all these movements is explained by Youssef M. Choueiri, who defines three varieties of fundamentalism in Islam (revivalism, reformism, and radicalism): "Finally, whatever definition is adopted in a study that aspires to understand the characteristics of fundamentalism, one particular chain of reasoning links revivalism, reformism, and radicalism. It is their rejection of **secularism** in all its schools and movements that marks the movements and serves to highlight their fundamentalist constructions."[10] One can echo Choueiri's words and apply them to the religious fundamentalism found not only in Islam but also in Christianity, Judaism, and Hinduism. We are clearly in post-Enlightenment times when we think like fundamentalists of any persuasion.

Although adherence to secularism makes it fashionable to be disdainful of fundamentalism and its ideal of a life of faith, it cannot be so easily dismissed. A brief exploration of ideological alternatives may help to explain why religious fundamentalism has attracted significant followers, in spite of the alleged irrationality of this from the viewpoint of Marx, Freud, and Nietzsche, to name but three critics of religious belief. With an end to understanding some of the philosophical terrain surrounding fundamentalism, one should keep in mind the following three metaphysical perspectives: (i) perennial naturalism; (ii) critical anti-realism, with its linkage to pluralism and relativism; and (iii) theism, with its logical inconsistencies and evidential weakness.

Naturalism, as a school of thought, maintains that knowledge is rooted in experience and logic, while **humanism** is a secular philosophy that emphasizes the needs and interests of human beings. **Critical anti-realism** is a reflective metaphysical position claiming that reality is constructed by humans rather than something existing independently of humans; **pluralism** and **relativism** are products of anti-realism, maintaining as they do that theories about the world are multiple, non-convergent and subjective. Finally, **theism** is a metaphysical position that attributes the origin of the cosmos to a supreme being (Allah, Yahweh, God, Atman) said to be omnipotent, omniscient, and good, notwithstanding pain, suffering, and evil in the world, and notwithstanding the thin evidentiary basis on which the belief is founded.

Given that, at least from the point of view of some contemporaries, perennial naturalism, so defined, has not led to the promised land described by Kant, to wit, "release from self-incurred tutelage,"[11] and given that critical anti-realism has led to a relativism that challenges traditional values such as the prohibition on homosexuality or abortion, theism looks attractive to many individuals. Moreover, a particular version of theism, one grounded in literalism of sacred texts, is attractive to those who qualify as fundamentalist Muslims, Christians, Jews, or Hindus. A fertile point of departure for our discussion of fundamentalism is its Islamic version, which has made fundamentalism transparently relevant to contemporary politics. We shall, accordingly, begin our discussion there.

Islamic Fundamentalism: Background

Islam was established by the prophet Muhammad (570–632). Upon his death the position of the leader of the new religion was assumed by his companion, Abu Bakr, and then his sons, Omar and Osman. Following the death of Osman by poisoning, Ali, the prophet's cousin (Ali ibn Abi Talib, c. 598–661), was finally selected as the caliph or leader of those who followed the teachings of Muhammad. Ali ruled only five years, and upon his death a struggle broke out between Ali's direct male descendant and those who admired the first three caliphs: Abu Bakr, Omar, and Osman. The result of this struggle was the formation of two sects in the bosom of Islam, Shi'ism and Sunnism. Doctrinal differences between these two groups—which have led to sectarian violence—may be outlined as follows:

- Shi'ism represents the partisans of Ali, and therefore reveres the 12 imams, as Ali and his descendants are called. Shi'ites believe that it is possible to remove the stains of sin through living a simple and devout life, as well as through suffering. Shi'ism is attractive to the poor and downtrodden, who anticipate the emergence of divine wisdom with the return of Mahdi (the twelfth imam). It is attractive to the poor because the re-emergence of divine wisdom represents the purification of society, the inauguration of truth and justice. To the dispossessed, Shi'ism represents a message of hope.

- Sunnism represents the followers of the Sunnah, or tradition, and does not revere Ali or his descendants. Unlike Shi'ism, Sunnism sees history as moving away from the ideal community that was present during the era of the four caliphs. Moreover, Sunnism lacks the messianic and emotional overtones of Shi'ism.[12]

Both Shi'ism and Sunnism have their political or fundamentalist sides. In the case of Shi'ism this is found largely in the inspirational movement of Muqtada al-Sadr in Iraq and Sayyed Hassan Nasrallah (1960–) and the Hezbollah in Lebanon. In the case of Sunnism, this side is found in Wahhabism, but also in the movements headed by supporters of Syed Abul Ala Maududi, the Muslim Brotherhood, Hamas, the Deobandi, the Taliban, Hizb-ut-Tahrir, and more recently Boka Haram and Al-Shabaab.

Islamic Fundamentalism: Its Beginning

A number of factors have contributed to the rise of modern Islamic fundamentalism, and it is helpful to have these in mind before looking at the content of the ideology. Among the more notable factors are foreign occupation, humiliation, and repression; the aversion of Arabs and Muslims alike to further calamities after their 1967 defeat in the war with Israel, a defeat attributed to the inadequate belief on the part of Muslims; the process of urbanization; the universal crisis of modernity; and finally, the legitimization Islam provides for political rule in the absence of established institutions and in the presence of unelected rulers.[13] Each of these will now be examined.

Foreign occupation, humiliation, and repression. Islamic fundamentalism is rooted not only in the breakup of the **Ottoman Empire** following World War I, but also in the rise to power of Britain, France, the United States, and the USSR following World War II. From the perspective of fundamentalists these powers functioned as totalitarian, colonialist regimes and it was against this that numerous intellectual Muslims argued, proposing, as an alternative, pan Islamism to counter the military and commercial expansionism of the West and the Soviet Union. One of the biggest grievances Islamic fundamentalists had in connection with this expansionism was the loss of sovereignty (*hakimiya*), which meant, among other things, the loss of governing themselves according to Islamic law. In short, Western military expansionism changed the world order, with capitalism following in its wake. The end result was Muslim countries falling into the hands of European and American colonialists, with the perceived victimization of Muslims, their rulers, territories, laws, and economies.[14] This perceived victimization from foreign domination generated, unsurprisingly, humiliation and a sense of repression.[15]

Defeat by Israel. Israel's defeat of Egypt, Jordan, and Syria in the Six-Day War of 1967 was in many ways a disaster in the Arab world. For some Arabs it was more than this. For them it was *the* disaster of the Arab world and Muslim world, exemplified by the loss of the holy city of Jerusalem.[16] Moreover, for many Arabs who shared this belief, the most compelling explanation of the turn of events was to be found either in the inferiority of Islam as a religion or in the infidelity of its believers. Forced to choose between these two options, many Arabs chose the second. In this way, then, the revival of Islam was given a start in the late 1960s.[17]

Of course, not all Arabs, to say nothing about all Muslims, felt the same way about the turn of events in the 1967 war. For them, the loss of Jerusalem was a disaster—even *the* disaster, perhaps, next to the United Nations partition of Palestine in 1948 and the subsequent founding of the state of Israel. However, its explanation lay not in infidelity on the part of the Arabs but in the lack of proper secular leadership given by Gamal Abdel Nasser of Egypt (1918–1970). The loss of Jerusalem, and Nasser's death, led to a competition for the "'mantle of leadership in the Arab state system."[18] Hafez al-Assad of Syria (1930–2000), Mu'ammer Gaddafi of Libya (1942–2011), and Saddam Hussein (1937–2006) all jostled for the position previously held by Nasser as leader of the Arab world. Nasser might have gone but Nasserism had *not*, for all three would have affirmed "pan-Arabism, secular and revolutionary politics, and the search for an Arab power capable of defeating Israel and challenging Western influence in the Arab world."[19] In the meantime, Anwar Sadat (1918–1981), Nasser's successor, was able to regain a measure of Arab pride by claiming victory in the Yom Kippur War of 1973. Nothing would seriously challenge this secular approach to politics in the Arab world until the late 1970s. Sadat's 1979 peace treaty with Israel—negotiated at Camp David with the help of US President Jimmy Carter—was harshly criticized in the Arab world and led to Egypt's suspension from the Arab League. Then came the Iranian Revolution of 1979, led by Ayatollah Khomeini and his Shi'ite followers. The revolution in Iran, a non-Arab state, coupled with the assassination of Sadat by a member of the Muslim Brotherhood,[20] signalled the revival of fundamentalist Islam in a bold way. These events were symptomatic of underlying social changes that would impact Palestine, Lebanon, Jordan, Israel, Syria, Egypt, Iraq, and Saudi Arabia in years to come.

Urbanization. A third factor contributing to the revival of fundamentalist Islam was the process of development or urbanization. The 1960s, 1970s, and 1980s saw an increase in the urban populations in Egypt, Iran, Iraq, Jordan, Kuwait, Lebanon, Saudi Arabia, Syria, and South Yemen.[21] In these countries the rate of urbanization exceeded the rate of industrialization, with the result that many people were marginalized. The new urban dwellers were made to feel as though they did not belong, and Islam became more passionately adopted by city dwellers as a remedy for their anonymity. As James Piscatori aptly says, "There does seem to be a general connection between the sense of not belonging and a return to religion."[22]

Modernity. A fourth factor that has contributed to the revival of Islam is the crisis of modernity. What exactly is this crisis? For Islamic fundamentalists, it represents a societal breakdown in the institutions that have traditionally provided meaning to one's life. Urbanization and industrialization, coupled with a revolution in knowledge, communication, and transportation, have resulted in pools of individuals being cut off from the traditional roots that have anchored their lives. Central among the institutions challenged by modernity have been religious institutions (mosques, churches, synagogues, temples) in all of their many forms. The erosion of other institutions, such as the family, the school, and parental authority, simply raised the question of meaning more acutely in the minds of those who were not the clear beneficiaries of secular ideas. This has led one commentator to say, with plausibility, "In response to the deracination and threats of cultural extinction associated with modernization processes, religious experience seeks to restore meaning to life."[23] The result has been a search by religious believers, including Muslims, for old rites of incorporation, to find old ways to address the cognitive dissonance of the present. The crisis of modernity is a crisis of identity. In the absence of something new to help define themselves, people—especially the marginalized—are returning to religion.

Legitimization of political rule. The fifth and final factor contributing to the revival of Islam is the new importance of ideology among governing elites in Arab countries that are in search of legitimacy. Faced with the Iranian Revolution that displaced the Shah and the Pahlavi family, ruling elites in Arab states in the Middle East encountered a completely new realignment that revealed weakness in the principal Arab states.[24] Saudi Arabia was particularly vulnerable, and its ruling family, the House of Sa'ud, was forced to play not only its oil card, which represented money and power, but also its Islamic card as the guardian of the holy sites of Mecca and Medina. The House of Sa'ud decided to do this in order to contain the influence of Iran in the Middle East and Persian Gulf.[25] But it was not just the elites in Saudi Arabia that sought legitimacy in Islam. The same can be said of governments in Egypt under Sadat and his successor, Hosni Mubarak, who used Islamic *fatwas* (religious decrees) or Islamic newspapers; Ja'far Numayri of Sudan (1930–2009), who accommodated the Muslim Brotherhood; and King Hussein of Jordan (1935–1999), who emphasized his descent from the Prophet[26]—all for the purpose of legitimizing their regimes.

The presence of a fundamentalist Iran, then, changed the politics of the Middle East and North Africa. It meant that Arab countries had to be on guard not only against secular Arab regimes such as Iraq, but also against religiously revived Arab and Persian regimes that could exploit demographic weaknesses. These demographic weaknesses included the special case of large Shi'ite populations in Iraq and Saudi Arabia. It is little wonder that the Arab states sought to legitimize the status quo in revived religious terms.

Having provided an overview of the emergence of contemporary Islamic fundamentalism, we will now take a closer look at three of its movements: Wahhabism, the Muslim Brotherhood, and Khomeini-inspired Shi'ism.

Islamic Fundamentalism: al-Wahhab

Wahhabism was born in the eighteenth century under the inspiration of Muhammad ibn 'Abd al-Wahhab in Saudi Arabia, but even Ibn 'Abd al-Wahhab had his radical predecessors, one of whom was Ahmad Ibn Taymiyyah (1263–1328). Ibn Taymiyyah declared total war on Sufism (Muslim mysticism) and Shi'ism, as well as Greek philosophy.[27] Al-Wahhab himself was a native of Najd (in present-day Saudi Arabia) who became dedicated to the cause of reform in Islam, a religion he thought had sunk into impiety. Owing to this, he began a campaign of purification to denounce innovations and superstitions that had become attached to Islam. In 1747 he received the support of the House of Sa'ud, which became his secular champion.[28]

For Western readers, one aspect of the history of al-Wahhab is particularly intriguing. In his rise to power as an Islamic spiritual leader, he was covertly assisted by a British spy nicknamed Humphrey who had been sent by Britain to Arab countries for the purpose of destabilizing the Ottoman Empire.[29] The British often used the strategy of divide and conquer and at this time wished to sow seeds of discontent between the Arabs and the Turks, and this Humphrey ably did by convincing al-Wahhab of al-Wahhab's religious significance for Islam and of the need to reform the ways of Muslims so as to conform to the teaching of the Prophet. The hope of the British and Humphrey was that this religious reformer would help to bring sectarian divisions in Islam, especially those that would split Arabs and Turks.[30] In this matter the British seemed to have succeeded admirably. Whether they are in present times pleased with the result seems very much to be doubted.

An influential successor of al-Wahhab was Sayyid Abul-Ala Maududi (1903–1979), an Indian Muslim who revered Ibn Taymiyyah and who claimed that the entire Muslim community was characterized by unbelief. Maududi, a journalist, endorsed political revolution and was instrumental in the founding of the Community of Islam (Jamaat-i-Islami) in India, a group that has incited violence in Kashmir. The last of the important followers of Wahhabism is Abdullah Azzam (1941–1989), a Palestinian who fled the West Bank when it was occupied by Israel in 1967. In Jordan he was a professor of religious law, and subsequently he moved to Saudi Arabia, where he hoped to generate a passion among young Arabs for jihad (holy war).[31] Figures such as Ibn Taymiyyah, Abdullah Azzam, and those found in between provide an understanding of Wahhabism. With its religious zeal and commitment to jihad, Wahhabism forms the ideological backbone of Al-Qaeda and now ISIS, as well as Boko Haram in Nigeria and Al-Shabaab in Somalia and Kenya. Wahhabism is anything but a dated religious relic—it is a movement and ideology that combats anything in its path.

Core Teachings

The core teachings of Wahhabism amount to a "strict and exclusive adherence to the plain sense of the Qur'an and the sunnah."[32] It rejects corruption and laxity, as well as the cultural richness of the medieval Islamic empire. Further, it rejects mystical piety in addition to alien philosophy and theology. Generally, Wahhabism, like the Salafi movement under Ibn Taymiyyah, seeks to strip away all innovations and to restore Islam to its pristine state as found in the day of the Prophet. Accordingly, it favours "extreme textual literalism" and rejects the four traditional schools of law in Sunni Islam.[33] Moreover, it opposes the worship of the Prophet Muhammad, condemns Muslims for praying at the shrines of holy men, criticizes the practice of marking graves, emphasizes the unity of God, and denounces all non-Sunni groups as hypocrites.[34] Finally, with its "ardent zeal," Wahhabism, at least in earlier times in the 1920s, went so far as to condemn as "heretical contraptions of the devil" the then "modern" means of communication, such as the telephone and wireless.[35] The sophisticated use by such groups as ISIS of mainstream and social media for propaganda and recruitment would suggest that modern communications are no longer "heretical contraptions."

Association with the House of Sa'ud

Wahhabism emerged in 1747 as the religious champion of a purified Sunni Islam and as the religious ally of the secular House of Sa'ud. As a movement and ideology, Wahhabism continued to expand, and in 1801 Wahhabists crushed the city of Karbala, Iraq, a holy Shi'a city, before taking both Mecca and Medina. Clearly, in Wahhabism there was to be no accommodation of Shi'ism, a point worth remembering in the present context of the ISIS fight with Shi'ites in Iraq and Syria. Forces of the Ottoman Sultan Mahmud II, under the leadership of the Egyptian Muhammad Ali and his son Ibrahim, took back both Mecca and Medina before defeating the Wahhabis decisively in 1818. Nonetheless, Wahhabism has, since that date, enjoyed periodic success, if only through the success of affiliated movements such as the Muslim Brotherhood, Hamas, the Deobandi, the Taliban, and Hizb-ut-Tahrir.

In the late twentieth century and early part of the twenty-first century, Wahhabism has been encouraged by various political and military successes: in resisting the West in the battle for the control of the Suez Canal in 1956; in shocking the West in the oil crisis of 1973; and in encouraging young middle-class males in urban areas of Saudi Arabia to take up the "separatist, supremacist, intolerant and brutalizing curriculum of Wahhabism"[36] and serve as mujahideen or sacred soldiers in the jihad in Afghanistan. Of course, more recent involvement of Wahhabism and its offshoots on a geopolitical scale includes the Al-Qaeda attacks of 11 September 2001 at the Twin Towers of the World Trade Center in New York City and on the Pentagon in Arlington, Virginia; attacks inside Iraq and Saudi Arabia in 2003 and 2004; the attack on the Madrid commuter train in 2004 killing 191 people and wounding 1,800 individuals; the Al-Shabaab attack on 21 September 2013 at the Westgate Mall, Nairobi, Kenya, which resulted in the death of 70 civilians, six security guards, and 175 injured;[37] the Boko Haram abduction of nearly 300 girls in April 2014 from a girls' school in Chibok, Nigeria; and the Al-Shabaab attack in March 2015 on a Christian university in northern Kenya resulting in the death of 148 individuals. All of these actions show a boldness and resolution on the part of Wahhabism and its affiliates to carry out bloodletting on a wide scale against innocent people.

Accretions of Islam

Wahhabism excoriates the features of Islam that are extraneous to it, denounces Shi'ism almost as fervently as it does other religions, and gains political support from the House of Sa'ud dating back to 1747. The hatred characteristic of Wahhabis and their religious and political affiliates, such as Al-Qaeda, is found in a letter attributed to Abu Musab al-Zarqawi (1966–2006), the late leader of Al-Qaeda in Iraq, who allegedly said of Shi'as that they are a more pernicious enemy than the Americans, and the best strategy for poor, weak, and sleepy Sunnis is to strike their religious and military cadres to preclude the transfer of power to a Shi'a-dominated democracy.[38] Finally, there is no doubt that, historically, Wahhabism found its political support in the House of Sa'ud. As George Antonius (1891–1941), the doyen of early twentieth-century Arab studies, says, referring to the agreement struck between al-Wahhab and the House of Sa'ud, "[al-Wahhab] found an ally in a scion of the House of Sa'ud, who accepted his teaching and became his secular champion."[39]

In promoting *tawhid*, or the oneness of God, Wahhabism rejects any semblance of worshipping anything other than Allah, including visitation to graves of saints or the celebration of the saints' birthdays. And it endorses the deeply conservative Hanbali school of legal Sunni jurisprudence.[40] In addition, Wahhabism unconditionally rejects divorce, alcoholism, drug addiction, nervous disorders, and crimes, as well as a weakening of parental authority, liberation of women, a questioning of the authority of the clergy, and a general drift towards individualism. In summary, Wahhabism is characterized ideologically by the following traits: it emphasizes (i) the oneness (*tawhid*) of Allah; (ii) the ideals of the Prophet and his companions; (iii) Hanbali jurisprudence, and intolerance of other religious groups within Islam, even to the point of legitimizing attacks on them.[41]

Islamic Fundamentalism: al-Banna and Qutb

Another radical Islamic organization, this one based in Egypt, is that of the **Muslim Brotherhood**, a Wahhabi-related religious group. It came into being under the leadership of Hasan al-Banna (1906–1949), who based his ideology on three basic principles: (i) Islam is a comprehensive system; (ii) Islam emanates from the Qur'an and the Prophetic Tradition; and (iii) Islam is applicable to all times and all places. Al-Banna "declared his movement to be the inheritor, and catalyst, of the most activist elements in Sunni traditionalist and reformist thinking.[42] The Muslim Brotherhood was founded in 1928 for the purpose of offsetting the negative effects of Westernization and secularism in Egyptian society. It aimed to do this by emphasizing the importance of a return to the "true" Islam, very much in the spirit of Wahhabism. And as a part of its means of achieving the true Islam, it supported anti-missionary, anti-colonial, and anti-Zionist endeavours.[43] The challenge for al-Banna was to encourage Egyptians to tap into the riches of modernity's potential while avoiding its moral depravity. In 1949 al-Banna was assassinated and the Muslim Brotherhood became, over the next few years, more militant.

The person who acted to carry on al-Banna's mission of social transformation was Sayyid Qutb (1906–1966), who became well known as the major theorist of Islamism and jihad. After spending two years in America from 1948 to 1950, he came to the conclusion that, notwithstanding its remarkable achievements, the United States had forgotten to balance material and spiritual needs, was therefore "exhausted," and could not be looked to for guidance on what constituted "humanity."[44] The period spent in the United States acted to confirm Qutb in his ideological conviction that there was a sharp line separating Islamic and misguided, permissive societies.[45] He came to the firm belief that Islam was more than a matter of personal piety—it was something that prescribed a whole new social order. What he had witnessed in the United States was a materialism and a lack of prudery that he felt had resulted in a devastating erosion of the country's moral character, caused by capitalist individualism.[46] He returned to Egypt in 1950, but was arrested in 1954 for encouraging subversive activities. Qutb then spent the next 10 years in prison, during which he wrote on the need for social reform in Egypt by means of eliminating by force the "infidel" government that dominated Egypt. Shortly after his release from prison in 1964, he was rearrested on charges of conspiring to assassinate President Nasser, and executed.[47]

Leadership and World Welfare

In Qutb's ideology, Islam is a creed for leadership and world welfare. History before Islam is steeped in depravity, or *jahiliyyah* (ignorance), when the spirit of man had become debased and the roots of humanity were destroyed by "a criminally luxurious and wasteful life" as well as by hopelessness and despair. The birth of Islam gave it, according to Qutb, a role in the "reconstruction of humanity" by liberating the human soul from superstitions, banalities, disease, and degradation. While Qutb thinks of Islam as pre-eminently a faith that inspires leadership, the real test of its mettle is proven when Muslims assume responsibility for the trusteeship of mankind, something he thinks Muslims have done in the past but more recently have failed to do. There is, he believes, a sharp contrast between the spirit of Islam and the spirit of materialism, and materialism prevails when the standards and norms inspired by Allah are displaced by debased appetites. Thus, argues Qutb, the time has come when the world could turn to Islam for leadership to replace this tired depravity. In his opinion, Egypt should seek freedom and social justice by looking to Islam, and in the process turn its back on two other unsatisfactory models for development: capitalism and communism. His intent is to lead Egyptians back to Islam with a constitution guided by the *shariah* law so that it could avoid the comic carnival of fashions produced by following foreign models imported from Russia, the United States, and Europe. In the transition from the present Islam and the future of Islam, Qutb aims to educate Muslims about the spirit of fanaticism that he thinks prevails in Europe (and presumably elsewhere in the West) against Islam. He attributes this fanaticism against Islam to two sources: (i) the poisoning of the European mind during the Crusades, a poisoning that caused a distorted view of Islam, and (ii) the recognition by European and American crusaders that the Islamic spirit acts as a bulwark against Western imperialism.[48]

Islamic Fundamentalism: Shi'ism and Ayatollah Khomeini

As previously stated, a great divide exists at the heart of Islam between Sunnis and the Shi'ites. The discussion up to now has focused almost exclusively on the former. There are two reasons for this. First, the Sunnis comprise about 85 per cent of all Muslims, while the Shi'ites comprise but 15 per cent. Second, in the years following the 9/11 attacks, Sunni groups such as Al-Qaeda, Al-Shabaab, and Boko Haram, all Wahhabi in nature, have become jihadists and as such destabilizing forces in the geopolitical world. One has only to recall terrorist events of recent years—even recent days—to appreciate this point. For the most part, Shi'ite militant activities have been restricted to Iraq and Lebanon, with no other threat posed to the outside world. Of course, the outside world has been seized by the possibility of a nuclear Shi'a Iran, but this worry exists at the state level and not at the level of terrorists or armed militias who happen to be Shi'a. For these reasons our attention has focused on Sunni militants.

Nonetheless, Shi'ism is not a force to discount. It has had and continues to have ideological significance. By way of entry into our discussion of the Shi'a, one can say that they are little known and little understood.[49] Shi'a form a majority of the population in Iran, Iraq, and the island of Bahrain. In Saudi Arabia they form a minority, often viewed by Sunni rulers with suspicion. Finally, in Azerbaijan there is a Shi'a majority, and in India, Pakistan, and Afghanistan a minority. On the global stage outside of Iran, their presence is felt most in Lebanon through Hezbollah and in Iraq through the utterances of the radical cleric Muqtada al-Sadr.[50]

What follows is a discussion of the Shi'a perspective, especially as it has been captured in the writings, speeches, and action of Ayatollah Ruhollah Khomeini, the mullah who bided his time in exile in the 1970s waiting for the Pahlavi dynasty of the Shah to fall. Before looking at some of the ideas expressed by the Ayatollah—ideas whose influence is still felt—we should fix firmly in our minds the characteristics of his Islamic revival. We should bear in mind in outlining these characteristics that Shi'ism as a movement, within Islam, has at its best functioned as "a beacon of hope for the poor, the weak, and the forsaken" and "a vanguard of hope for revolutionary uprising and the restoration of earthly justice."[51]

Five Central Tenets

Khomeini's fundamentalism, his political Islam, has at least five general characteristics, some of which it shares with Wahhabism. It subscribes to the following:

i. Islam is a comprehensive way of life for living in the modern world.

ii. Present-day failures of Muslim societies are attributable to a turning away from Islam and a turning towards the West.
iii. Muslims should reject the tenets of the Western ideology, including secularism, pluralism, and individualism.
iv. Ordinary Muslims must renew themselves through dedication, training, and struggle.
v. Patriarchal families should be nurtured so as to control and segregate women.[52]

It was against the background of these ideas that the Ayatollah worked while in exile towards the overthrow of the Shah, Mohammad Reza Pahlavi (1919–1980), and his regime. While Khomeini was in Paris in 1978, political repression continued unabated in Iran under the leadership of SAVAK, the Shah's secret police. This repression, when coupled with the Shah's dependence on the United States, the silencing of the press, and ever-present corruption, led to a particularly unstable situation in Iran. The situation was further exacerbated when the Shah's agricultural policies resulted in the displacement of many rural people and their eventual migration to the cities. The overall effect was an unemployment and housing crisis, made still worse by the sharp contrast between the rich and the poor. This fed into Shi'a rhetoric over martyrdom and the idea of doing battle against an unjust state. Cries for social justice were made in different quarters, but to no avail. In December 1978 a huge demonstration against the Shah's regime occurred and, conjoined with mutinies in the military, was followed in February 1979 with the return of Khomeini to Iran. While emphasizing social justice in much the same way as the Muslim Brotherhood or Qutb, Khomeini gave a greater role to the *ulama*, the learned of Islam, and thereby allowed for more pluralism than found in the writings of Sayyid Qutb or Hasan al-Banna.[53]

Colonialism and Imperialism

Ayatollah Khomeini, while being a religious figure, was primarily concerned with social and political issues in Iran.[54] It would be correct to say of him that over the years his thinking revealed a view of religion as a useful tool for teaching political and social ends.[55] High on his political and social agenda were colonialism and imperialism, to both of which we now turn.

Khomeini is adamantly opposed to the corrupting influences of outside governments that have broken the Muslim people into several groups.[56] He attributes this fragmentation of Muslims to imperialists and colonialists, including missionaries, Jews, Russians, Englishmen, Americans,[57] and Austrians. The plan of these individuals is "to keep us in our backward state, to preserve our pathetic way of life, so that they can exploit the tremendous wealth of our underground resources, of our land, and of our manpower."[58] Khomeini's protest of colonialism and imperialism seems to be a diffuse protest against foreign states because of (i) the influence foreign practices have come to have in Iran (e.g., theatres, dancing, and music); (ii) the direct activities of groups (e.g., missionaries) from other countries; and (iii) the specific actions of Christians and Jews. He seems to have a particular hostility towards Jews, and accuses them of being "the source of all anti-Islamic libels and intrigues."[59] Owing to the imperialistic actions of agents of Christianity, Zionism, and Bahaism, Khomeini thinks that Muslims have no alternative but to set up a true Islamic government, thereby overthrowing those pseudo-Muslim governments put in place by foreign powers.

Islamic Government

During the 1960s, Khomeini slowly began to change his views on Islamic government. Prior to this he had felt that clerics should limit their activity to giving legal and moral guidance on condition that the state's authorities enforce the law of Islam. However, during the latter part of the decade, Khomeini changed his views on the grounds that the Shah threatened the authority of the clerics, pursued secular policies, and finally—perhaps most importantly—started a campaign to have pre-Islamic Persian identity trump Shi'ism.[60] Faced with these events, Khomeini reasoned that the clerics should no longer remain content in the role of moral guides, but should become executive rulers. In fact, he goes so far as to say that clerics should have the primary power in judicial, legislative, and executive matters. Part of this executive rule would include one supreme *marja'* or religious guide, and one *faqih* (jurist) or supreme leader, who would have something like the divine spark of the imams. In affirming the validity of a moral guide, Khomeini exposed himself to the charge of presumptuousness, a charge to which he responded by drawing upon utilitarian, mystical, and traditional ideas. Khomeini proved himself to be sufficiently persuasive at this time, probably owing to his piety and courage,[61] that he not only succeeded in evading these charges successfully, but in fact attracted millions of Shi'ites in Iran to his way of thinking: Islamic government requires validation or permission from a living *faqih*.[62] The challenge to the Shah's regime, and to any constitutional regime similar to it, was obvious. Khomeini in effect rejected secular constitutionalism on the grounds that it fostered deceptions cultivated by "Western maniacs" who were nothing other than servants of imperialism.[63] Secular constitutionalism was out, theocracy was in.

The Role of Women

The views of Ayatollah Khomeini on women are, for the most part, quite extreme. He claims that women should be denied the franchise on the grounds that it is contrary to the *shariah*. In a nutshell, he feels that seclusion is the proper condition for women. They should not be brought into political offices for the reason that such action will lead to a paralysis in the offices. Nor does he want them to be allowed into provincial offices for the reason that they will turn everything upside down. Furthermore, he argues against granting equality to women in the matter of inheritance and divorce on the grounds that such is contrary to the precepts of Islam. With respect to all of the above conservative stances, Khomeini bases his position on an interpretation of Islamic law suggesting that women lack intellectual maturity and that freedom encourages sexual openness that will undermine Islam.[64]

On the subject of marriage, adultery, and conjugal relations, Khomeini has the following to say. In the event that a woman has contracted a continuing marriage, she has no right to go outside the home without her husband's permission, and she must be prepared to fulfill any of his desires. In exchange for such "total submission," the husband is obliged to provide his wife with food, clothing, and shelter. Further, a woman must hide her hair and her body from the eyes of men.[65]

With this understanding of Islamic fundamentalism in mind, that is, with the understanding of Islam as offered by al-Wahhab and his successor Maududi, by al-Banna and Qutb, and finally by Ayatollah Khomeini, we can now move on to another form of religious fundamentalism, that is, Christian fundamentalism.

Christian Fundamentalism

The story of Christian fundamentalism is largely the story of American Christian fundamentalism, though our discussion easily could be extended to Canada, Australia, and New Zealand.[66] American Christian fundamentalism is rooted, some think, in the **Great Western Transmutation**.[67] The GWT, as it is called, is said by its proponent, Marshall Hodgson (1922–1968), to be the irreversible occurrence of industrialization in the West at the end of the eighteenth century.[68] But we can give greater focus to the notion of Christian fundamentalism by understanding that the term "fundamentalism" comes from a series of 12 booklets called *The Fundamentals*, published between 1909 and 1915 and distributed free of charge by two US oil millionaires to Sunday schools throughout the country. The purpose of these booklets was to neutralize liberal thinking in Protestant churches in America—a liberalism that, it was believed, undermined the eternal truths of Christianity. These truths included the infallibility of the Bible, the Virgin birth, the miracles, the resurrection of Jesus, and the substitutionary view of Atonement.[69]

The religious groups in Christianity that fundamentalists opposed were not simply liberal Protestants, but also Roman Catholics, Mormons, Jehovah's Witnesses, and Christian Scientists. Clearly, though, the main fight fundamentalists had was with liberals inside the Christian churches, for liberalism represented modernity, and it was modernity that fundamentalists opposed. One of the defining moments between the fundamentalists and the modernists was a sermon delivered by Harry Emerson Fosdick in 1922 entitled "Shall the Fundamentalists Win?"[70] Fosdick claims that fundamentalism is essentially illiberal and intolerant, largely owing to its intransigence on the so-called "eternal" truths of Christianity. What he presents as an alternative is what amounts to an integration of modern ideas with religious ones: "We must be able to think our modern life clear through in Christian terms and to do that we must be able to think our Christian life clear through in modern terms."[71] Fosdick, a liberal and modernist, does not believe in the compartmentalization of human knowledge, and he is willing to expose his faith to the challenge of new knowledge. In his comment, Fosdick anticipates views on fundamentalism that would later be held: Christian fundamentalism is an orientation against the ideology of modernism.[72] In more recent times, Kevin Phillips has carried Fosdick's ideas further by raising concern about the religious right or Christian fundamentalism in the United States, a fundamentalism that, in his opinion, is anti-intellectual and inclined towards disenlightenment. This awakens concern in him owing to the role he believes this has played in the decline of world economic powers in the past, including Rome, Hapsburg Spain, the Dutch Republic, Britain, and now the United States. Of the five criteria that link these economic powers to decline, according to Phillips, three are closely tied to Christian fundamentalism. The five criteria are:

- public concern over cultural and economic decay;
- growing religious fervour;
- rising commitment to faith over reason and a downplaying of science;
- anticipation of an imminent second coming or Armageddon; and
- hubris-driven military overreach.

Of these five criteria, the second, third, and fourth are clearly features of Christian fundamentalism;[73] arguably, the other two are as well. Of course, none of this shows that

Phillips is correct, but his remarks do show that Fosdick's concern and position are being articulated in the present day.

What Christian fundamentalism advocates is a literal reading of the scriptures, a belief in atonement, a belief in the resurrection, and a belief in the second coming.[74] Writers in this theological camp, such as Jerry Falwell, Tim LaHaye, Francis Schaeffer, Pat Robertson, and long-time Senator Jesse Helms, tend to view the United States as God's New Israel. They attribute cultural corruption in the United States to humanists[75] who lived during the period from the Renaissance to the Enlightenment.[76] Such humanists are thought to include St Thomas Aquinas, Erasmus, Kant, Rousseau, Voltaire, Hegel, and Kierkegaard,[77] as well as the theologians Ferdinand Christian Baur, Albrecht Ritschl, and Friedrich Schleiermacher.[78] The humanism that became victorious during this historic period contributed, in their opinion, to a "rampant rationalism," which facilitated doubt and religious skepticism.[79] What have to be combatted, therefore, so they think, are atheism, secularism, and humanism as philosophical imports from Europe.[80] Some modern Jeremiahs, such as Jerry Falwell, believe that humanists in the United States have captured political power, and, owing to this, he and other fundamentalists are bent on reversing this tendency.[81] Tim LaHaye (1926–), a confidant of US President George W. Bush, boldly asserts that humanists, whether politicians, government officials, or educators, do not think like pro-moral Americans, and therefore are not fit to govern.[82] In what follows, attention will focus on the thoughts of one of these Christian fundamentalists, Jerry Falwell. He has been selected because of the skill with which he has advanced his ideological concerns, and because of the clarity of his position.

Jerry Falwell

Beginning in 1979, a new movement of fundamentalism came into existence in the United States—the Moral Majority, an organization headed by Jerry Falwell (1933–2007), a dynamic and articulate speaker.[83] Under his leadership, Protestant fundamentalism became politicized, denouncing the old Christian attitude of pietism and non-involvement in worldly affairs.[84] Though the Moral Majority disbanded in 1989, other groups, such as the Christian Coalition of America led by Pat Robertson (1930–), picked up where it left off. Falwell was able to move the Christian right from being merely passive to become assertive, and at times close to impositional.[85] Passive fundamentalism is characterized by a quiet "indwelling" and "minding one's own business," whereas assertive fundamentalism is characterized by "strident assertions of a condemnatory or judgemental sort," and impositional fundamentalism is characterized by "transcendent sanction" and "imposition"[86] of personal values on the larger society. Falwell's Moral Majority certainly took the Christian right from the first to the second of these positions, and possibly to the third, especially in its dealings in such policy areas as abortion, divorce, homosexuality, school prayer, and evolution.

Among the critics of the Moral Majority was Bob Jones III (1939–), whose family had founded the fundamentalist Bob Jones University in South Carolina. Jones protested that Falwell and his organization—an organization comprising diverse groups such as the Roman Catholics, Mormons, and Jehovah's Witnesses—were attempting to correct the immorality of the United States, when it should have been focusing on the cause of this immorality, sin.[87] To be sure, the association of the fundamentalist Falwell with Roman Catholics, Mormons, and Jehovah's Witnesses is odd, given the antipathy fundamentalism had to these groups during the 1920s and at the inception of the movement. And to be sure, Falwell's focus on secular immorality rather than sin might seem a bit theologically skewed. Nonetheless, he seems to have recognized a strategic value to joining ranks in this way, even if it made for some historical and theological impurity. So joining ranks it was, and for the purpose of combatting secular humanism in all its immorality! The result was something called neo-fundamentalism.[88]

The focus of the Moral Majority under Falwell's leadership was on selected public policy areas, including abortion, the Equal Rights Amendment, prayer in the schools, and textbook legislation. The tendency of Falwell to emphasize such visible public policy issues drove Bob Jones Jr to say of Falwell that he was, as far as Biblical Christianity was concerned, the most dangerous person in the United States.[89] There was a reason for Jones to be concerned about Falwell, for the latter, through his Moral Majority, had a huge audience to address by means of televangelism, and he would address this audience about moral issues rather than theological ones. Nonetheless, Falwell continued to speak out. But he spoke out on these issues against the background of a particular view of history. To this we will now turn before addressing his ideas on public policy.

Dispensationalism

Fundamentalists subscribe to a view of history, **dispensationalism**, according to which history is divided up into seven eras or dispensations whose character has already been fixed by God. This view asserts that the last dispensation will consist of Christ's Second Coming, inaugurating his thousand-year reign over humanity. This general view of history has two interpretations, one being post-millennial and the other being pre-millennial. Post-millennialists claim that a state of perfection would be achieved before Christ's return, while the pre-millennialists believe that perfection would not be achieved before this event. In the result, those subscribing to the former view have more positive outlook on humankind than the latter.[90] Jerry Falwell belongs to those subscribing to the second, or pre-millenial, view. This is a dark view of the world, one of chaos and decay, in which Jews return to Zion, the anti-Christ comes, and the final battle of Armageddon takes place.[91] It is worth noting that interest in dispensationalism, of the type associated with Jerry Falwell, increased following the Six-Day War in 1967. This war and its outcome attracted support by Christian fundamentalists for Israel.

Abortion

The decision of the US Supreme Court in *Roe v. Wade* in 1973 was a turning point for many right-wing Protestants in the United States. It certainly was for Jerry Falwell. His reaction to this decision on the constitutionality of abortion is captured in the following statement: "I couldn't believe that seven justices of the Court could be so callous about the dignity of human life."[92] Even prior to this time Falwell had preached on the subject of abortion. He appealed to Biblical verses in an attempt to demonstrate the opposition of God to abortion, claiming that it was part of the pre-millennial period of the end of time signified by immorality and social decay.[93] However, prior to 1981, Falwell did not make abortion a *cause célèbre*, but instead treated it as one among other sins. By 1980, in his work *Listen, America!*, Falwell offers his first extended examination on the subject, and he follows up on this in 1981 by discussing abortion as a practice that runs counter to the sanctity and dignity of human life.[94] It is not until 1986, however, in *If I Should Die Before I Wake*, that he presents his best-known attack on the practice of terminating a pregnancy. There he argues for the primacy of the fetus–God relationship and, correspondingly, of the independence of the fetus from the mother. In later tracts, Falwell provides a list of what he calls "proof texts" from the Bible that "demonstrate" the opposition of God to abortion.[95] On the basis of the scripture, Falwell led the Moral Majority on a campaign against abortion that joined forces with two other organizations, the Religious Roundtable and the Christian Voice. Together, these three organizations formed the New Christian Right, which proved to be instrumental in the election of Ronald Reagan in 1980 and a strong influence on the Republican platform of 1984, established as its convention. As a result, the party decided to make opposition to abortion a condition of judicial appointments.[96]

The Equal Rights Amendment

In 1972, a proposal to amend the US Constitution was initiated for the purpose of giving equal rights to women. Section 1 of the Equal Rights Amendment (ERA) read: "Equality or rights under the law shall not be denied or abridged by the United States or by any State on account of sex." Under Article V of the US Constitution, the amendment was required to be ratified by three-quarters (i.e., at least 38) of the country's state legislatures, but although Article V imposed no time limit for ratification, a deadline was given in this case. By the early 1980s, the deadline had passed, and the attempt to complete the required ratification had failed. Among several key opponents of this amendment was the conservative political activist and anti-feminist, Phyllis Schlafly (1924–), who exploited the anger that sex-neutral words (such as the word "person") evoked and ran a successful campaign against the amendment under the banner of STOP-ERA.[97]

For our purposes, however, the opposition to the amendment mounted by Jerry Falwell is of special interest. For him, the ratification process was nothing short of a plebiscite on feminism, feminism itself being nothing but another manifestation of secularism and relativism.[98] For Falwell, the ERA, as part of the feminist cause, struck at the very foundation of the American social structure. Its basic flaw was that it ran counter to the mandate that "the husband is the head of the wife, even as Christ is head of the Church" (Ephesians 5:23).[99] Opposing the public issue of equal rights for women became a matter of salvation for Falwell, who believed that wives who lived their lives according to the values of the ERA would not admit to the leadership of their husbands, thereby destroying the proper relationship with God.[100] In this reading, the ERA amounted to an almost demonic tampering with human relationships that were close to the relationship of Christ with his church. The role of women, for Falwell, was unambiguously defined by the Bible, and this role represented a source of values that ran against any analysis of gender and gender roles as something merely of human creation. As pointed out by others, Falwell effectively endorsed views expressed by fundamentalists in 1910 in subscribing to "natural fixed relationships" in which one submits to another in the fear of God.[101]

Prayer in the Schools

It has been said that modern Biblical critics submit the Bible to history and find it wanting, while dispensationalists submit history to the Bible and find it wanting.[102] One of the ways in which Christian fundamentalists sought to preserve contact with the Bible was through school prayer, including the Lord's Prayer. Jerry Falwell has been a leading advocate of school prayer. Following the terrorist attacks of 11 September 2001, Falwell is reported by the *New York Times* to have said that federal courts, having legalized abortion and banned school prayer, had so weakened the United States in a spiritual fashion that the nation was exposed to terrorist attacks.[103] According to him, the collective endeavours of "many secularists during the past generation resulting in the expulsion [of God] from our schools and from the public square, has left us vulnerable."[104]

Falwell's attack on the federal courts continued unabated one month later, when he explicitly addressed the issue of school prayer. For Falwell, the suicide attacks in New York City and Washington should have made Americans reconsider the secular path down which they had walked. For this reason, he supported Texas Governor Rick Perry's decision to ignore the US Supreme Court's ban on organized school prayer. According to Falwell, in speaking to the Court's decision, "Many, including me, believe that fateful decision launched the onset of descent in American education. Our nation's schools have replaced God with moral relativism and situational ethics in the nearly four decades following that decision."[105]

School Textbooks and Evolution

During the 1980s in the United States, the religious right, including Jerry Falwell's Moral Majority, managed to move the Republican Party in a conservative direction, not only on issues like abortion and the ERA, but also on the influence of secular textbooks on children in public schools.[106] Through the religious right, efforts were made to control the curricula so as to "play down" evolution and require instruction in creationism.[107] The success of these efforts was sufficient to arouse the interest of civil liberties groups and educational organizations in launching a counterattack. One such organization was People for the American Way (PFAW),[108] which was concerned about Falwell's political arm and "alarmed at the rhetoric that the religious right groups were using as they attacked public education."[109] It is evident that Falwell was successful in moving the public policy agenda to the right with respect to school textbooks and the subject of creationism and with respect to sex education in public schools.[110] He and his organization were instrumental in inspiring at least three textbook controversies affecting education in many parts of the United States. Three jurisdictions where controversies erupted were Texas and the Texas Board of Education, involving reading material in biology that discussed evolution rather than creationism; Hawkins County in Tennessee, involving readings on overpopulation and pollution published by Holt, Rinehart and Winston; and Mobile, Alabama, involving a charge that books ranging from Shakespeare's *Macbeth* to those on drug prevention promoted unconstitutionally the religion of secular humanism.[111]

Christian Fundamentalism: Domestic Policy

The religious right in the United States during the time of Jerry Falwell had a significant impact on some areas of domestic policy, especially those areas touching on abortion, the Equal Rights Amendment, prayer in school, and finally, school textbooks and evolution. The discussion could be expanded to include other domestic public policy areas, including same-sex marriage, gay rights generally, and stem cell research. Without exploring these latter fields, the evidence in the other policy areas makes clear that the religious right carried its dogmatic passions well beyond what could be called the passive stage of religious fundamentalism and into the assertive stage. We need only think here of the textbook controversies to make this point. But at times, actions evidently encouraged by Falwell moved individuals like Governor Rick Perry of Texas to defy openly the decision of the US Supreme Court with regard to school prayer. At this juncture the religious right came very close to moving beyond active fundamentalism to impositional fundamentalism—in effect, they took constitutional matters into their own hands and imposed self-made law on others.

Christian Fundamentalism: Foreign Policy

The Christian right in the United States—that is, Christian fundamentalism in that country—continued to exert an influence on the social policy of the George W. Bush administration in the fields of gay rights, abortion, and same-sex marriage. But it is in the foreign policy field that the fundamentalists had their most significant influence. Michael Lienesch captures this point very nicely: "When it comes to formulating foreign policy, those in the New Christian Right consider American support for Israel to be an absolute requirement."[112] This position seems axiomatic of Christian fundamentalists, and is reflected in the remarks of Falwell et al.: "To stand against Israel is to stand against God."[113] At the same time, one should add this represents a patronizing dimension to support of Jews, Judaism, and Israel. Christian fundamentalists such as Tim LaHaye see Jews as Christ-killers,[114] and believe that Israel will be redeemed as the remaining Jews become Christians.[115] Obviously, in this point of view, if the Jews of Israel were to be driven into the sea, as Islamic jihadists would have it, they would not be around to become Christians and Israel could not be redeemed.

These qualifications notwithstanding, American Christian fundamentalists extol the virtues of support for Israel. In a vicarious way, this means that they support the actions of the Israeli government, which, as indicated below, have been frequently influenced by a group of Jewish fundamentalists, Gush Emunim. Putting all of this together, the picture that emerges is one of American foreign policy on Israel being influenced by the Christian right in the United States, and the Christian right policy being driven by deference to the Israeli government. When this is coupled with the fact of Israeli government policy being driven by Jewish fundamentalism, as espoused by Gush Emunim and other groups, one sees that American foreign policy is influenced importantly by Jewish fundamentalism, making the collision with Islam even more dangerous than it would otherwise be. The details of this argument will be worked out more closely as we consider Jewish fundamentalism below.

Jewish Fundamentalism

Jewish fundamentalism has its own claim to contemporary political significance. This is largely owing to the role played by the Jewish sect called Gush Emunim ("Bloc of the Faithful") and to another influential group called Chabad Lubavitch. Though the former of these organizations no longer exists,[116] it, together with the Chabad Lubavitch, which does very much exist, exerted a powerful influence on Israeli domestic and international politics over the past 40 years. Before analyzing the ideologies of each of these, we need to say something more about the attitude of the Christian right in the US towards Israel, describe briefly the background to the birth of Israel, and consider Hasidism as a movement that predated more recent Jewish fundamentalism.

Israel and the Christian Right

The story of the Israel and the Christian right in the United States is largely the story of Israel and Jerry Falwell. Although recognizing that Christian fundamentalists had a reputation of being anti-Semitic, by the 1980s Falwell approved of a different attitude emerging among pastors of fundamentalist congregations—an attitude that saw them supporting Israel. In Falwell's own words, the reason for this change was simply that the creation of the state of Israel is "the single greatest sign indicating the imminent return of Jesus Christ."[117] Falwell was a leader in bringing about this change in attitude, a fact not lost on the Israeli government of Prime Minister Menachem Begin. In 1981 Begin awarded Falwell the Jabotinsky Medal in recognition of his influence on US President Reagan and for the constructive image of Israel he created for American conservative Christians.[118] So there was clear acknowledgement by the Begin government of the influence Falwell had on US politics and, importantly, active encouragement of this by the Israeli government. Other facts that show linkage between the Israeli government and Falwell, and between Falwell and the US government and its foreign policy towards Israel, include the following: Begin's attempt to encourage Falwell to mute the criticism in the West about Israel's bombing of Iraq in 1981; Falwell's testimony before the US House of Representatives' Foreign Affairs Committee on behalf of Israel in 1984; Falwell's receipt of a private plane as a gift from Israel; Falwell's address to Americans for a Safe Israel at its annual conference in 1984; Falwell's address to the conservative Rabbinical Assembly in Miami in 1995, where he said he would mobilize 70 million Christians for Israel; Falwell's conversion of Senator Jesse Helms of North Carolina into one of Israel's biggest allies; Falwell's arrangement of a meeting between Prime Minister Benjamin Netanyahu and in excess of a thousand influential Christian fundamentalists in 1998; and, in the same year, Falwell's address to the National Unity Coalition for Israel where, in the presence of Netanyahu, he argued against the internationalization of Jerusalem.[119] These facts speak to a linkage between the Israeli influence on the Christian right and the Christian right's influence on the US foreign policy. Shortly, we shall see the influence of the Jewish fundamentalists on the Israeli government, thereby solidifying an influence on the Christian right and on US foreign policy with respect to Israel, especially in connection in its conflict with the Palestinians.

Zionism and the Birth of the State of Israel

The attempt to create a national homeland for Jews began in Europe near the end of the nineteenth century under the banner of Zionism. Following the defeat of Jews by the Babylonians in the sixth century BCE, Jews found themselves living in an "ever-widening Diaspora."[120] Under the rule of Muslims in the Middle East after the spread of Islam, Jews and Christians occupied a secondary status. But things were much less appealing for Jews in Europe. Massacres of Jews in Christian Europe in the **First Crusade** were followed by decrees suppressing, expelling, and ghettoizing Jews. Many Jews, owing to these decrees, escaped and settled in Eastern Europe. But by the eighteenth century things seemed to improve and Jews followed the lead of the philosopher Moses Mendelssohn and became engaged in the public arena of culture, arts, and literature. By 1791 Jews were accorded citizenship in France and by 1858 they had gained the same status in England. Soon after this things began to turn in a regressive direction. Three events characterize the next 30 years: first, Eugen Duehring, a German philosopher and economist, against whom Marx wrote a scathing attack, publicly attacked Jews and urged European states to cancel their civil rights and to ghettoize them once again; Richard Wagner, of operatic fame, effused anti-Semitism; and finally, a pogrom was unleashed in Russia in 1881 resulting in the destruction of 160 Jewish villages from the Black Sea to the Baltic Sea.[121] It seems as though European and Russian societies were caught off guard by the effect of their original liberal views, inspired by the Enlightenment, in granting rights to Jews, and they soon came to fear Jewish success and its ability to identify Jews. In the result **anti-Semitism** soon became a feature of the social landscape.

In this context the "Dreyfus affair" occurred in 1894 in France when Alfred Dreyfus, a Jewish army captain, was charged with selling military secrets to the Germans. Owing to the irregularity of the legal proceedings to which Dreyfus was subjected, coupled with the anti-Semitism of the allegations to which he was exposed, this was a trial that would go down in infamy.[122] Its importance for present purposes, however, is that the Austrian Jewish journalist Theodor Herzl (1860–1904) covered the trial on behalf of his newspaper in Vienna, and what he witnessed convinced Herzl of the need to establish a Jewish state. Devoting his remaining life to this cause, he became known as the father of Zionism.[123] It was this movement and the Enlightenment that Hasidism opposed.

Hasidism and the Definition of a Jew

Before moving on to Gush Emunim and Chabad Lubavitch, we first need to form some understanding of Jewish fundamentalism in general.[124] According to its advocates, being a Jew means three things: (i) living by the commandments of the Torah (the *mitzvoth*); (ii) obeying the directives of the sages who have been ordained to determine the **halakha**; and finally, (iii) believing in the truth of everything the Torah teaches, as specified by the interpretation of scholars.[125] The spiritual model for Jewish fundamentalists, those subscribing to this definition of being a Jew,[126] was established by Hasidism, which had its roots in Eastern Europe of the eighteenth century. In the last 300 years, Hasidism has conducted an ongoing battle by its *rebbes* or *zaddiks*, sometimes called "fools for God," against the spirit of the Enlightenment. From the perspective of the *rebbes* of Hasidism, the Enlightenment represented a move away from the true tradition of Jews. It therefore stood not for freedom but for exile, a latter-day Babylon.[127] The Enlightenment is thus seen as leading Jews astray. But worse than the Enlightenment, according to Hasidic Jews, was Zionism, which—with its ideology of establishing a Jewish state—put Judaism on a secular path. Hasidism, then, is opposed to the Enlightenment and Zionism.[128]

Division between Jewish Orthodoxy and Rabbi Kook

The story of Jewish fundamentalism is still not complete. In addition to Hasidism there stood the movement of Jewish Orthodoxy[129] established in the eighteenth century, again in reaction to the Enlightenment. And, indeed, it went on to oppose Zionism on the grounds of its being a secular ideology—for the most part.[130] The Agudat Israel movement—modelled on an organization founded by the Orthodox Rabbi Samson Raphael Hirsch (1808–1888)—opposed Zionism.[131] And so, in a tentative way, did the Mizrahi

Orthodox Jews. But this was not true of the followers of Orthodox Rabbi Abraham Isaac Kook (1865–1935) and his Gush Emunim movement. Rabbi Kook came to Palestine from Lithuania in the early 1900s. Rabbi Kook, otherwise called Rav Kook, "placed extraordinary emphasis on *hitnahlut* or the resettling of the Land of Israel."[132] All interpretations of Judaism were subordinated by him to *hitnahhlut*. Nation-building became for Rav Kook a "religious task" validated by Jewish history. Nor was opposition to Zionism true of the Orthodox Haredim, the extreme movement of Jewish religious belief, especially the Ashkenazi Haredim or Chabad Lubavitch. The views of the Gush Emunim and Chabad Lubavitch movements will now be examined.

Messianic Expectations of the Gush Emunim

Rabbi Kook and the Gush Emunim movement were inspired by Rabbi Moshe Nachmanides (1194–1270), who argued in favour of the proposition that Jews should emigrate and conquer the land of Israel.[133] Nachmanides became the inspiration of the Gush Emunim, and of Rabbi Kook and his son Rabbi Zvi Yehuda Kook (1891–1982), who had, it seems, some of the charisma of the *rebbes*, or righteous ones, of Hasidism. The Kooks instilled in their followers enthusiasm and ecstasy for the coming of the Messiah rather than Talmudic consolation. Such enthusiasm and ecstasy are predicated on the belief that the settling of Israel will hasten the arrival of the Messiah.[134] The Gush Emunim, while not being the only sect that could possibly be described as expressing Jewish fundamentalism, is undoubtedly one of the most significant sects in this regard. Some might be inclined also to include the Kach Party of Rabbi Meir Kahane (1932–1990) as expressing Jewish fundamentalism, and though there is some truth in this, Kahane's Kach Party has never had the "impact on Israeli political culture that Gush Emunim enjoys,"[135] or that the Chabad Lubavitch presently enjoys. Since our present concern is with Jewish fundamentalism as it relates to current political culture, we can safely ignore the "sabre-rattling" Kahane movement.[136]

Metaphysical Beliefs of Gush Emunim

The Bloc of the Faithful, as previously indicated, were the driving force in establishing settlements in the Jordan Valley. These settlements include Beit El (population 3,600), Ofra (population 1,800), Shilo (population, 1,500), Eli (population 1,500), and Elon Moreh (population 1,500). Moreover, they were established as an act of defiance against the plan prohibiting the establishment of settlements in areas with concentrations of Arab populations. As far as the Gush Emunim are concerned, Greater Israel is non-negotiable. But an understanding of this position of Gush Emunim can only be had by taking a close look at three oaths that the Talmud, the authoritative text of Orthodox Jews, imposes on them.

According to the Talmud, two of these oaths conflict with the basic tenets of Zionism, the ideology that advocates the formation of a Jewish state in the Middle East. These oaths are (i) Jews should not rebel against those who are non-Jews; (ii) Jews should not migrate to Palestine before the coming of the Messiah. The third oath states that Jews should refrain from praying too hard so as to avoid having the Messiah come before his appointed time. Many famous rabbis have affirmed these three propositions, and have urged Orthodox believers to do the same. These rabbis included Shmuel, Eliezer, Ezra of Spain, Eibshutz, Hirsch, and Teitelbaum, and covered a period from the ninth century until the nineteenth century. One exception to the list of rabbis who subscribed to these three oaths, especially the oath pertaining to migration, was Nachmanides, whose teachings, as indicated above, became the spiritual fount of both the **National Religious Party** (founded in 1956) and the religious sect Gush Emunim. According to them, the three oaths apply only in pre-messianic times, and since the present time is marked by the beginning of redemption the three oaths do not apply. In other words, the pre-messianic era is giving way to cosmic time, called the beginning of redemption, and, therefore, the three oaths can be set aside. The construction of the Talmud and historic events in this way allows Rabbi Kook and his son, as well as the Gush Emunim, to support Zionism in a way in which its nemesis, the Haredim, cannot.[137]

The resolve of the Gush Emunim to push for settlements in the Jordan Valley had the support of many of the major figures of Israel's modern state, including Menachem Begin, Moshe Dayan, Yitzhak Shamir, Shimon Peres, and Ariel Sharon.[138] What the Gush Emunim believes, following the teachings of the Kooks, is that, as a nation, Israel is already redeemed, and that there are three stages to messianic redemption: (i) return from the Diaspora to the Land; (ii) a national reconstruction that would welcome a joining together of the People and the Land; and (iii) a repentance of love, which would "usher in the Messianic era."[139] The Kooks believe that the world stands at the beginning of messianic times, and the redemption of the land of Israel is essential for the world's redemption.[140] They go further, in fact, claiming that all people, friend or foe, have a role to play in bringing about the redemption to the world, thereby allowing a redemptive role for secular Jews and Arabs. However, the spirit of these claims vanished with the beginning of the Second Intifada.[141] According to Avishai Margalit, a renowed philosopher at the Hebrew University, the view of the Gush Emunim changed with the onset of the Second Intifada, and all the talk of harmony with the Arabs vanished. From that point on the view of the Gush Settlers was: "It is either us or them."[142]

Social and Moral Beliefs of Gush Emunim

It is perhaps helpful to list some of the social and moral beliefs to which the Gush Emunim and National Religious Party subscribe. Many of these were inspired by the Kooks, father and son. The former was a person of considerable Talmudic competence, while the second was a person of considerable charismatic personality. As a political messianic group with mystical tendencies, Gush Emunim has as its underlying premise the belief that, since the beginning of the Zionist enterprise, and since the Six-Day War, Israel has lived in a transcendental world.[143]

The Gush Emunim has a strong dislike of Western culture, including its rational and democratic elements, and also a strong dislike of non-Jews.[144] According to the late Dr Uriel Tal, professor of modern Jewish history at Tel Aviv University, this dislike evinces itself in the assertion of Rabbi Yehuda Amital, an outstanding Gush leader, that the Yom Kippur War of 1973 was directed against all gentiles.[145] Speaking of the 1973 war, Amital says, "The gentiles are fighting for their mere survival as gentiles, as the ritually unclean. Iniquity is fighting its battle for survival."[146]

On the subject of the return of any of the conquered territory, the position of the younger Rabbi Kook is quite simple: the Jewish people are prohibited from handing over any part of the land of Israel. Rabbi Kook says, "I tell you explicitly that the Torah forbids us to surrender even one inch of our liberated land."[147] In light of the apparent sacredness of this conquered land, there is, evidently, no room for compromise.¹⁴⁸ Further, according to Rabbi Kook, in speaking of the occupied territories conquered by Israel, "There are no conquests here and we are not occupying foreign lands; we are returning to our home, to the inheritance of our ancestors. There is no Arab land here, only inheritance of our God—and the more the world gets used to this thought the better it will be for them and for all of us."¹⁴⁹ And, again, he says, "Some argue that there are Arab lands here. It is all a lie and a fraud! There are absolutely no Arab lands here."¹⁵⁰

As for religious detachment, Rabbi Kook the elder maintains that Jews should be politically involved and should not stand aloof, as had been the practice in the past. For this reason, the followers of Kook do not frown on secular dress, or secular education, and have been passionate in their support for the military. Many of the followers have been officers in Israel's select units. For Gush Emunim, Jewish people are unique. Finally, on the subject of criminal law, Rabbi Israel Ariel, a Gush Emunim leader, claims, deferring to the Jewish theologian Maimonides (1135–1204), "It follows from Maimonides' words that a Jew who killed a non-Jew was exempt from human judgment, and has not violated the prohibition on murder."¹⁵¹

With this understanding of Gush Emunim in mind, we can now turn our attention to the second influential fundamentalist Jewish sect.

Views of the Chabad Lubavitch

It is not easy to consolidate the religious views of the Chabad Lubavitch, notwithstanding the fact that it is a significant movement in Judaism. What can be said is the following. It is a 250-year-old Brooklyn-based Hasidic, ultra-Orthodox movement¹⁵² that is fast becoming the face of Jewish Orthodoxy for both the Jewish people and the general public.¹⁵³ Heading this movement after 1951, Menachem Mendel Schneerson (1902–1994) rejected Rabbi Kook's affirmation of Zionism, which asserted the coming into existence of Israel as a state signalled the coming of the redemptive messianic age.¹⁵⁴ Lubavitch Hasidism is "a branch of the general Hasidic movement that emerged in the mid-eighteenth century in the forests of Poland."¹⁵⁵ Those Hasidics who subscribe to the Lubavitch beliefs maintain nothing short of a literal interpretation to the Torah—an interpretation that asserts the derivation of all human knowledge, including science, from the Torah.¹⁵⁶ Their world view derives from the Hasidic concept of creation, which in turn is based on the mystical teachings of the sixteenth-century Kabbalist master, Isaac Luria.¹⁵⁷ Lubavitchers embrace the idea of love for all Jews, which is implemented by attempting to kindle the godly spark in Jewish souls, but they have "widened their appeal," beginning in the early 1980s, to include non-Jews.¹⁵⁸ Lubavitchers encourage all people—Jews and non-Jews—to follow the seven laws God gave to Noah: no idolatry, no blasphemy, no sexual perversion, no murder, no theft, no cruelty to animals, and the creation of courts of justice.¹⁵⁹ Though Lubavitchers have widened their appeal to non-Jews, their Hasidism leads them to assert that Jews have a "special relationship" with each other and that the purest way of expressing one's love of God is to help another Jew.¹⁶⁰ This position is reflected in *Eyes Upon the Land*, a Chabad publication, where it says "although all humans are created 'in the image of g_d' and every life must be cherished, the Torah teaches Jews to place Jewish life as the highest priority."¹⁶¹ The purpose of the Lubavitch outreach program throughout the world is to "make it as easy as possible for a Jew to live more Jewishly."¹⁶² And "unlike missionary work in other religions, Chabad focuses only on Jews, and, in accordance with Jewish tradition, has no interest in converting non-Jews to the faith views."[163] In addition, as *Eyes Upon the Land* makes clear, followers of Rebbe Schneerson believe "The whole of the Holy Land accordingly belongs to the Jewish people."[164] And further, "God's promise is the only justification for Jewish claim to the Holy Land that cannot be easily refuted by Arabs, American and/or others."[165] These beliefs sometimes result in violent political action taken by their members, as illustrated by the following episode. On 25 February 1994, Baruch Goldstein—a physician and West Bank settler from Brooklyn, New York, and follower of Lubavitcher Rebbe Menachem Mendel Schneerson, who at that time headed the Chabad movement—entered a Muslim prayer hall at the Cave of the Patriarchs in Hebron, where he shot and killed 29 people, including children, and wounded many others before survivors of the massacre beat him to death.[166]

With the end of reaching every Jew in the world, Chabad Lubavitch has sought the support of the rich, famous, and powerful. The following political and cultural icons have been convinced that the Chabad is a movement of import. These supporters have included Bob Dylan, Jon Voight, Whoopi Goldberg, Al Gore, Jimmy Carter, Vladimir Putin, Joseph Lieberman, Elie Wiesel, Herman Wouk, Chaim Potok, Benjamin Netanyahu, Robert F. Kennedy, Rudolph Giuliani,[167] Margaret Thatcher, Alfonse D'Amato, Newt Gingrich, Menachem Begin, Shimon Peres, and Ariel Sharon.[168] Several of these, if not many, were inspired by the work of Schneerson, the head of the Chabad movement in the United States. This list of notable people shows the influence that Chabad Lubavitch has had, in US and Israeli politics, an influence that has cut across at least Jewish and Christian lines.

Political Implications of Gush Emunim and Chabad Lubavitch

Among the settlers in the occupied territories, Chabad Lubavitch is one of the most resolute groups,[169] a point perhaps illustrated by the Goldstein terrorist attack. From this it can be seen that Jewish fundamentalism in two of its guises (the Gush Emunim and Chabad movements) stands at the vortex of Middle East politics. Each of these movements, in its own way, has contributed to changing Israel's settlement policy. And here one sees ideology in action. There can be no doubt, in light of this, that Jewish fundamentalism acts as an obstacle to a political compromise in the Arab–Israeli conflict.[170]

Middle East politics as a whole, moreover, is balanced precariously between Islamic fundamentalists and Jewish fundamentalists, between the Wahhabists on the one hand, and Gush Emunim and Chabad Lubavitch on the other, with Christian fundamentalists weighing in on the side of the latter. With this in mind it is time to turn attention to another form of fundamentalism, this one found in India.

Hindu Fundamentalism

Hinduism is India's principal religion and entered India with the arrival of the Aryan invaders around 1500 BCE. About 82 per cent of all Indians identify themselves as Hindu, 12 per cent as Muslims, 2 per cent as Christians, and 2 per cent as Sikhs.[171] In contrast to Western religions, such as Judaism, Islam, and Christianity, Hinduism, which means "the belief of the people of India," does not hold firmly to fixed views of God but adopts a relaxed attitude to theological matters.[172] The oldest of the Hindu scriptures, dating from 1200 to 800 BCE, is found in the Vedas, and the world view adopted there addresses topics such as the nature of humanity, the substance of the universe, the three realms (earth, atmosphere, and heaven), the basis of cosmic order, and the ultimate source of things.[173]

We shall not focus on the ancient history of Hinduism. Our present concern is more recent developments. During the Middle Ages, India was subjected to an invasion by Muslims, people who proceeded for five centuries to control the subcontinent of India. By 1700, although many parts of India were under the sway of Islam, Muslim power was exhausted and India largely remained Hindu in spirit.[174] Following 1707, with the death of the Muslim Mogul emperor Aurangzeb, the Mogul Empire "declined rapidly," leaving a power vacuum eventually filled by the British starting with the British East India Company in 1757.[175] British rule in India manifested itself clearly in the economic institutions the British brought to the country, as well as in the educational institutions they introduced.[176] This British rule continued unimpeded until the latter part of the nineteenth century with the formation of the **Aryan Society** (Arya Samaj), whose leader, Swami Dayananda Saraswati (1824–1883), proclaimed that India should affirm its allegiance to the Vedas alone, denounce hereditary occupational castes, accept the Vedas as the source of all truth (scientific and religious), and believe that the Vedas record the first religion of humanity. It should be noted that the Aryan Society was "bitterly hostile" to external cultural influences on India.[177] The Aryan Society was a mild prelude to the emergence of ultra-nationalism in India that occurred under its first great political leader, Bal Gangadhar Tilak (1856–1920), who established a new public festival in honour of the god Ganesha, the elephant-headed son of Siva, for the purpose of bringing anti-British songs to the people of India. This was the first major attempt "to create a politicized Hindu ritual."[178] Tilak favoured the creation of a popular patriotism that presented a historical narrative depicting India's past as the "degradation of its once great religion and people."[179] In the fullness of time his ideas resulted in the establishment of the cultural society, the Hindu Mahasabha, which in turn resulted in the formation of the Indian People's Party.[180] The belief of the cultural society and subsequent party was that India must be preserved by affirming a fivefold unity: one land, one race, one religion, one culture, and one language.[181] This nationalistic affirmation is Hinduism's version of fundamentalism.

The Rise of Hindu Fundamentalism

One of the most important developments of a political nature in India during the 1990s was the rise of extreme Hindu fundamentalism, better known simply as Hindu nationalism.[182] The rise of virulent nationalism, accompanied by the "growing power" of the lower castes, occurred at the same time as economic liberalization, when reform by the government of India brought about a significant increase in consumerism and middle-class affluence.[183] With considerable confidence we can say that the roots of present-day Hindu nationalism (from 1990 onward) can be found in the religious reform movements, as they are called, of the British colonial period. These reforms included, as indicated above, the transforming of the **Ganesha** annual festival from a private affair to a public one "intended as a manifestation of religious revivalism, as well as a means to mobilize the Hindu population against both the British and the Muslims."[184] It needs to be emphasized that this new ritual of Ganesha is "an adaptation of an already existing ritual, partly so that it can be represented as a natural continuation or extension of traditional practice."[185] And it should be emphasized with the same vigour that, since Hindu unity is the purpose of the public festival, the ritual or deity must have wide appeal among Hindus.[186] It turns out that Ganesha is "an effective symbol of Hindu unity" for the simple reason that he "bridges the gap between the great and little dieties."[187]

This same Hindu nationalism or fundamentalism was largely responsible for the actions of Hindu activists who in 1992 sought to clear the site of a Muslim mosque at Ayodhya for the purpose of erecting a new temple. This site is the alleged birthplace of **Rama**, the Ramjanmabhumi.[188] Rama, in the mythology of Hinduism, was a mortal king "who was elevated to the status of an avatar of Vishnu."[189] The destruction of the Muslim mosque at this site is a subject to which we shall shortly return. This event, coupled with a later event, has contributed to a virulent form of Hindu fundamentalism.

The Tragedy of Godhra in the Western State of Gujarat

On 27 February 2002 an express train in India arrived in the station of Godhra, Gujarat. This train carried Hindu pilgrims who had just visited Ayodhya in honour of the god Rama. It is well known to scholars and visitors to this part of India that Ayodhya "has been a focal point of Hindu anti-Muslim feeling for several decades,"[190] a matter illustrated by the previous account of the destruction by Hindu nationalists of the Muslim mosque on the same site. The pilgrims in 2002 had attempted unsuccessfully to construct a Hindu temple and their lack of success resulted in an angry mood among the passengers on the train.

Upon arrival of the train in Godhra, arguments arose between passengers on the train and Muslim vendors. Hindu pilgrims from the train attacked some of these vendors because they refused to utter words of praise to the god Rama. Fifteen minutes after the train left the station, a train car ignited and burst into flames resulting in the death of about 60 persons (men, women, and children), most of them Hindus. Blame for this was attributed, without forensic support, to Muslims. The following days were filled with violence throughout the state of Gujarat carried out by Hindus who shouted Hindu rights slogans such as "Hail Ram" and expressions such as "Kill," "Destroy," and "Slaughter." According to one account, more than 2,000 Muslims, including women and children, were killed.[191] The same account estimated that other losses to Muslims included the following: 100,000 houses, 1,100 hotels, 15,000 businesses, 3,000 handcarts, and 5,000 vehicles.[192] Further, it has been alleged that the then leader of the Shiv Sena nationalist group said that the Muslims were a cancer to India and should be removed.[193] In addition, "Many scholars and commentators have accused the state government [of Gujarat] of being complicit in the attacks."[194] As one commentator remarked, "Beyond the tragedy, the problem for the BJP [Bharatiya Janata Party] was that the State's chief minister, Narendra Mody [Modi], is its party man who was accused by the opposition of doing nothing to stop the carnage at best, or encouraging the Hindus against the Muslims at worst."[195] Some critics went so far as to compare Modi's actions in connection with Godhra with those of Slobodan Milosevic's genocide in Bosnia.[196] Wherever the truth lay in this regard, Human Rights Watch was sufficiently convinced to accuse the state of a cover-up in its role in the violence. And, so it seems, the US government had enough misgivings to deny a visa to Modi and a resolution was submitted in the US House of Representatives condemning Modi for inciting religious persecution.[197]

According to Martha Nussbaum, particularly noteworthy of the aforementioned killings were the mass rapes and mutilations of women that occurred. There is no need for us to go into the details of this here. Suffice it to say, according to Nussbaum, the typical killing of women occurred only after they had been gang-raped, tortured, and then burned to death.[198] The story illustrates the fanaticism of Hindu fundamentalism. Apparently, the fanaticism of the Hindu right was recognized by voters in India when they elected a new parliamentary government subsequent to the Gujarat massacre—a government that distanced itself from the "forces of persecution and violence."[199]

Hindu Fundamentalism and Nationalism

Hindu fundamentalism has religious, cultural, and political dimensions.[200] While it had its beginnings in the 1870s, more recent developments, commencing in 1925, are more pertinent to the present discussion. Noteworthy is the RSS (Rashtriya Swayamsevak Sangh), which came into existence in 1925 as an organization in strong support of Hindutva and is "the only organization [in India] which has consistently geared itself to micro level politics, getting into almost every sphere of activity which influences social and political life."[201] One of the official publications of the RSS reveals the nationalistic perspective at the heart of Hindu fundamentalism: only Hindus could free Hindustan (India) and only they could save Hindu culture.[202] For those who followed Vinayak Damodar Savarkar (1883–1966), the founder of RSS, the ideology of **Hindutva** (literally, "Hindu-ness") comprised an affirmation of a common nationality, common race, and common culture or civilization.[203] Those who followed Savarkar affirmed "a coherent and powerful pattern of concepts" that has "acquired the undisputed status of the manifesto of Hindu fundamentalism."[204] Owing to the fact that Christians and Muslims, in the opinion of Savarkar and the RSS, do not look upon India as the Holy Land, they are excluded from sharing a common nationality with the rest of the people living in India. Furthermore, while claiming to be a cultural organization and denying being a religious one, the RSS goes out of its way to have as its "reference points" Hindu festivals, Hindu rituals, and Hindu scriptures.[205] Incrementally, Hindu fundamentalism converged on nationalism and nationalism on Hindu fundamentalism. Some claim that, "According to the RSS ideology, Hindu nationalism provides the antidote to false Nehruvian secularism."[206] More will be said about this secularism in a moment. What needs to be understood just now is the convergence of Hindu fundamentalism and nationalism.

More recent developments involving the RSS include its sponsoring a national organization in India to carry out its cultural agenda. This organization, established in 1964, is the World Hindu Council or Vishva Hindu Parishad (VHP), which listed its objectives in a pamphlet in 1982. These objectives included strengthening the Hindu society, welcoming back those who had left the Hindu fold, protecting the Hindu values of life, and rendering social services to humanity at large.[207] This organization sought "to recover low-caste and untouchable persons who have converted to 'non-indigenous' faiths."[208] In addition, it sought to prohibit the slaughter of cows as well as the preservation and veneration of the Hindi language.[209]

In RSS literature, the Hindu Mahassbha (presently non-existent), the Jana Sangh, the BJP, and the VHP are referred to as "the Hindutva family" (Sangh Parivar).[210] The Sangh Parivar seems to have been most directly implicated in the destruction of the Muslim mosque Babri Masjid in the Indian city of Ayodhya. On 6 December 1992 some 200,000 mobilized Hindu fundamentalists from the Sangh Parivar, including VHP members, "systematically attacked and destroyed the Babri Masjid."[211] The Muslim mosque and the thought-to-be ruins of the Hindu temple of Rama beneath it "proved an excellent symbol around which to rally certain militant Hindus of the Sangha parivara."[212] Undoubtedly, a politicization of Hindu sentiment has occurred in India "through the symbolic manipulation of the Babri Majjid and other sites where mosques supplanted temples in medieval times"[213]—a politicization that "has been the preoccupation of the BJP and its militant quasi-political ally, the Vishwa Hindu Parishad."[214]

What the foregoing shows is that the RSS and the organizations it has spawned (e.g., the BJP and the VHP) represent an ideology that valorizes the national culture of India.[215] As others have said, "Here one sees again the equation of nationality (rashtriya) with Hindutva. To deny that one is Hindu is tantamount to denying that one is Indian."[216] The RSS and its affiliates, such as the BJP, opposed secularism, especially that advocated by Jawaharlal Nehru (1889–1964), who was the first Indian Prime Minister following independence in 1947 and held office until his death in 1964. In the place of secularism it advocated "positive secularism," which amounted to guaranteed nationalism and national integration at the same time that it was grounded in the Indian cultural heritage, or for want of a better word, grounded in Hindutva.[217] A significant consequence of all of this is simply the displacement of Muslim and Christian influences in the body politic and an attempt to displace a previously prevailing philosophy of secularism defined as a non-religious philosophy that tolerated all religions without making any religion part of the state apparatus or constitution. Here Hindu fundamentalism collided with Nehruvian secularism, a real secularism, in contrast with the pseudo-secularism of the BJP. Worth noting as well is the shift that has occurred "in the making of the *ideal* Hindu woman."[218] Near the end of the 1970s and in the early 1980s, the Indian women's movement attended to issues such as rape, bride burning, and dowry, many of which "challenged the patriarchal power structures within a broad liberal framework."[219] It seems now, however, that through the influence of Hindutva and Hindu fundamentalism this feminist movement has been redirected in such a way that it no longer challenges the presuppositions of a patriarchal society but instead challenges the influence of Islam and Muslims in India.[220] Under the watchful eyes of Hindu fundamentalism, Hindu women can engage in protest marches and roadblocks along with their Hindu male counterparts, but their opposition is aimed not at old restrictions on women but at difficulties associated by them with the Muslim population.

It is important to say once again, as said in the case of Muslims, Christians, and Jews, that the fanaticism of which we speak here applies only to some Hindus. Not all Hindus are religious nationalists in the extreme. Some are. Some are not. Here we speak of those who fall under the umbrella of Hindutva as an ideology "associated with the resurgence of religious styles, not only in the forms of retrieval from the past, but also developed into new creations, ready to be used for religious purposes."[221] One other cautionary note is this. While Hindu fundamentalism and nationalism, as two sides of one coin, exist in India, they do not "exist uniformly throughout the whole country."[222] For instance, there is a sharp contrast to the way Hindu fundamentalism exists in West Bengal, an eastern state, and in Gujarat, a western state. Peaceful co-existence exists along religious lines in the former, whereas, as indicated above in connection with the butchery that followed the train tragedy, fragmentation and animosity exist between Hindu and Muslim in the latter.[223] Hindu fundamentalism, while present throughout India, has greater traction in some areas than in others.

Conclusion

Looking back on the review of Islamic, Christian, Jewish, and Hindu fundamentalism, one sees common threads running through all of them. All of these are conservative ideologies that aim to preserve traditions—arguments sustained through time. All are inclined to a literalism of the sacred text. All have a patriarchal bent. And all reject the values of the Enlightenment: rationalism, humanism, and secularism. Freedom from self-incurred tutelage is not something sought by these fundamentalists. If anything, freedom is thought to be adverse to the well-being of humans. Rather, deference to traditions, the practices of the past, is advocated.

The line of argument pursued, whether Islamic, Christian, Jewish, or Hindu, is all cut from much the same cloth. Adherents subscribe to the **inerrancy** of scripture and base their belief on the further belief of the revealed nature of the text. In none of these cases is the conviction regarding the revealed nature of the text based on anything that would count as an approximation to scientific evidence. Notwithstanding the shakiest of epistemological foundations, fundamentalists of all faiths have no hesitation in drawing conclusions from these foundations. Moreover, these are conclusions about which they have a sense of psychological certainty, whether in connection with some future state of affairs (e.g., after death) or with some established government policy or international affair.

The line of argument pursued by all four kinds of fundamentalists is the following: certainty can be derived from alleged facts for which there is little in the way of hard evidence. From the perspective of fundamentalists, the revealed nature of the text is self-authenticating. And from the perspective of believers, the lives lived by those inspired by the text act to confirm to them the truth of the revelation. This confirmation is augmented, from the perspective of the believers, by the testimony in the text of the occurrence of miracles and amazing deeds. But what should not be lost sight of in all of this is how the line of argument is anchored in the immediate and unreasoned acceptance of the word of Allah, God, Yahweh, or the Vedas. Finally, one should keep in mind that for fundamentalists, their acceptance of so-called revealed truth is situated in the broader context of tradition as defined by those who preceded them.

Evaluation: The Strengths of Religious Fundamentalism

1. Religious fundamentalists are undoubtedly correct that major changes have begun to affect society through the impact of science, consumerism, and technology. Many of these changes have been in the area of values connected with the family, sexual relationships, and general deference to authority. And there seems little doubt that changes in this area have had the effect of producing a measure of uncertainty in the minds of people living in societies where the values have been eroded. A return to conventional religious values, if this could be willed, would increase the sense of security and diminish the sense of uncertainty that has accompanied their erosion. All of this would have the further effect of creating more clarity in the area of public policy regarding pornography, drug control, homosexuality, marriage, and criminal law. In addition, more certainty in public policies would tend to have the effect of stabilizing institutions and reducing corruption in them.

Evaluation: The Weaknesses of Religious Fundamentalism

1. The arguments for Allah's existence, God's existence, Yahweh's existence, and Atman's existence have been subjected to thorough and exhaustive philosophical

assessment, and have been found wanting. This means that no compelling argument for their existence or probable existence has been given, and therefore there is no good reason to believe in their existence. That they are logical possibilities does not make them probable, and, as the argument from evil below demonstrates, they are in any case most improbable. The lack of credibility in the existence of Allah, God, Yahweh, and Atman has the effect of eroding credibility of the morality, self-righteousness, solidarity, and loyalty of those who subscribe to such a metaphysical belief.

2. A return to the values of religious fundamentalism in its various guises would necessitate a return to the traditional beliefs persons had about themselves and their place in the universe in earlier times. However, since one normally does not control one's beliefs, but instead absorbs them from the outside world, it is irrational to try to will oneself into this anachronistic world. So the fact that reality appears less certain today than in the past, owing to science, consumerism, and technology, does not give anyone a reason to believe that it is possible to go back to the past. At this point, what we believe and what we desire come apart at the seams.[224]

The connection between values and beliefs referred to above needs some elaboration. Roughly, beliefs about the world rest upon evidence and upon deep metaphysical principles that include views on causation, personal identity, and space and time, to name a few. As science and philosophy advance, less and less room seems left for the postulation of gods or Allah, God, Yahweh, or Atman, and hence those entities have no explanatory role to play. It is little wonder, then, that changes in our metaphysics have produced changes in values that presupposed these very beliefs. Hence there have been changes in humans' thinking about abortion, divorce, gay rights, patriarchal power, and so on. Fundamentalists are correct in recognizing one source, an important source, of these changes, but they err in thinking that persons can voluntarily wish their way back to these values.

3. There are inconsistencies among the four fundamentalisms considered here. For example, Islam, Judaism, and Hinduism do not endorse the notion of the Trinity; Judaism does not see Muhammad as a prophet or subscribe to the tradition of the sunnah; Christians do not venerate the practices of the Torah; and none of these religions see the Vedas as sacred scripture. Moreover, even allowing for what Searle and others have called a cluster theory of reference, the inconsistencies cannot be removed simply by saying "Allah," "God," "Yahweh," and "Atman" refer to the same being. The stories told around each of these terms are just too different.[225] Hence, since these fundamentalisms decry relativism of truth, it follows that not all of the fundamentalisms can be true. None of Islamic, Christian, Jewish, or Hindu fundamentalism shows a way to mediate among the conflicting claims of each. All the religious claims put forth are advanced on the grounds of traditional belief in revealed religion. None has epistemic priority over the other. So how is one to judge among the conflicting claims of the Wahhabis, the Gush Emunim, the American Christian right, or Hindu nationalists? There seems no rational way to separate out the true from the false in this domain, and one has as much chance of being wrong as being right in adhering to a particular religion.

4. If it is acceptable to believe truths on the grounds that they form part of a tradition of faith and are revealed, then it is acceptable to believe any truths on these

grounds. So if fundamentalists wish to defend their choice of belief on the grounds of tradition and revelation, then the same defence is open to any fanatic, including a Nazi. If the Qur'an can be appealed to, if the New Testament can be appealed to, if the Torah can be appealed to, and if the Vedas can be appealed to on the grounds of their belonging to a sacred canon and revelation, then so can *Mein Kampf*. This conclusion seems very unappealing, but fundamentalists must answer it if they are to be regarded seriously. This is the proper response to those who might be tempted to follow the school of thought called reformed epistemology,[226] which denies any need for religious commitment to be supported on the grounds of evidence. According to this school of thought, just as our sensory beliefs are not held on the basis of philosophical argument and are not inferred from anything, so, it is claimed, belief in God and the "great truths of the Gospel" are quite properly held as basic beliefs, and the standard demand for evidence to justify them is improper. Clearly, if this works for those who subscribe to reformed epistemology, it works for those who subscribe to non-reformed National Socialism.

5. How, it can be asked, can Allah, Yahweh, God, or Atman, who is all-loving, omnipotent, and omniscient, permit evil to exist, especially when this evil is not that which is caused by persons? This is the kind of question all respectable religious thinkers have had to face, but alas, none has responded in a way that looks at all convincing. Even adopting the metaphysics of Leibniz and thinking of evil in the context of possible worlds, it really does seem difficult to construe the facts of this world in such a way that this amounts to the best of all possible worlds. Even granting that much evil in the world is caused by the misuse of our freedom, clearly, a great deal is completely unrelated to the use of our freedom: animal suffering, natural disasters, and disease. Unless one adopts the fanciful position of someone like Christian Science founder Mary Baker Eddy (1821–1910), who thought evil the result of our misconceived thoughts, evil stares us in the face as an irrationality.[227] Our best bet is to acknowledge its existence and do the best we can to move on. What one cannot do with intellectual facility, and probably not with honesty, is to affirm its existence and that of Allah, God, Yahweh, or Atman at the same time. Unless one is completely prepared to sacrifice reason, it is impossible to overcome this objection. Fundamentalism must founder when it encounters the raw fact of gratuitous evil in the world.

6. Fundamentalism has a morally offensive nature in its four guises. It expects its adherents to adopt a set of behavioural practices (e.g., take back the land promised by Yahweh, shun homosexuals, cover women's faces, keep women in traditional roles, kill non-believers, refrain from indulging in singing, refrain from dancing) based on faith, with no rational substructure. Breach of these practices may result in a charge of immorality, infidelity, and damnation. There is in this something that is more than morally odd. It is morally outrageous that a person would be damned to eternal torment simply because he or she failed to act in a certain way on the basis of a belief lacking in evidential support. Allah, God, Yahweh, or Atman as the creator, *ex hypothesi*, designed persons to believe those things that are supported by evidence; accordingly, we have been programmed to believe those things that have evidence in their favour, and not to believe those things lacking evidence in their favour. To crosswire our biological programming, and thus to believe those things for which there is

no evidence and to disbelieve those things for which there is evidence, is the recipe for an early death (as LSD users who tried flying from skyscrapers discovered, for example). Given that for all practical purposes we have been programmed in this way, it would be morally outrageous for an omnipotent and omniscient being to condemn those who refused to follow behavioural codes whose only support was some alleged revealed text, that is, whose only support was absence of evidence. To be condemned to eternal damnation for this reason, when one is programmed this way, would be a moral outrage given that the executioner would also have been the designer.

7. The choice fundamentalists give non-believers is an artificial choice: either the order in the world arises from chance or from Allah, God, Yahweh, or Atman. But as Richard Dawkins points out, the choices are greater: either the order in the world arises by chance, or is the work of some transcendent being, or arises from natural selection. This complicates the story the fundamentalist wishes to tell, for denying the role played by chance does not thereby entail affirming the existence of a designer.[228]

8. A kind of madness in all this bodes ill for the future, but this madness—and the future—will not be remedied until reason prevails. With the emergence of these four religious movements, a new kind of sectarianism confronts humanity, namely, global religious sectarianism. So what is to be done to deal with this new sectarianism? An answer to this question is found in an unlikely place: the writings of the Scottish economist Adam Smith. In his *Wealth of Nations*, Smith provides an antidote to the dysfunctionality of sectarian religion. The antidote is twofold: the study of science and philosophy, and the frequency and gaiety of public diversions.[229] Through these non-violent means, Smith thinks that "whatever was unsocial or disagreeably rigorous in the morals of all the little sects into which the country is divided" might be corrected.[230] Given the precarious position of global politics, it may be time to reconsider the suggestions of this great economist as a means of regaining the high ground in the conflicts in the Middle East as well as in India with extreme nationalists, and in public policy areas such as abortion, equal rights, prayers in schools, and school textbooks.

9. All four versions of fundamentalism have a problem with democracy. Whereas democracy tends in the direction of compromise and pluralism, fundamentalism tends in the direction of intolerance and homogeneity. It prefers the simplicity of a black-and-white world view, with none of the complexity of grey areas to confuse and complicate—or refute—that world view. The conflict here is really between religious commitment and political allegiance, and this conflict in views has recently been brought to light by some writers.[231] Whether one is an Islamic fundamentalist, a member of the Chabad Lubavitch, or a follower of Jerry Falwell's Moral Majority, democratic compromises are frowned upon. Perhaps this was the reason Tim LaHaye fought so bitterly with Falwell over the latter's immersing himself in public policy issues in the United States, and why Jewish fundamentalists of some persuasion have distanced themselves from subscribing to Zionism.

10. Political religious fundamentalists defer to divine law, and thereby encourage the dismissal of domestic and international law. It is for this reason that Yehoshafat Harkabi, sometime professor of international relations at Hebrew University in Jerusalem

and former adviser to Menachem Begin, says, while speaking of religious extremists, "International law, public opinion, the United Nations, the superpowers—for the religious extremist none of these matter."[232] Such a rejection of the rule of law is a recipe for domestic and international conflict and chaos.

11. In a powerfully argued and extensively researched book entitled *The Tenacity of Unreasonable Beliefs: Fundamentalism and the Fear of Truth*, Solomon Schimmel uses archaeological, historical, literary, textual, philosophical, and scientific evidence to argue effectively against Jewish, Christian, and Islamic fundamentalism. His arguments are simply too lengthy to summarize here, but they do stand as a testament to the soft sand upon which the edifice of these three fundamentalisms (excluding Hinduism, which he does not address) are built. For the purpose of illustrating the compelling nature of his reasoning in the area of religious belief, two examples are given. First, he points out that the implications of modern evolutionary theory and neuropsychology are in conflict with traditional Orthodox (but one could also add Christian and Muslim) beliefs regarding the following: the "soul" as distinct from the body; humans being created in the "image of God"; and "free will." These concepts, he correctly asserts, are no longer plausible as descriptions of humans and human nature.[233] Second, he argues, effectively, that a reading of Michael Coogan's *The Old Testament: A Historical and Literary Introduction to the Hebrew Scriptures* (2006), James Kugel's *How to Read the Bible* (2007), and Richard Elliott Friedman's *The Bible with Sources Revealed* (2003) "will find in these books . . . a wealth of information and concepts that should enable [the reader] to conclude that the MSPM [multi-source post-Mosaic] theory has been demonstrated to be true beyond a reasonable doubt—even if not beyond *unreasonable* doubt."[234]

Related Websites

Human Religions. "The Causes of Fundamentalism, Intolerance and Extremism in World Religions, and Some Solutions."
www.humanreligions.info/fundamentalism.html

O'Leary, Dakota. "Christian Fundamentalists Are Driving Our State into the Dark Ages." Church and State, 1 Feb. 2013.
http://churchandstate.org.uk/2013/02/christian-fundamentalists-are-driving-our-country-into-the-dark-ages/

Olson, Roger E. "What Is 'Fundamentalism' and Who Is a 'Fundamentalist'?" Patheos, 12 Feb. 2013.
www.patheos.com/blogs/rogereolson/2013/02/what-is-fundamentalism-and-who-is-a-fundamentalist/

Rand Corporation. "Religious Fundamentalism."
www.rand.org/topics/religious-fundamentalism.html

Religious Tolerance.org. "'Fundamentalism' in Christianity & Islam."
www.religioustolerance.org/reac_ter9.htm

Further Readings on Religious Fundamentalism

Aldovandri, Carlo. *Apocalyptic Movements in Contemporary Politics: Christian and Jewish Zionism*. New York: Palgrave Macmillan, 2014.

Aldridge, Alan. *Religion in the Contemporary World: A Sociological Introduction*. Cambridge: Polity Press, 2013.

Amore, Roy C., Willard Gurden Oxtoby, and Amir Hussain. *World Traditions: Western Traditions*. Toronto: Oxford University Press, 2014.

Bebbington, D.W., and David Ceri Jones, eds. *Evangelicalism and Fundamentalism in the United Kingdom during the Twentieth Century*. New York: Oxford University Press, 2013.

Bokhari, Kamran, and Farid Senzai. *Political Islam in the Age of Democratization*. New York: Palgrave Macmillan, 2013.

Brekke, Torkel. *Fundamentalism: Prophecy and Protest in the Age of Globalization*. New York: Cambridge University Press, 2012.

Choueiri, Youssef M. *Islamic Fundamentalism: The Story of Islamist Movements*. New York: Continuum, 2010.

Cook, Michael. *Ancient Religions, Modern Politics: The Islamic Case in Comparative Perspective*. Princeton, NJ: Princeton University Press, 2014.

Gleis, Joshua L., and Benedetta Berti. *Hezbollah and Hamas: A Comparative Study*. Baltimore: Johns Hopkins University Press, 2012.

Gregory, Brad S. *The Unintended Reformation: How a Religious Revolution Secularized Society*. Cambridge, MA: Belknap Press of Harvard University Press, 2012.

Halveson, Jeffry R., Lloyd H. Goodall, and Steven R. Corman. *Master Narratives of Islamist Extremism*. New York: Palgrave Macmillan, 2011.

Hamilton, Marci, and Mark J. Rozell. *Fundamentalism, Politics, and the Law*. New York: Palgrave Macmillan, 2011.

Inbari, Motti. *Messianic Religious Zionism Confronts Israeli Territorial Compromises*. New York: Cambridge University Press, 2012.

Koessel, Karrie J. *Religion and Authoritarianism: Cooperation, Conflict and the Consequences*. New York: Cambridge University Press, 2014.

Madigan, Patricia. *Women and Fundamentalism in Islam and Catholicism: Negotiating Modernity in a Globalized World*. New York: Peter Lang, 2011.

Patterson, David. *A Genealogy of Evil: Anti-Semitism from Nazism to Islamic Jihad*. Cambridge: Cambridge University Press, 2011.

Shay, Shaul. *Global Jihad and the Tactic of Terror Abduction: A Comprehensive Review of Islamic Terror Organizations*. Brighton, UK: Sussex Academic Press, 2014.

Smith, Robert O. *More Desired Than Our Own Salvation: The Roots of Christian Zionism*. New York: Oxford University Press, 2013.

Soguk, Nevzat. *Globalization and Islamism*. Lanham, MD: Rowman & Littlefield, 2011.

Tibi, Bassam. *Islamism and Islam*. New Haven: Yale University Press, 2012.

Turner, John. *Religious Ideology and the Roots of the Global Jihad: Salafi Jihadism and International Order*. Basingstoke, UK: Palgrave Macmillan, 2014.

14 Secularism

Learning Objectives

- To learn about the roots of secularism.
- To recognize the difference between secularism and secularization.
- To acknowledge the contributions of various writers to the development of secularism.
- To understand the political significance of secularism.

A secular age is one in which enchantment disappears. It is an age no longer populated by gods, sirens, ghosts, spirits, demons, or goblins. But it is more than this, for it is an age in which the goal of human prosperity and success is of greatest importance. This latter point is made with force by Charles Taylor when he says "a secular age is one in which the eclipse of all goals beyond human flourishing becomes conceivable; or better, it falls within the range of the imaginable life for masses of people."[1] So there are two components to secularism as found in such an age: (i) the enchanted world dies, and (ii) humans conceive of their lives in terms of well-being. The result is a "humanistic alternative to faith."[2]

Secularism is the nemesis of religious belief, especially religious fundamentalism, which opposes the principles of the Enlightenment. We have seen this in the previous chapter in our discussion of Islamic, Christian, Jewish, and Hindu fundamentalism. Perhaps a recent event will make clearer in our minds the extent of the antipathy sometimes felt by some fundamentalists towards secularism. Secular bloggers in Bangladesh have been killed for promoting scientific ideas and for taking a critical approach towards religion. Such is the case of Avijit Roy, the founder of the blog Mukto Mona, a site for Bangladeshi atheists, who was attacked and killed by a machete-wielding individual while leaving a book fair in Dhaka, Bangladesh, in February 2015. His wife, Rafida Ahmed, received serious head injuries and the loss of her thumb in the same attack, which was suspected as having been carried out by religious militants.[3] Of course, not all fundamentalists are moved to carry out such attacks, neither in Bangladesh nor elsewhere, but the incident is an indication of how serious the ideas of secularism are taken by some believers. It is to a better understanding of these ideas that we now turn.

At the outset we need to sort out some confusion regarding the terms "secularization" and "secularism." Secularization, like commercialization, industrialization, liberalization, and modernization, is a *process* that works to establish practices or institutions in society. It need not be conceived of as an intentional or deliberative process but rather simply as something that happens, given the shape of the historical landscape at the time. In contrast, secularism, very much like commercialism, industrialism, liberalism, and modernism, refers to developed practices or institutions that are already established. It would not be misleading to say that secularization leads to secularism. However, it would be misleading to follow some scholars who say that secularization refers to a historical process whereas secularism is the name of an *ideology*. According to one such scholar, Harvey Cox, secularization implies a historical process where society and culture are delivered from religious control and metaphysical world views.[4] Here Cox is on solid ground. However, he errs when he says secularism is an *ideology*, a new closed world view that functions like a religion.[5] As we shall see, those who consider themselves secularists are simply persons who advocate grounding beliefs on evidence. That these same people are strong advocates of the scientific method in attempting to determine whether evidence exists to prove the existence of, for example, phlogiston gas or neutrinos, does not show that secularism is an ideology. It would show this only if these same individuals held their beliefs about evidence and the scientific method as *incorrigible*. But this is not the case with such individuals. Secularists are prepared to abandon their beliefs if these beliefs are not fruitful or productive. If, for instance, the scientific method did not result in success, then these same individuals would abandon it. At most, all one can say here about secularism is that it could be an ideology if it gets into the wrong hands. More accurate would be a description of it as political philosophy with the potential of being ideological.

In the pages that follow the evolution of secularism will be traced, beginning with the eminent Scottish philosopher, David Hume (1711–1776), and then moving on to the Danish existentialist, Søren Kierkegaard (1813–1855), the Austrian founder of psychoanalysis, Sigmund Freud (1856–1939), and the German-American Paul Tillich (1886–1965), who attempted to give a non-enchanted interpretation to Christian belief. The chapter will conclude by considering the thoughts of the British atheist, Richard Dawkins (1941–) and with a brief examination of comments of the British philosopher, J.L. Mackie (1917–1981). The intent here is to show the gradual intellectual evolution of secular ideas and values. A starker picture of the emergence of secularism could be painted by focusing on individuals such as Karl Marx, Friedrich Nietzsche (1844–1900), and Jean-Paul Sartre (1905–1980), but this would conceal the way in which this new political outlook came to be adopted. It came in an evolving way, not abruptly.

Central Beliefs of Secularism

- The cosmos is to be understood in terms of natural processes.
- Beliefs in supernatural entities, including gods, demons, nymphs, sirens, ghosts, witches, and other non-empirically established entities, are to be rejected.
- Public policy, whether domestic or international, should not be founded on supernatural beliefs.

The forces that helped shape the rise of secularism were twofold: the rise of science and the Protestant reformation. These two developments have been discussed in Chapter 1 and so only need to be summarized here. The rise of modern science gave humankind tools for understanding the cosmos far surpassing the understanding that had preceded it. This increasing understanding helped in demythologizing previous attempts at explaining events. As suggested above, gone were the sirens, ghosts, and spirits of the conjectured world. And in place of these things came the physics of Galileo and later. Newton with the postulations of mass, force, gravity, inertia, and so on as these concepts applied to matter. Thomas Hobbes (1588–1679) in the seventeenth century reflected and awakened this interest in modern science by attacking belief in invisible things such as fairies, ghosts, and gods, belief he attributed to man's fear when there was nothing to "accuse" as the source of evil or good.[6] Hobbes thought if the superstitious fear of spirits were taken away, "men would be much more fitted than they are for civil obedience."[7] He was, as it were, one of the first moderns to condemn the enchanted world and praise the world of empirical and mathematical sciences. The effect, according to him, would be not just better science but a better and more peaceful society.

The Protestant reformation added its own impetus to the development of secular society. Simply put, the break in the authority of the Roman Catholic Church, owing to the rise of various sects and denominations, naturally raised the question of "ownership of truth in religious matters." The priesthood of all believers meant that hierarchies could be circumvented and individual appeals could be made directly to God. But whose "truth" was to be accepted in these highly decentralized times? Inevitably, this would lead to hostilities between sects and even inquisitions, but the end result would be an uneasy feeling among all believers that their "truth" might not be as secure as originally thought. Once this uncertainty was raised it was inevitable that reflective individuals such as Hobbes and later Hume would raise philosophical questions about the credibility of such "truths" regardless of where they were quartered. When this matter of credibility is coupled with the general assault on idolatry by reformers, enchantment (which would include idolatry) was clearly threatened, or at least challenged.

So two forces helped to shape the rise of secularism, namely, the scientific revolution that began with Copernicus and Galileo, and the Protestant reformation that began with John Huss (1369–1415), Ulrich Zwingli (1484–1531), Martin Luther (1483–1546), and John Calvin (1509–1564). While there were undoubtedly other changes in the social context, such as the rise of the modern state, these two forces paved the path to disenchantment and the ridding of belief in gods, sirens, ghosts, goblins, and spirits.

The following discussion focuses on secularism inside European communities or those historically connected with them as found in North America, South America, and Australia. Predominantly, these have been Christian societies. Secularism as it has been defined above is more firmly established in these communities than it is in communities grounded in Islam, Judaism, or Hinduism. Herein lies the motivation for looking at the phenomenon of secularism inside what have previously been Christian communities; the motivation does not lie in giving preferential treatment to Christianity or Christian societies. This does not mean that secularism is not an issue in Muslim or Hindu societies. Indeed, as seen in the previous chapter, secularism is a debated notion and practice in India. Nonetheless, as a political stance, secularism is more entrenched in societies that have been predominantly Christian than in others. For this reason, we choose to look at the emergence of this political philosophy in this context.

David Hume

Though we have already described the conservative aspect of David Hume's philosophy in Chapter 3, there remain additional things to say about his attitude towards **natural religion**. Hume's analysis of natural religion, conceived as the tradition that believes Christian religious beliefs are but "extensions of scientific knowledge," as found in his *Dialogues Concerning Natural Religion* (published posthumously in 1779), results in the complete rebuttal of the cosmological and design arguments. The first of these deals with the alleged necessity of postulating a God for the purpose of explaining motion in the cosmos, while the second argues for the existence of a designer of the cosmos, an argument that Kant subsequently found the most tempting of all proofs for the existence of God. Most of the *Dialogues* focus on the design argument and it will occupy our attention in what follows.

The *Dialogues* comprise the thrust and counter-thrust arguments of three characters—Demea, Cleanthes, and Philo—as they deal with the notion of intentional design. Much speculation exists around the question of whether any of these individuals represents the view of David Hume. Fortunately, we do not have to adjudicate this dispute here. What can be said, as Terence Penelhum makes clear, is simply that through his writings, including the *Dialogues*, Hume discredits the tradition of natural religion utterly.[8] In the process he demolishes the argument from design. The cogency of Hume's reasoning here cannot be elucidated in all its grandeur, but by giving a brief overview of the positions adopted by Demea, Cleanthes, and Philo we can comprehend better the strength of Hume's argument.

Demea represents orthodoxy and a belief in a priori proofs of God's existence, Cleanthes represents the empirical theologian, and Philo the skeptic.[9] The considered opinion seems to be that Philo speaks best for the views of Hume, though one should emphasize that not all critics agree with this interpretation.[10] We shall stand by the considered opinion and use it to spell out Hume's views. Worth bearing in mind here is the very structure of this writing of Hume, for it has a remarkable similarity to the structure used by Plato in his writing as well as by George Berkeley in his. This similarity allows Hume the opportunity of teasing out subtle features of the argument from design.

For his part Demea makes the claim that whatever exists must have a cause and that this forces one to concede the existence of a Being who carries the reason for his existence in himself and who cannot be supposed not to exist without expressing a contradiction.[11] This argument turns out to be a blend of the **cosmological** and **ontological arguments**, the former relying on the existence of a necessary being to explain causality, and the latter relying on the apparent contradiction in denying the existence of a being who cannot be supposed not to exist. These arguments are found in the writings of Thomas Aquinas and Anselm, respectively. Hume, through Cleanthes, dispenses with Demea's macro argument by saying simply, "The words, therefore, *necessary existence*, have no meaning; or, which is the same thing, none that is consistent." The ground is now cleared to examine the way Hume, through Philo, dismantles the argument from design as advanced by Cleanthes.

Cleanthes presents the argument from design early in the *Dialogues*. Briefly, his argument is the following. Look around the world and you will find it to be but one great machine. By all the rules of analogy we are led to infer that the causes of the world and machines resemble each other and that therefore the Author of Nature is similar to the mind of man.[12] Penelhum has summarized Philo's first round of criticisms to this argument, a round that includes four main counterpoints.[13] First, the argument relies on a weak analogy for it compares the whole universe with human artifacts. Second, the comparison is odd for it compares the whole universe with "selected parts of it." Third, it is arbitrary to pick out intelligence as the sole source of order. Fourth, knowledge of cause and effect is derived from identifying the regularity of one kind of phenomenon being succeeded by another kind, and therefore the universe, not being a kind, is not subject to such alleged causal reasoning.[14] In the second round Philo draws out the undesirable anthropomorphic conclusions. These conclusions include the fact that the mind or intelligence needed to create the universe would "have all the limitations consistent with its product," the flaws of the universe would reveal imperfections in the designer, the world could have been created by many gods, and finally, God's mind, if like ours, could be mortal and belong to a god with a body.[15]

Hume's final position as found in Part XII of the *Dialogues* does give some comfort to Cleanthes and other religious believers, for he says, notwithstanding the position articulated so ably by Philo, that true religion suggests a "vague deistic belief" in an intelligent force causally responsible for the universe.[16] But even if one accepts that Hume is speaking honestly through Philo and wants to resurrect in some form the design argument, the most that can be claimed here in defence of so-called "true religion" is that deism is plausible. And if Taylor is correct in his analysis of deism in the eighteenth century, this amounted to a "shift towards the primacy of the impersonal order."[17] Accordingly, God relates to us "by establishing a certain order of things, whose moral shape we can easily grasp"[18] provided we are not led astray by superstitious ideas. The grace of God is no longer required, not even in our "fallen condition," in order for our reason to discern the correct path to follow. Clearly, the role of God diminishes to being creator and judge at the end of times. In our daily lives his role is pushed to the edge.

In conclusion, we can say that Hume attacks the design argument with overwhelming success while acknowledging the plausibility of a form of deism. While this is not secularism full blown, it stands as a halfway house to this same objective. God's role in the daily life of individuals has been marginalized. Evidently the world Hume imagines is less enchanted than the world of many of his predecessors, one notable exception being Thomas Hobbes.

Søren Kierkegaard

European philosophy was dominated during the latter part of the eighteenth century and early part of the nineteenth century by the philosophy of Georg Hegel (1770–1831). Two important schools of philosophy—Marxism and existentialism—arose following the hegemonic period of Hegelian thought. In Chapter 5 we looked at, among other things, Marx's attack on religion and his consideration of the criticism of religion made by David Strauss and Ludwig Feurerbach. Marx was wholly sympathetic with this attack, as is evident when he says, "Religion is only the illusory sun about which man revolves so long as he does not revolve about himself."[19] He goes on to say, almost immediately, that "The immediate task of philosophy, which is in the service of history, is to unmask human self-alienation in its *secular form* now that it has been unmasked in its *sacred form*."[20] Here Marx draws a contrast between the sacred and the secular. His contrast parallels the one marked earlier between the enchanted and the disenchanted worlds. It is easy to see, therefore, that Marx stands on the side of secularism. His reasons for taking this stance are twofold: religion is illusory and religion contributes to self-alienation. Clearly these are related points but they do stand separately.

Though something has already been said about Marxism, nothing has been said about **existentialism**. This school of thought includes Søren Kierkegaard, Friedrich Nietzsche, Karl Jaspers (1883–1969), Martin Heidegger (1889–1976), and Jean-Paul Sartre. Briefly, existentialism focuses on the role of individuals in the choices they make under conditions of freedom. Related themes include guilt, bad faith, despair, meaninglessness, absurdity, and hope. Nietzsche, Heidegger, and Sartre could function as figures on the road to secularism, but Kierkegaard stands out as a better transitional figure for he clearly has his feet still very much planted in the nineteenth century and in an enchanted tradition. Nonetheless, there are intimations in his writing that bear upon the secular and disenchantment. So it is to Kierkegaard that we now turn.

Kierkegaard lived a short life of 42 years. Yet during this time he wrote prolifically in the philosophical realm and delivered splendid sermons. So one might say there were two very different strands to his thinking. Conventionally, he is seen as an unqualified Christian thinker, yet there is something in his writing that suggests otherwise—or at least, that he is a new kind of Christian thinker with a foot in the secular world or at least the disenchanted world. Of Kierkegaard's philosophical writings, none stands taller than his *Concluding Unscientific Postscript*. It explores two different themes, objective truth and subjective truth.

The *Postscript* is divided into two books. Book One pertains to the objective problem concerning Christianity, while Book Two pertains to the subjective problem of becoming a Christian. The objective problem is a question of the truth of Christianity from the point of view of history. Accordingly, anyone interested in this question looks at historical evidence in support of Christian doctrine but in the process is left with only an approximation of the truth as the Scriptures and the Church are examined. Kierkegaard remarks, "for nothing is more readily evident than that the greatest attainable certainty with respect to anything historical is merely an approximation."[21] Kierkegaard believes there is "incommensurability" between approximation and eternal happiness, the goal of the Christian, and that this incommensurability makes the result unacceptable. Historical evidence is simply too weak a foundation for the stuff of faith.

Book Two develops the theme of subjective truth and the problem of becoming a Christian. In essence, it deals with the question of how an individual may participate in the eternal happiness promised by Christianity.[22] Well into the *Postcript* Kierkegaard offers a definition of subjective truth: "An objective uncertainty held fast in an approximation-process of the most passionate inwardness is the [subjective] truth."[23] Subjectivity, for Kierkegaard, is inwardness and at the same time the truth.[24] With this definition in mind, Kierkegaard offers a developmental theory of personality that in many respects is secular in nature. Inwardness is a key notion in this theory and Kierkegaard postulates that this inwardness is to be understood against the background of three different stages of development of human personality. These stages are the aesthetic stage, the ethical stage, and the religious stage. All of these manifest progressive ways in which a person finds meaning in life.

The aesthetic stage is a life of freedom and hedonism. It is represented by Don Juan of Mozart's opera of the same name, by Faust of Goethe's writing, and by Ahasuerus, the Wandering Jew of medieval Christian legends.[25] These individuals are all lost in the immediate situation and in the course of time find their activities ultimately tedious and boring. The result is a "staling of existence" that culminates in despair.[26] Almost axiomatic in Kierkegaard's thinking is his claim that, in life, "the important thing is not to cultivate one's mind but to mature one's personality."[27] And to mature one's personality is to aim for the most holy of things: the unifying personality.[28] There is no unified personality in the aesthetic stage, but instead there is born multifariousness and a fragmentation of time into disjointed, unappealing moments. It is not surprising that Kierkegaard believes, under the circumstances, that this stage of life ends in despair.

The next stage is the ethical one. This is, for Kierkegaard, the first serious either/or: it is the first serious occasion when the personality has a choice of moving on and maturing in the direction of integration. But Kierkegaard makes clear in *Either/Or* that the act of choosing is essentially an ethical act and does not surface in the aesthetic stage.[29] And then he adds, a few pages later, that the choice of either/or does not denote a choice between good and evil, but rather a choice between good and evil on the one hand and the exclusion of good and evil on the other.[30] It is a question of under what "determinants" a person wishes to contemplate and live life.[31] According to Kierkegaard's theory of personal development, there are three manifestations—marriage, vocation, and friendship—of this new stage of life in which seriousness and the assumption of responsibility play a role. It is not that any individual in such a relationship conducts himself or herself in an ethical way so much as it is that these same individuals consider themselves in terms of the good and the bad. In other words, these are relevant categories for them in a way they are not for the person in the aesthetic stage.

The final stage in development of personality for Kierkegaard is the religious, something he divides into Religion A and Religion B. Of both of these he says, "the distinguishing mark of religious action is suffering."[32] The logic of Kierkegaard's thinking is simply this: religiosity is inwardness and inwardness is suffering, and therefore religiosity is suffering. According to his logic, talk about fortune and misfortune is simply talk found in the aesthetic view of life and is forgetful of Jesus's invitation to a religious discourse: "Come hither all ye who labor and are heavy laden."[33] In the person's struggle for eternal happiness Kierkegaard sees suffering as "essential" to religious life.[34] From Kierkegaard's perspective existence is a kind of illness,[35] and unsurprisingly attaches suffering to it to those who have eyes to see. But he moves on to attribute something else to Religion A, namely, guilt. For this Danish thinker, consciousness of guilt turns out to be the first deep plunge into existence,[36] and this consciousness is like a yoke around the neck of humans from which they can never escape.[37] The importance or priority of guilt for Kierkegaard cannot be arrived at by numerical computations, but is something felt in the soul of humans in their striving for eternal happiness. Once again, as in the case of suffering, guilt for Kierkegaard is found in inwardness and hence is a form of religious expression.[38]

Kierkegaard goes on to say that an awareness of Religion A must be present in the individual before one can become aware of the content of Religion B.[39] So one should not think of the former as being trumped by the latter. Nonetheless, B does go further than A; its content can be best understood as equivalent to faith: faith in the idea that God has appeared as man in the form of Jesus. Once again, this existentialist sees faith as a deepening of the inwardness of humans in their wrestling with their eternal happiness. Faith turns out to be belief against understanding, and hence the paradoxical nature of Religion B.

What is striking about the so-called theology of Søren Kierkegaard is its disenchanted nature in the aesthetic, ethical, and Religion A stages of life. What is presented is largely a reduction of religious discourse to personal developmental discourse, at least until Religion B. Kierkegaard admits as much when he says, "Religiousness A can exist in paganism."[40] What is one to learn from all of this as far as secularity is concerned? It is simply that one of the most original Christian thinkers of the nineteenth century found it necessary to cultivate a new way of religious thinking, yet he did so by pushing enchantment further and further to the edges of one's life, and even then by making it accessible only to those who had the time to go on a deep spiritual journey through the inwardness of suffering and guilt. Secular ideas clearly were pressing in from all sides and Kierkegaard's innovative thinking is just one sign of this.

Sigmund Freud

There can be little doubt that Sigmund Freud is among the most original social scientists of the nineteenth and twentieth centuries. In addition there is little doubt about the clarity of his prose and the engaging nature of his thoughts. This can be said whether one disagrees with what he says. One is hard-pressed to find other writers of his time who write with such conviction, novelty, and transparency. Bertrand Russell and John Maynard Keynes may be possible rivals, but Freud is definitely a strong competitor.

In what follows my interest is not in attempting to canvass all the works of Freud, but instead simply to sample some things he has said in his two works *Totem and Taboo*[41] and *The Future of an Illusion*.[42] Of particular interest are some of his comments in *Totem and Taboo*, where he discusses at length the subject of animism. Freud appears to agree with the anthropology of such scholars as Herbert Spencer (1820–1903), J.G. Frazer (1854–1941), and Wilhelm Wundt (1832–1920) when he says in the course of the ages the human race has developed three systems of thought: animism, religion, and science.[43] Animism and religion clearly are the subject matter referred to earlier by Charles Taylor under the heading of enchantment. So we need to look at what Freud has to say about these two areas as species of enchantment. Only then will we see what role he played in moving Western thought in the direction of secularism.

For Freud, animism is, in its narrower sense, nothing other than the doctrine of souls, while in its wider sense it is the doctrine of spiritual beings in general.[44] According to Freud, the term "animism" was used by Wundt, Spencer, and others upon their realization of the view of nature and the universe held by so-called primitive races, that is, that spirits, both good and bad, populate the world and the "lesser" sentient and nonsentient entities on earth, and they in turn cause natural events. These spirits and demons, according to Freud, are simply projections of man's own emotional impulses.[45] Moreover, according to Freud, this view asserts that humans are inhabited by such spirits.[46] Freud is insistent in claiming that animism is a system of thought, indeed, the first complete theory of the universe.[47] For him it really amounts to a **Weltanshauung**, or world view—a world view that is perhaps the most consistent and exhaustive in giving a complete explanation of the nature of the universe.[48] In his discussion of animism Freud goes on to discuss sorcery, otherwise called the art of influencing spirits, and then magic, a branch of animistic technique.[49] Underlying animism, Freud suggests, is the observation or awareness of humans of sleep and dreams and, ultimately, of death.[50] Hobbes, long before Freud, suggests as much when he claims, at least of dreams, that humans' ignorance of how to distinguish dreams from vision and sense was the source of religions that affirmed the existence of satyrs, fawns, nymphs, fairies, ghosts, goblins, and witches.[51]

Freud and Hobbes concur on the importance of dreams in thrusting humans in the direction of enchantment.

Freud believes that the principle governing magic, in other words, the technique of animistic thought, is in effect the principle of "omnipotence of thought."[52] This is a phrasing he derived from his psychoanalytic practice while working with a man who suffered from obsessional ideas and who himself came up with the phrase by way of explanation of strange and uncanny events.[53] Freud makes use of this notion to link it to the three systems of thought previously mentioned: animism, religion, and science. He believes that at the animism stage, humans ascribe omnipotence to themselves, while at the religious stage they transfer it to the gods, and, finally, at the scientific stage they give up on it entirely, recognizing their smallness and submitting to death and the necessities of nature.[54] Freud elaborates further on this by saying the animistic phase corresponds to narcissism, the religious phase to the stage of choosing some external object for attachment as, for instance, one's parents, and the scientific stage to the renunciation of the pleasure principle and the turning to the external world for the object of one's desires.[55] In short, for Freud, animism came to primitive man as something natural, as an occasion when he projects the structural conditions of his own mind onto the external world. Science, for Freud, only arose after humans realized their ignorance of the world and the necessity of getting to know it.[56]

Totem and Taboo is an exemplary piece of Freud's writing that focuses on animism in a narrow sense. It is a sense that fits into the category of enchantment, as described by Charles Taylor. However, the second phase, as identified by Freud, is mankind's attempt at developing a system of thought based in a structured religion, and it too fits Taylor's definition. This system of thought is examined thoroughly by Freud in his *The Future of an Illusion*, and in this work we can understand better his more complete view on enchantment and, by implication, on secularism.

Freud makes an early declaration of his position with regard to religion in *The Future of an Illusion*. He asserts that religious ideas have arisen from the need to defend oneself against the superior force of nature and from the urge to rectify the deficiencies in civilization.[57] But he adds that these same ideas, with pretenses of containing elements of the highest importance, are not the products of experience or the end result of thinking. Rather, they are illusions or wish fulfillments whose strength is found solely in the strength of these wishes.[58] He adds, by way of clarification, that what he has in mind when he speaks of illusions here is something derived from human wishes.[59] Freud concludes that when we call a belief an illusion we disregard its relation to reality owing to the fact that an illusion does not ground itself in verification.[60] And then he boldly declares that scientific work is the only work that will lead us to the reality outside ourselves—in the absence of this, we are stuck in subjectivity.[61] While Freud does not aim to assess the truth-value of religious ideas or doctrines, he suggests quite strongly that the illusory nature of these beliefs—coupled with our understanding of the historic conditions surrounding the birth of these doctrines and those who created them—will cause a marked displacement of these beliefs in our lives.[62] Consequently, an unmistakable situation has arisen today, thinks Freud, in which "religion no longer has the same influence on people that it used to" because people find its promises "less credible."[63] The explanation for this, according to Freud, is simply "the increase of scientific spirit in the higher strata of human society."[64] It is Freud's opinion that civilization has little to fear from educated people, for in them religious motives will be replaced by secular motives and thus they will proceed unobtrusively.[65] Here Freud puts secularism squarely on display and links it to civilization and the scientific method. It is worth noting that this psychoanalytic theorist warns of possible dangers, notably the danger that may arise when the uneducated, who lack scientific understanding, unleash their fury upon those who threaten their religious beliefs.[66] This does not mean that Freud fails completely to acknowledge the worth of certain religious doctrines, but it does mean that he believes it is time to cease putting forward religious doctrines as the "reasons for the precepts of civilization."[67] He believes these doctrines are historical residues—neurotic relics to be replaced by the results of rational thinking.[68]

There can be no doubt that Freud disavows any association with the enchanted world. In this respect he does so much more categorically than Kierkegaard. Freud is clearly on the side of science and objectivity—of climbing outside the mind to see what is there in the external world. Kierkegaard is still very much immersed in subjectivity—hence the name of his *Unscientific Postcript*. Nonetheless, both of these intellectuals move in the direction of a study of humans and their psychology and both, though particularly Freud, carry us well down the road to a secular world. It is time to see how this story plays out with other writers, including a much respected Protestant theologian.

Paul Tillich

The impact of Kierkegaard on Christian thinkers who followed him was deep and penetrating. Two theologians affected by his thinking were Rudolf Bultmann (1884–1976) and Paul Tillich. The former, as a New Testament scholar, embarked on the task of demythologizing the New Testament for the purpose of showing that mythological thinking obscures the qualitative difference between man and God.[69] We need not explore Bultmann's thinking here, but it is worth remarking that he began to take Christian thought away from conventional orthodox Christian views of the enchanted. Of greater interest is the work of Paul Tillich.

Tillich's magnum opus is his *Systematic Theology*. Of particular interest in our pursuit of the topic of secularization and its impact on Christian thinking is the section of this work entitled "The Meaning of 'God'."[70] In spite of the historical scholarship and philosophical reflections that colour the pages of Tillich's opus—scholarship covering such topics as "Existence and the Christ," "Life and the Spirit," and "History and the Kingdom of God"[71]—it is difficult to come to any other conclusion about Tillich's theology other than it is all premised on his notion of God. And to summarize his position with unavoidable bluntness we need to say that for Tillich "God" is "the name for that which concerns man ultimately."[72] According to Tillich "whatever concerns a man ultimately becomes god for him."[73] Still later he says, "The being of God is being-itself."[74] Still later he adds, "Many confusions in the doctrine of God and many apologetic weaknesses could be avoided if God were understood first of all as being-itself or as the ground of being."[75] We are thus left with the following result: Tillich's treatment of all theological topics rests on his notion of God as a person's ultimate concern or as being-itself. These are not, in fact, the same notions so we need to analyze the implications of his claims. First, if God is simply one's ultimate concern, which would vary from one person to another, God turns out to be something quite different from that which is referred to in the Bible, where God is demonstrably anthropomorphic, modelled on persons in all their regalia. So on the first understanding of "God," Tillich simply changes the meaning to something that is reductive and for all practical purposes very secular. He eschews enchantment even more than Kierkegaard, at least when considering Kierkegaard's views on Religion B. Second, if God is being-itself or the ground of being, we are squarely in the world of Parmenides when he talks about "Being is, non-being is not." Tillich points to being-itself, hardly something whose existence would be contested, and takes it to be God. Yet, once again this is not a personal being. Instead, it is either a way of referring to existence abstractly considered or, in the spirit of Wittgenstein, to "all that is the case."[76] Neither of these is a very attractive outcome. And neither of these views, of being-itself or of ground of being, amounts to a form of deism discussed by Hume, still less to a form of conventional religious belief. In the end, one is not left with the enchanted when talking of being-itself or the ground of being.

The brevity of these remarks on Tillich should not be seen as a deliberate attempt to show him disrespect. Rather, they are meant to show how ingenious thinking will not suffice to save this new interpretation of Christian ideas from the charge of secularism. The idea of receiving grace from being-itself or from one's ultimate concern is burdened by confusion and obfuscation. Here, Tillich's ingenuity gets the better of him. What triumphs in the end is secularism: the eschewing of enchantment. There are no gods, demons, spirits, goblins, and satyrs. The world becomes, instead, one in which persons inwardly struggle, to use the title of another of Tillich's books, to have *The Courage to Be*.[77]

Richard Dawkins

An ethnologist and evolutionary biologist, Richard Dawkins taught for many years at Oxford University. In recent years he has been a strong advocate of secularism and has gained notoriety among religious believers for *The God Delusion*. In the opening pages of this book Dawkins makes clear that he is against supernaturalism in all its forms, by which he means he is against the God Hypothesis.[78] By taking aim at this hypothesis Dawkins attacks the belief in a superhuman, supernatural intelligence who deliberately designed and created the universe. Like Freud, Dawkins concludes, after an extensive survey of the facts, that belief in God is delusional.[79] Although he concentrates his criticism on monotheistic religions, he openly attacks belief in gods of all shape and size inasmuch as they are all supernatural beings.[80] It is Dawkins's attack on all form of supernaturalism that makes him a secularist in the spirit of Charles Taylor. In brief, Dawkins is effectively against enchantment.

Having considered different religious views within his object of criticism, Dawkins proceeds to discuss the presence of secularism in the thoughts of the founding fathers of the United States, and here he includes George Washington, John Adams, Thomas Jefferson, and James Madison. Dawkins argues rather convincingly that the founding fathers were secularists in the sense that they "believed in keeping religion out of politics."[81] While he admits that some of these may have been deists, in the sense discussed by Hume, he does not think the God Hypothesis is much more likely under this interpretation of "God" than under any other. In all its forms, he thinks, the Hypothesis is unnecessary.[82] In passing, Dawkins addresses the claim that we cannot disprove the God Hypothesis and responds by saying we cannot disprove the existence of orbiting teapots.[83] But Dawkins does not believe this should make us believe in orbiting teapots, nor should it make us believe in God or gods. But what about extraterrestrial intelligence? Here Dawkins pauses to distinguish between superhuman and supernatural, the former being the product of the evolutionary process and the latter, presumably, of conjecture.[84] While he is prepared to concede the possible existence of the former, he is not prepared to do the same for the latter. And at this point he launches into a slight digression to attack the established philosophical arguments for the existence of God.

Dawkins reviews the standard arguments for the existence of God: the unmoved mover, the uncaused cause, the cosmological argument, the argument from degree, the argument from design (Paley's argument), the ontological argument, the argument from personal experience, the argument from scripture, the argument from admired religious scientists, Pascal's Wager, and Bayesian Arguments.[85] It should be noted that, in passing, Dawkins refers approvingly to the philosophical critique of theism given by the late John L. Mackie of Oxford University.[86] Comments later in this chapter will make clear Mackie's stance. Following his overview of arguments for God's existence, Dawkins goes on the offensive by arguing against God's existence. He does this by acknowledging the improbability of God's existence given a choice between design being the source of ordered life and natural selection being the source of ordered life.[87] Chance and design fail as answers to the improbability of ordered life. Chance, for Dawkins, is not an answer because it is simply a restatement of the problem. And design is not an answer because it raises the question of who designed the designer. Instead, we are left with natural selection as "not only a workable solution, [but] a solution of stunning elegance and power."[88] And it is so, he thinks, because natural selection is a cumulative process and breaks the problem of improbability up into small pieces, so that each of the small pieces may be "slightly improbable" but not "prohibitively so."[89] The creationist misses the point completely, thinks Dawkins, because he treats "the genesis of statistical improbability" as a single event, rather than cumulative. When the single event is broken down into atomic bits, as it were, the statistically improbable becomes less than prohibitively improbable. Natural selection, according to Dawkins, acts like a crane (machine) rather than a skyhook. It builds things from the bottom up rather than the top down. In this way both design from above and chance are eliminated in favour of natural selection. From these considerations Dawkins concludes that the God Hypothesis is "untenable" and that "God almost certainly does not exist."[90] In this way he argues for secularism: the repudiation of enchantment. Gone are the gods of polytheistic and monotheistic traditions. They are as expendable as cosmic teapots.

One other aspect of Dawkins's thinking still needs to be discussed. It pertains to his comments on the new moral *Zeitgeist*. Dawkins attempts to summarize the principles of the good life, principles he claims are the New Ten Commandments or moral consensus. He takes these straight off an atheist's website and are as follows:

- Do not do to others what you do not want done to you.
- Strive to cause no harm.
- Treat human beings, other living things, and the world in general with love, honesty, faithfulness, and respect.
- Do not overlook evil, but allow for forgiveness.
- Seek to learn new things.
- Test all things.
- Respect the right of others to disagree with you.

- Form independent opinions on the basis of reason and experience.
- Question everything.[91]

While these are principles of ethics that Dawkins endorses along with many others, he also adds a few principles of his own:

- Enjoy your sex life and allow others to enjoy theirs.
- Do not discriminate or oppress on the basis of sex, race, or species.
- Do not indoctrinate children.
- Value the future time scale longer than your own.[92]

Whether Dawkins is correct in asserting that a *Zeitgeist* in many societies is moving in the direction of consensual ethics, in other words, moving in the direction of a consensus around ethical principles, does not matter at this point. What matters is that he asserts as much and that these principles make no reference to enchanted beings. There is no reference to Yahweh, God, Allah, Atman, Poseidon, Atlas, Aphrodite, satyrs, sirens, ghosts, goblins, or any other spiritual entity so strongly excoriated by Thomas Hobbes. What Dawkins gives us is an ethics of consensus that is largely atheistic or de-spiritualized. In this sense Dawkins embraces secularism by denying the existence of anything supernatural, such as God or gods,[93] and by affirming the existence of ethical principles that are free of spiritual baggage and grounded in affirmations of the good life for any decent human being.[94] While this does not take us all the way to the flourishing life described by Taylor above, it certainly takes us a long way in this direction. It is worth noting in concluding our discussion of Dawkins that he quotes from Dan Dennett of Tufts University when the latter says the appeal to natural selection or "crane talk" provides an unrebuttable refutation to the existence of God that is as effective to today as when it was used by Cleanthes in Hume's *Dialogues Concerning Natural Religion* a couple of centuries earlier.[95]

J.L. Mackie

The ideas of the Oxford University philosopher John Mackie are fitting ones for wrapping up our discussion of secularism. His *Ethics* is a tour de force that deserves consideration in this regard. The subtitle of his work is *Inventing Right and Wrong*, which clearly describes the main idea of the book. Morality is invented, not discovered in nature. It is something reached through accommodation of one person with another and through the application of reason: the rationality of acting morally. Mackie actually speaks of it as one branch of practical reason, the other being the rationality of pursuing one's own long-term interests.[96] Mackie does not have a lot to say about secularism but what he says amounts to a sound presentation of a secularist's perspective in the field of ethics. Briefly, Mackie contends that the attempt to ground morality on the existence of God is bound to fail. He claims there is no cogent positive argument for the existence of God, that the problem of evil amounts to an insuperable difficulty for any standard theism, that the advance of science makes the appeal to God as an explanatory hypothesis completely unnecessary and implausible, and that no revelation has reliable credentials.[97] In the absence of a believable theism upon which to base ethics, we have no alternative but to appeal to "a purely secular morality."[98]

Conclusion

As indicated at the beginning of this chapter, Charles Taylor provides a description of the two main ingredients of secularism: first is the death of the enchanted world and second is the realization among humans that they conceive of life in terms of well-being or, to put it somewhat differently, the realization by humans of "the eclipse of all goals beyond human flourishing."[99] We should understand here that the pursuit of this well-being or flourishing is no longer seen as a way of following or glorifying God and is not conceived as enabled by God.[100] Such is the nature of secularism.

The foregoing discussion has included a survey of diverse thinkers from the time of David Hume to the present. These thinkers included Hume, Kierkegaard, Freud, Tillich, Dawkins, and Mackie. While it would be incorrect to say that their respective positions on deep philosophical issues lead one inevitably towards secularism as defined by Taylor, their positions do all tend in that direction, at least with respect to the move towards disenchantment. In the case of Hume this is self-evident in his skepticism as found in the remarks of Cleanthes; in the case of Kierkegaard this is apparent in his reinterpretation of Christian belief and religious stance, pushing this belief to the edge of a personality theory in psychology; in the case of Freud this is evident in his interpretation of religious belief as illusory and largely unhealthy; in the case of Tillich this is found in his reinterpretation of God as the disenchanted ground of being and being-itself; in the case of Dawkins it is located in his interpretation of religious belief as delusional; and in the case of Mackie it is discovered in his assertion of the untenability of Christianity, if not all religious belief. There is a tendency in all these cases for religious belief to be marginalized or simply rejected. It is certainly rejected by Hume, Freud, Dawkins, and Mackie. This is less true of Kierkegaard and Tillich, but in the latter's case not much of an enchanted being exists in the ground of being or being-itself. In the case of Kierkegaard there is a recognition of the futility of basing one's belief on empirical evidence, and hence for at least Christian beliefs to survive they must be generated by a leap of faith—but only at the third stage of human development and then only in Religion B or the second half of this third stage. Religious belief on this developmental theory has been clearly marginalized.

But what of Taylor's claim that secularism embraces the idea of human flourishing? Of the claim that this flourishing or well-being, not in the glory of God or derived from him/her, is a second feature of secularism? This notion of well-being or flourishing is as old as Aristotle and was very much at home in the writings of the ancients. But can we locate it in the writings of the aforementioned writers? It is not in any obvious way traceable in Hume's writings, and certainly not in Freud's. In his case the inconsolable self sought refuge in the comfort of the psychoanalyst, but hardly with the expectation of finding a flourishing life—rather, merely to free the self of those things that made life unbearable. This still falls short of flourishing or well-being. For Kierkegaard, life is a sickness unto death, and while he seeks eternal happiness (one might say well-being), most of what Kierkegaard discusses deals with matters that are the antithesis of well-being: despair, guilt, suffering, and meaninglessness. This leaves us with Tillich, who does hold out the promise of health in the individual when he/she lives a life of faith and love: health and salvation for Tillich are one and the same, "being the elevation of man to the transcendent unity of the divine life."[101] So there is some presence of flourishing or well-being in Tillich's thought. Perhaps the one writer who is most upbeat about human well-being is Richard Dawkins, who does see the species in its different *Zeitgeists* moving forward consensually to better times. And this affirmation of flourishing and well-being is, I think, implicit in the principles of ethics that he enunciates in lay terms. It may not quite be the same standard of Aristotle, but it is a close second.

What these writers show is a marked tendency to carry the flag of secularism forward with respect to disenchanting the world. What Hume, Freud, Dawkins, and Mackie offer us is a world without God. The Christian theologians Kierkegaard and Tillich offer us a reinterpretation of the religious life that excludes any philosophically interesting and debatable notion of God, per Tillich, or, per Kierkegaard, a radically transformed understanding of religious life that effectively marginalizes religious belief except at the end of a long pilgrimage.

The record of these same individuals on the flourishing life or well-being is certainly more checkered. They do not speak with one voice about this subject and so it is difficult to conclude that one message is to be gleaned from all of this. On the evidence of these writers, one may ask: Has secularism rooted itself deeply, at least in Western societies? The answer would seem to be affirmative in the matter of disenchantment but more equivocal in the case of well-being or flourishing. Does this mean that secularism has not established itself in Western societies? Or does it mean that Taylor has simply added too much to the concept of secularism? This is a debate that others will undoubtedly pursue in the future and not one that needs to be settled here and now. It is sufficient to point out that at the very least, so far as Western civilization goes, the first limb of secularism is well entrenched. It is unlikely that Hume, for one, would be surprised or disappointed by the result.

Evaluation: The Strengths of Secularism

1. Secularism as a political philosophy or movement rests upon scientific methodology that gives rise to evidence-based public policies. As a political philosophy it begins to free itself from the tentacles of ideologies, which, by definition, are held to be incorrigible. It largely rests upon empirical principles, and this allows for theoretical constructs that can be confirmed through their predictive capacity and can be rejected through their lack of explanatory power.

2. Secularism provides a measuring rod of truth that, if applied judiciously, could resolve conflicts based on religion in a reasonable way. Since many conflicts, both old and new, have been based on religious differences, mankind for once stands the chance of liberating itself from gratuitous suffering caused by war rooted in religious differences. Here one can think of Christian conflicts between Protestants and Catholics, conflicts between Muslims and Christians, conflicts between Hindus and Muslims, and conflicts between Sunni and Shi'a Muslims. The disease of religious self-righteousness, which ideological entrenchment gives rise to, is effectively eliminated by an appeal to reason and a common yardstick. The ditching of belief in sirens, ghosts, gods, demons, satyrs, and other spiritual entities is a narrow pass that mankind must walk through and could walk through to reach this tranquil land.

3. Secularism allows us to face the problems of mankind in a direct and uncluttered way. Marx had a point here when he says that the immediate task of philosophy is to

unmask human self-alienation in its secular form once it has been unmasked in its sacred form. As a political philosophy, secularism frees the hands of its supporters to analyze institutions rationally and objectively, to see how and in what way they contribute to the well-being of individuals. Such institutions would include those, often defended by conservatives, such as the church, mosque, temple, synagogue, marriage, the judicial system, the constitutional system, and educational system.

Evaluation: The Weaknesses of Secularism

1. Prominent among the weaknesses of secularism is the naive belief that reason can prevail politically. This perhaps is most evident in the optimism of Dawkins, who sees a moral consensus emerging among humans—moreover, he imagines a moral consensus that emerges owing to its non-religious foundation. Adam Smith is aware of a problem in this domain. Smith suggests, as indicated in the chapter on classical liberalism, that religious sects had to be handled either through scientific or philosophical education or, more probably, through diversionary practices such as festivities that preoccupied the common man. Given that only a small percentage of humans will be inclined to adopt a scientific or philosophical attitude towards ordinary affairs, it is difficult to see a moral consensus emerging that can be used as a foundation for public policy-making. This seems to leave only diversionary activities sponsored by the state to remedy this problem. But this, in turn, presupposes an accepted political philosophy among the majority, something not likely to happen. The mistake of Dawkins here is to believe either (i) that humans are becoming more rational, or (ii) that nothing need be done to accommodate the fact that humans are not becoming more rational. Dostoevsky long ago suggested that the idea of humans becoming more rational simply sticks in one's throat. It does seem a non-starter. And this leads us to the conclusion of saying nothing needs to be done to move forward to consensus, itself a rather implausible position. Needless to say, not all secularists subscribe to Dawkins's optimism and so not all secularists are tarred with the same brush. But the naïveté here is a practical problem for secularism.

2. Another weakness of secularism, at least as described by Taylor, is its second pillar or plank. Let us call this the human flourishing plank or plank of well-being. At least in the Western world, it seems true to say that the disenchantment process has resulted in less interest and accommodation of religious beliefs, as in the case of changes to legislation regarding divorce, abortion, homosexuality, and the use of soft drugs. Hence, once belief in enchanted beings disappeared, many moral prohibitions went with it. But this does not mean that humans, again in the Western world, thereby bought into well-being or flourishing life. It seems instead, if they have bought into anything, they have bought into consumerism. This attachment to consumerism should come as no surprise to those familiar with the writings of Joseph Schumpeter, especially his *Capitalism, Socialism and Democracy*.[102] Schumpeter recognizes the capitalist nature of the West, as we must, and says the following: "The fundamental impulse that sets and keeps the capitalist engine in motion comes from the new consumer goods, the new methods of production or transportation, the new markets, the new forms of industrial organization that capitalist enterprise creates."[103] Here he affirms, among other things, the integral nature of consumerism to the capitalist system, and it is precisely

this economic system that prevails in the secular societies recognized by Taylor. What follows from this is something simple but deeply at odds with Taylor's affirmation of the second plank or pillar of secularism—namely, that secularists are not focusing on well-being or flourishing but on the purchase of material goods. Only if one sees this fixation on material goods as identical with well-being, an untenable supposition, can one say with Taylor that Western societies have arrived at secularism as he defines it. Given the definition, one has to conclude it is implausible to affirm that secularism has been established. The simple solution here to what we can call Taylor's problem is simply to give up on the second plank when describing secularism.

3. Secularism, also following Taylor, claims that the West has moved towards relinquishing its belief in enchantment. But this claim does not comport well with some contemporary developments. Writing in the summer of 2013 Adam Frank, a professor of physics and astronomy at the University of Rochester, laments the intransigence of a large part of the population in the United States to confront things scientifically. He asserts that in 1982, 44 per cent of Americans believed in creationism while today 46 per cent believe in it. He asserts that in 1989, 63 per cent of Americans understood that climate change was a problem whereas 25 years later this figure has dropped to 58 per cent. Moreover, he asserts anti-vaccine campaigners have brandished discredited studies that attempt to link vaccination with autism.[104] Here we see not movement in the direction of the affirmation of science but rather a retreat in the direction of enchantment. So even the first plank of Taylor's secularism is subject to review.

Related Websites

BBC. "Secularism." 27 Oct. 2009.
www.bbc.co.uk/religion/religions/atheism/types/secularism.shtml

Brooks, David. "Kicking the Secularist Habit." *The Atlantic*, Mar. 2003.
www.theatlantic.com/magazine/archive/2003/03/kicking-the-secularist-habit/302680/

Canadian Secular Alliance
http://secularalliance.ca/

National Secular Society. "What is Secularism?"
www.secularism.org.uk/what-is-secularism.html

Secularism and Non-Religion
www.secularismandnonreligion.org/

Further Readings on Secularism

Beiner, Ronald. *Civil Religion: A Dialogue in the History of Political Philosophy*. New York: Cambridge University Press, 2011.
Berlinerblau, Jacques, Sarah Fainberg, and Aurora Nou. *Secularism on the Edge: Rethinking Church–State Relations in the United States, France, and Israel*. New York: Palgrave Macmillan, 2014.

Bilgrami, Akeel. *Secularism, Identity, and Enchantment.* Cambridge, MA: Harvard University Press, 2014.

Black, Brian, and Gavin Hyman. *Confronting Secularism in Europe and India: Legitimacy and Disenchantment in Contemporary Times.* London: Bloomsbury Academic, 2014.

Cady, Elizabeth Linell, and Elizabeth Shakman Hurd. *Comparitive Secularisms in a Global Age.* New York: Palgrave Macmillan, 2010.

Calhoun, Craig, Mark Jurgens Meyer, and Jonathon VanAntwerpen. *Rethinking Secularism.* New York: Oxford University Press, 2011.

Cimino, Richard P., and Christopher Smith. *Atheist Awakening: Secular Activism and Community in America.* New York: Oxford University Press, 2014.

Cooper, Julie E. *Secular Powers: Humility in Modern Political Thought.* Chicago: University of Chicago Press, 2013.

Dawson, Lorne L., and Paul Bramadat. *Religious Radicalization and Secularization in Canada and Beyond.* Toronto: University of Toronto Press, 2014.

Dressler, Markus, and Arvind Pal-Singh Mandair. *Secularism and Religion-Making.* New York: Oxford University Press, 2011.

Glendon, Mary Anne, and Rafael Alvira. *Religion and Civil Society: The Changing Faces of Religion and Secularity.* Hildesheim, Germany: Olms, 2014.

Hertzke, Allan D. *The Future of Religious Freedom: Global Challenges.* New York: Oxford University Press, 2013.

Hurd, Elizabeth Shakman. *The Politics of Secularism in International Relations.* Princeton, NJ: Princeton University Press, 2008.

Jakobsen, Janet R., and Anne Pelligrini. *Secularisms.* Durham, NC: Duke University Press, 2008.

Kuru, Ahmet T. *Secularism and State Policies toward Religion: The United States, France and Turkey.* Cambridge: Cambridge University Press, 2009.

Mancini, Susanna, and Michel Rosenfield, eds. *Constitutional Secularism in an Age of Religious Revival.* Oxford; New York: Oxford University Press, 2014.

Neuman, Justin. *Fiction beyond Secularism.* Evanston, IL: Northwestern University Press, 2014.

Pritchard, Elizabeth A. *Religion in Public: Locke's Political Ideology.* Stanford, CA: Stanford University Press, 2014.

Requejo Coll, Ferran, and Camil Ungureanu. *Democracy, Law and Religious Pluralism: Secularism and Post-Secularism.* New York: Routledge, 2014.

Saas, C. "Muslim Headscarf and Secularism in France." *European Journal of Migration and Law* 3, 3–4 (2001): 453–6.

Scherer, Matthew. *Beyond Church and State: Democracy, Secularism, and Conversion.* New York: Cambridge University Press, 2013.

Selby, Jennifer A. *Questioning French Secularism: Gender Politics and Islam in a Parisian Suburb.* New York: Palgrave Macmillan, 2012.

Shah, Timothy-Samuel, Alfred C. Stephan, and Monica Duffy-Toft. *Rethinking Religion and World Affairs.* New York: Oxford University Press, 2012.

Slater, Michael R. *Pragmatism and the Philosophy of Religion.* Cambridge: Cambridge University Press, 2014.

Snyder, Jack L. *Religion and International Relations Theory.* New York: Columbia University Press, 2011.

Turner, Bryan S. *Religion and Modern Society: Citizenship, Secularization and the State.* Cambridge: Cambridge University Press, 2011.

Weir, Todd H. *Secularism and Religion in Nineteenth Century Germany: The Rise of the Fourth Confession.* New York: Cambridge University Press, 2014.

15 Conclusion

Prior to the events associated with the Enlightenment, three pivotal events occurred in modern world history: the scientific revolution, the Protestant Reformation, and the birth of the modern national state. While the roots of these three events preceded the seventeenth century, they reached new and critical phases in that era. These events forced humans to think about their political role in the cosmos in terms of individualism, authority, legitimacy, the state, liberty, equality, and human rights.

The first to think of these topics in a somewhat new way was Thomas Hobbes, but John Locke, more than any other figure, turned political thinking in a completely new direction. As a member of the Royal Society of London, Locke was very much aware of science, or natural philosophy as it was then called. Locke's empiricism was an inspiration of his scientific interests, but his interest in political authority was itself, at least in part, a product of his empiricism. He wanted to know the origin of political authority, and this interest was in part rooted in his attachment to the spirit of the times—namely, science. Locke's ideas on politics were more affected by the three aforementioned shifts in European thought and political structure than were those of Hobbes, for besides his scientific empiricism, Locke understood only too well, in a way that Hobbes did not, that the Protestant Reformation killed absolutism and that the authority of the emergent modern nation-state demanded explanation. Once Locke opened the door to philosophical questions on the authority of the state, it was just a matter of time until someone of Adam Smith's stature began to dig more deeply into some of the economic notions embedded in the account given by Locke.

What happened after Locke and Smith need not be described again here. Unpredictable ideologies were born to deal with changing circumstances brought on in part by the pluralism in confessions of faith, by growing commercialization, and by accelerating technological growth and industrialization based on scientific insights. All of these took place in an environment of a consolidated network of nation-states. The new ideologies competed, and continue to compete, for the same epistemic space; they all seek to attract believers. Unlike political philosophies, which do not aim to influence government policy but to facilitate detached reflection on the basic ideas behind such policies, ideologies aim to influence people and to mobilize them into action. Ideologies have as one of their functions the influence of public policies. This is one of the major reasons for being interested in such ideas. Because political ideologies influence public policies, it is desirable that we have some idea which of these are credible and which are not. A comparative study of this type allows one to understand better how to respond to government action both domestically and internationally.

Our study of competing political ideologies has revealed that some of them are rationally unacceptable and, in this sense, not credible. Among those that are not credible, for reasons offered in the respective evaluations, are the following: anarchism, Fascism, fundamentalism, and Marxism. To say that these are not rationally acceptable and do not warrant belief does not mean, of course, that they are not followed, in some instances by millions of individuals around the world. It is simply to say that as political ideologies they are either illogical or bereft of supporting evidence. Take the cases of fundamentalism and Fascism. These are ideologies based on unusual beliefs about the world: original sin, immaculate conception, resurrection, the need for salvation, the purity of the Aryan race, the belief in race, the incorrigibility of the Fuehrer or Il Duce, the veneration of war, and spiritual monism. Faced with these two ideologies, it is easy to agree with the remarks of the editor of *Harper's* to the effect that "[c]hildren unfamiliar with the world in time become marks for the dealers in fascist politics and quack religions."[1] Fail to nurture children on natural history and human history and the results, in the end, can be quite heartbreaking: religious wars or xenophobic national wars occur that cause grief to millions of people, or domestic policies take a regressive turn, costing people health and happiness and security. It is best to be done with these ideologies.

But what of the other ideologies that are listed as not credible in the light of reason? What about Marxism? Can anything be said to support that claim that Marxism is credible as a political ideology in the present world? It seems unlikely. Marxism, with its materialistic monism coupled with its inability to see the adaptability of capitalism to changing modes of production, to the formation of unions, to the issues of human rights, and even to environmental degradation,[2] is simply not supportable as a political ideology. Added to this list of Marxist weaknesses are its affirmation of violence and its propensity, through the dictatorship of the proletariat, to give rise to totalitarian and brutal regimes such as those of Joseph Stalin, Mao Zedong, and Pol Pot. John Maynard Keynes may have overstated the matter, but he was not far wrong when he said, "But Marxian Socialism must always remain a portent to the historians of Opinion—how a doctrine so illogical and dull can have exercised so powerful and enduring an influence over the minds of men, and, through them, the events of history."[3]

And what of anarchism? As engaging and imaginative as are the anarchistic ideas of Godwin, Proudhon, Bakunin, Goldman, Kropotkin, Goodman, and Bookchin, these ideas, collectively or independently, do not amount to a credible ideology. The existence of the anarchism of the Doukhobors of British Columbia proves at most only that this ideology can be sustained as the ideology of cells or sects within a vibrant political state. So the very success of Doukhobor anarchism is dependent on the rule of law, legislatures, bureaucracies, and military/police. But the most serious problem with this ideology generally is its inability to come to grips with the development of larger protective associations, including those that would qualify as what Robert Nozick calls ultraminimal or minimal states. Such groups, for reasons of security, will certainly arise and displace small groups standing at the base of anarchism. Among these larger groups will be those that are exploitive and unjust, promoting some of the very conditions that anarchists wish to avoid in governed societies.

Having disposed of the four aforementioned ideologies, what is one to say of the remaining ones: classical liberalism, conservatism, reform liberalism, democratic socialism, pacifism, feminism, environmentalism, neo-liberalism/libertarianism? Let us begin with some of the more vulnerable ideologies in this list.

Notwithstanding the engaging defence of conservatism presented by writers from David Hume, to Michael Oakeshott, and finally to Roger Scruton, the compelling impression one is left with is that conservatism, as "the politics of delay" and the ideology of deference to tradition, offers a magnified rationalization for the status quo in the interest of those who are its beneficiaries. Deference to tradition and veneration of delay turn out to be, in some societies, a recipe for the justification of such odious practices as slavery, male domination, and commercial whale hunting. The fact that conservatism would justify such practices is sufficient to condemn it for its moral insensitivity and inflexibility. In addition, given the critical nature of environmental problems, the frequency of sexual assaults against women and children, and the extent of global poverty, to take but three examples, a politics of delay is indefensible. In this sense, conservatism is not an ideology that warrants belief.

The assessment of pacifism is more challenging. It would be too blunt a criticism to say that pacifism is an ideology that does not work or cannot function. Obviously Mohandas Gandhi and Martin Luther King Jr were very effective in making this ideology work and function in modern times. In addition, both Aldous Huxley and Bertrand Russell make a compelling case regarding the catastrophic implications of nuclear war and the attractiveness of non-violence, while Ursula Franklin presents a coherent account of Quaker principles of anti-militarism and non-violence and effectively ties these matters to issues of technology and feminism. Pacifism is a political ideology that has been carefully thought out by those who advocate it. This much can be said. But can we say more? Can we say that it is credible?

Two things raise serious concerns here and tell against a positive answer. The first is that anti-militarism is rooted in many instances in religious belief. Without the inspiration of a religion to lean on, a person would be very hard-pressed to have the courage and determination and faith to practise non-violence. This can be said despite the atheism of Huxley and Russell. It is no accident that those who have practised pacifism effectively have been those with deep religious convictions. In a secular age, such as found in present-day industrialized democratic states, there is insufficient inspiration provided by religion to give strength to pacifism. The second thing that needs to be said is that, though non-violence and anti-militarism can work in some situations, there are many situations where the evidence suggests strongly that pacifism will not work. A government or state confronting drug cartels, human trafficking, and those who generally do not respect life would be hard-pressed to make non-violence work effectively. And an individual person, alone in a dark alley on a Saturday night in a big North American city, would be better off, on many occasions, taking action against an adversary than simply being non-violent. So it seems that, all things considered, pacifism is not credible.

What we are left with are the following ideologies: classical liberalism, reform liberalism, democratic socialism, feminism, neo-liberalism/libertarianism, and environmentalism, as well as the philosophical stance of secularism.

Classical liberalism and neo-liberalism/libertarianism are, as it were, two peas in the same pod. The one is the intellectual parent of the other, and so it makes sense to treat them together. The political ideology of John Locke and Adam Smith has been improved upon and sharpened by the likes of Friedrich Hayek, Mancur Olson, Robert Nozick, and Jan Narveson. Despite the rather obvious fact that nothing these advocates say addresses in a meaningful fashion the serious difficulties associated with capitalism, such as exploitation of the weak and vulnerable, decent housing for the homeless, health and education for the marginalized, gender inequality, hierarchical domination, global poverty, and pollution, nonetheless their defence of liberty (including economic liberty) as the engine of economic success seems incontrovertible. The one hook on which such liberals and libertarians hang their hat is liberty, especially economic liberty. While much can be said in defence of this liberty (even by the democratic socialist Anthony Giddens) and in defence of the ideologies that support it, the list of public goods left unaddressed by classical liberalism and neo-liberalism/libertarianism is long. At the end of the day, the list is simply too long to provide a credible starting point for political debate in the twenty-first century.

By way of contrast, reform liberalism, as advocated by Green, Hobhouse, Hobson, Dewey, and Keynes, recognizes the institutional weaknesses of classical liberalism and thereby of neo-liberalism/libertarianism in failing to prevent indecent, if not perverse, inequalities in societies vainly supported by the entitlement theory. Hobhouse, Hobson, Dewey, Keynes, and Rawls have endorsed the idea of some restrictions being placed on individual liberty in order that a communal good be realized. Seen against the toxic nature of gross inequalities in societies, this position or political ideology is defensible, especially given that as an ideology it stops short of endorsing the use of violence for remedying social ills. In addition to this, reform liberalism has the advantage of affirming tolerance through multiculturalism, as does Kymlicka, and arguing persuasively in favour of a pluralistic explanation standing at the foundation of any plausible social theory. Here, reform liberalism replaces the material monism of Marxism and the spiritual monism of Fascism with a powerful pluralism. So reform liberalism is credible.

As for democratic socialism, as seen above, this ideology stretches from utopian socialists such as Owen and Bernstein, to Tawney, to Nove, to Hampshire, and to Self. What all of these writers appear to share is a belief that, under their system, goods would be distributed in such a way that their usefulness would be maximized to promote human well-being. They all share, in their own idiom, the goal of ridding the world of the evils of want, disease, ignorance, squalor, and idleness. Underlying their position (with the exception of utopian socialists) is the idea that public goods are not achievable by individual efforts alone, but only through some centralized control and regulation. Correctly, most democratic socialists argue that equality is an ideal at which the state must aim. This is an ideal dating from Rousseau and the French Revolution, and affirms the close connection between liberty and social equality. One does not have to agree with all the subtleties of this ideology to see that it is rationally supportable. The writings of Tawney and Joseph Schumpeter, along with others listed above, are persuasive in showing democratic socialism to be a credible ideology in affirming the fundamental role played by economic forces in any social theory and in affirming the attraction of non-violence over violence in achieving more justice and liberty for citizens. This one can say, notwithstanding the difficulties this ideology has with transitional, workability, and transformational issues.

As for feminism, this ideology breaks new ground in providing insight into the public/private distinction, the gender/sex distinction, hierarchical domination, sexual equality, global poverty, and horizontal solidarity, as well as into the ethic of care. And feminism offers analytical insight into the ethic of care by focusing on three axes: universality versus particularity, respect for humanity as a whole versus respect for the individual, and finally, rights versus responsibilities. What is advocated by feminists here is, on balance, credible: it stands up to the criticism of reason. Feminism has advanced a long way since the days of Betty Friedan, and it is not a parochial movement. It has many things to say of relevance to both domestic and global politics by taking an active interest in both the hierarchical domination of women within a given society as well as in what could be called the horizontal solidarity of the marginalized in industrialized and poor societies. It also takes an active interest in the domination of poor states by rich ones, a domination that affects women and children disproportionately. The contributions of contemporary scholars such as Alice Schwarzer, Luce Irigaray, Carol Gilligan, Susan Okin, Martha Nussbaum, Val Plumwood, Nel Noddings, and Ayaan Hirsi Ali make a compelling case for the credibility of feminism in addressing human interests and needs that begin with the family and move outward.

Even if one limited the discussion of environmentalism to the *World Scientists' Warning to Humanity*, it would be sufficient to demonstrate the breadth and depth of this ideology. And it would be sufficient to demonstrate quite convincingly its sustainability. What environmentalism presents—setting aside arguable excesses in the form of deep ecology and transpersonal ecology—is a robust ideology that offers much insight on the gravity of the environmental situation. Whether one is talking about the accident at Bhopal, India, or at Chernobyl, Ukraine, or about the accelerated pace of the elimination of species of plants and animals, or the degradation of the atmosphere, water resources, oceans, soils, forests, and living species, environmentalism captures it all and argues forcefully and convincingly for the need to establish a global strategy to deal with a crisis at hand. Environmentalism is very much a credible ideology, as the contributions of Muir, Leopold, Carson, Næss, Bahro, Bookchin, and Fox make clear.

Leaving aside secularism for the moment, we are left, then, with four credible ideologies: reform liberalism, democratic socialism, feminism, and environmentalism. It is time to engage in a debate involving these four credible ideologies. Whatever the exact terms of the debate among advocates of these ideologies, there is a framework of mathematics/logic, science, and common sense and other beliefs that should serve as the background of this debate. This framework, following the American philosopher Willard Van Orman Quine (1908–2000), takes the form of a spider's web or a series of concentric circles; at the centre of this spider's web lie beliefs of which we are most sure.[4] The framework is one of epistemological holism. Among the most centrally located beliefs are those of self-awareness, awareness of others, the external world, causation, and induction. Let us call these Moorian beliefs, after the famous Cambridge common-sense philosopher, G.E. Moore (1873–1958). Also anchored near the centre are the rules of logic and mathematics, including the rules of modus ponens and modus tollens, as well as the rules of Boolean algebra and various geometries. Further removed from the centre are other types of beliefs about the world, and in ever-increasing distance from the centre are those found in the following disciplines: physics, chemistry, biology, geology, psychology, economics, history, sociology, and politics. If Quine is correct, and he seems to be, even beliefs held near the centre of this web can be dislodged.[5] This makes it look as though there is no foundation to our beliefs in general, and that all is relative. But this conclusion is precipitous and itself unwarranted. That something near the centre might be dislodged does not show that it will be, or that it will occur easily. The fact is that beliefs near the centre and even those at some distance from the centre are not easily relocated. A global postmodernist, who endorses relativism, may wish to dismiss the idea of the centrality and foundational nature of some beliefs, but to this one can reply by saying that such a postmodernist view "has not yet been built"[6] and is implausible if it chooses to make truth relative to culture, or social class, or gender, or sexual preference.[7] We are left instead with the Quinian framework, which, while not endorsing certainty, does show the difficulty of abandoning any one of the central claims.

Quine's web of belief provides the framework for adjudicating the worthiness of the beliefs found in all ideologies. Whether in the end the Moorian common-sense beliefs can be replaced by scientific beliefs is not something that needs to be determined here. Over 50 years ago, Wilfrid Sellars made it clear that some unresolved tension exists between the common-sense image (what he called the manifest image) of man-in-the world and the scientific image of man-in-the world,[8] but there is no doubt that in assessing the credibility of ideologies, scientific beliefs and Moorian common-sense beliefs stand like two sentinels guarding a pass through which all ideologies must go. The web of belief, outlined by Quine, makes for a useful framework in future assessments of feminism, environmentalism, reform liberalism, and democratic socialism.

What role in this debate is played by the political philosophy of secularism? As already stated in the chapter on secularism, this political stance is not, in fact, an ideology. The reason for this is simple: it is subject to refutation, is corrigible, and is falsifiable. The secularist asserts quite categorically that there is no evidence in favour of belief of things not empirically verified. The secularist therefore discounts the existence of supernatural entities. However, the secularist is prepared to abandon disbelief in the face of contrary evidence. From this perspective, feminists, environmentalists, reform liberals, and democratic socialists could all be secularists. The secularist could adopt any one of these perspectives but nothing in that individual's secularism demands that she or he do so. As someone largely espousing scientific values and rational thought, the secularist says nothing about topics we have discussed in connection with political ideologies: human nature, rebellion, justice, liberty, equality, origin of the state, political obligation, community, power, ends of government, preferred forms of government, rights, change, and violence. The secularist may indeed have views on each of these but not as a feature of her or his secularism. What is rejected, however, are those ideologies, notably religious fundamentalism, that presuppose the existence of things unverified. In a sense, secularism as a political philosophy is topic neutral with respect to those listed above and, in a sense, could be said to stand very near the centre of Quine's web of belief.

Appendix A
Scatter Diagram of Political Ideologies

Table A.1 Definitions of the Scatter Diagram of Political Ideologies

CL	classical liberalism
Cons	conservatism
RL	reform liberalism
M	Marxism
Comm	communism
DS	democratic socialism
FS	fascism
PF	pacifism
A	anarchism
LT	libertarianism
PC	public choice
RSFM	radical/social feminism
LFM	liberal feminism
PMFM	postmodern feminism
E	environmentalism
HFN	Hindu Fundamentalism
IFN	Islamic fundamentalism
JFN	Jewish fundamentalism
CFN	Christian fundamentalism

Appendix A

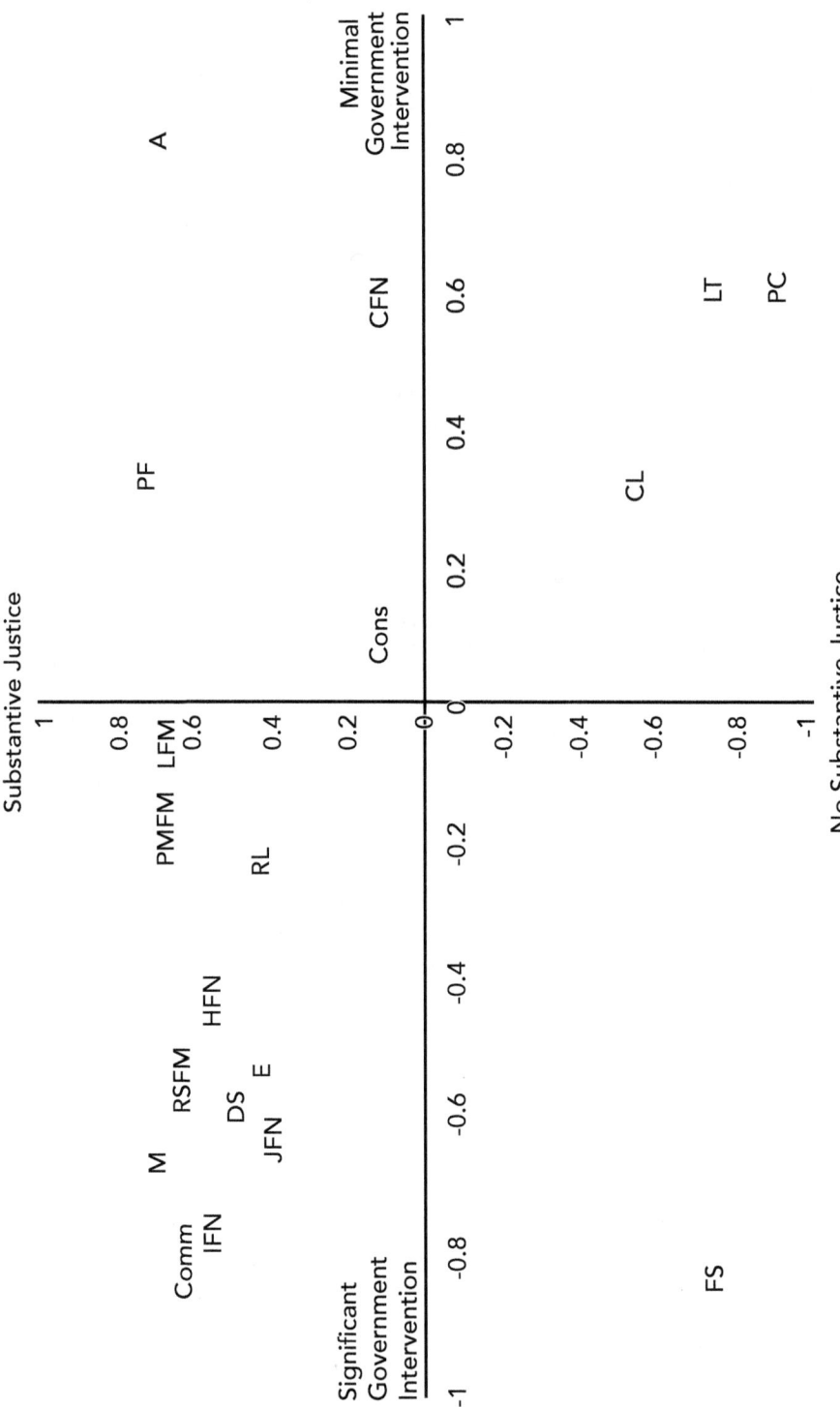

Figure A.1 Scatter Diagram of Political Ideologies

Appendix B
Comparing Political Ideologies

	Classical Liberalism	Reform Liberalism	Conservatism	Marxism
Human Nature	rational, self-interested, and acquisitive	rational, self-interested, acquisitive, not self-sufficient	intricate, passionate, and corrupted	plastic, not self-sufficient, influenced by social system
Origin of State	the social contract	the social contract	convention	class conflict
Political Obligation	desirable, though room for civil disobedience	required, though room for civil disobedience	required	required
Liberty	negative liberty	positive liberty	negative liberty	liberty for all only found in classless society
Equality	political and civil equality	political and civil equality, some economic and social equality	inequality in regard to economic and social matters	equality only in classless society
Community	downplayed in favour of individual and his or her rights	considered in shaping life of individual	emphasized through the preservation of institutions as the wisdom of the species	emphasized over individual
Power	constitutional power, democratically endorsed	constitutional power, democratically endorsed	constitutional power, democratically endorsed	dictatorship of the proletariat
Justice	procedural justice	procedural justice and some substantive justice	fairness embracing procedural justice	social, both procedural and substantive
Ends of Government	prevention of harm; night watchman approach	cultivation of the person	safeguarding tradition	classless society
Preferred Form of Government	democratic and subject to the rule of law	democratic and subject to the rule of law	aristocratic	dictatorial under the rule of the proletariat
Economic Organization	gold standard, competitive labour market, laissez-faire, dominant role played by individual	dominant role played by individual, but role for government in areas of public goods	market-driven	centralized planning, state-run
Rights	affirmation of life, liberty, and property	mixture of rights and utilities	subordinate to prudence	debunked as projections of class interests
Change	acceptable	acceptable and encouraged	unacceptable	acceptable when revolutionary
Violence	rejected except in case of rebellion	rejected except in case of unusual conditions	rejected	promoted

continued

Most of the headings for this diagram have been inspired by the work of Lyman Tower Sargent, found in his *Contemporary Political Ideologies: A Comparative Analysis*, 12th ed. (Belmont, Calif., and Toronto: Thompson/Wadsworth, 2003), pp. 15–16.

	Fascism	Feminism	Fundamentalism	Environmentalism
Human Nature	irrational, emotional	androgynous	corrupted, in need of salvation	anthropocentric
Origin of State	power, coercion, and social fitness	male domination of women	divine source	cultural product
Political Obligation	compliance required by leadership principle	compliance with just laws required	mandatory as inspired by God, Allah, Yahweh, Atman	mandatory when ecologically sound
Liberty	no individual liberty	liberty for all only found in genderless society	subject to conditions of faith	extended to all sentient beings, where possible
Equality	inequality based on leadership principle	equality in political and civil matters, as well as most economic and social matters	inequality especially for those outside the faith, but sometimes social inequality within the faith	equality in regard to interests and welfare of thing in question
Community	emphasized over individual	mixture of communitarianism and individualism	communitarianism trumps individualism	communitarianism trumps individualism
Power	dictatorial power	constitutional power, democratically endorsed along sexless lines	divine right of the state	constitutional power, democratically endorsed
Justice	interest of the strongest	based on sexual equality	faith-based	fairness in treatment of all forms of life
Ends of Government	dominance, empire-building	justice/ethic of care	faith-driven society	encouragement for biodiversity
Preferred Form of Government	dictatorial under the rule of the strongest	democratic and constitutionally based	theocratic	democratic and constitutionally based
Economic Organization	corporative economy	private enterprise and public regulations	market economy	market economy guided by tough regulations that guard sentient beings and environment generally
Rights	ridiculed as projections of liberal thinking	affirmation of gender neutrality of rights	restrictions on liberties	environmental constraints on liberty
Change	acceptable when revolutionary	acceptable when reversing discrimination	acceptable in reactionary way	acceptable when it furthers ecological agenda
Violence	promoted	rejected	promoted in some versions	generally rejected

	Pacifism	Neo-Liberalism and Libertarianism	Anarchism	Democratic Socialism
Human Nature	corrigible	acquisitive, self-interested	benign	corrigible, generally decent
Origin of State	protective instinct and thirst for power	convention/social contract	desire for power	convention, desire for protection
Political Obligation	usually desirable, but room for civil disobedience	mandatory	not obligatory, to be shunned when possible	compliance required, but room for civil disobedience
Liberty	extended to all humans	negative liberty	natural liberty	positive liberty
Equality	equality in political, civil, economic, and social spheres	political and civil equality	equality in all spheres usually endorsed	equality in political, civil, economic, and social spheres
Community	communitarianism trumps individualism	individualism trumps communitarianism	individualism trumps communitarianism	communitarianism trumps individualism
Power	constitutional power, democratically endorsed	constitutional power, democratically endorsed	individual power only	democratically endorsed and constitutionally based
Justice	procedural and substantive	procedural	procedural and substantive	flourishing life
Ends of Government	peace	prevention of harm to persons	personal fulfillment	collective and individual fulfillment
Preferred Form of Government	democratic and constitutionally based	democratic and constitutionally based	no government	democratically based
Economic Organization	market economy	market economy	market economy	centralized planning coupled with tempered free market
Rights	utility trumps rights in name of peace	rights trump utility	right to liberty takes priority	utility trumps rights
Change	acceptable when it averts violence	acceptable when it minimizes government	acceptable when it eliminates the state	acceptable when it contributes to equality
Violence	rejected	affirms violence in protecting rights	affirmed against the state	rejected

Note: Secularism adopts a position of neutrality with respect to the above headings, with the one caveat that no reference can be made to metaphysical entities such as gods, ghosts, goblins, or other such invisibles that are not empirically verified.

Glossary

Note: This glossary includes highlighted terms in the text as well as additional terms that act as semantic markers to assist those undertaking further research.

absolutism A form of government in which all political power is concentrated in the hands of either one or a few individuals.

abstract rights Rights divorced from history and tradition, singled out for praise by French Revolutionaries, and for criticism by the conservative Edmund Burke.

activism The struggle for social change. Examples include participation in the anti-Vietnam War movement, the struggle for the decriminalization of abortion, the civil disobedience advocated by Mohandas Gandhi, and the civil rights movement in the United States in the 1960s.

affirmative action Programs that ameliorate the conditions of disadvantaged individuals or groups, including those that suffer owing to race, national or ethnic origin, colour, religion, sex, age, or mental or physical disability.

agenda Term used by Jeremy Bentham in contrast to "non-agenda." Keynes asserts that the chief task of economists is to distinguish afresh those things comprising the agenda—namely, those things that are of priority to the government of the day. Again, according to Keynes, the companion task for politics and politicians is structuring a form of government that shall be capable of fulfilling the agenda.

ahimsa School of thought derived from Buddhism and Jainism that practises harmlessness, from which are derived—according to Aldous Huxley—both humanitarianism and pacifism. Cf. *satyagraha*.

alienation Being estranged from one's essential nature, work, or fellow human beings. This idea played a role in the writings of Georg Hegel and Karl Marx.

Al-Qaeda A decentralized, global network of Sunni Islamic terror cells founded by Osama bin Laden (1957–2011), the son of a wealthy Saudi Arabian entrepreneur. Al-Qaeda, which translates as "the Base," emerged in the 1980s during the waning days of the Cold War in response to the Soviet Union's 1979 invasion and occupation in Afghanistan, and gained global prominence in the 1990s and 2000 through a series of attacks, most notably on New York and Washington, DC, on 11 September 2001. The death of bin Laden at the hands of US Special Forces in 2011 has by all accounts weakened Al-Qaeda and its global jihad (holy war) agenda.

Al-Shabaab "The Youth," a Somalia-based jihadist terrorist group with allegiance to the militant Al-Qaeda. It has carried out many attacks, including those at the Westgate Centre in Nairobi, Kenya, on 21 September 2013 and at Garissa University College in Garissa, Kenya, on 2 April 2015, at both of which numerous innocent individuals lost their lives.

altruism Contrasts with egoism and manifests a concern for the interests and welfare of others. Like egoism, it can be interpreted normatively or psychologically: according to the former, people should be concerned for the interests and welfare of others; according to the latter, people are by nature so concerned.

anarchism Political ideology that advocates the abolition of authority on the grounds that coercion is evil. Without government, it aims to achieve social harmony. By the end of the nineteenth century, many anarchists became interested in the revolutionary potential of anarcho-syndicalism or revolutionary trade unionism.

androcentrism Literally, "male-centred." Feminists, whether liberal, socialist, or radical, oppose male-centredness in society for the adverse effect it has on women economically, politically, and socially.

androgyny The condition of possessing both male and female characteristics. It implies that humans are sexless persons and that therefore sex is irrelevant to social and political roles. Some feminists claim that one goal for the future should be the cultivation of individuals who are androgynous.

anti-Semitism Discrimination against Jews. This discrimination became institutionalized in the Third Reich in Germany during the years 1933–45.

antithetical ideals Ideals that are opposed. Liberty and equality are examples of antithetical ideals.

apartheid Racial segregation of blacks, whites, and "coloureds," especially as practised by the National Party in South Africa from 1948 to 1994.

Arabization The process by which people between the Euphrates River and the Arabian Peninsula transmitted their linguistic and racial features to conquered lands of Syria, Iraq, Persia, Turkestan, Egypt, Afghanistan, and Gibraltar from two centuries before the Christian era down to the ninth century CE.

Arab Spring A period of political turmoil across the Arab Middle East that witnessed the demise of several totalitarian regimes that had clung to power for decades, often with the help of Western nations that had coddled them for economic and strategic reasons. This phase began with a peaceful revolution in Tunisia, which then spread to Egypt, where protestors, aided by the Internet, forced the resignation of long-time ruler Hosni Mubarak. But this pattern did not repeat elsewhere, particularly in Libya, where a civil war had preceded the death of long-time ruler Mu'ammer Gaddafi.

aristocracy Rule by the best, usually comprising the elite or prominent citizens. One of six constitutional regimes as identified by Aristotle, the others being monarchy, polity, tyranny, oligarchy, and democracy.

Aryans In Nordic mythology, a pure-blooded and noble race of Northern Europe, especially those of German stock. Belief in this mythology served as the background for belief in Aryan supremacy as found in the Nazi Party.

Aryan Society Otherwise called "Arya Samaj," a Hindu organization founded in 1875 for the purpose of purifying Hindu religion. It affirmed the ultimate authority of one formless, omniscient God, the source of all knowledge and the authority of the Vedas.

atheistic materialism Position that affirms the centrality of material or natural forces in explanation of social phenomena while rejecting the belief in a god or gods.

autarky An economic policy that emphasizes self-sufficiency through the reduction of imported goods. In pre-Nazi Germany this idea was used by Johann Gottlieb Fichte and Friedrich List to explain the failures of economic policies based on free trade and to attack the positions of Adam Smith, Richard Cobden, and David Ricardo.

authority Legitimate political power.

autonomy and reciprocity Presupposition of classical and neo-liberal economists. This presupposition, at least as developed by James Buchanan, implies the normative claim to the effect that all persons in the trading context are natural equals, each one assumed to be equally capable of making exchanges and living with the consequences.

Banlieue Revolt (2005) A series of violent clashes between French police and youth that occurred in the poorer suburbs of Paris and other French cities in 2005. The riots—which lasted some 20 nights from late October through the middle of November that year—caused extensive property damage and two deaths. It also exposed the deep cracks between the mainstream of French society and its growing underclass of disaffected, unemployed Muslim youth of North African and Middle Eastern heritage.

barely visible family The minimal recognition given the family in John Rawls's *A Theory of Justice*. Rawls gives this minimal recognition in spite of his assumption that families are not only just but also are where moral development takes place in the first instance. Susan Okin finds this minimalism on the part of Rawls counterintuitive and in need of serious modification.

Bhagavad-Gita Song of the Lord, one of the classic writings of Hinduism composed *c*. 100 BCE. Its composition came after that of the Upanishads, composed between 600–200 BCE.

biocentrism Theory that places all life forms on the same ethical level. It condemns anthropocentrism for placing humans at the centre of ethical considerations in the cosmos.

biodiversity A term that allows the scientific community to describe the variability of life forms and ecosystems. The concept serves as a measure of ecological health and sustainability. The Amazon rainforest qualifies as a region of high biological diversity; a mono-cultural tree plantation would rank low in terms of biodiversity.

BJP Abbreviation for Bharatiya Janata Party, one of the major political parties and movements in India, established in 1951. The BJP favoured making Hindi the national language.

Boko Haram Islamic political movement in northeast Nigeria, Chad, Niger, and Cameroon. As a group it has been responsible for killing at least 5,000 civilians and for kidnapping children, including 276 schoolgirls at Chibok, Nigeria, in April 2014. Thus far, Nigerian security forces have been ineffective in combatting the terrorist activities of this group, which comprises between 7,000 and 10,000 individuals.

Bolshevism Derived from the Russian word *bolshinstvo* meaning "majority." In 1903, the Russian Social Democratic Labour Party split into two groups. The Bolsheviks, headed by Vladimir Ilyich Lenin, were radical and endorsed the use of violence; the Mensheviks, or "minority," were moderate in outlook.

bourgeoisie Term used by Marx to refer to the owners of the means of production (land, banks, natural resources) in a capitalist society. It was this class that emerged to challenge the old feudal class. Used loosely, it refers to the middle class. Cf. *proletariat*.

Brundtland report The informal name of the groundbreaking 1987 environmental report produced by the UN Commission on Environment and Development, after the Commission chair, Norwegian Prime Minister Gro Harlem

Brundtland. The report, *Our Common Future*, introduced the concept of sustainable development, and pushed global environmental problems up the political agenda and prepared the path for a series of international conferences on environment such as the Rio Conference in 1992.

bureaucracy One of five parts of the state, the others being the executive, legislature, judiciary, and military/ police. Normally, it comprises the non-elected administrative arm of the state.

caged virgin A term used by Ayaan Hirsi Ali to symbolize the subservience of women in Muslim societies, and more specifically to symbolize the sexual obsession of the patriarchal Muslim world with virginity, resulting in some societies in the predominance of female circumcision.

caliphate The designation an Islamic state. Presently the ISIS radical group is attempting to establish a caliphate in Iraq and Syria.

capabilities approach As advanced by Martha Nussbaum, an incomplete account of social justice that draws special attention to "minimum core social entitlements." These entitlements include those pertaining to bodily health, bodily integrity, thought, and emotions. Nussbaum supports this position and maintains that it is but one species of the human rights approach.

capitalism An economic system in which the means of production and the mechanics of distribution are controlled by a narrow class of property owners. It is predicated on competition, free trade, and the absence of monopoly control. In Adam Smith's writings it is clearly distinguished from two other economic systems: mercantilism and physiocracy.

caste A rigid hereditary class system—often associated with Hinduism in India—where sharp social divisions, as determined by occupations, are strictly enforced.

catallactic perspective Economic perspective, spoken of by James Buchanan, claiming that market organization replaces hierarchical organization. "Market outcomes" and "market ends," as they are called, simply emerge from the interactions of "interdependent choosers" within a structure of rules that "define the parameters of the game." On this view, the anarchism feared by Thomas Hobbes can be avoided, not by requiring an all-powerful and hierarchical sovereign power but a market backed by a limited sovereign who enforces the laws of property and contract.

Chabad Lubavitch A 250-year-old Hasidic movement. It has gained prominence and influence under the direction of the late Rebbe Menachem Mendel Schneerson of Brooklyn, New York. Under his tutelage the organization has grown from a small post-war community of Russian Hasidism to an influential global Hasidic organization.

Christian fundamentalism American religious movement that subscribes to the following beliefs: the virgin birth of Jesus, the inerrancy of scripture, a special theory of atonement, and the second coming of Jesus as a denouement of history.

civil disobedience Non-violent resistance of the law. This was advocated by Henry David Thoreau and William Lloyd Garrison in the United States, Leo Tolstoy in Russia, and most famously Mohandas Gandhi in India during the independence movement against the British in the 1940s. It was also used by Martin Luther King Jr in the civil rights movement in the United States during the 1960s.

civil rights Usually coupled with political rights to embrace those rights found in liberal constitutions: the right to freedom of speech, association, the press, conscience, and religion, and the right to vote (suffrage). These rights are contrasted with economic and social rights as applied to property, health, education, and employment.

civil society The domain of autonomous groups or associations that stand at arm's length from government. Such groups would include families, churches, unions, and clubs.

classical liberalism The version of liberalism advocated by John Locke and Adam Smith and resuscitated by neo-liberals such as Milton Friedman and Robert Nozick. Under this version of liberalism, the rights of individuals to life, liberty, and property are emphasized.

class struggle The contradiction identified by Marx as the fundamental mechanism explaining change in history. During the phase of capitalism, the capitalists, or bourgeoisie, dominated the proletariat, according to Marx. The former represented the owners of the means of production and the latter represented those who were exploited, namely, the workers.

Cold War The period that roughly lasted from 1946 to 1991 during which the former Soviet Union and the United States competed for global influence as the respective leaders of the Eastern (socialist) and the Western (capitalist) blocs. This competition unfolded through a series of direct political confrontations between the two superpowers, as well as a series of proxy wars between some of their respective allies in the developing post-colonial world in places such as Vietnam, the Korean Peninsula, Africa, and the Middle East. The Cold War threatened to turn "hot" on at least one major occasion—the Cuban Missile Crisis (1962)—when the prospect of Soviet nuclear missiles stationed off the American mainland in Cuba pushed both nations to the edge of a nuclear conflict. It would have likely destroyed planetary life as both nations maintained massive arsenals under the deterrence doctrine of Mutually Assured Destruction (MAD). The Cold War ended with the dissolution of the Soviet Union, whose state-run economy had failed to keep up with its more productive American competitor.

collective rights The view that the community is a self-originating source of moral, social, and historical claims. As argued by Kymlicka, such alleged rights or claims were the source of some of the opposition among Aboriginal peoples to Canadian Prime Minister Pierre Trudeau's White Paper of 1969. In a nutshell, this opposition expressed clearly the conflict between individualism and collectivism.

collectivism Following Friedrich Hayek, the organizing of the whole of society and its resources for a unitary end and the rejection of autonomous spheres that affirm the supremacy of individuals' ends.

colour-blind constitution Following Kymlicka, the removal of all legislation differentiating among people in terms of race and ethnicity.

common purpose Common good, general welfare, or general interest.

communism Political ideology, distinct from democratic socialism, advocating the use of violence by the vanguard of the proletariat, or intelligentsia, to overturn the dominance of the bourgeoisie. Marx was the most famous proponent of this ideology, though others included Lenin, Leon Trotsky, Mao Zedong, and Fidel Castro.

Communist Manifesto One of the central sources of Marxism, the ideology bearing the name of German philosopher Karl Marx (1818–1883). Published in 1848 during a revolutionary period in European history, this text written by Marx and his collaborator Friedrich Engels (1820–1895), argues that the "history of all hitherto existing society is the history of class struggles." The text introduced terms such as "proletariat" and "bourgeoisie" to a wider audience in detailing the nature, evolution, and (predicted) decline of capitalism. This work remains one of the most influential and referenced sources of political commentary and analysis.

communitarianism A political philosophy that emphasizes the role of community and tradition in defining the interests and rights of persons. This position has classical roots in Plato and Aristotle, but more recently it has been advanced by Alasdair MacIntyre.

comparative advantage Theory of Adam Smith, developed by David Ricardo, that nations should play upon their strengths by trading that which they produce efficiently and importing that which they do not.

consequentialism A moral school of thought that assesses the morality of actions by the extent to which they contribute to the realization of the good, conceived as including happiness or pleasure and, importantly, values other than these, e.g., self-realization and the appreciation of beauty.

conservatism Political philosophy wedded to the idea of preserving traditions, practices, and institutions. Edmund Burke is the most famous proponent of this view, though it is also advanced by David Hume and many others.

constitutionalism Belief in government working within the framework of a constitution that defines general principles of government institutions such as the legislature, executive, and judiciary. Sometimes, though not always, these general principles will specify political rights.

convention Unwritten law that lacks legal enforcement but includes various political, social, and economic penalties if not followed. Conventions play a particularly important role in the life of states, whose political institutions draw inspiration from the parliamentary traditions of the United Kingdom, where conventions are treated as if they were codified laws.

conventionalism School of moral thought maintaining that morality is grounded in practices that have evolved without the need of some contract. Non-moral examples of evolving practices include the use of money and the use of language.

corporativism (corporatism) Type of socio-political system used in Italy under Benito Mussolini with his vision of the corporate state. Under this theory, business interests and labour interests should be incorporated into the processes of government. In this way, the interests of labourers, managers, state, and nation are brought together.

cosmological argument Argument aimed at proving the existence of God as a first uncaused cause or unmoved mover of the cosmos. This argument was famously advanced by Thomas Aquinas.

crimes against humanity A concept introduced by the Greek jurist Nicolas Politis for the purpose of international prosecution of Turkish authorities in connection with atrocities they committed against the Armenian people at the end of the nineteenth century and beginning of the twentieth century. Other countries—from Germany and other Nazi-occupied nations during World War II to, more recently, Cambodia, Rwanda, and the former Yugoslavia—have witnessed such crimes. Cf. *war crimes*.

critical anti-realism Metaphysical position that claims reality is something constructed by humans rather than something existing independently of them. Pluralism and relativism are products of this position.

critical symptoms of decline As suggested by Kevin Phillips, concern over cultural and economic decay, growing religious fervour, rising commitment to faith over reason, popular anticipation of a millennial time frame, and strategic and military over-reach.

Crusades Christian military expeditions or holy wars initiated in Europe to take control of the Holy Land from Muslims. Eight such expeditions occurred from 1095 to 1212. In 1095, Pope Urban II encouraged Christian men of Europe to support the plight of their eastern Christian brothers as well as the movement of pilgrims to Jerusalem by recovering the sacred land of their lord.

Cultural Revolution Movement in China launched by Mao Zedong in 1966 to purge the country of his opponents. The Red Guard comprised the leaders of this movement. Cf. *Maoism*.

Das Kapital A text that contains many of the central positions held by German philosopher Karl Marx (1818–1883), the main founder of the political ideology bearing his name. *Das Kapital* explores and eviscerates various aspects of capitalism in laying out an extensive critique that continues to enjoy support and has courted controversy since 1867, when the first of what would eventually become four volumes appeared. The opening volume arguably qualifies as the most important, since it includes central elements of Marxist theory about the role of economics as the driving force of history. It is also the only one that appeared during Marx's lifetime. Collaborator and benefactor Friedrich Engels (1820–1895) published the remaining volumes posthumously.

deep ecology Radical environmentalism whose advocates, such as Arne Næss, focus on what they consider to be the roots of environmental despoliation. These roots extend to the anti-social aspects of industrialization, whether under capitalism or Marxism.

democracy Derived from the Greek word *demokratia*, meaning "rule by the people." In contemporary discussions this takes two forms: participatory democracy and representative democracy, the former found in some city-states of ancient Greece, and the latter found in present-day industrialized Western nations. According to Thomas Paine, democracy should strive to bring out the genius in everyone.

democratic centralism Lenin's theory that the central leadership of the Communist Party of the Soviet Union is to permit open discussions prior to, but not after, policy decisions. It affirmed the need for subordination to properly constituted authority.

democratic revolution As advocated by Peter Self, a revolution that extends democratic practices to institutions other than the state, aspires to more economic equality, and encourages the responsible exercise of rights by citizens.

democratic socialism A political ideology originating in the nineteenth century in response to the social problems created by the Industrial Revolution and the inability of classical liberalism to address these problems. It emphasizes equality, especially economic equality, as an ideal.

demography Strictly, writing about the *demos*, or people. It is a field of study that examines human populations in terms of their structure (e.g., age, sex, marital status) and dynamics (e.g., births, deaths, and migratory habits).

dialectic The art of critical examination into the truth of an opinion. Plato's dialectical thinking made use of the method of questions and answers. Hegel's dialectical idealism postulated a struggle between the thesis and the antithesis of an idea. Marx turned Hegel's dialectic on its head and established a position called "dialectical materialism," in which material things (such as classes of persons) formed the entities that engaged in the struggle as thesis and antithesis. In the thinking of both Hegel and Marx, the dialectical struggle resulted in a new synthesis being reached, which in turn formed the thesis of a new struggle.

dialectical materialism Marx's conception of social systems driven by modes of production and property relations. These causal forces influence law, religion, art, and philosophy, among other things, in a dialectical or Hegelian fashion.

dialectical naturalism A term that American philosopher Murray Bookchin coined to highlight the interplay between social and ecological problems. As such, dialectical naturalism stands in philosophical opposition to the dialectical materialism informing Marxism, since it ignores ecological concerns in framing history as the outcome of economic forces. Dialectical naturalism challenges this perspective in linking human existence to ecological limits.

dictatorship of the proletariat According to Marx and Lenin, the transitory period of rule by the proletariat that follows the overthrow of the bourgeoisie. During this time, the proletariat would have to be vigilant in suppressing attempts by the bourgeoisie to re-establish its dominance. Cf. *immiseration of the proletariat*.

difference A value espoused by some feminists, notably Irigaray and Gilligan, to affirm the distinction between women and men. Such feminists see talk of equality between the sexes as talk of sameness and the consequential elimination of those very qualities in women that should be affirmed.

difference principle A principle advocated by the liberal philosopher John Rawls according to which the lowest individual endowment is maximized. Hence, *ceteris paribus,* social goods should be distributed equally unless unequal distributions have the effect of normally providing an advantage to the poor and unless all members of society have equal chances of acquiring greater-than-average shares of social goods.

direct foreign investment (DFI) The outflowing of capital, sometimes, though not always, to poor countries with cheap labour.

disaster capitalism Following Naomi Klein, raids on the public sphere in the aftermath of catastrophic events such as Hurricane Katrina. Disaster capitalism views disasters as presenting market opportunities.

dispensationalism Christian fundamentalist view of history according to which history is divided up into seven dispensations or parts, whose character is fixed by God.

division of labour The practice of specialization in labour, noted and advocated by Adam Smith and David Ricardo in the eighteenth and nineteenth centuries but also recognized by Plato in *The Republic,* written in the early part of the fourth century BCE.

doctrine of surplus value A concept critical to the understanding of Marxism. Marx argues that the success of capitalism lies in its ability to accumulate the value, which workers create in excess of their labour costs. Entrepreneurs collect this "surplus" as profit, then reinvest portions of it into additional production capacities, thereby improving their potential to accumulate additional investment capital, not to mention profits.

dogma of heterosexuality According to Schwarzer, a culturally induced belief that ensures male sexual monopoly.

dominant protective association In the absence of government, the dominant association that exists to protect the interests of certain persons. Churches, unions, and gangs are examples of such associations that exist even in the presence of government. Cf. *protective association.*

ecology The study of the interactions of organisms with their physical environment and with each other.

economic determinism The theory that economic matters (e.g., modes and relations of production) determine social and political matters (e.g., legal and religious institutions).

egalitarianism School of thought that affirms a principle of procedural and substantive equality.

elitism Belief in rule by a minority justified either on the grounds of merit or on the grounds of inevitability, other forms of leadership being inefficient, impractical, or unattainable.

Enabling Act Legislation passed in March 1933 in Germany that transferred all legislative powers to Hitler's cabinet, including the power to amend the constitution. The third clause of the bill provided that laws enacted by the government (cabinet) should be drafted by the Chancellor (Hitler) and should come into effect the day after publication.

Enlightenment An intellectual movement of the eighteenth century in Europe that aimed to rid persons of their self-incurred subordination. It promoted the understanding of the universe, society, and humans based on reason and empirical research. Immanuel Kant is perhaps its most famous proponent.

environmentalism Political philosophy that advocates heightened sensitivity for the environment, popularly referred to by the use of the adjective "green." Its advocates range from proponents of moderate change to those such as the organization Greenpeace and deep ecologists, who are more aggressive in their approach.

equality One of three ideals of the French Revolution—the other two being liberty and fraternity (i.e., brotherhood)—that has found its way into constitutions of liberal societies as a protected ideal. It applies most frequently to the idea of procedural rather than substantive equality. Cf. *legal and political equality.*

equal liberty principle A principle advanced by John Rawls guaranteeing all members of liberal society equal political liberties, liberties of conscience, property rights, and legal rights.

essentialism Philosophical position asserting that the essence of any natural kind found in the sciences comprises a set of characteristics required of members of that kind. Applied to inanimate things, such as chemical elements, this position works better than it does when applied to biological species, such as humans, especially in light of Darwin's theory of evolution. Specifically applied to the human species, essentialism maintains that humans have an essence that exists independent of free choice. Cf. *existentialism.*

ethic of care Position of some feminists that women differ from men, with the former having an ethic of responsibility and relations in contrast to an ethic of justice and rights.

European Union Union of 27 counties in Europe. It evolved from the European Coal and Steel Community, the Common Market, and Euratom in the 1950s. Today, in many parts of Europe, it allows for free movement of goods, services, and labour and most recently makes use of a common currency, the euro.

events of 9/11 A shorthand reference for the attacks on New York and Washington, DC, by Al-Qaeda on 11 September 2011. The attacks began when 19 suicide terrorists of Arab-Muslim background seized four commercial passenger jets. The hijackers eventually crashed three of the planes into their intended targets—two planes hitting the twin towers of World Trade Center complex in New York and a third plane striking the Pentagon outside Washington. A fourth plane intended for Washington, DC, crashed in rural Pennsylvania after passengers rose against the hijackers. The Republican administration of US President George W. Bush responded to this particular event—which claimed some 3,000 victims that day—with its global War on Terror.

exchange Following Bastiat, the calculation made by all to discontinue direct production when obtaining it indirectly saves time and money.

exchange value According to Irigaray, a use-value or commodity our society or culture attaches to women and upon which our society is based.

existentialism Philosophical school of the twentieth century that emphasized freedom, individuality, and the human condition generally. Captured nicely in Jean-Paul Sartre's phrase that "we are what we choose to be."

externalities The effects on third parties resulting from transactions between two other parties under the conditions of a free market. Such externalities might include diseconomies (e.g., pollution, congestion, and ugliness) or economies (e.g., reliable postal services and efficient urban transportation).

factionalism Adverse division among the citizenry. This division results in the promotion of the interests of some citizens against the interests of the wider community.

Fascism A political ideology and movement, established by Benito Mussolini in 1919, calling for the abandonment of liberal and communist ideals, and the adoption of totalitarian ideals of leadership, ethnonational unity, irrationality, the leadership principle, and the corporate state.

federalism A constitutional system in which legislative powers are divided between a central government and regional governments at the state or provincial level. Accordingly, the citizens are subject to the legislative authority of two levels of government.

feminism A political ideology and movement that aims to advance the interests of women. Several philosophical positions have emerged from this movement, including liberal, socialist, and radical ones. These positions vary in how they deal with the dichotomy between public man and private woman, patriarchy, and sex and gender.

feminist empiricism A form of empiricism that attempts to combat inimical and androcentric-centred epistemology. Some feminists, such as Lorraine Code, reject feminist empiricism in favour of "middle-ground" empiricism that affirms "mitigated relativism" and "realism."

feudalism The peculiar association of vassalage with fief-holding established in the Carolingian Empire (ninth century CE) and that spread subsequently from the Frankish kingdom to Italy, Spain, Germany, England, Scotland, and Ireland. It was a social system of rights of lords and duties of vassals based on land tenure and personal relationships.

Fidesz A political party in Hungary. The emergence of Fidesz dates back to the concluding days of the Cold War, when Hungary became one of the first Soviet satellites to stage free, democratic elections. Political, economic, and social developments inside and outside of Hungary have subsequently pushed the party to the conservative side of the political spectrum, where it employs nationalistic rhetoric with great success to secure votes. During the most recent parliamentary election, it secured about two-thirds of the electorate.

final solution A Nazi euphemism for the organized extermination of European Jews during World War II. While German special forces (*Kampf einsatzgruppen*) might have killed up to one million Jews during the early years of the war as the German army was advancing across Europe, efforts took an organized and deadlier turn in early 1942 at the Wannsee Conference, where high-level Nazi officials signed off on an action plan to accelerate the killings by organizing them along industrial scales through the use of mass extermination camps such as the infamous Auschwitz.

First Crusade The first of a number of expeditions led by Christian states in Europe against Muslims, which commenced in 1095 and resulted in crusader strongholds in Antioch, Tripoli, and Jerusalem.

fiscal policy The spending and revenue-producing (e.g., taxation) policy of a government. As an example, Keynesian economics (economics based on the ideas of John Maynard Keynes) promoted increased spending and lower taxes when unemployment was high, and reduced spending and increased taxes when inflation was high.

forces of production Equivalent to modes of production in Marxist thinking. Accordingly, the forces of production work on property relations to produce, jointly, the superstructure comprising law, religion, philosophy, family, entertainment, etc.

freedom Made up of negative and positive freedom. The former refers to the absence of constraints imposed by the state, and the latter refers to the existence of opportunities to develop one's self.

free market A system of economic exchanges that features the near-absence of state regulation and interference. Proponents of this concept, which has never existed and may never exist in its ideal form, are skeptical if not hostile towards measures such as taxes, regulations of various sorts, and state participation in industry. They instead favour a laissez-faire attitude in economic matters based on the writings of Scottish philosopher Adam Smith.

free rider problem A problem that arises when the use of goods or benefits by someone who has not contributed to their production or creation cannot be excluded. In such a situation, it is no longer rational for such a person to contribute to the production of such goods.

French Revolution A revolution in France, beginning in 1789, that aimed to limit the powers of the monarchy and the privileges of the aristocracy and clergy. Though based on the ideals of liberty, equality, and fraternity, it quickly gave way to a reign of terror during which many were sent to the guillotine. Edmund Burke's *Reflections on the Revolution in France* was a treatise aimed at showing the strengths of conservatism against the principles of revolution.

Fuehrer Literally, "leader." In National Socialism of the Third Reich, it referred to the chief or supreme leader—i.e., Adolf Hitler. The equivalent of this position in Fascism was Il Duce—i.e., Mussolini.

fuehrerprinzip Leadership principle adhered to in Nazi Germany and Fascist Italy that required absolute obedience to the leader and correspondingly to his subordinates as in a military chain of command.

fundamentalism Ideology that emphasizes the basic ideas of a creed and the literal interpretation of sacred texts. Examples can be found in at least four major world faiths: Judaism, Christianity, Hinduism, and Islam.

futurists A group of artists whose various works informed not only modern art during the first half of the twentieth century but also Fascism. While their contributions varied, they took their name from the Futurist Manifesto penned by Italian writer Filippo Tommaso Emilio Marinetti (1876–1944) in 1909. The movement that would eventually bear the name of Marinetti's manifesto embraced modern technology and war in attacking the perceived decadence and liberalism of European society, then teetering on the edge of World War I. Marinetti himself would later serve Benito Mussolini as a cabinet minister and front-line soldier in Russia.

Gaia hypothesis View that the totality of all organic beings and their inorganic surroundings form a self-regulating system of immense complexity that functions as if it were alive itself. First developed by British scientist and physician James Lovelock (1919–), the hypothesis draws inspiration from Gaia, the bearer of all things in Greek mythology. While the scientific community initially challenged this argument, its level of acceptance has increased since its initial appearance in the 1960s.

Ganesha In Hinduism, the god of wisdom and remover of obstacles.

gender Roles women and men play in society. Cf. *sex*.

General Agreement on Tariffs and Trade (GATT) Trade regime established in 1948 to reduce trade barriers through the operation of the most-favoured-nation principle. Superseded, through the final, Uruguay Round of the GATT, by the more formalized and institutionalized World Trade Organization (WTO) in 1995.

Genocide Convention A resolution that the United Nations General Assembly adopted in 1948 to prevent and punish genocide. The convention legally defines genocide, incorporates it into international law, and spells out a punishment mechanism. The convention was a response to the Holocaust of World War II but also earlier genocides such as Armenian Genocide during and after World War I.

globalization The drive of corporations and capitalists to maximize profit through deregulation and international trade law.

global war on terror A series of measures with which the United States responded to the events of 9/11, when the Islamic terror network of Al-Qaeda successfully attacked the World Trade Center in New York and the Pentagon—symbols of America's commercial and military supremacy. Notable elements of this response included: the 2001 invasion of Afghanistan, whose Islamic fundamentalist government had offered Al-Qaeda moral and material support in staging the initial attacks; the 2003 invasion and occupation of Iraq, which the United States had falsely accused of maintaining so-called weapons of mass destruction (WMDs); and the legally sanctioned limitation if not outright suspension of various civil rights for the purpose of apprehending suspected terrorists and preventing future acts of terror through measures such as the Patriot Act, extraordinary rendition, and "enhanced interrogation techniques" such as water-boarding. Critics of this global war have argued that it has undermined the moral and economic standing of the United States.

gnosticism A syncretic religious and philosophical movement in the second century CE that emphasized esoteric knowledge. This knowledge (*gnosis*) was of the mysteries of the universe, and through gnosis came the power to overcome the demons of the universe and to answer such questions as "Whence evil?" and "Whither man?"

government In a broad sense, the central mechanisms of the state: the executive, the legislature, the bureaucracy, and the judiciary. A strikingly different definition is given by Frédéric Bastiat: government is the great fiction, through which everybody endeavours to live at the expense of everyone else.

Great Society An ambitious but unrealized agenda proposed by Democratic President Lyndon B. Johnson in the 1960s to drain the remaining pools of poverty in the United States. Developed during a period of unprecedented American political influence abroad and economic prosperity at home, this blueprint for reform followed in the ideological footsteps of the New Deal. But its success was questionable from the very start as it clashed with the challenges of the Vietnam War and the emerging conservatism of Republican Senator Barry Goldwater, whose extremist defence of personal virtues such as individual responsibility left no room for the perceived vices of the welfare state.

Great Western Transmutation Term coined by Marshall Hodgson to refer to the irreversible occurrence of cultural change, including industrialization, that occurred at the end of the eighteenth century. Cf. *Industrial Revolution*.

growing inequality of income Considered by neo-liberals to erode the support for the competitive market. Neo-liberals see job losses as an old problem in new dress, but believe growing inequality of income to be a new problem that must be addressed by policy action where appropriate. The policy action that neo-liberals endorse turns on better education and the easing of immigration.

Guantanamo Bay detention camp Detention camp and interrogation complex for individuals suspected of being (Islamic) terrorists, located within the US naval base at Guantanamo Bay, Cuba. Opened after the events of 9/11 in 2001 and the American-led war against the Taliban in Afghanistan, with nearly 800 detainees originally imprisoned there, the site with its peculiar legal status has become synonymous with American excesses in its interrogation tactics. While the treatment of prisoners has improved in the aftermath of various court rulings and political pressure, the site remains a controversial part of the American response to so-called Islamic terrorism. The Obama administration intends to close the base in 2016—it first sought to in 2009—but complex legal and political issues remain regarding the disposition of the remaining detainees, who number about 90.

Gujarat, India Site of gruesome attacks on Muslims by Hindus in 2002, resulting in more than 2,000 deaths.

Gush Emunim Hebrew for "Bloc of the Faithful." Political movement in Israel inspired by Rabbi Avraham Kook and his son, Rabbi Yehuda Kook. As a group, it is responsible for many of the settlements in territory occupied by Israel after the Six-Day War of 1967.

halakha Hebrew expression for "proper way." It refers to the accumulated laws and ordinances as they evolved from Old Testament times.

Hamas Islamic political organization active in Gaza. Ideologically influenced by the Muslim Brotherhood.

harm The effect of causing deterioration in the functioning of something. A notion heavily relied on by utilitarians, harm is too often confused with pain caused to a sentient being. Plato gives a better account of this notion than do utilitarians by advancing a functional definition.

Hasidism Sect of Orthodox Judaism that originated in eighteenth-century Poland under the tutelage of Rabbi Israel ben Eliezer (c. 1700–1760). His teachings emphasized prayer, piety, and joyful observance of God's commandments. The ideas of Hasidism are in some cases rooted in Jewish mysticism (the Kabbalah).

Hezbollah "Party of God," backed by Iran and active in Lebanon. Its present leader is Sayyed Hassan Nasrallah. It aims to eliminate Western colonialism, establish an Islamic state in Lebanon, and bring people to justice for crimes committed in Lebanon's civil war.

Hindutva Hinduness. A whole ideology has been established under this label by the BJP and VHP in India.

holism A term introduced by Jan Smuts of South Africa to refer to our understanding of the interconnectedness of the ecosystem. This is sometimes contrasted by environmentalists with an atomistic or linear approach to the ecosystem.

Holocaust Literally, "wholesale sacrifice" or "destruction." The first wholesale slaughter of a people in the twentieth century occurred in 1915 when more than a million—perhaps a million and a half—Armenians were killed by Turkish authorities. The second such slaughter occurred under the Nazis and the Third Reich of Adolf Hitler when six million Jews were exterminated under a program called the "Final Solution."

Homo economicus Simply, "economic man." Those who subscribe to the view that man is economic by nature assert that humans are ineluctably driven by the desire of endless accumulation. The thematic connection between this view of human nature and human tendencies towards greed or pleonexia, as discussed by Plato, is obvious.

hubris A term that signals the absence of humility and the abundance of arrogance. The term often appears in classical Greek literature to describe humans who dared to challenge the gods, only to experience some form of deserving retribution (nemesis). Modern uses of the term often refer to individuals whose ambitions far exceed their actual abilities.

humanism A secular philosophy that emphasizes the basic needs and interests of human beings. This idea was extant during classical times but was rediscovered during the Renaissance.

ideologue Intransigent supporter of an ideology.

imagination The faculty of humans Adam Smith emphasizes in developing his theory of moral sentiments. Pity or compassion, for Smith, depends on our own ability to imagine ourselves in the situation in which others find themselves. As he says, imagination is the source of our fellow-feeling for the misery of others.

immiseration of the proletariat Impoverishment of the working class. Marx thought that capitalism would, by virtue of economic competition, cause systemic downward mobility, eventually leading to its overthrow by the proletariat. Democratic socialists such as Eduard Bernstein and R.H. Tawney do not subscribe to this, thereby drawing a distinction between Marxists and democratic socialists. Cf. *dictatorship of the proletariat*.

imperialism The practice of a country acquiring and administering colonies and dependencies. Lenin thought imperialism to be the highest stage of capitalism. At its zenith, imperialist nations included Great Britain, Belgium, France, the Netherlands, and Portugal.

individualism Liberal view that asserts that individuals are the ultimate units of moral worth. Keynes's view explains the rise of individualism as attributable to ideas of natural liberty, social compact, toleration, utility, and rational self-love. Friedrich Hayek adds to the above, claiming that the whole of the philosophy of individualism is based on the impossibility of any person surveying more than a limited number of human needs. Thus, he concludes, the ends about which any person can have concerns will always be but a small fraction of all the needs of humans.

indivisibility Under public choice theory, the idea that benefits produced for one person are available to a wider group as well.

industrial absolutism According to Justice Brandeis of the United States Supreme Court, a form of authority that is quasi-governmental. This form of authority, possessed by industrialists, is thought by some to give rise to a private jurisdiction and relations between owners and workers that resembles that between rulers and subjects.

Industrial Revolution Dramatic industrial change in the eighteenth and nineteenth centuries that profoundly influenced the politics of modern man. This period witnessed the transformation of the modes of production from handcrafted work to mechanization, and still later to automation. The Industrial Revolution was the product of the rise of modern science, beginning with the foundation of professional scientific bodies, such as the Royal Society of London in 1660. Cf. *Great Western Transmutation*.

inerrancy A belief in religious fundamentalism that all sacred scriptures, being divinely inspired, are without error.

institutions Rule-governed structures in society. These include public institutions, such as courts, schools, and governmental and administrative units, as well as private institutions, such as the Red Cross, Exxon, and the Royal Bank of Canada.

International Monetary Fund (IMF) Established together with the World Bank under the Bretton Woods system in 1944. This organization was originally created to help ensure stability of foreign exchange. In contemporary times, the organization assists debtor and developing states. Often the assistance to debtor states is tied to the introduction by the debtor state of particular policies. A good example of this occurred under Anwar Sadat of Egypt in the early 1980s, who accepted loans from the IMF in exchange for removing subsidies for bread in Egypt—an action that eventually led to his assassination. Another example is presently underway as the IMF, together with the European Central Bank and the European Commission, aim to salvage the euro by demanding a "trimming" of the sovereign debt of Greece in exchange for economic bailouts. Initially, the agreement establishing the IMF worked on a gold exchange standard but this was discarded in 1978 in favour of allowing member states the freedom to choose their own system of exchange rate.

Invisible Committee The (so-far) anonymous authors of *The Coming Insurrection*, an anarchist text first published in France but popular throughout several Western countries. Several media accounts have linked this group with the Tarnac Nine, a group of middle-class French graduate students accused of plotting to commit various acts of terrorism.

invisible hand Notion advanced by Adam Smith to describe the convergence of individual and public interest in a free market society. It is sometimes thought to be the tendency of supply and demand towards self-correction. Economist John Maynard Keynes criticized this doctrine as unproved and almost certainly false.

iron law of oligarchy Theory of Robert Michel that organizations are controlled by the few active people in them because of the requirements of efficiency and organization.

iron law of wages Theory of David Ricardo to the effect that owners of the means of production, the capitalists, would pay the workers no more than was needed to survive.

ISIS caliphate Islamic State in Iraq and Syria; also known as ISIL (Islamic State of Iraq and the Levant), and, more commonly in the West today, Daesh. ISIS is a radical Muslim group aiming to control Iraq and Syria in the name of the Sunni version of Islam. The 2003 American war on Iraq and the failure of real power-sharing between Shi'ites and Sunnis in Iraq after the fall of Saddam Hussein resulted in the formation of ISIS.

Islamization Initially a term applied to the transformation of Middle East and North African societies under the influence of a new spiritual force called Islam in the eighth century CE. In contemporary times it is a term that populists in Europe and North American use to warn their respective societies against the perceived spread of radical Islamist ideology by recent immigrants from Arab-Muslim nations. More broadly, it assumes that Muslim practices, beliefs, and values are incompatible with what populists such as Geert Wilders have called Judeo-Christian traditions. This fear has encouraged the emergence of populist parties in several European countries and contributed to the 2011 massacre of 69 mostly young Norwegians at a youth camp at the hands of Anders Behring Breivik, who earlier the same day bombed a government building in Oslo, killing eight people.

Jim Crow A short-hand term for the body of laws that denied black Americans various political, social, and economic rights during the period that lasted from the mid-1870s to mid-1960s. Jim Crow laws segregated black Americans from white Americans by creating supposedly "separate but equal" public institutions and facilities. Attempts to break this institutionalized racism advanced in the 1950s thanks to legal rulings (*Brown v. Board of Education*) and the personal courage of figures such as Rosa Parks and Dr Martin Luther King Jr. This movement reached a temporary apex in the mid-1960s when the Democratic administration of Lyndon B. Johnson passed several groundbreaking pieces of legislation such as the Civil Rights Act (1964).

justice Along with courage and wisdom, considered by the Greeks to be one of the fundamental virtues. As a principle of right conduct it is usually thought of along procedural and substantive lines, the former applying to how one is treated (e.g., the recipient of due process) and the latter applying to the distribution of scarce goods.

Kristallnacht An episode of anti-Semitic violence, which the Nazi government of Germany orchestrated on 9 November 1938. The effects of this particular pogrom extended through several days and marked a sharp escalation in the state-sanctioned terror against Germans of Jewish ancestry. Whereas previous measures had added up to legalized discrimination, the Night of Broken Glass foreshadowed the regime's use of violence to solve what it euphemistically called the "Jewish problem."

labour theory of value An idea put forward by David Ricardo, stating that prices of goods are proportional to the value of labour embodied in them.

laissez-faire Literally, "let things be." This is a principle of capitalism espoused by Adam Smith according to which economic activity should be free of government interference. Smith was, accordingly, against protectionism.

law of nations Laws relating to the association between nations. In contemporary terms, the law of nations is known as international law with Hugo Grotius its most famous founder.

laws of nature In the study of human nature, laws that are discoverable by the use of reason alone. Thomas Hobbes is one of the more famous advocates of such laws, but others noteworthy in this regard include Plato, Aristotle, and Locke.

League of Nations International organization established in 1920 under a covenant of the Treaty of Versailles, which ended World War I. Precursor of the United Nations. The idea of the League was found in US President Woodrow Wilson's Fourteen Points, although the US Senate refused to ratify the Treaty or join the League.

lebensraum German word meaning "living space." The term was used by the Nazis between 1933 and 1945 as a slogan to justify German acquisition of territory, particularly in Eastern Europe.

legal and political equality The possession of the same legal and political rights by all members of a political community. For legal equality, these would normally include the right to procedural justice, the right to be secure against unreasonable search and seizure, and the right not to be subject to cruel and unusual treatment or punishment. For political equality, these would usually include freedom of conscience, of thought, of association, and of religion.

legitimacy Rule or governance that is justified by some principle of right or justice. According to Max Weber, the main principles were charisma, tradition, and rationality/legality.

liberalism A political philosophy emphasizing the rights of individuals within society. The first version of this philosophy—classical liberalism—was articulated by John Locke, who favoured the rights of individuals to life, liberty, and property, and by Adam Smith, who favoured economic freedoms. The second, later version—reform liberalism—was spelled out by T.H. Green, John Dewey, and John Maynard Keynes, who believed that political institutions should facilitate the goal of personal self-realization.

libertarianism A late twentieth-century anti-statist political philosophy. Economic and social freedoms, coupled with an unregulated free market, rank high among its ideals. As a political philosophy it shares much with public choice theory. This position has been advanced by Robert Nozick and Jan Narveson, both of whom advocate the widest possible domain of freedom for the individual. It differs from anarchism in that it subscribes to the notion of the minimal state.

Lockean proviso Argues that a permanent property right in a previously unowned thing is unacceptable if the position of those who are no longer at liberty to use that thing is thereby worsened. This proviso originates with Locke, who argues that in the appropriation process there must be "enough and as good left in common for others."

Maoism Political philosophy of Mao Zedong, who adapted Marxist ideas to serve China's needs. The term is sometimes used to refer to the cult surrounding Chairman Mao, a cult that reached its climax in the Cultural Revolution, launched by Mao in 1966.

March on Rome An insurrection that allowed Benito Mussolini to come to power in October 1922.

market failures Economic problems that arise from an unregulated free market system. Such problems include pollution, ugliness, and congestion.

Marxism School of political thought advocated by Karl Marx and Friedrich Engels and developed by Lenin and others. According to this ideology, the modes of production and property relations constitute the economic foundation upon which are built the political and legal superstructures. In the capitalist phase of history, which follows the aristocratic phase, Marxists believe the bourgeoisie controls the means of production—control that will not be released into the hands of the proletariat except by revolution.

materialism In political theory, the belief that natural resources and modes of production are the primary explanation of social and political structures and activity. In philosophical theory, the belief that the mind can be reduced, without residue, to the brain.

Mein Kampf Book that Nazi leader Adolf Hitler published in mid-1920s. Part autobiography, part political blueprint, part anti-Semitic tirade, Hitler wrote portions of *Mein Kampf* ("My Struggle") while serving a relatively light prison sentence for his treasonous role in the Beer Hall Putsch (1923), a failed attempt by a group of German politicians and former military leaders to seize power during the early years of the Weimar Republic, the period of parliamentary democracy that defined Germany from the end of World War I in 1918 to 1933, when Hitler seized power through a combination of electoral politics and political violence and intimidation.

Mensheviks Literally, "the minority." These individuals, followers of Georgi Plekhanov (1857–1918), were more consistent followers of Marx than were the Bolsheviks. They believed socialism would be established in Russia only after the establishment of capitalism. For Lenin and the Bolsheviks, this was too slow. Cf. *Bolshevism*.

mercantilism Economic theory common in the fifteenth and sixteenth centuries, and advocated by some as late as the eighteenth century. According to this theory, the power of a given country is determined by its wealth as measured in gold and silver reserves. State power could thus be enhanced by monopolizing these precious metals. Adam Smith argued forcefully against this theory in *The Wealth of Nations*.

meritocracy System in which social position and advancement are measured by ability and industry. In Western democratic countries, typically the public or civil service is predicated on merit, thereby impeding nepotism or patronage.

metaphysics A term used to describe the branch of philosophy that studies the fundamental nature of existence and reality or the most general features of the world. The term itself originated with an editor of Aristotle, who used it to describe a collection of works that had appeared after Aristotle's *Physics*. But these observations hardly describe the complexities and controversies that characterize this field—complexities and controversies touching on topics like the nature of the mind, freedom and determinism, causality, the nature of time, and personal identity.

militarism The glorification of military force by the state. Practical consequences of this sentiment may include substantial economic and political privileges for members of the military at the expense of other groups, and a heightened willingness to use military force in the pursuit of political goals. Militarism counts as one of the defining characteristics of Fascist regimes, but may also wax and wane in less totalitarian societies according to their circumstances.

modes of production Techniques of production, including those that are agricultural and those that are industrial.

monetarism School of economic thought that claims that the control of money supply is the most important mechanism in the control of the national economy and inflation. ·

Moral Majority A political organization founded in 1979, largely through the initiative of Jerry Falwell, for the purpose of having an effective body that could lobby government from an evangelical Christian point of view. It ceased to exist in 1989.

multiculturalism A movement and idea, in response to nationalism, that emphasizes cultural pluralism and group-differentiated rights. According to Will Kymlicka, multiculturalism as an idea is sometimes made use of by liberals against a conformist view of culture, and sometimes made use of by conservatives to support a conformist view of minority culture.

multilateralism In international affairs, a commitment to many nation-states in the joint pursuit of specific goals, as contrasted with unilateralism, bilateralism, and trilateralism.

Munich Agreement The agreement made among France, Germany, Italy, and the United Kingdom in 1938 that provided for the cession of parts of Czechoslovakia to Germany.

Muslim Brotherhood A Muslim movement established in 1928 in Egypt by Hasan al-Banna for the purpose of offsetting the negative effects of Westernization and secularism in Egyptian society.

myth of vaginal orgasm According to Alice Schwarzer, the dogma of the "sexual monopoly of men over women," which in turn provides "the foundation of the public monopoly of male society over women."

nation A group of people sharing a common language, ethnic background, history, and culture.

National Action Committee on the Status of Women (NAC) Canadian women's advocacy group founded in 1971 and largely funded by government. It became a target for cost-cutting neo-liberal governments in the 1990s and 2000s and lost funding as its white middle-class leadership was replaced by more strident visible minority leaders, but has continued as an umbrella organization supported primarily through private sources.

nationalism The veneration of the idea of the nation by a group of people who share ethnic, linguistic, historical, and religious backgrounds. Nationalism played an important role in the Balkans in the nineteenth century and in Africa in the twentieth century. In more recent years nationalism has reared its head in the former Yugoslavia, Chechnya, and East Timor, and less violently in Spain and Quebec. Sometimes this term is confused with patriotism—the love of one's homeland. The earliest mention of the term "nationalism" is in the work of Johann Gottfried Herder in 1774.

National Religious Party The political face of the Gush Emunim.

natural law Principles discoverable by reason that pertain to human conduct. It precedes all enacted law. Its advocates include Thomas Hobbes and his younger contemporary Samuel Pufendorf (1632–1694).

natural religion Religious belief based on empirical evidence, famously dissected by David Hume in his *Dialogues Concerning Natural Religion*.

natural rights Rights that people have simply as human individuals. The theory of natural rights emerged to provide political safeguards for the individual.

negative liberty The freedom one has when unconstrained by government. Cf. *positive liberty*.

neo-liberalism Political philosophy that reverts back to the economic and political ideals of classical liberalism, and couples these with the practices of deregulation, privatization, and monetarism. Equivalent to neo-conservatism.

new capitalism The twenty-first century attempt by the financial elite to roll back egalitarian gains. As described by Linda McQuaig, the effort to reverse egalitarian gains is but a return to laissez-faireism, or old capitalism, with the addition of international treaties that help to establish an "unfettered capitalism" as legally binding.

New Deal The totality of political and economic reforms that Democratic President Franklin Delano Roosevelt initiated and implemented in the United States during the 1930s to relieve and reverse the effects of the Great Depression. Some measures proved to be successful in creating employment for millions of American who lost everything in the wake of the 1929 stock-market crash that had triggered the Great Depression; other policies were less effective in the face of political and judicial resistance.

New Economic Policy (NEP) Introduced in the Soviet Union by Lenin in 1921 to rebuild the economy. It resulted in a temporary withdrawal from centralization and doctrinaire thinking. Freedom of trading and overtime for workers were permitted, as was the privatization of agriculture and small factories.

night watchman Metaphorical image used to

capture the role classical liberals, neo-liberals, and libertarians assign to the state. Accordingly, the state plays the role of ensuring the protection of the rights of life, liberty, and possessions.

nihilism The radical rejection of values as found in morality, order, and authority. This idea was advanced by Friedrich Nietzsche (1844–1900).

niqab Face veil commonly worn by women in some Muslim societies.

non-excludability Under public choice theory, the idea that goods, if supplied to one group, cannot be restricted to the people who organized its provision.

normative discourse Discourse that evaluates the moral element in persons' actions by means of criteria for what is right, wrong, good, or bad.

NSDAP Acronym for National sozialistische Deutsche Arbeiter partei, the German National Socialist German Workers' Party. The "Nazi" party emerged in 1920 out of the short-lived German Workers' Party, one of the countless nationalistic groups that had sprung up on far-right fringes of Germany's political spectrum following the end of World War I and the emergence of the Weimar Republic. Adolf Hitler eventually became its undisputed leader after he had become aware of it through his work as a government informant.

nulla poena sine lege Latin for "no penalty without a law."

Nuremberg Laws A body of laws that the ruling Nazi government of Germany passed in 1935 to legalize social Darwinistic ideas about eugenics (racial hygiene). Primarily but not exclusively, the laws turned Germans of Jewish ancestry into second-class citizens subject to humiliating treatment. While this particular community had been facing various repressions and restrictions since the Nazis had risen to power in 1933, the Nuremberg Laws institutionalized this pattern of state-sanctioned force and lowered the societal threshold for actions that eventually culminated in the Holocaust.

Nuremberg tribunals A series of trials that prosecuted and punished the surviving leaders of Germany's Nazi regime following the end of World War II. Convened in the spiritual capital of the Nazi movement, the tribunals broke new ground in international law by holding leading politicians and generals personally accountable for their actions, particularly Germany's war of aggression. It also introduced new ideas such as the concept of crimes against humanity in the aftermath of the Holocaust. While the tribunals—particularly the main trial against leading figures such as Hermann Göring—have faded into historical memory, their methodology and outcomes have significantly shaped the evolution of international law and its application in events since World War II.

ontological argument An argument aimed at proving the existence of God as a necessary being, that is, as a being whose existence cannot be denied except by asserting a contradiction. First advanced by St Anselm (1033–1109), this argument has had a checkered history with those affirming its self-evidence and others denying its rationality.

original position A hypothetical position advanced by John Rawls for determining principles of fairness. The position assumes a veil of ignorance, as free and equal citizens engage in co-operation in attempting to determine the principles by which they will live together.

Ottoman Empire Major Muslim power that controlled southeastern Europe, the Middle East, and North Africa from the thirteenth century until the early part of the twentieth century. The empire established itself in a significant way with the seizure of much of what was Byzantium in 1453.

pacifism A school of thought that believes in the non-violent opposition to the use of violence and injustice in any form. It has religious and anarchistic roots dating back to early Christianity and such figures as Tertullian and Origen.

Palestinian cause The aspiration among Palestinians to return to their homeland following their displacement in 1948 when the state of Israel was established following the end of the British colonial mandate of control for Palestine. This aspiration has given rise to the call of a "right of return" among Palestinian groups, both in the West Bank and in Gaza.

palingenetic From Greek, meaning having the attribute of being reborn or regenerated. In politics, it represents the desire to create a new political order following a period considered corrupt or decadent.

Pareto principle A principle claiming that any change in welfare must be acceptable to all those affected by it. Named after the Italian economist and sociologist Vilfredo Pareto.

Paris Commune The name of the revolutionary body that ruled Paris from March through May of 1871. This council, whose leading members represented a wide range of Marxist, socialist, and anarchist factions, rose to power during the power vacuum that had appeared following the defeat of France during its war (1870–1) with Prussia, leading to the formation of the German Reich. Regular government forces eventually ended this interregnum by storming the defensive barricades that had appeared throughout the city.

parliamentary system Sometimes called the Westminster system of government. This system

embraces a parliamentary executive and opposition with a significant role ascribed to the latter. The Westminster model contrasts with the American congressional model insofar as the executive in the American model is not based in the legislature.

participatory democracy A form of democracy in which those affected by decisions participate directly in making them. This form is usually contrasted with representative democracy.

Party for Freedom A Dutch populist party, whose agenda reflects many of the political positions held by comparable organizations across Western and Northern Europe. Defining policy positions include a marked hostility towards Islam, immigrants generally but especially from Muslim-Arab countries, and supranational organizations such as the European Union.

patriarchal government Form of government attacked by John Locke as illegitimate. Government by the patriarchs is government by the head of the family, the father. Locke's attack was directed at Robert Filmer, who attempted to legitimize the growth of government through God's license to Adam to govern Eve.

patriarchy Literally, "rule by the father." As a social system it represents the domination of women by men, and as such is strongly opposed by feminists.

perennial inflationary pressure Ongoing and inevitable inflationary pressures for higher wages. According to Joseph Schumpeter, this pressure results from high-level unemployment in capitalist society, which in turn leads to the weakening of the social framework and, curiously, to the breakdown of the capitalist society. Hence Schumpeter's turn of phrase "creative destruction."

permanent revolution A theory of Leon Trotsky (1879–1940) that promoted the idea that revolution should be continuous and international in scope. The effect of this was to institutionalize revolution.

petite difference According to Schwarzer, the biological difference possessed by men—a penis—but lacked by women that is made to have ideological consequences. These ideological consequences are rooted, however, not in biology but in culture and represent, "in every generation," identification with "dominance and subjection."

phallocentrism According to Plumwood, Schwarzer, and other feminists, a feature of contemporary discourse that places supreme importance on the male sex organ. They wish to uproot this feature and return the masculine to its own language, leaving open possibilities of a different language that would give women their own voice.

phallomorphism According to Irigaray, the shape of the phallus that our civilization privileges at the expense of women.

physiocracy An economic theory advocated by a French physician, François Quesnay, in the eighteenth century. According to this theory, the wealth of a nation consists in the consumable goods produced by the labour of that society, where the only productive labour is that which is employed upon the land. Agriculture is thus considered the key industry in the economy.

pluralism A theory maintaining that political power is distributed among interest groups in a civil society. Such groups include unions, churches, professional organizations, and ethnic groups. Accordingly, government policy is the result of the resolution of conflict among these groups.

plutocracy Literally, "rule by the wealthy." Aristotle claimed that oligarchy (rule by the few) is nothing but plutocracy.

polygamy Practice of marriage or mating where one person (male or female) has more than one spouse/mate/partner. Most commonly this involves a single male with several or many female partners (polygyny), although sometimes women have multiple spouses or mates (polyandry). John Stuart Mill examines the practice of polygamy in connection with the Mormons of the nineteenth century in his discussion of liberty.

positive liberty The liberty one has when impediments to self-realization, such as poverty and disease, are removed through government action. Cf. *negative liberty*.

positivism A philosophical perspective about the nature of scientific knowledge and research methodology. Subscribers of this perspective argue that knowledge of every kind should emerge exclusively through the use of value-neutral, quantitative observations and verifications. This view holds the scientific method in high esteem and rejects more subjective conceptions of reality.

postmodernism A school of thinking that rejects the values of the Enlightenment (truth, objectivity, value, facts, and meaning) and replaces them with consensus and subjectivism.

pragmatism A theory of knowledge distinct from rationalism and empiricism. It was advocated by William James, Charles Sanders Peirce, and John Dewey. In political theory, it refers to the practice of determining political action on the basis of practical and expedient factors rather than on the basis of rigid principles.

prisoner's dilemma A rational choice dilemma that arises when individually rational behaviour turns out to be jointly inefficient because it leads to an outcome or result that each agent prefers less than another.

procedural justice Justice that prescribes the manner in which duties, rights, and responsibilities are exercised and enforced in a court of law. Cf. *substantive justice*.

progressive taxation A system of taxation in which the percentage of income tax paid increases with one's earned income.

proletariat The class of wage earners with no property who subsist through the sale of their labour. In Marx's dialectical materialism, the proletariat would ultimately be victorious over the bourgeoisie, but only after a violent revolution. Cf. *bourgeoisie*.

property The institution of ownership. It is divided, typically, into private and public, with the former owned by individual persons and the latter owned by the state. The right to private property has been a cornerstone of liberal thinking since Locke. The institution of property is thoroughly examined by Plato in *The Republic* and by Aristotle in *Politics*.

property relations Relations of production that during stable times influence the ideology as found in law, politics, religion, art, and philosophy, and that during unstable times come into conflict with the techniques or modes of production. Property relations form part of the substructure of the social system.

protective association A term used by Robert Nozick to refer to protective organizations that naturally spring into existence in a state of nature such as that described by Thomas Hobbes and John Locke. Contemporary illustrations of such associations include gangs in urban areas, where the state, through its law enforcement agency, has lost control—i.e., where there is a no man's land.

public choice theory A theory that represents the invasion of economists in the neo-classical tradition into the domain of political science. Supporters of this position, such as Mancur Olson, argue that all organizational life can be dissolved into the competing interests of individuals.

public goods Goods whose benefit is indivisible. Illustrations of this are national defence and public health.

public sector Sector of the economy embracing services rendered by the state, including education, transportation, health, and postal services. These and other services are subject to attack by libertarians and public choice theorists.

Quakers Religious Society of Friends; Christian group originating in mid-seventeenth-century England and the American colonies, also known as the Friends. They advocate silent waiting for the "inward light" in the search for God. In addition, they were known for being non-violent advocates of social reform under the leadership of George Fox. In this respect, they represented a rediscovery of pacifism rather than its continuation.

Qur'an The holy manuscript of Muslims.

radicalism A political philosophy looking for far-reaching and sometimes immediate change. Marxists and the Jacobins of the French Revolution are illustrative of this school of thinking.

Rama In Hinduism, a mortal king elevated to the status of an avatar of Vishnu.

reactionary The intransigent resistance to change, or, occasionally, the desire to return to the past.

realism A metaphysical position affirming the existence of an independent and objective world.

realism and romance in sexual politics Contrast identified by Kate Millett between the approaches to sexual politics as found in the writings of J.S. Mill and John Ruskin from the nineteenth century.

reform liberalism A version of liberalism that developed during the nineteenth and twentieth centuries. T.H. Green of England was the first spokesperson of this movement, with John Dewey of the United States and J.M. Keynes of England soon following. What these three thinkers shared was a recognition of the importance of individual liberties and of the need for forceful state action to create conditions favourable to the enhancement of these liberties.

Regina Manifesto Manifesto of the Co-operative Commonwealth Federation as adopted in Regina, Saskatchewan, in 1933. It promoted principles regulating production, distribution, and exchange that aimed at satisfying human needs rather than making a profit.

relativism Epistemological position that denies the existence of an objective and independent world. Mitigated relativism endorses a modified form of this position by affirming a form of objectivity conditioned by historic and natural matters rooted in time and place. In other words, things are not unequivocally objective.

Renaissance The rebirth of arts and sciences following the medieval period in Europe. It is usually associated with the humanistic works of Erasmus and the rediscovery, mediated by the Arabs, of the works of Plato and Aristotle. The forces of secularism and individualism began to dominate in a way they had not since the classical period. Noteworthy among the emerging class of humanists of this period were the likes of Leonardo da Vinci, Giotto, Michelangelo, Botticelli, and Titian.

representative democracy A form of democracy in which elected candidates represent people in constituencies. It contrasts with participatory democracy, in which each citizen is free to participate in the decision-making of public policy.

republicanism Constitutional form of government. Republics stand in contrast to monarchies in lacking a monarch as head of state but possessing a political or quasi-political figure as commander-in-chief.

revolution Radical or dramatic social change in a country. Illustrations of such events include the French, American, Russian (Bolshevik), and Chinese Communist revolutions.

rights Justifiable legal or moral claim to something or to some practice. Positively enacted rights are those created by legislation, while natural rights are those which has by virtue of being a human being or sentient creature. Both Hobbes and Locke made use of the notion of natural rights, and in time this notion became incorporated into the American Declaration of Independence. Still later, it became a clarion call of many constitutions and in the United Nations Universal Declaration of Human Rights (1948). The notion is slow to emerge in political thinking, with hardly a trace of it to be found in the writings of Plato or Aristotle.

RSS Abbreviation for Rashtriya Swayamsevak Sangh, a cultural organization that applies itself to micro politics in every field in India.

sapere aude Literally, "dare to know." This was Immanuel Kant's motto of the Enlightenment.

satyagraha A philosophy of Mohandas Gandhi that excludes the use of violence and embraces civil disobedience and non-co-operation. Cf. *ahimsa*.

scientific image of the world A term Wilfrid Sellars applies to a view of the world derived from the postulation of imperceptible entities and principles pertaining to them that help to explain the behaviour of these entities. The scientific image is constructed making use of different procedures to connect theoretical entities, via different instruments, to intersubjectively accessible features of the manifest world. Sellars contrasts the scientific image with the manifest image of the world.

secularism Position denouncing religious values while affirming rational ones. Religious fundamentalism opposes it as atheistic, materialistic, and focused on a "transient and temporary reality."

Seneca Falls Convention A conference held in 1848 in Seneca Falls, New York, that marked the birth of the American women's rights movement. The Convention adopted Elizabeth Cady Stanton's Declaration of Sentiments and called for female suffrage.

Sephardim Jews who have gone to Israel from Arab lands. The ancestors of these people originally lived in Spain, but were expelled by Ferdinand and Isabella in 1492.

Sermon on the Mount The discourse of Jesus, as found in Matthew 5–7, which sets forth the principles of Christian ethics. It includes the beatitudes, Jesus's naming of those who are blessed—including the meek, the merciful, and the peacemakers.

sex Biological differences that separate men and women. Cf. *gender*.

shariah The religious law of Islam. Drawn from various sources including the Qur'an, this code covers a wide range of public and private matters among Muslims. Several Muslim nations recognize *shariah* as the solitary source of civil and criminal law, often doling out penalties deemed to be harsh and barbarous by Western observers. Other Muslim nations have combined *shariah* with elements of Western-style jurisprudence.

Shi'ism A sect of Islam found in Iran and Iraq that believes it is possible to remove the stains of sin through living a simple and devout life, as well as through suffering. It is especially attractive to the poor and dispossessed. Cf. *Sunnism*.

social contract The hypothetical agreement found at the base of civil society, according to Hobbes, Locke, and Rousseau, but disputed by Hume. This agreement moves persons from a state of nature—with a life that is "nasty, brutish, and short"—to a civil or political society.

social Darwinism A school of thought that attempts to transfer Charles Darwin's ideas regarding natural selection in biology to the cultural, social, and economic domains. Herbert Spencer, in the nineteenth century, and William Graham Sumner, in the twentieth century, promoted this school of thought.

social ecology Theory advanced by Murray Bookchin claiming that the natural world represents first nature, while the cultural, social, and political world represent second nature. The second emerges out of the first by a process of evolution, and gives rise to the present ecological crisis. Evolution has conferred a responsibility on human beings as part of second nature.

socialism Political philosophy that approves of public ownership of the means of production. Frequently the result of this is the nationalization of key industries or modes of transportation.

social responsibility Obligation to contribute to the common good. In a democracy, a balance, if not a tension, exists between social responsibility and individual liberty.

Soviet Union (Union of Soviet Socialist Republics) A former Marxist-socialist territorial state in Eurasia that existed from 1922 to 1991. The state emerged after the Bolsheviks under the leadership of Vladimir Lenin had consolidated their political and territorial control following the events of the Russian Revolution (1917) and Russian Civil War (1917–22). The state, which succeeded the Imperial Russian Empire of the Romanov dynasty, played a crucial role during the twentieth century, first as a member of the military alliance that defeated

Nazi Germany during World War II, then as the central antagonist to the United States during the Cold War.

state The executive and legislative branches of government, together with the bureaucracy, judiciary, and military/police.

state of nature Hobbesian and Lockean term that refers to the pre-political condition of humanity. Out of this condition emerges a social contract between a sovereign and his or her people (Hobbes) and among equally free individuals (Locke).

substantive justice Called "distributive justice" by Aristotle; the distribution of goods according to principles of fairness. Cf. *procedural justice*.

substructure Applies to the techniques or modes of production and the property relations in a Marxist analysis of society. Cf. *superstructure*.

suffrage The right to vote in electing public officials. The Seneca Falls Convention in 1848 represented the first major initiative in the United States to advance women's right to vote, and similar initiatives occurred in other countries such as Canada and the United Kingdom. But historically the issue of suffrage has extended not only to women but also to other identifiable groups, including blacks in South Africa and the United States, First Nations people in Canada, those who are not property owners, and, in some jurisdictions, convicted prisoners and ex-convicts. With the demise of apartheid in South Africa in the early 1990s, the advance of the civil rights movement in the United States in the early 1960s, and amendments to the Indian Act in Canada in 1960, the franchise was extended in these countries to different recognizable groups.

Sunnism The dominant sect of Islam that embraces the traditional social and legal practices of the Muslim community. Cf. *Shi'ism*.

superstructure The dimension of social life explained in terms of the means of production and property relations. According to Marxists, it includes religion, law, philosophy, culture, and the family. Cf. *substructure*.

survival of the fittest A term that English philosopher Herbert Spencer (1820–1903) coined in attempting to extend Charles Darwin's theory of evolution into social realms. This extension earned Spencer posthumous membership in the school of social Darwinism. Its various European and North American members argued that human societies must abide by the same laws as other non-human life forms. This view—which echoes but abuses Darwin's concept of natural selection—informed nineteenth-century imperialism, the eugenics (racial hygiene) movement of the early twentieth century, and German aggressions and atrocities (the Holocaust of European Jews) during the 1930s and 1940s in the quest for *lebensraum* (living space).

sustainable development A pattern of economic development that considers ecological limits. While definitions for this concept vary, the Brundtland report of 1987 defines it as "development that meets the needs of the present without comprising the ability of future generations to meet their own needs." The usage of this concept, which challenges previous assumptions about the possibility of limitless growth, has since expanded beyond its initial environmental context into other public policy fields.

syndicalism Trade unionism. It specifically refers to the version of trade unionism before 1914 in Spain and Italy.

TC Abbreviation for theological correctness. The term is inspired by its secular counterpart, PC, or political correctness.

Temple Mount Mount Moria; the most sacred site of Judaism and the third most sacred site of Islam, located in Jerusalem. In 1966 a group of Orthodox rabbis affirmed that Jews were allowed to enter the Temple Mount. The First Temple in Judaism was destroyed in 586 BCE, while the Second Temple was built in 516 BCE and destroyed in 70 CE. The hope of the members of the Temple Mount Faithful is to build the next temple on Mount Moria.

theism Belief in the existence of a god. Monotheism is the most common version of this in the Middle East and Western world.

theocracy Rule by the priestly class, or rule by those who emphasize religious beliefs in political decision-making.

theory of evolution A scientific explanation of the diversity and changes in biological life. It rests on the writings of English naturalist Charles Darwin (1809–1882), who argued in his groundbreaking publication *On the Origin of Species* (1859) that all past and present forms of life share a common ancestry, from which they evolved in separate directions through natural selection, a process that favours populations capable of adapting to their circumstances. Lacking any knowledge of genetics, Darwin developed his theory by careful observation of natural life, most famously through his journey to the Galapagos Island, a Pacific archipelago about 1,000 kilometres off the coast of Ecuador. While the scientific community of Darwin's era initially treated his views with hostility, they have since become widely accepted, despite rearguard challenges from theories that favour a religious element such as creationism or intelligent design.

Third Reich The Nazi regime in Germany from 1933 to 1945. The passing of the Enabling Act in March 1933 ended the Weimar Republic and established a new political order in Germany. The First Reich was the Holy Roman Empire (962–1806) and the Second Reich was the German Empire (1871–1918). Hitler expected the Third Reich to last a thousand years.

Third Way Efforts by social democratic parties to re-address their policies in the post-1989 period in Europe. According to Anthony Giddens, the Third Way can be viewed as progressivism.

Third World The developing countries of Africa, Asia, and Latin America. The first and second worlds comprise the industrialized democratic countries and the Soviet bloc countries led by the Communist Party.

toleration A moral dimension that reached a critical phase in European civilization during the Protestant Reformation. In contemporary times, following the works of J.S. Mill and John Rawls, discussions pertaining to it have focused on specifying how far liberal peoples are to tolerating non-liberal people's practices. The urgency of addressing this issue has arisen at the centre of the talk of the clash of civilizations and fear of the Islamization of Europe.

totalitarianism A political system in which all aspects of the community are controlled by the state. This control includes that over fundamental institutions such as schools, churches, courts, families, the workplace, and even recreational organizations. Such a system typically emerges at the far right of the political spectrum.

traditional principles of justice A notion addressed by John Rawls in his later writings. Rawls presents eight traditional principles that he takes to be standard principles of justice found among free and democratic societies. Many of these principles are drawn from writings in international law.

Treaty of Versailles Agreement that formally ended World War I between the victorious Allies (led by United States, the United Kingdom, and France) and defeated Germany. The treaty, which served as the centre plank of the post-war settlement, imposed a range of penalties on Germany, including the loss of her overseas colonies, the loss of territory along her eastern and western frontiers, restrictions on the size and composition of her military, and extensive reparation payments. The treaty also included the so-called War Guilt Clause (Article 231), which assigned Germany responsibility for the damages caused during the war. German nationalistic forces used the perceived harshness of these provisions to undermine the Weimar Republic.

"Twenty-Five Points" A political action agenda proposed by Adolf Hitler in 1920 in which he foreshadowed many of the militaristic, racist, and later genocidal policies that would define the Nazi regime that ruled Germany from 1933 to 1945. The program appeared when the National Socialist German Workers' Party (NSDAP) still existed under the label of the German Workers' Party (DAP).

United Nations Charter The treaty that founded the United Nations on 26 June 1945. Signed in San Francisco by the original member countries, the treaty describes the structure of the UN and its various bodies in spelling out organizational principles, purposes, and procedures. As of 2016, the United Nations has 193 member states.

utilitarianism A school of ethics claiming that the value of actions is to be assessed in terms of their ability to produce pleasure or pain. Early members of this school included Jeremy Bentham, James Mill, and John Stuart Mill. According to Bentham, the proper course of action was always that which produced the greatest happiness for the greatest number.

Utopia An ideal state or condition, which English humanist, philosopher, and political adviser Thomas More first coined in the early sixteenth century to describe an imaginary, far-off island with a perfect political system. This definition has since expanded to encompass creative and critical imaginations of future social, political, and technological worlds. Scholars, for example, describe Marxism as utopian, because it foresees unlimited material prosperity in lamenting current conditions. In this sense, utopian thought qualifies as contemporary social criticism.

VHP Abbreviation for Vishva Hindu Parishad. This pan-Hindu organization was established in 1964 for the purpose of bringing all Hindu sects and groups under one banner. The common identity of all Hindus is what the VHP emphasizes.

volk Literally, "the people." National Socialists attached mythological significance to this term and its referent, grafting on to the German people deeds and accomplishments of epic proportion.

Voltaire Francois-Marie Arouet (1694–1778), French Enlightenment figure who wrote extensively on philosophical topics, including optimism in philosophy, which he lampooned in his criticism of theodicy in his famous *Candide*.

vouchers In neo-liberal thought, state-endorsed coupons redeemable at either public or private institutions for purposes such as health and education. Both Milton Friedman and Alan Greenspan support the use of vouchers, at least in the field of education.

Wahhabism Sunni Islamic movement that emerged in 1747 under Ibn Abd al-Wahhab. It advocates the excoriating of anything extraneous to Islam, including Shi'ism.

war crimes Acts of soldiers or civilians that may be considered breaches of the laws or customs of war. At the conclusion of World War II, international military tribunals were established—one in Germany and one in Japan—to investigate crimes against peace, war crimes, and crimes against humanity as committed by Germany and Japan and their allies. Cf. *crimes against humanity*.

welfare state A political state with a social safety net in the form of social programs such as employment insurance, old age security, medical coverage, and assistance to those who are individually challenged.

Weltanschauung German for "world view." This notion features prominently in German philosophy and in the history of philosophy.

World Trade Organization (WTO) Successor organization to the General Agreement on Tariffs and Trade, established in 1995 through the final GATT negotiations, the Uruguay Round. This body aims to support the principles of neo-liberalism. Among the WTO's basic provisions are: concessions offered to one member must be available to other members; tariff-binding provisions can be reduced but not increased; products that enter from abroad must be treated the same as domestically produced goods; and countervailing and anti-dumping duties can be imposed to counter subsidies and dumping.

World War II The (so far) most devastating and destructive conflict in human history, whose political, social, economic, and demographic consequences can still be felt today. Spanning the globe, historians estimate that the conflict could have caused up to 80 million casualties. Key causes include the geopolitical instability that characterized the decade that followed World War I and the Great Depression of 1929. This combination of events paved the path for the emergence of expansionist totalitarian regimes in Europe (Nazi Germany, Fascist Italy) and Asia (imperial Japan). This Berlin–Rome–Tokyo "Axis" eventually launched a series of aggressive wars in their respective spheres of influence. German aggression in Europe also featured a genocidal dimension (cf. *Holocaust*). An alliance, which at its height included the British Commonwealth, the Soviet Union, and the United States, eventually succeeded in defeating this agenda due to superior military leadership and resources, including the inaugural use of nuclear weapons against Japanese targets during the waning days of the war, which also set the stage for the Cold War.

yeshiva School that instructs in Judaic learning. Its origins date back to 500–300 BCE to the time of the Men of the Great Assembly.

Zionism A Jewish nationalist movement and ideology whose goal was/is the creation and maintenance of a Jewish state in Palestine. This movement originated in Eastern Europe during the nineteenth century, and the first Zionist Congress was convened in 1897 by Theodor Herzl.

Notes

Chapter 1: Introduction
1. Some writers, such as Michael Freeden, have recently challenged the idea of placing ideologies on an axis of left and right. Whatever his misgivings, however, one can fine-tune the criteria used in this placement of ideologies in such a manner that the idea continues to have conceptual value. See Freeden, *Ideology: A Very Short Introduction* (Oxford: Oxford University Press, 2003), 79. In this case, the suggested criterion is the extent of government involvement in the individual's life that is promoted by the ideology in question.
2. A more complete list of topics included under the descriptive component is suggested by Lyman Tower Sargent in his *Contemporary Political Ideologies: A Comparative Analysis*, 12th edn (Belmont, CA, and Toronto: Thomson/Wadsworth, 2003), 15–16. A modified version of this more complete list is used as the basis for Appendix B, Comparing Political Ideologies.
3. Karl Marx and Friedrich Engels, *The Communist Manifesto* (1848; reprint, Oxford: Oxford University Press, 1992), 39.
4. Adolf Hitler, "Long Live Fanatical Nationalism," in *Political Ideologies*, comp. James A. Gould and Willis H. Truitt (New York: Macmillan, 1973), 119; originally published in *Volkischer Beobachter*, 23 Sept. 1928.
5. See I. Bernard Cohen, *The Birth of a New Physics*, rev. and updated edn (New York: Norton, 1985), 24–5, for a detailed discussion of the influence of Copernicus's ideas.
6. Ibid., 24.
7. Galileo's sin was insisting that his hypothesis was about how things actually are. Postmodernists such as the American philosopher Richard Rorty (1931–2007) seem to maintain the cultural reverse of this, claiming that scientific truths are just what researchers in physics departments happen to favour.
8. Ibid., 54, 81.
9. Ibid., 85.
10. One of the most elegant and concise summaries of scientific activity during the seventeenth century is provided by the fine English historian H.A.L. Fisher when he says, "The seventeenth century, which opens with the glowing dreams of Francis Bacon, closes with Isaac Newton's precise demonstration that the whole universe is one vast mechanism. Between these two names lies a long and splendid chapter of English scientific work, beginning with Harvey's discovery of the circulation of the blood in 1624 (reached only because he tested all his theories by experiment), carried on by Robert Boyle's epoch-making work in chemical science, illustrated by the foundation of the Royal Society, and giving to England a place in the intellectual life of Europe, which the insular reputation of a Shakespeare or a Milton could not have secured." See Fisher, *A History of Europe*, vol. 1 (London: Collins, 1935), 648.
11. It is worth noting that C.B. Macpherson has no difficulty in describing Locke's political thought as a liberal ideology. See Macpherson's editorial comments in his introduction to Locke's *Second Treatise of Government* (Indianapolis: Hackett Publishing Co., 1980), xxi.
12. Crane Brinton, John B. Christopher, and Robert Lee Wolff, *A History of Civilization*, 2nd edn, vol. 1 (Englewood Cliffs, NJ: Prentice-Hall, 1958), 496. Reform movements that preceded Luther's initiative included those of John Wyclif and Jan Hus.
13. Ibid.
14. Antonio Cassese, *International Law*, 2nd edn (Oxford: Oxford University Press, 2005), 24. Hans Morgenthau is in agreement with this interpretation of the Treaty of Westphalia when he says, "The rules of international law were securely established in 1648, when the Treaty of Westphalia brought the religious wars to an end and made the territorial state the cornerstone of the modern state system." See Morgenthau, *Politics among Nations: The Struggle for Power and Peace*, 5th edn (New York: Alfred A. Knopf, 1978), 280.
15. Brinton et al., *History of Civilization*, 555.
16. See Cassese, *International*, 23, for his discussion of J.R. Strayer's views to this effect.
17. Ibid., 24.

18. For a discussion of these points, see S.E. Finer, *The History of Government from the Earliest Times*, vol. 3 (Oxford: Oxford University Press, 1997), 1473–84.
19. See ibid., esp. 1475, 1484, for Finer's arguments concerning this.
20. There might be a tendency on the part of some scholars to commence a study of modern ideologies in the eighteenth century, owing to the start of the Industrial Revolution during this time. Finer asserts rather boldly but persuasively, "The fact is that industrialization was the most significant event in world history since agriculture succeeded food-gathering and hunting over 5,000 years before" (p. 1608). From his perspective, the industrial and technological revolution begins around 1770 and ushers in "an entirely new phase of world history" (pp. 1608–9). Without wishing to diminish the force of Finer's comment here, one might add that the industrial and technological revolution had its roots in the rise of modern science in 1660. For this reason it seems more justifiable to link the rise of modern science and the occurrence of the Industrial Revolution and to credit these linked events, in part, with transforming world history. The full story of the starting point of this transformation is told in terms of the rise of modern science, the Reformation, and the emergence of the modern nation-state in the seventeenth century.
21. Ibid., 1542.
22. Aleksandr I. Solzhenitsyn, *The Gulag Archipelago, 1918–1956: An Experiment in Literary Investigation, I–II*, trans. Thomas P. Whitney (New York: Harper and Row, 1973), 69–70.

Chapter 2: Classical Liberalism

1. For a discussion of how new, cheap technologies have led to a new generation of entrepreneurs, see "Entrepreneurialism Has Become Cool" and "Global Heroes," *The Economist*, 14–20 Mar. 2009, pp. 6 and 3, under the title, "A Special Report on Entrepreneurship." It is worth noting that although Meg Whitman served as president of eBay for 10 years, she did not actually found the company, which began as a website started by Pierre Omidyar. Of the other figures mentioned, Richard Branson is the sole founder of his enterprise, while both Steve Jobs and Larry Page co-founded their companies (Jobs with Steve Wozniak, Page with Sergey Brin). An excellent example of the entrepreneurial spirit is Michael Dell, who founded his computer company out of his university dorm room in 1984 and is *still* running it.
2. The Thirty Years' War concluded with the Peace of Westphalia in 1648. Following this treaty, the overpowering influence of two poles of authority—the Pope, as head of the Catholic Church, and the Emperor, as head of the Holy Roman Empire—was gradually diminished and replaced by the growing authority of the state. See Antonio Cassese, *International Law*, 2nd edn (Oxford: Oxford University Press, 2005), 22–5.
3. See Peter Jones, *Rights* (London: Macmillan, 1994), 78, for a discussion of this point.
4. S.E. Finer makes these points in connection with liberalism in the nineteenth century, but it is obvious that they were present in a nascent form in the seventeenth century. See Finer, *The History of Government from the Earliest Times*, vol. 3 (Oxford: Oxford University Press, 1997), 1570–1.
5. The story is complicated here. Industrialization in Britain and Belgium was in advance of its time and may have facilitated constitutionalization in those two states. Elsewhere on the Continent, constitutionalization was the achievement of liberals prior to industrialization. See ibid., 1609–10.
6. Steven Erlanger, "Did Liberalism Win? It's Not Clear," *International New York Times*, 14 Sept. 2015, 7.
7. Ibid.
8. Serge Schmemann, "Testing the Limits of Western Ideals," *International New York Times*, 14 Sept. 2015, 6.
9. John Locke, *The Second Treatise of Government*, ed. Thomas P. Peardon (1690; reprint, New York: Macmillan, 1989), Chap. IV, para. 22.
10. Ibid.
11. Ibid., Chap. IX, paras 124, 125, 126, 128.
12. Ibid., Chap. IV, para. 22.
13. Thomas Hobbes, *Leviathan* (1651; reprint, Oxford: Oxford University Press, 1996), Chap. XIII, para. 9.
14. Locke, *Second Treatise*, Chap. III, para. 19, Chap. II, paras 6, 7.
15. Ibid., Chap. III, para. 19.
16. The obvious point should be repeated here. Hobbes experienced the English Civil

War shortly before he wrote *Leviathan*, whereas Locke experienced it when he was comparatively young and roughly 50 years before he wrote his *Second Treatise*. The result is a picture of man drawn by Locke that is much more benign than that drawn by Hobbes. The most obvious explanation of this is their historic proximity to the Civil War.
17. Locke, *Second Treatise*, Chap. II, para. 6.
18. Ibid., Chap. IX, para. 124. The great Canadian political theorist C.B. Macpherson affirms the importance of property rights for Locke when he claims: "Everyone sees that Locke's assertion and justification of a natural individual right to property is central to his theory of civil society and government." See Macpherson, *The Political Theory of Possessive Individualism* (Oxford: Oxford University Press, 1962), 197.
19. Locke, *Second Treatise*, Chap. II, para. 15.
20. Ibid., Chap. III, para. 21.
21. Nozick has worked this out in some detail in *Anarchy, State, and Utopia* (New York: Basic Books, 1974), Chap. 2.
22. Cassese, *International Law*, 73.
23. Some may wish to say that there is no executive power in the state of nature for Locke. This is mistaken.
24. Locke is aware that besides the magistrates, the legislature acts as an umpire for disputes. He speaks of "[c]ivil society being a state of peace amongst those who are of it, from whom the state of war is excluded by the umpirage which they have provided in their legislative, for the ending all differences that may arise amongst any of them" (*Second Treatise*, Chap. XIX, para. 212).
25. Here Locke's terminology differs from its use in Chap. IX, para. 123, where "property" means "life, liberty, and possessions." This change of meaning in Locke is something one has to live with.
26. The names for these criteria come from Macpherson, *Political Theory*, 199–203.
27. Locke, *Second Treatise*, Chap. V, para. 33. The third criterion also comes to be known as the "Lockean proviso," which reads roughly: no initial appropriation can occur if it makes others worse off. See Nozick, *Anarchy, State, and Utopia*, 178–82; Jan Narveson, *The Libertarian Idea* (Peterborough, ON: Broadview Press, 2001), 176–7.
28. Locke, *Second Treatise*, Chap. V, para. 49.
29. According to Locke, God gave the world to "the use of the industrious and rational." Ibid., Chap. V, para. 34.
30. Ibid., Chap. V, para. 40.
31. Ibid., Chap. V, para. 50.
32. Ibid., Chap. V, para. 46.
33. Ibid., Chap. V, para. 50. The only brake that Locke applies to this is that it not injure others. But it is unclear how much he wishes to read into the notion of injury.
34. Adam Smith, *The Nature and Causes of the Wealth of Nations*, ed. Kathryn Sutherland (1776; reprint, Oxford: Oxford University Press, 1993), IV, i, 277.
35. Locke, *Second Treatise*, Chap. VIII, paras 96, 97.
36. Ibid., Chap. VIII, paras 97, 98.
37. Ibid., Chap. VIII, para. 98.
38. Ibid., Chap. VIII, para. 119.
39. Ibid.
40. Ibid.
41. Ibid., Chap. VIII, para. 121.
42. Ibid., Chap. VIII, para. 122.
43. Macpherson, *Political Theory*, 252.
44. Locke, Chap. XIX, paras 224, 225, and 226.
45. Locke, Chap. XIX, para. 230.
46. Hereafter cited as *Wealth of Nations*.
47. For an extensive discussion of this and related points, see Charles L. Griswold Jr, *Adam Smith and the Virtues of Enlightenment* (Cambridge: Cambridge University Press, 1999), 259–310.
48. Smith, *Wealth of Nations*, II, iii, 203. It is striking how similar this comment is to that of Hobbes, when he says, "I put for a general inclination of all mankind, a perpetual desire of power after power, that ceaseth only in death." Hobbes, *Leviathan*, Part I, Chap. 11, para. 2.
49. Smith, *Wealth of Nations*, II, iii, 205.
50. Adam Smith, *The Theory of Moral Sentiments*, ed. Knud Haakonssen (1759; reprint, Cambridge: Cambridge University Press, 2002), IV, 1.10. Smith claims, "And it is well that nature imposes upon us in this manner. It is this deception which rouses and keeps in continual motion the industry of mankind." See also Griswold, *Adam Smith*, 262, where he says, in discussing *The Theory of Moral Sentiments*, that "Smith also argued that it [happiness] is governed by 'deception' of the imagination. The deception consists in the belief that by attaining all of those good things we strive for we will be happy

51. Smith, *Wealth of Nations*, I, i, 15.
52. Emma Rothschild and Amartya Sen, "Adam Smith's Economics," in *The Cambridge Companion to Adam Smith*, ed. Knud Haakonssen (Cambridge: Cambridge University Press, 2006), 323.
53. Smith, *Wealth of Nations*, II, ii, 185.
54. Ibid., I, v, 37. He says, "But though labour be the real measure of the exchangeable value of all commodities, it is not that by which their value is commonly estimated."
55. Ibid., V, i, 440.
56. Ibid., V. i., p. 441.
57. Ibid.
58. Ibid.
59. Gore Vidal, *Julian* (Bungay, England: Reprint Society of London, 1964), 262. The strategy of "circuses over bread," however, is not always welcome. A case in point involves Toronto's bids to host the 1996 and 2008 Olympic Summer Games. Both bids were opposed by anti-Games activists who had organized under the name "Bread Not Circuses" to draw attention to the fact that money should be spent on fighting poverty and hunger rather than a multi-million dollar sporting event.
60. Smith, *Wealth of Nations*, IV, ii, 289.
61. Stephen Holmes has provided, in a brilliant study, some telling points in favour of the claim that Hobbes offers a normative theory of self-interest. This notwithstanding, Holmes is mistaken when he says, "The classical liberal theory of self-interest must be reinterpreted as a normative doctrine, therefore, and not a descriptive one." See Holmes, *Passions and Constraint: On the Theory of Liberal Democracy* (Chicago: University of Chicago Press, 1995), 4. Whatever may be the truth of Holmes's remarks in connection with Hobbes, they do not fit Smith, who, more than anyone else, is the paragon of a classical liberal. And this is true even though he offers a descriptive account of self-interest.
62. Smith, *Wealth of Nations*, IV, ii, 289–92.
63. Ibid., IV, ii, 289.
64. Ibid., IV, ii, 292.
65. Ibid.
66. Ibid., IV, ii, 294, 301.
67. Ibid., IV, ii, 292.
68. Ibid., IV, ii, 292–3.
69. Smith does not directly confront a point made by Farley Mowat when he said of Northmen who came to Scotland in the seventh century that "[m]arauding tended to be much more profitable than trading. A raider had no need to invest capital in trade goods; nor did he have to content himself with whatever the other fellow might choose to offer in exchange. A third and even more cogent reason for preferring raiding to trading was that few things acquired by way of trade could surpass in value a commodity best acquired by force." See Mowat, *The Farfarers: Before the Norse* (Toronto: Seal Books, 1998), 139.
70. Smith, *Wealth of Nations*, IV, ii, 299.
71. Ibid., IV, i, 286.
72. Ibid.
73. Ibid.
74. Ibid., IV, vii, 345.
75. Smith (ibid., IV, vii, 341) seems to oppose the use of religion to make this injustice right when—describing the Council of Castile's plans for the Amerindians encountered by Columbus—he says, "The pious purpose of converting them to Christianity sanctified the injustice of the project."
76. Smith (ibid., IV, vii, 359) recognizes that the sole purpose of the maintenance of colonies is monopoly control. Mercantilism is logically tied to both monopoly control and colonization.
77. Ibid., IV, vii, 346.
78. Smith affirms the existence of rights when he talks about the "sacred rights of mankind" and "respect for the rights of one another." Ibid., IV, vii, 346, 364.
79. Locke, *Second Treatise*, Chap. I, para. 3; Smith, *Wealth of Nations*, V, i, 407.
80. Locke, *Second Treatise*, Chap. V, para. 34.
81. Griswold, *Adam Smith*, 265.
82. Smith, *Wealth of Nations*, IV, ix, 388.
83. See Kathryn Sutherland's editorial comments in Smith, *Wealth of Nations*, 574, n. 388. Evidently Smith was dissuaded from dedicating his book to him owing to Quesnay's death.
84. Smith, *Wealth of Nations*, IV, ix, 390. The other two great inventions were the invention of writing and the invention of money.
85. Ibid., IV, ix, 388.
86. Ibid.
87. Ibid., IV, ix, 392.
88. Ibid., IV, ix, 380.

89. Ibid., IV, vii, 346.
90. Kant actually entered the university in 1740, and was technically a student for the next 15 years. During this period he was obliged to interrupt his education for some eight years because of his financial situation; he worked as a private tutor in the Königsberg area, although continuing his scholarly research and publishing two short works in addition to the *General History.*
91. Immanuel Kant, "What Is Enlightenment?" in *On History,* trans. Lewis White Beck et al. (1784; reprint, Indianapolis: Bobbs-Merrill, 1963), 3.
92. Ernst Cassirer, *The Philosophy of the Enlightenment,* trans. Fritz C.A. Koelln and James P. Pettegrove (Boston: Beacon Press, 1951), 7.
93. Hans Reiss, ed., *Kant's Political Writings,* trans. H.B. Nisbet (Cambridge: Cambridge University Press, 1970), 3.
94. Ibid.
95. The Enlightenment was a period of European intellectual history in the seventeenth and eighteenth centuries during which intellectuals affirmed the power of reason to lead to progress and happiness.
96. Immanuel Kant, *Groundwork of the Metaphysics of Morals,* trans. H.J. Paton (1785; reprint, New York: Harper and Row, 1964), 96. This is the third version of the categorical imperative of Kant. The first version reads: "So act that your will can regard itself at the same time as making universal law through its action"; the second reads: "So act as if you were through your maxims a law-making member of the kingdom of ends." See ibid., 88, 89, 100.
97. See Reiss, ed., *Kant's Political Writings,* 23, for this formulation.
98. Ibid., 25.
99. Ibid.
100. Ibid., 26–7.
101. Ibid., 28.
102. Smith, along with the physiocrats, sees perfect liberty as the only effectual expedient for the greatest annual reproduction. See Smith, *Wealth of Nations,* IV, ix, 388–9.
103. Ibid., V, iii, 459.
104. Ibid., IV, vii, 350.
105. See John Dwyer, "Virtue and Improvement: The Civic World of Adam Smith," in *Adam Smith Reviewed,* ed. Peter Jones and Andrew S. Skinner (Edinburgh: Edinburgh University Press, 1992), 192, for this descriptive label applied to Smith.
106. Smith, *Wealth of Nations,* V, iii, 459.
107. Ibid., I, ii, 21–2.
108. Ibid., I, ii, 22.
109. Ibid.
110. See Rothschild and Sen, "Adam Smith's Economics," 321–2, for an elaboration on this point.
111. Ibid., 321.
112. Smith, *Wealth of Nations,* V, i, 429.
113. Ibid., V, i, 431, 435.
114. For an extensive and able discussion of this problem, see Alec Nove, *The Economics of Feasible Socialism* (London: George Allen and Unwin, 1983).
115. Peter Self, *Rolling Back the Market: Economic Dogma and Political Choice* (New York: St Martin's Press, 2000), 46.
116. See ibid., 43–8, for a discussion of Hayek's views. See also F.A. Hayek, *The Road to Serfdom* (London: Routledge and Kegan Paul, 1944).
117. Smith, *Wealth of Nations,* I, viii, 65.
118. Self, *Rolling Back the Market,* 43–8.
119. See ibid., 44, for a discussion of Hayek's view. See also Friedrich A. Hayek, *Economic Freedom* (Oxford: Basil Blackwell, 1991), 388, where he speaks about the "mirage of social justice," claiming that in a market economy "the whole conception of social or distributive justice is empty or meaningless." This is but another way of rejecting merit or desert as useful notions.
120. Smith, *Wealth of Nations,* V, i, 407.
121. Rothschild and Sen, "Adam Smith's Economics," 349–50.
122. Smith, *Wealth of Nations,* I, viii, 78–83; IV, vii, 338ff.
123. Ibid., IV, vii, 364.
124. Smith, *Wealth of Nations,* IV, vii, 341.
125. See Rothschild and Sen, "Adam Smith's Economics," 350.
126. This is the question Self leaves for the classical liberal to answer.
127. Locke, *Second Treatise,* Chap. VI, para. 52ff.
128. See Sutherland's introduction to Smith, *Wealth of Nations,* xxxiii.
129. Ibid.

Chapter 3: Conservatism

1. Bruce Bawer, "Heirs to Fortuyn? Europe's Turn to the Right," *Wall Street Journal,* 23 Apr. 2009, http://online.wsj.com/article/SB124043553074744693.html.
2. Konstanty Gebert, "Poland Shouldn't Shut

Out Refugees," *International New York Times*, 10 Sept. 2015, 6.
3. Ibid.
4. Ibid.
5. Rick Lyman, "Rift Emerges in Europe as East Resists Migrants," *International New York Times*, 14 Sept. 2015, 4.
6. Dakshana Bascaramurty, "Woman at Centre of Niqab Debate Says She's Educated, Not Oppressed," *Globe and Mail*, 8 Oct. 2015.
7. Daniel Leblanc, "Heated Battles Fuel Final Debate," *Globe and Mail*, 3 Oct. 2015, A3.
8. David Hume, *A Treatise of Human Nature* (1739), reprint ed. L.A. Selby-Bigge (Oxford, Clarendon Press, 1888), Book III, Part III, s. I, 577.
9. Ibid., Book III, Part II, s. I, 477.
10. Ibid., Book III, Part II, s. I, 484.
11. Ibid.
12. Ibid., Book III, Part II, s. I, 481.
13. Ibid.
14. Ibid., Book III, Part II, s. I, 483.
15. Ibid.
16. The difference between a social contract and a convention is not trivial. The former, as this expression is used by Locke and Rousseau, implies consent on the part of those who are party to it; the latter does not imply consent. To the contrary, Hume says that "this convention is not of the nature of a promise." It seems that, for Hume, a convention is what results from a general sense of common interest expressed as an agreement without the interposition of a promise. See ibid., Book III, Part II, s. II, 490. This should be contrasted with what Locke says in the *Second Treatise*, paras 95–9, and with what Rousseau says in the *Social Contract*, Chap. VI.
17. Hume, *Treatise*, Book III, Part II, s. II, 485.
18. Ibid., Book III, Part II, s. II, 489.
19. Ibid., Book III, Part II, s. II, 490.
20. Ibid.
21. Ibid.
22. Ibid.
23. Ibid., Book III, Part II, s. II, 490–1.
24. Ibid., Book III, Part II, s. II, 487.
25. Ibid., Book III, Part II, s. II, 489.
26. Ibid.
27. Ibid., Book III, Part II, s. II, 494.
28. Ibid., Book III, Part II, s. II, 495.
29. Ibid., Book III, Part II, s. II, 501.
30. Ibid., Book III, Part II, s. II, 491.
31. Ibid., Book III, Part II, s. II, 497.
32. David Hume, "On Suicide" (1777), in *Selected Essays*, ed. Stephen Copley and Andrew Edgar (Oxford: Oxford University Press, 1993), 322.
33. Hume, *Treatise*, Book III, Part II, s. II, 489.
34. Ibid., Book III, Part II, s. II, 498.
35. Ibid., Book III, Part II, s. II, 496.
36. Ibid., Book III, Part II, s. II, 489.
37. Ibid., Book III, Part II, s. II, 485, 491.
38. Ibid., Book III, Part II, s. II, 490.
39. Ibid.
40. This conclusion is hardly surprising, given the richly textured empiricism of Hume in the rest of his philosophical writings.
41. Donald W. Livingston, *Hume's Philosophy of Common Life* (Chicago: University of Chicago Press, 1984), 333.
42. For an insight into T.S. Eliot's conservatism, especially as it pertains to the possibility of a Christian society, see his *Christianity and Culture* (New York: Harcourt, Brace, and World, 1949).
43. For an insight into Eric Voegelin's conservatism, see his *The New Science of Politics* (Chicago: University of Chicago Press, 1952).
44. Livingston, *Hume's Philosophy*, 330.
45. Ibid., 332.
46. Ibid., 333.
47. Edmund Burke, *Reflections on the Revolution in France* (1790; reprint, Oxford: Oxford University Press, 1993), 58–9.
48. Ibid., 61.
49. Ibid., 59.
50. Ibid.
51. Ibid., 185.
52. Ibid.
53. Ibid., 249.
54. Ibid., 59.
55. Ibid.
56. Ibid., 96.
57. Ibid., 97.
58. Ibid., 60.
59. Ibid.
60. Ibid., 61.
61. Ibid.
62. Ibid., 62.
63. Ibid., 60.
64. Ibid.
65. See ibid., 168–70, where he contrasts the ways of the French Revolution with his ways; the former combines reform with abolition and destruction, the latter with preservation, circumspection, and caution.
66. Ibid., 56, 57, 69, 90, 91, 92.

67. Ibid., 58.
68. Noel O'Sullivan, *Conservatism* (New York: St Martin's Press, 1976), 84.
69. Burke, *Reflections*, 91.
70. Quoted by O'Sullivan, *Conservatism*, 13. The letter was written by Burke as a response to attacks on him by the Duke of Bedford and the Earl of Lauderdale.
71. Burke, *Reflections*, 170.
72. Ibid.
73. O'Sullivan, *Conservatism*, 22.
74. Burke, *Reflections*, 90–1. Here Burke definitely contrasts with Hume, who did not see humans as intrinsically religious.
75. Ibid., 185.
76. Ibid.
77. Ibid., 169.
78. Alasdair MacIntyre, *Whose Justice? Which Rationality?* (Notre Dame, IN: University of Notre Dame Press, 1988), 12.
79. MacIntyre (ibid., 8) claims that Burke, along with John Henry Newman, "are explicitly concerned with tradition as their subject matter." It seems more correct to say that Burke is implicitly concerned with tradition, for he rarely articulates his position in terms of this notion.
80. Burke, *Reflections*, 171.
81. O'Sullivan, *Conservatism*, 27.
82. Anthony Quinton, "Conservatism," in *A Companion to Contemporary Political Philosophy*, eds Robert E. Goodin and Philip Pettit (Oxford: Basil Blackwell, 1993), 244.
83. Michael Oakeshott, *Rationalism in Politics* (London: Methuen, 1962), 168. See also Quinton, "Conservatism," 247, who challenges the claim that conservatism is not an ideology. As well, see Stephen Nathanson, *Economic Justice* (Upper Saddle River, NJ: Prentice-Hall, 1998), 8, 28, for the linkage between theory and ideology.
84. Oakeshott, *Rationalism*, 168.
85. Ibid., 169.
86. Ibid., 172.
87. Ibid., 173–83.
88. Ibid., 183.
89. Ibid.
90. Ibid., 184.
91. Ibid., 188–9.
92. Ibid., 192.
93. Ibid., 195. Oakeshott's inclusion of Pascal and Montaigne illustrates the conservative tendency of philosophic skepticism, which both of them espouse.
94. Roger Scruton, *A Political Philosophy* (London: Continuum, 2006), ix.
95. Ibid., 62.
96. Ibid., 1–29, 34, 62, 67, 83, 89, 121. Scruton (p. 141) speaks of "a refusal to accept the sacred in the only form that has actually been offered to us." He also speaks (p. 142) of the vanishing of the religious virtues of innocence, piety, and shame that accompany the evaporation of the sacred.
97. Ibid., 117.
98. Ibid., 108.
99. Ibid., ix.
100. Ibid.
101. Ibid.
102. Roger Scruton, *Culture Counts* (New York: Encounter Books, 2007), 2.
103. Scruton, *Political Philosophy*, 2, 20, 22.
104. Ibid., 34–7.
105. Ibid., 41–6.
106. Ibid., 83–4.
107. Ibid., 88–91.
108. Ibid., 96.
109. Ibid., 96–100.
110. Ibid., 131–5, 139–40.
111. See Scruton, *Culture Counts*, 75–82, esp. 78, and Scruton, *Political Philosophy*, 103–17, especially 106–11. But it should be noted that Scruton may be incorrect in thinking this does represent a return to the Enlightenment. Scruton seems to think, for example, that religion is to be valued as a social glue, whereas the Enlightenment questioned religion in the face of its social utility. It is not clear whether Scruton understands that this may be a problem for him, for he does go so far as to acknowledge, "The Enlightenment . . . also cleared away the mist of religious doctrine." See Scruton, *Culture Counts*, 81.
112. Quinton, "Conservatism," 245.
113. Hume's view is that the psychological mechanisms of sympathy ensure that we are "mirrors of each other." He thinks each of us internalizes the attitudes that others have towards us—hence our sense of ourselves is a product of the perception outsiders have of us. See Hume, *Treatise*, 369.
114. See Arnold J. Toynbee, *A Study of History* (Oxford: Oxford University Press, 1960). He sums up the nature of the breakdown under three points: a failure of creative power in the creative minority, a withdrawal of allegiance and mimesis on the part of the majority, and

a loss of social unity in the society as a whole. See Toynbee, *Study of History*, 923–4.
115. See Jared Diamond, *Guns, Germs, and Steel: The Fates of Human Societies* (New York: Norton, 1999). Diamond explores, among other things, an evolutionary account of the unequal distribution of wealth and power across societies and civilizations.
116. A.C. Grayling, *The Heart of Things: Applying Philosophy to the 21st Century* (London: Phoenix, 2005), 233.
117. Oakeshott, *Rationalism*, 174.
118. Run mainly by the Catholic and Anglican churches, the schools also had as their goal the conversion of Native children to Christianity.
119. It overruled *Plessy v. Ferguson*, 163 U.S. 537, 16 S.Ct. 1138, 41 L.Ed. 256 (1896), which interpreted the Fourteenth Amendment in a way consistent with separate but equal treatment. See *Brown v. Board of Education of Topeka*, 347 U.S. 483, 74 S.Ct. 686, 98 L.Ed. 873 (1954), and the judgment on relief ("*Brown II*"), 349 U.S. 294, 75 S.Ct. 753, 99 L.Ed. 1083 (1955). Judge Garrity's obituary in the *New York Times*, 18 Sept. 1999, includes information on his busing decision, and on citizen opposition to both it and the judge; see http://www.nytimes.com/1999/09/18/us/judge-w-arthur-garrity-jr-is-dead-at-79.html.
120. Burke, *Reflections*, 62.
121. Ibid., 60–1.
122. Alan Sokal and Jean Bricmont, *Intellectual Impostures: Postmodern Philosophers' Abuse of Science* (London: Profile Books, 1998).
123. Judith Butler, "Contingent Foundations: Feminism and the Question of Postmodernism," in *Feminists Theorize the Political*, eds Judith Butler and Joan W. Scott (New York: Routledge, 1992), 3–21.
124. Jacques Derrida, "Of Grammatology: Exergue," in *Jacques Derrida: Basic Writings*, ed. Barry Stocker (London: Routledge, 2007), 46.
125. Scruton, *Culture Counts*, 70.
126. Scruton, *A Political Philosophy*, 117.
127. Scruton, *Culture Counts*, 81.
128. See Robert Nozick, *Invariances* (Cambridge, MA: Harvard University Press, 2001), 54. For his definition of relative truths, see p. 19; for his finding that the social-relativist claim about truth is "highly implausible," see p. 60.
129. Daniel Stoffman, "An Ideology, Not a Fact," *Globe and Mail*, 22 Aug. 2009, A11.
130. Oakeshott, *Rationalism*, 176.
131. Ibid., 172.
132. Burke, *Reflections*, 137.
133. Adam Smith, *The Nature and Causes of The Wealth of Nations*, ed. Kathryn Sutherland (1776; reprint, Oxford: Oxford University Press, 1993), I, ii, 23.
134. See Quinton, "Conservatism," 257, for an elaboration of organicism.
135. Thomas Paine, *The Rights of Man* (1791; reprint, Oxford: Oxford University Press, 1995), 90–3.
136. John Stuart Mill, *On Liberty* (1859; reprint, Oxford: Oxford University Press, 1991), 64–5.
137. Ibid., 78.

Chapter 4: Reform Liberalism

1. While it is correct to say that "the Industrial Revolution got into its stride only after 1780," the revolution was largely a nineteenth-century phenomenon. See George Lichtheim, *Imperialism* (Harmondsworth, England: Penguin Books, 1971), 49.
2. Four developments helped produce the Industrial Revolution of the nineteenth century: the use of power-driven machines in production; increased efficiency in the production of coal, steel, and iron; the construction of railroads; and the expansion of banking facilities. See Crane Brinton, John B. Christopher, and Robert Lee Wolff, *A History of Civilization*, 2nd edn, vol. 2 (Englewood Cliffs, NJ: Prentice-Hall, 1958), 189.
3. David Moberg, "The Meltdown Goes Global: It Is Time to Rethink Capitalism," *In These Times*, 15 Apr. 2009, http://www.inthesetimes.com/article/4361/the-meltdown_goes_global.
4. Josh Gerstein, "Obama: The Beginning of the End," *Politico.com*, 18 Feb. 2009, http://www.politico.com/news/stories/0209/18958.html.
5. Paul Krugman, "The M.I.T. Gang," *International New York Times*, 25–26 July 2015, 9.
6. Ibid.
7. Ibid.
8. Ibid.
9. Paul Krugman, "Zombies against Medicare," *International New York Times*, 28 July 2015, 11.
10. Nick Malkoutzis, "How Serious a Threat to Democracy Is Inequality?" *Kathimerini*, 16 Sept. 2015, 3.

11. John Stuart Mill, *On Liberty* (1859), reprint ed. and introd. John Gray (Oxford: Oxford University Press, 1991), 15.
12. Ibid., 5.
13. See C.B. Macpherson, *The Life and Times of Liberal Democracy* (Oxford: Oxford University Press, 1977), 52–5, and John Plamenatz, *Man and Society*, vol. 2 (London: Longmans, 1963), 254–5, for discussion of differences between Bentham and John Stuart Mill.
14. See Peter Jones, *Rights* (London: Macmillan, 1994), 78, where he says that "the association between natural rights and social contract was no accident."
15. Mill, *On Liberty*, 13–14.
16. Ibid., 14.
17. Ibid., 104.
18. John Gray, introduction to Mill, *On Liberty*, xviii.
19. This is a distinction drawn by Isaiah Berlin in his *Four Essays on Liberty* (Oxford: Oxford University Press, 1969), 118–72, esp. 122.
20. Mill, *On Liberty*, 116.
21. See ibid., 117, where he says, "and if the parent does not fulfil this obligation, the State ought to see it fulfilled."
22. John Stuart Mill, *Principles of Political Economy* [1848] and *Chapters on Socialism* [1879], reprint ed. and introd. Jonathan Riley (Oxford: Oxford University Press, 1994), 377–8.
23. Mill, *Chapters on Socialism*, 436.
24. Mill, *Principles*, Bk. II, Chap. 1, s. 3, 14–15.
25. Ibid., Bk. IV, Chap. 6, s. 2, 126.
26. T.H. Green, "Liberal Legislation and Freedom of Contract," in *Works of T.H. Green*, 2nd edn, ed. R.L. Nettleship, vol. 3 (London: Longmans, Green, and Co., 1888), 370–1.
27. Ibid., 372.
28. Ibid., 374.
29. Peter Self, *Rolling Back the Market: Economic Dogma and Political Choice* (New York: St Martin's Press, 2000), 38–9.
30. L.T. Hobhouse, *Liberalism* (1911; reprint, Westport, CT: Greenwood Publishers, 1980), 1.
31. Ibid., 77–107.
32. Ibid., 108.
33. Ibid., 108–9.
34. J.A. Hobson, *Confessions of an Economic Heretic* (London: George Allen and Unwin, 1938), 196.
35. Ibid., 204.
36. Ibid., 192.
37. Ibid., 195.
38. J.A. Hobson, *Economics and Ethics* (London: D.C. Heath and Co., 1929), 213.
39. See Hobson, *Confessions*, 199.
40. Ibid.
41. Ibid.; Hobson, *Economics and Ethics*, 223.
42. Hobson, *Economics and Ethics*, 219.
43. Ibid., 221.
44. Hobson, *Confessions*, 210.
45. Hobson, *Economics and Ethics*, 167–8.
46. Hobson, *Economics and Ethics*, 213.
47. John Dewey, *Liberalism and Social Action* (New York: G.P. Putnam, 1935; reprint, New York: Capricorn Books, 1963), 56.
48. John Dewey, "The Future of Liberalism," *Journal of Philosophy* 32 (1935): 225.
49. Ibid., 226.
50. Ibid.
51. Ibid., 227.
52. Ibid.
53. Ibid.
54. Noel O'Sullivan, *Conservatism* (New York: St Martin's Press, 1976), 12.
55. Dewey, "The Future of Liberalism," 228.
56. Ibid.
57. Dewey, *Liberalism and Social Action*, 62.
58. Dewey, "The Future of Liberalism," 228.
59. Ibid., 229.
60. Dewey, *Liberalism and Social Action*, 63.
61. Ibid., 61.
62. Dewey makes the point, with force and conviction, that "[i]n the broad and final sense all institutions are educational in the sense that they operate to form the attitudes, dispositions, abilities and disabilities that constitute a concrete *personality*" (emphasis added). See Dewey, "Democracy and Educational Administration," *School and Society* 45 (1937): 460. See also p. 458, where he explicitly refers to the institutions of family, church, and school.
63. Ibid., 457.
64. Ibid., 458.
65. Ibid.
66. Ibid., 457.
67. Ibid., 461.
68. See Richard Wollheim, "Democracy," *Journal of the History of Ideas* 19 (1958): 225–42, esp. 241–2.
69. This problem is amply canvassed and assessed by Kenneth Arrow in his *Social Choice and Individual Values* (New York: Wiley, 1951). A contemporary discussion of Arrow's ideas can be found in Amartya Sen,

The Idea of Justice (Cambridge, MA: Belknap Press of Harvard University Press, 2009), 92–3, 110, 279–81, 314, 410.
70. A classic case of this occurred in Canada with the wartime internment of Japanese Canadians. See *Co-operative Committee on Japanese Canadians v. Attorney General for Canada*, [1947] A.C. 87, a decision by the Judicial Committee of the Privy Council.
71. For a discussion of these four weaknesses in democracy, see Wollheim, "Democracy," 236–7.
72. John Maynard Keynes, "Am I a Liberal?," in *Essays in Persuasion: The Collected Writings of John Maynard Keynes*, vol. 9 (London: Macmillan, 1931; reprint, Cambridge: Cambridge University Press, 1972).
73. Ibid., 297–8.
74. Ibid., 301.
75. Ibid., 305. That Keynes saw himself as a liberal is revealed in his comment, "Yet—all the same—I feel that my true home, so long as they offer a roof and a floor, is still with the Liberals." See Keynes, "Liberalism and Labour," in *Essays in Persuasion*, vol. 9, 309.
76. Dewey, "Democracy and Educational Administration," 458–9.
77. Keynes, "Am I a Liberal?," 306.
78. Ibid., 301.
79. Ibid., 300. His reason for so thinking is that future governments, he believes, will have to take on many duties they avoided in the past.
80. Ibid., 302. The motifs picked up here by Keynes are very similar to those dealt with by Bertrand Russell in his excellent book, *Marriage and Morals* (London: George Allen and Unwin, 1929). Writing only four years after Keynes's address on liberalism, Russell discusses, among other things: marriage, prostitution, trial marriage, the family, divorce, eugenics, and population. Given that both Russell and Keynes were at Cambridge University in the 1920s, it is quite possible that cross-fertilization of ideas occurred.
81. Keynes, "Am I a Liberal?," 302.
82. Keynes, "Am I a Liberal?," 303. The notions of fairness and reasonableness (distinct from rationality) have re-emerged in the writings of John Rawls. See Rawls, *A Theory of Justice* (Oxford: Oxford University Press, 1972).
83. Keynes, "Am I a Liberal?," 304.
84. Ibid. Keynes is himself quoting from Professor Commons, though he gives no citation.
85. John Maynard Keynes, "The End of Laissez-Faire," in *Essays in Persuasion*, vol. 9, 282.
86. Ibid.
87. The explanation for the success of these principles lies, thinks Keynes, in the rhetorical skills of economic textbooks, in the weakness of the opponents of these principles, notably protectionism and Marxism, and finally in the conformity between the principles and the needs and wishes of the business world of the day, notably the captains of industry.
88. Ibid., 287–8.
89. So named after Friedrich von Hayek (1899–1992), the Austrian economist and political philosopher, who affirmed individualism and the market.
90. Ibid., 288.
91. Ibid.
92. Ibid., 289.
93. Ibid.
94. Ibid., 290.
95. Ibid., 291.
96. Ibid.
97. Ibid., 292. The dissemination of data on a great scale comes close to, but is not quite identical with, the practice of transparency so applauded in neo-liberal circles.
98. Ibid.
99. Ibid. Keynes speaks normatively here, for he says, "I do not think that these matters should be left entirely to the chances of private judgement and private profits, as they are at present" (emphasis added).
100. Ibid.
101. Of the Conservative Party, Keynes says, "How could I bring myself to be a Conservative? They offer me neither food nor drink—neither intellectual nor spiritual consolation." Keynes, "Am I a Liberal?," 296.
102. Rawls actually says of justice that it is the first virtue of social institutions. See Rawls, *A Theory of Justice*, 3.
103. Ibid., 19.
104. Ibid., 12. See also p. 137.
105. Ibid., 17.
106. Ibid.
107. Ibid., 136.
108. Ibid., 19.
109. Ibid., 143.
110. Ibid., 137.
111. Ibid., 60 ff.
112. Ibid., 131.
113. Ibid., 132.

114. Ibid., 133.
115. Ibid., 134.
116. Ibid., 135.
117. Ibid., 250.
118. Ibid., 60.
119. It has been persuasively argued that not only does the liberty principle take priority over the difference principle, but that the difference principle itself is really two principles (the difference principle and the fair opportunity principle), with the fair opportunity principle taking priority over the difference principle. See Jonathan Wolff, "In Front of the Curtain," *Times Literary Supplement*, 7 Mar. 2008, 10–11.
120. Rawls, *A Theory of Justice*, 60, 61, 250. See also Stephen Nathanson, *Economic Justice* (Upper Saddle River, NJ: Prentice-Hall, 1998), 82–8, esp. 87.
121. Rawls, *A Theory of Justice*, 61.
122. Ibid.
123. Ibid.
124. Nathanson, *Economic Justice*, 87.
125. Rawls, *A Theory of Justice*, 73.
126. John Rawls, *The Law of Peoples* (Cambridge, MA: Harvard University Press, 1999), 3–4.
127. Ibid., 14.
128. Will Kymlicka, *Liberalism, Community, and Culture* (Oxford: Clarendon Press, 1989), 1.
129. Will Kymlicka, *Contemporary Political Philosophy: An Introduction*, 2nd edn (Oxford: Oxford University Press, 2002), 338.
130. Ibid., 338.
131. See ibid., 345.
132. See ibid., 347.
133. See ibid., 349.
134. See ibid., 368.
135. See ibid., 369.
136. See ibid., 333.
137. Ibid., 328.
138. Ibid., 267–8, 312–13.
139. Ibid., 312–13.
140. Vic Satzewich and Lloyd Wong, eds, *Transnational Identities and Practices in Canada* (Vancouver: University of British Columbia Press, 2006), xi.
141. Lloyd Wong and Vic Satzewich, "Introduction: The Meaning and Significance of Transnationalism," in Satzewich and Wong, eds, *Transnational Identities and Practices*, 1.
142. Ibid.
143. Sedef Arat-Koc, "Whose Transnationalism? Canada, 'Clash of Civilizations' Discourse, and Arab and Muslim Canadians," in Satzewich and Wong, eds, *Transnational Identities and Practices*, 216–17.
144. Rawls, *The Law of Peoples*, 14.
145. See T.H. Green, "Lectures on the Principles of Political Obligation," in *Works of T.H. Green*, vol. 3, 351, where he says, "There ought to be rights, because the moral personality . . . ought to be developed; and it is developed through rights."
146. See John Rawls, *Justice as Fairness: A Restatement* (Cambridge, MA: Harvard University Press, 2001), esp. 94–134, where he examines the difference principle and basic equal liberties principle against the background of the two traditions of utilitarianism and social contractarianism.
147. Plamenatz, *Man and Society*, vol. 2, 267.
148. See Herbert Spencer, *The Man versus the State* (1884; reprint, Oxford: Penguin Books, 1969), 66–7.
149. Rawls, *The Law of Peoples*, 361.
150. Dewey, *Liberalism and Social Action*, p. 27.
151. Self, *Rolling Back the Market*, 50.
152. Hobhouse, *Liberalism*, 108.
153. See the penetrating discussion of Hare and Rawls by J.L. Mackie, *Ethics: Inventing Right and Wrong* (Harmondsworth, England: Penguin, 1977), 92–7.
154. See Jones, *Rights*, 58–65, esp. 61, for a discussion of this second point.
155. Self, *Rolling Back the Market*, 48.
156. Ibid., 43.
157. C. Wright Mills, *The Marxists* (Harmondsworth, England: Penguin Books, 1962), 31.

Chapter 5: Marxism

1. All these factors are identified by Kevin Phillips in his *Bad Money: Reckless Finance, Failed Politics, and the Global Crisis of American Capitalism* (New York: Viking, 2008), 207.
2. See Leo Panitch, "Thoroughly Modern Marx," *Foreign Policy* (May/June 2009), http://www.foreignpolicy.com/story/-cms.php?story%20id=4856&print=1; Christopher Hitchens, "The Revenge of Karl Marx," *The Atlantic* (Apr. 2009), http://www.theatlantic.com/doc/200904/hitchens-marx.
3. Leo Panitch is Canada Research Chair in comparative political economy at York University in Toronto, while Christopher Hitchens was an *Atlantic* contributing editor and a *Vanity Fair* columnist.

4. Hans-Werner Sinn, "Why Greece Should Leave the Eurozone," *International New York Times*, 27 July 2015, 8.
5. Yanis Varoufakis, *The Global Minotaur: America, Europe, and the Future of the Global Economy* (London: Zed Books, 2013), 17.
6. Ibid., 18.
7. Ibid., 34–5.
8. Authorship of *The Communist Manifesto*, for example, is ascribed to both Marx and Engels. As Engels, however, stated in the preface to the German edition of 1883: "The basic thought running through the Manifesto . . . belongs solely and exclusively to Marx."
9. The text of *Capital* was written by Marx between 1863 and 1883 (vol. 1: 1867; vol. 2: 1863–78; vol. 3: 1863–83). The volumes were published in German in the following years: 1867 (vol. 1); 1885 (vol. 2); and 1894 (vol. 3).
10. Karl Marx, *On the Jewish Question* (1843), in *The Marx-Engels Reader*, ed. Robert C. Tucker (New York: Norton, 1972), 24.
11. Ibid., 26.
12. Ibid., 32–3.
13. This appears to be one of the first mentions of the public/private distinction in Western philosophical thinking. It is a distinction about which feminists have much to say.
14. Ibid., 33.
15. Ibid., 44.
16. Ibid., 38 (where he quotes approvingly from Bauer), 44.
17. Ibid., 46.
18. Ibid., 47.
19. Karl Marx, *Contribution to the Critique of Hegel's Philosophy of Right: Introduction* (1843), in *The Marx-Engels Reader*, 11.
20. Marx's awareness of the relevance of Feuerbach and Strauss to the issue of religion and human self-alienation is found in his writings *Theses on Feuerbach* (1845), *The German Ideology* (1845–6), and *The Economic and Philosophic Manuscripts* (1844), reproduced in part in *Marx: Selections*, ed. Allen W. Wood (New York: Macmillan, 1988).
21. For a thorough canvassing of the serious discussions that ensued in the nineteenth century concerning the historicity of Jesus, and for D.F. Strauss's role in these discussions, see the much neglected work of Albert Schweitzer, *The Quest of the Historical Jesus* (1906; reprint, New York: Macmillan, 1962), 68–120. Schweitzer, an intellectual force in his own right, drives home the point that Strauss's literary work "is one of the most perfect things in the whole range of learned literature," and one that produced "a storm of controversy." Schweitzer humorously adds, when speaking of Strauss's book *The Life of Jesus* (1835), "The fertilising rain brought up a crop of toad-stools," implying the barren nature of the immediate debate that followed. See Schweitzer, *Quest of the Historical Jesus*, 96.
22. It is difficult not to believe that Marx was influenced by the "biting scorn" Strauss showed his opponents. Here is one comment by Strauss, directed against the thoughts of a pastor at Tubingen: "This offspring of the legitimate marriage between theological ignorance and religious intolerance, blessed by a sleep-walking philosophy, succeeds in making itself so completely ridiculous that it renders any serious reply unnecessary." Quoted ibid., 97.
23. Marx, *Contribution to Critique of Hegel*, 12.
24. Ibid.
25. Karl Marx and Friedrich Engels, *The Communist Manifesto* (1848; reprint, Oxford: Oxford University Press, 1992), 3.
26. Some of the philosophical background to this comment of Marx is in order. Thomas Hobbes maintains, "The value, or worth of a man, is as of all other things, his price." Hobbes, *Leviathan* (1651; reprint, Oxford: Oxford University Press, 1996), Chap. 10. In contrast, Immanuel Kant maintains, "In the kingdom of ends everything has either a *price* or a *dignity*." Kant makes use of the exclusive disjunction here: ends have dignity or price, but not both; price admits of equivalence and replacement, dignity does not. Kant, *Groundwork of the Metaphysic of Morals*, trans. H.J. Paton (1785; reprint, New York: Harper and Row, 1964), 102. Marx seems to believe that in the bourgeois or capitalist society, Hobbes's view triumphs; but his indignation, found throughout the *Manifesto* and other writings, suggests that he believes Kant's view should triumph. However, since Marx is very careful in his use of normative discourse, how one should interpret Marx in getting at his "true meaning" is problematic. This issue will raise its head later in this chapter.
27. Marx and Engels, *The Communist Manifesto*, 5–7.

28. Ibid., 21.
29. See the author's preface, where he says, "My dialectic method is not only different from the Hegelian, but is its direct opposite." Karl Marx, *Capital* (1867–94; reprint, New York: Modern Library, 1906), 25.
30. Marx and Engels, *The Communist Manifesto* 21.
31. Ibid., 3.
32. Marx must have been influenced by Adam Smith here. Smith says, "The discovery of America and that of a passage to the East Indies by the Cape of Good Hope, are the two greatest and most important events recorded in the history of mankind." Smith, *The Nature and Causes of the Wealth of Nations*, ed. Kathryn Sutherland (1776; reprint, Oxford: Oxford University Press, 1993), Book IV, vii, 363.
33. Marx and Engels, *The Communist Manifesto*, 6, 10, 23.
34. Ibid., 15.
35. Ibid. Marx says, "The modern labourer, on the contrary, sinks deeper and deeper below the conditions of existence of his own class."
36. Ibid., 23.
37. Ibid., 13, 17, 39.
38. Karl Marx, *A Contribution Toward a Critique of Political Economy*, S.W. Ryazanskaya, trans. (New York: Internatioal Publishers, 1975), p. 20–1.
39. Marx's words are: "At a certain stage of development, the material productive forces of society come into conflict with the existing relations of production or—this merely expresses the same thing in legal terms—with the property relations within the framework of which they have operated hitherto." Marx, *Critique of Political Economy*, 21.
40. Ibid.
41. Aristotle, *Politics* (Oxford: Oxford University Press, 1995), Book III.9, 1280a7.
42. This is a point reaffirmed in Marx, *Capital*, 15, where he says, "My stand-point, from which the evolution of the economic formation of society is viewed as a process of natural history, can less than any other make the individual responsible for relations whose creature he socially remains, however subjectively he may raise himself above them."
43. See Marx, *Critique of Political Economy*, 21.
44. Marx, *Capital*, 837.
45. Ibid., 13.
46. Ibid., 695. As he says, "Even Malthus recognises over-population as a necessity of modern industry, though, after his narrow fashion, he explains it by the absolute overgrowth of the labouring population, not by their becoming relatively supernumerary."
47. Ibid., 509.
48. Ibid., 494–5.
49. Ibid., 322.
50. Ibid., 712.
51. Ibid.
52. Ibid., 714.
53. Ibid., 754ff.
54. Marx is at pains to show the parallel between his undertaking in *Capital* and those of other scientists. Hence he says, when speaking of political economy and economic forms, "To the superficial observer, the analysis of these forms seems to turn upon minutiae. It does in fact deal with minutiae, but they are of the same order as those dealt with in microscopic anatomy." Ibid., 12. He continues by pressing the analogy between the activity of the physicist and his own activity.
55. Robert C. Tucker, ed., *The Marx-Engels Reader* (New York: Norton, 1972), xxxiii.
56. The words of Robert Tucker are instructive here: "Value judgements resting on moral convictions abound in Marx and Engels. Thus they not only analyze exploitation and the division of labour in society, but morally condemn these phenomena as evil. Yet, there is almost no abstract discussion of ethics in their voluminous writings." Ibid., 666.
57. Marx, *Capital*, 668.
58. Karl Marx, *Inaugural Address of the Working Men's International Association* (1864), in *The Marx-Engels Reader*, 380.
59. Ibid., 380–1.
60. Karl Marx, *The Civil War in France* (1871), in *The Marx-Engels Reader*, 527.
61. Ibid., 570.
62. Ibid., 574.
63. Karl Marx, *Speech at the Anniversary of the People's Paper* (1856), in *The Marx-Engels Reader*, 428.
64. One of the strongest advocates of this interpretation of Marx is Allen Wood. He says, "Far from criticizing capitalism on the basis of rights or principles of justice, Marx does not even believe that capitalism is an unjust system." Shortly thereafter he says, "That capitalism should turn out to be just for Marx should therefore not surprise us." See Allen W. Wood, "The Marxian Critique of Justice," in *Marx, Justice, and History*, eds Marshall Cohen, Thomas Nagel, and Thomas

Scanlon (Princeton, NJ: Princeton University Press, 1980), 13.
65. Ibid., 13. Wood says that for Marx, justice turns out be "the highest expression of the rationality of social facts from the juridical point of view."
66. Ibid., 32.
67. Ibid., 14–15.
68. Ibid., 16.
69. Ibid.
70. Ibid., 18.
71. This contrasts with the view taken by Pruzan. See Elliot R. Pruzan, *The Concept of Justice in Marx* (New York: Peter Lang, 1989), 6.
72. Allen W. Wood, *Marx Selections* (New York: Macmillan, 1988), 13. Clearly, Wood speaks pejoratively about all ideologies here, but does not offer an explanation for so speaking. Chapter 1, offers the beginning of an explanation: ideologies tend to be dogmatic and incorrigible. Wood needs to offer some explanation that does not at the same time demolish his position on Marx, though it is far from clear that the explanation rooted in incorrigibility is available to him.
73. Wood, "Marxian Critique," 35.
74. Ibid.
75. Ibid., 40.
76. Ibid., 41.
77. These two arguments are reconstructions by P.G. Peffer of arguments given by Allen W. Wood. See Peffer, *Marxism, Morality, and Social Justice* (Princeton, NJ: Princeton University Press, 1990), 340–1, 349.
78. Friedrich Engels, *On Morality* (1878), in *The Marx-Engels Reader*, 667.
79. Ibid., 667–8.
80. As Tucker says, however, in his assessment of Engels's *Anti-Dühring* (1878), "The mode of reasoning seems more distinctively characteristic of Engels' mind, however, than Marx's." See Tucker, *The Marx-Engels Reader*, 666.
81. But note C. Wright Mills's point: "Marx's view of class consciousness is, however, as utilitarian and rationalist as anything out of Jeremy Bentham." See Mills, *The Marxists* (Harmondsworth, England: Penguin, 1962), 113.
82. Karl Marx, *The Economic and Philosophic Manuscripts* (1844), in *The Marx-Engels Reader*, 60.
83. Ibid.
84. Ibid., 60–1.
85. Bertell Ollman, *Alienation: Marx's Conception of Man in Capitalist Society* (Cambridge: Cambridge University Press, 1971), 151; Marx, *Manuscripts*, 61.
86. Marx, *Manuscripts*, 63.
87. Marx says, rather surprisingly, that private property is the product, the result, the necessary consequence, of alienated labour. He draws an analogy with the gods, which he thinks are the effect, not the cause, of intellectual confusion. See ibid., 65. He admits that later, in the cases of both gods and property, the relation becomes reciprocal, i.e., private property produces alienation, and intellectual confusion produces gods.
88. Ibid., 58.
89. Ibid.
90. Ibid.
91. Ibid., 59.
92. Ibid.
93. Ibid., 66.
94. Ibid., 70.
95. Ibid.
96. Ollman, *Alienation*, 132.
97. Marx and Engels, *The Communist Manifesto*, 26.
98. Ollman, *Alienation*, 134.
99. Karl Marx, *The Economic and Philosophic Manuscripts* (1844), in *Marx Selections*, 44.
100. Marx and Engels, *The Communist Manifesto*, 19–20.
101. John Plamenatz, *Man and Society*, vol. 3 (London: Longman, 1992), 204.
102. See Mills, *The Marxists*, 85, for this account of the notion of exploitation.
103. Robert R. Alford and Roger Friedland, *Powers of Theory* (Cambridge: Cambridge University Press, 1985), 271.
104. See ibid., 272, for an elaboration on these and other points.
105. Pluralism is a theoretical position on the decision-making process that claims that persons' interests are articulated by different interest groups and that government policy is simply the result of compromises among the competing interests of these groups.
106. Marx and Engels, *The Communist Manifesto*, 23.
107. See Peter Alter, *Nationalism* (London: Edward Arnold, 1985), 1–9, for a discussion of definitions of nationalism. He points out correctly that this term was first introduced by Herder in 1774.
108. Ibid., 4–5.

109. Ibid., 152.
110. Eduard Bernstein, *Evolutionary Socialism* (1909; reprint, New York: Schocken Books, 1961), 212.
111. R.H. Tawney, *Equality*, 4th edn (London: Unwin Books, 1964), 69.
112. Alec Nove, *The Economics of Feasible Socialism* (London: George Allen and Unwin, 1983), 1.
113. Mills, *The Marxists*, 104.
114. Ibid., 105.
115. Varoufakis, *The Global Minotaur*, 18.
116. Mills, *The Marxists*, 122.
117. Ibid., 123.

Chapter 6: Democratic Socialism

1. While the intent of Marx is clear here, he sometimes blunts his sharp points by talking about critical-utopian socialism and communism at one and the same time. See Karl Marx and Friedrich Engels, *The Communist Manifesto* (1848; reprint, Oxford: Oxford University Press, 1992), 34.
2. Ibid., 33.
3. Ibid.
4. Ibid., 35.
5. Ibid.
6. Ibid., 35–6.
7. Ibid., 36–7.
8. Nick Malkoutzis, "How Serious a Threat to Democracy Is Inequality?" *Kathimerini*, 16 Sept. 2015, 3.
9. Stephen Lewis, "A Socialist Takes Stock," *CCPA Monitor* 21, 8 (Feb. 2015): 24.
10. "Berning Up," *The Economist*, 10–16 Oct. 2015, 25.
11. Ibid.
12. Ibid.
13. Owen says, when speaking of "those great evils of which all now complain," that "[i]t will then be seen that the foundation on which these evils have been erected is ignorance." See his *A New View of Society* (1813–14; reprint, Toronto: Penguin Books, 1991), 64.
14. C. Wright Mills, *The Marxists* (Harmondsworth, England: Penguin Books, 1962), 132–3. And Bernstein makes clear here that revolution entails violence: "In general, one may say here that the revolutionary way (always in the sense of revolution by violence) does quicker work." See ibid., 182–3.
15. For Bernstein this dualism "consists in this, that the work aims at being a scientific inquiry and also at proving a theory laid down long before its drafting." See his *Evolutionary Socialism* (1909; reprint, New York: Schocken Books, 1961), 209.
16. Bernstein remarks (ibid., 210), "But, as Marx approaches a point when that final aim enters seriously into the question, he becomes uncertain and unreliable. Such contradictions then appear as were shown in the book under consideration, for instance in the section on the movement of incomes in modern society. It thus appears this great scientific spirit was in the end a slave to doctrine."
17. Ibid., 202.
18. Ibid., 212. As for the immiseration of the proletariat, Bernstein (p. 219) says, "We have to take working men as they are. And they are neither so universally pauperized as was set out in the *Communist Manifesto*, nor so free from prejudices and weaknesses as their courtiers would make us believe."
19. Bernstein deplores capitalism as such, notwithstanding his belief that it is an evolving system of socialism. See ibid., 221.
20. R.H. Tawney, *Equality*, 4th edn, rev. (London: Unwin Books, 1964), 164.
21. Ibid.
22. Ibid., 78.
23. Ibid.
24. Bernstein says, "And in this mind, I, at the time, resorted to the spirit of the great Konigsberg philosopher, the critic of pure reason, against the cant which sought to get a hold on the working-class movement . . . I did this in the conviction that social democracy required a Kant who should judge the received opinion and examine it critically with deep acuteness." Bernstein, *Evolutionary Socialism*, 185.
25. Tawney, *Equality*, 173.
26. Ibid., 172. Earlier (p. 166), Tawney says, "The problem of liberty, therefore, is necessarily concerned, not only with the political, but also with economic, relations."
27. Ibid., 168.
28. J.M. Winter and D.M. Joslin, eds, *R.H. Tawney's Commonplace Book* (Cambridge: Cambridge University Press, 1972), 53.
29. David A. Reisman, *Tawney, Galbraith, and Adam Smith: State and Welfare* (New York: St Martin's Press, 1982), 44.
30. Tawney, *Equality*, 46.
31. Ibid., 46–7.
32. Ibid., 48–9.
33. Ibid., 49.

34. Ibid., 167. "The extension of liberty from the political to the economic sphere is evidently among the most urgent tasks of industrial societies."
35. Ibid., 166.
36. Quoted approvingly by Tawney: ibid., 169.
37. C.A.R. Crosland, *The Future of Socialism* (New York: Schocken Books, 1956), 67.
38. Ibid., 68.
39. Ibid., 71–6.
40. Ibid., 77.
41. Ibid.
42. Alec Nove, *The Economics of Feasible Socialism* (London: George Allen and Unwin, 1983), 1.
43. Ibid., xii.
44. Ibid.
45. Ibid., 1.
46. Ibid., 5–7. Nove also makes the point that there are positive externalities such as efficient transportation, reliable postal services, and attractive flowers in a neighbour's garden. In addition, he notes that there seems to be an increase of the instances in the modern world in which externalities matter. See ibid., 5–6.
47. Ibid., 197.
48. Ibid., 200.
49. Ibid., 227–8.
50. Ibid., ix, xi.
51. Stuart Hampshire, *Innocence and Experience* (Cambridge, MA: Harvard University Press, 1989), 11.
52. Ibid., 12.
53. Sometimes Hampshire talks about the good life and sometimes the human good. See ibid., 13, 106.
54. Ibid., 13.
55. Ibid., 169.
56. Ibid., 108–87.
57. Ibid., 73.
58. Ibid., 169.
59. Ibid., 55.
60. Ibid., 183.
61. Ibid.
62. Ibid., 184–5.
63. Ibid., 185.
64. Ibid., 108.
65. Ibid., 185.
66. This statement is translated as: "A society in which justice and morality were banished would not evidently be able to subsist." Vilfredo Pareto (1848–1923) was an Italian economist and sociologist known for applying mathematics to economic analysis and for tracing the interaction between masses and elites.
67. Anthony Giddens, *The Third Way: The Renewal of Social Democracy* (Cambridge: Polity Press, 1998), 27–8.
68. Ibid., 26.
69. Ibid., 101–11.
70. Sir William Beveridge was famous for *The Pillars of Security* (New York: Macmillan, 1943), in which he spoke of the five giant Evils: Want, Disease, Ignorance, Squalor, and Idleness (pp. 49–51). José Harris, author of the definitive biography, claims that Beveridge does not fit under the label "socialist," "liberal," or "capitalist." Bearing in mind the quasi-socialist overtones of Beveridge's thinking, Giddens comes close to denying this, as does Crosland, *The Future of Socialism*, 81–2. See José Harris, *William Beveridge: A Biography*, 2nd edn (Oxford: Clarendon Press, 1997), 304.
71. Giddens, *Third Way*, 111. Imperial Germany was opposed to laissez-faire economics and proceeded to set up the prototype of the welfare state. This is a point that will be pursued in the next chapter, "Fascism and National Socialism."
72. Ibid., 127–8.
73. Ibid., 65.
74. One is reminded here of the crisis in democracy that Walter Lippmann sounded some 60 years ago. See Walter Lippmann, *The Public Philosophy* (New York: Mentor Books, 1956).
75. Giddens, *Third Way*, 72–7.
76. Ibid., 134.
77. Ibid., 130.
78. Ibid., 136.
79. Ibid., 94.
80. Ibid., 95.
81. These are points made by Peter Self, "Socialism," in *A Companion to Contemporary Political Philosophy*, ed. Robert E. Goodin and Philip Pettit (Oxford: Blackwell, 1993), 336.
82. A point made by Self: ibid., 337.
83. Again, this point is made effectively by Self: ibid., 338–53.
84. Ibid., 339.
85. Hampshire, *Innocence and Experience*, 185.
86. Peter Self makes the insightful comment that moral purpose is a necessary condition of all successful causes. If he is correct, it would seem in the case of socialism that both equality and justice are essential conditions. See Self, "Socialism," 337.

87. Nove, *Economics of Feasible Socialism*, 227.
88. Ibid., 200.
89. Ibid., 227.
90. Ibid., 199, 202.
91. Jad Adams, "A Small Person," *Times Literary Supplement*, 24 Apr. 2009, 22.
92. Robert Taylor, "Europe's Divided Left," *Dissent* 56, 2 (Spring 2009): 7.
93. Ian Buruma, "What Became of the Israeli Left?" *The Guardian*, 23 Oct. 2003, 1, http://www.guardian.co.uk/world/2003/oct/23/israel.
94. Stephen Nathanson, *Economic Justice* (Upper Saddle River, NJ: Prentice-Hall, 1998), 39.
95. Ibid.
96. Peter Self, *Rolling Back the Market: Economic Dogma and Political Choice* (New York: St Martin's Press, 2000), 181.
97. Nathanson, *Economic Justice*, 39.
98. Thomas Hobbes, *Leviathan* (1651; reprint, Oxford: Oxford University Press, 1996), Part I, c. 15, para. 21.
99. Tawney, *Equality*, 173.
100. Hampshire, *Innocence and Experience*, 183.
101. Those that might not be embraced would include the suggestions of Arne Næss and Warwick Fox. See Chapter 12, "Environmentalism."
102. See Self, *Rolling Back the Market*, 183, for this summary of causes.
103. These excellent points are made by Self: ibid., 184.
104. See Chapter 11, "Feminism," and the viewpoints of Martha Nussbaum and Susan Okin.
105. Nove, *Economics of Feasible Socialism*, xi.
106. Joseph A. Schumpeter, *Capitalism, Socialism, and Democracy*, 3rd edn (New York: Harper and Row, 1950), 167.
107. Ibid.
108. Ibid.
109. Ibid., 168.
110. Ibid., 82–3.
111. Adam Smith, *The Nature and Causes of the Wealth of Nations*, ed. Kathryn Sutherland (1776; reprint, Oxford: Oxford University Press, 1993), I, ii, 22.
112. Nathanson, p. 48.
113. See Nathanson, *Economic Justice*, 48, for this point.
114. Giddens, *Third Way*, 43–4.
115. Richard Pares, *The Historian's Business, and Other Essays* (Oxford: Clarendon Press, 1961), 9.

Chapter 7: Fascism and National Socialism

1. David Crossland, "Neo-Nazi Threat Growing Despite NPD Cash Woes," *Spiegel Online International*, 19 Mar. 2009, http://www.spiegel.de/international/germany/0,1518,614209,00.html.
2. Ibid.
3. Madhur Singh, "The Fiery Hindu Nationalist Who's Roiling Indian Politics," *Time*, 29 Apr. 2009, http://www.time.com/time/printout/0,8816,1894617,00.html.
4. Anna Porter, "Fascism: The Next Generation," *Globe and Mail*, 9 May 2009, F1, F4, F9; Marton Dunai, "Four Jailed for Neo-Nazi Killing Spree That Terrified Hungary's Roma," Reuters, 6 Aug. 2013, http://www.reuters.com/article/us-hungary-roma-killings-ruling-idUSBRE97508920130806. See also Siobhán Dowling, "Neo-Fascist Magyar Garda Is 'Hungary's Shame'," *Spiegel Online International*, 27 Aug. 2007, http://www.spiegel.de/international/germany/0,1518,502184,00.html.
5. Porter, "Fascism," F4.
6. Marsha Lederman, "He's Dangerous, Sure: But Comparing Trump to Hitler Is Surely Wrong," *Globe and Mail*, 19 Mar. 2016, A2.
7. Ibid.
8. Pascal Mercier, *Night Train to Lisbon* (New York: Grove Press, 2008).
9. Roger Griffin, *The Nature of Fascism* (London: Routledge, 1991), 86.
10. Ibid., 97.
11. Ibid., 63.
12. Ibid.
13. Benito Mussolini, *The Political and Social Doctrine of Fascism*, trans. Jane Soames (London: Hogarth Press, 1933), 18. The original publication of this manuscript was as an article for the fourteenth volume of *Enciclopedia Italiana* in 1932 (actually ghostwritten by the philosopher of Fascism, Giovanni Gentile).
14. Ibid., 17. What he claims is that "Liberalism only flourished for half a century."
15. The notion of perpetual peace gained its currency from the writings of Immanuel Kant, "Perpetual Peace," in *On History*, ed. Lewis White Beck (1795; reprint, New York: Bobbs-Merrill, 1963), 85ff.
16. Mussolini released two Decalogues during his lifetime, the first in 1934 and the second in 1938. In the Decalogue of 1934, proposition 1, he says, "Know that the Fascist

and in particular the soldier, must not believe in perpetual peace." See Mussolini, "The Fascist Decalogue," in James A. Gould and Willis H. Truitt, comps, *Political Ideologies* (New York: Macmillan, 1973), 106.
17. Adolf Hitler, speech in Essen, 22 Nov. 1926; published in *Volkischer Beobachter* as "Only Force Rules," 26 Nov. 1926.
18. Adolf Hitler, speech in Chemnitz, 2 April 1928; published in *Volkischer Beobachter* as "Originality Plus Brutality," 7 Apr. 1928.
19. Adolf Hitler, speech in Munich, 22 September 1928; published in *Volkischer Beobachter* as "Long Live Fanatical Nationalism," 23 Sept. 1928.
20. Hitler, "Only Force Rules."
21. Griffin, *Nature of Fascism*, 101–2.
22. Mussolini, *Political and Social Doctrine of Fascism*, 13.
23. Ibid.
24. Alan Bullock, *Hitler* (Harmondsworth, England: Pelican Books, 1962), 263.
25. See ibid., 266–70, for a vivid description of these and related events.
26. Ibid., 406.
27. Lyman Tower Sargent suggests as much when he says, "In the nineteenth and early twentieth centuries, reason and science were the central tenets of liberal and Marxist approaches to social change, and irrationalism specifically rejects those approaches. Fascism and National Socialism reject the application of reason and science to social problems and use myth, emotion, and hate as tools of manipulation." See Sargent, *Contemporary Political Ideologies*, 11th edn (Toronto: Harcourt Brace, 1999), 189. The author would like to acknowledge that several of the thematic headings of this chapter are drawn from Sargent's work.
28. Mussolini, *Political and Social Doctrine of Fascism*, 23.
29. Ibid., 21.
30. Ibid.
31. Ibid., 21–2.
32. Ibid., 22.
33. Ibid., 22–5.
34. Peter Alter, *Nationalism*, trans. Stuart McKinnon-Evans (London: Edward Arnold, 1989), 51.
35. Ibid., 52.
36. Hitler, *Mein Kampf*, trans. Ralph Manheim (Boston: Houghton Mifflin, 1999), 76.
37. Ibid., 10.
38. Ibid., 336.
39. Ibid., 339.
40. Ibid., 397.
41. Ibid., 426.
42. See Bullock, *Hitler*, 403, where he remarks, "As soon as Hitler began to think and talk about the organization of the State it is clear the metaphor which dominated his mind was that of an army.... It was from the Army that he took the Fuehrerprinzip, the leadership principle, upon which the Nazi Party and later the National Socialist State, were built."
43. Benito Mussolini, "The Fascist Decalogue," in Gould and Truitt, comps, *Political Ideologies*, 106. There is surely some irony here in Mussolini claiming that he is always right, and then turning about to revise his 1934 Decalogue in the version of 1938.
44. Paul Brooker, "The Nazi Fuehrerprinzip: A Weberian Analysis," *Political Science* 37 (1985): 51.
45. Allan Todd, *The European Dictatorships* (Cambridge: Cambridge University Press, 2002), 127.
46. Peter Neville, *Mussolini* (London: Routledge, 2004), 104–5.
47. Ibid., 105.
48. Ibid., 53–7.
49. Brooker, "Nazi Fuehrerprinzip," 57–8.
50. The fundamental aspect of this law for Hitler's regime is recognized by Bullock, *Hitler*, 266.
51. The Kroll Opera House became the meeting place of the Reichstag members after the Reichstag was torched on 27 February 1933.
52. Ibid., 270.
53. Ibid., 269.
54. Ibid., 277.
55. See ibid., 279–96. Of particular importance during this time is the Deutschland Pact of April 1933 in which Hitler and the Army generals reached agreement on the Army's oath of allegiance to the Chancellor, the suppression of Roehm's plans to remodel the Army, and finally the inviolability of the Army (ibid., 290).
56. Ibid., 279.
57. As cited ibid., 274–5.
58. Brooker, "Nazi Fuehrerprinzip," 51.
59. See the entry under "Darwinism" in the *Encyclopedia of Philosophy*, ed. Paul Edwards (New York: Macmillan and Free Press; London: Collier Macmillan, 1967), vol. 1, 297–8.

60. Greta Jones, *Social Darwinism and English Thought* (Brighton, England: Harvester Press; Atlantic Highlands, NJ: Humanities Press, 1980), 157.
61. Houston Stewart Chamberlain, *Foundations of the Nineteenth Century*, vol. 1, trans. John Lees (New York: John Lane; London: The Bodley Head, 1912), 251–7.
62. Ibid., 271.
63. T.H. Huxley, "Emancipation—Black and White," in *Lay Sermons, Addresses, and Reviews* (London: Macmillan, 1870), 23–4; originally published in *The Reader,* 20 May 1865.
64. Oswald Spengler, *The Hour of Decision*, trans. C.F. Atkinson (New York: Knopf, 1934), 202, quoted in Paul Hayes, *Fascism* (New York: Free Press, 1973), 27.
65. Eugen Duehring, *Die Judenfrage als Racen-, Sitten-, und Culturfrage* (Karlsruhe and Leipzig: Reuther, 1881), quoted in Hayes, *Fascism*, 28.
66. Mussolini, *Political and Social Doctrine of Fascism*, 16.
67. In translation the argument runs as follows: None but members of the nation may be citizens of the state. None but those of German blood, whatever their creed, may be members of the nation. No Jew, therefore, may be a member of the nation. See Adolf Hitler, "The Twenty-Five Points" (1920), in Gould and Truitt, comps, *Political Ideologies*, 113–15.
68. Adolf Hitler, "Struggle—The Source of Strength," *Volkischer Beobachter*, 21 Nov. 1927.
69. Hitler, "Originality Plus Brutality."
70. Hitler, *Mein Kampf*, 232.
71. Ibid., 303.
72. Ibid., 447.
73. For a summary and analysis of the racial overtones of *Mein Kampf*, see Griffin, *Nature of Fascism*, 97.
74. Ibid., 97–8.
75. Brooker, "Nazi Fuehrerprinzip," 50.
76. Hannah Arendt, *Eichmann in Jerusalem: A Report on the Banality of Evil* (Harmondsworth, England: Penguin Books, 1977), 83.
77. Ibid.
78. Alexander De Grand, *Italian Fascism: Its Origins and Development* (Lincoln: University of Nebraska Press, 1982), 113.
79. Ibid., 115.
80. It is said that Mussolini's Italy was masculine and warlike, placing women in a limited, subservient, and biological role. See Neville, *Mussolini*, 106.
81. De Grand, *Italian Fascism*, 115.
82. Neville, *Mussolini*, 208. As Neville (p. 117) points out, however, Mussolini had none of the hostility to Jews that Hitler held. In fact, Mussolini is recorded as saying that the small Jewish community had been loyal during the war, and had been good citizens on the whole.
83. De Grand, *Italian Fascism*, 115.
84. Ibid.
85. MacGregor Knox, *Common Destiny: Dictatorship, Foreign Policy, and War in Fascist Italy and Nazi Germany* (Cambridge: Cambridge University Press, 2000), 99.
86. Bullock, *Hitler*, 734. Some resistance still existed, however, in the churches and the army. It was from individuals in these institutions that plans were hatched to assassinate Hitler. See ibid., 734–7.
87. Ingo Müller, *Hitler's Justice: The Courts of the Third Reich*, trans. Deborah Lucas Schneider (Cambridge, MA: Harvard University Press, 1991), 43.
88. Scott Horton, "State of Exception," *Harper's* 315 (July 2007): 80–1.
89. Müller, *Hitler's Justice*, 140.
90. H.W. Koch, *In the Name of the Volk: Political Justice in Hitler's Germany* (London: I.B. Tauris and Co., 1989), 15.
91. Ibid., x and 21.
92. Ibid., x.
93. Müller, *Hitler's Justice*, 140–3.
94. Fabian von Schlabrendorff, *The Secret War against Hitler* (1965; reprint, Boulder, CO: Westview Press, 1994), 54.
95. Müller, *Hitler's Justice*, 144–5.
96. Ibid., 145.
97. Ibid., 150.
98. H.J. Hahn, *German Thought and Culture: From the Holy Roman Empire to the Present Day* (Manchester: Manchester University Press, 1995), 60.
99. J.N. Noakes and G. Pridham, eds, *Nazism: A History in Documents and Eyewitness Accounts, 1919–1945*, vol. 1 (New York: Schocken Books, 1983), 476.
100. Müller, *Hitler's Justice*, 71–4.
101. The Gestapo was the Prussian secret state police established by Goering. See Bullock, *Hitler*, 278.
102. Edward Crankshaw, *Gestapo: Instrument of*

Tyranny (1956; reprint, London: Greenhill Books, 1990), 89.
103. Schlabrendorff, *Secret War*, 81.
104. Crankshaw, *Gestapo*, 71.
105. Schlabrendorff, *Secret War*, 55.
106. Bullock, *Hitler*, 308.
107. Goering's speech at Frankfurt-on-Main, 3 Mar. 1933, N.D. [Nuremberg Documents] 1856-PS. Quoted ibid., 264.
108. Noakes and Pridham, *Nazism*, 537.
109. Ibid., 476.
110. Schlabrendorff, *Secret War*, 48–9.
111. Bullock, *Hitler*, 751.
112. Hayes, *Fascism*, 89.
113. For Aristotle, the polis is the final and perfect association, formed from a number of villages. The polis is believed to be self-sufficient. See Aristotle, *Politics* (Oxford: Oxford University Press, 1995), Book I.2, 1252b27.
114. Hayes, *Fascism*, 90.
115. Ibid., 92.
116. Ibid., 100.
117. Ibid., 90.
118. Ibid., 96.
119. Griffin, *Nature of Fascism*, 101. The word "palingenetic" comes from Greek "palin" (again) and "genesis" (birth). See ibid., 32–3.
120. Ibid., 76.
121. Ibid.
122. Todd, *European Dictatorships*, 117.
123. Philip Morgan, *Italian Fascism, 1919–1945*, 2nd edn (Houndmills, England: Palgrave Macmillan, 2004), 157.
124. Ibid.
125. Ibid.
126. See Neville, *Mussolini*, 112.
127. Morgan, *Italian Fascism*, 159.
128. Ibid.
129. Ibid., 161.
130. Bullock, *Hitler*, 278.
131. Ibid.
132. See Griffin, *Nature of Fascism*, 75, for his synopsis of people's feelings with respect to Italian Fascism.
133. Ibid., 105–6.
134. See ibid., 69.
135. Niccolò Machiavelli, *The Discourses* (1531; reprint, Oxford: Oxford University Press, 1997), 161–2.
136. Mussolini, *Doctrine of Fascism*, 11.
137. Thomas Hobbes, *Leviathan* (1651; reprint, Oxford: Oxford University Press, 1996), Part I, Chap. 15, para. 21.
138. Griffin, *Nature of Fascism*, 42.
139. Ibid., 43.
140. See Mussolini, *Doctrine of Fascism*, 18, for this description of liberalism. The Gordian knot to which he refers is that knot described in an apocryphal story in which Alexander the Great was challenged to untie a knot that could not be untied. He severed the knot by cutting it in two with his sword. The story alleges that Gordius, King of Phrygia and father of Midas, dedicated his chariot to Zeus, fastening the yoke to a pole with a knot of bark. An oracle had foretold that whoever untied the knot would rule both Europe and Asia. See Gilbert Meadows, *An Illustrated Dictionary of Classical Mythology* (London: Jupiter Books, 1978), 106.
141. Mussolini, *Doctrine of Fascism*, 18.
142. Ibid., 24.
143. See Alter, *Nationalism*, 13, where he summarizes the view of one of the most expert scholars of modern nationalism, Hugh Seton-Watson, who makes this claim.
144. Ibid., 14–15.
145. Gerhard von Glahn, *Law among Nations: An Introduction to Public International Law*, 7th edn (Boston: Allyn and Bacon, 1996), 148–9.
146. Bullock, *Hitler*, 264.
147. Ibid., 308.
148. On Pareto, see Chapter 6, note 66, where his statement is also translated.
149. Griffin, *Nature of Fascism*, 72.
150. Ibid., 76.
151. Hayes, *Fascism*, 100.
152. For more on *Entartete Musik*, see *Music and the Holocaust*, http://holocaustmusic.ort.org/.
153. Obituary: Romano Mussolini, *Vancouver Sun*, 4 Feb. 2006, C10.
154. Ibid.
155. Plato, *The Republic* (Oxford: Oxford University Press, 1994), 401 d.
156. See Michael H. Kater, *Different Drummers: Jazz in the Culture of Nazi Germany* (Oxford: Oxford University Press, 2003).

Chapter 8: Pacifism

1. Jenny Teichman, *Pacifism and the Just War: A Study in Applied Philosophy* (Oxford: Basil Blackwell, 1986), 7–8. These she refers to as the types identified by the theologian John Yoder (1927–1997), who stands in the Mennonite tradition.
2. Ibid., 9.
3. Violence hereinafter is thought of as "a considerable or destroying use of force

against persons or things." This definition is extracted from Ted Honderich's definition of political violence. See his *Violence for Equality: Inquiries in Political Philosophy* (Harmondsworth, England: Penguin Books, 1980), 23.
4. Teichman maintains, "The doctrine of the just war is the most important philosophical rejoinder to pacifism." While Teichman is correct in what she says, there is conceptual value in understanding that terrorism and pacifism stand as contraries. Clearly, like all contraries, such as hot and cold, there is a condition that stands in between pacifism and terrorism, namely, the just war. Teichman, *Pacifism and the Just War*, 46.
5. See Seth Mydans, "Monks' Protest Is Challenging Burmese Junta," *New York Times*, 24 Sept. 2007, http://www.nytimes.com/2007/09/24/world/asia/24myanmar.html.
6. Kazuaki Nagata, "Both Sides on Constitutional Change Hold Rallies," *Japan Times*, 4 May 2009, http://search.japantimes.co.jp/cgi-bin/nn20090504a3.html.
7. "Japan Wrestles with Pacifism," *International New York Times*, 21 July 2015, 6.
8. Ibid.
9. David D. Kirkpatrick and Mayy El Sheikh, "Brotherhood Divided over Strategy of Nonviolence," *International New York Times*, 6 Aug. 2015, 1.
10. Ibid., 1, 4.
11. Peter Brock, *A Brief History of Pacifism from Jesus to Tolstoy*, 2nd edn (Syracuse, NY: Syracuse University Press, 1992).
12. W.H.C. Frend, *The Early Church* (Philadelphia: Lippincott, 1966), 74. Years later, Jean-Jacques Rousseau was to express a position not too dissimilar to that of Celsus in maintaining that the Christian religion was deeply opposed to the social spirit. See Rousseau, *The Social Contract* (1762; reprint, Oxford: Oxford University Press, 1994), 163.
13. Christians did enjoy the benefits of the Roman state at this time. The great persecutions did not begin until much later, in 303 CE, lasting until 312. See Frend, *The Early Church*, 128–38.
14. Ibid., 73; Brock, *Brief History of Pacifism*, 11. Brock says, "Celsus was a pagan philosopher who, writing around 178 AD, had blamed Christians for undermining the security of the Empire by refusing to defend it by arms."
15. Frend, *The Early Church*, 73.
16. Brock, *Brief History of Pacifism*, 13.
17. Ibid.
18. Ibid., 14. As he says, John Hus the reformer was not a pacifist. It is worth noting, too, that Leo Tolstoy was familiar with the writings of Chelčický and spoke affectionately of them.
19. Ibid., 22.
20. Mennonites and Hutterites emigrated to Canada and the United States years later. They still function actively in these countries, with Hutterites remaining largely in agricultural settings and Mennonites living in both urban and rural areas.
21. Ibid., 40.
22. Ibid., 42.
23. Even Teichman, who views pacifism as anti-militarism, does concede, in the case of Penn and Pennsylvania, that in dealing with Native peoples Penn rejected the use of war; although he accepted the use of the force of the magistracy, he attempted to keep this to a minimum. So it would seem that, even for Teichman, pacifism for the Quakers meant more than just anti-militarism, otherwise why keep the use of force by the magistracy to a minimum? See Teichman, *Pacifism and the Just War*, 21–2.
24. Peter Brock, *The Quaker Peace Testimony: 1660 to 1914* (York, UK: Sessions Book Trust, 1990), 28.
25. D. Elton Trueblood, *The People Called Quakers* (New York: Harper and Row, 1966), 187.
26. This influence is acknowledged by Mulford Q. Sibley, *The Quiet Battle* (Boston: Beacon Press, 1963), 25. However, Horsburgh sees things differently. See H.J.N. Horsburgh, *Non-Violence and Aggression: A Study of Gandhi's Moral Equivalent of War* (London: Oxford University Press, 1968), 84, n. 2: "Thoreau is, of course, one of the small company of Western writers who exerted an influence on Gandhi. Ruskin and Tolstoy are others." Sibley sees Thoreau influencing Tolstoy and Gandhi while Horsburgh sees Thoreau and Tolstoy influencing Gandhi.
27. Howard Zinn, *A People's History of the United States* (New York: HarperCollins, 2003), 156. Emerson was also unenthusiastic about Thoreau's sojourn at Walden Pond. At Thoreau's funeral, he lamented Thoreau's lack of ambition in preferring to be "captain of a huckleberry party" rather than turning his talents to the betterment of society. See

Shannon L. Mariotti, "Thoreau, Adorno, and the Critical Potential of Particularity," in Jack Turner, ed., *A Political Companion to Henry David Thoreau* (Lexington: University Press of Kentucky, 2009), 415.
28. Henry Thoreau, "Civil Disobedience," in Sibley, *The Quiet Battle*, 29.
29. The Mexican-American War commenced on 25 April 1846, and centred on annexation by the United States of all land up to the Rio Grande. This was a war triggered by the United States under the leadership of James Polk. In the words of Colonel Ethan Allen Hitchcock, commander of the 3rd Infantry Regiment, "I have said from the start that the United States are the aggressors." See Zinn, *A People's History*, 151.
30. Thoreau, "Civil Disobedience," 28.
31. What non-violent actions amount to is best explained below in the discussion of Mohandas Gandhi and his doctrine of *satyagraha*.
32. Nicholas V. Riasanovsky, *A History of Russia*, 4th edn (New York: Oxford University Press, 1984), 442–3, for more details on Tolstoy's life, his criticism of civilization, and his call for the abandonment of violence.
33. Leo Tolstoy, "On the Negro Question," in *Tolstoy's Writings on Civil Disobedience and Non-Violence* (New York: Signet Books, 1967), 281. A letter written to Vladimir Chertkov, Tolstoy's protege and secretary, in January 1904, it was first published as an Introduction to *A Short Biography of William Lloyd Garrison*, co-authored by Chertkov and Florence Holah (London: Free Age Press, 1904).
34. Tolstoy, "On the Negro Question," 284.
35. Ibid., 283.
36. Again, the form of this non-violent resistance is best explained by Gandhi and his *satyagraha* doctrine.
37. Ibid. The connection between Garrison and Tolstoy is really one of two independent moralists coming to the same conclusions, much like the connection between Leibniz and Newton and the discovery of the calculus. See Brock, *Brief History of Pacifism*, 72–3.
38. Leo Tolstoy, "Nikolai Palkin," in *Tolstoy's Writings on Civil Disobedience and Non-Violence*, 198.
39. Ibid., 196.
40. Editor's Note in M.K. Gandhi, *Non-Violent Resistance* (New York: Schocken Books, 1951), iii.
41. Gandhi, *Non-Violent Resistance*, 3.
42. Ibid.
43. Ibid., 56.
44. It is to be recalled that Teichman misses this point when she says, "And again the common feature of these pacifisms is anti-war-ism." Teichman, *Pacifism and the Just War*, 9.
45. For an exploration of these and related ideas, see Horsburgh, *Non-Violence and Aggression*, 31–2. Horsburgh also makes clear (in Chapter 2) that *satyagraha* cannot be understood simply as a technique of non-violent resistance and as severed from its ethico-religious roots. These ethico-religious roots were both Christian and Hindu.
46. Gandhi, *Non-Violent Resistance*, 6. He asserts that the suffragettes employ passive resistance.
47. Ibid., 3.
48. Ibid., 4.
49. Joan V. Bondurant, *Conquest of Violence: The Gandhian Philosophy of Conflict*, rev. edn (Berkeley: University of California Press, 1965), 36–7.
50. Hartal is the voluntary closing of shops and businesses, usually for 24 hours. See ibid., 36 (first footnote).
51. Ibid., 36.
52. Gandhi, *Non-Violent Resistance*, 4. He later remarks, "We dare not pin our faith solely on civil disobedience. It is like the use of a knife to be used sparingly if at all." Ibid., 173.
53. See Horsburgh, *Non-Violence and Aggression*, 62–5, for an elaboration of these points.
54. Ibid., 65.
55. Gandhi, *Non-Violent Resistance*, 57.
56. Bondurant, *Conquest of Violence*, vii.
57. Ibid., 16.
58. There is an issue as to whether Gandhian non-violence could be defended without religious backing.
59. Ibid., 32.
60. Gandhi, *Non-Violent Resistance*, 79–81.
61. Albert Schweitzer, *Indian Thought and Its Development*, trans. Mrs. Charles E.B. Russell (London: Hodder and Stoughton, 1936), 79. It should be noted, drawing from the later chapter on environmentalism, that it is a short step from the doctrine of non-violence or *ahimsa* to the doctrine of reverence for life. It seems that Schweitzer may have been influenced in his search for a new ethical principle by the ideas and life of Gandhi.

62. See Bondurant, *Conquest of Violence*, 23–4.
63. Thomas Merton, ed., *Gandhi on Non-Violence* (Navajivan, India: New Directions, 1965), 23.
64. Aldous Huxley, ed., *An Encyclopaedia of Pacifism* (London: Chatto and Windus, 1937).
65. Ibid., 39.
66. The term "conflict" is broader in meaning than "violent conflict." It should be so understood in the case of Huxley and his use of the term.
67. Ibid., 40.
68. Ibid., 70–1.
69. Ibid., 48–9.
70. Ibid., 48.
71. Ibid., 49.
72. Ibid.
73. Ibid., 51.
74. Later commentators and academics would talk of "soft power" in this context.
75. Ibid., 52.
76. Ibid., 57.
77. Ibid., 58.
78. Ibid., 62.
79. Ibid., 59.
80. Ibid.
81. Ibid.
82. Ibid., 116–19.
83. Ibid., 40.
84. Ibid., 55. He draws a distinction between two senses of "imperialism": (i) the advantage of one nation ruling over, guiding, and developing a number of other nations, and (ii) the system of empires as found in Great Britain, France, Belgium, Portugal, the Netherlands, and Italy.
85. Ibid., 12–13.
86. Ibid., 12 and 55. Of the aforementioned empires, Huxley says (p. 55), "These empires were acquired for a variety of reasons—as a source of raw material, as an outlet for surplus population and surplus production, as a source of profit to a small class of speculative financiers."
87. Ibid., 39.
88. Ibid., 24.
89. Ibid., 47.
90. Bertrand Russell, *Which Way to Peace?* (London: Michael Joseph, 1936), 134.
91. Note here that Russell does not think of pacifism as a way of life, as does Huxley, but as a policy. However, he later admits that war resistance is not so much political but, like religion, a matter of personal conviction. Ibid., 134, 220.
92. Ibid., 211.
93. Ibid.
94. Ibid., 212.
95. Ibid., 140.
96. Ibid., 144. Notice how this differs from the list provided by Thomas Hobbes, which comprises competition, diffidence, and glory. See Hobbes, *Leviathan* (1651; reprint, Oxford University Press: Oxford, 1996), 82, Part I, c.13.
97. Bertrand Russell, *Prophecy and Dissent: 1914–16*, vol. 13 of *The Collected Papers of Bertrand Russell*, ed. Richard A. Rempel (London: Unwin Hyman, 1988), 150.
98. Ibid., 144.
99. Ibid., 148, 151.
100. Russell, *Which Way to Peace?*, 145. Recall that Adam Smith had similar critical remarks to make about Britain's colonialism. See Adam Smith, *The Nature and Causes of the Wealth of Nations*, ed. Kathryn Sutherland (1776; reprint, Oxford: Oxford University Press, 1993), IV, vii.
101. Russell, *Which Way to Peace?*, 145–6.
102. Ibid., 146.
103. Ibid., 223.
104. Ibid., 140, 203.
105. Ibid., 204.
106. Ibid., 205.
107. Ibid., 219.
108. Ibid., 220.
109. Bertrand Russell, *Pacifism and Revolution: 1916–18*, vol. 14 of *The Collected Papers of Bertrand Russell*, ed. Richard A. Rempel (London: Routledge, 1995), 203.
110. Ibid., 196.
111. Ibid., 204.
112. Ibid., 196–7.
113. Ibid., 147–51. Russell adds (p. 151), "I think both the right and the duty of self-defence result from too material a conception of what constitutes human and national welfare."
114. The Russell-Einstein Manifesto was issued at a press conference in London on 9 July 1955. See http://www.pugwash.org/about/manifesto.htm.
115. Ronald W. Clark, *The Life of Bertrand Russell* (New York: Alfred A. Knopf, 1976), 555.
116. Ibid., 556.
117. Bertrand Russell, *Human Society in Ethics and Politics* (1954; reprint, London: Routledge, 1992), 229. This is an implied reference to

the activities of US Senator Joseph McCarthy (1908–1957). As Andrew G. Bone notes, "Russell had been an outspoken critic of the Wisconsin Senator's anti-Communist demagogy ever since his rise to national prominence in 1950." See Bone, ed., *Man's Peril: 1954–55*, vol. 28 of *The Collected Papers of Bertrand Russell* (London: Routledge, 2003), 121. Earlier in *Human Society in Ethics and Politics*, Russell makes the following observation (p. 156): "Christians ever since have followed the mob rather than the Founder of their religion. Nor have those who are not Christians been in any way behindhand. [Soviet Premier Georgy] Malenkov and Senator McCarthy are both carrying on the good work in the spirit of the mob which demanded the Crucifixion." He adds (p. 217), "When people think of Christianity as helping fight the Russians, it is not the Quaker type of Christianity that they have in view, but something more in the style of Senator McCarthy."
118. See the comments of Michelle Swenarchuk in the Introduction to Ursula Franklin, *The Ursula Franklin Reader: Pacifism as a Map* (Toronto: Canada Council for the Arts, 2006), 3. In 1984, Franklin became the first woman professor at the University of Toronto to be named a University Professor, 18 years after that title was established. In 2001, she and three other retired professors (including the biographer Phyllis Grosskurth) launched a class action lawsuit against the university on behalf of retired women professors and librarians who had, over the years, been paid less than male colleagues with the same qualifications. This historic pay equity challenge was settled a year later when the university agreed to compensate some 60 retired women professors.
119. Franklin, *Ursula Franklin Reader*, 1.
120. Ibid., 46–7.
121. Ibid., 49–51.
122. Ibid., 102.
123. Ibid. Jane Addams, who co-founded Hull House in Chicago, the first settlement house in the US, won the Nobel Peace Prize in 1931. Sylvia Pankhurst, the daughter of two labour and women's rights activists, was a leading figure in the suffragette movement and later supported Ethiopia in its struggles against Fascist Italy.
124. Ibid., 100.
125. Ibid., 101.
126. Ibid., 2.
127. Similar things could be said of Gandhi and King regarding the linkage between their pursuit of peace and justice.
128. Ibid., 190–1.
129. For an excellent overview of pacifism, see Robert Holmes and Barry L. Gan, eds, *Nonviolence in Theory and Practice*, 2nd edn (Long Grove, IL: Waveland Press, 2005).
130. See Antonio Cassese, *International Law*, 2nd edn (Oxford: Oxford University Press, 2005), 400.
131. Huxley, *An Encyclopaedia of Pacifism*, 49.
132. Martin Luther King Jr, "Letter from Birmingham Jail," in Holmes and Gan, eds, *Nonviolence in Theory and Practice*, 102.
133. A.C. Grayling, *The Heart of Things: Applying Philosophy to the 21st Century* (London: Phoenix, 2005), 135.
134. Ibid.
135. Jan Narveson, "Pacifism: A Philosophical Analysis," *Ethics* 75 (1965): 259–71.
136. Ibid., 265.
137. Ibid., 266.
138. Ibid.
139. Jan Narveson, "Pacifism: A Philosophical Analysis," in *Moral Problems: A Collection of Philosophical Essays*, ed. James Rachels (New York: Harper and Row, 1975), 360. This is a slightly revised version of Narveson's paper, cited above.
140. This action prompted the rising political star Pierre Trudeau to call Pearson the "defrocked Priest of Peace." See Richard Gwyn, *The Northern Magus: Pierre Trudeau and Canadians* (Markham, ON: PaperJacks, 1981), 63.

Chapter 9: Anarchism

1. Dylan Penner, "Why Vote?" *CCPA Monitor* (Sept./Oct. 2015): 16.
2. These are three traits which George Woodcock identifies. See Woodcock, *Anarchism* (Harmondsworth, England: Penguin Books, 1962), 37.
3. Ibid., 40–1.
4. See Murray Bookchin, *The Ecology of Freedom: The Emergence and Dissolution of Hierarchy*, 4th edn (Oakland, CA: AK Books, 2005), 269.
5. For his observations on the changing nature of education in England in the seventeenth century, see Lawrence Stone, *The Causes of the English Revolution, 1529–1642* (London: Routledge and Kegan Paul, 1972), 96–7.

6. See Yannis Palaiologos, *The 13th Labour of Hercules: Inside the Greek Crisis* (London: Portobello Books, 2014), Chap. 10.
7. Ibid., 225.
8. Ibid., 223.
9. Ibid., 226–7.
10. Ibid., 227.
11. Ibid.
12. See Woodcock, *Anarchism*, 57.
13. Percy Bysshe Shelley, "Song to the Men of England," in George B. Woods et al., eds, *The Literature of England*, 4th edn (Chicago: Scott, Foresman and Co., 1958), vol. 2, 254. An annotation to the poem on the same page states that it was "inspired by Shelley's interest in the Manchester Massacre, an attack by soldiers upon a crowd assembled in St. Peter's Field at Manchester, August 16, 1819, to petition Parliament for a redress of grievances regarding taxation and representation." Interestingly, Friedrich Engels was a great admirer of Shelley, and called him "the genius, the prophet," a poet who, with Byron, found most of his readers "in the proletariat." See Engels, *The Condition of the Working Class in England*, ed. Victor Gordon Kiernan (Harmondsworth, England: Penguin Books, 1987), 245.
14. In fact, Godwin has a long list of arguments against subscribing to social contractarianism. See Godwin, *Enquiry Concerning Political Justice*, ed. K. Codell Carter (1793; reprint, Oxford: Oxford University Press, 1971), Book III, Chap. 2.
15. Godwin, "Summary," *Enquiry Concerning Political Justice*, 13. For evidence of his utilitarianism, see Book III, Chap. 3, 111.
16. Godwin, *Enquiry*, Book I, Chap. 2, 20.
17. Ibid., Book I, Chap. 4, 35.
18. Ibid., Book I, Chap. 5, 42.
19. Godwin, "Summary," 13–14.
20. Godwin, *Enquiry*, Book VIII, Chap. 3, 291–4.
21. Ibid., Book V, Chap. 24, 222.
22. Ibid., Book V, Chap. 22, p. 216.
23. William Godwin and Mary Wollstonecraft, by all reports, were happily married and maintained separate households. The marriage ended tragically with Mary's death following the birth of their only child, Mary Godwin.
24. Notwithstanding Godwin's affirmation of natural law and free love, he was nothing short of incensed when his daughter, Mary, eloped with Percy Shelley in 1814.
25. See the introduction to Pierre-Joseph Proudhon, *What is Property?*, ed. and trans. Donald R. Kelley and Bonnie G. Smith (1840; reprint, Cambridge: Cambridge University Press, 1994), xi, xii.
26. Ibid., 14.
27. Proudhon is more than a casual empiricist here. Science is something he takes seriously, in much the way that Hobbes did. And underlying his commitment to science is his firm belief in its mathematical foundation. He remarks, aphoristically, "Numbers rule the world," something he thinks is as true for the moral and political world as it is for the molecular and sidereal. See ibid., 117.
28. Ibid., 32–3.
29. Ibid., 86.
30. Ibid.
31. Ibid., 88.
32. Ibid., 122–69.
33. Pierre-Joseph Proudhon, *General Idea of the Revolution in the Nineteenth Century*, trans. John Beverley Robinson (1851; reprint, London: Pluto Press, 1989), 59.
34. Ibid., 105.
35. Proudhon claims that Rousseau in fact "understood nothing of the social contract." See ibid., 113.
36. Ibid., 112, 126.
37. Ibid., 170.
38. Pierre-Joseph Proudhon, *The Principle of Federation*, trans. Richard Vernon (1863; reprint, Toronto: University of Toronto Press, 1979), 5.
39. Ibid., 8–9.
40. Ibid., 11.
41. Ibid., 39.
42. Ibid., 43.
43. Ibid., 72.
44. See Woodcock, *Anarchism*, 151.
45. Mikhail Bakunin, *Statism and Anarchy*, trans. and ed. Marshall S. Shatz (1873; reprint, Cambridge: Cambridge University Press, 1990), 137.
46. Ibid., 137.
47. Ibid., 141–2.
48. Ibid., 178.
49. Ibid.
50. Ibid., 182.
51. Ibid., 178. And again on p. 135 he remarks, "We revolutionary anarchists are … enemies of the state and any form of statehood."
52. Ibid., 13, 26.
53. Ibid., 20.

54. Ibid., 136–7.
55. Ibid., 205.
56. See Woodcock, *Anarchism*, 171–86, for a brief history of Kropotkin's formative anarchistic years.
57. Ibid., 171–97.
58. Peter Kropotkin, *Mutual Aid: A Factor of Evolution* (1902; reprint with foreword by Ashley Montagu (Boston: Extending Horizons Books, 1955), 227.
59. Ashley Montagu, foreword to Kropotkin, *Mutual Aid*, 5. Kropotkin's emphasis on spontaneity is reminiscent of Hayek's in his defence of neo-liberalism. See Chapter 10, "Neo-Liberalism and Libertarianism."
60. Just as Malthus had written his *Essay on the Principle of Population* in response to Godwin. See the introduction to Godwin, *Enquiry*, xii.
61. Woodcock, *Anarchism*, 201.
62. Kropotkin, *Mutual Aid*, 228.
63. Ibid.
64. Ibid., 229.
65. Ibid., 14–15.
66. Barnett Newman, foreword to Peter Kropotkin, *Memoirs of a Revolutionist* (1899; reprint, New York: Grove Press, 1968), xi.
67. Kropotkin, *Mutual Aid*, 255.
68. Ibid., 236.
69. Montagu, foreword to ibid., i.
70. George Woodcock and Ivan Avakumovic, *The Doukhobors* (Toronto: McClelland and Stewart, 1977), 131.
71. Ibid., 131.
72. Ibid. As noted in note 33 of Chapter 8, Chertkov was Tolstoy's protege and secretary, the recipient of Tolstoy's letter "On the Negro Question."
73. Woodcock and Akakumovic, *The Doukhobors*, 131.
74. Alice Wexler, *Emma Goldman in Exile: From the Russian Revolution to the Spanish Civil War* (Boston: Beacon Press, 1989), 10.
75. Emma Goldman, *Living My Life*, 2 vols (1931; reprint, New York: Dover, 1970), vol. 1, 83–107.
76. Ibid., vol. 1, 143.
77. Ibid., vol. 1, 206.
78. Ibid., vol. 1, 207–13.
79. Ibid., vol. 1, 335.
80. The federal Anarchist Exclusion Act followed passage of legislation in New York State—the Criminal Anarchy Act of 1902—that had targeted Goldman. She had been arrested after the McKinley assassination because it was known that a speech she had given in Cleveland four months earlier had been attended by Leon Czolgosz, the unemployed Polish-American factory worker who fatally shot McKinley. Czolgosz had spoken briefly to Goldman at the event, asking for advice on reading materials. In jail, he repeatedly denied Goldman's involvement in the assassination, and she was eventually released after two weeks of detention.
81. Ibid., vol. 2, 555.
82. Ibid., vol. 2, 613.
83. Ibid., vol. 2, 622.
84. Ibid., vol. 2, 640.
85. Ibid., vol. 2, 755.
86. Percival Goodman and Paul Goodman, *Communitas: Means of Livelihood and Ways of Life* (Chicago: University of Chicago Press, 1947), 1–2.
87. See ibid., 10–15.
88. Ibid., 59.
89. Ibid., 110–13.
90. Ibid., 130.
91. Paul Goodman, "Reflections on the Anarchist Principle," in *Political Ideologies*, eds Matthew Festenstein and Michael Kenny (Oxford: Oxford University Press, 2005), 374–5.
92. Ibid., 373–4.
93. Goodman, "Anarchism and Revolution," in *Political Ideologies*, ed. Festenstein and Kenny, 374–5.
94. Ibid., 374.
95. Goodman and Goodman, *Communitas*, 125.
96. Woodcock, *Anarchism*, 18–29.
97. "Strike in Guadeloupe Escalates into Rioting," *New York Times*, 17 Feb. 2009, http://www.nytimes.com/2009/02/17/world/europe/17iht-france.4.20259662.html.
98. Woodcock, *Anarchism*, 29.
99. Adam Smith, *The Nature and Causes of the Wealth of Nations*, ed. Kathryn Sutherland (1776; reprint, Oxford: Oxford University Press, 1993), V, i, 408.
100. Ibid., IV, v, 330.
101. John Stuart Mill, *On Liberty* (1859; reprint, Oxford: Oxford University Press, 1992), 121.
102. John Locke, *Second Treatise of Government*, ed. and introd. C.B. Macpherson (1690; reprint, Indianapolis: Hackett Publishing Co., 1980), Chap. VII, para. 81, 44.
103. Mancur Olson, *The Logic of Collective Action: Public Goods and the Theory of Groups* (Cambridge, MA: Harvard University Press, 1965), 131.

104. Robert Nozick, *Anarchy, State, and Utopia* (New York: Basic Books, 1974), 12–18. Nozick lists three steps in the evolution of such protective associations; the third, curiously, results in a federal judicial system, in some ways paralleling Kropotkin's idea of federalism.
105. The story here is more complicated than it first appears. Olson would have it that Kropotkin is naive in this matter, yet a close examination of *Mutual Aid* reveals that Kropotkin has done his historical homework and found evidence of mutual aid communes. Hence he says, "After passing through the savage tribe, and next through the village community, the Europeans came to work out in medieval times a new form of organization, which had the advantage of allowing greater latitude for individual initiative, while it largely responded at the same time to man's need of mutual support. A federation of village communities, covered by a network of guilds and fraternities, was called into existence in the medieval cities. . . . immense results [were] achieved under this new form of union—in well-being for all, in industries, art, science, and commerce." See Kropotkin, *Mutual Aid*, 224.
106. Jan Narveson makes use of the example of the Vikings, who benefited from the "depredations of such people as the Franks, the Goths, and the Anglo-Saxons." See Narveson, *The Libertarian Idea* (Peterborough, ON: Broadview Press, 2001), 177–81.
107. See Finer, *The History of Government from the Earliest Times*, vol. 3 (Oxford: Oxford University Press, 1997), 1298–1300, for these points and others.
108. This is a position presented 30 years ago by the distinguished international lawyer Richard Falk for the purpose of attempting its rebuttal. See Falk, "Anarchism and World Order," in *Nomos XIX: Anarchism*, ed. J. Roland Pennock and John W. Chapman (New York: New York University Press, 1978), 63–87.

Chapter 10: Neo-Liberalism and Libertarianism

1. Jan Narveson, *The Libertarian Idea* (Peterborough, ON: Broadview Press, 2001), 8.
2. Andrew Romano, "Last of the True Believers?," *Newsweek*, 25 Apr. 2009, http://www.newsweek.com/id/195088.
3. Nora Loreto, "Canada's Youth: From Passivism to Activism," CCPA *Monitor* (Sept./Oct. 2015): 41–2.
4. Heather Mallick, "The Nixon of the North: How Stephen Harper Ruined Canada," *Harper's* 331 (Oct. 2015): 67–8.
5. Isaiah Berlin, "Two Concepts of Liberty," in *Four Essays on Liberty* (Oxford: Oxford University Press, 1969), 122.
6. Ibid., 131.
7. Ibid.
8. See Peter Self, *Rolling Back the Market: Economic Dogma and Political Choice* (New York: St Martin's Press, 2000), 37, for this observation, as well as Freeden for a sympathetic account of same. See Michael Freeden, *Ideologies and Political Theory: A Conceptual Approach* (Oxford: Oxford University Press, 1996), 141–54.
9. Herbert Spencer, *The Man versus the State* (1884; reprint, Oxford: Penguin Books, 1969), 67.
10. For an excellent discussion of the collapse of old-style liberalism, see E.H. Carr, *What Is History?* (Harmondsworth, England: Penguin Books, 1961), 31–55, esp. 38. This is a book sadly neglected by political philosophers and political scientists.
11. Self, *Rolling Back the Market*, 40.
12. See Peter Self, *Political Theories of Modern Government: Its Role and Reform* (London: Unwin Hyman, 1985), 49, where he acknowledges that the main carriers of this invasion are the public choice theorists. However, it is obvious that he thinks of Hayek as an economist whose influence on politics and the political victories of negative liberals is substantial. See Self, *Rolling Back the Market*, 52.
13. Friedrich A. Hayek, *The Road to Serfdom* (Chicago: University of Chicago Press, 1944), 20–1.
14. Ibid., 36.
15. Ibid.
16. Ibid., 93.
17. We shall see shortly how this contrasts with the position taken by public choice theorists.
18. Ibid., 59.
19. Ibid., 72–87.
20. Ibid., 60.
21. Ibid., 101.
22. Ibid., 101–2.
23. Ibid., 240.
24. Friedrich Hayek, "Economic Freedom and

Representative Government," in Friedrich Hayek, *Economic Freedom* (Oxford: Basil Blackwell, 1991), 383ff.
25. Ibid., 383.
26. Ibid., 385.
27. Ibid.
28. Ibid., 388.
29. Ibid.
30. Ibid., 389.
31. Ibid.
32. Ibid.
33. These points are well summarized by Patrick Dunleavy, *Democracy, Bureaucracy and Public Choice: Economic Explanations in Political Science* (Toronto: Prentice-Hall, 1991), 30–3. According to Dunleavy (p. 31), Olson believes that benefits are indivisible if benefits produced for one person are available for a wider group as well; as well, goods are non-excludable if goods supplied for one group cannot be restricted to the people who organized their provision. Dunleavy's summary is clearer than Olson's but is consistent with what Olson says in Chapter 1 of his book, cited immediately below.
34. Mancur Olson, *The Logic of Collective Action: Public Goods and the Theory of Groups* (Cambridge, MA: Harvard University Press, 1965), 5.
35. Hence Olson quotes with approval the view of R.M. MacIver when he says, "every organization presupposes an interest which its members all share." Ibid., 8.
36. See ibid., 45, where he claims that small groups function without inducements and that this is owing to individual actions of a member of the group being noticeable to other members in the group. On the other hand, large groups, especially those with significant lobbying organizations, make use of selective incentives such as coercion or positive inducements. See ibid., 132–3.
37. Olson admits that even in the case of small groups, the collective good will not "ordinarily be provided on an optimal scale," but that this suboptimality or inefficiency will be worse for large groups than for small groups. See ibid., 34–6.
38. Ibid., 35.
39. For an updated version of Olson's ideas, see Dunleavy, *Democracy, Bureaucracy and Public Choice*, 30–2.
40. Ibid., 31.
41. This is a point made with vivid clarity by Olson, *Logic of Collective Action*, 127.
42. Mancur Olson, *The Rise and Decline of Nations* (New Haven: Yale University Press, 1982), 18.
43. Ibid., 13.
44. See ibid., 48.
45. Ibid., 236.
46. Ibid., 177–8, 236–7.
47. Ibid., 131.
48. For a clear and concise discussion of the New Right model of the public choice theory, see Dunleavy, *Democracy, Bureaucracy and Public Choice*, 36–8, 43.
49. With suitable substitutions for differences in nomenclature, this point is consistent with that advocated by Schumaker et al. See Paul Schumaker, Dwight C. Kiel, and Thomas Heilke, *Great Ideas/Grand Schemes: Political Ideologies in the Nineteenth and Twentieth Centuries* (Toronto: McGraw-Hill, 1996), 60.
50. Adam Smith, *The Nature and Causes of the Wealth of Nations*, ed. Kathryn Sutherland (1776; reprint, Oxford: Oxford University Press, 1993), IV, ii.
51. Robert Nozick, *Anarchy, State, and Utopia* (New York: Basic Books, 1974), 6–9, 18–22.
52. Ibid., 33.
53. Ibid., 26–35, 48–53. It is here that Nozick makes clearest a connection between redistribution and side constraints.
54. Ibid., 113–19.
55. Ibid., 149.
56. Ibid., 151–60.
57. Narveson, *Libertarian Idea*, 166.
58. Ibid., 131, 137–8, 140–1, 145–6.
59. Ibid., 148.
60. Ibid., 152.
61. Ibid., 148.
62. Ibid., 166.
63. Ibid., 14.
64. Ibid., 158. Narveson attributes the distinction to Arthur Ripstein. Ibid., 155.
65. Ibid., 180.
66. By "negative right" Narveson means that "someone else has a duty to refrain from preventing someone else from doing something." Ibid., 58.
67. Ibid., 165.
68. Ibid.
69. Ibid., 59.
70. Ibid., 154.
71. Ibid., 175.
72. Ibid.
73. Ibid.

74. Ibid.
75. Pareto-dominance requires that any change in welfare should be acceptable to all those affected by it. For further discussion, see note 78 below.
76. Ibid., 177.
77. Ibid., 155.
78. Ibid., 177. Narveson seems to use the expression "Pareto-dominance" in the way in which Mancur Olson uses the expression "Pareto-optimal." According to Olson, Pareto-optimality is achieved when the group gain is maximized. See Olson, *Logic of Collective Action*, 27. A weak version of Pareto's principle is given by Peter Self when he says, "[the principle] states merely that a welfare change ought not to leave any individual worse off." See Self, *Political Theories of Modern Government*, 75. Another formulation of this principle is given by Self when he says, "The Pareto principle requires that any change in welfare should be acceptable to all those affected by it." See Self, *Rolling Back the Market*, 70.
79. Narveson, *Libertarian Idea*, 179.
80. It seems passing strange that Narveson's considerations lead us to the topic of collective action, the very starting point of the discussion for Mancur Olson's considerations of public choice theory. See Olson, *Logic of Collective Action*, Chaps 1, 2, 5.
81. Narveson, *Libertarian Idea*, 179.
82. Farley Mowat gives three reasons why raiding might be more profitable than trading: (i) a raider does not have to invest capital in trade goods; (ii) a raider does not have to content himself with whatever the other person might choose to offer in exchange; and (iii) few things acquired by way of trade could surpass in value a commodity acquired by force. See Farley Mowat, *The Farfarers: Before the Norse* (Toronto: Seal Books, 1998), 139. This point also is made above in Chapter 2, "Classical Liberalism," when discussing Adam Smith; see Chapter 2, note 76.
83. Narveson, *Libertarian Idea*, 180–1, 187ff.
84. Dunleavy, *Democracy, Bureaucracy and Public Choice*, 36.
85. Ibid.
86. Narveson, *Libertarian Idea*, 180.
87. Ibid., 187–336. And one should be reminded that Nozick emphasizes that any state more extensive than the minimal state is unjustified because it violates people's rights. Nozick, *Anarchy, State, and Utopia*, 149.
88. Karl Marx, *Capital*, trans. Samuel Moore and Edward Aveling, ed. Frederick Engels (New York: Modern Library, 1906), 12.
89. See Alec Nove, *The Economics of Feasible Socialism* (London: George Allen and Unwin, 1983), 5, for a discussion of these externalities.
90. Will Kymlicka, *Contemporary Political Philosophy: An Introduction*, 2nd edn (Oxford: Oxford University Press, 2002), 102.
91. Joseph Schumpeter, *Capitalism, Socialism, and Democracy*, 3rd edn (New York: Harper and Row, 1950), 139.
92. Ibid., 141–2.
93. Self, *Political Theories of Modern Government*, 50.
94. Ibid., 51.
95. This is a point well developed by Self: ibid., 52.
96. Ibid., 53.
97. This bloated version of rational egoism is a well-ridden horse in introductory ethics classes. It is time to put it out of its misery. At the end of the day, distinctions—whatever they are called—have to be made between desires that are self-absorbing or self-centred, and those that are other-centred. Even if all action is motivated by the desires, or needs, of an individual rather than also by duties, at least some of these desires are other-centred. And here we need not just think of the Mother Teresas, but of the many publicly spirited individuals who do yeoman service in the communities in which we reside or who work tirelessly in building the institutions in which we conduct our lives.
98. See ibid., 57–8.
99. See ibid., 54.
100. Self makes these points in an elegant fashion. See ibid., 63.
101. Ibid., 189.
102. Self develops these ideas more fully. See ibid., 77–8, 189–92.
103. Narveson, *Libertarian Idea*, 270.
104. Nozick, *Anarchy, State, and Utopia*, 39.
105. Ibid., 38.
106. Narveson, *Libertarian Idea*, 69.
107. Kymlicka, *Contemporary Political Philosophy*, p. 158.
108. See Self, *Political Theories of Modern Government*, 8, 48–78; Dunleavy, *Democracy, Bureaucracy and Public Choice*, 258–9.

109. These questions are a paraphrase of queries suggested by Kymlicka, *Contemporary Political Philosophy*, 158.
110. The comments here are but a modified version of the ideas presented by Dunleavy in *Democracy, Bureaucracy and Public Choice*. He remarks (p. 258), "Much of the recent discussion of economic explanations in political science has not been helpful. Too many contributions still seem to have been written simply to convey an evangelistic fervour that somehow—in the future—public choice is about to transform our understanding. Yet as a research programme, the field is getting long in the tooth while its empirical applications remain at best weakly defined." Peter Self is also sensitive to the non-empirical nature of public choice theory. He maintains, "Public choice theories usually build upon economic or logical models of rational behaviour which distinguish them from the more empirical theories associated with the studies of pluralism, corporatism and bureaucracy." See Self, *Political Theories of Modern Government*, 208.
111. Nozick, *Anarchy, State, and Utopia*, 178.
112. These points are laid out in compelling fashion by Kevin Phillips, *Bad Money: Reckless Finance, Failed Politics, and the Global Crisis of American Capitalism* (New York: Viking, 2008), 97, 207.

Chapter 11: Feminism

1. Andrew Heywood, *Political Ideologies: An Introduction* (London: Macmillan Education, 1992), 217.
2. Margaret Atherton, "Cartesian Reason and Gendered Reason," in *A Mind of One's Own: Feminist Essays on Reason and Objectivity*, eds Louise M. Antony and Charlotte Witt (Boulder, CO: Westview Press, 1993).
3. Heywood, *Political Ideologies*, 218.
4. Interestingly, in 1923 the original text of the Equal Rights Amendment (ERA) was drafted by the American suffragist activist Alice Paul to mark the seventy-fifth anniversary of the Seneca Falls Convention and its Declaration of Sentiments. Six decades later, the ERA—although passed by Congress—was unable to get ratification in the required 38 states. As discussed in Chapter 13, "Religious Fundamentalism," the American Christian right actively opposed the ERA because it ran counter to the belief—said to be based on scripture—that women were subordinate to men.
5. Rand Dyck, *Canadian Politics*, 4th edn (Scarborough, ON: Nelson Thomson, 2004), 305–6, and Alison Prentice et al., *Canadian Women: A History* (Toronto: Harcourt Brace Jovanovich-Holt, 1988), 282–3.
6. Dyck, *Canadian Politics*, 130.
7. *Edwards et al. v. Attorney General for Canada*, [1930] A.C. 124, 1 D.L.R. (P.C.). This decision by the Privy Council in Great Britain (popularly known as the "Persons Case") overturned a Supreme Court of Canada ruling in 1927 that women were not persons under the British North America Act.
8. It needs to be kept in mind that though the franchise was extended both federally and provincially in Canada during this time, minority groups were discriminated against until 1960, when the last disenfranchised citizens—First Nations—were finally allowed to vote in federal elections without forgoing their treaty rights.
9. See John Stuart Mill, *On Liberty* (1859); reprint ed. and introd. John Gray (Oxford: Oxford University Press, 1991).
10. Simone de Beauvoir, *The Second Sex* (1949; reprint, London: New English Library, 1960), 9.
11. Ibid.
12. See Ruth Gavison, "Feminism and the Public/Private Distinction," *Stanford Law Review* 45 (1992): 10, for an affirmation of the centrality of the public/private distinction in feminist thought. The author is indebted to Will Kymlicka for pointing out the importance of this article. See Kymlicka, *Contemporary Political Philosophy: An Introduction*, 2nd edn (Oxford: Oxford University Press, 2002), 421.
13. Will Kymlicka identifies three topics for analysis: (i) sexual equality and sexual discrimination, (ii) the public and the private, and (iii) an ethic of care. He deals effectively with each of these. The intent of the present writing is to show feminism to be more wide-ranging than these three topics suggest. See Kymlicka, *Contemporary Political Philosophy*, 377–8.
14. Stephen Kirchner, "German Feminism: Playing Dirty," *Time*, 18 June 2008, http://www.time.com/time/magazine/article/0,9171,1815720,00.html.
15. See Selin Grit, "Turkey Rallies over Murder of Woman Who 'Resisted Rape'," 15

Feb. 2015, www.bbc.com/news/world-europe-31476978; "Rape in India: 2012 Delhi Gang Rape in Jharkhand," *Wikipedia*.
16. Lynne O'Donnell and Rahim Faiez, "Protesters March for Woman Killed by Mob," *Globe and Mail*, 24 Mar. 2015, A12.
17. Denise Balkisoon, "A Very Dangerous Woman," *Globe and Mail*, 18 Apr. 2015, F3.
18. "El Salvador Woman Pardoned: Guadalupe Was Sentenced to 30 Years for Suffering a Miscarriage," *The Candle* 14, 1 (Spring 2015): 6.
19. Manfred Ertel, "Iceland's Women Reach for Power," *Spiegel Online International*, 22 Apr. 2009, http://www.Speigel.de/international/Europe/0,1518,620544,00,html.
20. Catherine Rampell, "As Layoffs Surge, Women May Pass Men in Job Force," *New York Times*, 5 Feb. 2009, http://www.nytimes.com/2009/02/06/business/06women.html.
21. Paul Schumaker, Dwight C. Kiel, and Thomas Heilke, *Great Ideas/Grand Schemes: Political Ideologies in the Nineteenth and Twentieth Centuries* (Toronto: McGraw-Hill, 1996), 402.
22. Alice Schwarzer, "The Function of Sexuality," in *Oppression of Women*, reprinted in *German Feminist Writings*, eds Patricia A. Herminghouse and Magda Mueller (New York and London: Continuum, 2001), 226. Schwarzer at times leans on other ideas of Firestone, specifically the following four demands: the freeing of women from the tyranny of reproduction by every means possible; economic and political autonomy for women and children; the complete integration of women and children into society; and the sexual freedom of women and children. See Shulamith Firestone, *The Dialectic of Sex* (London: Paladin, 1970), 192–5.
23. Schwarzer, "Function of Sexuality," 223.
24. Ibid.
25. Ibid.
26. Ibid., 224.
27. Ibid.
28. Ibid.
29. Ibid.
30. Ibid., 225.
31. Ibid., 226.
32. Ibid.
33. Ibid.
34. Ibid., 225–6.
35. Margaret Whitford, *Luce Irigaray: Philosophy in the Feminine* (London and New York: Routledge, 1991), 10.
36. Ibid., 12.
37. Ibid.
38. Ibid., 16–17.
39. Ibid., 17. It should be kept in mind that Plato in the *Republic* recognizes that the major part of the human mind is the desirous part, which he distinguishes from the reasoning and passionate parts. So others before the Enlightenment clearly acknowledged the power of non-rational forces in the human psyche. See Plato, *Republic* (Oxford: Oxford University Press, 1994), 153–5.
40. Luce Irigaray, *The Sex Which Is Not One* (Ithaca, NY: Cornell University Press, 1985), 159.
41. Ibid., 86.
42. Ibid., 159.
43. Ibid., 72.
44. Ibid.
45. Ibid., 73.
46. Ibid., 74.
47. Ibid.
48. Ibid., 161.
49. Ibid., 31.
50. Ibid., 170.
51. Ibid., 184–5.
52. Ibid., 192.
53. Ibid., 26.
54. Carol Gilligan, *In a Different Voice: Psychological Theory and Women's Development* (Cambridge, MA: Harvard University Press, 1982), 164.
55. Selma Sevenhuijsen, "Justice, Moral Reasoning, and the Politics of Child Custody," in *Equality Politics and Gender*, eds Elizabeth Meehan and Selma Sevenhuijsen (London: Sage, 1991), 97.
56. Augusto Blasi, "Kohlberg's Theory and Moral Motivation," in *The Legacy of Lawrence Kohlberg*, ed. Dawn Schrader (San Francisco: Jossey-Bass, 1990), 51.
57. Harvey Siegel, "On Using Psychology to Justify Judgements of Moral Adequacy," in *Lawrence Kohlberg: Consensus and Controversy*, eds Sohan Modgil and Celia Modgil (London: Falmer Press, 1986), 67.
58. Ibid., 68–70.
59. Gilligan, *In a Different Voice*, 21.
60. Ibid., 20.
61. Ibid., 21.
62. Sevenhuijsen, "Justice, Moral Reasoning," 97.
63. Carol Gilligan, "Remapping the Moral Domain," in *Reconstructing Individualism: Autonomy, Individuality, and the Self in Western*

Thought, eds Thomas Heller, Morton Sosna, and D.E. Wellberry (Stanford, CA: Stanford University Press, 1986), 238.
64. Gilligan, *In a Different Voice*, 17.
65. Gilligan, "Remapping the Moral Domain," 237–41.
66. Susan Okin, *Women in Western Political Thought* (Princeton, NJ: Princeton University Press, 1979), 4.
67. Ibid., 9. One might add to what Okin says by claiming that these philosophers generally analyzed the state and society without saying much about women.
68. Susan Okin, *Justice, Gender, and Family* (New York: Basic Books, 1989), 14.
69. Ibid., 91. Whether the tradition to which she refers is the whole (Western?) political tradition or simply the liberal tradition is unclear, but at the very least it includes the latter.
70. Ibid., 90.
71. Ibid., 90–102.
72. Ibid., 6.
73. Ibid., 93, 97.
74. Ibid., 108, 170.
75. Ibid., 108–9.
76. Ibid.
77. Ibid., 6–7.
78. Ibid., 14, 170.
79. Ibid., 179–85.
80. Ibid., 175, 176, 180.
81. Ibid., 171.
82. Martha Nussbaum, "The Future of Feminist Liberalism," in *Social and Political Philosophy: Classical Western Texts in Feminist and Multicultural Perspectives*, 3rd edn, ed. James P. Sterba (Belmont, CA: Wadsworth, 2003), 549–69.
83. Ibid., 553, 557.
84. Ibid., 550–5.
85. Ibid., 556.
86. Ibid., 563–4.
87. Ibid., 559.
88. Ibid., 557–9.
89. Ibid., 560.
90. Ibid., 561.
91. Ibid.
92. Ibid., 562.
93. Carol J. Adams and Lori Gruen, eds, *Ecofeminism: Feminist Intersections with Other Animals and the Earth* (London: Bloomsbury, 2014), 1.
94. Val Plumwood, *Feminism and the Mastery of Nature* (London and New York: Routledge, 1993), 1–2.
95. Ibid., 7.
96. Ibid., 166–8, 182–9.
97. The ethic of care also stands in contrast to rights-based ethics, an ethics that Plumwood thinks has "acquired an exaggerated importance in ethics as part of the public sphere and the masculine." Ibid., 172–3.
98. Ibid., 168.
99. Ibid., 168–9.
100. Ibid., 170.
101. Ibid., 183.
102. Ibid., 174.
103. See Warwick Fox, *A Theory of General Ethics: Human Relationships, Nature, and the Built Environment* (Cambridge, MA: MIT Press, 2006).
104. Plumwood, *Feminism and the Mastery of Nature*, 179.
105. Plumwood believes that dualisms such as culture/nature, reason/nature, male/female, mind/body, master/slave, reason/emotion are closely associated with domination and accumulation. See ibid., 42–3.
106. See Adams and Gruen, eds, *Ecofeminism*, 1.
107. Nel Noddings, *Women and Evil* (Berkeley, CA: University of California Press, 1989), 1.
108. Noddings believes that traditional ethical systems ignore many questions that are important to women. See ibid., 187.
109. Ibid., 183–7.
110. Ibid., 186.
111. Nel Noddings, *Peace Education: How We Come to Love and Hate War* (Cambridge: Cambridge University Press, 2012), 112–14.
112. Noddings, *Women and Evil*, 187.
113. Ibid., 178.
114. Ibid.
115. Ibid.
116. Ibid., 179.
117. Ibid., 182.
118. Ibid., 183.
119. Ibid., 187.
120. Ibid.
121. Ibid., 188.
122. Ibid., 189.
123. Ibid., 192.
124. Ibid., 197.
125. Ibid., 199–205.
126. Noddings, *Peace Education*, 119.
127. Ayaan Hirsi Ali, *The Caged Virgin: An Emancipation Proclamation for Women and Islam* (New York: Free Press, 2006), ix–xi.
128. Ibid., 2–7.
129. Ibid., 34.
130. Ibid., 17.

131. Ibid., 19.
132. Ibid.
133. That Hirsi Ali sees Islamic fundamentalism as an ideology is evident in her remarks on 9/11 where she speaks of the ideology that fuelled the terrorists of that event. See ibid., 36.
134. Ibid., 19.
135. Ibid., 20.
136. Ibid.
137. Ibid., 23.
138. Ibid., 26.
139. Ibid.
140. Ibid.
141. Ibid.
142. Ibid., 27–8.
143. Ibid., 28–9.
144. Ibid., 33.
145. Ibid., 35.
146. Ibid., 35.
147. Ibid., 36–8.
148. Ibid., 38.
149. Ibid., 37–41.
150. Ibid., 12–14.
151. Ibid., 14.
152. Ayaan Hirsi Ali, *Heretic: Why Islam Needs a Reformation Now* (New York: HarperCollins, 2015), 235.
153. Ibid., 234–5.
154. Ibid., Chap. 6, "Social Control Begins at Home."
155. See Wittgenstein's comments where he makes a similar point in connection with the notion of generalizing about similarities. Ludwig Wittgenstein, *Philosophical Investigations* (Oxford: Basil Blackwell, 1963), para. 67: "And the strength of the thread does not reside in the fact that some one fibre runs through its whole length, but in the overlapping of many fibres."
156. A good example of such a mechanism is found in the organization Canadian Women for Women in Afghanistan. This organization provided relief efforts for women in Afghanistan, and three of its members were killed by the Taliban on 13 August 2008.
157. John Rawls, *A Theory of Justice* (Oxford: Oxford University Press, 1972), 490.
158. Gilligan, *In A Different Voice*, 19.
159. Rainer Maria Rilke, *Letters to a Young Poet* (New York: Norton, 1934), 167.
160. The writer wishes to acknowledge his debt to R.L. Bowman for drawing to his attention the importance of Rilke's ideas on relationships in this context.
161. For a clear and analytic treatment of Kant and the principles of the Enlightenment, see Ernst Cassirer, *The Philosophy of the Enlightenment* (Boston: Beacon Press, 1951).
162. Adam Smith, *The Theory of Moral Sentiments* (New York: Cambridge University Press, 2002), Part II, Chap. II, 1, 97.
163. Ibid., Part VI, Conclusion, 6, 311.
164. Noddings, *Peace Education*, 112.
165. Kate Millett, *Sexual Politics* (New York: Ballantine Books, 1969), 1–12.
166. Ibid., 30.
167. For informative background material on Arabization and Islamization, see George Antonius, *The Arab Awakening: The Story of the Arab National Movement* (London: Hamish Hamilton, 1938).

Chapter 12: Environmentalism

1. James K. Boyce, "Rethinking Extinction: Toward a Less Gloomy Environmentalism," *Harper's* 331 (Nov. 2015): 67–75, esp. 71.
2. Ibid., 68.
3. Ibid., 72.
4. Bhopal Medical Appeal advertisement, *The Observer*, 5 June 2005, 16.
5. For a legal evaluation of this accident, see C.M. Abraham and Sushila Abraham, "The Bhopal Case and the Development of Environmental Law in India," *International and Comparative Law Quarterly* 40 (1991): 334. Other accounts claim that more than 3,500 people died and more than 150,000 people were injured. See Robert Paehlke, ed., *Conservation and Environmentalism: An Encyclopedia* (New York: Garland, 1995), 71.
6. Bhopal Medical Appeal advertisement.
7. Two that spring to mind here are the nuclear disaster at Chernobyl, Ukraine, on 26 April 1986, and the Sandoz warehouse disaster at Basel, Switzerland, on 1 November 1986.
8. Robert Pollin, "Doing the Recovery Right," *The Nation*, 28 Jan. 2009, http://www.thenation.com/doc/20090216/pollin/print?rel=nofollow.
9. See Ramachandra Guha, *Environmentalism: A Global History* (Don Mills, ON: Longman, 2000).
10. Ibid., 4.
11. Ibid., 5–6. A good Victorian example of literary reaction to pollution is Charles Dickens's *Our Mutual Friend* (1865), where both the river and piles of human refuse are symbols dominating the novel.

12. Guha repeats the assertion, first made by author Thomas De Quincey, that Wordsworth walked some 175,000 miles during his lifetime.
13. Guha, *Environmentalism*, 13. One can only speculate on what his thoughts would have been had he witnessed the tragedy of Bhopal.
14. Ibid., 15. This view contrasts with that of Karl Marx and Friedrich Engels, who saw the city and the country quite differently: "The bourgeoisie has subjected the country to the rule of the towns. It has created enormous cities, has greatly increased the urban population as compared with the rural, and has rescued a considerable part of the population from the idiocy of rural life." See *The Communist Manifesto* (1848; reprint, Oxford: Oxford University Press, 1992), 7.
15. Ibid.
16. Query: where does Adam Smith stand on the matter of the desirability of the multiplication of wants?
17. Guha, *Environmentalism*, 20.
18. Ibid., 25.
19. Ibid., 25–6.
20. Ibid., 26.
21. Ibid., 30. Notice here how Guha slips into the idiom of "ideology" in connection with environmentalism, notwithstanding his apparent aversion to this idiom earlier in the book, where he talks of environmentalism as a movement. See ibid., 5, 31, 43.
22. Ibid., 37.
23. Ibid., 45.
24. Ibid., 46. Smuts coined the term **holism**, a reference to the interconnectedness of the ecosystem.
25. Ibid., 50–2. There is an intimation in Muir's writings, especially in his writings inspired by pantheism, of a "reverence for life" principle. This very phrase was used by Albert Schweitzer in *Civilization and Ethics*, 3rd edn (London: Adam and Charles Black, 1949), though any influence of Muir on Schweitzer is unknown.
26. Environmental historian Roderick Nash, as quoted in John M. Meyer, *Political Nature: Environmentalism and the Interpretation of Western Thought* (Cambridge, MA: MIT Press, 2001), 23. Leopold's significant contribution to the field of wildlife management inspired environmental groups in the United States.
27. Guha, *Environmentalism*, 57.
28. The ideas of biodiversity will be discussed below in connection with the writings of Anne and Paul Ehrlich.
29. It is interesting to note, especially in light of the thematic connection between Muir and Albert Schweitzer, that Carson dedicated her book to Albert Schweitzer, who had stated: "Man has lost his capacity to foresee and forestall. He will end by destroying the earth." See Rachel Carson, *Silent Spring* (New York: Fawcett Crest Books, 1962).
30. Ibid., 16.
31. Ibid., 18.
32. Ibid., 25.
33. Ibid., 41.
34. Ibid., 44.
35. Ibid., 59.
36. Ibid., 199.
37. Ibid., 231.
38. Later supporters of ecologism would say that Carson was guilty of speciesism by looking at things from the human perspective.
39. Ibid., 261–2.
40. World Commission on Environment and Development (WCED), *Our Common Future* (Oxford: Oxford University Press, 1987), 43.
41. Ibid., 27. This clearly leaves the Commission open to the charge of speciesism.
42. Ibid., 32–3.
43. Ibid., 49–65.
44. Ibid., 310.
45. Ibid.
46. Ibid., 311.
47. Union of Concerned Scientists, *World Scientists' Warning to Humanity* (18 Nov. 1992), reproduced in Paul R. Ehrlich and Anne H. Ehrlich, *Betrayal of Science and Reason: How Anti-Environmental Rhetoric Threatens Our Future* (Washington, DC: Island Press, 1996), 242–50.
48. Ibid., 244–5.
49. Ibid., 246.
50. Robert E. Goodin, *Green Political Theory* (Cambridge: Polity Press, 1992), 185.
51. Ibid., 183.
52. Ibid., 191.
53. The expression comes from Amory Lovins, a student of Schumacher, who objected to using high technology to solve simple problems. In its entirety, the expression reads: "using nuclear fission to boil water is like using a chainsaw to cut butter."
54. Ibid., 193–8.
55. Ibid., 198–9.
56. Some would question whether these ideals

57. Ibid., 199–202.
58. Ibid., 44.
59. Ibid., 43. The deep ecology view of value is one of intrinsic value. Curiously, John Locke at times recognizes such a view when he refers to "the intrinsic value of things" and "the natural intrinsic value." See Locke, *Second Treatise of Government*, ed. and introd. C.B. Macpherson (Indianapolis: Hackett Publishing Co., 1980), paras 37, 43. Normally, he affirms either the labour theory of value or the market theory of value.
60. Goodin, *Green Political Theory*, 22–7.
61. Ibid., 54–77.
62. John Barry, *Environment and Social Theory*, 2nd edn (London: Routledge, 2007), 11.
63. Næss's position is discussed below in greater detail.
64. In this regard, see Andrew Dobson's discussion of Barry in his *Green Political Thought*, 4th edn (London: Routledge, 2007), 191.
65. Barry, *Environment and Social Theory*, 313.
66. Ibid., 295–7.
67. Ibid., 308–12.
68. Ibid., 312.
69. E.F. Schumacher, *Small Is Beautiful: A Study of Economics as if People Mattered* (New York: Harper and Row, 1973), v. Schumacher is quoting from Aldo Leopold's *A Sand County Almanac* (1949). The Alhambra is the palace fortress and garden of the Moorish monarchs of Granada in the Andalusian area of Spain. It dates back to the fourteenth century.
70. Arne Næss, *Ecology, Community, and Lifestyle: Outline of an Ecosophy*, trans. and rev. David Rothenberg (Cambridge: Cambridge University Press, 1989), 29. This book is based on Næss's *Økologi, samfunn, og livsstil* (Oslo: Universitetsforlaget, 1976).
71. Dobson, *Green Political Thought*, 25.
72. Ibid., 3.
73. Ibid., 2–3.
74. Ibid., 3.
75. Ibid., 5.
76. Ibid., 5, 28.
77. Ibid., 189.
78. Ibid., 42–3.
79. Ibid., 43.
80. Ibid., 51.
81. Ibid., 202.
82. Ibid.
83. Warwick Fox, *Toward a Transpersonal Ecology: Developing New Foundations for Environmentalism* (Boston: Shambhala, 1990; reprint, Albany: State University of New York Press, 1995).
84. Warwick Fox, *A Theory of General Ethics: Human Relationships, Nature, and the Built Environment* (Cambridge, MA: MIT Press, 2006), 14.
85. Fox, *Transpersonal Ecology*, 198.
86. Ibid.
87. Ibid., 217.
88. Fox does not make clear why we are seeking as expansive a self as possible. Plausibly, he might suggest that the answer is self-evident, in the way in which Aristotle might say it is self-evident that we seek happiness.
89. Ibid., 249.
90. Ibid., 267–8.
91. Fox, *Theory of General Ethics*, 55.
92. Ibid., 59.
93. Ibid.
94. Rainer Maria Rilke, *Letters to a Young Poet*, trans. Joan M. Burnham (reprint, Novato, CA: New World Library, 2000), 67.
95. Fox, *Theory of General Ethics*, 9–10.
96. Ibid., 67–8.
97. Ibid., 78–82.
98. Ibid., 300–1.
99. Ibid., 203.
100. Ibid., 107.
101. Ibid., 108–9.
102. Ibid., 80–1.
103. Ibid., 89.
104. Ibid., 302–5. See Chap. 6 for Fox's theory of contexts.
105. As pointed out by E.P. Thomson in the introduction to Bahro, *Socialism and Survival* (cited below), 7.
106. Rudolf Bahro, *Socialism and Survival*, trans. David Fernbach (London: Heretic Books, 1982), 38–9. See Isaiah 33:4: "Your plunder, O nations, is harvested as by young locusts; like a swarm of locusts men pounce on it."
107. Bahro, *Socialism and Survival*, 57.
108. Bahro admits that he has left scientific socialism behind and has embraced utopian socialism. See *From Red to Green: Interviews with New Left Review*, trans. Gus Fagan and Richard Hurst (London: Verso, 1984), 220: "From scientific socialism I have returned to utopian socialism, and politically I have moved from a class-dimensional to a populist-dimensional orientation."
109. Bahro, *Socialism and Survival*, 65.

110. Ibid., 28.
111. Ibid., 58–9.
112. Murray Bookchin, *The Philosophy of Social Ecology: Essays on Dialectical Naturalism*, 2nd edn, rev. (Montreal: Black Rose Books, 1995), xi.
113. Ibid., 119.
114. Ibid., 30–1. This is a big assumption on the part of Bookchin.
115. Ibid., 119.
116. Ibid., 120.
117. Ibid., 140.
118. Ibid.
119. Ibid., 136.
120. Ibid., 140.
121. Ibid., 33, 138.
122. Even the US government (which, under George W. Bush, proved reluctant to acknowledge climate change as a fact) has most recently come out in support of placing polar bears on the endangered species list because of melting ice caps—one of the signs of climate change.
123. For the listing of these headings, see Peninah Neimark and Peter Rhoades Mott, eds, *The Environmental Debate: A Documentary History* (Westport, CT: Greenwood Press, 1999), Introduction.
124. Donella H. Meadows et al., *The Limits to Growth* (Washington: Potomac Associates, 1972); Ehrlich and Ehrlich, *Betrayal of Science and Reason*, 71–2. As for Thomas Malthus, one should point out that he took aim at William Godwin, the anarchist, and his perfectibilist vision of human society in the matter of population. See T.R. Malthus, *An Essay on the Principle of Population* (1798; reprint, Oxford: Oxford University Press, 1993).
125. Ehrlich and Ehrlich, *Betrayal of Science and Reason*, 243.
126. Sandra Postel and Brian Richter, *Rivers for Life: Managing Water for People and Nature* (Washington, DC: Island Press, 2003), 14–16.
127. Deborah J. Pain, Andrew Meharg et al., "Levels of Cadmium and Zinc in the Soil and Plants Following the Toxic Spill from a Pyrite Mine, Aznalcollar, Spain," *Ambio* 32 (2003): 52–7.
128. Walter Wagner et al., "Sustainable Watershed Management: An International Multi-Watershed Study," *Ambio* 31 (2002): 2.
129. International Energy Agency (IEA), "Energy and Poverty," *IEA Bulletin* 44 (2002): 24.
130. For a full discussion and analysis of the ecological disaster at the Alberta tar sands, see William Marsden, *Stupid to the Last Drop: How Alberta Is Bringing Environmental Armageddon to Canada (and Doesn't Seem to Care)* (Toronto: Alfred A. Knopf, Canada, 2007).
131. Neimark and Mott, *Environmental Debate*, 273.
132. Eberhard Renner, "The Black Triangle Area—Fit for Europe?" *Ambio* 31 (2002): 231.
133. There are many such examples, including land-sourced pollutants from urban and industrial refuse that find their way into the ocean. See A.D. McIntyre, "Marine Pollution," in *World Guide to Environmental Issues and Organizations*, ed. P. Brackley (Harlow, England: Longman Current Affairs, 1999), 96.
134. Aaron Schwabach, "The Sandoz Spill: The Failure of International Law to Protect the Rhine from Pollution," *Ecology Law Quarterly* 16 (1989): 445–7.
135. Wynet Smith, "Undercutting Sustainability: The Global Problem of Illegal Logging and Trade," *Journal of Sustainable Forestry* 19 (2004): 10.
136. Sagar Krupa, "Atmosphere and Agriculture in the New Millennium," *Environmental Pollution* 126 (2003): 293.
137. Paul and Anne Ehrlich, "The Value of Biodiversity," *Ambio* 21 (1992): 225.
138. Boris Worm and David Vanderzwaag, "High-Seas Fisheries: Troubled Waters, Tangled Governance, and Recovery Prospects," *Behind the Headlines*, 1 Sept. 2007, http://www.thefreelibrary.com/High-seas+fisheries%3a+troubled+waters%2c+tangled+governance%2c+and...-a0170279120.
139. For an account of these and other accidents, see H.B. McCullough, "How Best to Drain the Alchemist's Cauldron: A Study of Marine Pollution in Australia," *Australian Journal of Political Science* 29 (1994): 73ff.
140. They have compelling things to say on the economic front as well. See, for instance, Amy Sinden, "The Economics of Endangered Species: Why Less Is More in the Economic Analysis of Critical Habitat Designations," *Harvard Environmental Law Review* 28 (2004): 129.
141. Thomas L. Friedman, *Hot, Flat, and Crowded: Why We Need a Green Revolution and How It Can Renew America* (New York: Farrar, Straus and Giroux, 2008).

142. See Antonio Cassese, *International Law,* 2nd edn (Oxford: Oxford University Press, 2005), Chap. 23.
143. Thomas Hobbes, *Leviathan* (1651; reprint, Oxford: Oxford University Press, 1996), Part 2, Chap. 18, para. 20.

Chapter 13: Religious Fundamentalism

1. Thomas Meyer, *Identity Mania: Fundamentalism and the Politicization of Cultural Differences* (London: Zed Books, 1997), 17.
2. Other things to be said of fundamentalism include a tendency for it to use a selective interpretation of traditions. See Rhys H. Williams, "Movement Dynamics and Social Change: Transforming Fundamentalist Ideology and Organization," in *Accounting for Fundamentalisms*, eds Martin E. Marty and R. Scott Appleby (Chicago: University of Chicago Press, 1994), 805. Others have described fundamentalism as a systematically distorted form of communication. See Meyer, *Identity Mania*, 25.
3. Lloyd Geering, *Fundamentalism: The Challenge to the Secular World* (Wellington, NZ: St Andrew's Trust for the Study of Religion and Society, 2003), 17–18.
4. Jeff Sharlet, "Jesus Killed Mohammed: The Crusade for a Christian Military," *Harper's* 318 (May 2009): 31-43, esp. 35.
5. See "2002 Gujarat Riots," *Wikipedia*. Accessed 28 Apr. 2015. See also Martha C. Nussbaum, "Body of the Nation: Why Women Were Mutilated in Gujarat," *Boston Review*, 29 July 2004.
6. "Boko Haram Kidnapping," *Wikipedia*. Accessed 13 May 2015.
7. "Al-Shabaab," *Wikipedia*. Accessed 13 May 2015.
8. The settlers think of themselves as occupying lands that were historically Jewish lands. See M. Feige, *Settling in the Hearts: Jewish Fundamentalism in the Occupied Territories* (Detroit: Wayne State University Press, 2009).
9. The idea, often talked about by government officials, of a "quick fix," or "degrading the enemy," or "eliminating the enemy" in connection with these messy political and military situations, upon reflection, can only strike one as absurd. It reminds one of the fanfare that accompanied pronouncements from Western governments about the "war on drugs." No one could possibly have believed rationally that the war on drugs was anything but a mug's game. There was simply too much money on the side of the "bad guys" for this to be anything but a phony war.
10. Youssef M. Choueiri, *Islamic Fundamentalism* (Boston: Twayne, 1990), 12.
11. This was Kant's definition of "enlightenment," a term that surfaces in surprising ways in discussions by fundamentalists. See Immanuel Kant, "What Is Enlightenment?" in *On History* (1784), reprinted and trans. Lewis White Beck et al. (New York: Bobbs-Merrill, 1963), 3–10.
12. Information in the two bulleted items is taken from Andrew Heywood, *Political Ideologies: An Introduction* (London: Macmillan Education, 1992), 167–8. For independent confirmation of accuracy of this summary, see Niels C. Nielsen Jr et al., *Religions of the World* (New York: St Martin's Press, 1983), 615–22, 647–55. See also Alfred Guillaume, *Islam*, 2nd edn (Harmondsworth, Middlesex: Penguin Books, 1956), 111–27.
13. All but the first of these reasons come from James P. Piscatori, *Islam in a World of Nation-States* (London: Cambridge University Press, 1986), 26–34. I have modified the second reason given by Piscatori from "process of development" to "process of urbanization," since the second of these better expresses what he goes on to discuss. The reason that turns on foreign occupation, repression, and humiliation is suggested by Sayed Khatab, *Understanding Islamic Fundamentalism: The Theological and Ideological Basis of al-Qa'ida's Political Tactics* (Cairo and New York: American University in Cairo Press, 2011), 20–5.
14. For a more complete analysis of these points, see Khatab, *Understanding Islamic Fundamentalism*, 20–4.
15. For a first approximation of resentment felt in the Islamic world towards US intervention in Muslim countries, see Khalil-ur-Rehman, "Islamic Fundamentalism," *The Dialogue* 6, 2 (2011): 93–104. See especially p. 95, where he says, "The American occupations of Afghanistan and Iraq have further reinforced the anti-American centre of gravity. . . . The Islamic world is under assault since centuries and remains so . . . America is no more a Republic, or City on the Hill. It is neo-Rome, Obama or no Obama, for these Trilateralist symbols symbolize imperialism."

16. Piscatori, *Islam in a World of Nation-States*, 26, calls this event "al-nakba," meaning "the disaster."
17. See Khatab, *Understanding Islamic Fundamentalism*, 81–2, for the assertion that after the defeat of the Arabs in the Six-Day War, a revival of Islam occurred among Muslims—a revival right-wing in orientation.
18. See the excellent discussion of the shifting sands of leadership in the Arab world in the late twentieth century in Cary Fraser, "In Defense of Allah's Realm: Religion and Statecraft in Saudi Foreign Policy Strategy," in *Transnational Religion and Fading States*, eds Susanne Hoeber Rudolph and James Piscatori (Boulder, CO: Westview Press, 1997), 221–40, esp. 221.
19. Ibid., 221.
20. The assassination of Sadat was carried out by a brother of one of the Muslim Brotherhood incarcerated by Sadat for instigating food riots. These riots broke out in response to Sadat's removal of bread subsidies as a condition for receiving IMF loans. As discussed later in the chapter, the Muslim Brotherhood was formed in the early part of the twentieth century by Hassan al-Banna.
21. Piscatori, *Islam in a World of Nation-States*, 27.
22. Ibid., 28.
23. Susanne Hoeber Rudolph, "Introduction: Religion, States, and Transnational Civil Society," in *Transnational Religion and Fading States,* eds Rudolph and Piscatori, 1.
24. See Fraser, "In Defense of Allah's Realm," 228–9, for a discussion of this point.
25. Ibid., 226.
26. Piscatori, *Islam in a World of Nation-States*, 32.
27. For a recent study of the historic background of Islamic radicalism, see Stephen Schwartz, *The Two Faces of Islam: The House of Sa'ud from Tradition to Terror* (New York: Random House, 2002), esp. Chaps 2 and 3. For the specific target of Taymiyyah's attack, see p. 55.
28. One of the best historical accounts of the Wahhabi movement is found in George Antonius's masterpiece, *The Arab Awakening: The Story of the Arab National Movement* (London: Hamish Hamilton, 1938), esp. 21–34.
29. See Khatab, *Understanding Islamic Fundamentalism*, 59.
30. Ibid., 56–65. Khatab recounts the story as given by Humphrey of his telling al-Wahhab of a dream he had of the Prophet. In the alleged dream the Prophet refers to al-Wahhab as his namesake and deputy in worldly and religious matters. Ibid., 62.
31. See Schwartz, *Two Faces of Islam*, 160.
32. Nielsen et al., *Religions of the World*, 668.
33. See Roger Hardy, *The Muslim Revolt: A Journey through Political Islam* (London: Hurst and Co., 2010), 97–8.
34. See Tariq Ali, *The Clash of Fundamentalisms: Crusades, Jihads and Modernity* (London and New York: Verso, 2003), 73–4.
35. Antonius, *Arab Awakening*, 338.
36. Schwartz, *Two Faces of Islam*, 155.
37. Mahmood Mamdani, "Senseless and [Sensible] Violence: Mourning the Dead at Westgate Mall," *Al Jazeera*, 26 Sept. 2013, http://www.aljazeera.com/indepth/opinion/2013/09/senseless-sensible-violence-mourning-dead-at-westgate-mall-2013925632 53438882.html.
38. "The History of Shia Muslims: Why the Aggravation?" *The Economist*, 6–12 Mar. 2004, 41. Al-Zarqawi was obviously an unwanted person in Iraq, from the United States' point of view. He and alleged foreign fighters in Iraq were the target of a US aerial attack in mid-May 2004. See Alan Freeman, "Bush to Outline 'Clear Strategy', for Iraq," *Globe and Mail*, 22 May 2004, A10. Further evidence of the hostility towards the Shi'ites originating from Wahhabis is found in the words Sunni sheik Hamed al-Ali posted on his website. He condemned the Shi'ite day of martyrdom "as the world's biggest display of heathens and idolatry." See "History of Shia Muslims: Why the Aggravation?"
39. Antonius, *Arab Awakening*, 22.
40. Peter Mandaville, *Global Political Islam* (London: Routledge, 2007), 152–3.
41. Ibid., 153–4.
42. Hamid Enayat, *Modern Islamic Political Thought* (Austin: University of Texas Press, 1982), 85. Note that al-Banna does not see himself standing in the Shi'ite tradition, but in the Sunni tradition. This is consistent with the claims made subsequently, namely, that Wahhabism is an offshoot of Sunnism and an adversary of Shi'ism.
43. Mandaville, *Global Political Islam*, 69–70.
44. Sayed Khatab, *The Political Thought of Sayyid Qutb: The Theory of Jahiliyyah* (London: Routledge, 2006), 142.

45. Ibid., 146.
46. Mandaville, *Global Political Islam*, 77.
47. Ibid., 78.
48. Sayyid Qutb, "The Present and Future of Islam," in *Readings in Political Ideologies since the Rise of Modern Science*, eds H.B. McCullough and Wolfgang Depner (Oxford: Oxford University Press, 2013), 312–16.
49. Hardy, *The Muslim Revolt*, 36.
50. See ibid. for more details.
51. Hamid Dabashi, *Shi'ism: A Religion of Protest* (Cambridge, MA: Belknap Press of Harvard University Press, 2011), 301–2.
52. F. Volker Greifenhagen, "Islamic Fundamentalism(s): More Than a Pejorative Epithet?" in *Contesting Fundamentalisms*, eds Carol Schick, JoAnn Jaffe, and Ailsa M. Watkinson (Halifax: Fernwood, 2004), 68–70.
53. See Vanessa Martin, *Creating an Islamic State* (London: I.B. Tauris, 2000), 146–50.
54. Ervand Abrahamian, *Khomeinism: Essays on the Islamic Republic* (Berkeley: University of California Press, 1993), 16.
55. Daniel Brumberg, *Reinventing Khomeini: The Struggle for Reform in Iran* (Chicago: University of Chicago Press, 2001), 5. Brumberg goes so far as to describe Khomeini's view of religion as utilitarian instrumentalism.
56. Clive Irving, *Sayings of the Ayatollah Khomeini* (New York: Bantam Books, 1980), 8.
57. See Abrahamian, *Khomeinism*, 23, where he quotes Khomeini as saying, "The American capitalists are scheming to take over Iran's resources." See also Martin, *Creating an Islamic State*, 62, where she claims, "Khomeini also attacked the deprivation and neglect of the poor and asserted that the government acted only in the interests of foreign powers, principally the USA and Israel."
58. Irving, *Sayings of the Ayatollah*, 9.
59. Ibid., 8, 13.
60. Brumberg, *Reinventing Khomeini*, 81–2.
61. With respect to his piety and courage, see Martin, *Creating an Islamic State*, 57, 66.
62. Brumberg, *Reinventing Khomeini*, 82–3.
63. Ibid., 83.
64. Martin, *Creating an Islamic State*, 60–1.
65. Irving, *Sayings of the Ayatollah*, 100, 101, 105.
66. For a discussion of Christian fundamentalism in Australia and New Zealand, but not Canada, see Douglas Pratt, "Religion and Terrorism: Christian Fundamentalism and Extremism," *Terrorism and Political Violence* 22 (2010): 438–56.
67. Bruce B. Lawrence, *Defenders of God: The Fundamentalist Revolt against the Modern Age* (New York: Harper and Row, 1989), 48–58, 153.
68. Ibid., 47–8.
69. Geering, *The Challenge to the Secular World*, 6.
70. The claim that this sermon was a defining moment is presented in Harriet A. Harris, *Fundamentalism and Evangelicals* (Oxford: Oxford University Press, 1998), 30.
71. Harry Emerson Fosdick, *Shall the Fundamentalists Win? A Sermon Preached at the First Presbyterian Church, New York, May 21, 1922* (reprint, New York: Riverside Church Archives, 1999), 5.
72. Richard Antoun, *Understanding Fundamentalism: Christian, Islamic, and Jewish Movements*, 2nd edn (Lanham, MD: Rowman & Littlefield, 2008), 117.
73. Kevin Phillips, "Church, State, and National Decline," in *Readings in Political Ideologies since the Rise of Modern Science*, eds H.B. McCullough and Wolfgang Depner (Oxford: Oxford University Press, 2013), 307–11.
74. Michael Lienesch, *Redeeming America: Piety and Politics in the New Christian Right* (Chapel Hill: University of North Carolina Press, 1993), 15.
75. According to Jerry Falwell et al., the fundamentalist Tim LaHaye identifies the five basic tenets of humanism as (i) atheism, (ii) evolution, (iii) amorality, (iv) autonomy of man, (v) one-world socialism. See Jerry Falwell, Ed Dobson, and Edward E. Hindson, eds, *The Fundamentalist Phenomenon: The Resurgence of Conservative Christianity* (Garden City, NY: Doubleday, 1981), 199.
76. Lienesch, *Redeeming America*, 141, 158–9.
77. Ibid., 158–60.
78. See Lawrence, *Defenders of God*, 161. Many of these names surface in connection with German New Testament scholarship, which was the first effort to engage in a serious textual criticism of the holy scriptures. See Albert Schweitzer, *The Quest for the Historical Jesus* (reprint, New York: Macmillan, 1962).
79. Lienesch, *Redeeming America*, 159.
80. Ibid., 161.
81. Ibid., 166.
82. Tim LaHaye, *The Battle for the Mind* (Old Tappan, NJ: Fleming H. Revell, 1980), 45–6, quoted in Lienesch, *Redeeming America*, 169.
83. For insight into the regional origins of Falwell's movement, see Daniel K. Williams,

"Jerry Falwell's Sunbelt Politics: The Regional Origins of the Moral Majority," *Journal of Policy History* 22 (2010): 125. http://muse.jhu.edu/journals/journal_of_policy_history/v022/22.2wil.
84. Harris, *Fundamentalism and Evangelicals*, 332.
85. The adjectives "passive," "assertive," and "impositional" are suggested by Pratt, "Religion and Terrorism."
86. See ibid., 443, 444, 446, 448.
87. Harris, *Fundamentalism and Evangelicals*, 332.
88. Harris gives a helpful account of the emergence of neo-fundamentalism. See ibid., 44–5.
89. Ibid., 45.
90. Stuart Sim, *Fundamentalist World: The New Dark Age of Dogma* (Toronto: Icon Books, 2004), 80–3.
91. JoAnne Jaffe, "With Us or With the Terrorists," in *Contesting Fundamentalisms*, eds Carol Schick, JoAnne Jaffe, and Ailsa M. Watkinson (Halifax: Fernwood, 2004), 114.
92. Susan Friend Harding, *The Book of Jerry Falwell: Fundamentalist Language and Politics* (Princeton, NJ: Princeton University Press, 2000), 195.
93. Ibid., 194. He also appealed to Biblical verses (e.g., Leviticus 18:22 and Romans 1:26–28) to show the immorality of homosexuality.
94. Falwell et al., *Fundamentalist Phenomenon*, 195–8.
95. Jerry Falwell, *If I Should Die Before I Wake* (Nashville, TN: Thomas Nelson, 1986).
96. Harding, *Book of Jerry Falwell*, 304.
97. Antoun, *Understanding Fundamentalism*, 107. In 1967, Shlafly founded the conservative anti-feminist group Eagle Forum. Its Canadian counterpart, founded in 1983, is REAL Women (Realistic, Equal, Active, for Life), which describes itself as an "alternative women's movement." While recognizing women's advances in the workplace, the organization also supports the right of women to be full-time mothers and homemakers. In addition to its pro-family, pro-life stance, REAL Women opposes same-sex marriage.
98. Donald G. Mathews, "'Spiritual Warfare': Cultural Fundamentalism and the Equal Rights Amendment," *Religion and American Culture* 3 (1993): 140.
99. Ibid.
100. Ibid.
101. Ibid., 141.
102. Harding, *Book of Jerry Falwell*, 237.
103. Gustav Niebuhr, "U.S. 'Secular' Groups Set Tone for Terror Attacks, Falwell Says," *New York Times*, 14 Sept. 2001, http://www.nytimes.com/2001/09/14/national/14FALW.html.
104. Ibid.
105. Jerry Falwell, "Defending Prayer in School," Listen America. WorldNetDaily Exclusive Commentary, 27 Oct. 2001, http://www.wnd.com/index.php?fa=PAGE.view&pageId=11457.
106. Marsha Nye Adler, "The Politics of Censorship," *Political Science and Politics* 21 (1988): 19.
107. Former Alaska governor Sarah Palin, the Republican vice-presidential candidate in the 2008 US election, has spoken in support of teaching creationism alongside evolution theory in schools. "Teach both," she said. "You know, don't be afraid of information." See "Who Is Gov. Palin?" *Washington Post*, 3 Sept. 2008, A14.
108. People for the American Way was founded by the television producer Norman Lear (of *All in the Family* fame).
109. Adler, "Politics of Censorship," 19.
110. Falwell et al., *Fundamentalist Phenomenon*, 200–1, see sex education as "pornographic brainwashing."
111. Adler, "Politics of Censorship," 19–22.
112. Lienesch, *Redeeming America*, 230.
113. Falwell et al., *Fundamentalist Phenomenon*, 215.
114. Lienesch, *Redeeming America*, 232.
115. Ibid., 231.
116. See Feige, *Settling in the Hearts*, 280: "Gush Emunim does not exist anymore as an organization."
117. David S. New, *Holy War: The Rise of Militant Christian, Jewish, and Islamic Fundamentalism* (Jefferson, NC: McFarland and Co., 2002), 39.
118. Ibid., 40.
119. See ibid., 39–41.
120. For a detailed account of this and the history of Jews after their defeat, see Rollin Armour Sr, *Islam, Christianity, and the West: A Troubled History* (Maryknoll, NY: Orbis Books, 2003), 146–66.
121. See ibid., 149–50. In May 1882 the Temporary Laws came into effect in Russia. These determined where Jews could live and settle, prohibited owning land, and banned them from universities, professions, and civil service work.

122. The Dreyfus affair is famous for the involvement of the novelist Emile Zola, whose defence of Dreyfus was published as an open letter to the President of France on the front page of the newspaper *L'Aurore* on 13 January 1898. Given the title "J'accuse . . . !" Zola's letter did just that, accusing the French Army of anti-Semitism in its prosecution of Dreyfus. Convicted of criminal libel, Zola fled to England to avoid imprisonment, but was later pardoned and allowed to return to France. Dreyfus was eventually exonerated by the Supreme Court in 1906.
123. Jackie Kuikman, "Jewish Fundamentalisms and a Critical Politics of Identity: The Makings of a Post-Zionist Discourse," in *Contesting Fundamentalisms*, eds Carol Schick, JoAnn Jaffe, and Ailsa Watkinson, 49.
124. Generally, three attitudes prevail in Israel towards religion: (i) Orthodox, (ii) traditional, and (iii) secular. Israeli religious Jews (i.e., Orthodox) divide into moderate (religious national) and extreme (Haredim). The Haredim itself divides into a party of Eastern European origin (the Ashkenazi Haredim or Chabad Lubavitch) and a party of Middle Eastern origin (the Sephardim Haredim). The religious national Jews organize into the National Religious Party (NRP), the party of the Gush Emunim. See Israel Shahak and Norton Mezvinsky, *Jewish Fundamentalism in Israel* (London: Pluto Press, 1999), 7.
125. Lawrence, *Defenders of God*, 122.
126. The prognosis of Orthodox Jewish leaders is that the Jewish people are "likely to split into two within the next three decades over the question, Who is a Jew?" See David Landau, *Piety and Power: The World of Jewish Fundamentalism* (New York: Hill and Wang, 1993), 291. Clearly, this has significance for the state of Israel. Lawrence, *Defenders of God*, 130, sheds some light on this cleavage: "The fuller expression of Jewish fundamentalism only emerges when we consider its representation through both wings of Jewish Orthodoxy. They appear to be opposite: the non-Hasidic haredim, epitomized by Neturei Karta, and the quasi-Hasidic Gush Emunim. Moreover, the leaders of both groups are openly antagonistic to each other." One of the deep differences between these groups is that the Gush Emunim affirms the legitimacy of the state, while the Neturei Karta does not. Ibid., 128.
127. Ibid., 126. Hasidism has represented the complete antithesis of Jewish scholars such as Baruch Spinoza and Moses Mendelssohn, who embraced the Enlightenment.
128. The Hasidic Jews are not alone in opposing Zionism: Orthodox Jews also oppose it. See ibid., 126–7.
129. The cornerstones of Orthodox Judaism are the following: the direct descendant of the House of David will come and defeat the oppressor, rebuild the Temple, and reign in Jerusalem; as well, the messianic era will commence with the war of Gog and Magog. See Jerome R. Mintz, *Hasidic People* (Cambridge, MA: Harvard University Press, 1992), 348.
130. Lawrence, *Defenders of God*, 127.
131. S. Zalman Abramov, *Perpetual Dilemma: Jewish Religion in the Jewish State* (Rutherford, NJ: Fairleigh Dickinson University Press, 1976), 74. Hirsch's son-in-law, Solomon Breuer, was a co-founder of Agudat Israel.
132. Lawrence, *Defenders of God*, 129.
133. Shahak and Mezvinsky, *Jewish Fundamentalism*, 19.
134. Lawrence, *Defenders of God*, 129.
135. Ibid., 132.
136. Some would go further and discount Kahane as a fundamentalist. Such is the position of Bruce Lawrence when he says "Rabbi Meir Kahane remains a counterfeit fundamentalist." Ibid.
137. Shahak and Mezvinsky, *Jewish Fundamentalism*, 18–20.
138. For these facts and an elaboration on them, see Avishai Margalit, "Settling Scores," *New York Review of Books* 48 (2001): 20–4, esp. 20–1.
139. Lawrence, *Defenders of God*, 137.
140. Margalit, "Settling Scores," 21.
141. There is reason to think that the Second Intifada has hurt the Palestinians in other respects as well. See Daniel Pipes, "The Intifada Is Hurting the Palestinians," *National Post*, 20 Apr. 2004, A12. The Second Intifada, which began in September 2000, was the second Palestinian uprising against Israeli rule, marked by violent clashes and a high death toll on both sides (the word "intifada" translates as "uprising" or "resistance"). It is unclear what sparked the uprising, although some have blamed the failure of Israeli–Palestinian peace negotiations being hosted by US President Bill Clinton, and others cited

Ariel Sharon's visit to the area of the Al-Aqsa Mosque in the historic Old City section of Jerusalem.
142. Margalit, "Settling Scores," 22.
143. The best discussion of this is provided by Uriel Tal, "The Foundations of a Political Messianic Trend in Israel," *Jerusalem Quarterly* 35 (Spring 1985), http://www.geocities.com/alabasters_archive/messianic_trend.html. See para. 1 for his affirmation of this claim.
144. Shahak and Mezvinsky, *Jewish Fundamentalism*, 65.
145. Tal, "Foundations of a Political Messianic Trend," para. 9.
146. Ibid.
147. Quoted in Yehoshafat Harkabi, *Israel's Fateful Hour*, trans. Lenn Schramm (New York: Harper and Row, 1986), 145.
148. Tal, "Foundations of a Political Messianic Trend," para. 16.
149. Quoted in Harkabi, *Israel's Fateful Hour*, 145.
150. Quoted ibid., 146.
151. Quoted ibid., 150.
152. Sue Fishkoff, *The Rebbe's Army* (New York: Schocken Books, 2003), 10–11.
153. Ibid., 14.
154. Norton Mezvinsky and Joshua Kolb, "Eyes Upon the Land: Chabad Lubavitch in Israel," *Religious Studies and Theology* 32, 1 (2013): 9.
155. Fishkoff, *The Rebbe's Army*, 17.
156. Ibid., 23.
157. Ibid., 14, 19.
158. Ibid., 22.
159. Ibid.
160. Ibid., 21.
161. As quoted in Mezvinsky and Kolb, "Eyes Upon the Land," 13.
162. Fishkoff, *The Rebbe's Army*, 55.
163. Sharrona Pearl, "Exceptions to the Rule: Chabad-Lubavitch and the Digital Sphere," *Journal of Media and Religion* 13 (2014): 124.
164. Mezvinsky and Kolb, "Eyes Upon the Land," 15.
165. Ibid.
166. Kuikman, "Jewish Fundamentalisms," 55. Goldstein was buried in the Jewish settlement of Kiryat Arba, adjacent to Hebron, where he lived. Although Israeli forces destroyed the shrine that supporters set up at Goldstein's grave, it continues to be a pilgrimage site for Israeli extremists. See Harvey W. Kushner, *Encyclopedia of Terrorism* (Thousand Oaks, CA: Sage, 2002), 150; BBC News, "Graveside Party Marks Hebron Massacre," 21 Mar. 2000, http://news.bbc.co.uk/2/hi/middle_east/685792.stm.
167. Fishkoff, *The Rebbe's Army*, 12.
168. Ibid., 69.
169. Shahak and Mezvinsky, *Jewish Fundamentalism*, 61; Kuikman, "Jewish Fundamentalisms," 53.
170. This is a point made by Ian S. Lustick in 1993, but it is still true. See Lustick, "Jewish Fundamentalism and the Israeli-Palestinian Impasse," in *Jewish Fundamentalism in Comparative Perspective*, ed. Laurence J. Silberstein (New York: New York University Press, 1993), 104.
171. Krishna K. Tummala, "Democracy vs. Fundamentalism: Religious Politics of the Bharatiya Janata Part in India," in *Religious Fundamentalism in the Contemporary World: Critical Social and Political Issues*, ed. Santosh C. Saha (Lanham, MD: Lexington Books, 2004), 209.
172. Nielsen et al., *Religions of the World*, 90–1.
173. Ibid., 101–5.
174. Ibid., 174.
175. Ibid.
176. Ibid., 174–5.
177. Ibid., 177–8.
178. C.J. Fuller, *The Camphor Flame: Popular Hinduism and Society in India* (Princeton, NJ: Princeton University Press, 2004), 263.
179. Shabnum Tejani, *Indian Secularism: A Social and Intellectual History 1890–1950* (Bloomington: Indiana University Press, 2008), 96.
180. Nielsen et al., *Religions of the World*, 179.
181. Ibid.
182. For an elaboration on this point, see Fuller, *The Camphor Flame*, 263ff.
183. Ibid., 262.
184. Ibid., 263.
185. Ibid., 264.
186. Ibid., 265.
187. Ibid., 267.
188. Ibid., 261.
189. *Hindu Myths: A Sourcebook Translated from the Sanskrit* (London and New York: Penguin Books, 1975), 197.
190. Martha C. Nussbaum, "Body of the Nation: Why Women Were Mutilated in Gujarat," *Boston Review*, 29 July 2004, http://www.countercurrents.org/guj-nussbaum290704.htm.
191. Ibid.
192. "2002 Gujarat Riots," *Wikipedia*, https://en.wikipedia.org/wiki/2002_Gujarat_riots.

193. Ibid.
194. Ibid.
195. Tummala, "Democracy vs. Fundamentalism," 224.
196. Ibid.
197. "2002 Gujarat Riots," *Wikipedia*.
198. Nussbaum, "Body of the Nation."
199. Ibid.
200. M.T. Cherian, *Hindutva Agenda and Minority Rights* (Bangalore: Centre for Contemporary Christianity, 2007), 186.
201. Ibid., 187.
202. Ibid., 189.
203. T.N. Madan, *Secularism and Fundamentalism in India: Modern Myths, Locked Minds*, 2nd edn (Oxford: Oxford University Press, 2009), 219.
204. Ibid., 220.
205. Cherian, *Hindutva Agenda*, 191.
206. Ibid., 203.
207. Robert J. Stephens, "Hinduism in Independent India: Fundamentalism and Secularism," in *Contemporary Hinduism: Ritual, Culture, and Practice*, ed. Robin Rinehart (Santa Barbara, CA: ABC CLIO, 2004), 321.
208. Ibid., 322.
209. Ibid., 322–3.
210. Ibid., 319.
211. Ibid., 325.
212. Ibid.
213. Mehnaaz Momen, "Can Secular Liberal Politics Be Reincarnated in India?" *Journal of Asian and African Studies* 40 (2005): 250.
214. Ibid., 250.
215. Madan, *Secularism and Fundamentalism in India*, 227.
216. Stephens, "Hinduism in Independent India," 319.
217. Cherian, *Hindutva Agenda*, 220.
218. Momen, "Can Secular Liberal Politics Be Reincarnated," 251.
219. Ibid., 252.
220. Ibid., 252.
221. Ibid., 256.
222. Kunal Mukherjee, "Is Hindu Nationalism a Threat to Religious Minorities in Eastern India?" *The Round Table* 102 (2013): 455.
223. Ibid.
224. The relation of belief and desire as mental states is subtle and elusive. Though opposite in philosophic spirit, both Hume and Pascal recognized the way in which beliefs are influenced by desires and passions. But as Terence Penelhum says, "this in no way shows that we should think of beliefs as actions, and in particular it does not give sense to the suggestion that believing is something we can do to order." Terence Penelhum, *Reason and Religious Faith* (Boulder, CO: Westview Press, 1995), 50–1.
225. See Saul Kripke, *Naming and Necessity* (Cambridge, MA: Harvard University Press, 1972), 29–32, for a further discussion of referential problems in this context.
226. An advocate of this position is Alvin Plantinga. See his *Warranted Christian Belief* (New York: Oxford University, 2000).
227. For a philosophical analysis of this position, see H.B. McCullough, "Theodicy and Mary Baker Eddy," *Sophia* 14 (1975): 12–18.
228. See Richard Dawkins, *The God Delusion* (Toronto: Bantam, 2006), Chaps 3, 4. For a criticism of Dawkins's enthusiasm for his version of evolutionary theory, see Marilynne Robinson, "Hysterical Scientism: The Ecstasy of Richard Dawkins," *Harper's* 313 (Nov. 2006): 83–8.
229. Adam Smith, *The Nature and Causes of the Wealth of Nations*, ed. Kathyrn Sutherland (1776; reprint, Oxford: Oxford University Press, 1993), 440–1.
230. Ibid., V, ii, Art. 3, 440.
231. Hugo Heclo is one such writer. See Heclo, *Christianity and American Democracy* (Cambridge, MA: Harvard University Press, 2008).
232. Harkabi, *Israel's Fateful Hour*, 145.
233. Solomon Schimmel, *The Tenacity of Unreasonable Beliefs: Fundamentalism and the Fear of Truth* (Oxford and New York: Oxford University Press, 2008), 73.
234. Ibid., 232–3.

Chapter 14: Secularism

1. Charles Taylor, *A Secular Age* (Cambridge, MA: Belknap Press of Harvard University Press, 2007), 19–20.
2. Ibid., 77.
3. Affan Chowdhry, "Killings of Bloggers in Bangladesh Reverberate in Suburban Canada," *Globe and Mail*, 26 May 2015, A1, A4.
4. Harvey Cox, *The Secular City* (New York: Macmillan, 1967), 18.
5. Ibid.
6. Thomas Hobbes, *Leviathan* (1651; reprinted Oxford: Oxford University Press, 1996), Part I, c. 12, para. 6.

7. Ibid., Part I, c. 2, para. 8.
8. Terence Penelhum, *Hume* (London: Macmillan, 1975), 163.
9. Ibid., 180–1.
10. See ibid., 180ff., for evidence of this.
11. David Hume, *The Dialogues Concerning Natural Religion* (1779), reprinted in *Hume on Religion*, ed. Richard Wollheim (London: Fontana Library, 1963), Part ix.
12. Ibid., Part ii.
13. Penelhum, *Hume*, 184.
14. Ibid., 184–5.
15. Ibid., 186.
16. Penelhum makes this point with abundant clarity. See ibid., 194, 195.
17. Taylor, *Secular Age*, 221.
18. Ibid.
19. Karl Marx, *Contribution to the Critique of Hegel's Philosophy of Right: Introduction* (1843), in *The Marx-Engels Reader*, ed. Robert C. Tucker (New York: Norton, 1972), 12.
20. Ibid.
21. Søren Kierkegaard, *Concluding Unscientific Postcript* (Princeton, NJ: Princeton University Press, 1941), 25.
22. Ibid., 20.
23. Ibid., 182.
24. Ibid., 182–3.
25. George Price, *The Narrow Pass* (London: Hutchinson, 1963), 161–70.
26. Ibid., 168.
27. Søren Kierkegaard, *Either/Or*, vol. 2 (Garden City, NY: Anchor Books, 1959), 166.
28. Ibid., 164.
29. Ibid., 170.
30. Ibid., 173.
31. Ibid.
32. Kierkegaard, *Concluding Unscientific Postcript*, 387.
33. Ibid., 388, 392.
34. Ibid., 400.
35. Ibid., 403.
36. Ibid., 473.
37. Ibid., 475.
38. Ibid., 479.
39. Ibid., 494.
40. Ibid., 495.
41. Sigmund Freud, *Totem and Taboo* (London: Routledge and Kegan Paul, 1950).
42. Sigmund Freud, *The Future of an Illusion* (1927; Garden City, NY: Anchor Books, 1961).
43. Freud, *Totem and Taboo*, 77.
44. Ibid., 75.
45. Ibid., 92.
46. Ibid., 76.
47. Ibid., 77, 95.
48. Ibid., 77.
49. Ibid., 78.
50. See Ernst Cassirer, *An Essay on Man* (New Haven: Yale University Press, 1944), 84, for a discussion of the importance of death to mythical consciousness—a discussion that fits very nicely into Freud's treatment of animism.
51. Hobbes, *Leviathan*, Part I, c. II, para. 8.
52. Freud, *Totem and Taboo*, 85.
53. Ibid., 85.
54. Ibid., 88.
55. Ibid., 90.
56. Ibid., 91.
57. Freud, *Future of an Illusion*, 30.
58. Ibid., 37, 41, 47.
59. Ibid., 48.
60. Ibid., 49.
61. Ibid., 50.
62. Ibid., 52.
63. Ibid., 62.
64. Ibid.
65. Ibid., 63.
66. Ibid., 64. It is hard not to think of the excesses of contemporary religious fundamentalism in this context as illustrating the very point Freud wishes to make.
67. Ibid., 72.
68. Ibid.
69. See Shubert Ogden's Introduction to Rudolf Bultmann, *Existence and Faith* (New York: Living Age Books, 1960), 18–19.
70. Paul Tillich, *Systematic Theology*, vol. 1 (Chicago: University of Chicago Press, 1951), 211–34.
71. See Paul Tillich, *Systematic Theology*, vol. 2 (Chicago: University of Chicago Press, 1957) and Tillich, *Systematic Theology*, vol. 3 (Chicago: University of Chicago Press, 1963).
72. Tillich, *Systematic Theology*, vol. 1, 211.
73. Ibid.
74. Ibid., 235.
75. Ibid.
76. Tillich falls into confusion by failing to consider the philosophical literature on the theory of reference developed by Frege and Russell, to name but two illustrious thinkers. For a clear and compelling presentation of the topic of reference, see Peter Thomas Geach, *Reference and Generality* (Ithaca, NY: Cornell University Press, [1962] 1980).

77. Paul Tillich, *The Courage to Be* (New Haven: Yale University Press, 1952).
78. Richard Dawkins, *The God Delusion* (London and Toronto: Bantam Press, 2006), 16.
79. Ibid., 31.
80. Ibid., 36.
81. Ibid., 41.
82. Ibid., 43, 46.
83. Ibid., 69ff.
84. Ibid., 71. Dawkins does not use the word "conjecture" here but it does seem supported by the context.
85. For a different but supporting critical evaluation of some theologically based arguments for the existence of God, see Michael Martin, *The Case against Christianity* (Philadelphia: Temple University Press, 1991).
86. Dawkins, *God Delusion*, 82–3. Mackie's book is *The Miracle of Theism*.
87. Ibid., 119.
88. Ibid., 121.
89. Ibid.
90. Ibid., 158.
91. Ibid., 263–4.
92. Ibid., 264.
93. Ibid., 13–14, 35–6.
94. See Dawkins, *God Delusion*, 264, for his talk about decent persons and the good life.
95. Ibid., 157.
96. J.L. Mackie, *Ethics: Inventing Right and Wrong* (Harmondsworth, England: Penguin, 1977), 227.
97. Ibid., 232.
98. Ibid.
99. Taylor, *Secular Age*, 19.
100. Ibid., 84.
101. Tillich, *Systematic Theology*, vol. 3, 280.
102. Joseph A. Schumpeter, *Capitalism, Socialism and Democracy* (1942; reprint New York: Harper Perennial Modern Thought, 2008).
103. Ibid., 83.
104. See Frank's editorial opinion: Adam Frank, "The Age of Denial," *International Herald Tribune*, 23 Aug. 2013, 6.

Chapter 15: Conclusion

1. Lewis H. Lapham, "Notebook," *Harper's* 314 (May 2007): 10.
2. Even Walmart, one of the most successful department stores in the history of North America, has gone green, recognizing the compatibility of eco-friendly products, technology, and money-making. In brief, Walmart recognizes that it can make money by selling environmentally friendly products. See Mindy Fetterman, "Wal-Mart Grows 'Green' Strategies," *USA Today*, 24 Sept. 2006, http://www.usatoday.com/money/industries/retail/2006-09-24-wal-mart-cover-usat_x.htm.
3. John Maynard Keynes, *Laissez-faire and Communism* (New York: New Republic, 1926), 47–8.
4. W.V. Quine and J.S. Ullian, *The Web of Belief*, 2nd edn (New York: Random House, 1978).
5. A typical analytic sentence is "All bachelors are unmarried men." Is the so-called definitional truth of this called into question by the fact that there are now same-sex marriages? Possibly not, but the case is not clear. In any event, the example makes Quine's point that nothing is necessarily permanently true.
6. Robert Nozick, *Invariances: The Structure of the Objective World* (Cambridge, MA: Belknap Press of Harvard University Press, 2001), 54.
7. Ibid., 60.
8. Wilfrid Sellars, *Science, Perception and Reality* (London: Routledge and Kegan Paul, 1963), 1–40.

References

Books and Articles

Abraham, C.M., and Sushila Abraham. "The Bhopal Case and the Development of Environmental Law in India." *International and Comparative Law Quarterly* 40 (1991): 334–65.

Abrahamian, Ervand. *Khomeinism: Essays on the Islamic Republic.* Berkeley: University of California Press, 1993.

Adams, Carol J., and Lori Gruen, eds. *Ecofeminism: Feminist Intersections with Other Animals and the Earth.* London: Bloomsbury, 2014.

Adams, Jad. "A Small Person." *Times Literary Supplement*, 24 Apr. 2009, 22.

Adler, Marsha Nye. "The Politics of Censorship." *Political Science and Politics* 21 (1988): 18–24.

Alford, Robert R., and Roger Friedland. *Powers of Theory: Capitalism, the State, and Democracy.* Cambridge: Cambridge University Press, 1985.

Ali, Tariq. *The Clash of Fundamentalisms: Crusades, Jihads and Modernity.* London and New York: Verso, 2003.

Alter, Peter. *Nationalism.* Translated by Stuart McKinnon-Evans. London: Edward Arnold, 1989.

Antonius, George. *The Arab Awakening: The Story of the Arab National Movement.* London: Hamish Hamilton, 1938.

Antoun, Richard T. *Understanding Fundamentalism: Christian, Islamic, and Jewish Movements*, 2nd edn. Lanham, MD: Rowman & Littlefield, 2008.

Arat-Koc, Sedef. "Whose Transnationalism? Canada, 'Clash of Civilizations' Discourse, and Arab and Muslim Canadians." In *Transnational Identities and Practices in Canada.* Edited by Vic Satzewich and Lloyd Wong. Vancouver: University of British Columbia Press, 2006.

Arendt, Hannah. *Eichmann in Jerusalem: A Report on the Banality of Evil.* Harmondsworth, England: Penguin Books, 1977.

Aristotle. *Politics.* Oxford: Oxford University Press, 1995.

Armour, Rollin, Sr. *Islam, Christianity, and the West: A Troubled History.* Maryknoll, NY: Orbis Books, 2003.

Arrow, Kenneth. *Social Choice and Individual Values.* New York: Wiley, 1951.

Atherton, Margaret. "Cartesian Reason and Gendered Reason." In *A Mind of One's Own: Feminist Essays on Reason and Objectivity.* Edited by Louise M. Antony and Charlotte Witt. Boulder, CO.: Westview Press, 1993.

Auden, W.H. *Selected Poems.* New York: Vintage Books, 2007.

Bahro, Rudolf. *Socialism and Survival.* Translated by David Fernbach. London: Heretic Books, 1982.

——. *From Red to Green: Interviews with New Left Review.* Translated by Gus Fagan and Richard Hurst. London: Verso, 1984.

Bakunin, Mikhail. *Statism and Anarchy.* 1873. Reprint translated and edited by Marshall S. Shatz. Cambridge: Cambridge University Press, 1990.

Balkisoon, Denise. "A Very Dangerous Woman." *Globe and Mail*, 18 Apr. 2015, F3.

Barry, John. *Environment and Social Theory*, 2nd edn. London: Routledge, 2007.

Bascaramurty, Dakshana. "Woman at Centre of Niqab Debate Says She's Educated, Not Oppressed." *Globe and Mail*, 8 Oct. 2015.

Beauvoir, Simone de. *The Second Sex.* 1949. Reprint, London: New English Library, 1960.

Berlin, Isaiah. *Four Essays on Liberty.* Oxford: Oxford University Press, 1969.

Bernstein, Eduard. *Evolutionary Socialism.* 1909. Reprint, New York: Schocken Books, 1961.

Beveridge, William. *The Pillars of Security.* New York: Macmillan, 1943.

Bhopal Medical Appeal, advertisement in *The Observer*, 5 June 2005.

Blasi, Augusto. "Kohlberg's Theory of Moral Motivation." In *The Legacy of Lawrence Kohlberg: Consensus and Controversy.* Edited by Dawn Schrader. San Francisco: Jossey-Bass, 1990.

Bondurant, Joan V. *Conquest of Violence: The Gandhian Philosophy of Conflict*, rev. edn. Berkeley: University of California Press, 1965.

Bookchin, Murray. *The Philosophy of Social Ecology: Essays on Dialectical Naturalism*, 2nd edn. Montreal: Black Rose Books, 1995.

Boyce, James K. "Rethinking Extinction: Toward a Less Gloomy Environmentalism." *Harper's* 331 (Nov. 2015): 67–75.

Brinton, Crane, John B. Christopher, and Robert Lee Wolff. *A History of Civilization*, 2nd edn, vols. 1 and 2. Englewood Cliffs, NJ: Prentice-Hall, 1958.

Brock, Peter. *The Quaker Peace Testimony: 1660 to 1914.* York, England: Sessions Book Trust, 1990.

——. *A Brief History of Pacifism from Jesus*

to Tolstoy, 2nd edn. Syracuse, NY: Syracuse University Press, 1992.

Brooker, Paul. "The Nazi Fuehrerprinzip: A Weberian Analysis." *Political Science* 37 (1985): 50–72.

Brumberg, Daniel. *Reinventing Khomeini: The Struggle for Reform in Iran*. Chicago: University of Chicago Press, 2001.

Bullock, Alan. *Hitler: A Study in Tyranny*. Harmondsworth, England: Pelican Books, 1962.

Burke, Edmund. *Reflections on the Revolution in France*. Reprint, Oxford: Oxford University Press, 1993.

Butler, Judith. "Contingent Foundations." In *Feminists Theorize the Political*. Edited by Judith Butler and Joan W. Scott. New York: Routledge, 1992.

Candle, The. "El Salvador Woman Pardoned: Guadalupe Was Sentenced to 30 Years for Suffering a Miscarriage." 14, 1 (Spring 2015): 6.

Carr, E.H. *What Is History?* Harmondsworth, England: Penguin Books, 1961.

Carson, Rachel. *Silent Spring*. New York: Fawcett Crest Books, 1962.

Cassese, Antonio. *International Law*, 2nd edn. Oxford: Oxford University Press, 2005.

Cassirer, Ernst. *An Essay on Man*. New Haven: Yale University Press, 1944.

———. *The Philosophy of the Enlightenment*. Translated by Fritz C.A. Koelln and James P. Pettegrove. Boston: Beacon Press, 1951.

Chamberlain, Houston Stewart. *Foundations of the Nineteenth Century*, vol. 1. Translated by John Lees. New York: John Lane; London: Bodley Head, 1912.

Cherian, M.T. *Hindutva Agenda and Minority Rights*. Bangalore: Centre for Contemporary Christianity, 2007.

Choueiri, Youssef M. *Islamic Fundamentalism*. Boston: Twayne, 1990.

Chowdhry, Affan. "Killings of Bloggers in Bangladesh Reverberate in Suburban Canada." *Globe and Mail*, 26 May 2015, A1, A4.

Clark, Ronald W. *The Life of Bertrand Russell*. New York: Alfred A. Knopf, 1976.

Cohen, I. Bernard. *The Birth of a New Physics*, rev. and updated edn. New York: Norton, 1985.

Cox, Harvey. *The Secular City*. New York: Macmillan, 1967.

Crankshaw, Edward. *Gestapo: Instrument of Tyranny*. 1956. Reprint, London: Greenhill Books, 1990.

Crosland, C.A.R. *The Future of Socialism*. New York: Schocken Books, 1956.

Dabashi, Hamid. *Shi'ism: A Religion of Protest*. Cambridge, MA: Belknap Press of Harvard University Press, 2011.

Dawkins, Richard. *The God Delusion*. Toronto: Bantam, 2006.

De Grand, Alexander. *Italian Fascism: Its Origins and Development*. Lincoln: University of Nebraska Press, 1982.

Derrida, Jacques. "Of Grammatology: Exergue." In *Jacques Derrida: Basic Writings*. Edited by Barry Stocker. London: Routledge, 2007.

Dewey, John. *Liberalism and Social Action*. New York: G.P. Putnam, 1935; reprint, New York: Capricorn Books, 1963.

———. "The Future of Liberalism." *Journal of Philosophy* 32 (1935): 225–30.

———. "Democracy and Educational Administration." *School and Society* 45 (1937): 457–62.

Dobson, Andrew. *Green Political Thought*, 4th edn. London: Routledge, 2007.

Dunleavy, Patrick. *Democracy, Bureaucracy and Public Choice: Economic Explanations in Political Science*. Toronto: Prentice-Hall, 1991.

Dwyer, John. "Virtue and Improvement: The Civic World of Adam Smith." In *Adam Smith Reviewed*. Edited by Peter Jones and Andrew S. Skinner. Edinburgh: Edinburgh University Press, 1992, 190–217.

Dyck, Rand. *Canadian Politics*, 4th edn. Scarborough, ON: Nelson Thomson, 2004.

Economist, The. "The History of Shia Muslims: Why the Aggravation?" 6–12 Mar. 2004.

———. "A Special Report on Entrepreneurship." 14–20 Mar. 2009.

———. "Berning Up." 10–16 Oct. 2015, 25.

Edwards, Paul, ed. *Encyclopedia of Philosophy*, vol. 1. New York: Macmillan and Free Press; London: Collier Macmillan, 1967.

Ehrlich, Paul R., and Anne H. Ehrlich. "The Value of Biodiversity." *Ambio* 21 (1992): 219–26.

———. *Betrayal of Science and Reason: How Anti-Environmental Rhetoric Threatens Our Future*. Washington, DC: Island Press, 1996.

Eliot, T.S. *Christianity and Culture*. New York: Harcourt, Brace and World, 1949.

Enayat, Hamid. *Modern Islamic Political Thought*. Austin: University of Texas Press, 1982.

Engels, Friedrich. *The Condition of the Working Class in England*. 1845. Reprint edited by Victor Gordon Kiernan. Harmondsworth, England: Penguin Books, 1987.

———. *On Morality*. 1878. In *The Marx-Engels Reader*. Edited by Robert C. Tucker. New York: Norton, 1972.

Erlanger, Steven. "Did Liberalism Win? It's Not Clear." *International New York Times*, 14 Sept. 2015, 7.

Falk, Richard. "Anarchism and World Order." In *Nomos XIX: Anarchism*. Edited by J. Roland Pennock and John W. Chapman. New York: New York University Press, 1978.

Falwell, Jerry. *If I Should Die Before I Wake*. Nashville, TN: Thomas Nelson, 1986.

———, Ed Dobson, and Edward E. Hindson, eds. *The Fundamentalist Phenomenon: The Resurgence of Conservative Christianity*. Garden City, NY: Doubleday, 1981.

Fanon, Frantz. *The Wretched of the Earth*. New York: Grove Press, 1967.

Feige, M. *Settling in the Hearts: Jewish Fundamentalism in the Occupied Territories*. Detroit: Wayne State University Press, 2009.

Finer, S.E. *The History of Government from the Earliest Times*, vol. 3. Oxford: Oxford University Press, 1997.

Firestone, Shulamith. *The Dialectic of Sex*. London: Paladin, 1970.

Fisher, H.A.L. *A History of Europe*, vol. 1. London: Collins, 1935.

Fishkoff, Sue. *The Rebbe's Army*. New York: Schocken Books, 2003.

Fosdick, Harry Emerson. *Shall the Fundamentalists Win? A Sermon Preached at the First Presbyterian Church, New York, May 21, 1922*. Reprint, New York: Riverside Church Archives, 1999.

Fox, Warwick. *Toward a Transpersonal Ecology: Developing New Foundations for Environmentalism*. Boston: Shambhala, 1990. Reprint, Albany: State University of New York Press, 1995.

———. *A Theory of General Ethics: Human Relationships, Nature, and the Built Environment*. Cambridge, MA: MIT Press, 2006.

Frank, Adam. "The Age of Denial." *International Herald Tribune*, 23 Aug. 2013, 6.

Franklin, Ursula. *The Ursula Franklin Reader: Pacifism as a Map*. Introduction by Michelle Swenarchuk. Toronto: Canada Council for the Arts, 2006.

Fraser, Cary. "In Defense of Allah's Realm: Religion and Statecraft in Saudi Foreign Policy Strategy." In *Transnational Religion and Fading States*. Edited by Susan Hoeber Rudolph and James Piscatori. Boulder, CO: Westview Press, 1997.

Freeden, Michael. *Ideology: A Very Short Introduction*. Oxford: Oxford University Press, 2003.

Freeman, Alan. "Bush to Outline 'Clear Strategy' for Iraq." *Globe and Mail*, 22 May 2004, A10.

Frend, W.H.C. *The Early Church*. Philadelphia: Lippincott, 1966.

Freud, Sigmund. *Totem and Taboo*. London: Routledge and Kegan Paul, 1950.

———. *The Future of an Illusion*. 1927. Garden City, NY: Anchor Books, 1961.

Friedman, Thomas L. *Hot, Flat, and Crowded: Why We Need a Green Revolution and How It Can Renew America*. New York: Farrar, Straus and Giroux, 2008.

Fuller, C.J. *The Camphor Flame: Popular Hinduism and Society in India*. Princeton, NJ: Princeton University Press, 2004.

Gandhi, M.K. *Non-Violent Resistance*. New York: Schocken Books, 1951.

Gavison, Ruth. "Feminism and the Public/Private Distinction." *Stanford Law Review* 45 (1992): 1–45.

Geach, Peter Thomas. *Reference and Generality*. Ithaca, NY: Cornell University Press, [1962] 1980.

Gebert, Konstanty. "Poland Shouldn't Shut Out Refugees." *International New York Times*, 10 Sept. 2015, 6.

Geering, Lloyd. *Fundamentalism: The Challenge to the Secular World*. Wellington, NZ: St Andrew's Trust for the Study of Religion and Society, 2003.

Giddens, Anthony. *The Third Way: The Renewal of Social Democracy*. Cambridge: Polity Press, 1998.

Gilligan, Carol. *In a Different Voice: Psychological Theory and Women's Development*. Cambridge, MA: Harvard University Press, 1982.

———. "Remapping the Moral Domain." In *Reconstructing Individualism: Autonomy, Individuality, and the Self in Western Thought*. Edited by Thomas Heller, Morton Sosna, and D.E. Wellbery. Stanford, CA: Stanford University Press, 1986.

Godwin, William. *Enquiry Concerning Political Justice*. 1793. Reprint edited by K. Codell Carter. Oxford: Oxford University Press, 1971.

Goldman, Emma. *Living My Life*. 2 vols. 1931. Reprint, New York: Dover Publications, 1970.

Goodin, Robert E. *Green Political Theory*. Cambridge: Polity Press, 1992.

Goodman, Paul. "Anarchism and Revolution." In *Political Ideologies: A Reader and Guide*. Edited by Matthew Festenstein and Michael Kenny. Oxford: Oxford University Press, 2005.

———. "Reflections on the Anarchist Principle." In *Political Ideologies: A Reader and Guide*. Edited by Matthew Festenstein and Michael Kenny. Oxford: Oxford University Press, 2005.

Goodman, Percival, and Paul Goodman. *Communitas: Means of Livelihood and Ways of Life*. Chicago: University of Chicago Press, 1947.

Grayling, A.C. *The Heart of Things: Applying Philosophy to the 21st Century*. London: Phoenix, 2005.

Green, T.H. "Lectures on the Principles of Political Obligation." In *Works of Thomas Hill Green*, 2nd edn, vol. 3. Edited by R.L. Nettleship. London: Longmans, Green, and Co., 1888.

———. "Liberal Legislation and Freedom of Contract." In *Works of Thomas Hill Green*, 2nd edn, vol. 3. Edited by R.L. Nettleship. London: Longmans, Green, and Co., 1888.

Greifenhagen, F. Volker. "Islamic Fundamentalism(s): More Than a Pejorative Epithet?" In *Contesting Fundamentalisms*. Edited by Carol Schick, JoAnn Jaffe, and Ailsa M. Watkinson. Halifax: Fernwood, 2004.

Griffin, Roger. *The Nature of Fascism*. London: Routledge, 1991.

Griswold, Charles L., Jr. *Adam Smith and the Virtues of Enlightenment*. Cambridge: Cambridge University Press, 1999.

Guha, Ramachandra. *Environmentalism: A Global History*. Don Mills, ON: Longman, 2000.

Guillaume, Alfred. *Islam*, 2nd edn. Harmondsworth, Middlesex: Penguin Books, 1956.

Haakonssen, Knud, ed. *The Cambridge Companion to Adam Smith*. Cambridge: Cambridge University Press, 2006.

Hahn, H.J. *German Thought and Culture: From the Holy Roman Empire to the Present Day*. Manchester: Manchester University Press, 1995.

Hampshire, Stuart. *Innocence and Experience*. Cambridge, MA: Harvard University Press, 1989.

Harding, Susan Friend. *The Book of Jerry Falwell: Fundamentalist Language and Politics*. Princeton, NJ: Princeton University Press, 2000.

Hardy, Roger. *The Muslim Revolt: A Journey through Political Islam*. London: Hurst and Co., 2010.

Harkabi, Yehoshafat. *Israel's Fateful Hour*. Translated by Lenn Schramm. New York: Harper and Row, 1986.

Harris, Harriet A. *Fundamentalism and Evangelicals*. Oxford: Oxford University Press, 1998.

Harris, José. *William Beveridge: A Biography*, 2nd edn. Oxford: Clarendon Press, 1997.

Hayek, F.A. *The Road to Serfdom*. Chicago: University of Chicago Press, 1944.

———. "Economic Freedom and Representative Government." In *Economic Freedom*. Oxford: Basil Blackwell, 1991.

Hayes, Paul. *Fascism*. New York: Free Press, 1973.

Heclo, Hugh. *Christianity and American Democracy*. Cambridge, MA: Harvard University Press, 2008.

Heywood, Andrew. *Political Ideologies: An Introduction*. London: Macmillan Education, 1992.

Hindu Myths: A Sourcebook Translated from the Sanskrit. London and New York: Penguin Books, 1975.

Hirsi Ali, Ayaan. *The Caged Virgin: An Emancipation Proclamation for Women and Islam*. New York: Free Press, 2006.

———. *Heretic: Why Islam Needs a Reformation Now*. New York: HarperCollins, 2015.

Hitler, Adolf. "The Twenty-Five Points." In *Political Ideologies*. Compiled by James A. Gould and Willis H. Truitt. New York: Macmillan, 1973. Originally proclaimed in a speech at a meeting of the dap [Deutsche Arbeiterpartei] on 24 February 1920.

———. *Mein Kampf*. Translated by Ralph Manheim. Boston: Houghton Mifflin, 1999. First published in German in 1925–6.

———. "Only Force Rules." In *Political Ideologies*. Compiled by James A. Gould and Willis H. Truitt. New York: Macmillan, 1973. Originally published in *Volkischer Beobachter*, 26 November 1926.

———. "Struggle—The Source of Strength." In *Political Ideologies*. Compiled by James A. Gould and Willis H. Truitt. New York: Macmillan, 1973. Originally published in *Volkischer Beobachter*, 21 November 1927.

———. "Originality Plus Brutality." In *Political Ideologies*. Compiled by James A. Gould and Willis H. Truitt. New York: Macmillan, 1973. Originally published in *Volkischer Beobachter*, 7 April 1928.

———. "Long Live Fanatical Nationalism." In *Political Ideologies*. Compiled by James A. Gould and Willis H. Truitt. New York: Macmillan, 1973. Originally published in *Volkischer Beobachter*, 23 September 1928.

Hobbes, Thomas. *Leviathan*. 1651. Reprint, Oxford: Oxford University Press, 1996.

Hobhouse, L.T. *Liberalism*. 1911. Reprint, Westport, CT: Greenwood, 1980.

Hobson, J.A. *Economics and Ethics*. London: D.C. Heath and Co., 1929.

———. *Confessions of an Economic Heretic*. London: George Allen and Unwin, 1938.

Holmes, Robert L., and Barry L. Gan, eds. *Nonviolence in Theory and Practice*, 2nd edn. Long Grove, IL: Waveland Press, 2005.

Holmes, Stephen. *Passions and Constraint: On the Theory of Liberal Democracy*. Chicago: University of Chicago Press, 1995.

Honderich, Ted. *Violence for Equality: Inquiries in Political Philosophy*. Harmondsworth, England: Penguin Books, 1980.

Horsburgh, H.J.N. *Non-Violence and Aggression: A Study of Gandhi's Moral Equivalent of War*. London: Oxford University Press, 1968.

Horton, Scott. "State of Exception." *Harper's* 315 (July 2007): 80–1.

Hume, David. *A Treatise of Human Nature*. 1739. Reprint edited by L.A. Selby-Bigge. 3 vols. Oxford: Clarendon Press, 1888.

———. "On Suicide." 1777. In *Selected Essays*. Edited by Stephen Copley and Andrew Edgar. Oxford: Oxford University Press, 1993.

———. *The Dialogues Concerning Natural Religion*. 1779. Reprinted in *Hume on Religion*. Edited by Richard Wollheim. London: Fontana Library, 1963.

Huxley, Aldous, ed. *An Encyclopaedia of Pacifism*. London: Chatto and Windus, 1937.

Huxley, T.H. "Emancipation—Black and White." In *Lay Sermons, Addresses, and Reviews*. London: Macmillan, 1870. Originally published in *The Reader*, 20 May 1865.

International Energy Agency (IEA). "Energy and Poverty." *IAEA Bulletin* 44 (2002): 24–9.

International New York Times. "Japan Wrestles with Pacifism." 21 July 2015, 6.

Irigaray, Luce. *The Sex Which Is Not One*. Ithaca, NY: Cornell University Press, 1985.

Irving, Clive. *Sayings of the Ayatollah Khomeini*. New York: Bantam Books, 1980.

Johnson, Paul. "The Anti-Semitic Disease." *Commentary* (June 2005): 33–8.

Jones, Greta. *Social Darwinism and English Thought*. Brighton, England: Harvester Press; Atlantic Highlands, NJ: Humanities Press, 1980.

Jones, Peter. *Rights*. London: Macmillan, 1994.

Kant, Immanuel. "What Is Enlightenment?" 1784. In *On History*. Edited and translated by Lewis White Beck et al. New York: Bobbs-Merrill, 1963.

———. *Groundwork of the Metaphysics of Morals*. 1785. Translated by H.J. Paton. New York: Harper and Row, 1964.

———. "Perpetual Peace." 1795. In *On History*. Edited and translated by Lewis White Beck et al. New York: Bobbs-Merrill, 1963.

Keynes, John Maynard. "Am I a Liberal?" 1925. In *Essays in Persuasion: The Collected Writings of John Maynard Keynes*, vol. 9. London: Macmillan, 1931; reprint, Cambridge: Cambridge University Press, 1972.

———. "The End of Laissez-Faire." 1926. In *Essays in Persuasion: The Collected Writings of John Maynard Keynes*, vol. 9. London: Macmillan, 1931; reprint, Cambridge: Cambridge University Press, 1972.

———. *Laissez-Faire and Communism*. New York: New Republic, 1926.

———. "Liberalism and Labour." 1926. In *Essays in Persuasion: The Collected Writings of John Maynard Keynes*, vol. 9. London: Macmillan, 1931; reprint, Cambridge: Cambridge University Press, 1972.

Khalil-ur-Rehman. "Islamic Fundamentalism." *The Dialogue* 6, 2 (2011): 93–104.

Khatab, Sayed. *The Political Thought of Sayyid Qutb: The Theory of Jahiliyyah*. London: Routledge, 2006.

———. *Understanding Islamic Fundamentalism: The Theological and Ideological Basis of al-Qa'ida's Political Tactics*. Cairo and New York: American University in Cairo Press, 2011.

Kierkegaard, Søren. *Concluding Unscientific Postcript*. Princeton, NJ: Princeton University Press, 1941.

———. *Either/Or*, vol. 2. Garden City, NY: Anchor Books, 1959.

King, Martin Luther, Jr. "Letter from Birmingham Jail." In *Nonviolence in Theory and Practice*, 2nd edn. Edited by Robert L. Holmes and Barry L. Gan. Long Grove, IL: Waveland Press, 2005.

Kirkpatrick, David L., and Mayy El Sheikh. "Brotherhood Divided over Strategy of Nonviolence." *International New York Times*, 6 Aug. 2015, 1.

Knox, MacGregor. *Common Destiny: Dictatorship, Foreign Policy, and War in Fascist Italy and Nazi Germany*. Cambridge: Cambridge University Press, 2000.

Koch, H.W. *In the Name of the Volk: Political Justice in Hitler's Germany*. London: I.B. Tauris and Co., 1989.

Krauthammer, Charles. "The Neoconservative Convergence." *Commentary* (July–Aug. 2005): 21–6.

Kripke, Saul A. *Naming and Necessity*. Cambridge, MA: Harvard University Press, 1972.

Kropotkin, Peter. *Memoirs of a Revolutionist*. 1899. Reprint with foreword by Barnett Newman and preface by Paul Goodman. New York: Grove Press, 1968.

———. *Mutual Aid: A Factor of Evolution*. 1902. Reprint with foreword by Ashley Montagu. Boston: Extending Horizons Books, 1955.

Krugman, Paul. "For Richer." *New York Times Magazine*, 20 Oct. 2002, 67.

———. "The M.I.T. Gang." *International New York Times*, 25–26 July 2015, 9.

———. "Zombies against Medicare." *International New York Times*, 28 July 2015, 11.

Krupa, Sagar. "Atmosphere and Agriculture in the New Millennium." *Environmental Pollution* 126 (2003): 293–300.

Kuikman, Jackie. "Jewish Fundamentalisms and a Critical Politics of Identity: The Makings of a Post-Zionist Discourse." In *Contesting Fundamentalisms*. Edited by Carol Schick, JoAnn Jaffe, and Ailsa M. Watkinson. Halifax: Fernwood, 2004.

Kymlicka, Will. *Liberalism, Community, and Culture*. Oxford: Clarendon Press, 1989.

———. *Contemporary Political Philosophy: An Introduction*, 2nd edn. Oxford: Oxford University Press, 2002.

LaHaye, Tim. *The Battle for the Mind*. Old Tappan, NJ: Fleming H. Revell, 1980.

Landau, David. *Piety and Power: The World of Jewish Fundamentalism*. New York: Hill and Wang, 1993.

Lapham, Lewis H. "Notebook." *Harper's* 314 (May 2007): 10.

Lawrence, Bruce B. *Defenders of God: The Fundamentalist Revolt against the Modern Age*. New York: Harper and Row, 1989.

Leblanc, Daniel. "Heated Battles Fuel Final Debate." *Globe and Mail*, 3 Oct. 2015, A3.

Lewis, Stephen. "A Socialist Takes Stock." *CCPA Monitor* 21, 8 (Feb. 2015).

Lichtheim, George. *Imperialism*. Harmondsworth, England: Penguin Books, 1971.

Lienesch, Michael. *Redeeming America: Piety and Politics in the New Christian Right*. Chapel Hill: University of North Carolina Press, 1993.

Lippmann, Walter. *The Public Philosophy*. New York: Mentor Books, 1956.

Livingston, Donald W. *Hume's Philosophy of Common Life*. Chicago: University of Chicago Press, 1984.

Locke, John. *Second Treatise of Government*. 1690. Edited with an introduction by C.B. Macpherson. Indianapolis: Hackett, 1980.

———. *The Second Treatise of Government*. 1690. Edited by Thomas P. Peardon. New York: Macmillan, 1989.

———. *The Second Treatise of Government*. 1690. Reprint, Oxford: Oxford University Press, 1997.

Loreto, Nora. "Canada's Youth: From Passivism to Activism." *CCPA Monitor* (Sept./Oct. 2015): 41–5.

Lustick, Ian S. "Jewish Fundamentalism and the Israeli–Palestinian Impasse." In *Jewish Fundamentalism in Comparative Perspective: Religion, Ideology, and the Crisis of Modernity*. Edited by Laurence J. Silberstein. New York: New York University Press, 1993.

Lyman, Rick. "Rift Emerges in Europe as East Resists Migrants." *International New York Times*, 14 Sept. 2015, 4.

Machiavelli, Niccolò. *The Discourses*. 1531. Reprint, Oxford: Oxford University Press, 1997.

McCullough, H.B. "Theodicy and Mary Baker Eddy." *Sophia* 14 (1975): 12–18.

———. "How Best to Drain the Alchemist's Cauldron: A Study of Marine Pollution in Australia." *Australian Journal of Political Science* 29 (1994): 62–81.

McIntyre, A.D. "Marine Pollution." In *World Guide to Environmental Issues and Organizations*. Edited by Peter Brackley. Harlow, England: Longman Current Affairs, 1999.

———. "The Future of the Oceans." *IAEA Bulletin* 45 (2003): 41–5.

MacIntyre, Alasdair C. *Whose Justice? Which Rationality?* Notre Dame, IN: University of Notre Dame Press, 1988.

Mackie, J.L. *Ethics: Inventing Right and Wrong*. Harmondsworth, England: Penguin, 1977.

Macpherson, C.B. *The Political Theory of Possessive Individualism*. Oxford: Oxford University Press, 1962.

———. *The Life and Times of Liberal Democracy*. Oxford: Oxford University Press, 1977.

Madan, T.N. *Secularism and Fundamentalism in India: Modern Myths, Locked Minds*, 2nd edn. Oxford: Oxford University Press, 2009.

Malkoutzis, Nick. "How Serious a Threat to Democracy Is Inequality?" *Kathimerini*, 16 Sept. 2015, 3.

Mallick, Heather. "The Nixon of the North: How Stephen Harper Ruined Canada." *Harper's* 331 (Oct. 2015): 67–8.

Malthus, T.R. *An Essay on the Principle of Population*. 1798. Reprint, Oxford: Oxford University Press, 1993.

Mandaville, Peter. *Global Political Islam*. London: Routledge, 2007.

Margalit, Avishai. "Settling Scores." *New York Review of Books*, 20 Sept. 2001, 20–4.

Marsden, William. *Stupid to the Last Drop: How Alberta Is Bringing Environmental Armageddon to Canada (and Doesn't Seem to Care). Toronto: Alfred A. Knopf Canada, 2007.

Martin, Michael. *The Case against Christianity.* Philadelphia: Temple University Press, 1991.

Martin, Vanessa. *Creating an Islamic State.* London: I.B. Tauris, 2000.

Marx, Karl. *Contribution to the Critique of Hegel's Philosophy of Right: Introduction.* 1843. In *The Marx-Engels Reader.* Edited by Robert C. Tucker. New York: Norton, 1972.

———. *On the Jewish Question.* 1843. In *The Marx-Engels Reader.* Edited by Robert C. Tucker. New York: Norton, 1972.

———. *The Economic and Philosophic Manuscripts.* 1844. In *The Marx-Engels Reader.* Edited by Robert C. Tucker. New York: Norton, 1972.

———. *The Economic and Philosophic Manuscripts.* 1844. In *Marx Selections.* Edited by Allen W. Wood. New York: Macmillan, 1988.

———. *Speech at the Anniversary of the People's Paper.* 1856. In *The Marx-Engels Reader.* Edited by Robert C. Tucker. New York: Norton, 1972.

———. *A Contribution to the Critique of Political Economy.* 1859. In *The Marx-Engels Reader.* Edited by Robert C. Tucker. New York: Norton, 1972.

———. *Inaugural Address of the Working Men's International Association.* 1864. In *The Marx-Engels Reader.* Edited by Robert C. Tucker. New York: Norton, 1972.

———. *Capital.* 1867–94. [Originally published in German in 3 vols; vols 2 and 3 were edited and published by Friedrich Engels after Marx's death.] Reprint translated by Samuel Moore and Edward Aveling and edited by Frederick Engels. New York: Modern Library, 1906.

———. *The Civil War in France.* 1871. In *The Marx-Engels Reader.* Edited by Robert C. Tucker. New York: Norton: 1972.

——— and Friedrich Engels. *The Communist Manifesto.* 1848. Reprint, Oxford: Oxford University Press, 1992.

Mathews, Donald G. "'Spiritual Warfare': Cultural Fundamentalism and the Equal Rights Amendment." *Religion and American Culture* 3 (1993): 129–54.

Meadows, Donella H., et al. *The Limits to Growth.* Washington, DC: Potomac Associates, 1972.

Meadows, Gilbert. *An Illustrated Dictionary of Classical Mythology.* London: Jupiter Books, 1978.

Mercier, Pascal. *Night Train to Lisbon.* New York: Grove Press, 2008.

Merton, Thomas, ed. *Gandhi on Non-Violence.* Navajivan, India: New Directions, 1965.

Meyer, John M. *Political Nature: Environmentalism and the Interpretation of Western Thought.* Cambridge, MA: MIT Press, 2001.

Meyer, Thomas. *Identity Mania: Fundamentalism and the Politicization of Cultural Differences.* London: Zed Books, 1997.

Mezvinsky, Norton, and Joshua Kolb. "Eyes Upon the Land: Chabad Lubavitch in Israel." *Religious Studies and Theology* 32, 1 (2013).

Mill, John Stuart. *Principles of Political Economy and Chapters on Socialism.* 1848 (*Principles*); 1879 (*Chapters*).Reprint edited with an introduction by Jonathan Riley. Oxford: Oxford University Press, 1994.

———. *On Liberty.* 1859. Reprint edited with an introduction by John Gray. Oxford: Oxford University Press, 1991.

Millett, Kate. *Sexual Politics.* New York: Ballantine Books, 1969.

Mills, C. Wright. *The Marxists.* Harmondsworth, England: Penguin Books, 1962.

Mintz, Jerome R. *Hasidic People.* Cambridge, MA: Harvard University Press, 1992.

Momen, Mehnaaz. "Can Secular Liberal Politics Be Reincarnated in India?" *Journal of Asian and African Studies* 40 (2005).

Morgan, Philip. *Italian Fascism, 1919–1945,* 2nd edn. Houndmills, England: Palgrave Macmillan, 2004.

Morgenthau, Hans. *Politics among Nations: The Struggle for Power and Peace,* 5th edn, rev. New York: Alfred A. Knopf, 1978.

Mowat, Farley. *The Farfarers: Before the Norse.* Toronto: Seal Books, 1998.

Mukherjee, Kunal. "Is Hindu Nationalism a Threat to Religious Minorities in Eastern India?" *The Round Table* 102 (2013).

Müller, Ingo. *Hitler's Justice: The Courts of the Third Reich.* Translated by Deborah Lucas Schneider. Cambridge, MA: Harvard University Press, 1991.

Mussolini, Benito. *The Political and Social Doctrine of Fascism.* Translated by Jane Soames. London: Hogarth Press, 1933.

———. "The Fascist Decalogue." In *Political Ideologies.* 1934 and 1938. Compiled by James A. Gould and Willis H. Truitt. New York: Macmillan, 1973.

Næss, Arne. *Ecology, Community, and Lifestyle: Outline of an Ecosophy.* Translated and revised by David Rothenberg. Cambridge: Cambridge University Press, 1989.

Narveson, Jan. "Pacifism: A Philosophical Analysis." *Ethics* 75 (1965): 259–71.

———. "Pacifism: A Philosophical Analysis." In *Moral Problems: A Collection of Philosophical Essays*, 2nd edn. Edited by James Rachels. New York: Harper and Row, 1975.

———. *The Libertarian Idea*. Peterborough, ON: Broadview Press, 2001.

Nathanson, Stephen. *Economic Justice*. Upper Saddle River, NJ: Prentice-Hall, 1998.

Neimark, Peninah, and Peter Rhoades Mott, eds. *The Environmental Debate: A Documentary History*. Westport, CT: Greenwood Press, 1999.

Neville, Peter. *Mussolini*. London: Routledge, 2004.

New, David S. *Holy War: The Rise of Militant Christian, Jewish, and Islamic Fundamentalism*. Jefferson, NC: McFarland and Co., 2002.

Nielsen, Niels C., et al. *Religions of the World*. New York: St Martin's Press, 1983.

Noakes, J.N., and G. Pridham, eds. *Nazism: A History in Documents and Eyewitness Accounts, 1919–1945*, vol. 1. New York: Schocken Books, 1983.

Noddings, Nel. *Women and Evil*. Berkeley: University of California Press, 1989.

———. *Peace Education: How We Come to Love and Hate War*. Cambridge: Cambridge University Press, 2012.

Nove, Alec. *The Economics of Feasible Socialism*. London: George Allen and Unwin, 1983.

Nozick, Robert. *Anarchy, State, and Utopia*. New York: Basic Books, 1974.

———. *Invariances: The Structure of the Objective World*. Cambridge, MA: Belknap Press of Harvard University Press, 2001.

Nussbaum, Martha. "The Future of Feminist Liberalism." In *Social and Political Philosophy: Classical Western Texts in Feminist and Multicultural Perspectives*, 3rd edn. Edited by James P. Sterba. Belmont, CA: Wadsworth, 2003.

———. "Body of the Nation: Why Women Were Mutilated in Gujarat." *Boston Review*, 29 July 2004.

Oakeshott, Michael. *Rationalism in Politics, and Other Essays*. London: Methuen, 1962.

Obituary: Romano Mussolini. *Vancouver Sun*, 4 Feb. 2006, C10.

O'Donnell, Lynne, and Rahim Faiez. "Protesters March for Woman Killed by Mob." *Globe and Mail*, 24 Mar. 2015, A12.

Ogden, Shubert. "Introduction." In Rudolf Bultmann, *Existence and Faith*. New York: Living Age Books, 1960.

Okin, Susan. *Women in Western Thought*. Princeton, NJ: Princeton University Press, 1979.

———. *Justice, Gender, and the Family*. New York: Basic Books, 1989.

Ollman, Bertell. *Alienation: Marx's Conception of Man in Capitalist Society*. Cambridge: Cambridge University Press, 1971.

Olson, Mancur. *The Logic of Collective Action: Public Goods and the Theory of Groups*. Cambridge, MA: Harvard University Press, 1965.

———. *The Rise and Decline of Nations*. New Haven: Yale University Press, 1982.

O'Sullivan, Noel. *Conservatism*. New York: St Martin's Press, 1976.

Owen, Robert. *A New View of Society and Other Writings*. 1813–14. Reprint, Toronto: Penguin Books, 1991.

Paehlke, Robert, ed. *Conservation and Environmentalism: An Encyclopedia*. New York: Garland, 1995.

Pain, Deborah J., Andrew Meharg, et al. "Levels of Cadmium and Zinc in Soil and Plants Following the Toxic Spill from a Pyrite Mine, Aznalcollar, Spain." *Ambio* 32 (2003): 52–7.

Paine, Thomas. *The Rights of Man*. 1791. Reprint, Oxford: Oxford University Press, 1995.

Palaiologos, Yannis. *The 13th Labour of Hercules: Inside the Greek Crisis*. London: Portobello Books, 2014.

Pares, Richard. *The Historian's Business, and Other Essays*. Oxford: Clarendon Press, 1961.

Pearl, Sharrona. "Exceptions to the Rule: Chabad-Lubavitch and the Digital Sphere." *Journal of Media and Religion* 13 (2014).

Peffer, R.G. *Marxism, Morality, and Social Justice*. Princeton, NJ: Princeton University Press, 1990.

Penelhum, Terence. *Hume*. London: Macmillan, 1975.

———. *Reason and Religious Faith*. Boulder, CO: Westview Press, 1995.

Penner, Dylan. "Why Vote?" *CCPA Monitor* (Sept./Oct. 2015).

Phillips, Kevin. *Bad Money: Reckless Finance, Failed Politics, and the Global Crisis of American Capitalism*. New York: Viking, 2008.

———. "Church, State, and National Decline." In *Readings in Political Ideologies since the Rise of Modern Science*. Edited by H.B. McCullough and Wolfgang Depner. Oxford: Oxford University Press, 2013.

Pipes, Daniel. "The Intifada Is Hurting the Palestinians." *National Post*, 20 Apr. 2004, A12.

Piscatori, James P. *Islam in a World of Nation-States*. London: Cambridge University Press, 1986.

Plamenatz, John. *Man and Society*, vol. 2. London: Longmans, 1963.

Plantinga, Alvin. *Warranted Christian Belief.* New York: Oxford University Press, 2000.

Plato. *The Republic.* Oxford: Oxford University Press, 1994.

Plumwood, Val. *Feminism and the Mastery of Nature.* London and New York: Routledge, 1993.

Porter, Anna. "Fascism: The Next Generation." *Globe and Mail*, 9 May 2009, F1, F4, F9.

Postel, Sandra, and Brian Richter. *Rivers for Life: Managing Water for People and Nature.* Washington, DC: Island Press, 2003.

Pratt, Douglas. "Religion and Terrorism: Christian Fundamentalism and Extremism." *Terrorism and Political Violence* 22 (2010): 438–56.

Price, George. *The Narrow Pass.* London: Hutchinson, 1963.

Proudhon, Pierre-Joseph. *What Is Property?* Reprint edited and translated by Donald R. Kelley and Bonnie G. Smith. Cambridge: Cambridge University Press, 1994.

———. *General Idea of the Revolution in the Nineteenth Century.* 1851. Translated by John Beverley Robinson. Reprint, London: Pluto Press, 1989.

———. *The Principle of Federation.* 1863. Reprint translated by Richard Vernon. Toronto: University of Toronto Press, 1979.

Pruzan, Elliot R. *The Concept of Justice in Marx.* New York: Peter Lang, 1989.

Quine, W.V., and J.S. Ullian. *The Web of Belief*, 2nd edn. New York: Random House, 1978.

Quinton, Anthony. "Conservatism." In *A Companion to Contemporary Political Philosophy.* Edited by Robert E. Goodin and Philip Pettit. Oxford: Basil Blackwell, 1993.

Qutb, Sayyid. "The Present and Future of Islam." In *Readings in Political Ideologies since the Rise of Modern Science.* Edited by H.B. McCullough and Wolfgang Depner. Oxford: Oxford University Press, 2013.

Rawls, John. *A Theory of Justice.* Oxford: Oxford University Press, 1971.

———. *Collected Papers.* Edited by Samuel Freeman. Cambridge, MA: Harvard University Press, 1999.

———. *The Law of Peoples.* Cambridge, MA: Harvard University Press, 1999.

———. *Justice as Fairness: A Restatement.* Cambridge, MA: Harvard University Press, 2001.

Reisman, David A. *Tawney, Galbraith, and Adam Smith: State and Welfare.* New York: St Martin's Press, 1982.

Reiss, Hans, ed. and introd. *Kant's Political Writings.* Translated by H.B. Nisbet. Cambridge: Cambridge University Press, 1970.

Renner, Eberhard. "The Black Triangle Area—Fit for Europe?" *Ambio* 31 (2002): 231–5.

Riasanovsky, Nicholas V. *A History of Russia*, 4th edn. New York: Oxford University Press, 1984.

Rilke, Rainer Maria. *Letters to a Young Poet.* New York: Norton, 1934.

———. *Letters to a Young Poet.* Translated by Joan M. Burnham. Novato, CA: New World Library, 2000.

Robinson, Marilynne. "Hysterical Scientism: The Ecstasy of Richard Dawkins." *Harper's* 313 (Nov. 2006): 83–8.

Rothschild, Emma, and Amartya Sen. "Adam Smith's Economics." In *The Cambridge Companion to Adam Smith.* Edited by Knud Haakonssen. Cambridge: Cambridge University Press, 2006.

Rousseau, Jean-Jacques. *The Social Contract.* 1762. Reprint, Oxford: Oxford University Press, 1994.

Rudolph, Susanne Hoeber, and James Piscatori. *Transnational Religion and Fading States.* Boulder, CO: Westview Press, 1997.

Russell, Bertrand. *Prophecy and Dissent: 1914–16*, vol. 13 of *The Collected Papers of Bertrand Russell.* Edited by Richard A. Rempel. London: Unwin Hyman, 1988.

———. *Pacifism and Revolution: 1916–18*, vol. 14 of *The Collected Papers of Bertrand Russell.* Edited by Richard A. Rempel. London: Routledge, 1995.

———. *Marriage and Morals.* London: George Allen and Unwin, 1929.

———. *Which Way to Peace?* London: Michael Joseph, 1936.

———. *Human Society in Ethics and Politics.* 1954. Reprint, London: Routledge, 1992.

———. *Man's Peril: 1954–55*, vol. 28 of *The Collected Papers of Bertrand Russell.* Edited by Andrew G. Bone. London: Routledge, 2003.

Sargent, Lyman Tower. *Contemporary Political Ideologies: A Comparative Analysis*, 11th edn. Toronto: Harcourt Brace, 1999.

———. *Contemporary Political Ideologies: A Comparative Analysis*, 12th edn. Belmont, CA, and Toronto: Thomson/Wadsworth, 2003.

Satzewich, Vic, and Lloyd Wong, eds. *Transnational Identities and Practices in Canada.* Vancouver: University of British Columbia Press, 2006.

Schimmel, Solomon. *The Tenacity of Unreasonable Beliefs: Fundamentalism and the Fear of Truth.* Oxford and New York: Oxford University Press, 2008.

Schlabrendorff, Fabian von. *The Secret War against*

Hitler. 1965. Reprint, Boulder, CO: Westview Press, 1994.

Schmemann, Serge. "Testing the Limits of Western Ideals." *International New York Times*, 14 Sept. 2015, 6.

Schumacher, E.F. *Small Is Beautiful: A Study of Economics as if People Mattered*. New York: Harper and Row, 1973; London: Abacus, 1974.

Schumaker, Paul, Dwight C. Kiel, and Thomas Heilke. *Great Ideas/Grand Schemes: Political Ideologies in the Nineteenth and Twentieth Centuries*. Toronto: McGraw-Hill, 1996.

Schumpeter, Joseph A. *Capitalism, Socialism, and Democracy*. 1942. 3rd edn. New York: Harper and Row, 1950.

———. *Capitalism, Socialism, and Democracy*. 1942. 5th edn, introd. Tom Bottomore. London: Allen and Unwin, 1976.

———. *Capitalism, Socialism and Democracy*. 1942. Reprint, New York: Harper Perennial Modern Thought, 2008.

Schwabach, Aaron. "The Sandoz Spill: The Failure of International Law to Protect the Rhine from Pollution." *Ecology Law Quarterly* 16 (1989): 443–80.

Schwartz, Stephen. *The Two Faces of Islam: The House of Sa'ud from Tradition to Terror*. New York: Random House, 2002.

Schwarzer, Alice. "The Function of Sexuality." In *Oppression of Women*. Reprinted *German Feminist Writings*. Edited by Patricia A. Herminghouse and Magda Mueller. New York and London: Continuum, 2001.

Schweitzer, Albert. *The Quest for the Historical Jesus*. 1906; first English translation, 1910. Reprint, New York: Macmillan, 1962.

———. *Indian Thought and Its Development*. Translated by Mrs. Charles E.B. Russell. London: Hodder and Stoughton, 1936.

Scruton, Roger. *A Political Philosophy*. London: Continuum, 2006.

———. *Culture Counts: Faith and Feeling in a World Besieged*. New York: Encounter Books, 2007.

Self, Peter. *Political Theories of Modern Government: Its Role and Reform*. London: Unwin Hyman, 1985.

———. "Socialism." In *A Companion to Contemporary Political Philosophy*. Edited by Robert E. Goodin and Philip Pettit. Oxford: Blackwell, 1993.

———. *Rolling Back the Market: Economic Dogma and Political Choice*. New York: St Martin's Press, 2000.

Sellars, Wilfrid. "Philosophy and the Scientific Image of Man." In *Science, Perception, and Reality*. London: Routledge and Kegan Paul, 1963.

Sen, Amartya. *The Idea of Justice*. Cambridge, MA: Belknap Press of Harvard University Press, 2009.

Sevenhuijsen, Selma. "Justice, Moral Reasoning and the Politics of Child Custody." In *Equality Politics and Gender*. Edited by Elizabeth Meehan and Selma Sevenhuijsen. London: Sage, 1991.

Shahak, Israel, and Norton Mezvinsky. *Jewish Fundamentalism in Israel*. London: Pluto Press, 1999.

Sharlet, Jeff. "Jesus Killed Mohammed: The Crusade for a Christian Military." *Harper's* 318 (May 2009): 31–43.

Sibley, Mulford Q., ed. *The Quiet Battle: Writings on the Theory and Practice of Non-Violent Resistance*. Boston: Beacon Press, 1963.

Siegel, Harvey. "On Using Psychology to Justify Judgments of Moral Adequacy." In *Lawrence Kohlberg: Consensus and Controversy*. Edited by Sohan Modgil and Celia Modgil. London: Falmer Press, 1986.

Sim, Stuart. *Fundamentalist World: The New Dark Age of Dogma*. Toronto: Icon Books, 2004.

Sinden, Amy. "The Economics of Endangered Species: Why Less Is More in the Economic Analysis of Critical Habitat Designation." *Harvard Environmental Law Review* 28 (2004): 129–214.

Sinn, Hans-Werner. "Why Greece Should Leave the Eurozone." *International New York Times*, 27 July 2015, 8.

Smith, Adam. *The Theory of Moral Sentiments*. 1759. Reprint edited by Knud Haakonssen. Cambridge: Cambridge University Press, 2002.

———. *The Nature and Causes of the Wealth of Nations*. 1776. Reprint edited by Kathryn Sutherland. Oxford: Oxford University Press, 1993.

Smith, Wynet. "Undercutting Sustainability: The Global Problem of Illegal Logging and Trade." *Journal of Sustainable Forestry* 19 (2004): 7–30.

Sokal, Alan, and Jean Bricmont. *Intellectual Impostures: Postmodern Philosophers' Abuse of Science*. London: Profile Books, 1998.

Solzhenitsyn, Aleksandr I. *The Gulag Archipelago, 1918–1956: An Experiment in Literary Investigation, I–II*. Translated by Thomas P. Whitney. New York: Harper and Row, 1973.

Spencer, Herbert. *The Man versus the State*. 1884. Reprint, Oxford: Penguin Books, 1969.

Spengler, Oswald. *The Hour of Decision*. Translated by C.F. Atkinson. New York: Knopf, 1934.

Stephens, Robert J. "Hinduism in Independent India: Fundamentalism and Secularism." In *Contemporary Hinduism: Ritual, Culture, and Practice*. Edited by Robin Rinehart. Santa Barbara, CA: ABC CLIO, 2004.

Stoffman, Daniel. "An Ideology, Not a Fact." *Globe and Mail*, 22 Aug. 2009, A11.

Stone, Lawrence. *The Causes of the English Revolution, 1529–1642*. London: Routledge and Kegan Paul, 1972.

Tawney, R.H. *Equality*, 4th edn, rev. London: Unwin Books, 1964.

Taylor, Charles. *A Secular Age*. Cambridge, MA: Belknap Press of Harvard University Press, 2007.

Taylor, Robert. "Europe's Divided Left." *Dissent* 56, 2 (Spring 2009): 5–9.

Teichman, Jenny. *Pacifism and the Just War: A Study in Applied Philosophy*. Oxford: Basil Blackwell, 1986.

Tejani, Shabnum. *Indian Secularism: A Social and Intellectual History 1890–1950*. Bloomington: Indiana University Press, 2008.

Thoreau, Henry. "Civil Disobedience." In *The Quiet Battle: Writings on the Theory and Practice of Non-Violent Resistance*. Edited by Mulford Q. Sibley. Boston: Beacon Press, 1963.

Tillich, Paul. *Systematic Theology*, 3 vols. Chicago: University of Chicago Press, 1951, 1957, 1963.

——. *The Courage to Be*. New Haven: Yale University Press, 1952.

Todd, Allan. *The European Dictatorships: Hitler, Stalin, Mussolini*. Cambridge: Cambridge University Press, 2002.

Tolstoy, Leo. "On the Negro Question." 1904. Reprinted in *Tolstoy's Writings on Civil Disobedience and Non-Violence*. New York: Signet Books, 1967.

——. "Nikolai Palkin." 1906. Reprinted in *Tolstoy's Writings on Civil Disobedience and Non-Violence*. New York: Signet Books, 1967.

Toynbee, Arnold J. *A Study of History*. Abridgment by D.C. Somervell. Oxford: Oxford University Press, 1960.

Trueblood, D. Elton. *The People Called Quakers*. New York: Harper and Row, 1966.

Tummala, Krishna K. "Democracy vs. Fundamentalism: Religious Politics of the Bharatiya Janata Part in India." In *Religious Fundamentalism in the Contemporary World: Critical Social and Political Issues*. Edited by Santosh C. Saha. Lanham, MD: Lexington Books, 2004.

Union of Concerned Scientists. *World Scientists' Warning to Humanity*, 18 Nov. 1992. Reproduced in Paul R. Ehrlich and Anne H. Ehrlich, *Betrayal of Science and Reason: How Anti-Environmental Rhetoric Threatens Our Future*. Washington, DC: Island Press, 1996.

Varoufakis, Yanis. *The Global Minotaur: America, Europe, and the Future of the Global Economy*. London: Zed Books, 2013.

Vidal, Gore. *Julian*. London: Random House, 1976.

Voegelin, Eric. *The New Science of Politics: An Introduction*. Chicago: University of Chicago Press, 1952.

Von Glahn, Gerhard. *Law among Nations: An Introduction to Public International Law*, 7th edn. Boston: Allyn and Bacon, 1996.

Wagner, Walter. "Sustainable Watershed Management: An International Multi-Watershed Study." *Ambio* 31 (2002): 2–13.

Washington Post. "Who Is Gov. Palin?" 3 Sept. 2008, A14.

Wexler, Alice. *Emma Goldman in Exile: From the Russian Revolution to the Spanish Civil War*. Boston: Beacon Press, 1989.

Whitford, Margaret. *Luce Irigaray: Philosophy in the Feminine*. London and New York: Routledge, 1991.

Williams, Daniel K. "Jerry Falwell's Sunbelt Politics: The Regional Origins of the Moral Majority." *Journal of Policy History* 22 (2010).

Williams, Rhys H. "Movement Dynamics and Social Change: Transforming Fundamentalist Ideology and Organizations." In *Accounting for Fundamentalisms: The Dynamic Character of Movements*, vol. 4 of *The Fundamentalist Project* (1991–). Edited by Martin E. Marty and R. Scott Appleby. Chicago: University of Chicago Press, 1994.

Winter, J.M., and D.M. Joslin, eds. *R.H. Tawney's Commonplace Book*. Cambridge: Cambridge University Press, 1972.

Wittgenstein, Ludwig. *Philosophical Investigations*. Oxford: Basil Blackwell, 1963.

Wolff, Jonathan. "In Front of the Curtain." *Times Literary Supplement*, 7 Mar. 2008, 10–11.

Wollheim, Richard. "Democracy." *Journal of the History of Ideas* 19 (1958): 225–42.

Wong, Lloyd, and Vic Satzewich. "Introduction: The Meaning and Significance of Transnationalism." In *Transnational Identities and*

Practices in Canada. Edited by Vic Satzewich and Lloyd Wong. Vancouver: University of British Columbia Press, 2006.

Wood, Allen W. "The Marxian Critique of Justice." In *Marx, Justice, and History*. Edited by Marshall Cohen, Thomas Nagel, and Thomas Scanlon. Princeton, NJ: Princeton University Press, 1980.

———. *Marx Selections*. New York: Macmillan, 1988.

Woodcock, George. *Anarchism*. Harmondsworth, England: Penguin Books, 1962.

Woodcock, George, and Ivan Avakumovic. *The Doukhobors*. Toronto: McClelland & Stewart, 1977.

World Commission on Environment and Development. *Our Common Future*. Oxford: Oxford University Press, 1987.

Worm, Boris, Edward B. Barbier, Nicola Beaumont, et al. "Impacts of Biodiversity Loss on Ocean Ecosystem Services." *Science* 314 (3 Nov. 2006): 787–90.

Zinn, Howard. *A People's History of the United States*. New York: HarperCollins, 2003.

Case Law

Brown v. Board of Education of Topeka, 347 U.S. 483, 74 S.Ct. 686, 98 L.Ed. 873 (1954); judgment on relief ("*Brown II*"), 349 U.S. 294, 75 S.Ct. 753, 99 L.Ed. 1083 (1955)

Co-operative Committee on Japanese Canadians v. Attorney General for Canada, [1947] A.C. 87 (P.C.)

Edwards et al. v. Attorney General for Canada, [1930] A.C. 124, [1930] 1 D.L.R. 98 (P.C.)

Plessy v. Ferguson, 163 U.S. 537, 16 S.Ct. 1138, 41 L.Ed. 256 (1896)

Roe v. Wade, 410 U.S. 113, 93 S.Ct. 705; 35 L.Ed. 2d 147 (1973)

Internet Sources

Bawer, Bruce. "Heirs to Fortuyn?: Europe's Turn to the Right." *Wall Street Journal*, 23 Apr. 2009. http://online.wsj.com/article/SB124043553074744693.html.

Buruma, Ian. "What Became of the Israeli Left?" *The Guardian*, 23 Oct. 2003. http://www.guardian.co.uk/world/2003/oct/23/israel.

Crossland, David. "Neo-Nazi Threat Growing Despite npd Cash Woes." *Spiegel Online International*, 19 Mar. 2009. http://www.spiegel.de/international/germany/0,1518,614209,00.html.

Dunai, Marton. "Four Jailed for Neo-Nazi Killing Spree That Terrified Hungary's Roma." Reuters, 6 Aug. 2013. http://www.reuters.com/article/us-hungary-roma-killings-ruling-idUSBRE97508920130806.

Ertel, Manfred. "Iceland's Women Reach for Power." *Spiegel Online International*, 22 Apr. 2009. http://www.spiegel.de/international/europe/0,1518,620544,00.html.

Falwell, Jerry. "Defending Prayer in School." *Listen America*. *WorldNetDaily Exclusive Commentary*, 27 Oct. 2001. http://www.wnd.com/index.php?fa=PAGE.view&pageId=11457.

Fetterman, Mindy. "Wal-Mart Grows 'Green' Strategies." *USA Today*, 24 Sept. 2006. http://www.usatoday.com/money/industries/retail/2006-09-24-wal-mart-cover-usat_x.htm.

Gerstein, Josh. "Obama: 'The Beginning of the End.'" *Politico.com*, 18 Feb. 2009. http://www.politico.com/news/stories/0209/18958.html.

Goldberg, Carey. "Judge W. Arthur Garrity Jr. Is Dead at 79." *New York Times*, 18 Sept. 1999. http://www.nytimes.com/1999/09/18/us/judge-w-arthur-garrity-jr-is-dead-at-79.html.

"Graveside Party Marks Hebron Massacre." *BBC News*, 21 Mar. 2000. http://news.bbc.co.uk/2/hi/middle_east/685792.stm.

Grit, Selin. "Turkey Rallies over Murder of Woman Who 'Resisted Rape.'" *BBC News*, 15 Feb. 2015. www.bbc.com/news/world-europe-31476978.

Hitchens, Christopher. "The Revenge of Karl Marx." *The Atlantic*, Apr. 2009. http://www.theatlantic.com/doc/200904/hitchens-marx.

Kirchner, Stephen. "German Feminism: Playing Dirty." *Time*, 18 June 2008. http://www.time.com/time/magazine/article/0,9171,1815720,00.html.

Mamdani, Mahmood. "Senseless and [Sensible] Violence: Mourning the Dead at Westgate Mall." *Al Jazeera*, 26 Sept. 2013, http://www.aljazeera.com/indepth/opinion/2013/09/senseless-sensible-violence-mourning-dead-at-westgate-mall-201392563253438882.html.

Moberg, David. "The Meltdown Goes Global: It Is Time to Rethink Capitalism." *In These Times*, 15 Apr. 2009. http://www.inthesetimes.com/article/4361/the_meltdown_goes_global.

Music and the Holocaust. http://holocaustmusic.ort.org/.

Mydans, Seth. "Monks' Protest Is Challenging Burmese Junta." *New York Times*, 24 Sept. 2007. http://www.nytimes.com/2007/09/24/world/asia/24myanmar.html.

Nagata, Kazuaki. "Both Sides on Constitutional Change Hold Rallies." *Japan Times*, 4 May 2009. http://search.japantimes.co.jp/cgi-bin/nn20090504a3.html.

Niebuhr, Gustav. "U.S. 'Secular' Groups Set Tone for Terror Attacks, Falwell Says." *New York Times*, 14 Sept. 2001. http://www.nytimes.com/2001/09/14/national/14FALW.html.

Panitch, Leo. "Thoroughly Modern Marx." *Foreign Policy* (May/June 2009). http://www.foreignpolicy.com/story/cms.php?story%20id=4856&print=1.

Pollin, Robert. "Doing the Recovery Right." *The Nation*, 28 Jan. 2009. http://www.thenation.com/doc/20090206/pollin/print?rel=nofollow.

Rampell, Catherine. "As Layoffs Surge, Women May Pass Men in Job Force." *New York Times*, 5 Feb. 2009. http://www.nytimes.com/2009/02/06/business/06women.html.

Romano, Andrew. "Last of the True Believers?" *Newsweek*, 25 Apr. 2009. http://www.newsweek.com/id/195088.

Russell-Einstein Manifesto. http://www.pugwash.org/about/manifesto.htm. Issued at a press conference in London, 9 July 1955.

Singh, Madhur. "The Fiery Hindu Nationalist Who's Roiling Indian Politics." *Time*, 29 Apr. 2009. http://www.time.com/time/printout/0,8816,1894617,00.html.

"Strike in Guadeloupe Escalates into Rioting." *New York Times*, 17 Feb. 2009. http://www.nytimes.com/2009/02/17/world/europe/17iht-france.4.20259662.html.

Tal, Uriel. "Foundations of a Political Messianic Trend in Israel." *Jerusalem Quarterly* 35 (Spring 1985). http://www.geocities.com/alabasters_archive/messianic_trend.html.

Wikipedia. "Rape in India: 2012 Delhi Gang Rape in Jharkhand." Accessed 28 Apr. 2015.

———. "2002 Gujarat Riots." Accessed 28 Apr. 2015.

———. "Boko Haram Kidnapping." Accessed 13 May 2015.

———. "Al-Shabaab." Accessed 13 May 2015.

Worm, Boris, and David VanderZwaag. "High-Seas Fisheries: Troubled Waters, Tangled Governance, and the Recovery Prospects." *Behind the Headlines*, 1 Sept. 2007. http://www.thefreelibrary.com/High-seas+fisheries%3a+troubled+waters%2c+tangled+governance%2c+and...-a0170279120.

Index

Abe, Shinzo, 158
abortion, 42, 198, 229, 281, 292–4
absolutism, 5–6, 49, 139
Académie des Sciences, 4
Adams, John, 323
Agudat Israel, 298
ahimsa, 164
Ahmed, Rafida, 313
al-Assad, Hafez, 283
al-Banna, Hassan, 279, 287
alienation, 92, 97–8, 100
Al-Qaeda, 285–6
al-Sadr, Muqtada, 279, 282, 288
Al-Shabaab, 279–80, 282, 285–6
Alternative in Eastern Europe, The (Bahro), 267
altruism, 220
al-Wahhab, Muhammed ibn 'Abd, 279, 284
American Revolution, 6
Amital, Yehuda, 300
Anabaptists, 5, 159
anarchism, 3, 179–201; and feminism, 229; central beliefs, 180; critique of, 210; eco-, 268–9; strengths of, 196–8; weaknesses of, 198–201, 332
Anarchy, State, and Utopia (Nozick), 211
animal rights, 221, 269
animism, 320–1
Anniversary of the People's Paper (Marx), 94
anthropocentrism, 263–4, 269
anti-immigration sentiment, 29–30
anti-militarism, 159–62, 164, 166–9, 171–2, 174; *see also* pacifism
anti-Semitism, 131, 143, 147, 188, 297–8
anti-statism, 188–90, 193, 211, 218
Antonius, George, 286
apartheid, 77
Arab League, 283
Arab Spring, 200–1

Ariel, Israel, 301
Aristotle, 4–5, 92
Aryan Society, 303
assertive fundamentalism, 292
Astell, Mary, 226
Atlee, Clement, 123
autarky, 132, 146–8, 153
autonomy: of individuals, 8, 22, 26, 119–20, 213; of institutions, 70, 117, 139
Azzam, Abdullah, 285

Bahrain, 288
Bahro, Rudolf, 267–8
Bakunin, Mikhail, 105, 186–9
Bangladesh, 313
banks, 70, 79
Barclay, Robert, 160
Barry, John, 260–1, 274
Bauer, Bruno, 87
Beck, Ludwig, 145
Begin, Menachem, 297, 300, 302, 311
Benn, Gottfried, 149
Bentham, Jeremy, 58, 94
Berkeley, George, 316
Berlin, Isaiah, 204
Bernstein, Eduard, 103, 109, 111–12
Beveridge, Sir William, 120
Bevin, Ernest, 123
Bhopal Medical Appeal, 253
biocentrism, 269
biodiversity, 252, 255, 271–3
birth control, 68, 198, 230
Blanchard, Oliver, 56
Boko Haram, 242, 279–80, 286, 288
Bolshevism, 98
Bookchin, Murray, 268–9, 273
Bormann, Martin, 145
bourgeois constitutionalism, 145
bourgeoisie, 86, 89–94, 102, 108, 184; petty, 108
Boyle, Robert, 4
Brandeis, Louis D., 114
Brandis, Dietrich, 254
Brazil, 9
Bricmont, Jean, 48

British East India Company, 303
Brock, Peter, 159
Brundtland report, 257–8
Brundtland, Gro Harlem, 257–8, 270, 275
Buddhism, 164–5, 261, 265
Bullock, Alan, 136, 149
Bultmann, Rudolf, 322
Burke, Edmund, 7, 29, 35–40, 45–8, 107
Bush, George W., 292, 296
Bush, Jeb, 57

Caged Virgin, The (Hirsi Ali), 241
Cairnes, J.E., 69
Calvin, John, 5, 315
Canada, 31, 191, 204, 227, 332
Canadian Charter of Rights and Freedoms, 74
Cantet, Laurent, 49
Capital (Marx), 86, 92
capitalism, 63, 95, 169, 207, 219–20; anti-, 190–1; lack of alternatives to, 128
Capitalism, Socialism, and Democracy (Schumpeter), 126–7, 328
Carlyle, Thomas, 108
Carpenter, Edward, 254
Carson, Rachel, 255–7, 261
Carter, Jimmy, 283, 302
Cassese, Antonio, 12, 274
Castro, Fidel, 98
censorship, 154
Chabad Lubavitch, 280, 296, 298–302
Chamberlain, Houston Stewart, 140
Chapters on Socialism (Mill), 60
Chelčický, Petr, 159
Chertkov, Vladimir, 191
China, 9, 98
Chinese Communist Revolution, 98
Choueiri, Youssef M., 280
Christian fundamentalism, 279, 291–6
Christian Voice, 294
City of Ladies (de Pisan), 226

civil disobedience, 157, 160, 162–3, 193
Civil War in France (Marx), 94–5
class struggle, 89–91, 96–7
class-based morality, 96–7
classical liberalism, 3-4, 8–27, 333–4; central beliefs, 10; strengths of, 23–4; weaknesses of, 9–10, 24–7
climate change, 270–2, 329
Clinton, Hilary, 132
colonialism, 19, 22, 26, 289
Commons, John R., 68
communism, 90, 98, 100, 107, 190; vs socialism, 108–9, 112
Communist Manifesto, The (Marx and Engels), 86, 89–91, 101, 107
Communitas (Goodman), 193–5
Community of Islam, 285
comparative advantage, principle of, 16–18
Concluding Unscientific Postscript (Kierkegaard), 318
conscientious objection, 167, 169, 193
conscription, 192
consent theory of value, 13
conservatism, 3, 7, 29–52, 333; and environmentalism, 43; central beliefs, 30; philosophic, 121; strengths of, 46–8; weaknesses of, 49–52
Constantine, 159
constitutionalism, 9, 23; bourgeois, 145
consumerism, 303, 328–9
contraception, 68, 198, 230
contractarianism, 32, 59, 214–6, 218, 249
Contribution to the Critique of Hegel's Philosophy of Right (Marx), 86, 88
Contribution to the Critique of Political Economy (Marx), 86, 89, 91, 98
conventionalism, 32–3
Coogan, Michael, 311
Copernicus, Nicholas, 4, 315
corporatism, 102, 114, 147–8
cosmopolitan pluralism, 121
Courage to Be (Tillich), 323

Cox, Harvey, 313
creationism, 295, 324, 329
Cripps, Stafford, 123
critical anti-realism, 281
Critique of Pure Reason (Kant), 20
Cromwell, Oliver, 5
Crosland, C.A.R., 114–16
Crusades, 297
cultural relativism, 42, 247

Dalton, Hugh, 123
D'Amato, Alfonse, 302
Darkness at Noon (Koestler), 1
Darré, Richard Walter, 149
Darwin, Charles, 140
Darwinism, 140, 324; social, 136, 140, 152
Dawkins, Richard, 310, 314, 323–7
Dayan, Moshe, 300
de Beauvoir, Simone, 227–8, 245
de Pisan, Christine, 226
de Quevedo, Miguel Ángel, 254
de Saint-Simon, Henri, 109
deep ecology, 238–9, 253, 259–64; criticism of, 269, 274
de-extinction, 252
deism, 317, 323
democracy: and capitalism, 219–20; and fundamentalism, 310; and reform liberalism, 77–8; Dewey on, 65–7, 77; Giddens on, 120–1; Hayek on, 207; Wollheim on, 66–7
democratic socialism, 3, 107–28, 334–5; central beliefs, 110; strengths of, 124–6; weaknesses of, 126–8
demographics, 92–3
Deobandi, 282
Derrida, Jacques, 48
desegregation, 47
Dewey, John, 55, 64–7, 77
dialectical materialism, 89, 101
Dialogues Concerning Natural Religion (Hume), 316–17
Diamantopoulou, Anna, 58
Dickens, Charles, 55

dictatorship, 9, 104, 133, 139, 180, 188; of the proletariat, 104–5
difference principle of justice, 72–3, 80–1
Diggers, 180–1
disarmament, 165–6, 168, 170, 174
dispensationalism, 293
Disraeli, Benjamin, 108
distributive justice, 118, 213
division of labour, 16–17, 24
Dobson, Andrew, 263–4, 274
dogmatism, 7
domestic policy, 3, 270, 295–6
Dostoevsky, Fyodor, 328
Douglas, Tommy, 122
Doukhobors, 191, 332
Draghi, Mario, 56
Dreyfus, Alfred, 298
Duda, Andrzej, 30
Duehring, Eugen, 141, 147, 152, 298
Dulles, John Foster, 170
Dworkin, Ronald, 55
Dylan, Bob, 302

eco-anarchism, 268–9
eco-feminism, 237–9
ecologism, 260–1, 263–8; proto-, 255–7; vs environmentalism, 263
ecology: social, 268–9; transpersonal, 264–7, 275
Economic and Philosophic Manuscripts, The (Marx), 86, 97
economic crisis, 56–7, 85–6, 224
economics, 8, 19–20, 23, 46, 56, 190; and determinism, 98–9, 101–2, 104; environmental, 261; Keynesian, 56, 68–9; laissez-faire, 16–18, 24, 56, 69, 210; neo-liberal, 208, 211; role in politics, 125, 128, 206, 208, 211, 218; socialist, 122; trickle-down, 72–3; wage-labour system, 13
Economics of Feasible Socialism, The (Nove), 116–17
Eddy, Mary Baker, 309

education, 47, 182, 240–1, 249, 294–5
Edwards, Henrietta Muir, 227
egalitarianism, 115–16, 122, 147, 260
Egypt, 287
Ehrlich, Anne, 273
Ehrlich, Paul, 273
Eichmann, Adolf, 142
Einstein, Albert, 170, 174
Eisenhower, Dwight D., 170
Eisner, Kurt, 143–4
Either/Or (Kierkegaard), 319
Elias, Alois, 144
Eliot, T.S., 35
Eltahawy, Mona, 229
emancipation: Bahro on, 267–8; Marx on, 87–8, 99, 109; of women, 230–1, 241
Emerson, Ralph Waldo, 161
Enabling Act, 134, 143
Encyclopedia of Pacifism, An (Huxley), 164
Enfranchisement of Women (Mill), 226
Engels, Friedrich, 86, 96–7
English Civil War, 5–6
Enlightenment: and Islam, 242–4, 249–50; Kant on, 8, 20–1, 23, 135, 145; opposition to, 231, 245, 249, 279, 298; Scruton on, 44
Enquiry Concerning Political Justice (Godwin), 181
entertainment, 17, 328
entitlement theory, 27, 213, 217, 223
environmental justice, 172
environmentalism, 3, 125, 252–75, 335; and conservatism, 43; and feminism, 237–9; central beliefs, 255; first wave, 253–4; reform, 257–8, 275; second wave, 253, 255; strengths of, 270–4; transitional, 258–9; vs ecologism, 263; weaknesses of, 274–5
Equal Rights Amendment, 279, 293–5
equality: and ethical socialism, 122; and liberty, 9, 125; Crosland on, 115; Giddens on, 120; Hampshire on, 118–9; Kant on, 22; Tawney on, 113
Essay Concerning Human Understanding, An (Locke), 4
Essence of Christianity (Feuerbach), 88
Estera, 30
ethic of care, 233–4, 238, 246
ethical socialism, 122
Ethics (Mackie), 325
ethics: environmental, 237–9; of virtue, 239; relational, 239–40; secular, 325
eugenics, 136, 140
Evolution of Parliament, The (Pollard), 113
existentialism, 100, 317–8
experimentalism, 65
extinction, 252
Eyes Upon the Land, 301–2

Falwell, Jerry, 292–7, 310
family, 121, 234, 235–7; and justice, 235–7; gender roles, 234, 294
Famous Five, 227
fascism, 3, 131–54; and nationalism, 132, 137–8; and racism, 140–3, 152; central beliefs, 133; strengths of, 149–50; weaknesses of, 150–4, 332
feasible socialism, 116–17
Female Eunuch, The (Greer), 228
female genital mutilation, 243
Feminine Mystique, The (Friedan), 227–8
feminism, 3, 226–50, 334–5; and anarchism, 229; and Marxism, 229; and pacifism, 171–2, 176; and socialism, 126; central beliefs, 228; eco-, 237–9; first wave, 226; opposition to, 294; second wave, 227–8; strengths of, 245–8; weaknesses of, 248–50
Feuerbach, Ludwig, 88–9, 99, 317
Fichte, Johann Gottlieb, 132, 147
final solution, 142
Firestone, Shulamith, 229, 245
Fisher, Stanley, 56

foreign policy, 3, 148, 296–7
Fosdick, Harry Emerson, 291–2
Fourier, Charles, 109
Fox, George, 160, 180
Fox, Warwick, 238, 264–7, 273
Frank, Adam, 329
Franklin, Ursula, 171–2, 173, 176, 333
Frazer, J.G., 320
free rider problem, 209
free trade, 6, 16–18, 42; opposition to, 102, 132, 146–7
freedom: and religious fundamentalism, 307; Giddens on, 120; Goodman on, 195; Green on, 61; Kant on, 21–23; neo-liberal concept of, 204, 211; *see also* liberty
Freisler, Roland, 144–5
French Legitimists, 108
French Revolution, 6, 38, 107, 185
Freud, Sigmund, 174, 232, 314, 320–2, 326–7
Frick, Henry Clay, 192
Friedan, Betty, 227–8, 245
Friedman, Richard Elliott, 311
Friedman, Thomas L., 274
Fuehrerprinzip, *see* leadership principle
fundamentalism, *see* religious fundamentalism
Fundamentals, The, 291
Future of an Illusion, The (Freud), 320–1

Gaddafi, Mu'ammer, 283
Galbraith, John Kenneth, 55
Galilei, Galileo, 4, 315
Gan, Barry, 173
Gandhi, Mohandas, 157, 162–4, 174, 254
Gandhi, Sonia, 132
Garrison, William Lloyd, 162
Gauthier, David, 214
gay rights, 295–6; *see also* homosexuality
Gell-Mann, Murray, 259
gender, 228, 230–1, 234–5, 239, 247–9

General History of Nature and Theory of the Heavens (Kant), 20
General Idea of the Revolution in the Nineteenth Century, The (Proudhon), 185
Genet, Jean, 250
Gentile, Giovanni, 149
Germany, 87, 94, 131–54
Gestapo, 145
Giddens, Anthony, 119–21, 128
Gilligan, Carol, 232–4, 245
Gingrich, Newt, 302
Giuliani, Rudolph, 302
Globke, Hans, 146
God Delusion (Dawkins), 323
Godwin, Mary, 181
Godwin, William, 180–3
Goebbles, Paul Joseph, 154
Goering, Hermann, 136, 142–3, 145
Goldberg, Whoopi, 302
Goldman, Emma, 179, 191–3, 199
Goldstein, Baruch, 302
Goodin, Robert E., 259–61
Goodman, Paul, 193–5
Gore, Al, 302
Gould, Stephen Jay, 259
government, 9, 11, 14–15; and property, 19, 183–4; and reform liberalism, 78; Burke on, 36, 38; Godwin on, 182; Green on, 61; Islamic, 289–90; Keynes on, 68, 70–1; night watchman, 12, 78, 204, 212; Oakeshott on, 41; overthrow of, 15–16; Proudhon on, 185
Grayling, A.C., 46
Great Western Transmutation, 291
Greece, 85, 180
Green political theory, 259–61
Green theory of value, 259–60
Green, T.H., 55, 61
Greer, Germaine, 228
Griffin, Robert, 135, 149
Guha, Ramachandra, 253
Guillaume, James, 189
Guizot, François, 184
Gulag Archipelago, The (Solzhenitsyn), 7

Gush Emunim, 280, 296, 298–302

Hamas, 280, 282
Hampshire, Stuart, 117–19
Harkabi, Yehoshafat, 310
Harm Principle, 59
Harper, Stephen, 204
Hasidism, 280, 297–9, 301
Hawking, Stephen, 259
Hayek, Friedrich, 25–6, 206–8, 220
Headscarves and Hymens (Eltahawy), 229
Hegel, Georg, 317
Heidegger, Martin, 149, 318
Helms, Jesse, 292, 297
Henry VIII, 5
Heretic (Hirsi Ali), 244
Herzl, Theodor, 298
Heydrich, Reinhard, 142, 144
Hezbollah, 280, 282, 288
Hindu fundamentalism, 280, 302–7
Hindutva, 305–6
Hirsch, Samson Raphael, 298
Hirsi Ali, Ayaan, 228, 237, 241–5, 247, 250
Hitchens, Christopher, 85
Hitler, Adolf, 131–54
Hizb-ut-Tahrir, 282
Hobbes, Thomas, 5, 9, 11, 174, 315, 317
Hobhouse, L.T., 55, 61–2
Hobson, J.A., 55, 62–4
Hodgkin, Dorothy Crowfoot, 259
Hodgson, Marshall, 291
Holland, 29–30, 49
Holmes, Robert, 173
Holocaust, 142
homosexuality, 192, 196, 230, 232; and conservatism, 29, 49; and marriage, 44, 52, 295; rejection of, 198, 230, 224, 281, 309
Hooke, Robert, 4
Horsburgh, H.J.N., 162
Hot, Flat, and Crowded (Friedmans), 274
Huber, Ernst Rudolf, 145
Huguenots, 5
human rights, 2, 75, 76, 247; and capitalism, 219; Universal Declaration of, 36

Human Rights Watch, 304
humanism, 122, 235, 281, 292–3; and justice, 235; Christian, 1; ethical, 163
Hume, David, 29, 31–5, 45–8, 314–17, 326–7
Hungary, 29–30, 132
Huss, John, 315
Hussein, Saddam, 283
Hutterites, 159
Huxley, Aldous, 164–7, 333
Huxley, T.H., 141

ideology, 2–3, 331–2
If I Should Die before I Wake (Falwell), 294
imperialism: and fascism, 133, 137, 147–8, 150–1; opposition to, 166, 288–90
impositional fundamentalism, 292
In a Different Voice (Gilligan), 232–3
independence, *see* autonomy
India, 132, 280, 303–7
individualism, 29, 61–3, 75, 120, 190, 206; objection to, 240, 286–7, 289
Industrial Revolution, 6, 55
inegalitarianism, 14, 16, 36, 50–1
Inquiry into the Nature and Cause of the Wealth of Nations, see Wealth of Nations, The
intentional design, 316
International Monetary Fund, 56
internationalism, 42, 124, 135, 206, 297
intuitionism, 214
invisible hand, 16–18, 212; critique of, 69
Iran, 279–80, 288–90
Iranian Revolution, 283–4
Iraq, 242, 279–80, 285–6, 288, 297
Irigaray, Luce, 231–2
Ishaq, Zunera, 31
ISIS (Islamic State in Iraq and Syria), 280, 285
Islam: and women, 241–5, 289–90; fundamentalism, 9, 242, 279, 281–90; Hirsi Ali on, 241–5

Israel, 124, 282–3, 285, 296–302
Italo-Ethiopian War, 139
Italy, 131–9, 141–3, 147–50

Jainism, 165
Jamaat-i-Islami, 285
Japan, 158
Jaspers, Karl, 318
Jefferson, Thomas, 323
Jesus, 88–9, 158–65, 291, 197, 319
Jewish fundamentalism, 280, 296–302
Jews, 87–9, 141–3, 280, 296–302
Jobbik, 132
Johnson, Lyndon B., 176
Jones, Bob, Jr, 292–3
just war doctrine, 157, 161
justice, 72–3, 80–1, 118–9; and education, 34; and environment, 172; and family, 235–7; and property, 32–3, 118–19, 125, 182–3; and technology, 172; as artificial virtue, 31–2; distributive, 118, 213; Hampshire on, 118–9; Hume on, 31–4; Marx on, 95–8; Rawls on, 72–3; under fascism, 143–6, 153; vs care, 233–4
Justice, Gender, and Family (Okin), 234

Kach Party, 299
Kahane, Meir, 299
Kant, Immanuel, 8–9, 20–7, 145; criticism of, 238
Kelsen, Hans, 143
Kennedy, Robert, 302
Kenney, Jason, 31
Kenya, 280
Keynes, John Maynard, 55, 67–71, 174–5, 332
Keynesian economics, 56, 68–9
Khomeini, Ayatollah Ruhollah, 279, 283–4, 288–90
Kierkegaard, Søren, 313, 317–20, 322, 326–7
King, Martin Luther, Jr, 157, 174
Knox, John, 5

Koestler, Arthur, 1
Kohlberg, Lawrence, 233
Kook, Abraham Isaac, 299–301
Kook, Zvi Yehuda, 299
Kopacz, Ewa, 30
Kropotkin, Peter, 189–91, 268
Krugman, Paul, 56–8
Krushchev, Nikita, 170
Kugel, James, 311
Kymlicka, Will, 49, 55–6, 73–5, 219

labour theory of value, 13, 17, 101
LaHaye, Tim, 292, 296, 310
laissez-faire, 16–18, 24, 56, 69, 210; critiques of, 78–9, 147
Laplace, Pierre-Simon, 20
law of nature, 10–11
Law of the Peoples, The (Rawls), 73
leadership principle, 138–40
Lederman, Marsha, 132
legalism, 200
Leibniz, Gottfried, 145, 309
Lenin, Vladimir, 98, 189, 193
Leopold, Aldo, 254–5, 261
Letters to a Young Poet (Rilke), 246
Levellers, 180
Leviathan (Hobbes), 5, 14, 151
Lewis, David, 109
Lewis, Stephen, 109
liberalism, 6, 20, 68, 127, *see also* classical liberalism, reform liberalism, neo-liberalism
Liberalism (Hobhouse), 61
Liberalism and Social Action (Dewey), 64
Libertarian Idea, The (Narveson), 214
libertarianism, 3, 203–24, 333–4; central beliefs, 205; characteristic tone of, 3; strengths of, 218–19; weaknesses of, 219–24
liberty: and equality, 9, 125; and tolerance, 52; Mill on, 58–60; natural, 10; negative, 60, 204; positive, 60, 204; Tawney on, 113; under anarchism, 196; *see also* freedom

liberty principle of justice, 72–3, 80–1
Lieberman, Joseph, 302
Lienesch, Michael, 296
List, Friedrich, 147
Listen, America! (Falwell), 293
living wage, 62
Locke, John, 4–16, 22–7, 198, 211; compared to Smith, 14, 18–19
Logic of Collective Action, The (Olson), 208–9
Loreto, Nora, 203
Luria, Isaac, 301
Luther, Martin, 5, 315

Machiavelli, 149
MacIntyre, Alasdair, 40
Mackie, John L., 313, 324–7
Macpherson, C.B., 15
Madison, James, 323
Mailer, Norman, 250
Maimonides, 301
majoritarianism, 14–15
Malcolm, Neill, 144
Mallik, Heather, 204
Man and Nature (Perkins), 254
Man versus the State, The (Spencer), 204
Manifesto of fascist Racism, The, 142–3
Mao Zedong, 98, 104, 332
March on Rome, 134
Margalit, Avishai, 300
Margulis, Lynn, 259
market theory of value, 1, 13–4, 16, 101
marriage, 43–4, 50, 52, 183, 198; same-sex, 44, 52, 295
Marsh, George Perkins, 254
Marshall, Alfred, 69
Marx, Karl, 86–105, 107–9, 184; *see also* Marxism,
Marxism, 3, 85–105, 332; and feminism, 229; central beliefs, 86; criticism of, 135–6, 149, 187–8; strengths of, 99–101; weaknesses of, 101–5, 332
Masham, Damaris, 226
materialism, 89–92, 101 136, 287
Maududi, Sayyid Abul-Ala, 285

Mavor, James, 191
Mayer, Julius, 193
Mayr, Ernst, 259
McClung, Nellie, 227
McKinley, William, 192
McKinney, Louise, 227
McNamara, Robert, 81, 176
Mein Kampf (Hitler), 137, 142
Memoirs of a Revolutionist (Kropotkin), 190
Mendelssohn, Moses, 297
Mennonites, 159–60, 171
mercantilism, 14, 18–19
Mercier, Pascal, 134
Mesiatz, Gennady, 259
metaphysical rights, 37–8
militarism, *see* war
Mill, Harriet Taylor, 226
Mill, John Stuart, 23, 55, 58–61, 187, 204; and feminism, 226–7, 234
Millett, Kate, 228, 250
Mills, C. Wright, 61, 82, 104
Modi, Narendra, 132
Mogul Empire, 303
Montagu, Ashley, 191
moral consensus, 324–5
Moral Majority, 279, 292–5, 310
Morris, William, 254, 267
Morrison, Herbert, 123
Morvai, Krisztina, 132
Moser, Johann Jakob, 145
Mubarak, Hosni, 284
Muir, John, 254–5, 261
multiculturalism, 49, 73–5, 80, 82, 242
Mumford, Lewis, 254
Murphy, Emily, 227
music, 154
Muslim Brotherhood, 158, 279–80, 283–8
Mussolini, Benito, 131, 134–8, 141–3, 147–54
Mutual Aid (Kropotkin), 190–1
Myanmar, 158

Nachmanides, Moshe, 299–300
Næss, Arne, 238, 261–3
Narveson, Jan, 175, 203, 214–17
Nasrallah, Sayyed Hassan, 282
Nasser, Gamal Abdel, 283
nation, definitions of, 152
national parks, 254

National Religious Party, 300
national socialism, *see* fascism
nationalism, 7, 102–3; and fascism, 132, 137–8; Hindu, 132, 280, 303–7
nation-state, 5–7, 9, 41–2, 331
natural laws, 64
natural rights, 64
natural selection, 324
naturalism, 281
Naumann, Friedrich, 147
negative liberty, 60, 204
Nehru, Jawaharlal, 306
neo-fundamentalism, 293
neo-liberalism, 203–24, 333–4; central beliefs, 205; strengths of, 218–19; weaknesses of, 219–24
neo-Nazism, 131–2
Netanyahu, Benjamin, 297, 302
new liberalism, 68
New Right, 210–11, 217
New Ten Commandments, 324–5
Newton, Isaac, 4
Niekisch, Ernst, 144
Nietzsche, Friedrich, 278, 318
Nigeria, 280
Night Train to Lisbon (Mercier), 134
night watchman, 12, 78, 204, 212
Noddings, Nel, 239–41, 245
Nove, Alec, 103, 116–17
Nozick, Robert, 12, 211–13, 332
nuclear weapons, 170, 173, 176, 255–7, 288
Numayri, Ja'far, 284
Nuremberg Laws, 143
Nuremberg tribunals, 142
Nussbaum, Martha, 235–7, 245–7

Oakeshott, Michael, 29, 40–1, 45–8, 50
Obama, Barack, 56, 253
Obstfeld, Maurice, 56
Okin, Susan, 234–5, 242, 245
Ollman, Bertell, 100
Olson, Mancur, 198–9, 208–11, 217
On Liberty (Mill), 23, 50, 58–9

On the Jewish Question (Marx), 86
On the Origin of Species (Darwin), 140
Orbán, Viktor, 30
Origen, 159
Ottoman Empire, 103, 282, 284–5
Owen, Robert, 109, 111–12, 172
Owen, Wilfrid, 162

pacifism, 3, 157–77; and feminism, 171–2, 176; and religion, 158–60, 177, 333; obstacles to, 168; strengths of, 173–6; weaknesses of, 176–7
Pahlavi, Mohammad Reza, 289
Paine, Thomas, 51
Palaiologos, Yannis, 180
Panitch, Leo, 85
Pankhurst, Emmeline, 227
Pankhurst, Richard, 227
Pareto, Vilfredo, 119
Paris Commune, 95
Parlby, Irene, 227
Parmenides, 323
passive fundamentalism, 292
Pauling, Linus, 259
Pearson, Karl, 140
Pearson, Lester B., 176
Peffer, R.G., 96–7
Penelhum, Terence, 316–17
Penn, William, 160
Penrose, Roger, 259
People's Court, 143–5
Peres, Shimon, 300, 302
Pesticides Action Network UK, 253
petty bourgeoisie, 108
Phillips, Kevin, 291–2
philosophic conservatism, 119, 121
philosophical materialism, 90
Philosophie de la Misère (Proudhon), 108
physiocracy, 20
Pinchot, Gifford, 254
Pirie, Madsen, 206
Piscatori, James, 283
Plamenatz, John, 101
Plato, 226, 316
Plumwood, Val, 237–9, 245

pluralism, 5, 69, 78, 128, 281, 334; cosmopolitan, 121; rejection of, 279
Pol Pot, 98, 104, 332
Poland, 29–30
Polanyi, John, 259
policy: domestic, 3, 270, 293–6; foreign, 3, 148, 296–7
Politics (Aristotle), 92
politics of delay, 42, 45, 47, 50, 333
Pollard, A.F., 113
Polytechneio uprising, 180
population: change, 140; control, 258–9, 262–3; growth, 93, 126, 207, 270–1; Keynes on, 71, 76, 78; statistics, 93
positive liberty, 60, 204
postmodernism, 44–5, 48–9, 335–6
Potok, Chaim, 302
Principles of Political Economy (Mill), 60
prisoner's dilemma, 214
proletariat, 89–91; dictatorship of, 104–5
property, 127, 179, 183; and government, 19, 183–4; and justice, 32–3, 118–19, 125, 182–3; co-operative, 122; Hume on, 33, 35; Locke on, 11, 13–5, 19; Marx on, 91–2, 98; Mill on, 60; Proudhon on, 184–5; relations, 91–2, 98–99, 108; rights, 13–15, 22, 58, 76, 203, 271
protective associations, 12, 212, 332
Protestantism, 5, 55, 122, 180, 291–3
proto-ecologism, 255–7
Proudhon, Pierre-Joseph, 105, 108, 184–6
psychoanalysis, 231–2, 278, 314, 321–2
public choice theory, 208, 217, 220
Puritans, 5
Putin, Vladimir, 302

Quakers, 159–61, 167, 171, 333
Quebec, 227
Quesnay, François, 20
Quine, Willard Van Orman, 335–6
Quinton, Anthony, 40, 45
Qutb, Sayyid, 287–8

Rabbinical Assembly, 297
racism, 47, 49, 140–3, 152
radicalism, 65, 77, 112, 180, 192–3, 280
rational egoism, 220
rationalism, 223, 292, 307
rationality, 214–20, 239; and justice, 95; and morality, 325
Rawls, John, 55, 71–3; criticism of, 234–5, 246
Reagan, Ronald, 206, 294
reason, 267, 325, 328; and anarchism, 185–6, 195; and classical liberalism, 11–12, 21–2; and conservatism, 35; and fascism, 136; and pacifism, 176; and philosophy, 89; and religion, 244, 291; Kantian, 21, 237–9, 217
Reflections on the Revolution in France (Burke), 35–6, 38, 40, 107
reform environmentalism, 257–8, 275
reform liberalism, 3, 55–82, 334–5; central beliefs, 56; strengths of, 76–80; vs. Socialism, 79–80; weaknesses of, 80–2
Reformation, 5, 315, 331
refugees, 29–31
relativism, 49, 281, 308; cultural, 42, 247; ethical, 247, 295
religion, 281: and pacifism, 158–60, 177, 333; and sexuality, 242–3; Burke on, 39; Franklin on, 171; Freud on, 320–2; Kierkegaard on, 319; Marx on, 87–9, 92, 317; natural, 316–17; Scruton on, 44; Smith on, 17, 310, 328; Strauss on, 88–9
religious fundamentalism, 3, 278–311; strengths of, 307; weaknesses of, 307–11, 332
Religious Roundtable, 294
Republic (Plato), 226

residential schools, 47
responsive theory of cohesion, 265–7, 273
rights, 14, 48, 64, 233–4; and reform liberalism, 75; animal, 221, 269; Burke on, 35–8; Locke on, 11, 14; metaphysical vs real, 37–8; Paine on, 51; to property, 13–15, 22, 58, 76, 185, 203, 271
Rights of Man (Paine), 51
Rilke, Rainer Maria, 246, 266
Rise and Decline of Nations, The (Olson), 209
Road to Serfdom, The (Hayek), 26, 206, 220
Robertson, Pat, 292
Roehm, Ernst, 145
Roma, 132
Rommel, Erwin, 146
Rosenberg, Alfred, 149
Rousseau, Jean-Jacques, 35, 173
Rousso, Alan, 58
Roy, Avijit, 313
Royal Society of London for the Improvement of Natural Knowledge, 4, 331
RSS (Rashtriya Swayamsevak Sangh), 305
rule of law: and classical liberalism, 9–10, 15, 19, 23; and conservatism, 35; and neo-liberalism, 206, 211
Ruskin, John, 254
Russell, Bertrand, 167–70, 333
Russell–Einstein Manifesto, 170
Russia, 9
Russian Revolution, 98, 121

Sadat, Anwar, 283–4
Sagan, Carl, 259
same-sex marriage, 44, 52, 295
Sand County Almanac, A (Leopold), 255
Sanders, Bernie, 109–10, 132
Sanford, Mark, 203
Sangh Parivar, 305
Saraswati, Swami Dayananda, 303
Sartre, Jean-Paul, 313, 318
Sassoon, Siegfried, 162
satyagraha, 162–4, 174
Saudi Arabia, 284

Savarkar, Vinayak Damodar, 305
Scalia, Antonin, 48
Schaeffer, Francis, 292
Schimmel, Solomon, 311
Schlalfly, Phyllis, 294
Schmitt, Carl, 143, 149
Schneerson, Menachem Mendel, 301–2
Schumacher, E.F., 259, 261
Schumpeter, Joseph A., 126–7, 219, 328
Schwarzer, Alice, 229–31, 245
Schweitzer, Albert, 164, 256, 261
science, 4–6; and anarchism, 184; and classical liberalism, 17, 21; and environmentalism, 254, 270; and fascism, 136, 138, 148, 150; and religious fundamentalism, 301, 303, 307; and secularism, 313–5, 321–2, 325
scientific conservation, 253–4
scientific method, 4–6, 90, 99, 314, 322
Scruton, Roger, 29, 41–8
Second Amendment, 48
Second Intifada, 300
Second Sex, The (de Beauvoir), 227
sectarianism, 310, 328
secularism, 313–29, 336; central beliefs, 313; positive, 306; rejection of, 280, 307; strengths of, 327–8; vs secularization, 313; weaknesses of, 328–9
segregation, 47, 77
Selassie, Haile, 150
Self, Peter, 220
Sellars, Wilfrid, 336
Seneca Falls Convention, 226
Sermon on the Mount, 158–9, 161, 165
Sexual Politics (Millett), 228
sexuality, 43, 230–1, 241–3; *see also* homosexuality
Shamir, Yitzhak, 300
shariah, 49
Sharon, Ariel, 300, 302
Shelley, Mary, 181
Shelley, Percy, 181

Shi'ism, 279, 281–6, 288–90, 327
Sierra Club, 254
Sifton, Clifford, 191
Silent Spring (Carson), 255, 261
Simons, Menno, 159
Six-Day War, 282, 293, 300
slavery, 161–2, 169
Small is Beautiful (Schumacher), 261
Smith, Adam, 6, 8–9, 16–20, 22–7, 197, 248; and neo-liberalism, 211; compared to Locke, 14, 18–19; critique of, 69, 147; and religion, 17, 310, 328
social contract, 9, 14, 24, 26–7, 36–7; original position, 71
social Darwinism, 136, 140, 152
social ecology, 42, 268–9
socialism: and feminism, 126; and liberalism, 127; critical-utopian, 109; democratic, 3, 107–28, 334–5; early, 7; ethical, 122; feasible, 116–17; Hobhouse on, 62; Hobson on, 63; Marx on, 107–9; petty-bourgeois, 108; Proudhon on, 108; "true", 108; vs communism, 108–9, 112; vs reform liberalism, 79–80
socialistic ecologism, 267–8
Sokal, Alan, 48
Solzhenitsyn, Aleksandr, 7
Spanish Civil War, 193, 199
Spencer, Herbert, 77, 204, 320
Spengler, Oswald, 141
Sprat, Thomas, 4
Stalin, Joseph, 98, 104, 332
Stanton, Elizabeth Cady, 226
state: minimal, 212–3; of nature, 10–12, 22, 58, 199, 212, 216; of war, 11; ultraminimal, 212–3; *see also* nation–state, government
Statism and Anarchy (Bakunin), 186
statistics, 93
Stiglitz, Joseph, 56
Strauss, David, 88–9, 317
Stuckart, Wilhelm, 146
student radicalism, 180

Subjection of Women, The (Mill), 226
Submission: Part I (van Gogh), 241
Suez Crisis, 176
suffrage, female, 226–7
Sufism, 284
Sullivan, Noel, 40
Sumner, William Graham, 140
Sunnism, 279, 281, 285–8
sustainable development, 257–8, 262, 270, 274–5
Sutherland, Kathryn, 26
Suu Kyi, Aun San, 158
Syria, 280
Systematic Theology (Tillich), 322

Taborites, 159
Tal, Uriel, 300
Taliban, 282
Tawney, R.H., 103, 112–14
Taylor, Charles, 73, 313, 320–1, 326–9
Taymiyyah, Ahmad Ibn, 284
televangelism, 293
Tenacity of Unreasonable Beliefs, The (Schimmel), 311
terrorism, 157, 242, 288, 295, 302
Tertullian, 159
Thatcher, Margaret, 206, 302
theism, 281, 324
theories of value: consent, 13; labour, 13, 17, 101; market, 1, 13–4, 16, 101; Green, 259–60
Theory of Justice, A (Rawls), 73, 234, 238, 246
Theory of Moral Sentiments, The (Smith), 16, 211, 248
Thierack, Otto, 144
Third Reich, 137, 139, 142–6
Third Way, 119–21, 128
Thoreau, Henry David, 160–1, 254
Thus Spoke Zarathustra (Nietzsche), 278
Tilak, Bal Gangadhar, 303
Tillich, Paul, 313, 322–3, 326–7
Tinbergen, Jan, 259
Tolstoy, Leo, 161–2
Tonegawa, Susumu, 259

totalitarianism, 138
Totem and Taboo (Freud), 320–1
transitional environmentalism, 258–9
transpersonal ecology, 264–7, 275
Treatise on Human Nature, A (Hume), 31, 34
Trudeau, Pierre, 55, 74
Trump, Donald, 132
Tsipris, Alexis, 85
Two Treatises of Government (Locke), 4, 6, 10–11

Ullyett, G.C., 257
Union Carbide, 253
unions, 102, 111, 192, 332
United States Forest Service, 254
Unity of Czech Brethren, 159, 171
Universal Declaration of Human Rights, 36
universities, 70, 79
urbanization, 282–3
utilitarianism, 58, 214

value, theories of, 1, 13–4, 16–17, 101
van den Bruck, Arthur Moeller, 137
van Gogh, Theo, 241
VanderZwaag, David, 273
Varoufakis, Yanis, 85, 104
Vehmgericht, 94
Verhaeghe, Paul, 204
Vesalius, Andreas, 4
Vidal, Gore, 17

Vindication of the Rights of Women, A (Wollstonecraft), 226
violence: against children, 47, 246–7; against women, 229, 243, 246–7; and fascism, 132, 135, 149; and justice, 119, 124; political, 65, 100, 180; rejection of, 109, 112, 126; sectarian, 281, 285, 304
virtues, artificial vs natural, 31–2
Vishva Hindu Parishad, 305
Voegelin, Eric, 35
Voight, Jon, 302
Volksgerichtshof, 143–5
von Braun, Wernher, 150
von Clausewitz, Carl, 173
von Humboldt, Alexander, 254
von Moser, Friedrich Karl, 145

Wagner, Richard, 187, 298
Wahhabism, 279, 282. 284–8
Waldenses, 159
war, 6, 10–12, 68, 173–5, 216, 332: anarchist view of, 182, 192–3; anti-, 158, 160–1, 167, 193; class, 135–6; critique of, 143; fascist view of, 134, 149–51; Franklin on, 171–2; Huxley on, 166; just, 157, 161; nuclear, 170, 255, 257; resisters, 166; Russell on, 167–8; women and, 240–1; *see also* individual wars
Washington, George, 323
Waszczykowski, Withold, 30

Wealth of Nations, The (Smith), 16–18, 20, 50, 78, 211, 310
Wels, Otto, 139
Westphalia, Treaty of, 6
Which Way to Peace? (Russell), 167
Wiesel, Elie, 302
Wilson, Edward O., 259, 272
Winstanley, Gerrard, 180
Wolff, Christian, 145
Wollheim, Richard, 66–7
Wollstonecroft, Mary, 181, 226
Women in Western Political Thought (Okin), 234
women: and Islam, 241–5, 289–90; and militarism, 171–2; in India, 306; Smith on, 26; under classical liberalism, 26; *see also* feminism
Wood, Allen, 95–7
Wordsworth, William, 254
World Bank, 81
World Hindu Council, 305
World Scientists' Warning to Humanity, 258–9, 270, 335
Worm, Boris, 273
Wouk, Herman, 302
Wundt, Wilhelm, 320

xenophobia, 49

Yom Kippur War, 283, 300
Young England, 108

Zhukovsky, Nicholas, 189
Ziegler, Adolf, 154
Zionism, 280, 289, 297–301
Zwingli, Ulrich, 5, 315